AF800385

Infosys Science Foundation Series

Infosys Science Foundation Series in Mathematical Sciences

Editors-in-Chief

Gopal Prasad, University of Michigan, Ann Arbor, USA

Irene Fonseca, Carnegie Mellon University, Pittsburgh, PA, USA

Associate Editors

Chandrashekhar Khare, University of California, Los Angeles, USA

Mahan Mj, Tata Institute of Fundamental Research, Mumbai, India

Manindra Agrawal, Indian Institute of Technology Kanpur, Kanpur, India

Ritabrata Munshi, Tata Institute of Fundamental Research, Mumbai, India

S. R. S. Varadhan, New York University, New York, USA

Weinan E, Princeton University, Princeton, USA

The **Infosys Science Foundation Series in Mathematical Sciences**, a Scopus-indexed book series, focuses on high-quality content in the domain of pure and applied mathematics, biomathematics, financial mathematics, operations research and theoretical computer science. With this series, Springer hopes to provide readers with monographs, textbooks, edited volume, handbooks and professional books of the highest academic quality on current topics in relevant disciplines. Literature in this series will appeal to a wide audience of researchers, students, educators and professionals across the world.

S. A. Edalatpanah · Farhad Hosseinzadeh Lotfi ·
Kristiaan Kerstens · Peter Wanke
Editors

Analytical Decision Making and Data Envelopment Analysis

Advances and Challenges

Springer

Editors
S. A. Edalatpanah
Department of Applied Mathematics
Ayandegan Institute of Higher Education
Tonekabon, Iran

Farhad Hosseinzadeh Lotfi
Department of Applied Mathematics,
Science and Research Branch
Islamic Azad University
Tehran, Iran

Kristiaan Kerstens
University of Lille
CNRS, UMR 9221—LEM—Lille
Économie Management
IESEG School of Management
Lille, France

Peter Wanke
COPPEAD Graduate Business School
Federal University of Rio de Janeiro
Rio de Janeiro, Brazil

ISSN 2363-6149 ISSN 2363-6157 (electronic)
Infosys Science Foundation Series
ISSN 2364-4036 ISSN 2364-4044 (electronic)
Infosys Science Foundation Series in Mathematical Sciences
ISBN 978-981-97-6971-1 ISBN 978-981-97-6972-8 (eBook)
https://doi.org/10.1007/978-981-97-6972-8

Mathematics Subject Classification: 91B06, 90B50, 90C08, 90C70, 03B52, 90C26, 68Q15

© The Editor(s) (if applicable) and The Author(s), under exclusive license to Springer Nature Singapore Pte Ltd. 2024

This work is subject to copyright. All rights are solely and exclusively licensed by the Publisher, whether the whole or part of the material is concerned, specifically the rights of translation, reprinting, reuse of illustrations, recitation, broadcasting, reproduction on microfilms or in any other physical way, and transmission or information storage and retrieval, electronic adaptation, computer software, or by similar or dissimilar methodology now known or hereafter developed.
The use of general descriptive names, registered names, trademarks, service marks, etc. in this publication does not imply, even in the absence of a specific statement, that such names are exempt from the relevant protective laws and regulations and therefore free for general use.
The publisher, the authors and the editors are safe to assume that the advice and information in this book are believed to be true and accurate at the date of publication. Neither the publisher nor the authors or the editors give a warranty, expressed or implied, with respect to the material contained herein or for any errors or omissions that may have been made. The publisher remains neutral with regard to jurisdictional claims in published maps and institutional affiliations.

This Springer imprint is published by the registered company Springer Nature Singapore Pte Ltd.
The registered company address is: 152 Beach Road, #21-01/04 Gateway East, Singapore 189721, Singapore

If disposing of this product, please recycle the paper.

Preface

He who knows all the answers has not been asked all the questions.
—Confucius

In today's complex and rapidly changing world, decision-making is a critical task that managers and decision-makers must navigate with precision and insight. Decision making (DM), i.e., multi-criteria decision-making (MCDM) or multi-attribute decision-making (MADM), is a sub-discipline of operations research (OR) that analyzes multiple conflicting criteria in decision-making problems considering the details as much as possible. Furthermore, data envelopment analysis (DEA) is a widely used nonparametric linear programming method for assessing the efficiency and productivity of decision-making units (DMUs). The theory and applications of DEA are spread over a wide area in production and beyond and are very diverse. DEA is also compared or combined with other disciplines. Over the past few years, researchers have developed several DM or DEA (DMDEA) methods to help decision-makers analyze and solve challenging problems. Consequently, it is appropriate to prepare an edited book to bring researchers working in these diverse fields on a common ground and share their experiences. In addition, this would be a chance to give direction to future challenges/trends related to DMDEA.

This book explores the theory and applications of DMDEA, encompassing deterministic and uncertain environments. It delves into combining DEA with machine learning techniques and the fusion of DEA models with various decision-making frameworks. The chapters cover various topics, from new modeling approaches to uncertainty handling and applications in diverse sectors.

The initial chapters provide foundational concepts and recent advancements in DEA. The chapter "Merging Data Envelopment Analysis and Structural Risk Minimization: Some Examples of Use of Multi-output Machine Learning Techniques on Real-World Data" discusses how DEA can be combined with machine learning techniques to handle multi-output scenarios, improving decision-making under real-world conditions. The chapter "A New Network Data Envelopment Analysis Model for Efficacy Evaluation of Decision-Making Units" introduces a new network DEA model for evaluating DMUs, considering the network structure of processes involved, specifically applied to the Iranian airline industry. The chapter "Possibilistic Network DEA Approach for Performance Evaluation of Two-Stage Decision Making Units Under Uncertainty" presents a method for evaluating DMUs under uncertainty by using a fuzzy network DEA model.

Subsequent chapters explore the application of DEA in various industries. The chapter "Managerial Ability in Indian Life Insurance Companies: A Comparison Based on DEA and DEAGP" evaluates managerial abilities in Indian life insurance companies by using DEA and goal programming methods. The chapter "Efficiency Appraisal and Classification of Flexible Random Factors" proposes methodologies for evaluating the efficiency of organizations incorporating stochastic and flexible elements. The chapter "Performance Evaluation of Indian Banking Financial Sector by Using DEA Approach" assesses the performance of Indian banks, identifying key factors influencing efficiency. The chapter "Application of Data Envelopment Analysis in Decision Making of Civil Engineering Problems" provides practical examples of DEA applications in civil engineering.

Further chapters address advanced topics in DEA, such as robust optimization and tri-level decision-making. The chapter "A Robust Optimization Approach for Estimating the Most Productive Scale Size in Uncertain Data Envelopment Analysis" presents a novel method for estimating productive scale size under uncertainty. The chapter "Goal Programming Method for Solving Tri-Level Data Envelopment Analysis" extends the DEA model to tri-level structures, demonstrating its application through an illustrative example. The chapter "Machine Learning Techniques and Efficiency Evaluation: A Survey of Methodological Contributions" surveys the integration of machine learning with DEA, highlighting key methodological contributions. The chapter "A Literature Review for Nonparametric Frontier Methods Applied to Portfolio Analysis" summarizes research on nonparametric frontier methods in portfolio performance evaluation.

The book also delves into specific decision-making models and optimization under uncertainty, incorporating advanced fuzzy set theories. The chapter "An Optimization Algorithm to Solve Imprecisely Defined Unconstrained Optimization Problem" discusses a fuzzy optimization algorithm for imprecisely defined problems. The chapter "Examining Dimensions and Critical Success Factors of Supply Chains Based on the Blockchain and Internet of Things (B-IoT)" evaluates critical success factors for implementing a smart supply chain using IoT and blockchain technologies. The chapter "A Multi-Objective Investment Selection Problem Using Fuzzy and Intuitionistic Fuzzy Approach" develops a multi-objective linear model for investment selection using fuzzy and intuitionistic fuzzy sets. The chapter "Revolutionizing Education: An Optimal MAGDM-Based e-Learning Approach for Curriculum Beyond the Classroom" proposes a multi-attribute group decision-making model for selecting the best e-learning websites. The chapter "Balanced Neutrosophic Fermatean Graphs with Applications" explores the application of balanced neutrosophic fermatean graphs in optimizing medical treatment delivery.

The chapter "TOPSIS-Based Entropy Measure for N-Valued Neutrosophic Trapezoidal Numbers and Their Application to Multi-Criteria Decision-Making Problems" develops a multi-criteria decision-making method using N-valued neutrosophic trapezoidal numbers. The chapter "A New Decision-Making Analysis Model Based on the Transformation of Picture Fuzzy Sets into Fuzzy Sets" proposes a transformation method for picture fuzzy sets to enhance their applicability in various industrial contexts. The chapter "An Enhanced Score Function for Quadripartitioned Single-Valued Neutrosophic Sets" introduces an enhanced score function for quadripartitioned single-valued neutrosophic sets, providing a multi-criteria decision-making method.

The book comprehensively explores DMDEA and its applications in various decision-making contexts. By presenting methodological advancements, real-world applications, and future research directions, it aims to equip researchers, practitioners, and decision-makers with the tools and knowledge needed to navigate the complexities of modern decision-making. Through its detailed chapters, readers will understand how DMDEA can be utilized to improve decision-making processes, address uncertainty, and optimize performance across different sectors. By combining DEA with other decision-making models and machine learning techniques, this book showcases the versatility and practical utility of DMDEA. It highlights the importance of integrating advanced fuzzy set theories, such as intuitionistic fuzzy sets, fermatean sets, and neutrosophic sets, in handling imprecise and uncertain data. The practical case studies and empirical applications provide valuable insights into implementing DMDEA in real-world scenarios, demonstrating its effectiveness in enhancing decision-making processes.

Thanks to the dedication and expertise of many individuals who made this book possible. We extend our heartfelt gratitude to the publishing team of Springer Nature for their invaluable guidance throughout the editorial process. We also wish to thank all the contributors for sharing their insights and research, enriching the content of this volume. Additionally, we deeply appreciate the reviewers for their diligent work in evaluating the chapters and ensuring the quality of this book. We believe the chapters presented here will provide our readers with substantial knowledge and inspiration for their studies and research in the field of DMDEA. We hope students and researchers will find this book both informative and enlightening.

Tonekabon, Iran S. A. Edalatpanah
Tehran, Iran Farhad Hosseinzadeh Lotfi
Lille, France Kristiaan Kerstens
Rio de Janeiro, Brazil Peter Wanke

Contents

Merging Data Envelopment Analysis and Structural Risk Minimization: Some Examples of Use of Multi-output Machine Learning Techniques on Real-World Data

Nadia M. Guerrero, Juan Aparicio, Raul Moragues, and Daniel Valero-Carreras

Abstract Data Envelopment Analysis (DEA) is nowadays a very famous nonparametric technique for the measurement of technical efficiency. It does so by building a production possibility set that satisfies certain microeconomic and mathematical axioms, such as free disposability in inputs and outputs and convexity, and determines the most conservative estimate of technical inefficiency of each assessed unit via the minimal extrapolation principle (i.e., the Occam's Razor view). Given a data sample and from a statistical point of view, this last axiom implies an estimation of technical inefficiency by exclusively minimizing the empirical error, resulting in overfitting to the data as a by-product. To overcome this statistical problem when the objective is measuring technical inefficiency beyond the data sample, a methodology has been recently introduced which follows the Structural Risk Minimization (SRM) principle. It controls both the empirical and the generalization (prediction) error of the model. This methodology, called Data Envelopment Analysis-based Machines (DEAM) was introduced for the single-output setting [(Guerrero, Aparicio, & Valero-Carreras 2022). Combining Data Envelopment Analysis and Machine Learning. Mathematics 2022, 10, 909]. In this chapter, we extend the DEAM approach for the estimation of production functions to the multi-output production framework,

N. M. Guerrero · J. Aparicio (✉) · R. Moragues · D. Valero-Carreras
Center of Operations Research (CIO), Miguel Hernandez University, Elche, Spain
e-mail: j.aparicio@umh.es

N. M. Guerrero
e-mail: nadia.guerrero@goumh.umh.es

R. Moragues
e-mail: rmoragues@umh.es

D. Valero-Carreras
e-mail: dvalero@umh.es

J. Aparicio
ValgrAI—Valencian Graduate School and Research Network of Artificial Intelligence, Valencia, Spain

© The Author(s), under exclusive license to Springer Nature Singapore Pte Ltd. 2024
S. A. Edalatpanah et al. (eds.), *Analytical Decision Making and Data Envelopment Analysis*, Infosys Science Foundation Series in Mathematical Sciences,
https://doi.org/10.1007/978-981-97-6972-8_1

evaluate technical efficiency with respect to a variety of measures, and illustrate its performance via some empirical applications. In this way, we provide some examples of use of multi-output machine learning techniques for measuring technical efficiency on real-world data.

Keywords Data envelopment analysis · Machine learning · Support vector regression · Structural risk minimization · Multi-output production frontiers

1 Introduction

Efficiency measurement is an area of research which has grown immensely since the original definition proposed by (Koopmans, 1951) and the first approaches to their measurement by Debreu and Farrell (Debreu, 1951; Farrell, 1957). Proposed techniques are often classified into parametric and nonparametric approaches, from which some of the most extended methods are Stochastic Frontier Analysis in the parametric family (Aigner et al., 1977; Meeusen & van Den Broeck, 1977), while in the nonparametric family, Data Envelopment Analysis (DEA) has become one of the most commonly used methodologies. The parametric approach usually assumes some functional form for the production function and aims to estimate the coefficients or parameters associated with this form, using a method such as the minimization of an error function. Upon this basis, it can apply statistical inference tools to the parameters, but it requires some assumptions on the distributions of the error terms and technical inefficiency. On the other hand, the nonparametric approach does not require an a priori assumption about the shape of the production function, nor does it require assumptions about the probability distributions associated with the error terms or the data generating process. Instead, nonparametric methodologies usually base their estimation on the satisfaction of certain properties of the underlying production process. Additionally, the nonparametric approaches have a more natural multi-output extension in comparison with the parametric approaches, which necessarily represent this more complex framework through an indirect notion: the distance function (Orea & Zofío, 2019).

When measuring efficiency, it is often measured with respect to some production possibility set or technology, which consists of those combinations of resources (inputs) and products (outputs) which are feasible to be produced by the production process under study. In particular, DEA is a nonparametric technique originally introduced in (Banker et al., 1984; Charnes et al., 1978) which is based on the microeconomic assumptions on the technology of convexity, envelopment of the data, free disposability of inputs and outputs, and the principle of minimal extrapolation. The family of DEA techniques also includes different estimations of the production possibility set, or technology, according to a variety of assumptions and choices, such as returns to scale.

Regardless of the particular form of the production technology, the measurement of efficiency pays particular interest to the efficient frontier of the technology, which consists of those points which cannot be improved while remaining feasible. In this context, the technical efficiency of a Decision Making Unit (DMU) is defined as the potential improvement of said unit while remaining in the technology (reaching the efficient frontier). However, there are multiple and varied paths to improvement which can be followed to reach efficiency, with a variety of properties being satisfied by various approaches. For example, some of the first approaches introduced were the Farrell or radial measures (Farrell, 1957). The input-oriented radial measure allowed for the equiproportional reduction of the inputs while leaving the outputs constant, while the output-oriented radial measure allows for the increase in outputs while leaving the inputs constant (Banker et al., 1984; Charnes et al., 1978). In particular, the Farrell measures keep the relative proportions of the inputs (outputs), or mix, constant. Another approach to measure efficiency, the Directional Distance Function (DDF), considers an a priori specified directional vector and projects DMUs along it (Chambers et al., 1998; Luenberger, 1992). These measures do retain certain properties of the original DMU, but they do not guarantee that the projection of the DMU in question is fully efficient, since there may be potential improvements to be made along some variables but not others, and they measure so-called weak efficiency. A stronger concept is that of strong or Pareto efficiency, where the units that the projections are made into do not allow for further improvement along any of their components without the worsening of another component. In order to overcome this limitation, measures such as the Russell measures were proposed which generalise the Farrell measures. The Russell measures are still oriented, but not radial. They allow the rescaling of different input (output) variables by different amounts (Färe & Lovell, 1978). Along these lines, an alternative formulation of the DEA models using slacks along individual variables (inputs and outputs) was introduced via the additive model (Charnes et al., 1985), which was later extended by the addition to weights to the slacks, and the introduction of a variety of Weighted Additive measures of efficiency such as (Cooper et al., 1999, 2011; Tone, 2001). All these measures rely on estimations of the underlying production technology and modify the permitted improvement paths of the DMUs.

Despite all its nice properties, DEA has been criticised for its nature as a descriptive tool. In particular, the use of the principle of minimal extrapolation is an approach which aims to minimize the distance from the frontier to the dataset, which is related to exclusively minimizing the empirical error (Esteve et al., 2020). This results in overfitting to the dataset being used and a potential lack of generalization to unseen data when the sample size is small. This has led authors to turn to areas such as statistical learning in order to attempt to perform statistical inference tasks on these datasets in order to estimate more robust efficiencies. One avenue of research in this direction is the study of the asymptotic properties of the DEA estimators such as consistency, rates of convergence, and bias (Kneip et al., 1998, 2008, 2011, 2015). Building upon this, bias correction methods have been developed using bootstrapping methodologies.

Another approach towards the attempts to overcome this limitation can be found in generalization theory, and the approaches to attempt to bind not only the empirical error but also the prediction or generalization error. In this area, a fruitful and interesting direction is the Structural Risk Minimization (SRM) principle, which attempts to obtain and minimize an upper bound on the expected risk over a hypothesis class (Vapnik, 1991). These types of bounds are called Probably Approximately Correct, since they are bounds which have a small probability of the bound failing (Probably) when the bound is achieved via a classifier which has a low error rate (Approximately Correct). Then, using these bounds, techniques are developed to minimize them. A family of estimators which are related to the SRM principle is that of Support Vector Machines (SVM) (Vapnik, 1998), which aim to minimize two factors: the value of the empirical risk and the generalization error. These factors control the bound on the expected risk. In particular, Support Vector Regression adapts the SVM family to regression problems.

Based on these concepts, a recent contribution (Guerrero et al., 2022) proposed an estimator called Data Envelopment Analysis-based Machines (DEAM) to estimate polyhedral technologies satisfying microeconomic axioms as in DEA except for the minimal extrapolation principle. In that article, the authors defined a piece-wise linear hypothesis class and provided a PAC bound for the fat-shattering dimension of this class. Using these bounds, they introduced a methodology inspired by Support Vector Regression, enabling it to control the generalization error of the model, thus allowing it to generalize to unseen data. Guerrero et al., however, only introduced the technique in a single-output scenario, which is a very limited production situation in practice.

In this chapter, we will extend the DEAM technique to estimate technical efficiency in multi-input multi-output contexts. This extension satisfies the microeconomic axioms of DEA except for the minimal extrapolation principle, and estimates, as in the original DEAM technique, production technologies which do not overfit to the data. Furthermore, we will tailor the most usual list of technical efficiency measures to be used in the case of resorting to DEAM for estimating the production technology. In this sense, we will provide the mathematical programming models that should be implemented. Finally, we will illustrate the performance of the new models, in comparison with DEA, through two real-world datasets.

The area of statistical learning is also related to machine learning. The worlds of efficiency estimation and machine learning have some similarities which have recently begun to be exploited in force, with a variety of authors attempting to use techniques to avoid overfitting in efficiency estimation via the use of machine learning techniques. Some early contributions toward this area can be seen in work of (Kuosmanen & Johnson, 2010), who introduced a piecewise linear estimator called Corrected Concave Nonparametric Least Squares. Nonparametric estimators using kernels were introduced in (Du et al., 2013), and a methodology involving quadratic and cubic splines was proposed in (Daouia et al., 2016). Methods involving decision trees were tailored to measure technical efficiency in (Aparicio et al., 2021; Esteve et al., 2020) and (Tsionas, 2022), and were enriched by bagging (bootstrap aggregating) techniques such as random forest (Esteve et al., 2023) or boosting methodologies such as gradient boosting in (Guillen et al., 2023). Support Vector

Regression-inspired methods were also introduced in (Valero-Carreras et al., 2021, 2022).

The rest of this chapter is structured as follows. Section 2 briefly reviews background concepts about Data Envelopment Analysis, measures of efficiency, and the DEAM technique. Section 3 extends DEAM to the context of multi-output production processes and enriches DEAM with the measurement of efficiency with respect to multiple measures of efficiency. Section 4 illustrates the efficiencies obtained by multi-output DEAM using two empirical examples with multiple outputs. Finally, Sect. 5 presents some conclusions obtained, and outlines some potential avenues for further research.

2 Background

We begin by setting up some notation. We will denote vectors using bold characters while scalars will be in italics. We will denote the scalar product of two vectors $\boldsymbol{a}, \boldsymbol{b}$ by $\boldsymbol{ab}$, while their component-wise product will be indicated by $\boldsymbol{a} \odot \boldsymbol{b}$. We now briefly introduce the basic concepts of Data Envelopment Analysis, including a variety of measures of efficiency, and we describe the Data Envelopment Analysis-based Machines (DEAM) methodology.

Data Envelopment Analysis is a nonparametric methodology to estimate the technical efficiency of a Decision Making Unit (DMU) from the information obtained about the inputs and outputs of some observations. We consider a set of n DMUs, where unit k takes inputs $\boldsymbol{x}_k = \left(x_k^{(1)}, \ldots, x_k^{(m)}\right) \in R_+^m$ in order to produce $\boldsymbol{y}_k = \left(y_k^{(1)}, \ldots, y_k^{(s)}\right) \in R_+^s$ outputs. The data will be arranged into a matrix $X = (\boldsymbol{x}_k)$ of inputs and a matrix $Y = (\boldsymbol{y}_k)$ of outputs, where each DMU is a column of these matrices. The production possibility set, or technology, is defined in general as:

$$T = \{(\boldsymbol{x}, \boldsymbol{y}) \in R_+^{m+s} : \boldsymbol{x} \text{ can produce } \boldsymbol{y}\}. \quad (1)$$

The technical efficiency of a DMU can be defined as the improvement in inputs and/or outputs which can be performed while remaining within the production technology. Of relevance to its measurement is a particular region of the technology called the weak efficient frontier of T:

$$\delta^W(T) = \left\{(\boldsymbol{x}, \boldsymbol{y}) \in T : \hat{\boldsymbol{x}} < \boldsymbol{x}, \hat{\boldsymbol{y}} > \boldsymbol{y} \Rightarrow \left(\hat{\boldsymbol{x}}, \hat{\boldsymbol{y}}\right) \notin T\right\}. \quad (2)$$

The weak efficient frontier of a technology consists of the points that are not strictly Pareto dominated by any other points in the technology. Other forms of the efficient frontier result in slightly different definitions, such as the strong efficient frontier of T, which consists of those points for which any improvement along any variable results in leaving the technology:

$$\delta^S(T) = \{(\boldsymbol{x}, \boldsymbol{y}) \in T : \hat{\boldsymbol{x}} \leq \boldsymbol{x}, \hat{\boldsymbol{y}} \geq \boldsymbol{y}, (\hat{\boldsymbol{x}}, \hat{\boldsymbol{y}}) \neq (\boldsymbol{x}, \boldsymbol{y}) \Rightarrow (\hat{\boldsymbol{x}}, \hat{\boldsymbol{y}}) \notin T\}. \tag{3}$$

Since the theoretical technology is unknown in practice, we will work with estimates of this technology. Under Variable Returns to Scale, the DEA estimate of the technology is as follows:

$$\widehat{T}_{DEA} = \{ (\boldsymbol{x}, \boldsymbol{y}) \in R_+^{m+s} : x \geq X\lambda, y \leq Y\lambda, \lambda \geq 0, \lambda 1 = 1 \} \tag{4}$$

In particular, $\widehat{T}_{DEA}$ is the smallest set containing the observations, which satisfies convexity and free disposability in inputs and outputs (Banker et al., 1984). Convexity of the technology means that, for any two DMUs $(\boldsymbol{x}_k, \boldsymbol{y}_k)$, $(\boldsymbol{x}_l, \boldsymbol{y}_l) \in \widehat{T}_{DEA}$, then any convex linear combination of them is also feasible, that is, $\lambda_k(\boldsymbol{x}_k, \boldsymbol{y}_k) + (1 - \lambda_k)(\boldsymbol{x}_l, \boldsymbol{y}_l) \in \widehat{T}_{DEA}, 0 \leq \lambda_k \leq 1$. Free disposability in inputs and outputs assumes that, if $(\boldsymbol{x}, \boldsymbol{y}) \in \widehat{T}_{DEA}$ then, whenever $\boldsymbol{x}' \geq \boldsymbol{x}$ and $\boldsymbol{y}' \leq \boldsymbol{y}$, we have $(\boldsymbol{x}', \boldsymbol{y}') \in \widehat{T}_{DEA}$. Due to the principle of minimal extrapolation, which is related to the selection of the smallest set satisfying the previous conditions, $\widehat{T}_{DEA}$ is a conservative estimate, which will fit the data perfectly at a frontier level, but will overestimate the technical efficiency of the DMUs, since the true efficient frontier will be slightly higher and unobserved. This is due to the property of minimal extrapolation, and it is a characteristic often denoted overfitting in the data-based modelling and machine learning literature. It usually means that an estimator fits the data so well that it may not generalise to new data, which was not used to train the estimator. This is especially a problem if the objective of the study is to state something about the underlying production function of the sector instead of evaluating and ranking exclusively the set of DMUs under assessment with respect to their performance. Under the statistical approach to production theory (Daraio & Simar, 2007), there is a Data Generating Process (DGP), which is unknown for the observers, which relates inputs to outputs. We only observe a sample of n possible combinations of these inputs and outputs. At this point, researchers could be interested in determining two alternative notions of technical efficiency: relative vs absolute efficiency (Aparicio & Esteve, 2022). Data Envelopment Analysis identifies the degree of relative technical efficiency of each DMU, that is, the degree of efficiency measured in comparative terms regarding the performance of exactly the observations in the sample. On the other hand, absolute technical efficiency is the performance determined with respect to the underlying DGP. It stands to reason that, when the sample size increases significantly, the two notions (approximately) coincide by invoking some property of consistency. But this is not true in the case of relatively small sample sizes. In certain real frameworks, calculating the relative technical efficiency of each DMU may not be the only goal of the study. For example, in the well-known PISA (Programme for International Student Assessment) survey by the OECD (Organisation for Economic Co-operation and Development), researchers play with information about a (random) sample of schools of each participant (country). In fact, data are provided by OECD in such a way that it is almost impossible to recognize the schools under study. Thus, the schools are anonymous for any external observer. Consequently, estimating the efficiency of these n anonymous units (schools) in the observed sample is not the only objective. Instead, a more useful task is to go beyond it and attempt to estimate the underlying (education) production function behind the data. The information obtained about the production technology will allow a decision maker to obtain guidance in practice about how to improve performance in the actual units (schools), instead of on this sample of anonymous observations, where it may not be very useful. In this context, determining absolute technical efficiency could make more sense than identifying relative technical efficiency. In particular, one of the real-world datasets that we will use to illustrate the performance of our model corresponds to information provided in the PISA report. Additionally, even in the case of having information about all the units that make up a given population (for example, all banks in Europe, all tax offices in a country, etc.), we could suppose, as it is usual to assume in Statistics, that these observations are a random sample of all the different combinations that we could have observed. Behind these observations is the DGP and we could be interested in assessing each DMU with respect to it rather than exclusively the observed performance of the remaining units in the population under evaluation. Although we recognize that, in this second scenario, researchers might be tempted to exclusively measure relative efficiency due to having data about all the elements of the population. In this sense, relative efficiency would work as a descriptive tool of the performance in the sample and the calculation of absolute efficiency could be seen as complementary information (determined from an inferential perspective). We will also illustrate our approach using a framework like the last one mentioned here.

With respect to $\widehat{T}_{DEA}$, or any production technology satisfying similar microeconomic axioms, a variety of measures of efficiency have been proposed, which relate to the distance of each DMU to the frontier (weak or strong). These are various ways of considering how to improve the efficiency of a DMU, which may be accomplished by increasing the produced outputs without increasing the required inputs, by producing the same outputs with fewer inputs, or a combination of these two approaches. We next present this variety of measures.

2.1 *Measures of Technical Efficiency in Efficiency Analysis*

In general terms, the technical efficiency level of a DMU k is defined as the distance between the input–output bundle $(\boldsymbol{x}_k, \boldsymbol{y}_k)$ and the so-called efficient frontier of a technology T, defined as those points whose efficiency cannot be increased without leaving the technology. The radial measures of efficiency are some of the first proposed methods for measuring technical efficiency (Farrell, 1957). The output-oriented radial measure (RO) maintains the inputs of each DMU constant while increasing every output by the same scalar value ϕ:

$$\phi(\boldsymbol{x}, \boldsymbol{y}) = max\{\phi : (\boldsymbol{x}, \phi\boldsymbol{y}) \in T\}. \tag{5}$$

Similarly, the input-oriented radial measure (RI) keeps the output values constant while scaling all inputs equiproportionally by a scalar θ (Banker et al., 1984). It is defined by:

$$\theta(\boldsymbol{x}, \boldsymbol{y}) = min\{\theta : (\theta \boldsymbol{x}, \boldsymbol{y}) \in T\}. \tag{6}$$

These measures have a radial orientation, as they scale all inputs or outputs by the same amount. They keep the mix of outputs (inputs) constant. Another approach, the directional distance function (DDF) (Chambers et al., 1998; Luenberger, 1992), considers the potential improvement along a direction specified by a nonzero vector $\boldsymbol{g} = \left(\boldsymbol{g}_0^x, \boldsymbol{g}_0^y\right)$, where $\boldsymbol{g}_0^x \in R_+^m$ and $\boldsymbol{g}_0^y \in R_+^s$, as a measure of inefficiency β of an input–output bundle $(\boldsymbol{x}, \boldsymbol{y})$ given by the following program:

$$\beta(\boldsymbol{x}, \boldsymbol{y}) = max\left\{\beta : \left(\boldsymbol{x} - \beta \boldsymbol{g}_0^x, \boldsymbol{y} + \beta \boldsymbol{g}_0^y\right) \in T\right\}. \tag{7}$$

Regarding the directional vector $\boldsymbol{g}$, in this chapter, we particularly use the values of the DMU itself, that is, $\boldsymbol{g} = (\boldsymbol{x}, \boldsymbol{y})$. The measures described so far, RI, RO and DDF, project DMUs to the weak efficient frontier of the technology in either a radial direction or a direction previously specified. At this stage, some extra improvement may still be possible, but not simultaneously in all inputs (outputs), by focusing on the strong efficient frontier.

Other proposals directly project DMUs to the strong efficient frontier. For example, an alternative model, which measures slacks independently along each variable, is the weighted additive (WA) model (Knox Lovell & Pastor, 1995). Using the weighted additive model, the Range Adjusted Measure (Cooper et al., 1999) is defined by choosing weights as follows. Let $R_j^- = \overline{x}_j - \underline{x}_j$ and $R_r^+ = \overline{y}_r - \underline{y}_r$ be the range of each variable. Then, the WA uses weights $\left(\boldsymbol{\alpha}_o^x, \boldsymbol{\mu}_o^y\right) \in R_{++}^{m+s}$, where $\boldsymbol{\alpha}_0^{x(j)} = \frac{1}{(m+s)R_j^-}$ and $\boldsymbol{\mu}_0^{y(r)} = \frac{1}{(m+s)R_r^+}$:

$$WA(\boldsymbol{x}, \boldsymbol{y}) = max\left\{\boldsymbol{\alpha}_0^x \boldsymbol{s}_0^x + \boldsymbol{\mu}_0^y \boldsymbol{s}_0^y \in R : \left(\boldsymbol{x} - \boldsymbol{s}_0^x, \boldsymbol{y} + \boldsymbol{s}_0^y\right) \in T, \left(\boldsymbol{s}_0^x, \boldsymbol{s}_0^y\right) \in R_+^{m+s}\right\}. \tag{8}$$

A generalization of the radial measures which we also consider are the Russell measures, which scale each input (output) by a different constant (Färe & Lovell, 1978). This allows for the identification of inefficiencies in some variables. The input-oriented Russell model (RUI) scales each input j by a scalar $0 \leq \theta^{(j)} \leq 1$, and is given by:

$$RUI(x, y) = min\left\{\frac{1}{m}\sum\nolimits_{(j=1)}^{m} \theta^{(j)} : (\theta \ominus x, y) \in T,\ 0 \leq \theta \leq 1\right\}. \tag{9}$$

Similarly, the output-oriented Russell model (RUO), which allows for the increase of each output by a different factor, is given by:

$$RUO(x, y) = max\left\{\frac{1}{s}\sum\nolimits_{r=1}^{s}\phi^{(r)} : (x, \phi \ominus y) \in T, \phi \geq 1\right\}. \tag{10}$$

The final measure that we consider is the Enhanced Rusell Graph (ERG) measure, introduced in (Pastor et al., 1999) and (Tone, 2001), which uses the ratio between the terms in the Russell Input and Output measures. This model is not linear, but it can be linearized using a slacks-based model via a standard transformation in the literature:

$$ERG(x, y) = min\left\{\left(\frac{1}{m}\sum\nolimits_{j=1}^{m}\theta^{(j)}\right)/\left(\frac{1}{s}\sum\nolimits_{r=1}^{s}\phi^{(r)}\right) : (\theta \ominus x, \phi \ominus y) \in T, \phi \geq 1, 0 \leq \theta \leq 1\right\}. \tag{11}$$

In this chapter, we adapt each of the measures presented to the proposed multi-output generalization of DEAM in (Guerrero et al., 2022). Also, we will compare the efficiency scores obtained by DEA and multi-output DEAM with respect to each measure in empirical examples. We remark that the comparisons between efficiency scores are only appropriate when comparing efficiencies calculated with respect to the same measure with respect to each model, since different measures have different properties and cannot be compared.

We remark here the different nature of some of the measures. The Radial Input and Russell input measures are input-oriented, such that values of 1 indicate technical efficiency, and the obtained efficiency values lie between 0 and 1. On the other hand, the Radial Output and Russell Output measures have the property that the efficient units attain the value 1, and larger values indicate lower efficiency, since their outputs can be increased by larger amounts while remaining feasible. The DDF and the WA measure can be considered measures of inefficiency, since efficient units achieve a score of 0, and larger values indicate less efficiency. Finally, the ERG provides values between 0 and 1, with this last value signaling efficiency.

2.2 Data Envelopment Analysis-Based Machines

We now present the basics of Data Envelopment Analysis-based Machines as introduced in (Guerrero et al., 2022), where the single-output multi-input model was stated. This technique is useful to estimate production technologies, without suffering from overfitting, via the implementation of bounds on the generalization error of the model following the Structural Risk Minimization (SRM) principle. The DEAM model is:

$$
\begin{aligned}
\underset{w,\beta,\delta,\xi,\xi\prime,u,v}{Min} \quad & u+v+C\left(\textstyle\sum_{i=1}^{n}\xi_i^2+\sum_{i=1}^{n}\xi_i\prime^2\right) \\
s.t. \quad & \\
& \|\boldsymbol{w}_i\|_1 \le u & \forall i=1,\ldots,n \quad (12.1) \\
& \beta_i \le v & \forall i=1,\ldots,n \quad (12.2) \\
& \delta_p y_i \le \boldsymbol{w}_p\boldsymbol{x}_i+\beta_p & \forall i,p=1,\ldots,n \quad (12.3) \\
& \boldsymbol{w}_i,\delta_i \ge 0 & \forall i=1,\ldots,n \quad (12.4) \\
& \boldsymbol{w}_i\boldsymbol{x}_i+\beta_i-\delta_i y_i \le \varepsilon+\xi_i & \forall i=1,\ldots,n \quad (12.5) \\
& \delta_i y_i-\boldsymbol{w}_i\boldsymbol{x}_i-\beta_i \le \varepsilon+\xi_i\prime & \forall i=1,\ldots,n \quad (12.6) \\
& \xi_i,\xi_i\prime \ge 0 & \forall i=1,\ldots,n \quad (12.7) \\
& \|(\boldsymbol{w}_i,\delta_i)\|_1 = 1 & \forall i=1,\ldots,n \quad (12.8) \\
& \boldsymbol{w}_i\boldsymbol{x}_i+\beta_i-\delta_i y_i \le \boldsymbol{w}_p\boldsymbol{x}_i+\beta_p-\delta_p y_i & \forall i,p=1,\ldots,n \quad (12.9)
\end{aligned}
\tag{12}
$$

This model is a Support Vector Regression-inspired model where the terms u and v are bounds to each of the components in the fat-shattering bound obtained for a class of piece-wise linear hypothesis classes in (Theorem 3, Guerrero et al., 2022). This model involves a number n of half-spaces (and corresponding hyperplanes), which estimate a polyhedral production technology via their intersection. The first two conditions (12.1) and (12.2) ensure that the bounds on the generalization error hold, using the 1-norm, which is linear, for consistency with (12.8). Constraint (12.3) guarantees that the estimated production technology envelops the data from above, by forcing each hyperplane to be above the data. Moreover, constraint (12.4) ensures free disposability (see (Kuosmanen & Johnson, 2010)). The constraints (12.5), (12.6) and (12.7) relate to the variables $\xi\prime s$, which, at optimum, can be interpreted as the l_∞ distance from the observation to a 'robust' definition of efficient frontier, which uses the notion of margin (here represented by ε). Given that this frontier is made up of hyperplanes, the distance is achieved in one of them. Finally, this hyperplane is guaranteed to be the one closest to the observation by restriction (12.9).

The DEAM model also involves two hyperparameters, C and ε, which will be chosen by cross-validation. The hyperparameter C weighs the terms in the objective function, which combines the empirical error term involving ξ and the bound term $u+v$. The other hyperparameter, ε, is a margin hyperparameter, which adds robustness to SVR and DEAM.

The technology estimated by the single-output DEAM is a piece-wise linear technology that can be defined as

$$
\hat{T}_{DEAM} := \left\{(x,\ y) \in R_+^{m+1} : \mathbf{w}_p^* x + \beta_p^* - \delta_p^* y \ge 0,\ \forall p \in \{1,\ \ldots,\ n\}\right\},
$$

given an optimal solution $(\{\mathbf{w}_p^*,\ \beta_p^*,\ \delta_p^*,\ \xi_p^*,\ \xi_p^{*'}\}_{p=1,\ldots,n},\ u^*,\ v^*)$ of model (12). This technology is the intersection of the half-spaces defined by the set of n hyperplanes identified by the model at optimum. It satisfies convexity and free disposability

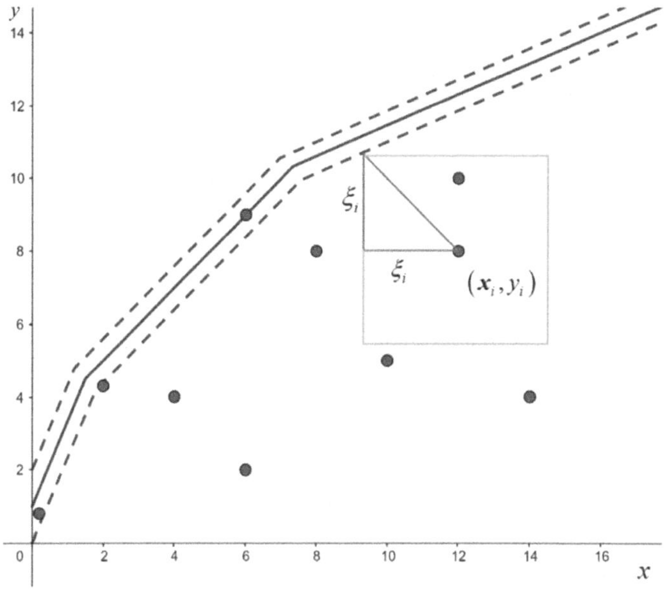

Fig. 1 Illustration of the DEAM estimation of a production function in a single-input single-output example

(Propositions 1 and 2, Guerrero et al., 2022) and includes all the observations. Consequently, it contains the DEA-estimated technology as a subset (Corollary 1, Guerrero et al., 2022).

Figure 1 illustrates the technology that can be estimated by DEAM in a single-input single-output example. The solid line represents the efficient frontier, whereas the dashed lines indicate its corresponding robust estimate (plus/minus the margin ε). The DEAM technology, i.e., the intersection between the non-negative orthant and the half-spaces defined from the hyperplanes, is a polyhedron. The technology contains all the DMUs, is a convex set and satisfies free disposability. However, it does not meet the minimal extrapolation principle. Additionally, the value of the variable ξ_i at optimum represents the least distance from DMU_i to the margin (using the l_∞-norm).

3 Methodology

In this section, we extend the DEAM model to the multi-output context. To do that, we will provide a natural extension of the single-output model by transforming the product of scalars δy into the product of corresponding vectors $\boldsymbol{\delta y}$. Accordingly, the multi-output DEAM model is as follows:

$$\begin{aligned}
\underset{w,\beta,\delta,\xi,\xi\prime,u,v}{Min} \quad & u + v + C\left(\sum_{i=1}^{n}\xi_i^2 + \sum_{i=1}^{n}\xi_{i}\prime^2\right) & & \\
s.t. \quad & & & \\
& \|\boldsymbol{w}_i\|_1 \leq u & \forall i = 1, \ldots, n \quad & (13.1) \\
& \beta_i \leq v & \forall i = 1, \ldots, n \quad & (13.2) \\
& \boldsymbol{\delta}_p \boldsymbol{y}_i \leq \boldsymbol{w}_p \boldsymbol{x}_i + \beta_p & \forall i, p = 1, \ldots, n \quad & (13.3) \\
& \boldsymbol{w}_i, \boldsymbol{\delta}_i \geq 0 & \forall i = 1, \ldots, n \quad & (13.4) \\
& \boldsymbol{w}_i \boldsymbol{x}_i + \beta_i - \boldsymbol{\delta}_i \boldsymbol{y}_i \leq \varepsilon + \xi_i & \forall i = 1, \ldots, n \quad & (13.5) \\
& \boldsymbol{\delta}_i \boldsymbol{y}_i - \boldsymbol{w}_i \boldsymbol{x}_i - \beta_i \leq \varepsilon + \xi_{i}\prime & \forall i = 1, \ldots, n \quad & (13.6) \\
& \xi_i, \xi_{i}\prime \geq 0 & \forall i = 1, \ldots, n \quad & (13.7) \\
& \|(\boldsymbol{w}_i, \boldsymbol{\delta}_i)\|_1 = 1 & \forall i = 1, \ldots, n \quad & (13.8) \\
& \boldsymbol{w}_i \boldsymbol{x}_i + \beta_i - \boldsymbol{\delta}_i \boldsymbol{y}_i \leq \boldsymbol{w}_p \boldsymbol{x}_i + \beta_p - \boldsymbol{\delta}_p \boldsymbol{y}_i & \forall i, p = 1, \ldots, n \quad & (13.9)
\end{aligned} \tag{13}$$

This model extends DEAM to the multi-output context by considering a number s of outputs, so that the hyperplanes envelop the data in every output simultaneously, where now, correspondingly, each $\boldsymbol{\delta}_p$ is a vector with s components. Its production technology is defined as the intersection of a number of at most n different hyperplanes estimated by the model, so that multi-output DEAM provides a convex, piece-wise linear technology which, given an optimal solution $(\{w_p^*,\ \beta_p^*,\ \delta_p^*,\ \xi_p^*,\ \xi_p^{*'}\}_{p=1,\ldots,n},\ u^*,\ v^*)$ of model (13), is defined by:

$$\widehat{T}_{DEAM} := \left\{(\boldsymbol{x}, \boldsymbol{y}) \in R_+^{m+s} : \boldsymbol{w}_p^* \boldsymbol{x} + \beta_p^* - \boldsymbol{\delta}_p^* \boldsymbol{y} \geq 0, \forall p \in \{1, \ldots, n\}\right\}.$$

This estimator satisfies the properties of envelopment of the data, convexity and free disposability of inputs and outputs, inherited from the single-output model.

Proposition 1. $\widehat{T}_{DEAM}$ is a convex set.

Proof. $\widehat{T}_{DEAM}$ is defined as the intersection of a set of half-spaces, which is a convex set. ■

Proposition 2. $\widehat{T}_{DEAM}$ satisfies free disposability of inputs and outputs.

Proof. Free disposability holds as $\boldsymbol{w}_i, \boldsymbol{\delta}_i \geq 0$ for all $i = 1, \ldots, n$, which is guaranteed by constraint (13.4). See (Kuosmanen & Johnson, 2010). ■

Proposition 3. $\widehat{T}_{DEAM}$ envelops the data. That is, $(\boldsymbol{x}_k, \boldsymbol{y}_k) \in \widehat{T}_{DEAM}$ for all $k \in \{1, \ldots, n\}$.

Proof. Let $(\boldsymbol{x}_k, \boldsymbol{y}_k)$ be an observation. Then, by constraint (13.3), $\boldsymbol{w}_p \boldsymbol{x}_k + \beta_p - \boldsymbol{\delta}_p \boldsymbol{y}_k \geq 0$ for all $p = 1, \ldots, n$. This guarantees that every hyperplane envelops the data from above. Thus, so does their intersection, $\widehat{T}_{DEAM}$. Therefore, $(\boldsymbol{x}_k, \boldsymbol{y}_k) \in \widehat{T}_{DEAM}$ ■.

By collecting these results together, we also satisfy the property that $\widehat{T}_{DEA} \subseteq \widehat{T}_{DEAM}$, in other words, the technology estimated by the multi-output DEAM estimator contains the DEA estimate of the technology as a subset. The hyperparameters

C and ε involved in the DEAM model will be tuned using a train-test split with a set of possible values for each hyperparameter.

Next, we adapt the list of most usual efficiency measures in DEA to be calculated with respect to the technology $\widehat{T}_{DEAM}$. The adaptation is performed by substituting $\widehat{T}_{DEAM}$ instead of the generic technology T in the corresponding definitions from Sect. 2. In particular, we show the models which calculate the efficiency of a generic input–output bundle $(\boldsymbol{x}_0, \boldsymbol{y}_0)$. We begin with the input-oriented radial measure (RI), which is calculated via the linear program:

$$\begin{aligned} min_{\theta,\boldsymbol{x},\boldsymbol{y}} \quad & \theta \\ s.t. \quad & \boldsymbol{x} \le \theta \boldsymbol{x}_o, \\ & \boldsymbol{y} \ge \boldsymbol{y}_o, \\ & \boldsymbol{w}_p^* \boldsymbol{x} + \beta_p^* - \boldsymbol{\delta}_p^* \boldsymbol{y} \ge 0,\ p = 1, \ldots, n \\ & \boldsymbol{x}, \boldsymbol{y} \ge 0 \end{aligned} \tag{14}$$

Similarly, the output-oriented radial measure (RO) is calculated using:

$$\begin{aligned} max_{\phi,\boldsymbol{x},\boldsymbol{y}} \quad & \phi \\ s.t. \quad & \boldsymbol{x} \le \boldsymbol{x}_o, \\ & \boldsymbol{y} \ge \phi \boldsymbol{y}_o, \\ & \boldsymbol{w}_p^* \boldsymbol{x} + \beta_p^* - \boldsymbol{\delta}_p^* \boldsymbol{y} \ge 0,\ p = 1, \ldots, n \\ & \boldsymbol{x}, \boldsymbol{y} \ge 0 \end{aligned} \tag{15}$$

We now adapt the DDF with directional vector $\boldsymbol{g} = \left(\boldsymbol{g}_o^x, \boldsymbol{g}_o^y\right) \in R_+^{m+s}$. Later, in the section devoted to the empirical applications, we will use the values of the DMU itself as components of the directional vector, that is, $\boldsymbol{g} = \left(\boldsymbol{x}_0, \boldsymbol{y}_0\right)$:

$$\begin{aligned} max_{\beta,\boldsymbol{x},\boldsymbol{y}} \quad & \beta \\ s.t. \quad & \boldsymbol{x} \le \boldsymbol{x}_o - \beta \boldsymbol{g}_o^x, \\ & \boldsymbol{y} \ge \boldsymbol{y}_o + \beta \boldsymbol{g}_o^y, \\ & \boldsymbol{w}_p^* \boldsymbol{x} + \beta_p^* - \boldsymbol{\delta}_p^* \boldsymbol{y} \ge 0,\ p = 1, \ldots, n \\ & \boldsymbol{x}, \boldsymbol{y} \ge 0 \end{aligned} \tag{16}$$

The next measure which we present is the Weighted Additive (WA) measure with weights $\left(\boldsymbol{\alpha}_o^x, \boldsymbol{\mu}_o^y\right) \in R_{++}^{m+s}$. In the applications shown in this chapter, we choose the weights corresponding to the Range Adjusted Measure, that is, we consider weights $\boldsymbol{\alpha}_0^{x(j)} = \frac{1}{(m+s)R_j^-}$ and $\boldsymbol{\mu}_0^{y(r)} = \frac{1}{(m+s)R_r^+}$, where $R_j^- = \overline{x}_j - \underline{x}_j$ and $R_r^+ = \overline{y}_r - \underline{y}_r$ are the ranges of values of each variable. The WA is calculated by solving the slacks-based linear model as follows:

$$\begin{aligned} max_{s_0^x, s_0^y, x, y} \quad & \alpha_o^x s_o^x + \mu_o^y s_o^y \\ s.t. \quad & x \le x_o - s_o^x, \\ & y \ge y_o + s_o^y, \\ & w_p^* x + \beta_p^* - \delta_p^* y \ge 0, \; p = 1, \ldots, n \\ & x, y, s_o^x, s_o^y \ge 0 \end{aligned} \tag{17}$$

The Russell Input measure (RUI) is calculated by solving:

$$\begin{aligned} min_{\theta, x, y} \quad & \frac{1}{m} \sum_{j=1}^{m} \theta^{(j)} \\ s.t. \quad & x^{(j)} \le \theta^{(j)} x_o^{(j)}, \quad j = 1, \ldots, m \\ & y \ge y_o, \\ & w_p^* x + \beta_p^* - \delta_p^* y \ge 0, \; p = 1, \ldots, n \\ & x, y \ge 0, \theta \le 1 \end{aligned} \tag{18}$$

Analogously, the Russell Output-oriented measure (RUO) has the following model:

$$\begin{aligned} max_{\phi, x, y} \quad & \frac{1}{s} \sum_{r=1}^{s} \phi^{(r)} \\ s.t. \quad & x \le x_o, \\ & y^{(r)} \ge \phi^{(r)} y_o^{(r)}, \quad r = 1, \ldots, s \\ & w_p^* x + \beta_p^* - \delta_p^* y \ge 0, \; p = 1, \ldots, n \\ & x, y \ge 0, \phi \ge 1 \end{aligned} \tag{19}$$

Finally, the Enhanced Russell Graph (ERG) measure requires a bit more work. It is a solution of the following nonlinear problem:

$$\begin{aligned} min_{\theta, \phi, x, y} \quad & \frac{\frac{1}{m} \sum_{j=1}^{m} \theta^{(j)}}{\frac{1}{s} \sum_{r=1}^{s} \phi^{(r)}} \\ s.t. \quad & x^{(j)} \le \theta^{(j)} x_o^{(j)}, \quad j = 1, \ldots, m \\ & y^{(r)} \ge \phi^{(r)} y_o^{(r)}, \quad r = 1, \ldots, s \\ & w_p^* x + \beta_p^* - \delta_p^* y \ge 0, \quad p = 1, \ldots, n \\ & x, y \ge 0, \phi \ge 1, \theta \le 1 \end{aligned} \tag{20}$$

This problem is not linear, but it can be converted into a linear problem by considering as a basis its associated slacks-based formulation (Tone, 2001):

$$\begin{aligned} min_{s_0^x, s_0^y, x, y} \quad & \frac{1 - \frac{1}{m} \sum_{j=1}^{m} \frac{s_o^{x(j)}}{x_o^{(j)}}}{1 + \frac{1}{s} \sum_{r=1}^{s} \frac{s_o^{y(r)}}{y_o^{(r)}}} \\ s.t. \quad & x \le x_o - s_o^x, \\ & y \ge y_o + s_o^y, \\ & w_p^* x + \beta_p^* - \delta_p^* y \ge 0, \; p = 1, \ldots, n \\ & x, y, s_o^x, s_o^y \ge 0 \end{aligned} \tag{21}$$

This model can be linearized using the method of (Charnes & Cooper, 1962), where they normalise the denominator to one via an auxiliary variable $\chi = \left(1 + \frac{1}{s}\sum_{r=1}^{s} \frac{t_o^{y(r)}}{y_o^{(r)}}\right)^{-1} > 0$. We then define transformed slack variables by $\boldsymbol{t}_0^x = \chi \boldsymbol{s}_0^x$ and $\boldsymbol{t}_0^y = \chi \boldsymbol{s}_0^y$, and substitute the original input and output vectors via $\widetilde{\boldsymbol{x}} = \chi \boldsymbol{x}$ and $\widetilde{\boldsymbol{y}} = \chi \boldsymbol{y}$. This results in the following linear problem in $\chi, \boldsymbol{t}_0^x, \boldsymbol{t}_0^y, \widetilde{\boldsymbol{x}}, \widetilde{\boldsymbol{y}}$, which we solve:

$$
\begin{array}{ll}
min_{\chi, t_o^x, t_o^y, \widetilde{x}, \widetilde{y}} & \chi - \frac{1}{m}\sum_{j=1}^{m} \frac{t_o^{x(j)}}{x_o^{(j)}} \\
s.t. & \chi + \frac{1}{s}\sum_{r=1}^{s} \frac{t_o^{y(r)}}{y_o^{(r)}} = 1, \\
& \widetilde{\boldsymbol{x}} \leq \chi \boldsymbol{x}_o - \boldsymbol{t}_o^x, \\
& \widetilde{\boldsymbol{y}} \geq \chi \boldsymbol{y}_o + \boldsymbol{t}_o^y, \\
& \boldsymbol{w}_p^* \widetilde{\boldsymbol{x}} + \chi \beta_p^* - \boldsymbol{\delta}_p^* \widetilde{\boldsymbol{y}} \geq 0, \; p = 1, \ldots, n \\
& \widetilde{\boldsymbol{x}}, \widetilde{\boldsymbol{y}}, \boldsymbol{t}_o^x, \boldsymbol{t}_o^y \geq 0, \\
& \chi \geq 0
\end{array}
\tag{22}
$$

Thus, we can calculate all six measures by solving linear programming models.

4 Computational Experiences

In this section, we illustrate the use of the multi-output DEAM model using two empirical datasets. We use these two examples to illustrate the efficiencies obtained with respect to the various measures introduced using both models, and the differences between DEAM and DEA.

The first dataset contains 51 schools located in the region of Madrid (Spain). The dataset comes from the Organisation for Economic Co-operation and Development (OECD), from its report on the quality of teaching in countries through the Programme for International Student Assessment (PISA) (OECD, 2014). The second dataset, used in (Aparicio et al., 2020), contains 44 DMUs. In this case, the DMUs are regional tax offices in Spain that oversee the tax collection in almost all Spanish provinces.

We calculate the efficiency of each DMU according to the six measures of efficiency presented in the previous section. These are the Radial measures (both input and output-oriented; RI and RO), the Directional Distance Function (DDF), the Weighted Additive (WA) measure, the Russell measures (RUI, RUO), and the Enhanced Russell Graph (ERG).

We recall that the input-oriented measures of efficiency (RI and RUI) have efficient units with a score of 1, and their range of possible values is (0,1]. Meanwhile, the output-oriented measures (RO and RUO) also have values of 1 for efficient units, but in these case inefficient DMUs have values strictly greater than 1. The DDF and WA are measures of inefficiency and thus efficient units achieve values of 0, while inefficient units attain strictly positive values. Finally, the ERG also has values in (0,1], with efficient units achieving the value 1.

The DEAM estimates of the efficiencies were obtained by first selecting the best hyperparameters from a grid of possible values. In particular, $C \in \{1,10,50,100,10^6\}$, while $\varepsilon \in \{0,0.001,0.01,0.1,0.2,0.3,0.4,0.5,1\}$. The dataset was split, at random, into a training set consisting of two thirds of the DMUs while the remaining third was reserved for the test set. Once the best hyperparameters were selected with this train-test split, the DEAM model was solved on the whole dataset and the efficiency of each DMU was calculated for each measure of efficiency.

The models were solved using a PC with an Intel® Core™ i7-8700 CPU 3.2 GHz with 6 cores, 32 Gigabyte of RAM and operating system Windows 10 Home 64 bit. CPLEX v12.10 was used to solve the optimization problems. DEAM spent 143 s on the first dataset, and 74 s for the second one.

4.1 Schools in Madrid

The first dataset that we consider comes from the education context. It is a dataset obtained from the PISA report by the OECD in 2012, where the DMUs are schools in the region of Madrid, in Spain. The inputs used are the quality of the educational resources of the school (SCMATEDU, x_1), the economic, social and cultural status index of the students (ESCS, x_2), and the number of teachers per (hundred) students (TEACHERS, x_3). This means that one indicator represents the physical resources available, one represents the socioeconomic status of the students, and one represents the human capital in each school. The variables used as outputs of the process are the scores in standardized tests in mathematics (PVMATH, y_1) and reading (PVREAD, y_2). The dataset is made up of 51 schools that were selected by the OECD at random as a representative sample of the schools in the region of Madrid. Note how, in this situation, it seems more interesting to determine absolute technical efficiency rather than relative technical efficiency, since we do not have information about all the schools in this region of Spain. Additionally, DEAM is able to provide certain insights on the education production function of the sector beyond the sample observed.

The efficiencies calculated by DEA and DEAM with respect to each measure are reported in Table 1. Each row indicates one DMU, with the final rows indicating the average efficiency obtained by each method and the number of DMUs considered efficient in each case. We observe a higher value of average inefficiency estimated by DEAM than DEA in all measures. This is because the DEA frontier is closer to the data than the DEAM frontier, as a consequence of the minimal extrapolation principle. In contrast, DEAM tries to estimate the actual education production function that is behind the generation of this particular sample of schools. Additionally, the differences in the average efficiency values range between 2 and 25%, with the latter attained at the DDF. Furthermore, Fig. 2 shows the distributions of the efficiencies measured by both methods.

Table 1 Results on the PISA dataset involving schools in Madrid

						DEA							DEAM						
DMU	x_1	x_2	x_3	y_1	y_2	RI	RO	DDF	WA	RUI	RUO	ERG	RI	RO	DDF	WA	RUI	RUO	ERG
1	2.547	5.28	7.669	538.1	540.12	0.943	1.010	0.009	0.065	0.912	1.011	0.911	0.896	1.054	0.035	0.110	0.888	1.071	0.880
2	3.886	5.61	8.355	526.55	541.01	0.774	1.056	0.051	0.226	0.725	1.066	0.724	0.770	1.140	0.088	0.240	0.715	1.158	0.705
3	3.43	3.91	0.719	462.92	435.57	1.000	1.000	0.000	0.000	1.000	1.000	1.000	1.000	1.000	0.000	0.002	0.996	1.000	0.989
4	3.079	4.52	5.569	482.7	504.57	0.907	1.064	0.043	0.121	0.857	1.083	0.843	0.900	1.078	0.049	0.127	0.834	1.090	0.829
5	5.576	4.27	9.219	475.03	490.62	0.879	1.124	0.068	0.346	0.622	1.124	0.611	0.840	1.159	0.089	0.357	0.609	1.174	0.601
6	3.618	5.34	7.858	515.33	497.42	0.790	1.102	0.079	0.256	0.733	1.115	0.707	0.790	1.134	0.085	0.259	0.717	1.188	0.698
7	2.73	4.83	7.426	522	501.03	0.893	1.038	0.029	0.137	0.864	1.066	0.831	0.893	1.054	0.036	0.145	0.842	1.111	0.822
8	3.43	3.56	8.293	466.25	462.29	1.000	1.000	0.000	0.000	1.000	1.000	1.000	1.000	1.000	0.000	0.009	0.988	1.000	0.961
9	3.43	4.55	5.504	521.99	528.37	0.962	1.023	0.015	0.053	0.925	1.028	0.924	0.953	1.027	0.017	0.065	0.902	1.031	0.891
10	3.618	4.31	7.843	439.71	477.43	0.876	1.176	0.079	0.278	0.712	1.187	0.677	0.872	1.195	0.091	0.283	0.680	1.203	0.664
11	5.576	5.89	8.247	575.22	596.57	1.000	1.000	0.000	0.000	1.000	1.000	1.000	0.859	1.087	0.054	0.233	0.773	1.092	0.773
12	3.824	4.24	12.55	476.09	485.35	0.873	1.117	0.065	0.296	0.660	1.127	0.639	0.867	1.119	0.073	0.311	0.643	1.169	0.633
13	4.352	5.64	8.055	502.06	491.3	0.721	1.145	0.126	0.350	0.639	1.157	0.627	0.721	1.208	0.127	0.354	0.629	1.249	0.618
14	4.352	5.6	6.407	563.5	559.93	0.912	1.020	0.019	0.104	0.898	1.021	0.898	0.888	1.064	0.041	0.131	0.857	1.072	0.851
15	4.352	3.76	10.241	399.56	462.14	0.947	1.070	0.030	0.235	0.765	1.141	0.703	0.930	1.143	0.051	0.266	0.707	1.188	0.664
16	3.618	4.89	7.341	488.98	475.76	0.808	1.148	0.096	0.265	0.695	1.166	0.689	0.806	1.150	0.096	0.269	0.684	1.196	0.677
17	4.352	4.48	6.818	527.74	518.22	0.944	1.041	0.025	0.155	0.826	1.049	0.812	0.943	1.042	0.025	0.177	0.808	1.071	0.794
18	2.73	4.03	7.979	506.97	517.54	1.000	1.000	0.000	0.000	1.000	1.000	1.000	1.000	1.000	0.000	0.021	0.920	1.000	0.973
19	2.353	4.98	8.432	487.05	489.73	0.910	1.101	0.072	0.202	0.837	1.103	0.783	0.875	1.132	0.087	0.206	0.762	1.144	0.763
20	3.252	4.53	8.139	485.73	488.29	0.868	1.114	0.073	0.214	0.736	1.134	0.732	0.866	1.114	0.074	0.218	0.717	1.154	0.717
21	3.824	4.79	6.677	557.72	558.29	0.995	1.002	0.001	0.016	0.962	1.005	0.962	0.993	1.003	0.002	0.050	0.948	1.017	0.933

(continued)

Table 1 (continued)

						DEA							DEAM						
DMU	x_1	x_2	x_3	y_1	y_2	RI	RO	DDF	WA	RUI	RUO	ERG	RI	RO	DDF	WA	RUI	RUO	ERG
22	3.618	3.89	9.254	481.47	484.08	0.955	1.039	0.021	0.102	0.826	1.046	0.825	0.943	1.056	0.030	0.129	0.783	1.079	0.802
23	4.061	4.91	11.801	518.66	520.18	0.835	1.089	0.062	0.279	0.652	1.090	0.639	0.830	1.095	0.062	0.283	0.646	1.152	0.635
24	3.252	4.06	8.379	455.6	490.63	0.936	1.106	0.042	0.148	0.797	1.112	0.769	0.935	1.133	0.048	0.179	0.783	1.137	0.757
25	3.824	5.16	4.889	535.09	515.14	0.932	1.021	0.016	0.084	0.927	1.030	0.920	0.906	1.049	0.032	0.100	0.880	1.063	0.874
26	3.252	3.86	10.131	450.2	465.29	0.966	1.095	0.033	0.143	0.810	1.095	0.788	0.966	1.115	0.034	0.171	0.780	1.116	0.766
27	5.576	4.17	7.986	544.77	531.85	1.000	1.000	0.000	0.000	1.000	1.000	1.000	1.000	1.000	0.000	0.012	0.999	1.000	0.970
28	3.252	5.37	7.253	559.58	530.52	0.977	1.005	0.005	0.063	0.943	1.026	0.925	0.924	1.040	0.026	0.134	0.909	1.091	0.875
29	3.252	5.35	8.157	514.38	507.43	0.789	1.093	0.071	0.229	0.744	1.094	0.726	0.789	1.130	0.083	0.233	0.726	1.178	0.714
30	5.576	4.39	7.39	492.08	515.49	0.911	1.083	0.048	0.284	0.697	1.085	0.688	0.867	1.105	0.067	0.288	0.682	1.122	0.679
31	3.43	4.46	7.458	492.5	480.55	0.882	1.095	0.059	0.209	0.744	1.129	0.736	0.880	1.095	0.059	0.213	0.731	1.142	0.725
32	4.762	4.04	5.155	480.81	467.74	0.953	1.054	0.025	0.160	0.708	1.054	0.708	0.933	1.062	0.033	0.176	0.697	1.094	0.701
33	4.061	5.08	6.193	574.48	569.54	1.000	1.000	0.000	0.000	1.000	1.000	1.000	0.994	1.003	0.002	0.014	0.991	1.011	0.985
34	3.683	5.13	8.432	489.58	476.31	0.770	1.160	0.109	0.307	0.659	1.171	0.652	0.768	1.174	0.109	0.310	0.644	1.232	0.639
35	4.061	4.7	5.61	557.63	551.83	1.000	1.000	0.000	0.000	1.000	1.000	1.000	1.000	1.000	0.000	0.002	1.000	1.000	0.995
36	3.43	4.81	7.838	477.37	516.09	0.840	1.100	0.082	0.219	0.748	1.125	0.727	0.833	1.150	0.093	0.223	0.728	1.157	0.713
37	2.73	4.17	8.429	518.05	560.68	1.000	1.000	0.000	0.000	1.000	1.000	1.000	1.000	1.000	0.000	0.000	1.000	1.000	0.957
38	4.061	4.53	7.326	520.44	517.37	0.918	1.055	0.036	0.170	0.795	1.063	0.776	0.918	1.055	0.037	0.176	0.780	1.088	0.768
39	3.252	5.69	6.572	551.23	559.5	1.000	1.000	0.000	0.000	1.000	1.000	1.000	0.900	1.053	0.034	0.108	0.896	1.054	0.887
40	2.906	4.58	8.432	478.26	487.24	0.886	1.128	0.083	0.213	0.760	1.132	0.744	0.886	1.129	0.084	0.217	0.730	1.164	0.726
41	2.353	4.25	8.705	503.51	500.29	0.989	1.028	0.011	0.098	0.879	1.059	0.853	0.989	1.029	0.011	0.113	0.846	1.070	0.846

(continued)

Table 1 (continued)

						DEA							DEAM						
DMU	x_1	x_2	x_3	y_1	y_2	RI	RO	DDF	WA	RUI	RUO	ERG	RI	RO	DDF	WA	RUI	RUO	ERG
42	3.252	4.22	7.727	472.39	472.68	0.914	1.112	0.059	0.195	0.744	1.137	0.736	0.911	1.113	0.060	0.213	0.722	1.152	0.710
43	3.43	4.11	9.615	476.23	475.28	0.910	1.092	0.049	0.193	0.716	1.118	0.709	0.910	1.096	0.057	0.218	0.700	1.152	0.693
44	2.142	4.31	6.509	518.9	541.13	1.000	1.000	0.000	0.000	1.000	1.000	1.000	1.000	1.000	0.000	0.007	0.990	1.000	0.993
45	4.352	4.78	6.03	531.72	566.63	1.000	1.000	0.000	0.000	1.000	1.000	1.000	0.981	1.010	0.007	0.070	0.941	1.029	0.911
46	2.547	5.13	8.432	500.74	555.01	1.000	1.000	0.000	0.000	1.000	1.000	1.000	0.867	1.055	0.039	0.134	0.845	1.089	0.833
47	3.43	4.11	7.759	478.77	489.54	0.927	1.082	0.040	0.139	0.763	1.089	0.753	0.922	1.084	0.044	0.166	0.758	1.113	0.739
48	2.547	5.51	6.587	552	542.14	1.000	1.000	0.000	0.000	1.000	1.000	1.000	0.987	1.006	0.004	0.050	0.976	1.017	0.962
49	3.43	4.63	7.24	531.27	546.76	0.942	1.030	0.020	0.077	0.868	1.031	0.868	0.939	1.031	0.021	0.098	0.853	1.044	0.846
50	3.824	4.87	5.82	499.34	529.09	0.899	1.051	0.036	0.154	0.828	1.086	0.817	0.875	1.074	0.047	0.160	0.812	1.094	0.807
51	3.079	4.35	7.865	483.38	517.75	0.922	1.086	0.051	0.150	0.808	1.089	0.789	0.916	1.096	0.057	0.153	0.788	1.100	0.776
MEAN						0.923	1.058	0.036	0.136	0.839	1.068	0.828	0.906	1.077	0.045	0.160	0.809	1.100	0.798
# Efficient DMUs						13	13	13	13	13	13	13	7	7	7	1	2	7	0

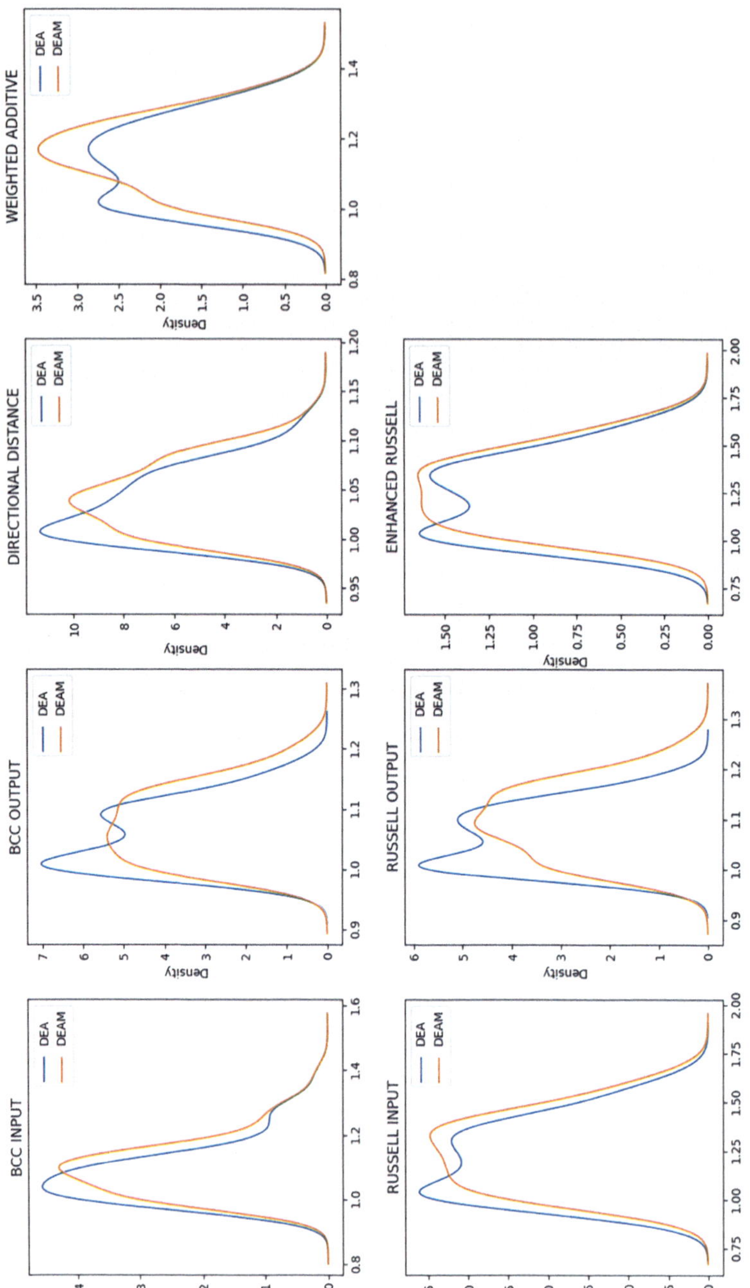

Fig. 2 Efficiency distributions measured by DEA and DEAM for the dataset of schools in Madrid

Regarding the number of DMUs classified as efficient by each method, we observe that DEAM has higher discriminating capability that DEA. DEAM classifies 7 or fewer DMUs as efficient while DEA classifies 13 DMUs as efficient, so that the number of efficient DMUs is reduced by almost a half. Every DMU considered efficient by DEAM was already considered efficient by DEA. We also observe that, with respect to certain measures, the number of DMUs considered efficient is even lower. These measures are the Weighted Additive (1 efficient DMU), Russell Input (2 efficient DMUs) and Enhanced Russell Graph (zero efficient units). Thus, we observe that DEAM can detect inefficiencies in certain components better than DEA in this application.

To illustrate the differences measured, we examine the estimated efficiencies of two schools in the dataset. The first school that we compare is school 46, which is considered efficient by DEA, but inefficient by DEAM. This school has above-average values of ESCS (5.13) and teachers per 100 students (8.432), but its educational resources are close to the minimum of the dataset (2.547). Its students attain scores slightly lower than the average in mathematics (500.74), while their scores in reading are high (555.01). With these values, this unit is considered efficient by DEA, while DEAM estimates its RI at 0.867. Its DEAM efficiency with respect to the RUI and ERG are below 0.85. Its WA is 0.134, which is slightly below the average of 0.160. The RO, DDF, RUO efficiency values of this DMU are closer to efficient. These values indicate that DEAM proposes that its inputs can be decreased by around 15% while still achieving similar outputs (test scores), but that, with the resources available, little further improvement on the test scores is possible. The second school that we observe in more detail is school 5, which has very high educational resources (5.576) and teachers (9.219), but its ESCS is below average (4.27). This school, despite the resources available, only achieves low scores in the standardized tests. In fact, this school obtains results below 490 in both subjects. These scores fall short of the average scores of the PISA overall dataset, which are 494 in reading and 496 in mathematics in 2012. This school is considered inefficient by both methods, but while DEA estimates at 0.879 its Radial input efficiency, DEAM evaluates it at 0.84. In this case, DEAM is capable of detecting further inefficiencies than DEA in all measures, but particularly with respect to the radial (RI and RO), DDF and Russell Output measures.

Due to the nature of the data as a sample of a larger dataset, another viewpoint in which we wish to focus is the possible perspective of a decision maker when faced with data not in the dataset. In this case, the estimation of absolute technical efficiency and information about the production function beyond the sample is useful. A decision maker, with data about a school potentially not in the observed sample, may be interested in evaluating it with respect to the estimated (education) production technology. In order to work with the DEAM estimated technology, one needs only the hyperplane parameters estimated by DEAM. Given these parameters, one can compare any point in the input–output space with this convex set by solving a system of linear equations and determining whether it satisfies each inequality. One possible case of interest is the allocation of educational resources and teachers to enable schools to obtain at least the overall average PISA scores in 2012, which are 494 in

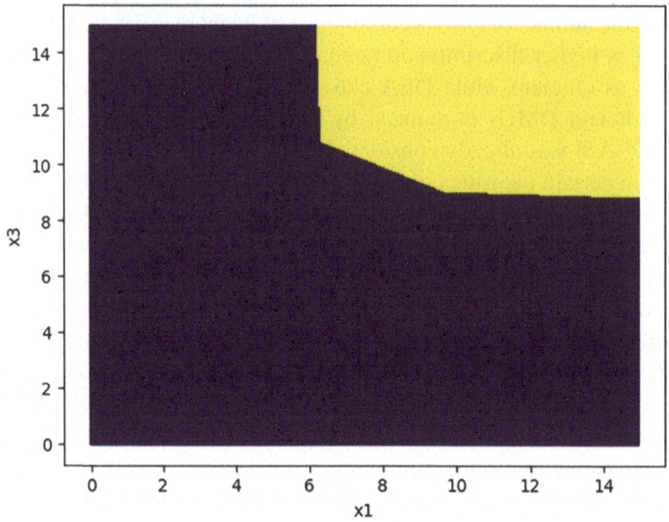

Fig. 3 DEAM level curve of feasible average PISA results given ESCS = 3.60

mathematics and 496 in reading. For this task, the ESCS of the students, which is determined by the area in which the school is located, is not easily modified, and can be considered fixed. For example, given a school with an ESCS close to the lowest observed value of 3.56, to allocate resources so that these scores were feasible with respect to the estimated production function. A hypothetical school with ESCS of 3.60 and average values in the remaining input cannot achieve these scores. Figure 3 represents the combinations of educational resources and teachers which yield these scores feasible. It can be observed that large values would be necessary, which are not present in any observed unit. Even a hypothetical allocation equal to the largest values in the observed sample, with $x_1 = 5.576$ and $x_3 = 12.55$, would not yield a feasible unit, given $x_2 = 3.60$. Figure 4 represents the feasible region with an ESCS value of 4.00, where the feasible region includes much lower values of allocated resources. Thus, an increase of around 10% in the ESCS of this hypothetical school would make it much easier to allocate resources towards reaching the proposed objective. Therefore, something else other than investment in teachers or resources is necessary, such as mid- or long-term changes in the socioeconomic fabric of the neighborhood, or a change in the production technology (new disruptive educational strategies), among other possibilities.

4.2 *Spanish Regional Tax Offices*

We now analyse the efficiency of tax offices from the regions (provinces) into which Spain is subdivided. This dataset can be found in (Aparicio et al., 2020). The data

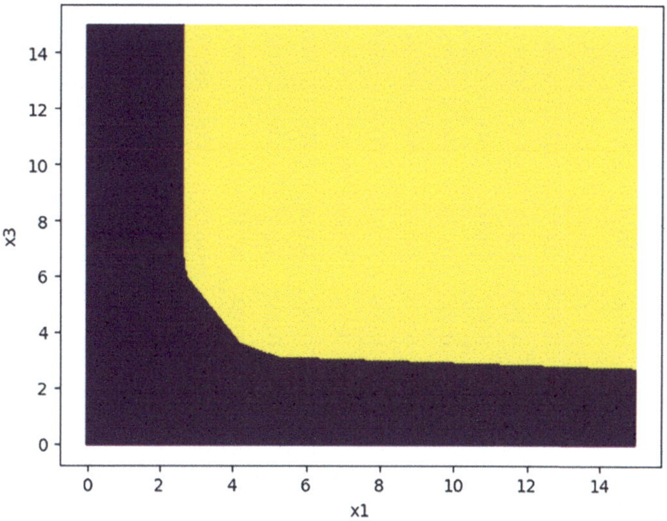

Fig. 4 DEAM level curve of feasible average PISA results given ESCS = 4.00

is from the year 2008. In this case, we consider three variables as inputs and two as outputs. There are two inputs related to labor: the number of tax inspectors and specialists (x_1) and the number of workers in the rest of the workforce (x_2). The third variable considered as an input (x_3) indicates the number of complaints against tax authority that have been positively resolved in favor of the taxpayers, showing mistakes by the tax office personnel. This is a bad output, that is, an output variable which is undesirable and thus it is a variable which a manager should aim to minimize, so this variable is considered as an input in our model, as in (Hailu & Veeman, 2000; Mahlberg & Sahoo, 2011). The outputs considered are the two main types of taxes which are collected by the offices under study: the inheritance and gift tax (y_1), and the real estate transfer tax settlements processed (y_2).

We report the results obtained in Table 2, where we indicate the estimated efficiencies for each DMU, as well as the average efficiency according to each measure, and the number of DMUs considered efficient. The average efficiency is deemed slightly lower by DEAM than by DEA with respect to all measures. Furthermore, we can observe that DEAM classifies 10 DMUs as efficient, while DEA considers 15 DMUs efficient, showing the higher discrimination capability of DEAM. These observations indicate that DEAM obtains estimates of efficiency that fit the data less closely, thus obtaining estimates of the production frontier that do not suffer from the overfitting problem of DEA.

Figure 5 then shows the density of the efficiencies measured, where we can see the higher average efficiencies obtained by DEAM, particularly in the cases of the Russell Input and Enhanced Russell Graph measures, which could already be observed in the PISA dataset.

Table 2 Results on the Spanish tax offices dataset

	DEA							DEAM						
DMU	RI	RO	DDF	WA	RUI	RUO	ERG	RI	RO	DDF	WA	RUI	RUO	ERG
ALMERIA	0.554	2.150	0.331	0.107	0.414	2.236	0.317	0.527	2.150	0.335	0.110	0.361	2.254	0.315
CADIZ	1.000	1.000	0.000	0.000	1.000	1.000	1.000	1.000	1.000	0.000	0.000	1.000	1.000	0.996
CORDOBA	0.523	1.994	0.323	0.069	0.412	2.132	0.378	0.523	1.994	0.323	0.070	0.369	2.157	0.354
GRANADA	0.653	1.609	0.224	0.103	0.456	1.671	0.448	0.653	1.609	0.224	0.104	0.451	1.671	0.446
HUELVA	0.521	2.473	0.377	0.064	0.393	2.565	0.290	0.506	2.474	0.379	0.069	0.317	2.569	0.287
JAEN	0.595	1.743	0.265	0.066	0.470	2.161	0.394	0.589	1.752	0.268	0.067	0.428	2.193	0.379
MALAGA	0.577	1.742	0.270	0.099	0.513	1.948	0.428	0.554	1.821	0.289	0.100	0.426	1.948	0.388
SEVILLA	0.739	1.305	0.156	0.138	0.537	1.504	0.518	0.739	1.385	0.156	0.139	0.532	1.504	0.514
HUESCA	1.000	1.000	0.000	0.000	1.000	1.000	1.000	1.000	1.000	0.000	0.000	1.000	1.000	1.000
TERUEL	1.000	1.000	0.000	0.000	1.000	1.000	1.000	0.932	1.180	0.049	0.004	0.589	1.261	0.561
ZARAGOZA	0.760	1.325	0.138	0.041	0.672	1.347	0.601	0.760	1.325	0.138	0.042	0.546	1.424	0.541
OVIEDO	1.000	1.000	0.000	0.000	1.000	1.000	1.000	1.000	1.000	0.000	0.000	1.000	1.000	1.000
BALEARES	0.977	1.024	0.012	0.022	0.821	1.034	0.821	0.930	1.075	0.036	0.024	0.771	1.124	0.768
CANTABRIA	0.862	1.156	0.073	0.024	0.704	1.493	0.531	0.862	1.156	0.073	0.026	0.603	1.493	0.512
ALBACETE	0.969	1.041	0.018	0.007	0.873	1.056	0.873	0.945	1.073	0.031	0.008	0.860	1.097	0.854
CIUDAD REAL	1.000	1.000	0.000	0.000	1.000	1.000	1.000	1.000	1.000	0.000	0.000	1.000	1.000	1.000
CUENCA	0.990	1.017	0.006	0.004	0.923	1.018	0.923	0.962	1.068	0.024	0.005	0.840	1.090	0.831
GUADALAJARA	1.000	1.000	0.000	0.000	1.000	1.000	1.000	0.995	1.007	0.003	0.004	0.943	1.017	0.935
TOLEDO	1.000	1.000	0.000	0.000	1.000	1.000	1.000	0.995	1.006	0.003	0.002	0.972	1.008	0.972
AVILA	1.000	1.000	0.000	0.000	1.000	1.000	1.000	0.978	1.061	0.016	0.004	0.799	1.074	0.748
BURGOS	0.879	1.167	0.070	0.014	0.757	1.373	0.649	0.870	1.184	0.077	0.015	0.683	1.412	0.647

(continued)

Table 2 (continued)

	DEA							DEAM						
DMU	RI	RO	DDF	WA	RUI	RUO	ERG	RI	RO	DDF	WA	RUI	RUO	ERG
LEÓN	0.975	1.026	0.013	0.010	0.943	1.292	0.774	0.969	1.033	0.016	0.011	0.922	1.308	0.743
PALENCIA	0.850	1.448	0.126	0.009	0.659	1.674	0.534	0.803	1.451	0.143	0.013	0.490	1.878	0.403
SALAMANCA	0.953	1.060	0.026	0.005	0.879	1.156	0.834	0.941	1.078	0.034	0.006	0.874	1.179	0.803
SEGOVIA	0.828	1.457	0.131	0.009	0.620	1.608	0.559	0.804	1.457	0.143	0.013	0.496	1.702	0.463
SORIA	1.000	1.000	0.000	0.000	1.000	1.000	1.000	1.000	1.000	0.000	0.001	1.000	1.000	0.905
VALLADOLID	0.745	1.462	0.164	0.033	0.551	1.574	0.471	0.745	1.462	0.164	0.034	0.516	1.574	0.466
ZAMORA	1.000	1.000	0.000	0.000	1.000	1.000	1.000	1.000	1.000	0.000	0.000	1.000	1.000	1.000
BARCELONA	1.000	1.000	0.000	0.000	1.000	1.000	1.000	1.000	1.000	0.000	0.000	1.000	1.000	1.000
GIRONA	0.825	1.244	0.105	0.013	0.724	1.245	0.707	0.818	1.246	0.105	0.014	0.565	1.256	0.562
LLEIDA	1.000	1.000	0.000	0.000	1.000	1.000	1.000	0.992	1.009	0.004	0.002	0.955	1.013	0.948
TARRAGONA	1.000	1.000	0.000	0.000	1.000	1.000	1.000	1.000	1.000	0.000	0.000	1.000	1.000	1.000
BADAJOZ	0.650	1.687	0.232	0.081	0.407	1.715	0.388	0.650	1.687	0.232	0.083	0.407	1.715	0.380
CACERES	0.955	1.077	0.029	0.006	0.795	1.077	0.795	0.928	1.124	0.046	0.009	0.775	1.126	0.775
A CORUÑA	0.722	1.410	0.166	0.055	0.588	1.527	0.528	0.722	1.410	0.166	0.057	0.543	1.539	0.518
LUGO	0.715	1.564	0.190	0.033	0.526	2.098	0.398	0.715	1.564	0.190	0.034	0.495	2.106	0.380
OURENSE	0.458	3.122	0.453	0.051	0.331	3.231	0.227	0.441	3.152	0.464	0.055	0.260	3.303	0.202
PONTEVEDRA	0.545	1.995	0.313	0.100	0.416	2.066	0.363	0.545	2.004	0.313	0.101	0.400	2.066	0.358
LA RIOJA	0.859	1.330	0.099	0.030	0.545	1.331	0.521	0.859	1.330	0.099	0.033	0.501	1.331	0.477
MADRID	1.000	1.000	0.000	0.000	1.000	1.000	1.000	1.000	1.000	0.000	0.000	1.000	1.000	1.000
MURCIA	0.470	2.029	0.366	0.142	0.397	2.194	0.359	0.470	2.169	0.366	0.146	0.380	2.196	0.352

(continued)

Table 2 (continued)

	DEA							DEAM						
DMU	RI	RO	DDF	WA	RUI	RUO	ERG	RI	RO	DDF	WA	RUI	RUO	ERG
ALICANTE	0.994	1.006	0.003	0.140	0.741	1.007	0.741	0.936	1.068	0.033	0.210	0.676	1.089	0.620
CASTELLÓN	0.905	1.108	0.051	0.089	0.655	1.299	0.544	0.893	1.122	0.057	0.090	0.654	1.304	0.536
VALENCIA	1.000	1.000	0.000	0.000	1.000	1.000	1.000	1.000	1.000	0.000	0.000	1.000	1.000	1.000
MEAN	0.842	1.336	0.108	0.036	0.744	1.423	0.703	0.831	1.356	0.114	0.039	0.691	1.454	0.658
# Efficient DMUs	15	15	15	15	15	15	15	10	10	10	9	10	10	8

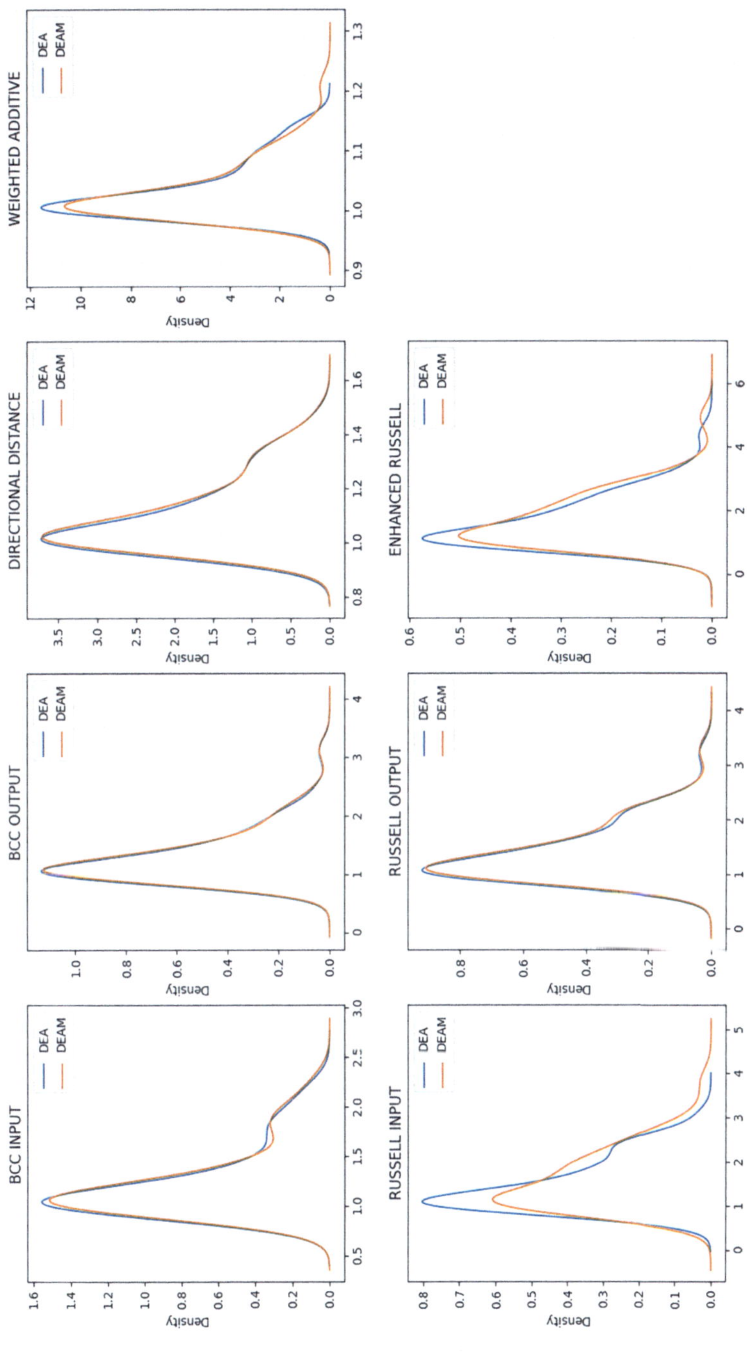

Fig. 5 Efficiency distributions measured by DEA and DEAM for the dataset of tax offices in Spain

As with the previous dataset, the units considered efficient by DEAM were already considered efficient by DEA, but the converse does not hold. The provinces which are considered efficient by DEA but not by DEAM include some of the provinces with the smallest populations, such as Teruel (0.932 RI) and Avila (0.978 RI), where the changes in efficiency are slightly higher, but also some larger provinces such as Guadalajara, Toledo, and Lleida, which are considered almost fully efficient by DEAM. For example, the differences between DEA and DEAM in the case of Lleida are smaller than 0.01 with respect to the RI, RO, DDF and RUO measures, with larger changes of up to 0.045 in the RUI measure and 0.052 in the ERG.

The largest changes in efficiency can be observed in Teruel, Alicante, Baleares, and Palencia. In particular, Alicante has a large variation between the measured efficiencies depending on the measure. DEAM considers this unit almost efficient in the output-oriented measures (RO and RUO) and the DDF, but it is the least efficient according to the WA and achieves efficiencies lower than 0.70 with respect to the RUI and ERG. These measures are capable of detecting inefficiencies in a single input, and it can be noted that this unit attains the maximum of the dataset in input x_3, with above average values in the remaining inputs and outputs.

5 Conclusions

In the nonparametric literature of efficiency estimation, one of the advantages of DEA and related estimators is the natural multi-output extension and interpretation of the models. However, methods such as DEA are descriptive in nature, and do not naturally work to perform inference. There have been recent contributions of models which combine DEA with machine learning principles (see, for example, (Kuosmanen & Johnson, 2010), (Du et al., 2013), (Esteve et al., 2020), (Valero-Carreras et al., 2021), (Olesen & Ruggiero, 2022)). A recent contribution, (Guerrero et al., 2022) proposed a technique, called Data Envelopment Analysis-based Machines (DEAM), which follows the Structural Risk Minimization principle in order to overcome the descriptive nature of DEA. This is achieved via the statement of theoretical bounds on both the empirical and generalization error of the model. However, the DEAM technique was only introduced in the single-output production context. In this chapter, we have extended DEAM to estimate efficiency in production processes with multiple outputs and multiple inputs while satisfying the properties of convexity, free disposability, and envelopment of the observed data, but not that of minimal extrapolation.

Moreover, we have described how some well-known measures of efficiency can be adapted to calculate efficiency with the multi-output DEAM technique. These include both oriented and non-oriented measures which calculate weak or Pareto efficiency, in a variety of possible orientations. We have illustrated this approach with applications to two real datasets in the education and tax collection contexts. In both cases, DEAM shows a higher discriminating power than DEA, classifying fewer DMUs as efficient than DEA, and obtaining efficiency scores which indicate lower efficiencies. This indicates that we obtain results which overcome the overfitting present in DEA, estimating production frontiers which are more robust. Furthermore, this can be understood as identifying more sources of inefficiency.

These additional sources of inefficiency can be observed in all the adapted measures, but they are highlighted even more with respect to some measures, such as the Weighted Additive, Russell Input and Enhanced Russell Graph measures, where DEAM classifies an even smaller number of units as fully efficient, thus being able to identify more inefficiencies with respect to these measures. These are slacks-based measures which measure Pareto efficiency, and can identify inefficiencies along individual variables, in the inputs (Russell Input) or in both inputs and outputs simultaneously (WA, ERG). More examples should be considered to evaluate whether this applies in general.

A limitation of the DEAM estimator is the intensive computational burden placed by cross-validation of the hyperparameters. This could be further explored and improved upon by the consideration of other methods for estimating the hyperparameters or by the simplification of models.

Finally, we mention some possible avenues for further research. Given the Structural Risk Minimization bounds on DEAM, a direction worth studying are the properties of asymptotic convergence and consistency results for DEAM (Christmann & Steinwart, 2007; Steinwart, 2002, 2005). Another possible direction worth considering is the extension of DEAM to work with panel data, evaluating the differences in efficiency arising from the changes in efficiency and productivity over time (efficiency change, scale efficiency change, technical change) (Tsionas, 2022). Another interesting generalization could consider the measurement and decomposition of the economic inefficiencies into their components (allocative, technical, etc.) (Aparicio & Zofío, 2023). Another potential avenue comes from the Support Vector Regression literature, where transformation functions are often considered which transform the input space into a higher-dimensional space allowing for better estimations and yielding more flexibility to the technique (Vapnik, 1998). Finally, with single-output estimation methods, there are often multiple proposed approaches to generalize them to the multi-output prediction context, and other such techniques could also be considered (Vazquez & Walter, 2003).

Acknowledgements The authors thank the grant PID2022-136383NB-I00 funded by MICIU/AEI/10.13039/501100011033 and by ERDF/EU. This work was also supported by the Generalitat Valenciana under Grant ACIF/2020/155. Additionally, J. Aparicio thanks the grant PROMETEO/2021/063 funded by the Valencian Community (Spain).

References

Aigner, D., Lovell, C. A. K., & Schmidt, P. (1977). Formulation and estimation of stochastic frontier production function models. *Journal of Econometrics, 6*(1), 21–37. https://doi.org/10.1016/0304-4076(77)90052-5

Aparicio, J., Cordero, J. M., & Díaz-Caro, C. (2020). Efficiency and productivity change of regional tax offices in Spain: An empirical study using Malmquist-Luenberger and Luenberger indices. *Empirical Economics, 59*(3), 1403–1434. https://doi.org/10.1007/s00181-019-01667-8

Aparicio, J., & Esteve, M. (2022). How to peel a data envelopment analysis frontier: A cross-validation-based approach. *Journal of the Operational Research Society, 1–15.* https://doi.org/10.1080/01605682.2022.2157765

Aparicio, J., Esteve, M., Rodriguez-Sala, J. J., & Zofio, J. L. (2021). The Estimation of Productive Efficiency Through Machine Learning Techniques: Efficiency Analysis Trees. In *International Series in Operations Research and Management Science* (Vol. 312, pp. 51–92). Springer. https://doi.org/10.1007/978-3-030-75162-3_3.

Aparicio, J., & Zofío, J. L. (2023). Decomposing profit change: Konüs, Bennet and Luenberger indicators. *Socio-Economic Planning Sciences, 101573.* https://doi.org/10.1016/J.SEPS.2023.101573

Banker, R. D., Charnes, A., & Cooper, W. W. (1984). Some models for estimating technical and scale inefficiencies in data envelopment analysis. *Management Science, 30*(9), 1078–1092. https://doi.org/10.1287/mnsc.30.9.1078

Chambers, R. G., Chung, Y., & Färe, R. (1998). Profit, directional distance functions, and Nerlovian efficiency. *Journal of Optimization Theory and Applications, 98*(2), 351–364. https://doi.org/10.1023/A:1022637501082

Charnes, A., & Cooper, W. W. (1962). Programming with linear fractional functionals. *Naval Research Logistics Quarterly, 9*(3–4), 181–186. https://doi.org/10.1002/nav.3800090303

Charnes, A., Cooper, W. W., Golany, B., Seiford, L., & Stutz, J. (1985). Foundations of data envelopment analysis for Pareto-Koopmans efficient empirical production functions. *Journal of Econometrics, 30*(1–2), 91–107. https://doi.org/10.1016/0304-4076(85)90133-2

Charnes, A., Cooper, W. W., & Rhodes, E. (1978). Measuring the efficiency of decision making units. *European Journal of Operational Research, 2*(6), 429–444. https://doi.org/10.1016/0377-2217(78)90138-8

Christmann, A., & Steinwart, I. (2007). Consistency and robustness of kernel-based regression in convex risk minimization. *Bernoulli, 13*(3), 799–819. https://doi.org/10.3150/07-BEJ5102

Cooper, W. W., Park, K. S., & Pastor, J. T. (1999). RAM: a range adjusted measure of inefficiency for use with additive models, and relations to other models and measures in DEA. *Journal of Productivity Analysis, 11*(1), 5–42. https://doi.org/10.1023/A:1007701304281.

Cooper, W. W., Pastor, J. T., Borras, F., Aparicio, J., & Pastor, D. (2011). BAM: A bounded adjusted measure of efficiency for use with bounded additive models. *Journal of Productivity Analysis, 35*(2), 85–94. https://doi.org/10.1007/s11123-010-0190-2

Daouia, A., Noh, H., & Park, B. U. (2016). Data envelope fitting with constrained polynomial splines. *Journal of the Royal Statistical Society. Series B: Statistical Methodology, 78*(1), 3–30. https://doi.org/10.1111/RSSB.12098.

Daraio, C., & Simar, L. (2007). *Advanced Robust and Nonparametric Methods in Efficiency Analysis* (Vol. 4). Springer US. https://doi.org/10.1007/978-0-387-35231-2.

Debreu, G. (1951). The coefficient of resource utilization. *Econometrica, 19*(3), 273. https://doi.org/10.2307/1906814

Du, P., Parmeter, C. F., & Racine, J. S. (2013). Nonparametric kernel regression with multiple predictors and multiple shape constraints. *Statistica Sinica*, 1347–1371.

Esteve, M., Aparicio, J., Rabasa, A., & Rodriguez-Sala, J. J. (2020). Efficiency analysis trees: A new methodology for estimating production frontiers through decision trees. *Expert Systems with Applications, 162*, 113783. https://doi.org/10.1016/j.eswa.2020.113783

Esteve, M., Aparicio, J., Rodriguez-Sala, J. J., & Zhu, J. (2023). Random forests and the measurement of super-efficiency in the context of free disposal hull. *European Journal of Operational Research, 304*(2), 729–744. https://doi.org/10.1016/J.EJOR.2022.04.024

Färe, R., & Lovell, C. A. K. (1978). Measuring the technical efficiency of production. *Journal of Economic Theory, 19*(1), 150–162.

Farrell, M. J. (1957). The measurement of productive efficiency. *Journal of the Royal Statistical Society. Series A (General), 120*(3), 253. https://doi.org/10.2307/2343100.

Guerrero, N. M., Aparicio, J., & Valero-Carreras, D. (2022). Combining data envelopment analysis and machine learning. *Mathematics, 10*(6), 909. https://doi.org/10.3390/MATH10060909

Guillen, M. D., Aparicio, J., & Esteve, M. (2023). Gradient tree boosting and the estimation of production frontiers. *Expert Systems with Applications, 214*, 119134. https://doi.org/10.1016/J.ESWA.2022.119134

Hailu, A., & Veeman, T. S. (2000). Environmentally sensitive productivity analysis of the Canadian pulp and paper industry, 1959–1994: an input distance function approach. *Journal of Environmental Economics and Management, 40*(3), 251–274. https://doi.org/10.1006/JEEM.2000.1124

Kneip, A., Park, B. U., & Simar, L. (1998). A note on the convergence of nonparametric Dea estimators for production efficiency scores. *Econometric Theory, 14*(6), 783–793. https://doi.org/10.1017/S0266466698146042

Kneip, A., Simar, L., & Wilson, P. W. (2008). Asymptotics and consistent bootstraps for Dea estimators in nonparametric frontier models. *Econometric Theory, 24*(6), 1663–1697. https://doi.org/10.1017/S0266466608080651

Kneip, A., Simar, L., & Wilson, P. W. (2011). A computationally efficient, consistent bootstrap for inference with non-parametric DEA estimators. *Computational Economics, 38*(4), 483–515. https://doi.org/10.1007/S10614-010-9217-Z

Kneip, A., Simar, L., & Wilson, P. W. (2015). When Bias kills the variance: central limit theorems for Dea and FDH efficiency scores. *Econometric Theory, 31*(2), 394–422. https://doi.org/10.1017/S0266466614000413

Koopmans, T. C. (1951). Efficient allocation of resources. *Econometrica, 19*(4), 455. https://doi.org/10.2307/1907467

Kuosmanen, T., & Johnson, A. L. (2010). Data envelopment analysis as nonparametric least-squares regression. *Operations Research, 58*(1), 149–160. https://doi.org/10.1287/opre.1090.0722

Knox Lovell, C. A., & Pastor, J. T. (1995). Units invariant and translation invariant DEA models. *Operations Research Letters, 18*(3), 147–151. https://doi.org/10.1016/0167-6377(95)00044-5

Luenberger, D. G. (1992). Benefit functions and duality. *J. Math. Econom., 21*(5), 461–481. https://doi.org/10.1016/0304-4068(92)90035-6

Mahlberg, B., & Sahoo, B. K. (2011). Radial and non-radial decompositions of Luenberger productivity indicator with an illustrative application. *International Journal of Production Economics, 131*(2), 721–726. https://doi.org/10.1016/J.IJPE.2011.02.021

Meeusen, W., & van Den Broeck, J. (1977). Efficiency estimation from cobb-douglas production functions with composed error. *International Economic Review, 18*(2), 435. https://doi.org/10.2307/2525757

OECD. (2014). *PISA 2012 Technical Report*.

Olesen, O. B., & Ruggiero, J. (2022). The hinging hyperplanes: An alternative nonparametric representation of a production function. *European Journal of Operational Research, 296*(1), 254–266. https://doi.org/10.1016/j.ejor.2021.03.054

Orea, L., & Zofío, J. L. (2019). Common methodological choices in nonparametric and parametric analyses of firms' performance. In *The Palgrave Handbook of Economic Performance Analysis* (pp. 419–484). Springer International Publishing. https://doi.org/10.1007/978-3-030-23727-1_12.

Pastor, J. T., Ruiz, J. L., & Sirvent, I. (1999). An enhanced DEA Russell graph efficiency measure. *European Journal of Operational Research, 115*(3), 596–607. https://doi.org/10.1016/S0377-2217(98)00098-8

Steinwart, I. (2002). Support vector machines are universally consistent. *Journal of Complexity, 18*(3), 768–791. https://doi.org/10.1006/JCOM.2002.0642

Steinwart, I. (2005). Consistency of support vector machines and other regularized kernel classifiers. *IEEE Transactions on Information Theory, 51*(1), 128–142. https://doi.org/10.1109/TIT.2004.839514

Tone, K. (2001). A slacks-based measure of efficiency in data envelopment analysis. *European Journal of Operational Research, 130*(3), 498–509. https://doi.org/10.1016/S0377-2217(99)00407-5

Tsionas, M. (2022). Efficiency estimation using probabilistic regression trees with an application to Chilean manufacturing industries. *International Journal of Production Economics, 249*, 108492. https://doi.org/10.1016/J.IJPE.2022.108492

Valero-Carreras, D., Aparicio, J., & Guerrero, N. M. (2021). Support vector frontiers: A new approach for estimating production functions through support vector machines. *Omega, 104*, 102490. https://doi.org/10.1016/j.omega.2021.102490.

Valero-Carreras, D., Aparicio, J., & Guerrero, N. M. (2022). Multi-output Support vector frontiers. *Computers & Operations Research, 143*, 105765. https://doi.org/10.1016/J.COR.2022.105765

Vapnik, V. (1991). Principles of risk minimization for learning theory. *Advances in Neural Information Processing Systems, 4*, 831–838.

Vapnik, V. (1998). *Statistical learning theory*. Wiley.

Vazquez, E., & Walter, E. (2003). Multi-output support vector regression. *IFAC Proceedings Volumes, 36*(16), 1783–1788. https://doi.org/10.1016/S1474-6670(17)35018-8

A New Network Data Envelopment Analysis Model for Efficacy Evaluation of Decision-Making Units

Hilda Saleh, Morteza Shafiee, and Sara Nakhjirkan

Abstract Assessing the performance of organizations has become a complex matter within the realm of management, considering the current global setting and its ever-changing nature. Although Data Envelopment Analysis (DEA) has been used as a powerful tool for the evaluation of decision-making units, in the traditional DEA models, these units are viewed as a black box, and therefore their internal relationships are generally ignored, assuming that the performance of DMUs is a function of selective inputs and outputs. Recently, there has been a great deal of research on multi-stage units, especially series and parallel units. However, research with a mixed structure is very limited with many studies unable to introduce the efficient unit. However, since in most real cases, the researcher deals with a series and parallel structure simultaneously, it is vital to develop a model of efficiency evaluation with efficient units. Thus, in the current paper, we attempted to solve the mentioned problems. At first, a mixed structure was introduced and then we developed a new model for a mixed structure. Also, the proposed model has the capability of introducing a relative-efficient unit. This is followed by an explanation of the methodology and development of a new network model to measure efficiency in the Iranian Airline Industry.

Keywords Airlines · Data envelopment analysis (DEA) · Network DEA · Performance evaluation

H. Saleh
Department of Mathematics, Faculty of Science, Central Tehran Branch, Islamic Azad University, Tehran, Iran

M. Shafiee (✉)
Department of Industrial Management, Economic and Management Faculty, Shiraz Branch, Islamic Azad University, Shiraz, Iran
e-mail: ma.shafiee277@gmail.com

S. Nakhjirkan
Department of Industrial and Systems Engineering, Isfahan University of Technology, Isfahan, Iran

© The Author(s), under exclusive license to Springer Nature Singapore Pte Ltd. 2024

S. A. Edalatpanah et al. (eds.), *Analytical Decision Making and Data Envelopment Analysis*, Infosys Science Foundation Series in Mathematical Sciences,
https://doi.org/10.1007/978-981-97-6972-8_2

1 Introduction

In today's global and dynamic environment, evaluating the performance of organizations has been a challenging issue in the field of management. Despite the intricacy inherent in organizations, they must possess the adaptability to fulfill their responsibilities towards both shareholders and stakeholders, and in addition, despite the dynamic economic and the uncertainty in the government's budget, the need for performance evaluation for the long-term survival of the organizations has become an inevitable necessity. Every entity necessitates an evaluation framework to comprehend the efforts and excellence of its endeavors, particularly within intricate and evolving settings. The absence of an evaluation and oversight mechanism within a company leads to a breakdown in communication both within and outside the organization. This eventually results in the demise of the company. The occurrence of organizational demise might not be readily apparent to managers since it does not happen instantaneously. Various research studies have consistently proven that the absence of an efficient feedback mechanism hinders the implementation of vital reforms required for the advancement, expansion, and enhancement of an organization's operations.

Efficiency measurement, especially in the last two decades, has been of great interest due to its importance in performance evaluation. Since 1957, when Farrell proposed a method for measuring efficiency, several comprehensive and fundamental improvements have been proposed in performance measurement (Farrell, 1957). The problems with the traditional performance appraisal systems led to a revolution in performance management so the researchers and users moved to create new performance appraisal systems to focus on current goals and environments. In this way, numerous appraisal techniques were developed to be used by various organizations. Out of all the existing methods for evaluating and analyzing performance, Data Envelopment Analysis (DEA) models prove to be highly effective in organizing and examining data. These models stand out due to their ability to gauge performance consistently over a period of time, without the need for any initial assumptions about efficiency frontier. (Tone & Tsutsui, 2014a). Therefore, such models are more widely used in performance evaluation, especially for comparing units in performance measurement.

DEA, a technique grounded in linear programming, offers a novel approach to assess both qualitative and quantitative aspects of decision-making units (DMUs). The concept of DEA originated from the innovative work of Charnes, Cooper, and Rhodes (CCR) in the late 1970s (Charnes et al., 1978). Later, in 1984, Banker and his colleagues presented a progressive variant of the CCR model, known as BCC, which introduced an evolutionary approach (Banker et al., 1984). Over the subsequent years, the DEA gained considerable recognition and attracted numerous researchers who explored its potential and devised diverse frameworks. Fundamentally, these frameworks diverge in their approach, feasibility, orientation, scalability, as well as the assortment of metrics employed.

The data envelopment analysis has been used as a powerful tool by researchers in a variety of fields, such as bank branch appraisal, university performance appraisal, location problems, and so on. In other words, DEA is an instrumental in assessing the performance of similar decision-making entities that operate with several inputs and outputs. Within conventional DEA models, decision-making units (DMUs) are regarded as a "black box". This issue warranting neglect of their internal dynamics. Consequently, it is commonly assumed that DMU performance is solely determined by primary inputs and final outputs, disregarding any internal relationships. That is why Färe and Grosskopf (1996) introduced the network DEA to deal with this problem. They believed that the conventional DEA models viewed the decision-making units as a "black box", in which inputs were directly converted to outputs and the internal structure of these units was not considered in the appraisal, while various processes of the organization should be examined at different stages and the successful sectors should be distinguished from the unsuccessful ones to help improve performance. However, the DMUs have a network framework. In actuality, organizations consist of complex multi-component structures in which the components are strictly interconnected to each other. Thus, to have a more powerful model, the internal relationships among components should be considered. Hence, network DEA models were proposed to break the black box and divide the DMU into several stages considering the internal relationships and network structure.

Various research studies have dedicated attention to NDEA, with the aim of devising a novel framework suitable for the distinct organizational network structure found in numerous organizations such as: (Färe & Grosskopf, 2000; Tone & Tsutsui, 2009). These network can be classified into three distinct groups: (1) Series Networks, (2) Parallel Networks, and (3) Mixed Networks.

Since DEA researchers have recently focused on network structures, their extended models have some problems. The main problem is that most models available in the literature are not capable of delivering efficient units and do not often introduce relative efficiency units. According to the DEA, this can be a big fault. Another problem is that, in the real world, we usually deal with a mixed structure. Thus, there exists a scarcity of studies examining this specific field and these models are not capable of introducing efficient units.

In this present paper, we aim to address the previously stated issues. At first, a mixed structure is introduced and then a new model for the mentioned mixed structure is developed, which is able to introduce an efficient unit. The arrangement of this paper is as follows: initially, an overview of network configuration is provided. This segment encompasses an examination of DEA and multi-stage DEA, along with their applications and related efficiency evaluation concepts. Subsequently, a detailed account of the methodology and creation of a new network model, designed to efficiency assessment, is presented. This novel model is then applied to the context of the Iranian Airline Industry. Finally, the concluding section offers insights and key findings.

2 Background

2.1 Series Networks

Let x_{jt} be the independent inputs, z_{jt} the intermediate products, and y_{jt} the independent outputs in each t_{th} stage of the j_{th} network. Figure 1 shows a multi-stage decision-making unit in a general mode. However, these units act only as a two-stage process in many modes.

Numerous investigations have thus far been carried out on the assessment of multi-stage series units. In one of the first studies in this field, using the concept of the non-participatory game as well as the geometric mean of the performance of the different stages, Yong et al. (2008) suggested a model for assessing the two-stage structures, in which a heuristic method was used to solve the proposed model.

In another study, Kao and Hwang suggested a model using the rational DEA model to assess two-stage processes with the aim of decomposing the overall performance of these processes and making the comparison of the efficiency of stages 1 and 2 possible (Kao & Hwang, 2008). Then, they employed the proposed model to assess the insurance companies in Taiwan. However, the image provided by this model has not been necessarily efficient. Chen et al. made certain alterations to this model. (Chen et al., 2009a) to make the image provided by the modified model efficient. Considering an independent input for stage 2, Li et al. (2012) assessed the performance of R & D units. Chen et al. (2009b) formulated the model by incorporating a convex of efficiencies of first and subsequent stages, which involved the consideration of both constant and variable returns to scale. Sahoo et al. (2014) investigated the decomposition of the technical efficiency by considering the independent sub-technology frontiers.

Due to the wide range of network structures in the real world, numerous practical investigations have been carried out within this particular domain. For instance, Paradi used the two-stage processes to assess the effectiveness of branches within the commercial banking sector (Paradi et al., 2011). Amado et al. integrated the network and BSC (Amado et al., 2012). Chen and Yan used the network data envelopment analysis to assess supply chains (Chen & Yan, 2011). In another study, Liu and Lu (2010) assessed and ranked the performance of the R&D division within Taiwan's research institutes that receive support from the government (Liu & Lu, 2010). Also,

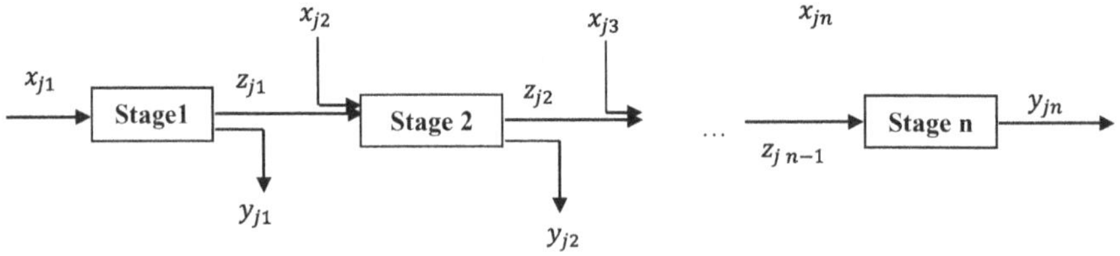

Fig. 1 A series network

Lu et al. (2012) assessed the US airlines using a two-stage DEA model (Lu et al., 2012).

In the common two-stage systems, the final output of the system is considered only as the output of stage 2, while in some cases the final output can also be considered as the output of stage 1. So, in such cases, it has a dual role (as input and output) for stage 2. Accordingly, using the concept of time-staged outputs, Aviles-Sacoto et al. (2015) put forward a new conceptual framework which they applied to evaluate the performance of business schools.

Using multi-objective programming, Despotis et al. (2016a) demonstrated a model to assess the performance of two-stage units to simultaneously maximize the efficiency of both stages. They obtained the Pareto optimal solution for the assessed network by presenting a Phase II model. Also, using "the composition approach", Despotis et al. (2016b) considered a bi-objective program to assess unique performance scores for a two-stage system.

In another study, Despotis et al. (2016c) used the "weak link" idea in supply chains and the "maximum-flow/minimum-cut problem" in networks to provide a model for assessing a two-stage unit and obtaining the Pareto optimal solution.

Additionally, some researchers have considered the use of the network models in real-life problems involving uncertainties and extended the models to specific data. Fukuyama and Weber (2010), inter alia, proposed a Slack-Based Measure (SBM) two-stage model to assess the performance of Japanese banks in the presence of undesirable outputs. In another study, Akther et al. (2013) used a two-stage DEA model to assess the performance of 21 banks in Bangladesh to maximize the desirable outputs and minimize the undesirable outputs. Using a bargaining game approach in DEA and proposing a fuzzy bargaining approach, Tavana et al. (2018) assessed the performance of two-stage units with fuzzy data. In addition, the two-stage DEA model with a carry-over variable was proposed by Ton et al. (2019) and the proposed model was used to assess the performance of insurance companies from 2008 to 2016. Kao and Liu (2019) expanded the concept of cross-efficiency to the two-stage DEA models. Ebrahimzadeh Shermeh et al. (2018) evaluated the performance of power companies using a series of networks DEA models. Fallah (2020) applied a two-stage NDEA to evaluate its effectiveness and productivity in petrochemical companies. To assess the performance of DMUs, Shafiee et al. (xxxx) utilized the NDEA model and BSC approach. Readers for more information, see (Despotis & Koronakos, 2014; Esfidani et al., 2020; Fang, 2020; Khovcyni & Eslami, 2021; Sahoo et al., 2021; Saleh & Rostamy, 2013; Saleh et al., 2011; Seyed Esmaeili et al., 2020; Shafiee et al., 2014).

2.2 Parallel Networks

In the actual environment, certain systems that are evaluated consist of separate sub-categories. Even though these sub-categories act autonomously and simultaneously, the overall efficiency of the entire system is influenced by the performance of each

Fig. 2 A parallel network

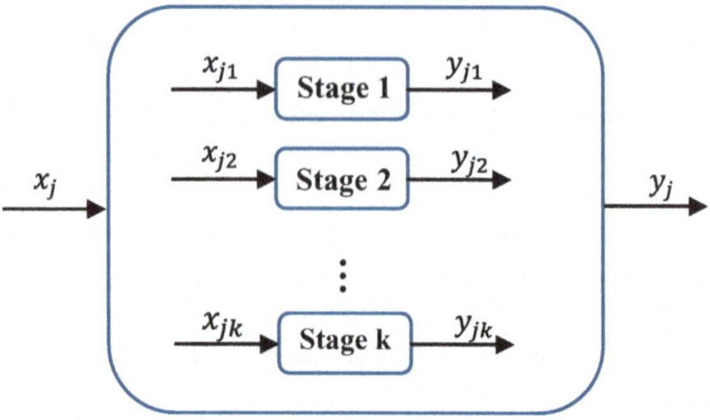

individual subset. To enhance comprehension of this issue, you can refer to the parallel network with k-stages depicted in Fig. 2.

In the real world, some of the systems assessed are made up of independent sub-sets. Although each of these sub-sets works independently and in parallel, the performance of the whole system is affected by the performance of each of them. Consider the k-stages parallel network shown in Fig. 2.

Where x_j and y_j are the initial input and the final output of the system, respectively. x_{jt} and y_{jt}, $t = 1, \ldots, k$, are independent inputs and outputs of each component. Many studies have so far been done on parallel networks. One of the first studies in this field was conducted by Castelli et al. (2004). In this investigation, three fundamental assumptions were considered to enhance network efficiency. These assumptions include: none of the stages share inputs and outputs, and there are no intermediate transfers among them. Kao (2009) presented a slack-based model to identify inefficiency resources in a parallel network as well as in each of the components. Thus, the inefficiency slack of the network could be explained by the inefficiency slacks of its components. Using the idea put forward by Bi et al. (2011), Bi et al. presented a model for resource allocation and target setting in parallel networks. Furthermore, building upon previous research on assessing the efficiency of parallel networks through both quantitative and qualitative metrics, Kao and Lin (2012) expanded the network frameworks by incorporating fuzzy data. In this research, the efficiency of chemistry departments in UK universities was evaluated by employing both quantitative and qualitative measures. To determine the range of efficiency, two bi-level programming problems were solved at varying α levels. Cook et al. (2010a) also proposed a model to assess multistage systems using additive efficiency decomposition. In another study, Du et al. first examined the existing DEA models and showed that these models can be categorized considering the participatory games in the game theory (2015a). They then presented a new model to assess parallel systems using "Stackelberg/leader–follower non-cooperative game". The important point in the models presented by Kao (2009) and (Du et al., 2015a) is the assumption that the initial input of the system is equal to the sum of the inputs of each of the components and that the final output of the system is equal to the sum of the outputs of each of the components. However, Gong et al. (Gong et al., 2018a) in a research on the Chinese manufacturing industry, shown that the assumption is not necessarily the case in some parallel systems. Therefore, they presented a new model to deal with this problem.

In addition, there has been a key assumption in the models presented for parallel networks that all components utilize the same inputs to generate the identical outputs and that there is no relationship between the sub-sets in a system. However, this assumption may not hold true in various practical scenarios. Therefore, Du et al. (Du et al., 2015b) expanded the existing network models to systems including non-homogenous sub-units. It is also assumed that sub-sets can be related to each other in this system. Readers can study (Ding et al., 2023; Gong et al., 2018b; Kremantzis et al., 2022; lo Storto, 2020; Park et al., 2022; Shi et al., 2021) for more information about parallel networks.

2.3 *Mixed Networks Structures*

The third category consists of mixed networks. These systems simultaneously include series and parallel structures. Consider a mixed network structure as in Fig. 3.

The complexity of these networks surpasses that of series and parallel configurations. It should be noted that less research has been conducted on mixed networks than on series and parallel networks. One of the studies on mixed networks was conducted by Tone and Tsutsui (2009), where they proposed a slack-based network DEA model to assess the mixed networks in three input-oriented, output-oriented, and non-oriented modes. The relationships between divisions in the fixed link and the free link mode were also discussed in this study. In another study (Tone & Tsutsui, 2014b), extending the dynamic NDEA model to the SBM model, Tone and Tsutsui measured the overall efficiency in different periods. They also analyzed the changes in network efficiency and each of the divisions in different periods. One of the critical challenges in the field of managerial decision-making is that there are multiple optimal solutions when multi-stage processes are assessed. In other words, a stage may be efficient when an optimal solution is used, but it may be inefficient when

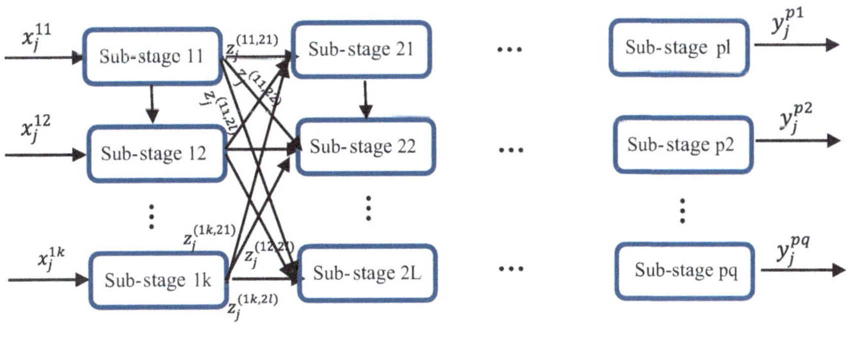

Fig. 3 A general mixed network

another optimal solution is used. Fukuyama and Mirdehghan (2012) dealt with this problem to identify the efficiency status of multi-stage systems using a two-phase procedure.

One of the key components in the mix networks is the two-stage configuration with a parallel-series internal framework. In their study, Ma et al. (2017) put forward a framework to evaluate a two-stage parallel-series system that used an autonomous input in the second stage. They then used a heuristic process to calculate the efficiency decomposition in this structure. In another study, Ma and Chen defined the coordination efficiencies in a parallel-series network (Ma & Chen, 2018). Zhou et al. (2018a) used a two-stage SBM DEA model with undesirable output to assess the parallel-series system with undesirable output in wastewater treatment systems in China. A different type of series–parallel multi-stage system was examined by Kao (2018) who showed that the efficiency of a system can be expressed as multiplied by a factor greater than one. Those interested can refer to (Yu & Fan, 2009; Zhou et al., 2018b; Barat et al., 2019; Kang et al., 2023) for more information about mixed networks.

As it was mentioned in the previous studies, research using the mixed structure is very limited, unable to introduce the efficient unit. Thus, this research dealt with the series and parallel structure simultaneously, to develop a model of efficiency evaluation and introduce efficient units. The main objective of this study was to create an innovative approach for determining the efficiency score within a mixed structure, ultimately allowing for the identification of relative efficiency unit.

3 A New Network DEA Model

Now, let's consider a collection of DMUs comprising *DMUj*, $j = 1, \ldots, n$, as Fig. 4.

Each DMU has a two-stage structure. The first and second stages have K and L sub-stage, respectively. For example, 2 l represents the lth sub-process of the second stage. The initial stage involves taking inputs (x) and generating an intermediate measure known as z. Subsequently, the following stage employs these intermediate measures (z) as inputs to produce outputs (y). x_{ij}^{1k} is ith input of the first stage and

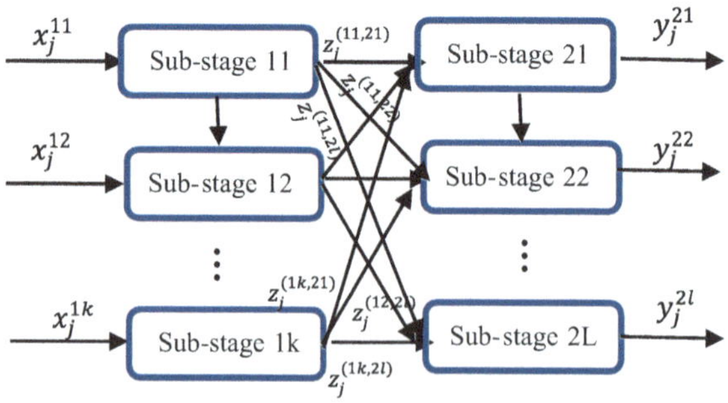

Fig. 4 A mixed network with two stages

kth sub-process of DMU_j.$z_{dj}^{(1k,2l)}$ shows, dth element of the intermediate measure between 1kth and 2lth sub-process of DMU_j. The two-stage structure in this paper can easily be extended to multi-stage structures.

The model presented in this research that is grounded on the concept of relative efficiency. Most researchers have suggested existing NDEA models based on predefined DEA models and changed them according to their needs. However, this approach will cause some problems. One of these deficiencies is that no existing NDEA model can compute relational efficiency and there might be no efficiency equal to 1 in the final results. Hence, the modelling process in this paper will start with a relational efficiency definition.

To make a relation between DMU efficiency and its sub-stage efficiencies, the following definition is used.

$$E_j = \overline{w}^1 E_j^1 + \bar{w}^2 E_j^2 \tag{1}$$

In Eq. (1), E_j is DMU_j efficiency which is a convex combination of E_j^1 and E_j^2. E_j^1 and E_j^2 are the efficiencies of the first and second stages, respectively. $\overline{w}^1$ and $\overline{w}^2$ represent the weights that they are assigned to the initial and subsequent stage. To define these weights, three specifications should be considered. First, their sum should be equal to one. Second, weights need to be defined in a way that the NDEA model can be linearized. Third, they should represent the size and importance of the stage. Hence, they can be defined by the input share that each stage uses (Cook et al., 2010b). Also when we deal with a network structure, using geometric and arithmetic means are appropriate approaches to defining the efficiency of DMUs, stages and sub-stage.

The efficiency of each stage is also defined as the convex combination of sub-stage efficiency. So Eq. (1) will be changed to Eq. (2). This definition can be generalized to multi-stage networks.

$$E_j = \overline{w}^1 E_j^1 + \overline{w}^2 E_j^2 = \overline{w}^1 \sum_k w^k E_j^{1k} + \overline{w}^2 \sum_l w^l E_j^{2l} \tag{2}$$

Sub-stage weights (w^k and w^l) also need to satisfy the three conditions mentioned above. w^k and w^l are defined as follows:

$$w^k = \frac{\sum_i v_i^{1k} x_{ij}^{1k}}{\sum_k \sum_i v_i^{1k} x_{ij}^{1k}} \tag{3}$$

and

$$w^l = \frac{\sum_k \sum_d \eta_d^{(1k,2l)} z_{dj}^{(1k,2l)}}{\sum_l \sum_k \sum_d \eta_d^{(1k,2l)} z_{dj}^{(1k,2l)}} \tag{4}$$

Accordingly, stages' weights are also defined as (5) and (6).

$$\overline{w}^1 = \frac{\sum_k \sum_i v_i^{1k} x_{ij}^{1k}}{\sum_k \sum_i v_i^{1k} x_{ij}^{1k} + \sum_l \sum_k \sum_d \eta_d^{(1k,2l)} z_{dj}^{(1k,2l)}} \tag{5}$$

$$\overline{w}^2 = \frac{\sum_k \sum_l \sum_d \eta_d^{(1k,2l)} z_{dj}^{(1k,2l)}}{\sum_k \sum_i v_i^{1k} x_{ij}^{1k} + \sum_k \sum_l \sum_d \eta_d^{(1k,2l)} z_{dj}^{(1k,2l)}} \tag{6}$$

Considering the explained relations, DMU_j efficiency will be as follows:

$$E_j = \frac{\sum_k \sum_l \sum_d \eta_d^{(1k,2l)} z_{dj}^{(1k,2l)} + \sum_l \sum_r u_r^{2l} y_{rj}^{2l}}{\sum_k \sum_i v_i^{1k} x_{ij}^{1k} + \sum_k \sum_l \sum_d \eta_d^{(1k,2l)} z_{dj}^{(1k,2l)}} \tag{7}$$

To yield the model, the first T.D.T model is written based on the definition of E_j in (7).

$$\max RE_o = \frac{\dfrac{\sum_k \sum_l \sum_d \eta_d^{(1k,2l)} z_{do}^{(1k,2l)} + \sum_l \sum_r u_r^{2l} y_{ro}^{2l}}{\sum_k \sum_i v_i^{1k} x_{io}^{1k} + \sum_k \sum_l \sum_d \eta_d^{(1k,2l)} z_{do}^{(1k,2l)}}}{\max\left\{ \dfrac{\sum_k \sum_l \sum_d \eta_d^{(1k,2l)} z_{dj}^{(1k,2l)} + \sum_l \sum_r u_r^{2l} y_{rj}^{2l}}{\sum_k \sum_i v_i^{1k} x_{ij}^{1k} + \sum_k \sum_l \sum_d \eta_d^{(1k,2l)} z_{dj}^{(1k,2l)}} \middle| j = 1, \ldots, n \right\}} \tag{8}$$

$$s.t$$

$$v_i^{1k}, \eta_d^{(1k,2l)}, u_r^{21} \geq 0$$

Using Charnes and Cooper's transformation (Charnes & Cooper, 1962), we have:

$$t = \frac{1}{\max\left\{ \dfrac{\sum_k \sum_l \sum_d \eta_d^{(1k,2l)} z_{dj}^{(1k,2l)} + \sum_l \sum_r u_r^{2l} y_{rj}^{2l}}{\sum_k \sum_i v_i^{1k} x_{ij}^{1k} + \sum_k \sum_l \sum_d \eta_d^{(1k,2l)} z_{dj}^{(1k,2l)}} \middle| j = 1, \ldots, n \right\}} \tag{9}$$

Thus, the final proposed model converts to the following model:

$$\begin{aligned}
\max\ RE_o &= \sum_k \sum_l \sum_d \eta_d^{(1k,2l)} z_{do}^{(1k,2l)} + \sum_l \sum_r u_r^{2l} y_{ro}^{2l} \\
s.t \\
&\sum_k \sum_i v_i^{1k} x_{io}^{1k} + \sum_k \sum_l \sum_d \eta_d^{(1k,2l)} z_{do}^{(1k,2l)} = 1, \\
&\sum_k \sum_l \sum_d \eta_d^{(1k,2l)} z_{dj}^{(1k,2l)} + \sum_l \sum_r u_r^{2l} y_{rj}^{2l} - \sum_k \sum_i v_i^{1k} x_{ij}^{1k} \\
&- \sum_k \sum_l \sum_d \eta_d^{(1k,2l)} z_{dj}^{(1k,2l)} \leq 0,\ j = 1, \ldots, n, \\
&v_i^{1k},\ \eta_d^{(1k,2l)},\ u_r^{2l} \geq 0.
\end{aligned} \tag{10}$$

Theorem 1 Suppose that *DMUo* is under evaluation by Model (10).

1.1 The objective function value of the model (10) is less than 1.

1.2 The efficacy of every individual stage and its corresponding sub-stages is less than 1.

1.3 DMU is efficient only if all stages and sub-stages are efficient.

Proof 1.1 We know that

$$\sum_k \sum_l \sum_d \eta_d^{(1k,2l)} z_{do}^{(1k,2l)} + \sum_l \sum_r u_r^{2l} y_{ro}^{2l} - \sum_k \sum_i v_i^{1k} x_{io}^{1k} - \sum_k \sum_l \sum_d \eta_d^{(1k,2l)} z_{do}^{(1k,2l)} \leq 0^{\cdot} \tag{11}$$

Also, we have:

$$\sum_k \sum_i v_i^{1k} x_{io}^{1k} + \sum_k \sum_l \sum_d \eta_d^{(1k,2l)} z_{do}^{(1k,2l)} = 1 \tag{12}$$

So:

$$\sum_k \sum_l \sum_d \eta_d^{(1k,2l)} z_{do}^{(1k,2l)} + \sum_l \sum_r u_r^{2l} y_{ro}^{2l} \leq 1. \tag{13}$$

Proof 1.2 It is evident ■.

Proof 1.3 It is evident ■.

Identifying weaknesses within sub-units is a crucial aspect when evaluating the performance of an organization. Various research works have explored the Network DEA models in the DEA literature. Nevertheless, many of these existing models possess limitations, particularly in determining the relative efficiency unit. In this section, we will face these problems.

Now, it is important to show that the proposed model always introduces an efficient unit. To show this property, we need to prove Lemma 1.

Lemma 1 If *DMUo* is an under-evaluation unit, then there is a constraint that it is binding at the optimal solution.

Proof Suppose that (v_i^{*1k}, $\eta_d^{*(1k,2l)}$, $\eta_d^{*(1k,2l)}$, u_r^{*2l}) is the optimal solution of the *Model* (10) and z^* is the optimal value for the objective function of the mentioned model. Now, suppose that these constraints:

$$\sum_k \sum_l \sum_d \eta_d^{\prime(1k,2l)} z_{do}^{(1k,2l)} + \sum_l \sum_r u_r^{21} y_{ro}^{21} - \sum_k \sum_i v_i^{1k} x_{io}^{1k} - \sum_k \sum_l \sum_d \eta_d^{(1k,2l)} z_{do}^{(1k,2l)} \leq 0, j = 1, \ldots, n \tag{14}$$

are not binding at this optimal solution. In other words:

$$\sum_{k}\sum_{l}\sum_{d}\eta_d^{\prime *(1k,2l)} z_{dj}^{(1k,2l)} + \sum_{l}\sum_{r} u_r^{*2l} y_{rj}^{2l} - \sum_{k}\sum_{i} v_i^{*1k} x_{ij}^{1k}$$
$$- \sum_{k}\sum_{l}\sum_{d}\eta_d^{*(1k,2l)} z_{dj}^{(1k,2l)} < 0, j = 1, ..., n \quad (15)$$

We know that $y_o^{21} \geq 0, y_o^{21} \neq 0$. So without loss of generality, we suppose that $y_{1o}^{21} > 0$ and define:

$$A = (v_i^{*1k}, \eta_d^{*(1k,2l)}, \eta_d^{*(1k,2l)}, u_1^{*21} + \varepsilon, u_2^{*21}, ..., u_{R_{21}}^{*21}, ..., u_1^{*2L}, u_2^{*2L}, ..., u_{R_{2L}}^{*2L}) \quad (16)$$

so that:

$$\varepsilon = \min \left\{ \frac{\begin{array}{c}\sum_k \sum_i v_i^{*1k} x_{ij}^{1k} + \sum_k \sum_l \sum_d \eta_d^{*(1k,\,2l)} z_{dj}^{(1k,2l)} \\ -\sum_k \sum_l \sum_d \eta_d^{*(1k,2l)}, z_{dj}^{(1k,2l)} - \sum_l \sum_r u_r^{2l} y_{rj}^{2l}\end{array}}{y_{1j}^{21}} \middle| j \in Q \right\} \quad (17)$$

Such that $Q = \{j \middle| y_{1j}^{21} > 0\}$. Therefore, A is a feasible solution for the *model* (10). It is evident that the value of the objective function for this feasible solution is greater than z^* and this is a contradiction.

So, one of the constraints of *Model* (10) is bounding at the optimal solution ■.

Theorem 2 If $DMU_1, ..., DMU_n$ are under-evaluation DMUs, then there exists at least one.

DMU that it is belong to relative efficient DMUs set.
there is at least one DMU that demonstrates a certain level of efficiency.

Proof Suppose $(v_i^{*1k}, \eta_d^{*(1k,2l)}, \eta_d^{*(1k,2l)}, u_r^{*2l})$ represent the optimal solution obtained from the *Model* (10) during assessment of DMU_o and the constraint related to DMU_Q is binding. In other words:

$$\sum_{k}\sum_{l}\sum_{d}\eta_d^{\prime *(1k,2l)} z_{dQ}^{(1k,2l)} + \sum_{l}\sum_{r} u_r^{*2l} y_{rQ}^{2l}$$
$$- \sum_{k}\sum_{i} v_i^{*1k} x_{iQ}^{1k} - \sum_{k}\sum_{l}\sum_{d}\eta_d^{*(1k,2l)} z_{dQ}^{(1k,2l)} = 0, \quad (18)$$

Now, we prove that DMU_Q is an efficient unit.

Suppose that $\sum_{k}\sum_{i} v_i^{*1k} x_{iQ}^{1k} + \sum_{k}\sum_{l}\sum_{d}\eta_d^{*(1k,2l)} z_{dQ}^{(1k,2l)} = \alpha$. We know that $\alpha > 0$. If $\alpha = 1$ then the proof is complete; otherwise, we have:

$$\sum_k \sum_l \sum_d \frac{\eta_d^{*(1k,2l)}}{\alpha} z_{dQ}^{(1k,2l)} + \sum_l \sum_r \frac{u_r^{*2l}}{\alpha} y_{rQ}^{2l} = 1 \tag{19}$$

and

$$\begin{aligned}
&\sum_k \sum_l \sum_d \frac{\eta_d^{\prime*(1k,2l)}}{\alpha} z_{dj}^{(1k,2l)} + \sum_l \sum_r \frac{u_r^{*2l}}{\alpha} y_{rj}^{2l} \\
&- \sum_k \sum_i \frac{v_i^{*1k}}{\alpha} x_{ij}^{1k} - \sum_k \sum_l \sum_d \frac{\eta_d^{*(1k,2l)}}{\alpha} z_{dj}^{(1k,2l)} \\
&\leq 0, j = 1, \ldots, n.
\end{aligned} \tag{20}$$

So $\left(\frac{v_i^{*1k}}{\alpha}, \frac{\eta_d^{*(1k,2l)}}{\alpha}, \frac{\eta_d^{*(1k,2l)}}{\alpha}, \frac{u_r^{*2l}}{\alpha}\right)$ is a feasible solution for the model (10) when DMU_Q is under evaluation. It is evident that:

$$\begin{aligned}
&\sum_k \sum_l \sum_d \frac{\eta_d^{\prime*(1k,2l)}}{\alpha} z_{dQ}^{(1k,2l)} + \sum_l \sum_r \frac{u_r^{*2l}}{\alpha} y_{rQ}^{2l} \\
&- \sum_k \sum_i \frac{v_i^{*1k}}{\alpha} x_{iQ}^{1k} - \sum_k \sum_l \sum_d \frac{\eta_d^{*(1k,2l)}}{\alpha} z_{dQ}^{(1k,2l)} = 0,
\end{aligned} \tag{21}$$

as a result:

$$\begin{aligned}
&\sum_k \sum_l \sum_d \frac{\eta_d^{\prime*(1k,2l)}}{\alpha} z_{dQ}^{(1k,2l)} + \sum_l \sum_r \frac{u_r^{*2l}}{\alpha} y_{rQ}^{2l} \\
&= \sum_k \sum_i \frac{v_i^{*1k}}{\alpha} x_{iQ}^{1k} + \sum_k \sum_l \sum_d \frac{\eta_d^{*(1k,2l)}}{\alpha} z_{dQ}^{(1k,2l)} = 1
\end{aligned} \tag{22}$$

Finally, we have

$$\sum_k \sum_l \sum_d \frac{\eta_d^{*(1k,2l)}}{\alpha} z_{dQ}^{(1k,2l)} + \sum_l \sum_r \frac{u_r^{*2l}}{\alpha} y_{rQ}^{2l} = 1 \tag{23}$$

Thus DMU_Q is a relative-efficient unit ■.

It is important to highlight that the suggested model has the potential to be expanded to a production system with multiple stages.

4 A Real Case Study

In this section, a related case study based on the proposed model has been set up. We utilize the innovative network model to assess the performance of Iranian airline companies. Since the late 1970s, many airline companies have shown real enthusiasm for the evaluation of their efficiency (Bauer, 1990). This interest has led to the use of several methods for efficiency evaluation by famous airlines; for example, they use some approaches such as the factor productivity approach (Barbot et al., 2008; Nyshadham & Rao, 2000; Oum & Yu, 1995), Stochastic Frontier Analysis (SFA) (Martín et al., 2009; Scotti et al., 2012); the Turn Quist total factor productivity index (Good et al., 1993; Wanke & Barros, 2016); and DEA models (Barros & Peypoch, 2009; Jain & Natarajan, 2015; Lozano & Gutiérrez, 2014; Zhu, 2011). Although there is much research on the efficiency and productivity of airlines all over the world, there is still a need for more sophisticated and advanced modelling.

It should be noted that DEA studies in the airline industry are very limited and the few studies that exist treat the decision-making units as a "black box, where inputs are processed into outputs (Barros & Peypoch, 2009; Jain & Natarajan, 2015). Although the use of DEA is a positive development in the evaluation of the airline industries, there are still some problems. The major problem is that network DEA models used in airline efficiency evaluation are unable to introduce the efficient units and identify the reference units. Another problem is that the DEA models in the airline industry tend to use a series network while in reality, the structures are mixed as series and parallel. Due to these problems, this research aims to assess the performance of Iranian airline companies. Figure 5 shows a framework for using the proposed model in the Iranian airline industry.

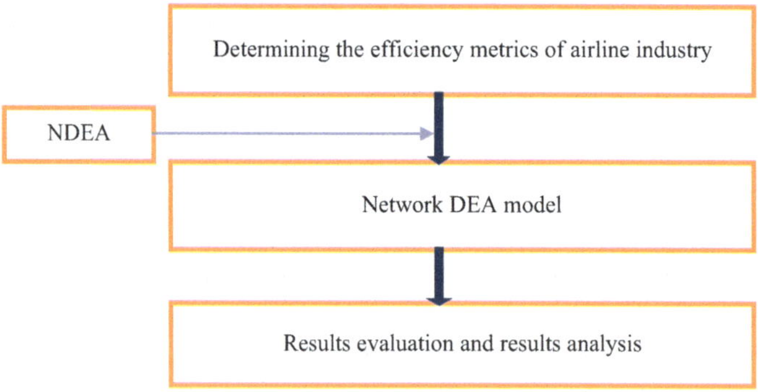

Fig. 5 Suggested performance assessment model of the Iranian airline industry

4.1 Determining the Efficiency Metrics of the Airline Industry

One of the most crucial factors of an efficient performance measurement system is the definition of the corresponding performance measures because these measures can guide managers in the process of decision-making. Since performance measures are selected based on the nature of the field study, they would vary in different situations. A review of the airline performance measurement literature shows great attention to cost-based performance measures. Ease of understanding makes it more welcomed by managers but its inflexibility and incompatibility with strategic focus motivated us to construct a new framework to cover these shortcomings.

Research in the airline industry is commonly classified into two distinct categories. The first category is classical strategic research, with a great deal of research available focusing on strategic variables such as:

- Focus on the core of the business.
- Internationalization.
- Load factor.

Another important category is productivity research. These studies use econometric methods to evaluate airline productivity. These two directions of research have two drawbacks:

- Most productivity research is confined to one airline or, ultimately, one country's airline. Therefore, the scope of these studies needs to be further developed to better reflect the global nature of airlines.
- The operational efficiency of an airline is often not addressed in strategic research. It is important to establish a connection between strategic questions and evaluating operational efficiency on a global scale. (Schefczyk, 1993).

Typically, assessments of airline performance can be classified into two groups. First, qualitative assessments take into account most of the indicators related to customers and services provided. Second, airline operations such as the number of passengers dislodged, income and expenses associated with operations as well as indicators such as occupancy rate, the number of people employed per seat, and so on.

The transportation research laboratory presents a report titled "Airlines Performance Indicators" annually, which analyzes the performance indicators of airlines worldwide, publishing the outputs and results of more than 50 airlines. Some of the issues they are looking at are fuel, manpower, profitability, occupancy, the number of people employed per kilometre seat, etc.

Schefczyk (1993) and Lemaitre (1998) have divided the performance criteria of airlines and airports into three categories: financial, marketing, and operational. Because operational and marketing indices are closely related, these criteria are taken into account in the literature simultaneously, and most studies have focused on the operational aspect.

Schefczyk (1993) used the DEA models to analyze and compare operational efficiencies in measuring the performance of 15 international airlines. One reason for choosing data envelopment analysis for performance evaluation is that this methodology is a nonparametric approach and does not require a relationship or function to link the inputs to the outputs. He presented a new approach to measuring performance. In this study, the inputs were divided into two categories: asset inputs, and cost inputs. The most important output of a passenger airline was the passenger income per kilometre, which generated capital through ticket sales by the commercial sector. Other outputs included cargo and other revenues. His model had 3 inputs and 2 outputs. Inputs included ton-kilometers, operating costs and non-flight-related assets. He divided the total operating income into two parts: passenger and non-passenger revenue and considered these two as outputs.

Tofallis (1997) applied the same indices and data but considered all inputs and outputs together, taking the related inputs and outputs and assigning an efficiency number to each segment using data envelopment analysis.

Feng and Wang (1997) introduced indices to assessment airlines based on financial ratios. In this research, the whole operation of the airline was divided into three parts: marketing, production, and operations and a total of 63 indicators were introduced to evaluate the sectors.

In his dissertation, Midkif (2000) examined all personnel activities for flying, from ticket sales to passenger departure from the airport. At MIT, Strina (2004) did her dissertation on analyzing US airline trends and performance. In this research, she studied some indicators such as occupation coefficient, labor productivity, and fleet productivity.

ICAO and IATA are two credible reference bodies that define standard indices for airlines and are accepted and used throughout the world. The number of indicators defined by IATA is large, and most of our managers use them to analyze the status of their lines to understand their position relative to their competitors. Indicators are ton-kilometer, carried passenger-kilometer, available passenger, number of carried passengers, occupancy coefficient, number of personnel per department and number of personnel per kilometer seat, operating income and expenses, number of accidents and incidents, operating income per carried ton-kilometers carried, fuel efficiency, average fleet age, and fleet utilization rate (Strina, 2006).

Wang (2006) analyzed the performance of Taiwan's airlines using MCDM and fuzzy sets. All of the indicators he considered were also financial ratios. But it is difficult to evaluate the performance of international airlines from their published financial information, as most airlines lease most of their aircraft. In addition, the differences between accounting and tax laws in different countries and the existence of large rental assets make the profit and loss statement and balance sheet information less relevant for performance comparisons. One solution is to use non-financial data. For example, the existing ton-kilometers index is much more accurate than flight depreciation which reflects the amount of aircraft capacity.

Barbot et al. (2008) calculated the efficiency and productivity of major airlines across different regions of the world using DEA and total factor productivity. Their model had 3 inputs and 3 outputs. Inputs included manpower (number of people

Table 1 The important indexes of Iranian airline efficiency evaluation

Raw	Index
1	Available ton-kilometer and passenger-kilometer
2	The mean age of fleet used
3	Passenger-kilometer revenue
4	Commercial and sales capacity
5	Repair and maintenance
6	The number of staff
7	Area of used buildings
8	Total costs
9	Airport coverage
10	Premium paid
11	Tone-kilometer revenue
12	Fuel cost
13	Navigation, landing and takeoff costs
14	Available seat-kilometer
15	Public and administrative expenses

working in the business core), fleet (number of active aircraft), and fuel (number of gallons consumed). Outputs were passenger-kilometers revenue, ton-kilometers shipped and other non-passenger and cargo operating revenues.

Now, to select significant variables that have more relationship with the efficiency of the Iranian airlines, we provide a full checklist consisting virtually of all variables (inputs and outputs) in the airline industry that previous studies used. Variables that we used in the checklist were distributed among experts of an Iranian airline. Also, we arranged an interview with the CEO of the Iranian airline where new variables that had serious effects on efficiency were added. In this stage, we had a checklist that was filtered by Iranian Airlines experts. The checklist consists of 15 elements, as illustrated in Table 1.

In this stage, a final checklist was designed based on these 15 indexes. A Likert five-choice checklist was used for final index identification. This checklist was distributed among 17 Iranian Airline CEOs. Since the checklist was based on quantitative indexes, a fuzzy method was used for the final measures selection. To reduce the inputs and outputs indexes and to identify index weights, a fuzzy method was used. In this paper, we used the triangular fuzzy numbers shown in Fig. 6. For example, the triangular fuzzy number for low is (0.1,0.3.0,5), where 0.1 and 0.5 are lower and upper bounds respectively and 0.3 is the middle of the fuzzy number. This approach can be used for the explanation of other fuzzy numbers in this paper.

Suppose that A is a triangular fuzzy number shown as $\left(\alpha\ m\ \beta\right)$. m is mean, α and β are left and right ranges, respectively. However, the fuzzy triangular average is obtained as follows:

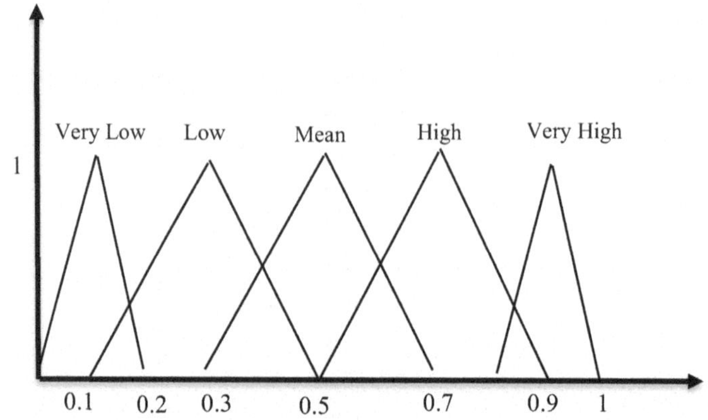

Fig. 6 Membership function of linguistic variables

$$A_{avg} = \frac{A_1 + \cdots + A_n}{n} = (\alpha_1, m_1, \beta_1) + \cdots + (\alpha_n, m_n, \beta_n)$$
$$= \left(\frac{1}{n}\sum_{i=1}^{n}\alpha_i, \frac{1}{n}\sum_{i=1}^{n}m_i, \frac{1}{n}\sum_{i=1}^{n}\beta_i\right) \quad (24)$$

The weighted triangular average is as follows:

$$A_{avg}^{w} = \frac{w_1A_1 + \cdots + w_nA_n}{w_1 + \cdots + w_n} \quad (25)$$

The approach the fuzzy coefficient is used to convert fuzzy coefficients to definite values. If there is a triangular fuzzy number, then the values of the total score are calculated from the following formulas. This method was developed by Chen and Huang (2008).

$$\mu_T(A) = \frac{m + \beta}{2(1 + \beta)} + \frac{m}{2(1 + \alpha)} \quad (26)$$

After collecting the questionnaires distributed among 17 managers, experts and CEOs, a definite number corresponding to each indicator was obtained to indicate its importance. The findings are illustrated in Table 2.

In presenting the model in this research, an attempt was made to consider all inputs and outputs related to operations because of the high score of the indexes. Only one point that must be considered is that the calculation of the sixth index of the checklist (the buildings used, the Rial value and the area to be used) in Iran itself requires extensive research work while the likelihood of achieving it is very low. As you can see, the least definite weight number obtained corresponds to this index, so we removed it according to the decision maker. Finally, 4 inputs and 2 outputs were determined. These inputs and outputs are reported in Table 3.

Table 2 The important indexes of Iranian Airline efficiency evaluation

Raw	Index	Very low	Low	Mean	High	Very high	β	m	α	μ_T
1	Available ton-kilometer and passenger-kilometer				3	14	0.982	0.865	0.747	0.713
2	The mean age of the fleet used		8	9			3.5	6.9	10.3	0.483
3	Passenger-kilometer revenue			5	8	4	0.865	0.688	0.512	0.644
4	Commercial and sales capacity	2	7	8			3.1	6.3	9.5	0.454
5	Repair and maintenance	2	10	5			2.5	5.7	8.9	0.428
6	Number of staff			5	9	3	0.859	0.676	0.494	0.639
7	Area of used buildings	2	10	5			0.523	0.335	0.147	0.428
8	Total costs		3	4	3	7	0.823	0.666	0.506	0.629
9	Airport coverage	5	3	9			3	5.9	8.8	0.432
10	Premium paid		7	8	2		3.7	7.1	10.5	0.491
11	Tone-kilometer revenue		2	9	2	4	0.770	0.594	0.418	0.595
12	Fuel cost		7	10			3.7	7.1	10.5	0.491
13	Navigation, landing and takeoff costs	2	5	10			3.5	6.7	9.9	0.471
14	Available seat-kilometer		4	6	3	4	0.759	0.582	0.409	0.588
15	Public and administrative expenses	2	10	5			2.5	5.7	8.9	0.428

Table 3 Inputs and outputs of Iranian airlines efficiency evaluation

Raw	Inputs	Raw	Outputs
1	Total costs	1	Tone-kilometer revenue
2	The number of staff	2	Passenger-kilometer revenue
3	Available ton kilometer and passenger-kilometer		
4	Available seat-kilometer		

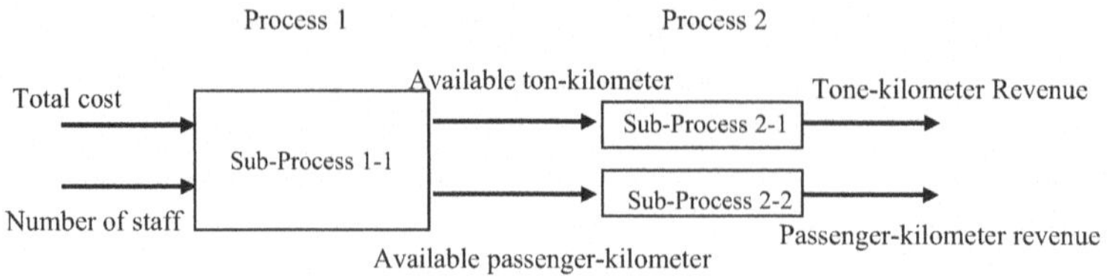

Fig. 7 The structure of inputs and outputs of Iranian airlines

By considering the inputs and outputs and interviewing some experts in this area, the network structure for processing inputs into outputs was determined. This network structure is based on the DEA model as shown in Fig. 7.

4.2 Performance Evaluation

Using *Model* (10), we evaluated Iranian airlines. The findings are presented in Table 4.

As can be seen airlines 2, 5, 11, and 12 are generally efficient and all their sub-stage are efficient as well. Also in process 1, all units are efficient. Thus, to improve their performance, airlines need to focus on processes. This issue is a confirmation of Theorem 1. Now for better comparison, these results are shown in Chart 1.

It is evident that unit 10 has the weakest overall performance. Also among the sub-stages 2–1 and sub-stages 2–2, units 5 and 9 have the weakest performance, respectively.

Table 4 The experts' opinion about the importance of Iranian airlines efficiency evaluation indexes

DMUs	Overall efficiency	Sub-process 1–1	Sub-process 2–1	Sub-process 2–2
1	0.918	1	1	0.916
2	1	1	1	1
3	0.873	1	1	0.871
4	0.764	1	1	0.734
5	1	1	1	1
6	0.799	1	1	0.047
7	0.898	1	1	0.89
8	0.919	1	1	0.918
9	0.961	1	0.199	1
10	0.516	1	0.67	0.1
11	1	1	1	1
12	1	1	1	1

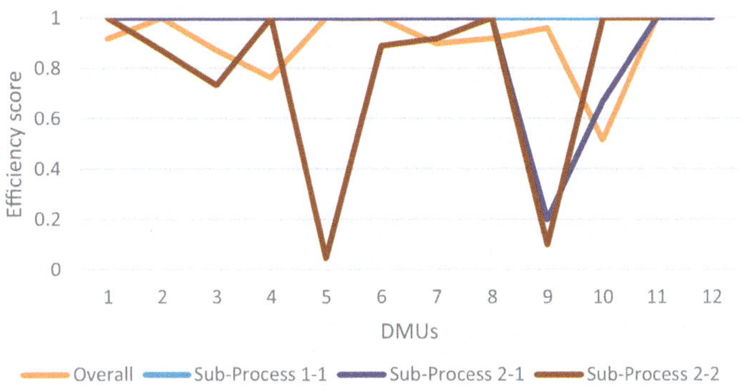

Chart 1 The results of performance evaluation

5 Conclusion

This paper focused on developing a new model for calculating the relative efficiency score in the mixed structure to introduce the relative efficient units. For empirical validity, we applied our method for the evaluation of Iranian airlines. So, to select significant variables that had a stronger relationship with the efficiency of considered Iranian airlines, we provided a full checklist consisting of virtually all variables (inputs and outputs) in the airline industry used in previous studies. Variables that we used in the checklist were distributed among experts of Iranian airlines. Also, we arranged an interview with the CEO of an Iranian airline, where new variables that had serious effects on the efficiency of Iranian airlines were added. After collecting the questionnaires distributed among 17 managers, experts and CEOs, a definite number corresponding to each indicator was obtained to indicate its importance. Finally, 5 inputs and 2 outputs were determined. By considering the inputs and outputs and interviewing some experts in this area, the network structure for processing inputs into outputs was determined. Using *Model* (10), we evaluated Iranian airlines and specified efficient and inefficient units. We suggest focusing on the alternative optimal solutions and the unique efficiency of each stage for further research.

References

Akther, S., Fukuyama, H., & Weber, W. L. (2013). Estimating two-stage network slacks-based inefficiency: An application to Bangladesh banking. *Omega, 41*(1), 88–96. https://doi.org/10.1016/j.omega.2011.02.009

Amado, C. A., Santos, S. P., & Marques, P. M. (2012). Integrating the data envelopment analysis and the balanced scorecard approaches for enhanced performance assessment. *Omega, 40*(3), 390–403. https://doi.org/10.1016/j.omega.2011.06.006

Aviles-Sacoto, S., Cook, W. D., Imanirad, R., & Zhu, J. (2015). Two-stage network DEA: When intermediate measures can be treated as outputs from the second stage. *Journal of the Operational Research Society, 66*(11), 1868–1877. https://doi.org/10.1057/jors.2015.14

Barros, C. P., & Peypoch, N. (2009). An evaluation of European airlines' operational performance. *International Journal of Production Economics, 122*(2), 525–533.

Bauer, P. W. (1990). Decomposing TFP growth in the presence of cost inefficiency, nonconstant returns to scale, and technological progress. *Journal of Productivity Analysis, 1*(4), 287–299. https://doi.org/10.1007/BF00160047

Barat, M., Tohidi, G., & Sanei, M. (2019). DEA for nonhomogeneous mixed networks. *Asia Pacific Management Review, 24*(2), 161–166.

Bi, G., Ding, J., Luo, Y., & Liang, L. (2011). Resource allocation and target setting for parallel production system based on DEA. *Applied Mathematical Modelling, 35*(9), 4270–4280. https://doi.org/10.1016/j.apm.2011.02.048

Barbot, C., Costa, Á., & Sochirca, E. (2008). Airlines performance in the new market context: A comparative productivity and efficiency analysis. *Journal of Air Transport Management, 14*(5), 270–274. https://doi.org/10.1016/j.jairtraman.2008.05.003

Banker, R. D., Charnes, A., & Cooper, W. W. (1984). Some models for estimating technical and scale inefficiencies in data envelopment analysis. *Management Science, 30*(9), 1078–1092.

Castelli, L., Pesenti, R., & Ukovich, W. (2004). DEA-like models for the efficiency evaluation of hierarchically structured units. *European Journal of Operational Research, 154*(2), 465–476. https://doi.org/10.1016/S0377-2217(03)00182-6

Charnes, A., & Cooper, W. W. (1962). Programming with linear fractional functionals. *Naval Research Logistics Quarterly, 9*(3–4), 181–186. https://doi.org/10.1002/nav.3800090303

Charnes, A., Cooper, W. W., & Rhodes, E. (1978). Measuring the efficiency of decision making units. *European Journal of Operational Research, 2*(6), 429–444. https://doi.org/10.1016/0377-2217(78)90138-8

Chen, L. H., & Huang, L. (2009). Portfolio optimization of equity mutual funds with fuzzy return rates and risks. *Expert Systems with Applications, 36*(2), 3720–3727.

Chen, C., & Yan, H. (2011). Network DEA model for supply chain performance evaluation. *European Journal of Operational Research, 213*(1), 147–155. https://doi.org/10.1016/j.ejor.2011.03.010

Chen, Y., Cook, W. D., Li, N., & Zhu, J. (2009b). Additive efficiency decomposition in two-stage DEA. *European Journal of Operational Research, 196*(3), 1170–1176. https://doi.org/10.1016/j.ejor.2008.05.011

Chen, Y., Liang, L., & Zhu, J. (2009a). Equivalence in two-stage DEA approaches. *European Journal of Operational Research, 193*(2), 600–604. https://doi.org/10.1016/j.ejor.2007.11.040

Cook, W. D., Liang, L., & Zhu, J. (2010a). Measuring performance of two-stage network structures by DEA: A review and future perspective. *Omega, 38*(6), 423–430. https://doi.org/10.1016/j.omega.2009.12.001

Cook, W. D., Zhu, J., Bi, G., & Yang, F. (2010b). Network DEA: Additive efficiency decomposition. *European Journal of Operational Research, 207*(2), 1122–1129. https://doi.org/10.1016/j.ejor.2010.05.006

Despotis, D. K., Koronakos, G., & Sotiros, D. (2016a). Composition versus decomposition in two-stage network DEA: A reverse approach. *Journal of Productivity Analysis, 45*(1), 71–87. https://doi.org/10.1007/s11123-014-0415-x

Despotis, D. K., Sotiros, D., & Koronakos, G. (2016b). A network DEA approach for series multi-stage processes. *Omega, 61*, 35–48. https://doi.org/10.1016/j.omega.2015.07.005

Despotis, D. K., Koronakos, G., & Sotiros, D. (2016c). The "weak-link" approach to network DEA for two-stage processes. *European Journal of Operational Research, 254*(2), 481–492. https://doi.org/10.1016/j.ejor.2016.03.028

Despotis, D. K., & Koronakos, G. (2014). Efficiency assessment in two-stage processes: A novel network DEA approach. *Procedia Computer Science, 31*, 299–307.

Ding, T., Zhang, Y., Zhang, D., & Li, F. (2023). Performance evaluation of Chinese research universities: A parallel interactive network DEA approach with shared and fixed sum inputs. *Socio-Economic Planning Sciences*, 101582.

Du, J., Zhu, J., Cook, W. D., & Huo, J. (2015a). DEA models for parallel systems: Game-theoretic approaches. *Asia-Pacific Journal of Operational Research, 32*(02), 1550008. https://doi.org/10.1142/S0217595915500086

Du, J., Chen, Y., & Huo, J. (2015b). DEA for non-homogenous parallel networks. *Omega, 56*, 122–132. https://doi.org/10.1016/j.omega.2014.10.001

Esfidani, S., Lotfi, F. H., Razavyan, S., & Ebrahimnejad, A. (2020). A slacks-based measure approach for efficiency decomposition in multi-period two-stage systems. *RAIRO-Operations Research, 54*(6), 1657–1671.

Ebrahimzadeh Shermeh, H., Alavidoost, M. H., & Darvishinia, R. (2018). Evaluating the efficiency of power companies using data envelopment analysis based on SBM models: A case study in power industry of Iran. *Journal of Applied Research on Industrial Engineering, 5*(4), 286–295.

Fallah, M. (2020). Efficiency, effectiveness and productivity of personnel's health in petrochemical companies. *Journal of Applied Research on Industrial Engineering, 7*(3), 280–286.

Fang, L. (2020). Stage efficiency evaluation in a two-stage network data envelopment analysis model with weight priority. *Omega, 97*, 102081.

Färe, R., & Grosskopf, S. (1996). Productivity and intermediate products: A frontier approach. *Economics Letters, 50*(1), 65–70. https://doi.org/10.1016/0165-1765(95)00729-6

Färe, R., & Grosskopf, S. (2000). Network DEA. *Socio-Economic Planning Sciences, 34*, 35–49. https://doi.org/10.1016/S0038-0121(99)00012-9

Farrell, M. J. (1957). The measurement of productive efficiency. *Journal of the Royal Statistical Society: Series A (general), 120*(3), 253–281.

Feng, C. M., & Wang, R. T. (2000). Performance evaluation for airlines including the consideration of financial ratios. *Journal of Air Transport Management, 6*(3), 133–142. https://doi.org/10.1016/S0969-6997(00)00003-X

Fukuyama, H., & Mirdehghan, S. M. (2012). Identifying the efficiency status in network DEA. *European Journal of Operational Research, 220*(1), 85–92. https://doi.org/10.1016/j.ejor.2012.01.024

Fukuyama, H., & Weber, W. L. (2010). A slacks-based inefficiency measure for a two-stage system with bad outputs. *Omega, 38*(5), 398–409. https://doi.org/10.1016/j.omega.2009.10.006

Good, D. H., Nadiri, M. I., Röller, L. H., & Sickles, R. C. (1993). Efficiency and productivity growth comparisons of European and US air carriers: A first look at the data. *Journal of Productivity Analysis, 4*(1), 115–125. https://doi.org/10.1007/BF01073469

Gong, Y., Zhu, J., Chen, Y., & Cook, W. D. (2018a). DEA as a tool for auditing: Application to Chinese manufacturing industry with parallel network structures. *Annals of Operations Research, 263*(1), 247–269. https://doi.org/10.1007/s10479-016-2197-1

Gong, Y., Zhu, J., Chen, Y., & Cook, W. D. (2018b). DEA as a tool for auditing: Application to Chinese manufacturing industry with parallel network structures. *Annals of Operations Research, 263*, 247–269.

https://www.icao.int/Pages/default.aspx.

IATA. (2006). World air transport statistics. Retrieved 20 November, 2020, from https://www.iata.org/en/publications/store/world-air-transport-statistics/.

lo Storto, C. (2020). Measuring the efficiency of the urban integrated water service by parallel network DEA: The case of Italy. *Journal of Cleaner Production, 276*, 123170.

Jain, R. K., & Natarajan, R. (2015). A DEA study of airlines in India. *Asia Pacific Management Review, 20*(4), 285–292.

Kao, C. (2018). Multiplicative aggregation of division efficiencies in network data envelopment analysis. *European Journal of Operational Research, 270*(1), 328–336. https://doi.org/10.1016/j.ejor.2017.09.047

Kao, C. (2009). Efficiency measurement for parallel production systems. *European Journal of Operational Research, 196*(3), 1107–1112. https://doi.org/10.1016/j.ejor.2008.04.020

Kao, C., & Lin, P. H. (2012). Efficiency of parallel production systems with fuzzy data. *Fuzzy Sets and Systems, 198*, 83–98. https://doi.org/10.1016/j.fss.2012.01.004

Kao, C., & Hwang, S. N. (2008). Efficiency decomposition in two-stage data envelopment analysis: An application to non-life insurance companies in Taiwan. *European Journal of Operational Research, 185*(1), 418–429. https://doi.org/10.1016/j.ejor.2006.11.041

Kao, C., & Liu, S. T. (2019). Cross efficiency measurement and decomposition in two basic network systems. *Omega, 83*, 70–79. https://doi.org/10.1016/j.omega.2018.02.004

Kang, C. C., Feng, C. M., Chou, P. F., Wey, W. M., & Khan, H. A. (2023). Mixed network DEA models with shared resources for measuring and decomposing performance of public transportation systems. *Research in Transportation Business & Management, 46*, 100828.

Khoveyni, M., & Eslami, R. (2021). Efficiency stability region for two-stage production processes with intermediate products. *Computers & Industrial Engineering, 151*, 106950.

Kremantzis, M. D., Beullens, P., Kyrgiakos, L. S., & Klein, J. (2022). Measurement and evaluation of multi-function parallel network hierarchical DEA systems. *Socio-Economic Planning Sciences, 84*, 101428.

Lemaitre, A. (1998). The development of performance indicators at airports: a management perspective. Paper presented at the 8th world conference on transport research. Amsterdam: Pergamon.

Lewis, H. F., & Sexton, T. R. (2004). Network DEA: Efficiency analysis of organizations with complex internal structure. *Computers and Operations Research, 31*(9), 1365–1410. https://doi.org/10.1016/S0305-0548(03)00095-9

Liu, J. S., & Lu, W. M. (2010). DEA and ranking with the network-based approach: A case of R&D performance. *Omega, 38*(6), 453–464. https://doi.org/10.1016/j.omega.2009.12.002

Li, Y., Chen, Y., Liang, L., & Xie, J. (2012). DEA models for extended two-stage network structures. *Omega, 40*(5), 611–618. https://doi.org/10.1016/j.omega.2011.11.007

Lozano, S., & Gutiérrez, E. (2014). A slacks-based network DEA efficiency analysis of European airlines. *Transportation Planning and Technology, 37*(7), 623–637.

Lu, W. M., Wang, W. K., Hung, S. W., & Lu, E. T. (2012). The effects of corporate governance on airline performance: Production and marketing efficiency perspectives. *Transportation Research Part E: Logistics and Transportation Review, 48*(2), 529–544. https://doi.org/10.1016/j.tre.2011.09.003

Martín, J. C., Román, C., & Voltes-Dorta, A. (2009). A stochastic frontier analysis to estimate the relative efficiency of Spanish airports. *Journal of Productivity Analysis, 31*, 163–176.

Ma, J., Qi, L., & Deng, L. (2017). Efficiency measurement and decomposition in hybrid two-stage DEA with additional inputs. *Expert Systems with Applications, 79*, 348–357. https://doi.org/10.1016/j.eswa.2017.03.016

Ma, J., & Chen, L. (2018). Evaluating operation and coordination efficiencies of parallel-series two-stage system: A data envelopment analysis approach. *Expert Systems with Applications, 91*, 1–11. https://doi.org/10.1016/j.eswa.2017.08.045

Midkif, A. H., Hansman, R. J., & Reynolds, T. G. (2004). *Air carrier flight operations* [No. ICAT-2004–3]. MIT International Center for Air Transportation.

Nyshadham, E. A., & Rao, V. K. (2000). Assessing efficiency of European airports: A total factor productivity approach. *Public Works Management & Policy, 5*(2), 106–114.

Oum, T. H., & Yu, C. (1995). A productivity comparison of the world's major airlines. *Journal of Air Transport Management, 2*(3–4), 181–195. https://doi.org/10.1016/0969-6997(96)00007-5

Paradi, J. C., Rouatt, S., & Zhu, H. (2011). Two-stage evaluation of bank branch efficiency using data envelopment analysis. *Omega, 39*(1), 99–109. https://doi.org/10.1016/j.omega.2010.04.002

Park, J., Lee, B. K., & Low, J. M. (2022). A two-stage parallel network DEA model for analyzing the operational capability of container terminals. *Maritime Policy & Management, 49*(1), 118–139.

Sahoo, B. K., Zhu, J., Tone, K., & Klemen, B. M. (2014). Decomposing technical efficiency and scale elasticity in two-stage network DEA. *European Journal of Operational Research, 233*(3), 584–594. https://doi.org/10.1016/j.ejor.2013.09.046

Saleh, H., Hosseinzadeh Lotfi, F., Toloie Eshlaghy, A., & Shafiee, M. (2011). A new two-stage DEA model for bank branch performance evaluation. In 3rd National Conference on Data Envelopment Analysis, Islamic Azad University of Firoozkooh.

Saleh, H., & Rostamy, M. M. (2013). Performance evaluation in bank branch with two-stage DEA model.

Sahoo, B. K., Saleh, H., Shafiee, M., Tone, K., & Zhu, J. (2021). An alternative approach to dealing with the composition approach for series network production processes. *Asia-Pacific Journal of Operational Research, 38*(06), 2150004.

Schefczyk, M. (1993). Operational performance of airlines: An extension of traditional measurement paradigms. *Strategic Management Journal, 14*(4), 301–317. https://doi.org/10.1002/smj.4250140406

Scotti, D., Malighetti, P., Martini, G., & Volta, N. (2012). The impact of airport competition on technical efficiency: A stochastic frontier analysis applied to Italian airport. *Journal of Air Transport Management, 22*, 9–15.

Seyed Esmaeili, F. S., Rostamy-Malkhalifeh, M., & Hosseinzadeh Lotfi, F. (2020). Two-stage network DEA model under interval data. *Mathematical Analysis and Convex Optimization, 1*(2), 103–108.

Shafiee, M., Lotfi, F. H., & Saleh, H. (2014). Supply chain performance evaluation with data envelopment analysis and balanced scorecard approach. *Applied Mathematical Modelling, 38*(21–22), 5092–5112.

Shafiee, M., Saleh, H., & Ziyari, R. (in Press). Projects efficiency evaluation by means data envelopment analysis and balanced scorecard. *Decisions and operations research*. https://doi.org/10.22105/DMOR.2020.229828.1150.

Shi, X., Emrouznejad, A., & Yu, W. (2021). Overall efficiency of operational process with undesirable outputs containing both series and parallel processes: A SBM network DEA model. *Expert Systems with Applications, 178*, 115062.

Strina, F. (2006). *US airline industry trends and performance 1999–2004: analysis of Form 41 data* (Master's thesis, Department of Aeronautics and Astronautics, Massachusetts Institute of Technology). Retrieved from http://hdl.handle.net/1721.1/35562.

Tavana, M., Khalili-Damghani, K., Arteaga, F. J. S., Mahmoudi, R., & Hafezalkotob, A. (2018). Efficiency decomposition and measurement in two-stage fuzzy DEA models using a bargaining game approach. *Computers and Industrial Engineering, 118*, 394–408. https://doi.org/10.1016/j.cie.2018.03.010

Tofallis, C. (1997). Input efficiency profiling: An application to airlines. *Computers and Operations Research, 24*(3), 253–258. https://doi.org/10.1016/S0305-0548(96)00067-6

Tone, K., Kweh, Q. L., Lu, W. M., & Ting, I. W. K. (2019). Modeling investments in the dynamic network performance of insurance companies. *Omega, 88*, 237–247. https://doi.org/10.1016/j.omega.2018.09.005

Tone, K., & Tsutsui, M. (2014a). Dynamic DEA with network structure: A slacks-based measure approach. *Omega, 42*(1), 124–131. https://doi.org/10.1016/j.omega.2013.04.002

Tone, K., & Tsutsui, M. (2014b). Dynamic DEA with network structure: A slacks-based measure approach. *Omega, 42*(1), 124–131.

Tone, K., & Tsutsui, M. (2009). Network DEA: A slacks-based measure approach. *European Journal of Operational Research, 197*(1), 243–252. https://doi.org/10.1016/j.ejor.2008.05.027

Wanke, P., & Barros, C. P. (2016). Efficiency in Latin American airlines: A two-stage approach combining virtual frontier dynamic DEA and simplex regression. *Journal of Air Transport Management, 54*, 93–103. https://doi.org/10.1016/j.jairtraman.2016.04.001

Wang, Y. J. (2008). Applying FMCDM to evaluate financial performance of domestic airlines in Taiwan. *Expert Systems with Applications, 34*(3), 1837–1845.

Yong, Z. H. A., Liang, L., & Xu, C. Y. (2008). Two-stage BCC model for cooperative efficiency evaluation using a geometric mean method. *Systems Engineering-Theory and Practice, 28*(10), 53-58. https://doi.org/10.1016/S1874-8651(10)60001-4.

Yu, M. M., & Fan, C. K. (2009). Measuring the performance of multimode bus transit: A mixed structure network DEA model. *Transportation Research Part e: Logistics and Transportation Review, 45*(3), 501–515.

Zhou, X., Luo, R., Yao, L., Cao, S., Wang, S., & Lev, B. (2018b). Assessing integrated water use and wastewater treatment systems in China: A mixed network structure two-stage SBM DEA model. *Journal of Cleaner Production, 185*, 533–546.

Zhu, J. (2011). Airlines performance via two-stage network DEA approach. *Journal of CENTRUM Cathedra: THe Business and Economics Research Journal, 4*(2), 260–269.

Zhou, X., Luo, R., Yao, L., Cao, S., Wang, S., & Lev, B. (2018a). Assessing integrated water use and wastewater treatment systems in China: A mixed network structure two-stage SBM DEA model. *Journal of Cleaner Production, 185*, 533–546. https://doi.org/10.1016/j.jclepro.2018.02.278

Possibilistic Network DEA Approach for Performance Evaluation of Two-Stage Decision Making Units Under Uncertainty

Pejman Peykani, Mostafa Sargolzaei, Farhad Hamidzadeh, Fatemeh Sadat Seyed Esmaeili, and Amir Takaloo

Abstract Uncertainty is a significant context to investigate when assessing entities. In the presence of imprecise and vague data, this study presents a novel method for evaluating the performance of decision-making units (DMUs) utilizing a network structure consisting of two stages. To present the fuzzy network data envelopment analysis (FNDEA) model, two-stage data envelopment analysis (TSDEA), chance-constrained programming (CCP), and possibilistic programming are employed. Furthermore, the possibilistic network data envelopment analysis (PNDEA) method can be utilized under various returns to scale (RTS) assumptions. To measure the performance of investment firms (IFs) using a two-stage structure that includes portfolio and operational management procedures, the developed fuzzy network DEA model is implemented. In addition, IFs like mutual funds (MFs) and investment organizations are extremely significant organizations to make investments in capital markets. Consequently, assessing the performance of these firms to identify efficient IFs and propose appropriate solutions for inefficient IFs is important. Finally, a real-world case study from the Tehran Stock Exchange is used, and the findings indicate that the developed model is effective.

P. Peykani (✉)
Department of Industrial Engineering, Faculty of Engineering, Khatam University, Tehran, Iran
e-mail: p.peykani@khatam.ac.ir; pejman.peykani@yahoo.com

M. Sargolzaei · A. Takaloo
Department of Finance and Banking, Faculty of Management and Accounting, Allameh Tabataba'i University, Tehran, Iran
e-mail: mostafa.sargolzaei@atu.ac.ir

A. Takaloo
e-mail: amirtakalloo@yahoo.com

F. Hamidzadeh · F. S. Seyed Esmaeili
School of Industrial Engineering, Iran University of Science and Technology, Tehran, Iran
e-mail: farhad.hamidzadeh@gmail.com

F. S. Seyed Esmaeili
e-mail: f_seyed@mail.iust.ac.ir

© The Author(s), under exclusive license to Springer Nature Singapore Pte Ltd. 2024
S. A. Edalatpanah et al. (eds.), *Analytical Decision Making and Data Envelopment Analysis*, Infosys Science Foundation Series in Mathematical Sciences,
https://doi.org/10.1007/978-981-97-6972-8_3

Keywords Two-stage structure · Investment firms · Data uncertainty · Fuzzy network data envelopment analysis · Possibilistic programming

1 Introduction

One of the data-driven approaches for evaluating the decision-making units' (DMUs) performance is data envelopment analysis (DEA), which converts several inputs into several outputs (Cooper et al., 2011; Peykani et al., 2020a, b, 2021b). In addition, DEA is a non-parametric approach that evaluates the DMUs' efficiency without requiring a production function (Liu et al., 2016; Omrani et al., 2022). Charnes et al. (1978), motivated by Farrell (1957), developed the DEA model for assessing the related DMUs group's efficiencies that utilize various inputs to generate various outputs with the constant returns to scale assumption. The presented approach had been described by Banker et al. (1984) for evaluating efficiencies with the variable returns to scale assumptions.

Notably, conventional and traditional DEA models disregard internal or linking activities, but in lots of real-world cases, DMUs could have the network or internal structures. On the other hand, traditional DEA structures were indicated as black boxes or whole units without providing any specific information regarding the internal components (Hosseinzadeh Hamidzadeh & Pishvaee, 2023; Lotfi et al., 2023). Black boxes DEA approaches do not provide suitable information to determine inefficiency (Henriques et al., 2020). Furthermore, there is a lack of clarity on what takes place regarding the black box DEA structures, and internal interactions utilized by the DEA have not yet been investigated (Tavana et al., 2018a, b). This paper performs an investigation of internal structures, taking into account the full structures of investment firms (IFs) rather than considering them as black boxes.

When using network data envelopment analysis (NDEA) structures for determining the DMUs' performance within real-world circumstances, it is crucial to take into account the element of uncertainty (Peykani et al., 2021a). Even a slight deviation or bias in values can lead to significant variations in final results (Peykani et al., 2018). To address this issue, one effective method is fuzzy network data envelopment analysis (FNDEA), which can accurately evaluate the DMUs' efficiency with network structures despite imprecise and vague data. FNDEA has gained popularity in recent years due to its ability to handle uncertainty and imprecision in data. It is particularly useful when coping with complex systems that have multiple inputs and outputs, as well as relations between them. FNDEA utilizes fuzzy set theory to demonstrate imprecise or vague data, which allows for a more accurate representation of real-world circumstances. This structure has been utilized in several fields, such as finance, healthcare, transportation, and manufacturing. In conclusion, FNDEA is a considerable tool for examining the efficiencies of DMUs with network structures while accounting for uncertainty and imprecision in data (Tavassoli & Farzipoor Saen, 2023). In the following sections, we will provide a short overview of some notable studies that have utilized FNDEA.

The data must be crisp by default in the basic DEA model. Subsequently, in real-world applications, the DEA model may confront imprecise and vague inputs and outputs. Thus, fuzzy DEA models were developed to address this issue. A fuzzy mathematical programming method, for the first time, was introduced by Sengupta (1992), including a collection of fuzzy theories towards the DEA approaches. Kao and Liu (2000) proposed an approach for evaluating the DMUs' efficiency within uncertain data. The α-cut method was utilized for transforming the FDEA model into a traditional crisp DEA approach. The approach developed by Saati et al. (2002), involved the description of a fuzzy DEA structure and the utilization of an α-level to transform the developed approach into an interval-based mathematical programming approach. Kao and Liu (2007) extended their previous method to encounter the missing value. For coping with the two-stage DEA network structure, Kao and Liu (2011) utilized the α-cut method when coping with fuzzy data, and utilized related method in Taiwan non-life insurance organizations. Hosseinzadeh Lotfi et al. (2009) expanded the utilization of multi-activity network DEA to include triangular fuzzy outputs and inputs. On the other side, they presented a function for ranking to suggest an equivalent crisp version of fuzzy DEA of multi-activity network. A network structure with two stages for fuzzy DEA that could evaluate dairy supply chains' agility performance under uncertain conditions was proposed by Khalili-Damghani et al. (2012). Furthermore, A three-stage structure using fuzzy DEA to assess the serial processes implementation, containing just-in-time (JIT) procedures, goals in dairy supply chains, and agility indices was described by Khalili-Damghani and Taghavifard (2012).

In the existence of fuzzy data, Lozano and Moreno (2013) expanded a DEA approach for twenty-four non-life insurance DMUs in Taiwan, considering a two-stage structure. Khalili-Damghani and Tavana (2012) described a FNDEA approach to assess efficiency in supply chains efficiency's agility. A two-stage DEA utilizing a fuzzy multi-objective programming approach for assessing the performance of United States bank holding companies was proposed by Wang et al. (2014). A new fuzzy network slack-based measure to assess the performance of supply chain networks considering reverse and forward logistics was developed by Momeni et al. (2014). Liu et al. (2016) described an approach for ranking the fuzzy two-stage efficiency DEA methods. In consideration of the fact that there are fuzzy data, Kao (2014) utilized α-cut and membership grade approaches to measure efficiency in network DEA models.

Lozano and Moreno (2014) adapted a variety of fuzzy DEA methods to the network DEA framework for managing fuzzy data where the DMUs are organized by a network framework. For assessing organizations in green supply chain management (GSCM), a novel network DEA approach that includes dual-role elements, fuzzy data, and undesirable outputs was presented by Mirhedayatian et al. (2014). Furthermore, for supply chain assessment investigation, a fuzzy supply chain DEA by integrating fuzzy intermediate measures within a triangular fuzzy membership function was developed by Xia et al. (2014). Additionally, a two-stage fuzzy network DEA approach based on Stackelberg game theory and utilizing it in the banking system was presented by Tavana and Khalili-Damghani (2014). In addition, a fuzzy dynamic network DEA method to assess airport functionality was described by Olfat et al. (2016).

It should be mentioned that a fuzzy network slacks-based measure approach to local power firms' evaluation in Iran using fuzzy data was developed by Shermeh et al. (2016). Thus, a dynamic network DEA approach within a fuzzy context was developed by Soltanzadeh and Omrani (2018). Additionally, for demonstrating the capabilities of the presented FNDEA approach, they utilized a study of Iran's airline industry as a case study. On the other side, a fuzzy DEA approach with a two-stage structure by utilizing a bargaining game method was described by Tavana et al., (2018a, b). The authors then utilized the presented approach for evaluating branches of Saman Bank's performance in Iran by taking into consideration the branches' levels of profitability and productivity.

A novel FNDEA model according to the fuzzy arithmetic method for travel and airport section benchmarking was proposed by Hatami-Marbini (2019). Additionally, a fuzzy network epsilon-based DEA technique to assess supply chain performance was developed by Li et al. (2019). In the situation of uncertainty, J.-Sharahi & Khalili-Damghani (2019) used fuzzy programming to setting targets and allocation of resources in NDEA. For assessing the two-stage DMUs performance, a double frontier fuzzy network DEA method was described by Amirteimoori et al. (2020). Shi et al. (2020) have published a Fuzzy network DEA method for evaluating the system efficiency utilizing Stackelberg game theory. Fathi and Farzipoor Saen. (2021) assessed sustainability of supply chains using hybrid approach including common set of weights (CSW) technique, double frontier fuzzy network DEA approach, and Malmquist productivity index (MPI).

A fuzzy double frontier NDEA approach for assessing the sustainability of supply chain was presented by Tavassoli et al. (2021). The developed model is a type of the radial DEA models and predicts the pessimistic and optimistic sustainability of supply chain. A fuzzy NDEA to assess the Iranian airlines' efficiency was developed by Heydari et al. (2020). A non-radial NDEA approach for evaluating the information technology influence on banking organizations, in the existence of fuzzy non-discretionary variables, was proposed by Hu et al. (2021). Tavassoli and Farzipoor Saen (2022) used a fuzzy slack-based measure NDEA approach to examine the effectiveness and transportation systems efficiency.

Pourbabagol et al. (2023) developed a new FNDEA approach according to necessity and possibility measures for assessing the performance of agile supply chains. Tavassoli and Farzipoor Saen (2023) also presented a novel non-radial FNDEA approach for assessing the Iranian combined cycle power plants' performance considering both parallel and series structures. The developed approach not only assesses the power plants' sustainability and their related elements but also evaluates the environmental and operational performance.

It should be noted that in fuzzy network DEA literature, the fuzzy arithmetic methodology, the α-level based methodology, the fuzzy ranking methodology, and the fuzzy type-2/random fuzzy set methodology have been utilized to cope with fuzzy data. The literature gap shows that the possibility approach, despite all its advantages and simplicity, is not used to present the FNDEA model so far. In conclusion, a new fuzzy network data envelopment analysis structure for various returns to scale assumptions utilizing chance-constrained programming and possibilistic programming will be developed in this paper. Notably, the presented approach has been utilized for modeling two-stage efficiency with intermediate measure in a single execution and in the existence of fuzzy data. On the other hand, this method is applied to a realistic dataset from the Tehran Stock Exchange (TSE) as a case study to evaluate the performance of the related investment firms (IFs).

The rest of this study is structured as follows. The basic network DEA approach structure under all returns to scale assumptions for a two-stage structure has been presented in Sect. 2. Then, the fuzzy network data envelopment analysis model according to possibilistic programming has been described in Sect. 3. The presented possibilistic network data envelopment analysis model in this paper is implemented for Tehran stock exchange real case study, and the findings will have been presented in Sect. 4. Lastly, the study conclusions and future research directions are described in Sect. 5.

2 Two-Stage DEA Model

The basic network DEA approach utilized in this paper is presented in this section. It should be mentioned that the two-stage structure is one of the most widely known types of network structures, and it has gained a lot of attraction in the network DEA literature. Figure 1 represents an extended two-stage structure graphically, which involves a set of G homogenous decision making units $\mathrm{DMU}_g\,(g = 1, ..., G)$ in which each DMU has A inputs $x_{ag}(a = 1, ..., A)$ in the first stage, B outputs $u_{bg}(b = 1, ..., B)$ (leakage variable) that leave the system's structure in its first stage, C intermediate variables $z_{cg}(c = 1, ..., C)$ that connect the first stage and second stage, D extra inputs $v_{dg}(d = 1, ..., D)$ in the second stage and lastly E outputs $y_{eg}(e - 1, ..., E)$ in the second stage.

This must be considered that according to the study by Chen and Zhu (2004), the network DEA method is proposed for measuring the performance of decision-making units and also sub decision making units (first stage and second stage) in a single model within outputs that leave the system in stage 1 and extra inputs that enter to the stage 2 for a two-stage structure. It should be considered that the two-stage DEA method for decision-making units under assessment (DMU_p) is as Model (1) where Q_1 and Q_2 are user-determined weights indicating the importance or preference towards the performance of two stages.

$$\text{Min } Q_1\Delta_p - Q_2\nabla_p \tag{1-1}$$

$$\text{S.t.} \sum_{g=1}^{G} x_{ag}\Theta_g \leq x_{ap}\Delta_p, \forall a \tag{1-2}$$

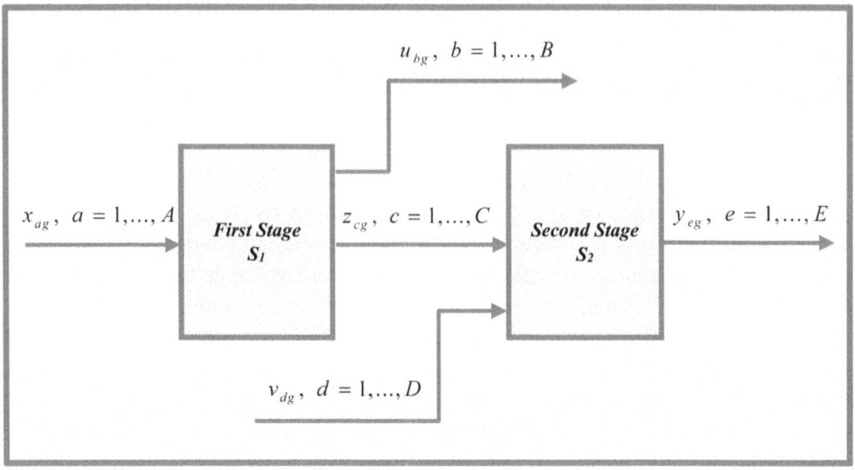

Fig. 1 The extended structure of two-stage network DEA model

$$\sum_{g=1}^{G} u_{bg}\Theta_g \geq u_{bp}, \forall b \tag{1-3}$$

$$\sum_{g=1}^{G} z_{cg}\Theta_g \geq \widehat{z}_{cp}, \forall c \tag{1-4}$$

$$\delta_1\left(\sum_{g=1}^{G}\Theta_g + \delta_2(-1)^{\delta_3}\Omega\right) = \delta_1 \tag{1-5}$$

$$\sum_{g=1}^{G} z_{cg}\Phi_g \leq \widehat{z}_{cp}, \forall c \tag{1-6}$$

$$\sum_{g=1}^{G} v_{dg}\Phi_g \leq v_{dp}, \forall d \tag{1-7}$$

$$\sum_{g=1}^{G} y_{eg}\Phi_g \geq y_{ep}\nabla_p, \forall e \tag{1-8}$$

$$\xi_1\left(\sum_{g=1}^{G}\Phi_g + \xi_2(-1)^{\xi_3}\mho\right) = \xi_1 \tag{1-9}$$

$$\Theta_g, \Phi_g \geq 0, \forall g \tag{1-10}$$

It should be mentioned that Δ_p^*, $1/\nabla_p^*$ and Δ_p^*/∇_p^* demonstrate the efficiency score of first-stage, efficiency score of second-stage, and overall efficiency of a DMU under evaluation, respectively. So, DMU under investigation will have total efficiency if it is efficient in the second and first stages simultaneously. Note that Ω and $\mho$ in Eqs. (1-5) and (1-9) are very small positive numbers, and in Model (1), $\widehat{z}_{cp}$ is an unknown decision variable.

As seen in Model (1), applying the Constraints (1-5) and (1-9), the described network DEA structure is capable of implementation in systems with different returns to scale (RTS). Thus, by setting binary parameters in these constraints as follows, the returns to scale are considered as different RTSs, such as constant returns to scale (CRS), variable returns to scale (VRS), non-decreasing returns to scale (NDRS), and non-increasing returns to scale (NIRS).

I. *If* $\delta_1 = \xi_1 = 0 \Rightarrow CRS$
II. *If* $\delta_1 = \xi_1 = 1 \,\&\, \delta_2 = \xi_2 = 0 \Rightarrow VRS$
III. *If* $\delta_1 = \xi_1 = 1 \,\&\, \delta_2 = \xi_2 = 1 \,\&\, \delta_3 = \xi_3 = 1 \Rightarrow NDRS$
IV. *If* $\delta_1 = \xi_1 = 1 \,\&\, \delta_2 = \xi_2 = 1 \,\&\, \delta_3 = \xi_3 = 0 \Rightarrow NIRS$

3 Possibilistic Network DEA Model

The FNDEA model will be proposed in this section based on possibility approach and CCP for coping with vague and imprecise data. Considering that all data are indicated by fuzzy numbers $\tilde{x}_{ag}(a = 1, \ldots, A)$, $\tilde{u}_{bg}(b = 1, \ldots, B)$, $\tilde{z}_{cg}(c = 1, \ldots, C)$, $\tilde{v}_{dg}(d = 1, \ldots, D)$, and $\tilde{y}_{eg}(e = 1, \ldots, E)$ within trapezoidal membership functions. Consequently, the following demonstrates Model (1) for fuzzy findings:

$$\text{Min } Q_1\Delta_p - Q_2\nabla_p \tag{2-1}$$

$$\text{S.t.} \sum_{g=1}^{G} \tilde{x}_{ag}\Theta_g \preceq \tilde{x}_{ap}\Delta_p, \forall a \tag{2-2}$$

$$\sum_{g=1}^{G} \tilde{u}_{bg}\Theta_g \succeq \tilde{u}_{bp}, \forall b \tag{2-3}$$

$$\sum_{g=1}^{G} \tilde{z}_{cg}\Theta_g \succeq \widehat{z}_{cp}, \forall c \tag{2-4}$$

$$\delta_1\left(\sum_{g=1}^{G} \Theta_g + \delta_2(-1)^{\delta_3}\Omega\right) = \delta_1 \tag{2-5}$$

$$\sum_{g=1}^{G} \tilde{z}_{cg} \Phi_g \leq \hat{z}_{cp}, \forall c \quad (2\text{-}6)$$

$$\sum_{g=1}^{G} \tilde{v}_{dg} \Phi_g \leq \tilde{v}_{dp}, \forall d \quad (2\text{-}7)$$

$$\sum_{g=1}^{G} \tilde{y}_{eg} \Phi_g \geq \tilde{y}_{ep} \nabla_p, \forall e \quad (2\text{-}8)$$

$$\xi_1 \left(\sum_{g=1}^{G} \Phi_g + \xi_2 (-1)^{\xi_3} \mho \right) = \xi_1 \quad (2\text{-}9)$$

$$\Theta_g, \Phi_g \geq 0, \forall g \quad (2\text{-}10)$$

For coping with vague and imprecise data in Model (2), possibilistic programming will be applied. The possibility theory, which was presented by Zadeh (1978), was an alternative to probability theory for dealing with particular types of uncertainty. In addition, a possibility method is a considerable approach for addressing the uncertainty resulting from the lack or absence of information regarding the model parameters' precise value in the fuzzy mathematical programming (Peykani et al., 2018, 2019, 2022a, c).

In fuzzy linear programming approaches, it must be emphasized that constraints could have been regarded as fuzzy events, and fuzzy coefficients could be considered to be fuzzy variables. Therefore, possibility theory could be used to identify the fuzzy constraint possibilities (Peykani et al., 2022c). Suppose $\tilde{\pi}$ and $\tilde{\varpi}$ be a variable of trapezoidal fuzzy on the space of possibility (Υ, $P(\Upsilon)$, Pos) and μ be a crisp number. It should be mentioned that the fuzzy events' possibility $\{\tilde{\pi} \leq \mu\}, \{\tilde{\pi} \geq \mu\}, \{\tilde{\pi} \leq \tilde{\varpi}\}$, and $\{\tilde{\pi} \geq \tilde{\varpi}\}$ are as Eqs. (3-1) to (3-4):

$$\text{Pos}\{\tilde{\pi} \leq \mu\} = \begin{cases} 1, \mathit{if}\, \pi_2 \leq \mu; \\ \dfrac{\mu - \pi_1}{\pi_2 - \pi_1}, \mathit{if}\, \pi_1 \leq \mu \leq \pi_2; \\ 0, \mathit{if}\, \pi_1 \geq \mu. \end{cases} \quad (3\text{-}1)$$

$$\text{Pos}\{\tilde{\pi} \geq \mu\} = \begin{cases} 1, \mathit{if}\, \pi_3 \geq \mu; \\ \dfrac{\pi_4 - \mu}{\pi_4 - \pi_3}, \mathit{if}\, \pi_3 \leq \mu \leq \pi_4; \\ 0, \mathit{if}\, \pi_4 \leq \mu. \end{cases} \quad (3\text{-}2)$$

$$\text{Pos}\{\tilde{\pi} \le \tilde{\varpi}\} = \begin{cases} 1, \textit{if}\, \pi_2 \le \varpi_3; \\ \dfrac{\varpi_4 - \pi_1}{\varpi_4 - \varpi_3 + \pi_2 - \pi_1}, \textit{if}\, \pi_1 < \varpi_4, \pi_2 > \varpi_3; \\ 0, \textit{if}\, \pi_1 \ge \varpi_4. \end{cases} \quad (3\text{-}3)$$

$$\text{Pos}\{\tilde{\pi} \ge \tilde{\varpi}\} = \begin{cases} 1, \textit{if}\, \pi_3 \ge \varpi_2; \\ \dfrac{\pi_4 - \varpi_1}{\pi_4 - \pi_3 + \varpi_2 - \varpi_1}, \textit{if}\, \pi_4 > \varpi_1, \pi_3 < \varpi_2; \\ 0, \textit{if}\, \pi_4 \le \varpi_1. \end{cases} \quad (3\text{-}4)$$

Considering the possibility measure, transforming fuzzy chance constraints on crisp counterpart ones in unique specific confidential level (λ) is equivalent to Eqs. (4-1) to (4-4):

$$\text{Pos}\{\tilde{\pi} \le \mu\} \ge \lambda \Leftrightarrow (1-\lambda)\pi_1 + (\lambda)\pi_2 \le \mu \quad (4\text{-}1)$$

$$\text{Pos}\{\tilde{\pi} \ge \mu\} \ge \lambda \Leftrightarrow (\lambda)\pi_3 + (1-\lambda)\pi_4 \le \mu \quad (4\text{-}2)$$

$$\text{Pos}\{\tilde{\pi} \le \tilde{\varpi}\} \ge \lambda \Leftrightarrow (1-\lambda)\pi_1 + (\lambda)\pi_2 \le (\lambda)\varpi_3 + (1-\lambda)\varpi_4 \quad (4\text{-}3)$$

$$\text{Pos}\{\tilde{\pi} \ge \tilde{\varpi}\} \ge \lambda \Leftrightarrow (\lambda)\pi_3 + (1-\lambda)\pi_4 \le (1-\lambda)\varpi_1 + (\lambda)\varpi_2 \quad (4\text{-}4)$$

So, the possibility measure is utilized to cope with vague and imprecise data and transform them into their crisp counterpart. It must be considered that α and β are confidential levels for fulfilling the constraints. The following represents the development of the novel FNDEA structure according to the possibility method:

$$\text{Min } Q_1\Delta_p - Q_2\nabla_p \quad (5\text{-}1)$$

$$\text{S.t. Pos}\left\{\sum_{g=1}^{G} \tilde{x}_{ag}\Theta_g \le \tilde{x}_{ap}\Delta_p\right\} \ge \alpha_a, \forall a \quad (5\text{-}2)$$

$$\text{Pos}\left\{\sum_{g=1}^{G} \tilde{u}_{bg}\Theta_g \ge \tilde{u}_{bp}\right\} \ge \alpha'_b, \forall b \quad (5\text{-}3)$$

$$\text{Pos}\left\{\sum_{g=1}^{G} \tilde{z}_{cg}\Theta_g \ge \hat{z}_{cp}\right\} \ge \alpha''_c, \forall c \quad (5\text{-}4)$$

$$\delta_1\left(\sum_{g=1}^{G}\Theta_g+\delta_2(-1)^{\delta_3}\Omega\right)=\delta_1 \tag{5-5}$$

$$\text{Pos}\left\{\sum_{g=1}^{G}\tilde{z}_{cg}\Phi_g\le\hat{z}_{cp}\right\}\ge\beta_c,\forall c \tag{5-6}$$

$$\text{Pos}\left\{\sum_{g=1}^{G}\tilde{v}_{dg}\Phi_g\le\tilde{v}_{dp}\right\}\ge\beta'_d,\forall d \tag{5-7}$$

$$\text{Pos}\left\{\sum_{g=1}^{G}\tilde{y}_{eg}\Phi_g\ge\tilde{y}_{ep}\nabla_p\right\}\ge\beta''_e,\forall e \tag{5-8}$$

$$\xi_1\left(\sum_{g=1}^{G}\Phi_g+\xi_2(-1)^{\xi_3}\mho\right)=\xi_1 \tag{5-9}$$

$$\Theta_g,\Phi_g\ge 0,\forall g \tag{5-10}$$

Now, by Eq. (4-1) to (4-4), a crisp counterpart of fuzzy chance constraints related to one unique confidential level and utilizing possibility measure is presented as follows:

$$\text{Min } Q_1\Delta_p-Q_2\nabla_p \tag{6-1}$$

$$\text{S.t.}\sum_{g=1}^{G}\left((1-\alpha_a)x^1_{ag}+(\alpha_a)x^2_{ag}\right)\Theta_g\le\left((\alpha_a)x^3_{ap}+(1-\alpha_a)x^4_{ap}\right)\Delta_p,\forall a \tag{6-2}$$

$$\sum_{g=1}^{G}\left((\alpha'_b)u^3_{bg}+(1-\alpha'_b)u^4_{bg}\right)\Theta_g\ge\left((1-\alpha'_b)u^1_{bp}+(\alpha'_b)u^2_{bp}\right),\forall b \tag{6-3}$$

$$\sum_{g=1}^{G}\left((\alpha''_c)z^3_{cg}+(1-\alpha''_c)z^4_{cg}\right)\Theta_g\ge\hat{z}_{cp},\forall c \tag{6-4}$$

$$\delta_1\left(\sum_{g=1}^{G}\Theta_g+\delta_2(-1)^{\delta_3}\Omega\right)=\delta_1 \tag{6-5}$$

$$\sum_{g=1}^{G}\left((1-\beta_c)z^1_{cg}+(\beta_c)z^2_{cg}\right)\Phi_g\le\hat{z}_{cp},\forall c \tag{6-6}$$

$$\sum_{g=1}^{G}\left(\left(1-\beta_d''\right)v_{dg}^1+\left(\beta_d''\right)v_{dg}^2\right)\Phi_g \le \left(\left(\beta_d''\right)v_{dp}^3+\left(1-\beta_d''\right)v_{dp}^4\right), \forall d \quad (6\text{-}7)$$

$$\sum_{g=1}^{G}\left(\left(\beta_e''\right)y_{eg}^3+\left(1-\beta_e''\right)y_{eg}^4\right)\Phi_g \ge \left(\left(1-\beta_e''\right)y_{ep}^1+\left(\beta_e''\right)y_{ep}^2\right)\nabla_p, \forall e \quad (6\text{-}8)$$

$$\xi_1\left(\sum_{g=1}^{G}\Phi_g+\xi_2(-1)^{\xi_3}\mho\right)=\xi_1 \quad (6\text{-}9)$$

$$\Theta_g, \Phi_g \ge 0, \forall j \quad (6\text{-}10)$$

Finally, the possibilistic network data envelopment analysis (PNDEA) structure that could be utilized within different returns to scale assumptions is proposed as Model (6).

4 Real-Life Case Study of Investment Firms

The developed possibilistic network DEA model in this section would be utilized to measure the TSE investment firms' performance. Investment firms like mutual funds (MFs) perform an indispensable task in the financial system's functioning. IFs utilize the funds gathered from investors in accordance with a defined investment strategy, and each investor will participate in the investment risks and rewards proportional to his ownership stake in the investment firms (Basso & Funari, 2016; Sarkar, 2022).

A two-stage DEA approach to evaluate the MF family's performance by regarding related portfolio and operational management procedures was described by Premachandra et al. (2012). In a study that was very similar to this one, Premachandra et al. (2016) used the network DEA method to evaluate the performance of the mutual fund industry. Subsequently, a two-stage structure for evaluating the implementation of mutual funds in the management of operations step by including overall investor cash flow like leakage variable was described by Galagedera et al. (2016). A network slack-based measure (NSBM) approach for measuring efficiency of mutual fund companies was applied by Sánchez-González et al. (2017). On the other side, a novel network DEA structure for mutual funds' performance assessment, taking into account the mutual funds' three-stage structure procedure considering resource, portfolio, and operational management was proposed by Galagedera et al. (2018). In the existence of uncertain data, Peykani and Mohammadi (2018) introduced an interval network data envelopment analysis (INDEA) method considering CRS and VRS assumptions that is capable to be utilized for performance evaluation of investment companies (ICs).

Then, a DEA approach with a structure consisting of two stages considering non-discretionary output within the operational management step in order to model social responsibility within MF implementation assessment was presented by Galagedera (2019). Galagedera et al. (2020) presented a network DEA structure for evaluating the MF performance from management of disbursement standpoint in the existence of non-discretionary input. In addition, Hsieh et al. (2020) proposed a two-stage network DEA approach to the performance evaluation of MFs, in which quality of decisions and capital magnetization are regarded to be two-stage processes of MFs. Peykani and Mohammadi (2020) used a window network data envelopment analysis (WNDEA) structure that can assess the performance of ICs considering panel data. On the other hand, a two-stage DEA structure to assess the precious metal mutual funds performance was applied by Tsolas (2020).

Fukuyama and Galagedera (2021) noted that data collected within mutual funds performance assessments utilizing the network DEA method is applicable and motivates real-world solutions to MF management related problems. Peykani et al. (2021a) described a novel FNDEA structure for measuring the performance and IFs ranking considering the two-stage procedure, including portfolio and operational management procedure. It should be noted that related findings extracted from the real-life case study indicate that the developed method has excellent performance. Last but not the least, a new robust network data envelopment analysis (RNDEA) structure to assess the mutual funds performance considering deep uncertainty was proposed by Peykani et al. (2024).

Table 1 provides an illustration of a more detailed categorization for the performance evaluation of mutual funds using network DEA. This classification takes into consideration the following three aspects: model from (multiplier or envelopment), modeling approach (NDEA method), and data type (crisp or uncertain). In the final row of Table 1, the details of this study are also provided.

As demonstrated in Fig. 2, the IF's total efficiency consists of two phases which the stage 1 indicates the procedure of management of operations, and the stage 2 indicates the procedure of management of portfolio.

It must be mentioned that financial data for 10 TSE investment firms were gathered from March 2021 to March 2022. After gathering data in the trapezoidal membership function, the presented possibilistic network DEA approach will be performed at various confidence levels while considering constant and variables returns to scale. Possibilistic NDEA approach findings for the first stage, second stage, and total, under CRS and VRS assumptions at different confidential levels from 0 to 100%, have been shown in Tables 2 and 3.

The PNDEA method results demonstrate that raising the confidential level from 0 to 1 for fulfilling the constraints decreases the objective function. Ultimately, according to the findings in Tables 2 and 3, the average scores of IFs across all confidence levels, as well as the ranking of IFs with VRS and CRS assumptions, are indicated in Table 4.

According to Table 4, IF 05 and IF 06 have the best operational management performance and portfolio management processes, respectively. Consequently, these two IFs can be considered as a benchmark for managers of other IFs. In addition, IF 05 has the first rank from an overall viewpoint in comparison with other IFs. It

Table 1 A review of network DEA and mutual funds studies

Author(s) (Publication Year)	Model form	NDEA modeling approach	Data type
Premachandra et al. (2012)	Multiplier	Additive efficiency decomposition	Crisp
Galagedera et al. (2016)	Multiplier	Additive efficiency decomposition	Crisp
Premachandra et al. (2016)	Multiplier	Additive efficiency decomposition	Crisp
Sánchez-González et al. (2017)	Envelopment	Slacks-based measure	Crisp
Galagedera et al. (2018)	Multiplier	Additive efficiency decomposition	Crisp
Peykani and Mohammadi (2018)	Envelopment	Production possibility set	Interval
Galagedera (2019)	Multiplier	Additive efficiency decomposition	Crisp
Hsieh et al. (2020)	Envelopment	Slacks-based measure	Crisp
Galagedera et al. (2020)	Envelopment	Production possibility set	Crisp
Peykani and Mohammadi (2020)	Multiplier	Additive efficiency decomposition	Crisp
Tsolas (2020)	Multiplier	Independent	Crisp
Fukuyama & Galagedera (2021)	Envelopment	Production possibility set	Crisp
Peykani et al. (2021a)	Multiplier	Additive efficiency decomposition	Fuzzy
Peykani et al. (2024)	Multiplier	Non-cooperative game	Interval
This study	Envelopment	Production possibility set	Fuzzy

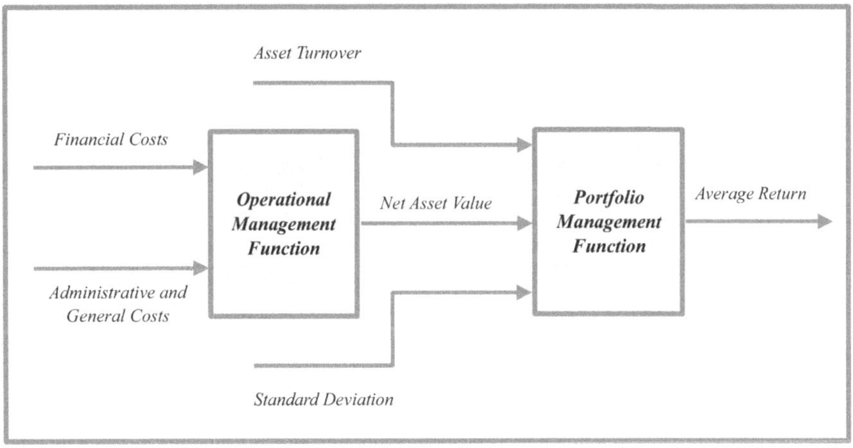

Fig. 2 Investment firms' structure

should be mentioned that IF 04 has the worst performance in all types of returns to scales.

Table 2 Results of the PNDEA model under CRS assumption

IFs		Confidence levels				
		0%	25%	50%	75%	100%
Operational management process (Stage 1)	IF 01	0.11021	0.11303	0.11591	0.11886	0.12188
	IF 02	0.09518	0.09762	0.10011	0.10266	0.10527
	IF 03	0.11499	0.11793	0.12094	0.12401	0.12716
	IF 04	0.03161	0.03241	0.03324	0.03408	0.03495
	IF 05	0.71507	0.73331	0.75198	0.77109	0.79065
	IF 06	0.09687	0.09934	0.10188	0.10447	0.10712
	IF 07	0.07672	0.07868	0.08068	0.08274	0.08484
	IF 08	0.20228	0.20745	0.21274	0.21816	0.22370
	IF 09	0.05185	0.05317	0.05453	0.05592	0.05734
	IF 10	0.07702	0.07898	0.08100	0.08306	0.08517
Portfolio management process (Stage 2)	IF 01	0.59540	0.62619	0.65850	0.69241	0.72801
	IF 02	0.18488	0.19444	0.20447	0.21499	0.22605
	IF 03	0.09463	0.09952	0.10466	0.11005	0.11571
	IF 04	0.07967	0.08379	0.08812	0.09266	0.09742
	IF 05	0.26651	0.28030	0.29477	0.30996	0.32590
	IF 06	0.66946	0.70408	0.74041	0.77855	0.81859
	IF 07	0.24654	0.25929	0.27268	0.28673	0.30148
	IF 08	0.03502	0.03683	0.03873	0.04073	0.04282
	IF 09	0.47107	0.49544	0.52102	0.54786	0.57604
	IF 10	0.39931	0.41996	0.44164	0.46440	0.48829

(continued)

Table 2 (continued)

IFs		Confidence levels				
		0%	25%	50%	75%	100%
Investment firms (Overall)	IF 01	0.06562	0.07078	0.07633	0.08230	0.08873
	IF 02	0.01760	0.01898	0.02047	0.02207	0.02380
	IF 03	0.01088	0.01174	0.01266	0.01365	0.01471
	IF 04	0.00252	0.00272	0.00293	0.00316	0.00340
	IF 05	0.19057	0.20555	0.22166	0.23900	0.25767
	IF 06	0.06485	0.06995	0.07543	0.08133	0.08769
	IF 07	0.01891	0.02040	0.02200	0.02372	0.02558
	IF 08	0.00708	0.00764	0.00824	0.00889	0.00958
	IF 09	0.02442	0.02634	0.02841	0.03063	0.03303
	IF 10	0.03075	0.03317	0.03577	0.03857	0.04159

5 Concluding Remarks and Future Research Directions

A new fuzzy network DEA model utilizing a possibility method and chance-constrained programming was developed in this study. This method was developed for a two-stage structure that has been expanded to contain leakage variables and additional inputs into the second step. Additionally, the Tehran stock exchange investment firms were also applied for demonstrating validation and solve the provided possibilistic network DEA approach. Notably, proposing the fuzzy network DEA model according to possibilistic programming has many innovations and contributions that are as follows: the capability to be applied under different return to scales, the ability to calculate two stages and total efficiency in a single implementation under uncertainty and the ability to use fuzzy network DEA for evaluating the performance of IFs. In order to describe future research directions of this study, the network DEA approaches for coping with uncertainty can be presented according to alternative methods in the related literature, such as robust optimization (Mardani Najafabadi et al., 2023; Peykani et al., 2024, 2022a, 2022b; Qu et al., 2022; Seyed Esmaeili et al., 2021; Shirazi & Mohammadi, 2019).

Table 3 The PNDEA model results under VRS assumption

	IFs	Confidence levels				
		0%	25%	50%	75%	100%
Operational management process (Stage 1)	IF 01	0.33961	0.35163	0.36409	0.37703	0.39047
	IF 02	0.72305	0.75145	0.78102	0.81182	0.84393
	IF 03	0.10426	0.10758	0.11101	0.11455	0.11822
	IF 04	0.10200	0.10525	0.10861	0.11208	0.11567
	IF 05	1.27363	1.32102	1.37027	1.42148	1.47475
	IF 06	0.15937	0.16531	0.17147	0.17789	0.18456
	IF 07	0.16271	0.16687	0.17113	0.17548	0.17994
	IF 08	0.81783	0.83876	0.86019	0.88212	0.90457
	IF 09	0.14927	0.15448	0.15989	0.16550	0.17132
	IF 10	0.17269	0.17710	0.18161	0.18622	0.19095
Portfolio management process (Stage 2)	IF 01	0.63947	0.67603	0.71471	0.75564	0.79899
	IF 02	0.39232	0.43323	0.48014	0.53434	0.59752
	IF 03	0.22362	0.22934	0.23518	0.24116	0.24729
	IF 04	0.09266	0.09503	0.09745	0.09993	0.10247
	IF 05	0.30089	0.30858	0.31644	0.32449	0.33273
	IF 06	0.81818	0.83908	0.86046	0.88235	0.90476
	IF 07	0.27869	0.28580	0.29309	0.30054	0.30818
	IF 08	0.04413	0.04526	0.04641	0.04759	0.04880
	IF 09	0.53228	0.56586	0.60172	0.64003	0.68101
	IF 10	0.40219	0.42587	0.45098	0.47764	0.50594
Investment firms (Overall)	IF 01	0.21717	0.23771	0.26022	0.28490	0.31198
	IF 02	0.28367	0.32555	0.37500	0.43379	0.50427
	IF 03	0.02331	0.02467	0.02611	0.02763	0.02923
	IF 04	0.00945	0.01000	0.01058	0.01120	0.01185
	IF 05	0.38322	0.40763	0.43361	0.46125	0.49069
	IF 06	0.13040	0.13871	0.14755	0.15696	0.16698
	IF 07	0.04535	0.04769	0.05016	0.05274	0.05545
	IF 08	0.03609	0.03796	0.03992	0.04198	0.04415
	IF 09	0.07945	0.08742	0.09621	0.10592	0.11667
	IF 10	0.06945	0.07542	0.08190	0.08895	0.09661

Table 4 The IFs average score and ranking according to PNDEA model

	Ifs	$Stage_1$		$Stage_2$		Overall	
		Score	Rank	Score	Rank	Score	Rank
Constant returns to scale (CRS)	IF 01	0.11598	4	0.65678	2	0.07675	2
	IF 02	0.10017	6	0.20393	7	0.02058	7
	IF 03	0.12101	3	0.10439	8	0.01273	8
	IF 04	0.03326	10	0.08788	9	0.00295	10
	IF 05	0.75242	1	0.29400	5	0.22289	1
	IF 06	0.10194	5	0.73848	1	0.07585	3
	IF 07	0.08073	8	0.27196	6	0.02212	6
	IF 08	0.21287	2	0.03863	10	0.00829	9
	IF 09	0.05456	9	0.51965	3	0.02857	5
	IF 10	0.08104	7	0.44049	4	0.03597	4
Variable returns to Scale (VRS)	IF 01	0.36457	4	0.71254	2	0.26240	3
	IF 02	0.78225	3	0.47688	4	0.38446	2
	IF 03	0.11112	9	0.23502	8	0.02619	9
	IF 04	0.10872	10	0.09739	9	0.01062	10
	IF 05	1.37223	1	0.31623	6	0.43528	1
	IF 06	0.17172	6	0.85988	1	0.14812	4
	IF 07	0.17123	7	0.29289	7	0.05028	7
	IF 08	0.86069	2	0.04638	10	0.04002	8
	IF 09	0.16009	8	0.59962	3	0.09714	5
	IF 10	0.18171	5	0.44955	5	0.08247	6

References

Amirteimoori, A., Azizi, H., & Kordrostami, S. (2020). Double frontier two-stage fuzzy data envelopment analysis. *International Journal of Uncertainty, Fuzziness and Knowledge-Based Systems, 28*(01), 117–152.

Banker, R. D., Charnes, A., & Cooper, W. W. (1984). Some models for estimating technical and scale inefficiencies in data envelopment analysis. *Management Science, 30*(9), 1078–1092.

Basso, A., & Funari, S. (2016). DEA performance assessment of mutual funds. *Data Envelopment Analysis: A Handbook of Empirical Studies and Applications*, 229–287. Springer, Boston, MA.

Charnes, A., Cooper, W. W., & Rhodes, E. (1978). Measuring the efficiency of decision making units. *European Journal of Operational Research, 2*(6), 429–444.

Chen, Y., & Zhu, J. (2004). Measuring information technology's indirect impact on firm performance. *Information Technology and Management, 5*(1/2), 9–22.

Cooper, W. W., Seiford, L. M., & Zhu, J. (2011). *Handbook on Data Envelopment Analysis*. Springer.

Farrell, M. J. (1957). The measurement of productive efficiency. *Journal of the Royal Statistical Society. Series A (General), 120*(3), 253.

Fathi, A., & Farzipoor Saen, R. (2021). Assessing sustainability of supply chains by fuzzy Malmquist network data envelopment analysis: Incorporating double frontier and common set of weights. *Applied Soft Computing, 113*, 107923.

Fukuyama, H., & Galagedera, D. U. A. (2021). Value extracting in relative performance appraisal with network DEA: An application to US equity mutual funds. *Data-Enabled Analytics: DEA for Big Data*, pp. 263–297. Cham: Springer International Publishing.

Galagedera, D. U. A. (2019). Modelling social responsibility in mutual fund performance appraisal: A two-stage data envelopment analysis model with non-discretionary first stage output. *European Journal of Operational Research, 273*(1), 376–389.

Galagedera, D. U. A., Watson, J., Premachandra, I. M., & Chen, Y. (2016). Modeling leakage in two-stage DEA models: An application to US mutual fund families. *Omega, 61*, 62–77.

Galagedera, D. U. A., Roshdi, I., Fukuyama, H., & Zhu, J. (2018). A new network DEA model for mutual fund performance appraisal: An application to U.S. equity mutual funds. *Omega, 77*, 168–179.

Galagedera, D. U. A., Fukuyama, H., Watson, J., & Tan, E. K. (2020). Do mutual fund managers earn their fees? new measures for performance appraisal. *European Journal of Operational Research, 287*(2), 653–667.

Hamidzadeh, F., & Pishvaee, M. S. (2023). A data envelopment analysis approach to evaluate efficiencies in organ allocation problem: A case study. *Journal of Industrial and Systems Engineering, 14*(4), 138–157.

Hatami-Marbini, A. (2019). Benchmarking with network DEA in a fuzzy environment. *RAIRO-Operations Research, 53*(2), 687–703.

Henriques, I. C., Sobreiro, V. A., Kimura, H., & Mariano, E. B. (2020). Two-stage DEA in banks: Terminological controversies and future directions. *Expert Systems with Applications, 161*, 113632.

Heydari, C., Omrani, H., & Taghizadeh, R. (2020). A fully fuzzy network DEA-range adjusted measure model for evaluating airlines efficiency: A case of Iran. *Journal of Air Transport Management, 89*, 101923.

Hosseinzadeh Lotfi, F., Jahanshahloo, G. R., Vahidi, A. R., & Dalirian, A. (2009). Efficiency and effectiveness in multi-activity network DEA model with fuzzy data. *Applied Mathematical Sciences, 3*(52), 2603–2618.

Hosseinzadeh Lotfi, F., Allahviranloo, T., Shafiee, M., & Saleh, H. (2023). Supply chain evaluation by network DEA. *Supply Chain Performance Evaluation: Application of Data Envelopment Analysis*, 329–417. Cham: Springer International Publishing.

Hsieh, H. P., Tebourbi, I., Lu, W. M., & Liu, N. Y. (2020). Mutual fund performance: The decision quality and capital magnet efficiencies. *Managerial and Decision Economics, 41*(5), 861–872.

Hu, C. K., Liu, F. B., Chen, H. M., & Hu, C. F. (2021). Network data envelopment analysis with fuzzy non-discretionary factors. *Journal of Industrial and Management Optimization, 17*(4), 1795–1807.

Sharahi, J. S., & Khalili-Damghani, K. (2019). Fuzzy type-II De-Novo programming for resource allocation and target setting in network data envelopment analysis: A natural gas supply chain. *Expert Systems with Applications, 117*, 312–329.

Kao, C., & Liu, S. T. (2007). Data envelopment analysis with missing data a reliable solution method. *Modeling Data Irregularities and Structural Complexities in Data Envelopment Analysis*, pp. 291–304. Springer, Boston, MA.

Kao, C., & Liu, S. T. (2000). Fuzzy efficiency measures in data envelopment analysis. *Fuzzy Sets and Systems, 113*(3), 427–437.

Kao, C., & Liu, S. T. (2011). Efficiencies of two-stage systems with fuzzy data. *Fuzzy Sets and Systems, 176*(1), 20–35.

Kao, C. (2014). Network data envelopment analysis with fuzzy data. *Studies in Fuzziness and Soft Computing*, pp. 191–206. Springer, Berlin, Heidelberg.

Khalili-Damghani, K., & Taghavifard, M. (2012). A three-stage fuzzy DEA approach to measure performance of a serial process including JIT practices, agility indices, and goals in supply chains. *International Journal of Services and Operations Management, 13*(2), 147–188.

Khalili-Damghani, K., Taghavifard, M., & Abtahi, A. R. (2012). A fuzzy two-stage DEA approach for performance measurement: Real case of agility performance in dairy supply chains. *International Journal of Applied Decision Sciences, 5*(4), 293–317.
Li, Y., Abtahi, A. R., & Seyedan, M. (2019). Supply chain performance evaluation using fuzzy network data envelopment analysis: A case study in automotive industry. *Annals of Operations Research, 275*(2), 461–484.
Liu, J. S., Lu, L. Y., & Lu, W. M. (2016). Research fronts in data envelopment analysis. *Omega, 58*, 33–45.
Lozano, S., & Moreno, P. (2013). A DEA model for two-stage systems with Fuzzy data. *IEEE International Conference on Fuzzy Systems*, 1–6. IEEE.
Lozano, S., & Moreno, P. (2014). Network fuzzy data envelopment analysis. *Performance Measurement with Fuzzy Data Envelopment Analysis*, pp. 207–230.
Mardani Najafabadi, M., Kazmi, H., Shirzadi Laskookalayeh, S., & Abdeshahi, A. (2023). Investigating the ability of fuzzy and robust DEA models to apply uncertainty conditions: An application for date palm producers. *Opsearch, 60*, 776–801.
Mirhedayatian, S. M., Azadi, M., & Farzipoor Saen, R. (2014). A novel network data envelopment analysis model for evaluating green supply chain management. *International Journal of Production Economics, 147*, 544–554.
Momeni, E., Tavana, M., Mirzagoltabar, H., & Mirhedayatian, S. M. (2014). A new fuzzy network slacks-based DEA model for evaluating performance of supply chains with reverse logistics. *Journal of Intelligent and Fuzzy Systems, 27*(2), 793–804.
Olfat, L., Amiri, M., Soufi, J. B., & Pishdar, M. (2016). A dynamic network efficiency measurement of airports performance considering sustainable development concept: A fuzzy dynamic network-DEA approach. *Journal of Air Transport Management, 57*, 272–290.
Omrani, H., Emrouznejad, A., Shamsi, M., & Fahimi, P. (2022). Evaluation of insurance companies considering uncertainty: A multi-objective network data envelopment analysis model with negative data and undesirable outputs. *Socio-Economic Planning Sciences, 82*, 101306.
Peykani, P., & Mohammadi, E. (2020). Window network data envelopment analysis: An application to investment companies. *International Journal of Industrial Mathematics, 12*(1), 89–99.
Peykani, P., Mohammadi, E., Pishvaee, M. S., Rostamy-Malkhalifeh, M., & Jabbarzadeh, A. (2018). A novel fuzzy data envelopment analysis based on robust possibilistic programming: Possibility, necessity and credibility-based approaches. *RAIRO-Operations Research, 52*(4–5), 1445–1463.
Peykani, P., Mohammadi, E., Emrouznejad, A., Pishvaee, M. S., & Rostamy-Malkhalifeh, M. (2019). Fuzzy data envelopment analysis: An adjustable approach. *Expert Systems with Applications, 136*, 439–452.
Peykani, P., Mohammadi, E., Farzipoor Saen, R., Sadjadi, S. J., & Rostamy-Malkhalifeh, M. (2020a). Data envelopment analysis and robust optimization: A review. *Expert Systems, 37*(4), e12534.
Peykani, P., Mohammadi, E., Jabbarzadeh, A., Rostamy-Malkhalifeh, M., & Pishvaee, M. S. (2020b). A novel two-phase robust portfolio selection and optimization approach under uncertainty: A case study of Tehran stock exchange. *PLoS ONE, 15*(10), e0239810.
Peykani, P., Mohammadi, E., & Emrouznejad, A. (2021a). An adjustable fuzzy chance-constrained network DEA approach with application to ranking investment firms. *Expert Systems with Applications, 166*, 113938.
Peykani, P., Farzipoor Saen, R., Seyed Esmaeili, F. S., & Gheidar-Kheljani, J. (2021b). Window data envelopment analysis approach: A review and bibliometric analysis. *Expert Systems, 38*(7), e12721.
Peykani, P., Memar-Masjed, E., Arabjazi, N., & Mirmozaffari, M. (2022a). Dynamic performance assessment of hospitals by applying credibility-based fuzzy window data envelopment analysis. *Healthcare, 10*(5), 876.
Peykani, P., Gheidar-Kheljani, J., Farzipoor Saen, R., & Mohammadi, E. (2022b). Generalized robust window data envelopment analysis approach for dynamic performance measurement under uncertain panel data. *Operational Research, 22*(5), 5529–5567.

Peykani, P., Hosseinzadeh Lotfi, F., Sadjadi, S. J., Ebrahimnejad, A., & Mohammadi, E. (2022c). Fuzzy chance-constrained data envelopment analysis: A structured literature review, current trends, and future directions. *Fuzzy Optimization and Decision Making, 21*(2), 197–261.

Peykani, P., & Mohammadi, E. (2018). Interval network data envelopment analysis model for classification of investment companies in the presence of uncertain data. *Journal of Industrial and Systems Engineering, 11*(Special Issue: 14th International Industrial Engineering Conference), 63–72.

Peykani, P., Emrouznejad, A., Mohammadi, E., & Gheidar-Kheljani, J. (2024). A novel robust network data envelopment analysis approach for performance assessment of mutual funds under uncertainty. *Annals of Operations Research, 339*(3), 1149–1175.

Pourbabagol, H., Amiri, M., Taghavifard, M. T., & Hanafizadeh, P. (2023). A new fuzzy DEA network based on possibility and necessity measures for agile supply chain performance evaluation: A case study. *Expert Systems with Applications, 220*, 119552.

Premachandra, I. M., Zhu, J., Watson, J., & Galagedera, D. U. A. (2012). Best-performing US mutual fund families from 1993 to 2008: Evidence from a novel two-stage DEA model for efficiency decomposition. *Journal of Banking & Finance, 36*(12), 3302–3317.

Premachandra, I. M., Zhu, J., Watson, J., & Galagedera, D. U. A. (2016). Mutual fund industry performance: a network data envelopment analysis approach. *Data Envelopment Analysis*, pp. 165–228. Springer, Boston, MA.

Qu, S., Feng, C., Jiang, S., Wei, J., & Xu, Y. (2022). Data-driven robust DEA models for measuring operational efficiency of endowment insurance system of different provinces in China. *Sustainability, 14*(16), 9954.

Saati, S. M., Memariani, A., & Jahanshahloo, G. R. (2002). Efficiency analysis and ranking of DMUs with fuzzy data. *Fuzzy Optimization and Decision Making, 1*(3), 255–267.

Sánchez-González, C., Sarto, J. L., & Vicente, L. (2017). The efficiency of mutual fund companies: Evidence from an innovative network SBM approach. *Omega, 71*, 114–128.

Sarkar, S. (2022). Performance evaluation of mutual funds using frontier methods. *Handbook of Production Economics*, pp. 1281–1307. Singapore: Springer Nature Singapore.

Sengupta, J. K. (1992). A fuzzy systems approach in data envelopment analysis. *Computers & Mathematics with Applications, 24*(8–9), 259–266.

Seyed Esmaeili, F. S., Rostamy-Malkhalifeh, M., & Hosseinzadeh Lotfi, F. (2021). A hybrid approach using data envelopment analysis, interval programming and robust optimisation for performance assessment of hotels under uncertainty. *International Journal of Management and Decision Making, 20*(3), 308–322.

Shermeh, H. E., Najafi, S. E., & Alavidoost, M. H. (2016). A novel fuzzy network SBM model for data envelopment analysis: A case study in Iran regional power companies. *Energy, 112*, 686–697.

Shi, X., Emrouznejad, A., Jin, M., & Yang, F. (2020). A new parallel fuzzy data envelopment analysis model for parallel systems with two components based on Stackelberg game theory. *Fuzzy Optimization and Decision Making, 19*(3), 311–332.

Shirazi, F., & Mohammadi, E. (2019). Evaluating efficiency of airlines: A new robust DEA approach with undesirable output. *Research in Transportation Business & Management, 33*, 100467.

Soltanzadeh, E., & Omrani, H. (2018). Dynamic network data envelopment analysis model with fuzzy inputs and outputs: An application for Iranian Airlines. *Applied Soft Computing, 63*, 268–288.

Tavana, M., & Khalili-Damghani, K. (2014). A new two-stage Stackelberg fuzzy data envelopment analysis model. *Measurement, 53*, 277–296.

Tavana, M., Izadikhah, M., Di Caprio, D., & Farzipoor Saen, R. (2018a). A new dynamic range directional measure for two-stage data envelopment analysis models with negative data. *Computers & Industrial Engineering, 115*, 427–448.

Tavana, M., Khalili-Damghani, K., Santos Arteaga, F. J., Mahmoudi, R., & Hafezalkotob, A. (2018b). Efficiency decomposition and measurement in two-stage fuzzy DEA models using a bargaining game approach. *Computers and Industrial Engineering, 118*, 394–408.

Tavassoli, M., & Farzipoor Saen, R. (2023). Sustainability measurement of combined cycle power plants: a novel fuzzy network data envelopment analysis model. *Annals of Operations Research*, 1–41.

Tavassoli, M., Fathi, A., & Farzipoor Saen, R. (2021). Assessing the sustainable supply chains of tomato paste by fuzzy double frontier network DEA model. *Annals of Operations Research*, 1–33.

Tavassoli, M., & Farzipoor Saen, R. (2022). A new fuzzy network data envelopment analysis model for measuring efficiency and effectiveness: Assessing the sustainability of railways. *Applied Intelligence, 52*(12), 13634–13658.

Tsolas, I. E. (2020). Precious metal mutual fund performance evaluation: A series two-stage DEA modeling approach. *Journal of Risk and Financial Management, 13*(5), 87.

Wang, W. K., Lu, W. M., & Liu, P. Y. (2014). A fuzzy multi-objective two-stage DEA model for evaluating the performance of US bank holding companies. *Expert Systems with Applications, 41*(9), 4290–4297.

Xia, Q., Liang, L., & Yang, F. (2014). Integrating fuzzy intermediate factors in supply chain efficiency evaluation. *Studies in Fuzziness and Soft Computing*, 243–254.

Zadeh, L. A. (1978). Fuzzy sets as a basis for a theory of possibility. *Fuzzy Sets and Systems, 1*(1), 3–28.

Managerial Ability in Indian Life Insurance Companies: A Comparison Based on DEA and DEAGP

Ram Pratap Sinha and Bahareh Vaisi

Abstract Although global life insurance industry experienced significant structural and technological changes over the past decade, it is expected to increase based on the next decade's outlook. The performance of life insurance companies is influenced by several factors, and managerial ability is a key facilitator for the companies aiming to gain a leadership position in insurance market. Thus managerial ability evaluation is essential for retaining and rewarding capable managers. Nevertheless, managerial ability is an intellectual capability that could not be measured directly. The present study provides an indirect measure of managerial ability of 22 Indian life insurers for the period 2013–14 to 2019–20. For efficiency evaluation of the life insurers both data envelopment analysis and goal programming have been used. In the second stage, the efficiency scores are regressed on several contextual variables (solvency ratio, market share, insurer size and insurer age). The results indicate that the influence of size and insurer age is statistically significant. We have derived estimates of managerial ability for the two methods of evaluation and the results are quite similar. Finally, we have validated the estimates of managerial ability by regressing return on total asset (an important measure of insurer performance) on managerial ability measurers and the regression coefficients are statistically significant.

Keywords Managerial ability · Data envelopment analysis · Data envelopment analysis-goal programming · Life insurance companies · Efficiency

JEL classification G22 · C44 · C67 · C88 · D22

R. P. Sinha (✉)
Economics, Government College of Engineering and Leather Technology, Kolkata 700106, India
e-mail: rampratapsinha39@gmail.com

B. Vaisi
Young Researchers and Elite Club, South Tehran Branch, Islamic Azad University, Tehran, Iran
e-mail: st_b_vaisi@azad.ac.ir

© The Author(s), under exclusive license to Springer Nature Singapore Pte Ltd. 2024

S. A. Edalatpanah et al. (eds.), *Analytical Decision Making and Data Envelopment Analysis*, Infosys Science Foundation Series in Mathematical Sciences,
https://doi.org/10.1007/978-981-97-6972-8_4

1 Introduction

In the nineties, many of the emerging economies initiated economic liberalization with a more important role for the non-government enterprises. A key feature of the process of economic liberalization has been deregulation of infrastructure industries including financial intermediaries like commercial banking and insurance. On a theoretical plane, support in favor of entry deregulation in industries earmarked for stringent government regulation came from (Averchand Johnson 1962; Stigler, 1971; Becker, 1983). Averchand Johnson (1962) pointed out that while formulating price controls on regulated monopoly industries, the use of rate of return criteria is likely to promote misallocation of resources. (Stigler, 1971) emphasized on the capture of regulation by interest groups. Becker (1983) advanced an analytical model of competition for political pressure groups who contend among themselves for obtaining benefits from the government.

Up to the 1980s, Indian financial sector was highly regulated and the life insurance sector was no exception. Directed credit allocation of credit and directed investment were two characteristic features of the regulated regime. However, since 1991, the government of India initiated LPG (Liberalization, Privatization and Globalization) policies and the Indian financial sector was among the first of the few sectors to experience deregulation. Since 1956, Indian life insurance sector had a monopoly market player. The Life Insurance Corporation of Indian and the regulated system continued up to 1999. Deregulation of the insurance market was implemented with the establishment of the Insurance Regulatory and Development Authority of India (IRDA) which issued guidelines for entry to the insurance sector. Between 1999–00 and 2019–20 the number of life insurers rose from 1 to 24. Between 2000 and 2020, life insurance penetration (insurance premium as percentage of GDP) increased from 1.77 to 3.20. At the same time, life insurance density (per capita premia in US $) improved from 9.9 in 2000 to 59 in 2020.

While the life insurance industry in India had a significant growth during the period under consideration, there are substantial inter-firm differences in performance. The purpose of the present study is to explain the performance differences in terms of managerial ability. From a resource based view of the productive firms, managerial ability serves a crucial role in explaining performance of the firm. Barney (1991) pointed out that firm resources are rare, valuable and cannot be substituted or imitated perfectly. Castanias and Helfat (1991, 2001) pointed out that the top management of firm is a valuable resource which enables them to generate rents. Adner and Helfat (2003) found strong linkage between managerial decisions and business performance. Holcomb et al. (2009) found that managers with higher degree of ability are capable of positively influencing resource productivity.

Given the importance of managerial capability in shaping the growth performance of business enterprises, several international research studies have attempted to provide quantitative measures of managerial ability for either the corporate sector in general or in industry specific cases. However, in the Indian context, there is a complete absence of published research literature relating to the evaluation of managerial ability of productive firms. The present study seeks to eliminate this research vacuum. To be specific, the objective of the current study is to provide a managerial ability measure (with validation) for the Indian life insurance companies. One finds, three alternative standpoints for estimating the influence of managerial ability on business performance: (i) evaluation of managerial ability on the basis of certain indicators of economic/financial performance, (ii) estimation of managerial fixed effects on the basis of job switches by corporate managers, and (iii) indirect evaluation of managerial ability from the regression residuals of efficiency estimates on the environmental (contextual) variables.

We have, however, adopted the three-stage approach advanced by Demerjian et al. (2012) which was further refined by Demerjian et al. (2013) and Demerjian, Lewis-Western and McVay (2020). We have also used inputs from Banker and Park (2020, 2021). The study banks on 154 firm-year observations involving 22 Indian life insurance companies over the period 2013–14 to 2019–20. The three stage approach that we have used for estimating and validating managerial ability involves the application of DEA (Data Envelopment Analysis) and DEAGP (Data Envelopment Analysis-Goal Programming) in the first stage for the estimation of insurer specific efficiency and the use of regression approach in the subsequent two stages for finding out the impact of the contextual variable (on efficiency) and validation of managerial ability respectively. The study has 5 sections and proceeds as follows. Following this introduction, Sect. 1 reviews the concerned literature. Section 2 outlines the methodology. Variables and data are described in Sect. 3. Section 4 states and discusses the results. Section 5 concludes.

2 Literature Review

In a modern productive organisation, ownership and control are divorced as the day to day activity of the productive firms are overseen by managers. The managers of business organizations act as agents of the business owners (principal). While the actions/efforts of agents are guided by the persuasion of individual interests, the proponents of agency theory assume that incentive compatible contracts can lead to alignment of the interests of the principals and agents.

The design of incentive compatible contracts requires knowledge of managerial ability/effort. While it is generally agreed that managerial talent is important in determining firm performance, the managerial efforts are not directly observable. In view of this, several research studies attempted to estimate managerial performance. Barr et al. (1993) estimated managerial quality using data envelopment analysis. The study considered (core) deposits, performing (earning) assets and (total) interest income as the three banking sector outputs and six input variables representing the resources required to operate a bank. Murthi et al. (1996) measured managerial performance through marketing and production performance of firms. Relative marketing performance in this study is the performance regarding ROI (return on investment) and company market share in terms of five inputs. The production efficiency (in relative terms) considers the ROI (return on investment) performance when compared to expenses regarding purchase procurement and manufacturing.

A second line of study considered the impact of (managerial) fixed effects on corporate performance in the context of the managers who switch jobs. Bertrand et al. (2003) investigated the managerial impact on corporate behavior and performance based on managers-firm matched panel data. They found that a major part of the variations in firm practices regarding investment, company financial policy and organization strategy can depend on the existence of managerial fixed effects in the relationship. Bamber et al. (2010) studied the influence of idiosyncratic fixed effects on the disclosure characteristics of the in-sample firms (for the period 1995–2005) and found that the impact of managers on corporate financial disclosure is significant. Baik et al. (2011) examined the linkage between managerial ability and managerial forecast and found that the accuracy of the earnings forecast issuance improves with CEO ability. Demerjian et al. (2012) provided an estimate of managerial ability in a more general context without restricting the sample of job switching managers. The study provided estimates of managerial ability in a multi stage evaluation approach including the computation of company-wise (relative) efficiencies in the first stage (obtained from DEA) based on their observed capability to produce revenues relative to the quantity and composition of productive resources used by the firms. The study showed that the company-specific measure of efficiency calculated in the first stage is influenced by several environmental variables including managerial ability. However, managerial ability is not an observed variable. Thus it is necessary to remove the impact of the observed environmental variables on firm level efficiency in order to find out the managerial ability component. The study accordingly eliminated the impact of other important determinants of company size, share in the market, positive (free) cash flow, the extent of product based diversification and geographic diversification, influence of time, industry impact and firm age on efficiency for identifying the managerial ability factor. As the non-explained section of firm efficiency may yet include the influence of other non-identified explanatory variables, it is necessary to execute test of result validation for knowing if the residual ability measure correctly represents managerial ability.

Several subsequent research studies examined the relationship between managerial ability and firm performance. Demerjian et al. (2013) evaluated the relationship between the quality of firm earnings and managerial ability. The study revealed that managers having higher degree of ability has a positive influence on the quality of firm earnings (e.g. persistent and higher earnings level, lesser number of earnings restatement, less error regarding provisions for non-performing assets etc.). Andreou et al. (2016) assessed the impact of managerial ability on creation of liquidity by commercial banks and their behavior regarding risk-taking. The study showed that managers having greater level ability are capable of creating more liquidity and assuming more business risk. However, during financial crisis periods, bank managers with greater managerial ability reduce credit creation. Cheung et al. (2017) studied the linkage between firm performance and managerial ability in relation to (managerial) discretion and the quality of monitoring. The study found that greater degree of managerial discretion enables managers with higher level of ability to positively influence firm performance when such discretion is monitored closely to control rent seeking incentives of the managers. Demerjian et al. (2020) examined if whether higher managerial ability impart more stability in earnings management or not. The outcome showed that managers with higher degree of ability exhibit higher probability of engaging in smoothing of earnings leading to better operational performance in subsequent periods. Kumar and Goswami (2021) examined the link between managerial capability and real earnings management of a panel of 108 non-financial firms for the period 2006 to 2017. Cheng and Zhang (2022) found a positive link between the managerial ability factor and company-specific risk of Chinese firms based on models with fixed effects. The positive impact of firms with superior managerial ability is, however, weakened with greater degree of idiosyncratic fluctuation. Khoo and Cheung (2022) scrutinized how managerial ability influences the decisions regarding corporate debt maturity and found that firms having managers of superior ability tend to take on more short-term debt financing. In another new study, Kumar and Zbib (2022) identified that not only firms having higher level of managerial ability had superior equity price reaction during the market failure during the onset of the Covid-19 pandemic but also they significantly had higher surplus cash.

The extant research studies on the insurance sector has mostly concentrated on the efficiency and productivity performance of the insurance companies. Kaffash et al. (2020) surveyed 132 published research studies (which appeared between 1993 and 2018) on the insurance sector with the application of data envelopment analysis. The reader is also referred to (Grmanová & Strunz, 2017; Gharakhaniet et al., 2018; Sinha, 2019; Anandarao et al., 2019; Aigbovo-Omoruyi, 2020; Ghosh, 2021; Mahad et al., 2021; Sinha, 2021; Suarez-Fernandez et al., 2021; Abdin et al., 2022) for the study of insurer efficiency performance. Banker, Amirteimoori and Sinha (2022) compared managerial ability of Indian and Iranian general insurers. However, with the exception of Cvetkoska et al. (2022), there are no known published studies on the estimation of managerial ability of the life insurance sector. In view of this, the current study seeks to fill this gap.

3 Research Methodology

In the current study, we seek to address the following research questions:

(i) How managerial ability of Indian life insurers has varied across the companies and over the period under observation?
(ii) What is the relationship of return on total asset with managerial ability i.e. between direct measure of performance with an indirect measure of managerial performance.

Evaluation of managerial ability necessitates efficiency estimation of the in-sample life insurers. For this, we have applied DEA and DEAGP methods. In the second step, the effect of contextual variables on the performance of companies to create a measure of managerial ability is eliminated, and in the third step, the constructed measure is used as an independent/dependent variable. The details of the above-mentioned structure, DEA/DEAGP modeling, managerial ability estimation, and their properties are discussed in the following paragraphs.

3.1 DEA Modeling for Efficiency Evaluation

In accordance with the adopted approach in the current study, the estimation of managerial ability at the firm level requires the evaluation of relative efficiency performance of the in-sample firms. Therefore, we have estimated firm efficiency performance using two non-parametric methods, DEA and DEAGP. An illustration (Fig. 1) is presented to better explain the computational procedure for technical efficiency scores.

Estimation of efficiency requires specification of the input–output framework. Let us consider a technology which converts a vector of m inputs (denoted by x) to output vector representing s outputs (denoted by y). The true technology is unknown to us. However, we adopt data driven approaches for estimating production frontier and firm level efficiency. We assume that the technology has the following two characteristics:

(a) The input and output vectors of the insurers are freely disposable. Thus if x_0 can produce a given level of output $\overline{y}$, it can also be produced by x_1 where $x_1 \geq x_0$. Similarly, if y_0 can be produced from $\overline{x}$, then y_1 is also producible from $\overline{x}$, provided $y_1 \leq y_0$.
(b) The technology is convex implying that convex combinations of observed production points are also feasible.

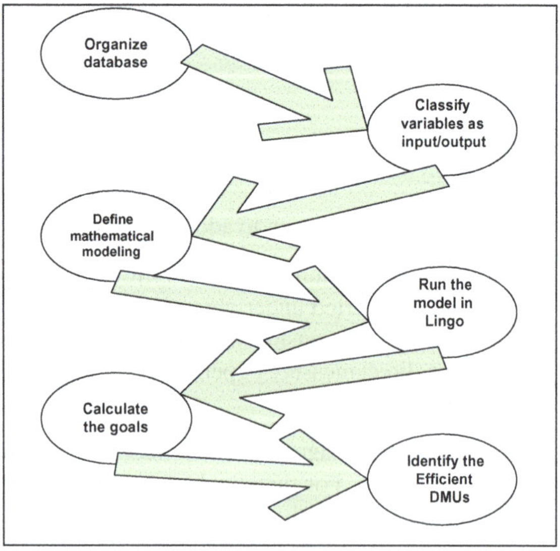

Fig. 1 Computational procedure for technical efficiency scores

Charnes et al. (1978) introduced the concept of DEA as method of performance benchmarking in the context of constant returns to scale. They introduced a ratio definition of efficiency by generalizing the single output to single input measure of efficiency to the case of multiple outputs and multiple inputs without assigning weights beforehand. Banker et al. (1984) extended the analysis in the context of variable returns to scale. In the present case, we have applied the BCC model for efficiency evaluation in the first stage. For a sample of n Decision Making Units (DMUs), the objective of an observed DMU) E_o is:

$$\max\ E_0 = \frac{\sum_{r=1}^{s} u_r y_{r0} + W}{\sum_{i=1}^{m} v_i x_{i0}} \tag{1}$$

$S.t.$

$$\begin{aligned} \frac{\sum_{r=1}^{s} u_r y_{rj} + W}{\sum_{i=1}^{m} v_i x_{ij}} &\le 1 && \text{j} = (1, 2, \ldots.., \text{n}) \\ & && \textit{where W is a free variable} \\ u_r &\ge 0 && r = (1, 2, \ldots.., s) \\ v_i &\ge 0 && i = (1, 2, \ldots.., m) \end{aligned}$$

The process is repeated for each of the n in-sample DMus. Let $E_0{}^*$ is the optimal efficiency value of the observed decision-making unit. If $E_0^* = 1$, then the DMU is efficient. Also, if $E_0^* < 1$, the DMU is inefficient. The obtained set of weights $(v,\ u)$, is different across DMus. This property of DEA sometimes lead to a failure in distinguishing between efficient and projected units especially when the sample size is small as for many inputs and outputs the optimal weights in DEA estimation become zero.

3.2 *DEAGP Modeling for Efficiency Evaluation*

For adding robustness to the outcome of our study, we have supplemented DEA estimation with Goal Programming for evaluating the efficiency of the observed decision making units. Let us explain the method briefly. Goal Programming method, introduced by Charnes et al. (1955), is a conventional technique in multi criteria decision making which uses the concept of minimizing deviations from the Goal in decision making. Suppose the objective function of Goal Programming is Z_j while g_j represents the goal. In case of frontier analysis, the weighted sum of outputs of an observed firm (DMU) cannot exceed the benchmark output,$u_0 y_0 + W \le UY$ and similarly the weighted sum of inputs cannot be lower than the benchmark level of input: $v_0 x_0 - W \le VX$. We can denote $d_j^+ = u_0 y_0 + W - UY$ and $d_j^- = u_0 y_0 - W - VX$. Then the multi criteria optimisation problem (model (2)) is converted to a single criterion optimisation problem which is presented below:

$$\min \sum_{j=1}^{n} d_j^+ + d_j^- \quad (2)$$

$S.t.$

$$Z_j - g_j = d_j^+ - d_j^- d_j^+, \ d_j^- \geq 0 \, j = 1, \ldots, n$$

In the present study, the DEA based Goal Programming model is formulated as follows:

$$\min \sum_{j=1}^{n} d_j^+ + d_j^- \quad (3)$$

$S.t.$

$$\begin{aligned} \frac{\sum_{r=1}^{s} u_r y_{rj} + W}{\sum_{i=1}^{m} v_i x_{ij}} + d_j^- - d_j^+ &= 1 \quad j = 1, \ldots, n \\ u_r &\geq 0 \quad r = 1, \ldots, s \\ v_i &\geq 0 \quad i = 1, \ldots, m \\ d_j^+, d_j^- &\geq 0 \quad j = 1, \ldots, n \end{aligned}$$

where, all the Goals are equal to unity (the ceiling level of efficiency). By solving the DEA-GP model (model (4)), u_r^* *and* v_i^* can be obtained as the Common Set of Weights. Thus the efficiency of all the DMUs can be estimated using the CSWs. For empirical studies on goal programming based DEA for evaluating efficiency refer Estellita Lins et al. (2004), Makuei et al.(2008), Alinezhad and Kiani (2009), Stewart (2010), Vaisi (2012), Vaisi and Ebrahimi (2015), Tavana et al. (2017) and Vaisi (2017).

3.3 Second and Third Stage Estimation

In the intermediate (second) stage of the estimation process, the efficiency scores generated from the first stage application of DEA are now regressed on the contextual variables which influence firm-specific efficiency except managerial ability (which cannot be estimated directly). Indirect estimates of managerial ability are available from the regression residuals of the second stage regression. In the final (third) stage the quantified relationship between managerial ability and other measures of performance is explored econometrically. Since the estimate of managerial ability might contains some unidentified factor, it is advisable to use the estimate (of managerial ability) as an explanatory variable and not as a dependent variable.

For the second and third stage estimation, we have used panel data models. This is because we have dependent and explanatory variables which spread across firms and time periods. There are three commonly used panel data models: (i) the pooled OLS (ordinary least squares) model, (ii) the fixed effects model and (iii) the random effects model. Pooled OLS is suitable only when firm-specific effects are all observable for all firms for the periods under observation. Fixed effects model is suitable when such effects are unobservable and the unobserved variables are correlated with the included variables. On the other hand, if the unobserved variables are uncorrelated with the observed variables then they can be included in the model disturbance term. In such a case, random effects model is suitable.

3.4 Managerial Ability Estimation

Corporate managers play a pivotal role in the process of decision making of the respective enterprises and consequently the significance of managerial ability in the revenue generation process cannot be undermined. Thus estimation of managerial ability is essential for retaining and rewarding capable managers. The efficiency measure generated by efficiency evaluation in the first stage may be affected by not only company-specific but also manager-specific efficiency drivers, and thus it might be over/under-state managerial ability.

As mentioned earlier, Demerjian et al. (2012) introduced an empirical measure of managerial ability from the DEA-generated firm efficiency measures by eliminating a number of firm-specific factors, industry effects and time specific effects, and proposed a practical measure of managerial ability based on the available financial data of the firms. Banker and Park (2020, 2021) in two studies pointed out that, the approach of Demerjian et al. (2012) made two important contributions to the managerial ability literature. First, their approach provided a method for measuring managerial ability which is an unobserved variable. Secondly, their study validated the measure by associating it with other measures of ability.

In the present study, the input, output, contextual and validating variable are described in Sect. 3. On the other hand, the estimates of managerial ability are provided and explained in Sect. 4.

4 Input and Output Variables and Data

4.1 Description of the Input and Output Variables

Estimation of insurer's efficiency and evaluation of the impact of environmental variables on the estimated efficiency outcomes require the identification of the relevant variables. Eling and Luhnen (2010) identified 3 principal forms of inputs that are utilised in the insurance industry: labor, business services & materials, and capital.

In the absence of adequate classified information about expenses on labor and business services & materials, we have considered Operating Expenses as the proxy input. In addition, we have taken Claims Incurred as the second input. These two indicate the total spending by the concerned insurer.

Leverty and Grace (2010) pointed out that in the financial services industry research studies, there are three standpoints for selecting outputs: (i) the (financial) intermediation approach, (ii) the user cost approach and (ii) the value added approach. Sealey and Lindley (1977) introduced the financial intermediation approach in the context of depository financial institutions. Brockett et al. (1998) viewed insurance companies as financial intermediaries which mobilise funds from the policyholders and deploy them in the capital market and from the income stream pays claims, taxes and other expenses. The user cost approach is due to Hancock (1985) which considers an indicator as an input or output depending on its net contribution to the insurer revenue. Grace and Timme (1992) and Berger et al. (2000) followed the value added approach as they considered an item as output if it provides significant value addition.

In the present context, our objective is to estimate managerial ability of the observed life insurers based on their ability to generate operating surplus. Consequently, we have taken Net Premium Income and Other Income (comprising of investment income) of the observed life insurers as the two outputs.

4.2 Data and Period of Analysis

For the present study, we have used secondary data for gathering information about the input, output and contextual variables. In specific, we have collected data from the IRDA Annual Reports for the period under observation and the Handbook on Indian Insurance Statistics for 2013–14, 2015–16, 2017–18, and 2019–20.

5 Results and Discussion

In this section, first, the technical efficiency and managerial ability of each period are determined separately. The results and analysis are given in the following subsections.

5.1 Efficiency Estimates

The first step towards the evaluation of managerial ability of the observed insurers is the computation of firm wise technical efficiency. In the present case, we have made efficiency estimates separately for each year under observation. Thus the frontiers are year-specific. The technology is assumed to be local implying the operation of variable returns to scale. Since we have deployed two methods including DEA-BCC (DEA based on Banker, Charnes and Cooper approach, 1984) and DEA-GP

(DEA based on Goal Programming) for the estimates of technical efficiency, Table 1 presents the average technical efficiency scores for the period 2013–14 to 2019–20. The efficiency scores vary between zero and 1.

According to the DEA-BCC method, mean efficiency scores of the observed life insurance companies during the period under observation varied between 44 and 57%. Looking at the year on year fluctuations, it is evidenced that mean efficiency improved between 2013–14 and 2014–15 but declined in the next year. Thereafter, it recorded secular improvement for the period 2016–17 to 2018–19. In comparison, the fluctuation in mean efficiency scores is more pronounced under the DEAGP method as the mean efficiency varied between 59 and 92% during the same period. Following this method, the mean efficiency score improved between 2013–14 and 2017–18 (as it climbed from 59% in 2013–14 to 92% in 2017–18) but declined thereafter (85% in 2018–19 and 81% in 2019–20). Figure 2 provides a graphical presentation of the movements in average efficiency scores under both methods for the aforementioned period.

Table 1 Mean efficiency estimates for the life insurance companies (2013–14 to 2019–20)

Method of efficiency estimation	2013–14	2014–15	2015–16	2016–17	2017–18	2018–19	2019–20
DEA-BCC	0.44	0.562	0.467	0.51	0.544	0.574	0.522
DEA-GP	0.589	0.726	0.73	0.786	0.92	0.853	0.811

Source Calculated

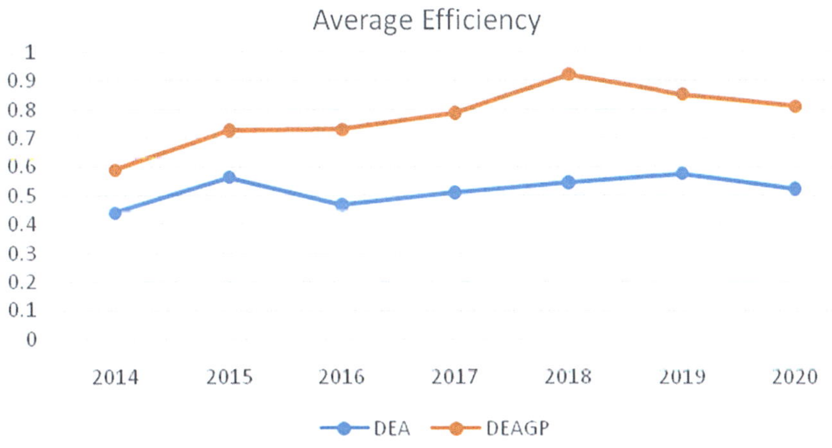

Fig. 2 Movements in average efficiency scores (2013–14 to 2019–20)

5.2 *Influence of Environmental Variables on the Efficiency Estimates*

The efficiency outcomes(scores) obtained from the utilisation of DEA-BCC and DEA-GP models in the first stage are influenced by both company-specific and manager-specific factors. Since we are interested in estimating managerial ability, we need to eliminate the influence of company-specific factors first. With this objective in mind, we have regressed the efficiency scores on the following four contextual variables: *Solvency Ratio*, *Market Share*, *Total Asset* and *Insurer Age* (in number of completed years). Since insurer efficiency scores represent a bounded dependent variable (having lower and upper bounds of 0 and 1 respectively), we have considered log of efficiency as the regressand. On the basis of the outcome of Hausman test, we have chosen fixed effect panel data model for the purpose of regression. Thus the regression model could be written as:

$$L_n(E_i) = \beta_0 + \beta_1(Solvency) + \beta_2(Market\ share) + \beta_3(LnTA) + \beta_4(Age) + u_i \quad (4)$$

Here $Ln(E_i)$ stands for log of efficiency score of the ith insurance company, Solvency represents solvency ratio, Ln TA represents log of total assets, and Age stands for insurer's age expressed in the number of years.

Tables 2 and 3 represent the coefficients of the regressors, standard error of the coefficient estimates and probabilities of type I error for the two regression models. Besides, the goodness of fit is indicated in terms of LSDV (Least Square Dummy Variable) R squared and the standard error of estimate. The tables indicate that insurer size has a positive and significant association with efficiency scores. Further, the coefficient of Market Share is statistically significant at 95% level of confidence for DEA-GP efficiency but non-significant for DEA-BCC efficiency scores. The coefficients of the remaining two explanatory variables are statistically insignificant for both the models.

5.3 *Estimates of Managerial Ability*

In the present context, the residual from estimating Eq. (5) is our measure of managerial ability. The mean managerial ability scores generated from the two methods are displayed in Table 4. The insurer wise estimates of managerial ability are included in Appendix, Tables A.1 and A.2. Figure 3 provides a graphical comparison of the outcomes.

Comparison of the estimates of managerial ability obtained from the application of DEA and DEAGP show that, the estimate of managerial ability based on DEA-BCC is higher than that of DEA-GP for 2014–15 to 2016–17 while the reverse is true for the remaining four years (2013–14 and for the period 2017–18 to 2019–20).

Table 2 Regression of DEA-BCC efficiency on the environmental variables

Particulars	Coefficient (β)	Standard error	Observed t value	Probability of having error of type 1 error
Intercept	−4.8015	0.4374	−10.98	<0.0001
Solvency	0.0092	0.0089	1.040	0.3103
Market share	0.9949	0.6424	1.549	0.1364
Log of the total asset	0.3087	0.0367	8.414	<0.0001
Insurer age	−0.0329	0.0122	−2.690	0.0137
LSDV R squared	0.6562			
Standard error of estimate	0.2800			

Source Calculated

Table 3 Regression of DEA-GP efficiency on the contextual variables

Particulars	Coefficient (β)	Standard error	Observed t value	Probability of having error of type 1 error
Intercept	−3.5669	0.4066	−8.773	<0.0001
Solvency	−0.0108	0.0130	−0.8340	0.4137
Market share	0.2883	0.5627	0.5124	0.6137
Log of the total asset	0.2454	0.0322	7.610	<0.0001
Insurer age	−0.01995	0.0094	−2.113	0.0468
LSDV R squared	0.6491			
Standard error of estimate	0.2708			

Source Calculated

Table 4 Managerial ability measure of insurance companies in India under DEABCC/DEAGP

Methods	Year						
	2013–14	2014–15	2015–16	2016–17	2017–18	2018–19	2019–20
DEA-BCC	−0.0955	0.6179	0.3583	0.1223	0.0242	−0.1579	−0.2194
DEA-GP	0.0055	0.0153	−0.0109	−0.0138	0.0298	−0.0407	0.0149

Source Calculated

5.4 Clustering of Life Insurers Based on Managerial Ability Scores

We have clustered the observed life insurance companies into two insurer groups on the basis of mean managerial ability scores. Group 1 comprises of 11 life insurers

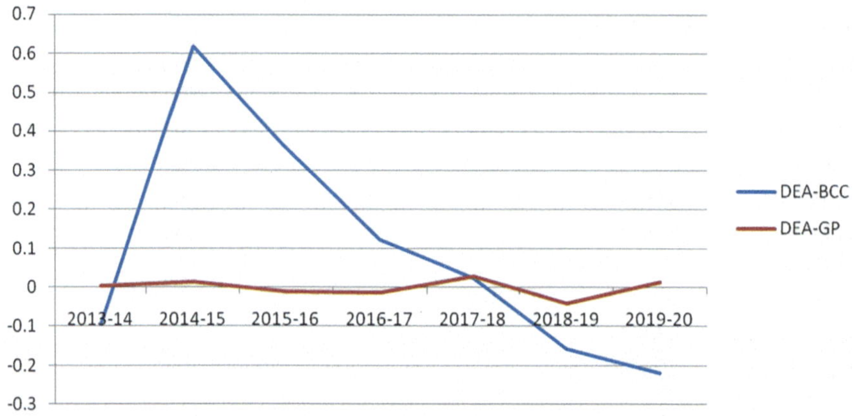

Fig. 3 Average managerial ability of Indian life insurers

(Canara HSBC OBC, India First, IDBI Federal, Star Union Dai-ichi, Tata AIA, Aviva Life, SBI Life, Aditya Birla Sun Life, Max Life, Shriram Life and Exide Life) who registered positive mean managerial ability for the seven year period. Group 2 includes the remaining 11 life insurers (LIC, Kotak Mahindra, PNB Metlife, HDFC Standard, ICICI Prudential,Pramerica, Bajaj Allianz, Bharti AXA, Reliance Nippon, Aegon and Future Generali) with negative mean managerial ability. The details are provided in Table 5.

5.5 *Relationship with Other Measures of Firm Performance*

Finally, we have estimated the relationship of another measure of firm performance—*Return on Total Asset-* with our estimated measure of Managerial Ability, by following the procedure introduced by Demerjian et al. (2012) for both methods (DEA-BCC and DEA-GP). The results are presented in Tables 6 and 7. The outcomes in both cases indicate strong positive linkage between Return on Total Asset and Managerial Ability.

Table 5 Clustering of life insurance companies based on managerial ability estimates

Group 1	Mean Managerial Ability—BCC Model	Mean Managerial Ability—DEAGP Model	Group 2	Mean Managerial Ability—BCC Model	Mean Managerial Ability—DEAGP Model
Canara HSBC OBC	0.3251	0.3793	LIC	–0.0001	–0.0001
India First	0.2887	0.3368	Kotak Mahindra	–0.0044	–0.0051
IDBI Federal	0.2334	0.2723	PNB Metlife	–0.0516	–0.0603
Star Union Dai-ichi	0.1316	0.1535	HDFC Standard	–0.0693	–0.0808
Tata AIA	0.1242	0.1449	ICICI Prudential	–0.0770	–0.0898
Aviva Life	0.1235	0.1441	Pramerica	–0.1040	–0.1214
SBI Life	0.1075	0.1254	Bajaj Allianz	–0.1201	–0.1401
Aditya Birla Sun Life	0.0773	0.0902	Bharti AXA	–0.2187	–0.2552
Max Life	0.0553	0.0645	Reliance Nippon	–0.2721	–0.3175
Shriram Life	0.0245	0.0285	Aegon	–0.3063	–0.3573
Exide Life	0.0129	0.0150	Future Generali	–0.3069	–0.3581
Mean Value	0.1367	0.1595	Mean Value	–0.1391	–0.1623

Source Calculated

Table 6 Regression of ROTA (return on total asset) on managerial ability (DEA-BCC model)

Particulars	Coefficient (β)	Standard error	Observed t value	Probability of having error of type 1 error
Intercept	0.00546207	3.95477e-012	1.381e + 009	<0.0001
Managerial ability	0.0228292	0.00553668	4.123	0.0005
LSDV R squared	0.3037			
Standard error of estimate	0.0210			

Source Calculated

Table 7 Regression of ROTA (return on total asset) on managerial ability (DEA-GP model)

Particulars	Coefficient (β)	Standard error	Observed t value	Probability of having error of type 1 error
Intercept	0.00546207	3.95458e-011	1.381e + 008	<0.0001
Managerial ability	0.0192772	0.00563894	3.419	0.0026
LSDV R squared	0.2459			
Standard error of estimate	0.0132			

Source Calculated

6 Conclusion

During the post-deregulation phase, Indian life insurance sector had significant growth. However, as is only to be expected, there is considerable heterogeneity in the growth rate of business across the life insurers. Managerial ability differentials proved crucial in the manifest performance of the insurers. The present study sought to provide estimates of this unobservable for 22 life insurers. For this, the study adopted a three-stage approach which analyses and decomposes insurance company performance. In specific, the present study follows the basic structure of Demerjian et al. (2012) wherein a measure of managerial ability is derived as the residual of second stage regression of the efficiency score estimates on important contextual variables representing insurer-specific factors. However, we have differed from the original study in three respects. First, we have applied the three stage approach in the context of a specific financial service industry instead of the entire business sector. Second, for getting robust results in the efficiency evaluation process, we have used DEAGP (in addition to DEA) which rely on common set of weights respectively for efficiency evaluation. Finally, the second stage analysis (regression of efficiency estimates on the environmental/contextual variables) also differs substantially from the original study undertaken the U.S. context.

The major outcomes of the present study are the following. First, the second stage regression outcomes imply that the relationship results are fairly robust across the two sets of efficiency scores derived from the application of DEA and DEAGP in the first stage. For both the cases it is found that insurer size and age are the two explanatory variables which influence insurer performance significantly. The impact of solvency ratio is negative but statistically insignificant. Secondly, the regression of Return on Total Asset on Managerial Ability shows that there is a strong positive relationship between the two implying that the indirect measure of performance (managerial ability) and direct measure of performance (return on total asset) are significantly related to each other. The results have significant practical importance as this will facilitate the incentive design process for corporate managers.

Our study is based on a period comprising of seven financial years. Further, we did not consider the influence of managerial ability on some other dimensions of insurer revenue like stability or smoothness. An extension of the study might provide more insights regarding the role of managerial ability in the growth trajectory of life insurers. Further, the study might extended to cases with undesirable inputs and outputs (Monzeli, 2020) which will be a novel extension of the extant literature.

Appendix

See Tables A.1 and A.2.

Table A.1 Insurer wise estimates of managerial ability (DEA Model)

Insurer	2013–14	2014–15	2015–16	2016–17	2017–18	2018–19	2019–20
Aditya Birla Sun Life	0.0036	0.41137	0.11396	0.06847	0.07268	–0.1289	0.18604
Aegon	–0.2348	–0.5305	–0.4848	–0.3855	–0.3043	–0.2039	–0.285
Aviva Life	0.1196	0.27666	–0.0474	0.21087	0.07464	0.23	0.52249
Bajaj Allianz	–0.2749	0.10012	–0.1312	–0.1066	–0.089	–0.3391	–0.1803
Bharti AXA	–0.4489	–0.4921	–0.3893	–0.3736	0.13471	0.03828	–0.1488
Canara HSBC OBC	0.6543	0.32997	0.12709	0.27666	0.29863	0.58895	0.32473
Exide Life	0.1811	–0.1107	–0.188	0.14083	0.10983	0.0128	0.04879
Future Generali	–0.2871	–0.2393	–0.5223	–0.4185	–0.5173	–0.1641	–0.2819
HDFC Standard	0.0647	–0.089	0.01425	–0.0107	–0.1531	–0.3112	–0.314
ICICI Prudentia	–0.3317	–0.0466	–0.0866	–0.0611	0.21623	–0.2289	–0.1563
IDBI Federal	0.0882	0.16686	0.29261	0.44635	0.31957	0.32014	0.40898
India First	0.7469	0.14776	0.36294	0.38556	0.21206	0.16583	–0.1478
Kotak Mahindra	–0.1391	0.171	0.07266	0.00486	–0.0693	–0.0707	0.18
LIC	–0.142	0.11256	0.17612	–0.0256	–0.0864	–0.0353	0.05818
Max Life	0.1898	0.15725	0.21804	0.0019	–0.051	–0.129	–0.0291
PNB Metlife	–0.0639	0.00429	–0.0912	–0.0883	–0.1004	–0.022	–0.1184
Pramerica	–0.142	–0.0492	–0.0496	–0.1596	–0.2246	–0.1031	–0.237

(continued)

Table A.1 (continued)

Insurer	2013–14	2014–15	2015–16	2016–17	2017–18	2018–19	2019–20
Reliance Nippon	–0.518	–0.3832	–0.4723	–0.1189	–0.145	–0.2674	0.76128
SBI Life	0.1426	0.28163	0.1462	0.05865	0.1125	0.01088	–0.0718
Shriram Life In	0.1556	–0.1233	–0.1696	–0.0588	0.16848	0.19889	–0.1649
Star Union Dai–ichi	0.2361	0.32088	0.024	0.03492	0.17268	0.13269	0.05025
Tata AIA	–0.0955	0.61789	0.35829	0.12228	0.02422	–0.1579	–0.2194

Source Calculated

Table A.2 Insurer wise estimates of managerial ability DEAGP model)

Insurer	2013–14	2014–15	2015–16	2016–17	2017–18	2018–19	2019–20
Aditya Birla Sun Life	0.117334	0.286408	0.061536	–0.01266	0.013395	–0.30513	0.32754
Aegon	–0.57869	–0.33418	–0.33147	–0.37594	0.100568	–0.26262	–0.20579
Aviva Life	0.247693	0.154953	–0.23846	0.178298	–0.02615	–0.14572	0.103062
Bajaj Allianz	0.147247	–0.04351	–0.00497	–0.00609	–0.26822	–0.28006	–0.10873
Bharti AXA	–0.68911	–0.3653	0.05643	–0.29571	0.390388	0.071693	0.003545
Canara HSBC OBC	0.552323	0.181025	–0.10492	0.101359	0.119326	0.821831	0.329858
Exide Life	0.203198	–0.07179	0.170871	0.220282	0.256164	–0.05491	0.060825
Future Generali	–0.42225	–0.15873	–0.16946	–0.19588	–0.08228	–0.15708	–0.18277
HDFC Standard	0.012317	–0.12213	0.01325	–0.08728	–0.21051	–0.25576	–0.23142
ICICI Prudentia	–0.08964	–0.09976	–0.2079	–0.17373	–0.20487	–0.16936	–0.14089
IDBI Federal	0.027956	0.330421	0.241383	0.430961	0.445414	0.377358	0.464269
India First	0.401261	–0.05645	0.056778	0.259473	0.07569	0.182216	–0.22257

(continued)

Table A.2 (continued)

Insurer	2013–14	2014–15	2015–16	2016–17	2017–18	2018–19	2019–20
Kotak Mahindra	–0.19511	0.17845	0.081844	0.010344	–0.10597	–0.02707	0.253007
LIC	0.265458	0.191854	0.138543	0.164915	–0.26585	–0.29404	–0.16309
Max Life	0.176547	0.261303	0.138981	0.02242	–0.10298	–0.06486	0.040693
PNB Metlife	0.10771	0.009791	0.103306	0.068168	–0.09093	–0.00425	–0.09302
Pramerica	–0.93163	–0.13367	0.177996	–0.30158	0.04462	–0.0453	–0.10813
Reliance Nippon	–0.25168	–0.38692	–0.57323	–0.22374	–0.08978	–0.36445	0.4787
SBI Life	0.443693	0.23311	–0.06744	–0.03087	–0.05588	–0.04218	–0.03729
Shriram Life In	0.07208	–0.17547	0.001863	–0.36081	0.229686	0.118023	–0.15657
Star Union Dai–ichi	0.383278	0.212974	0.011928	0.014151	0.254493	0.113313	0.045584
Tata AIA	0.120606	0.243961	0.202592	0.289715	0.229222	–0.10695	–0.12927

Source Calculated

References

Abdin, Z., Prabantarikso, R., Fahmy, E., & Farhan, A. (2022). Analysis of the efficiency of insurance companies in Indonesia. *Decision Science Letters, 11*(2), 105–112. https://doi.org/10.5267/j.dsl.2022.1.002

Adner, R., & Helfat, C. E. (2003). Corporate effects and dynamic managerial capabilities. *Strategic Management Journal, 24*(10), 1011–1025. https://doi.org/10.1002/smj.331

Aigbovo-Omoruyi, O. (2020). Efficiency of insurance industry in Nigeria: An application of data envelopment analysis. *Nigerian Journal of Risk and Insurance, 10*(1), 233–265.

Alinezhad, A., & Kiani, M. R. (2009). Practical common weights goal programming approach for technology selection. *Mathematical Sciences, 3*(2), 201–212.

Anandarao, S., Durai, S., & Goyari, P. (2019). Efficiency decomposition in two-stage data envelopment analysis: An application to life insurance companies in India. *Journal of Quantitative Economics, 17*(2), 271–285. https://doi.org/10.1007/s40953-018-0148-1

Andreou, P. C., Philip, D., & Robejsek, P. (2016). Bank liquidity creation and risk-taking: Does managerial ability matter? *Journal of Business Finance & Accounting, 43*(1–2), 226–259. https://doi.org/10.1111/jbfa.12169

Averch, H. & Johnson, L. L. (1962). Behavior of the firm under regulatory constraint. *American Economic Review, 52*(5), 1052–1069. https://www.jstor.org/stable/1812181.

Baik, B., Farber, D., & Lee, S. (2011). CEO ability and management earnings forecasts. *Contemporary Accounting Research, 28*(5), 1645–1668. https://doi.org/10.1111/j.1911-3846.2011.01091.x

Bamber, L., Jiang, J., & Wang, I. (2010). What's My Style? *The Influence of Top Managers on Voluntary Corporate Financial Disclosures, the Accounting Review, 85*(4), 1131–1162. https://doi.org/10.2308/accr.2010.85.4.1131

Banker, R., & Park, H. U. (2020). A statistical foundation for the measurement of managerial ability. University of Saskatchewan Working Paper.

Banker, R. D., Charnes, A., & Cooper, W. W. (1984). Models for the estimation of technical and scale inefficiencies in data envelopment analysis. *Management Science*, September, 1078–1092.

Banker, R. D.,Amirteimoori, A., & Sinha, R. P. (2022). An integrated data envelopment analysis and generalized additive model for assessing managerial ability with application to the insurance industry. *Decision Analytics Journal*. https://doi.org/10.1016/j.dajour.2022.100115.

Banker, R., & Park, H. U. (2021). Three-stage approach to analyze managerial ability. *Data Envelopment Analysis Journal, 5*(1), 27–54. https://doi.org/10.1561/103.00000034

Barney, J. B. (1991). Firm resources and sustained competitive advantage. *Journal of Management, 17*, 99–120. https://doi.org/10.1177/014920639101700108

Barr, R. S., Seiford, L. M., & Siems, T. F. (1993). An envelopment-analysis approach to measuring the managerial efficiency of banks. *Annals of Operations Research, 45*(1), 1–19. https://doi.org/10.1007/BF02282039

Becker, G. S. (1983). A theory of competition among pressure groups for political influence. *The Quarterly Journal of Economics, 98*(3), 371–400. https://doi.org/10.2307/1886017

Berger, A. N., Cummins, J. D., Weiss, M. A., & Zi, H. (2000). Conglomeration versus strategic focus: Evidence from the insurance industry. *Journal of Financial Intermediation, 9*(4), 323–362. https://doi.org/10.1006/jfin.2000.0295

Bertrand, M., & Schoar, A. (2003). Managing with style: The effect of managers on firm policies. *The Quarterly Journal of Economics, 118*(4), 1169–1208. https://doi.org/10.1162/003355303322552775.

Brockett, P. L., Cooper, W. W., Golden, L. L., Rousseau, J. J., & Wang, Y. (1998). DEA evaluations of the efficiency of organizational forms and distribution systems in the US property and liability insuranceindustry. *International Journal of Systems Science, 29*(11), 1235–1247. https://doi.org/10.1080/00207729808929612

Castanias, R. P., & Helfat, C. E. (1991). Managerial resources and rents. *Journal of Management, 17*(1), 155–171. https://doi.org/10.1177/014920639101700110

Castanias, R. P., & Helfat, C. E. (2001). The managerial rents model: Theory and empirical analysis. *Journal of Management, 27*(6), 661–678. https://doi.org/10.1177/014920630102700604

Charnes, A., Cooper, W. W., & Rhodes, E. (1978). Measuring the efficiency of decision making units. *European Journal of Operational Research, 429–44,*. https://doi.org/10.1016/0377-2217(78)90138-8

Charnes, A., Cooper, W. W., & Ferguson, R. O. (1955). Optimal estimation of executive compensation by linear programming. *Management Science, 1*(2), 138–151. http://www.jstor.org/stable/2627315.

Cheng, L., & Zhang, Y. (2022). Do able managers take more risks? *Journal of Innovation & Knowledge, 7*(2), 100182. https://doi.org/10.1016/j.jik.2022.100182

Cheung, K. T. S., Naidu, D., Navissi, F., & Ranjeeni, K. (2017). Valuing talent: Do CEOs' ability and discretion unambiguously increase firm performance. *Journal of Corporate Finance, 42*, 15–35. https://doi.org/10.1016/j.jcorpfin.2016.11.006

Cvetkoska, V., Eftimov, L., Ivanovski, I., & Kamenjarska, T. (2022). Measuring the managerial ability in the insurance companies in the republic of North Macedonia, Croatia, Serbia, and Slovenia, and identifying its determinants. *International Journal of Banking, Risk and Insurance, 10*(1). http://hdl.handle.net/20.500.12188/16476.

Demerijian, P., Lewis-Western, M., & McVay, S. (2020). How does intentional earnings smoothing vary with managerial ability? *Journal of Accounting, Auditing & Finance, 35*(2), 1–32. https://doi.org/10.1177/0148558X17748405

Demerjian, P., Lev, B., & McVay, S. (2012). Quantifying managerial ability: A new measure and validity tests. *Management Science, 58*(7), 1229–1248. https://doi.org/10.1287/mnsc.1110.1487

Demerjian, P., Lev, B., Lewis, M., & McVay, S. (2013). Managerial ability and earnings quality. *The Accounting Review, 88*(2), 463–498. https://doi.org/10.2308/accr-50318

Eling, M., & Luhnen, M. (2010). Efficiency in the international insurance industry: A cross-country comparison. *Journal of Banking & Finance, 34*(7), 1497–1509. https://doi.org/10.1016/j.jbankfin.2009.08.026

Estellita Lins, M. P., Angulo-Meza, L., & Moreira da Silva, A. C. (2004). A multi-objective approach to determine alternative targets in data envelopment analysis. *Journal of the Operational Research Society, 55*(10), 1090–1101. https://doi.org/10.1057/palgrave.jors.2601788
Gharakhani, D., Eshlaghy, A. T., Hafshejani, K. F., Mavi, R. K., & Lotfi, F. H. (2018). Common weights in dynamic network DEA with goal programming approach for performance assessment of insurance companies in Iran. *Management Research Review*. https://doi.org/10.1108/MRR-03-2017-0067
Ghosh, A. (2021). Analyzing efficiency of indian life insurance companies using DEA and SEM. *Turkish Journal of Computer and Mathematics Education (TURCOMAT), 12*(12), 3897–3919.
Grace, M. F., & Timme, S. G. (1992). An examination of cost economies in the United States life insurance industry. *Journal of Risk and Insurance, 59*(1), 72–103. https://doi.org/10.2307/253217
Grmanová, E., & Strunz, H. (2017). Efficiency of insurance companies: Application of DEA and Tobit analyses. *Journal of International Studies, 10*(3). https://doi.org/10.14254/2071-8330.2017/10-3/18.
Hancock, D. (1985). The financial firm: Production with monetary and nonmonetary goods. *Journal of Political Economy, 93*(5), 859–880. https://doi.org/10.1086/261339
Holcomb, T. R., Holmes, R. M., Jr., & Connelly, B. L. (2009). Making the most of what you have: Managerial ability as a source of resource value creation. *Strategic Management Journal, 30*(5), 457–485. https://doi.org/10.1002/smj.747
https://www.researchgate.net/profile/Ali-Emrouznejad/publication/321826067_RECENT_APPLICATIONS_OF_DATA_ENVELOPMENT_ANALYSIS/links/5af928f44585157136f39d2e/RECENT-APPLICATIONS-OF-DATA-ENVELOPMENT-ANALYSIS.pdf#page=222.
Kaffash, S., Azizi, R., Huang, Y., & Zhu, J. (2020). A survey of data envelopment analysis applications in the insurance industry 1993–2018. *European Journal of Operational Research, 284*(3), 801–813. https://doi.org/10.1016/j.ejor.2019.07.034
Khoo, J., & Cheung, A. (2022). Managerial ability and debt maturity. *Journal of Contemporary Accounting and Economics, 18*(1), 1–23. https://doi.org/10.1016/j.jcae.2021.100295.
Kumar, M., & Goswami, R. (2021). Managerial ability and real earnings management among indian listed firms. *Vision, 0*(0). https://doi.org/10.1177/09722629211046065.
Kumar, S., & Zbib, L. (2022). Firm performance during the Covid-19 crisis: Does managerial ability matter? *Finance Research Letters, 102720*,. https://doi.org/10.1016/j.frl.2022.102720
Leverty, J. T., & Grace, M. F. (2010). The robustness of output measures in property-liability insurance efficiency studies. *Journal of Banking & Finance, 34*(7), 1510–1524. https://doi.org/10.1016/j.jbankfin.2009.08.015
Mahad, N. F., Abd Aziz, N. A., Amin, F. A. M., & Mahyideen, J. M. (2021). An integrated DEA and PROMETHEE II method for complete ranking: An application in life-insurance sector. *Journal of Academic Research in Business and Social Sciences, 11*(10), 982–992. http://creativecommons.org/licences/by/4.0/legalcode.
Makuei, A., Alinezhad, A., Kiani, M. R., & Zohrehbandian, M. (2008). A goal programming method for finding common weights in DEA with an improved discriminating power for efficiency. *Journal of Industrial and Systems Engineering, 1*(4), 293–303.
Monzeli, A., Daneshian, B., Tohidi, G., Sanei, M., & Razavian, S. (2020). Efficiency study with undesirable inputs and outputs in DEA. *Journal of Fuzzy Extension and Applications, 1*(1), 73–80. https://doi.org/10.22105/jfea.2020.248018.1005
Murthi, B. P. S., Srinivasan, K., & Kalyanaram, G. (1996). Controlling for observed and unobserved managerial skills in determining first-mover market share advantages. *Journal of Marketing Research, 33*(3), 329–336. https://doi.org/10.1177%2F002224379603300307.
Roll, Y., Cook, W. D., & Golany, B. (1991). Controlling factor weights in data envelopment analysis. *IIE Transactions, 23*(1), 2–9. https://doi.org/10.1080/07408179108963835
Sealey, C. W., Jr., & Lindley, J. T. (1977). Inputs, outputs, and a theory of production and cost at depository financial institutions. *The Journal of Finance, 32*(4), 1251–1266. https://doi.org/10.1111/j.1540-6261.1977.tb03324.x

Sinha, R. P. (2019). Network DEA efficiency of Indian non-life insurance companies. *International Journal on Recent Trends in Business and Tourism (IJRTBT), 3*(3), 83–90.
Sinha, R. P. (2021). Two-stage data envelopment analysis efficiency of Indian general insurance companies. *Global Business Review, 09721509211047645*,. https://doi.org/10.1177/09721509211047645
Stewart, T. J. (2010). Goal directed benchmarking for organizational efficiency. *Omega, 38*(6), 534–539. https://doi.org/10.1016/j.omega.2010.01.004
Stigler, G. J. (1971). The theory of economic regulation. *The Bell Journal of Economics and Management Science, 3–21*. https://doi.org/10.2307/3003160
Suarez-Fernandez, S., Quiroga-Garcia, R., & Manzano-Perez, I. (2021). A comparison of DEA and SFA approaches: Application to the US non-life insurance market. *Applied Economics Journal, 28*(2), 107–127. https://so01.tci-thaijo.org/index.php/AEJ/article/view/242756.
Tavana, M., Shabanpour, H., Yousefi, S., & Saen, R. F. (2017). A hybrid goal programming and dynamic data envelopment analysis framework for sustainable supplier evaluation. *Neural Computing and Applications, 28*(12), 3683–3696. https://doi.org/10.1007/s00521-016-2274-z
Vaisi, B. (2012). The superiority of DEAGP in ranking decision making units over DEA-AHP method: Utilizing relative closeness to ideal decision making units. *Management Science Letters, 2*(8), 2903–2908.
Vaisi, B., & Ebrahimi, A. (2015). Utilizing computer simulation and DEAGP to enhance productivity in a manufacturing system. *International Journal of Data Envelopment Analysis, 3*(4), 857–866.
Vaisi, B. (2017). Productivity improvement in a manufacturing system using computer simulation: A comparison between DEA AND DEAGP in recent applications of data envelopment analysis, proceedings of the 15th international conference on Data Envelopment Analysis, University of Economics, Prague, Czech Republic.

Efficiency Appraisal and Classification of Flexible Random Factors

Monireh Jahani Sayyad Noveiri and Sohrab Kordrostami

Abstract Traditional data envelopment analysis (DEA) models assist in comprehending the performance of decision-making units (DMUs) in situations where a definitive set of inputs and outputs is available. However, in certain real-world scenarios, it becomes necessary to assess the performance of DMUs when dealing with flexible and random measures. Hence, in this chapter, we propose the utilization of two distinct methodologies, namely oriented and non-oriented chance-constrained DEA-based approaches, to evaluate the efficiency of diverse organizations incorporating both stochastic and flexible elements. The chance-constrained DEA-based patterns are transformed into deterministic mixed integer programming problems. A case study is used to estimate the relative efficiency and categorize flexible random variables by utilizing the proposed approach. According to the empirical evidence, efficiency levels exhibit no increment as risk levels increase. The utilization of stochastic observations is more informative when compared to the attainment of efficiency scores through precise measures.

Keywords Data envelopment analysis · Efficiency · Flexible measure · Random factors

1 Introduction

Classifying the performance measures and determining their role is vital to estimate the comparative efficiency of decision-making units (DMUs) in a rational way. There are some factors in many investigations with the ability to serve as either input or output that are categorized as flexible factors within the domain of academic literature on performance measurement.

M. Jahani Sayyad Noveiri · S. Kordrostami (✉)
Department of Mathematics, Lahijan Branch, Islamic Azad University, Lahijan, Iran
e-mail: sohrab.kordrostami@iau.ac.ir

© The Author(s), under exclusive license to Springer Nature Singapore Pte Ltd. 2024

S. A. Edalatpanah et al. (eds.), *Analytical Decision Making and Data Envelopment Analysis*, Infosys Science Foundation Series in Mathematical Sciences,
https://doi.org/10.1007/978-981-97-6972-8_5

The research conducted by Cook and Zhu (2007) pertained primarily to the consideration of flexible measures in data envelopment analysis (DEA). Their study involved the categorization of such measures through analysis at both the individual DMU position and the aggregate position in the multiplier form of DEA. The DEA is a non-parametric measure utilized to ascertain the comparative efficacy of DMUs that have various inputs and outputs. Amirteimoori and Emrouznejad (2011) presented a substitute approach based on DEA for handling flexible indicators into the envelopment structure. Toloo (2012) investigated alternative strategies for specifying the classification of flexible factors. Kordrostami and Jahani Sayyad Noveiri (2012) suggested the use of a DEA-based methodology for assessing the capability of DMUs in situations where flexible and negative parameters are present. Subsequently, Tavana (2020) introduced a directional distance model that is non-radial in nature, in order to effectively handle negative variables. Furthermore, the model was extended to accommodate situations where both negative and flexible measures are identified. Amirteimoori et al. (2013) posited that flexible slacks-based methodologies can be utilized in determining the comparative effectiveness of entities as well as in establishing the status of flexible measures. Subsequently, Bod'a (2020) formulated an alternative and flexible slacks-based measure framework. Tohidi and Matroud (2017) presented a different non-radial DEA technique for the categorization of flexible measures and the evaluation of returns to scale. In the research directed by Toloo et al., (2018a, 2018b), the assessment of the banking industry's performance in the context of flexible measures was carried out through the utilization of their non-radial directional distance approach. In the study conducted by Kordrostami et al. (2019), an examination of the efficiency of DMUs under circumstances involving data that is both flexible and integer-valued was carried out. Zarrin (2023) also presented another mixed-integer slacks-based measure DEA technique for measuring the efficiency of processes in attending flexible and integer factors. Kordrostami and Jahani Sayyad Noveiri (2021) evaluated the efficacy of entities characterized by factors that are bound, discrete, and adaptable. Ghiyasi and Cook (2020) examined the concept of flexible measures as it pertains to variable returns to scale (VRS) and proposed an aggregate model to facilitate their implementation. The categorization of performance measures and the proposal of related models were executed by Toloo et al. (2020) through the utilization of the epsilon function. Jahani Sayyad Noveiri et al. (2022) analyzed the multi-period efficiency of entities in the company of flexible indicators. Some scholarly investigations have also included flexible and indeterminate measures, as can be seen in the works of Kordrostami et al. (2014), Kordrostami and Jahani Sayyad Noveiri (2014), Toloo et al., (2018a, 2018b), and Joulaei et al. (2019). Sharifi et al. (2021) proposed a method for discerning the adaptable variable's role as an input or output by incorporating the likelihood of selecting such factor as input or output, with unequal probabilities, into the model. This method was applied to determine the optimal efficiency level. Some studies such as (Li et al., 2021; Hosseini Monfared et al., 2021a, 2021b; Hosseini Monfared et al., 2022) addressed the classification of flexible measures in the network processes with precise data. Furthermore, the changes of performance measures, including flexible measures, have been examined in studies directed by Jahani Sayyad Noveiri and Kordrostami (2023) and Jahani Sayyad Noveiri et al. (2023). Despite all the efforts made in order to analyze the performance and determine the role of flexible indicators, no research has been done for this purpose when random data is present. Therefore, it is necessary to consider the stochastic nature in investigating the efficacy and the function of flexible parameters.

Numerous production-focused DEA models utilizing stochastic programming have been devised to appraise the performance of DMUs within diverse fields. Olesen and Peteren (2016) managed an extensive assessment of the concept of stochastic DEA. The chance-constrained approach advanced by Charnes and Cooper (1959) has gained widespread adoption and is deemed among the most prevalent methodologies applied in contemporary research. Land et al. (1993) expanded the circumstances of probabilistic inputs and outputs by deploying chance-constrained programming. Cooper et al. (2002) proposed an expansion of chance-constrained DEA models to identify the locations where efficacious and inefficacious conduct may manifest with their probabilities. Cooper et al. (2004) provided chance-constrained DEA methodologies aimed at addressing the issue of congestion. In the realm of DEA, it has been noted that contemporary stochastic DEA models are not suitable for the assessment of flexible measures. However, when faced with uncertainty, there are indicators with an unfamiliar standing of inputs and outputs in numerous practical scenarios. For instance, deposits can be deemed as a flexible random parameter in assessing the efficacy of bank branches.

Accordingly, the objective of this chapter is to construct methodologies centered on DEA for the evaluation of the efficacy of a group of DMUs, as well as to categorize flexible random measurements in circumstances where there are random performance measurements. The present study expounds upon the flexible chance-constrained DEA approaches, which are available in both oriented and non-oriented forms. This is done through the lens of two distinct perspectives: individual DMU and aggregate ones. In order to perform model calculations, deterministic forms that possess equal characteristics are presented. Through the computation of these models, the flexible measures and stochastic efficiency of entities can be ascertained.

The subsequent sections of this examination are arranged in this way: Sect. 2 is dedicated to an exposition of the initial and fundamental models pertinent to the subject matter. In Sect. 3, a variety of DEA-based methodologies, both oriented and non-oriented in nature, are presented for the purpose of evaluating the comparative efficiency of frameworks that feature flexible, stochastic parameters. In Sect. 4, the designed technique is exemplified through the application of a data set. Section 5 discusses the implications and findings of the study, with particular attention given to the conclusions reached.

2 Flexible Measures and Stochastic DEA: A Brief Review

2.1 Flexible DEA Models

Consider a scenario where there exist D DMUs, denoted as $DMU_d(d = 1, ..., D)$ employing A inputs, represented by $e_{ad}(a = 1, ..., A; d = 1, ..., D)$, and generating B outputs, indicated as $g_{bj}(b = 1, ..., B; d = 1, ..., D)$. Moreover, a set of F flexible factors designated as $l_{fd}(f = 1, ..., F; d = 1, ..., D)$, is introduced which can serve as inputs or outputs. Amirteimoori and Emrouznejad (2011) introduced the following technology and input-oriented envelopment model aimed at evaluating the relative efficiency of a given unit, known as DMU_o, while categorizing flexible measures.

$$T = \{(e, g, l) : e \geq \sum_{d=1}^{D} \lambda_d e_d, g \leq \sum_{d=1}^{D} \lambda_d g_d, (either\, l \geq \sum_{d=1}^{D} \lambda_d l_d \; or \; l \leq \sum_{d=1}^{D} \lambda_d l_d),$$
$$\lambda_d \geq 0,\ d = 1, ..., D\} \tag{1}$$

$$\begin{aligned} & Min\ \theta \\ & s.t.\ \sum_{d=1}^{D} \lambda_d e_{ad} \leq \theta e_{ao}, a = 1, ..., A, \\ & \sum_{d=1}^{D} \lambda_d g_{bd} \geq g_{bo}, b = 1, ..., B, \\ & \sum_{d=1}^{D} \lambda_d l_{fd} \leq \theta l_{fo} + Mh_f, f = 1, ..., F, \\ & \sum_{d=1}^{D} \lambda_d l_{fd} \geq l_{fo} - M(1 - h_f), f = 1, ..., F, \\ & \lambda_d \geq 0, d = 1, ..., D, h_f \in \{0, 1\}. \end{aligned} \tag{2}$$

Model (2) has been formulated on the basis of the underlying premise of constant returns to scale (CRS). Furthermore, an assessment of the efficacy and the classification of flexible parameters within the variable returns to scale (VRS) framework can be conducted by imposing the constraint $\sum_{d=1}^{D} \lambda_d = 1$. The variable M is appropriately regarded as a positive number of a significant magnitude, while the variable h_f is classified as a binary entity. In the event that the optimal value h_f, represented as h_f^*, , amounts to zero (i.e. $h_f^* = 0$), the flexible factor is examined as the input and is treated in the form of the output only if $h_f^* = 1$. This condition governs the use and interpretation of the flexible measure. Subsequently, as posited by Cook and Zhu (2007), the application of the majority rule is employed in the categorization of the flexible metric, whilst the consideration of alternative optimal solutions necessitates an assessment based on the research of Toloo (2012). The efficient designation of the unit under scrutiny, denoted as DMU_o, is contingent upon the inherent condition that θ^* is equal to unity. Otherwise, it is determined as inefficient.

Tohidi and Matroud (2017) presented a non-oriented approach for the classification of flexible indicators, estimation of efficiency scores, and determination of the returns to scale state while assuming VRS in the following way:

$$\begin{aligned}
& Min \ \frac{\pi}{\eta} \\
& s.t. \ \sum_{d=1}^{D} \lambda_d e_{ad} \leq \pi e_{ao}, a = 1, 2, ..., A, \\
& \sum_{d=1}^{D} \lambda_d g_{bd} \geq \eta g_{bo}, b = 1, 2, ..., B, \\
& \sum_{d=1}^{D} \lambda_d l_{fd} \leq \pi l_{fo} + M h_f, f = 1, 2, ..., F, \\
& \sum_{d=1}^{D} \lambda_d l_{fd} \geq \eta l_{fo} - M(1 - h_f), f = 1, 2, ..., F, \\
& \sum_{d=1}^{D} \lambda_d = 1, \\
& h_f \in \{0, 1\}, f = 1, ..., F, \lambda_d \geq 0, d = 1, ..., D; \pi, \eta \geq 0.
\end{aligned} \tag{3}$$

The variables π and η are scalar quantities. The flexible measure indexed by f is regarded as an input when the optimum value h_f^* equals zero, while in cases where h_f^* equals one, it is considered as an output.

2.2 Chance—Constrained DEA

The incorporation of stochastic variables in DEA models is a significant feature of chance-constrained DEA. In the present subsection, a delineation of a specialized framework has been succinctly depicted (Cooper et al., 2002, 2004; Huang & Li, 2001; Land et al., 1993; Olesen & Petersen, 2016). Assuming the existence of

D DMUs, $DMU_d(d = 1, ..., D)$, each of which consumes A randomly determined inputs $\tilde{e}_{ad}(a = 1, \ldots, A)$, and produces B randomly determined outputs designated as $\tilde{g}_{bd}(b = 1, \ldots, B)$. Terms $\tilde{e}_{ao}$ and $\tilde{g}_{bo}$ show inputs and outputs of the entity under examination DMU_o. The method for defining a chance-constrained DEA under the CRS assumption is as the next way:

$$\begin{aligned} & E_\alpha^* = Min \ \ \theta_\alpha \\ & s.t. \\ & \quad p\left\{\sum_{d=1}^{D} \lambda_d \tilde{e}_{ad} \le \theta_\alpha \tilde{e}_{ao}\right\} \ge 1-\alpha, \ \ a = 1, ..., A, \\ & \quad p\left\{\sum_{d=1}^{D} \lambda_d \tilde{g}_{bd} \ge \tilde{g}_{bo}\right\} \ge 1-\alpha, \ \ \ b = 1, ..., B, \\ & \quad \lambda_d \ge 0, d = 1, ..., D. \end{aligned} \tag{4}$$

In compliance with model (4), the likelihood is represented by the variable p, while the chance restrictions require that the probability of breaching them does not surpass α.

Provided that inputs and outputs are governed by individual variables, $\tilde{e}_{ad} = e_{ad} + m_{ad}\xi$, $\tilde{g}_{bd} = g_{bd} + n_{bd}\tau$, it is plausible to transform model (4) into model (5).

$$\begin{aligned} & E_\alpha^* = Min \ \ \theta_\alpha \\ & s.t. \\ & -\Phi^{-1}(\alpha)(\sum_{d=1}^{D} \lambda_d m_{ad} - \theta_\alpha m_{ao}) \le \theta e_{ao} - \sum_{d=1}^{D} \lambda_d e_{ad}, \ \ a = 1, ..., A, \\ & -\Phi^{-1}(\alpha)(\sum_{d=1}^{D} \lambda_d m_{ad} - \theta_\alpha m_{ao}) \ge \sum_{d=1}^{D} \lambda_d e_{ad} - \theta_\alpha e_{ao}, \ \ a = 1, ..., A, \\ & -\Phi^{-1}(\alpha)(\sum_{d=1}^{D} \lambda_d n_{bd} - n_{bo}) \le \sum_{d=1}^{D} \lambda_d g_{bd} - g_{bo}, \ \ \ b = 1, ..., B, \\ & -\Phi^{-1}(\alpha)(\sum_{d=1}^{D} \lambda_d n_{bd} - n_{bo}) \ge g_{bo} - \sum_{d=1}^{D} \lambda_d g_{bd}, \ \ \ b = 1, ..., B, \\ & \lambda_d \ge 0, d = 1, ..., D. \end{aligned} \tag{5}$$

The mean values of inputs and outputs are represented by e_{ad} and g_{bd}, respectively. The symbols m_{ad} and n_{bd} are utilized to portray the standard deviations of the variables $\tilde{e}_{ad}$ and $\tilde{g}_{bd}$, individually. The function $\Phi^{-1}(\alpha)$ indicates the inverse of the standard normal distribution function, Φ. The stochastic variables ξ and τ are postulated to conform to the standard normal distribution in this instance. The stochastic efficiency of DMU_o, with respect to a predefined threshold α, is denoted by the condition E_α^*. DMU_o is called stochastic efficient for the predefined risk level α if $E_\alpha^* = 1$.

3 Efficiency Analysis with Flexible Random Factors

Suppose whole observations, inputs, outputs and flexible factors, are random indicators with a normal distribution. Considering $\tilde{e}_d = (\tilde{e}_{1d}, ..., \tilde{e}_{Ad}), \tilde{g}_d = (\tilde{g}_{1d}, ..., \tilde{g}_{Bd})$, and $\tilde{l}_d = (\tilde{l}_{1d}, ..., \tilde{l}_{Fd})$ as the vectors of random input, output, and flexible measures, the flexible stochastic technology can be shown in the following way:

$$T = \{(\tilde{e}, \tilde{g}, \tilde{l}) : \tilde{e} \geq \sum_{d=1}^{D} \lambda_d \tilde{e}_d, \tilde{g} \leq \sum_{d=1}^{D} \lambda_d \tilde{g}_d, (either\, \tilde{l} \geq \sum_{d=1}^{D} \lambda_d \tilde{l}_d \; or \; \tilde{l} \leq \sum_{d=1}^{D} \lambda_d \tilde{l}_d),$$
$$\lambda_d \geq 0, \; d = 1, ..., D\}. \tag{6}$$

In the subsequent discussion, various models are presented for the evaluation of the standing of flexible random factors within production systems. In order to pursue this objective, the present study endeavors to develop both oriented and non-oriented chance-constrained DEA methods with flexible parameters, with a focus on examining individual DMUs as well as the aggregate perspective. The purpose of such an approach is to categorize stochastic flexible measures and evaluate the stochastic efficiency of various processes.

3.1 *Oriented Flexible Chance-Constrained DEA Model*

Within this area of study, input-oriented flexible chance-constrained DEA models have been developed, with an emphasis placed on individual DMUs and aggregate efficiency considerations.

3.1.1 Individual DMU Perspective

In light of the aforementioned terms and technological advancements (6), the subsequent input-oriented chance-constrained technique is planned to address the challenges posed by production systems that exhibit flexible random measures:

$$
\begin{aligned}
& Min\ \ \theta \\
& s.t.\ \ p\left\{\sum_{d=1}^{D} \lambda_d \tilde{e}_{ad} \le \theta \tilde{e}_{ao}\right\} \ge 1-\alpha, a = 1, 2, \ldots, A, \\
& \qquad p\left\{\sum_{d=1}^{D} \lambda_d \tilde{g}_{bd} \ge \tilde{g}_{bo}\right\} \ge 1-\alpha, b = 1, 2, \ldots, B, \\
& either \\
& \qquad p\left\{\sum_{d=1}^{D} \lambda_d \tilde{l}_{fd} \le \theta \tilde{l}_{fo}\right\} \ge 1-\alpha, f = 1, 2, \ldots, F, \\
& or \\
& \qquad p\left\{\sum_{d=1}^{D} \lambda_d \tilde{l}_{fd} \ge \tilde{l}_{fo}\right\} \ge 1-\alpha, f = 1, 2, \ldots, F, \\
& \quad \lambda_d \ge 0, d = 1, \ldots, D.
\end{aligned}
\tag{7}
$$

By analyzing the variables l_{fo} and $\sigma_f^o(\lambda_d, \theta)$ as the mean value of $\tilde{l}_{fo}$ and the standard error of $\sum_{d=1}^{D} \lambda_d \tilde{l}_{fd} - \theta \tilde{l}_{fo}$, respectively, it can be determined that the following constraints pertain to flexible measures with the role of the input:

$$
\begin{aligned}
& p\left\{\sum_{d=1}^{D} \lambda_d \tilde{l}_{fd} \le \theta \tilde{l}_{fo}\right\} \\
& = p\left\{\frac{(\sum_{d=1}^{D} \lambda_d \tilde{l}_{fd} - \theta \tilde{l}_{fo}) - (\sum_{d=1}^{D} \lambda_d l_{fd} - \theta l_{fo})}{\sigma_f^o(\lambda_d, \theta)} \le \frac{-(\sum_{d=1}^{D} \lambda_d l_{fd} - \theta l_{fo})}{\sigma_f^o(\lambda_d, \theta)}\right\} \\
& \ge 1-\alpha
\end{aligned}
\tag{8}
$$

The normal distribution is evidently demonstrated by $\sum_{d=1}^{D} \lambda_d \tilde{l}_{fd} - \tilde{l}_{fo}$, thereby leading to the conclusion that:

$$
l_{fd} - \theta l_{fo} \le \Phi^{-1}(\alpha)\sigma_f^o(\lambda_d, \theta). \tag{9}
$$

Within the context of this discourse, Φ symbolizes the standard normal distribution, whereas Φ^{-1} represents its inverse. Similarly, alternative constraints pertaining to model (7) can be rephrased. As a result, it can be inferred that model (7) has been converted to model (10).

$$
\begin{aligned}
& Min \;\; \theta \\
& s.t. \;\; \sum_{d=1}^{D} \lambda_d e_{ad} - \theta e_{ao} \leq \Phi^{-1}(\alpha)\sigma_a^o(\lambda_d, \theta), a = 1, 2, ..., A, \\
& \qquad g_{bo} - \sum_{d=1}^{D} \lambda_d g_{bd} \leq \Phi^{-1}(\alpha)\sigma_b^o(\lambda_d), b = 1, 2, ..., B, \\
& either \\
& \qquad \sum_{d=1}^{D} \lambda_d l_{fd} - \theta l_{fo} \leq \Phi^{-1}(\alpha)\sigma_f^o(\lambda_d, \theta) f = 1, 2, ...F, \\
& or \\
& \qquad l_{fo} - \sum_{d=1}^{D} \lambda_d l_{fd} \leq \Phi^{-1}(\alpha)\sigma_f^o(\lambda_d), f = 1, 2, ..., F, \\
& \qquad \lambda_d \geq 0, d = 1, ..., D.
\end{aligned}
\tag{10}
$$

Currently, there exists an assumption that all stochastic performance measures are discerned individually through single factors. Specifically, this implies

$$
\tilde{e}_{ad} = e_{ad} + m_{ad}\xi, \;\; \tilde{g}_{bd} = g_{bd} + n_{bd}\tau, \;\; \tilde{l}_{fd} = l_{fd} + s_{fd}\upsilon.
$$

The variables e_{ad}, g_{bd} and l_{fd} represent the respective mean values of $\tilde{e}_{ad}$, $\tilde{g}_{bd}$ and $\tilde{l}_{fd}$. Furthermore, the standard errors of variables are displayed by m_{ad}, n_{bd} and s_{fd}. It is assumed that variables ξ, τ and υ are independent random variables conforming to the standard normal distribution. The present postulation has been deliberated to facilitate the conversion of model (10) into a linear problem. Assuming that the indicators e_{ad}, g_{bd}, l_{fd}, m_{ad}, n_{bd} and s_{fd} are non-negative, we have:

$$
\begin{aligned}
\sigma_a^o(\lambda_d, \theta) &= \left| \sum_{d=1}^{D} \lambda_d m_{ad} - \theta m_{ao} \right|, \\
\sigma_f^o(\lambda_d, \theta) &= \left| \sum_{d=1}^{D} \lambda_d s_{fd} - \theta s_{fo} \right|, \\
\sigma_b^o(\lambda_d) &= \left| \sum_{d=1}^{D} \lambda_d n_{bd} - n_{bo} \right| \;\; and \\
\sigma_f^o(\lambda_d) &= \left| \sum_{d=1}^{D} \lambda_d s_{fd} - s_{fo} \right|.
\end{aligned}
$$

Consequently, model (10) is substituted by model (11).

$$
\begin{aligned}
& Min \ \ \theta \\
& s.t. \ \ \sum_{d=1}^{D} \lambda_d e_{ad} - \theta e_{ao} \le \Phi^{-1}(\alpha)\left|\sum_{d=1}^{D} \lambda_d m_{ad} - m_{ao}\right|, a = 1, 2, \ldots A, \\
& \qquad g_{bo} - \sum_{d=1}^{D} \lambda_d g_{bd} \le \Phi^{-1}(\alpha)\left|\sum_{d=1}^{D} \lambda n_{bd} - n_{bo}\right|, b = 1, 2, \ldots, B, \\
& either \\
& \qquad \sum_{d=1}^{D} \lambda_d l_{fd} - \theta l_{fo} \le \Phi^{-1}(\alpha)\left|\sum_{d=1}^{D} \lambda_d s_{fd} - \theta s_{fo}\right|, f = 1, 2, \ldots, F, \\
& or \\
& \qquad l_{fo} - \sum_{d=1}^{D} \lambda_d l_{fd} \le \Phi^{-1}(\alpha)\left|\sum_{d=1}^{D} \lambda_d s_{fd} - s_{fo}\right|, f = 1, 2, \ldots, F, \\
& \qquad \lambda_d \ge 0, d = 1, \ldots, D.
\end{aligned} \tag{11}
$$

Also, it can be shown that models (11) and (12) are equivalent for the predetermined amount $\alpha \le 0.5$.

$$
\begin{aligned}
& Min \ \ \theta \\
& s.t. \ \ -\Phi^{-1}(\alpha)\left(\sum_{d=1}^{D} \lambda_d m_{ad} - \theta m_{ao}\right) \le \theta e_{ao} - \sum_{d=1}^{D} \lambda_d e_{ad}, a = 1, 2, \ldots, A, \quad (12.1) \\
& \qquad -\Phi^{-1}(\alpha)\left(\sum_{d=1}^{D} \lambda_d m_{ad} - m_{ao}\right) \ge \sum_{d=1}^{D} \lambda_d e_{ad} - \theta e_{ao}, a = 1, 2, \ldots, A, \quad (12.2) \\
& \qquad -\Phi^{-1}(\alpha)\left(\sum_{d=1}^{D} \lambda_d n_{bd} - n_{bo}\right) \le \sum_{d=1}^{D} \lambda_d g_{bd} - g_{bo}, b = 1, 2, \ldots, B, \quad (12.3) \\
& \qquad -\Phi^{-1}(\alpha)\left(\sum_{d=1}^{D} \lambda_d n_{bd} - n_{bo}\right) \ge g_{bo} - \sum_{d=1}^{D} \lambda_d g_{bd}, b = 1, 2, \ldots, B, \quad (12.4) \\
& either \\
& \qquad -\Phi^{-1}(\alpha)\left(\sum_{d=1}^{D} \lambda_d s_{fd} - \theta s_{fo}\right) \le \theta l_{fo} - \sum_{d=1}^{D} \lambda_d s_{fd}, f = 1, 2, \ldots, F, \quad (12.5) \\
& \qquad -\Phi^{-1}(\alpha)\left(\sum_{d=1}^{D} \lambda_d s_{fd} - \theta s_{fo}\right) \ge \sum_{d=1}^{D} \lambda_d l_{fd} - \theta l_{fo}, f = 1, 2, \ldots, F, \quad (12.6) \\
& or \\
& \qquad -\Phi^{-1}(\alpha)\left(\sum_{d=1}^{D} \lambda_d s_{fd} - \theta s_{fo}\right) \le \sum_{d=1}^{D} \lambda_d l_{fd} - l_{fo}, f = 1, 2, \ldots, F, \quad (12.7) \\
& \qquad -\Phi^{-1}(\alpha)\left(\sum_{d=1}^{D} \lambda_d s_{fd} - \theta s_{fo}\right) \ge l_{fo} - \sum_{d=1}^{D} \lambda_d l_{fd}, f = 1, 2, \ldots, F, \quad (12.8) \\
& \qquad \lambda_d \ge 0, d = 1, \ldots, D.
\end{aligned} \tag{12}
$$

Constraints (12.5)–(12.8) of model (12) can, furthermore, be substituted by constraints (13.5)–(13.8) of model (13).

$$
\begin{aligned}
& F^{\alpha *} = Min\ \theta \\
& s.t.\ \ -\Phi^{-1}(\alpha)\left(\sum_{d=1}^{D}\lambda_d m_{ad} - \theta m_{ao}\right) \le \theta e_{ao} - \sum_{d=1}^{D}\lambda_d e_{ad},\ a = 1, 2, \ldots, A, && (13.1) \\
& -\Phi^{-1}(\alpha)\left(\sum_{d=1}^{D}\lambda_d m_{ad} - \theta m_{ao}\right) \ge \sum_{d=1}^{D}\lambda_d e_{ad} - \theta e_{ao},\ a = 1, 2, \ldots, A, && (13.2) \\
& -\Phi^{-1}(\alpha)\left(\sum_{d=1}^{D}\lambda_d n_{bd} - n_{bo}\right) \le \sum_{d=1}^{D}\lambda_d g_{bd} - g_{bo},\ b = 1, 2, \ldots, B, && (13.3) \\
& -\Phi^{-1}(\alpha)\left(\sum_{d=1}^{D}\lambda_d n_{bd} - n_{bo}\right) \ge g_{bo} - \sum_{d=1}^{D}\lambda_d g_{bd},\ b = 1, 2, \ldots, B, && (13.4) \\
& -\Phi^{-1}(\alpha)\left(\sum_{d=1}^{D}\lambda_d s_{fd} - \theta s_{fo}\right) \le \theta l_{fo} - \sum_{d=1}^{D}\lambda_d s_{fd} + Mh_f,\ f = 1, 2, \ldots, F, && (13.5) \\
& -\Phi^{-1}(\alpha)\left(\sum_{d=1}^{D}\lambda_d s_{fd} - \theta s_{fo}\right) \ge \sum_{d=1}^{D}\lambda_d l_{fd} - \theta l_{fo} - Mh_f,\ f = 1, 2, \ldots, F, && (13.6) \\
& -\Phi^{-1}(\alpha)\left(\sum_{d=1}^{D}\lambda_d s_{fd} - s_{fo}\right) \le \sum_{d=1}^{D}\lambda_d l_{fd} - l_{fo} + M(1 - h_f),\ f = 1, 2, \ldots, F, && (13.7) \\
& -\Phi^{-1}(\alpha)\left(\sum_{d=1}^{D}\lambda_d s_{fd} - s_{fo}\right) \ge l_{fo} - \sum_{d=1}^{D}\lambda_d l_{fd} - M(1 - h_f),\ f = 1, 2, \ldots, F, && (13.8) \\
& \lambda_d \ge 0,\ d = 1, \ldots, D;\ h_f \in \{0, 1\}.
\end{aligned}
\qquad (13)
$$

Definition 1. For the predefined value α, the process under consideration, DMU_o, is called stochastically efficient if $F^{\alpha *} = 1$. Oppositely, it is inefficient. Also, the flexible factor is examined as the input if $h_f^* = 0$ and is treated as the output only if $h_f^* = 1$.

3.1.2 Aggregate Perspective

Cook and Zhu (2007) established a pattern for the overall categorization of each flexible parameter, whereby the preeminent choice among the entities, as previously discussed, is taken into account (i.e. the individual DMU perspective) and, alternatively, a viewpoint from the director of the consortium of DMUs (i.e. the aggregate perspective) is considered. The present inquiry designates the position of flexible measures through the utilization of the subsequent model:

The input-oriented chance-constrained model (14) is applied in order to analyze the efficacy rates of a given set of entities. Within this framework, the flexible parameter is scrutinized in terms of its classification as an input or output component. To elucidate, the determination of the placement of flexible parameters is accomplished without reliance on the consensus decision of the majority. In the event that the optimal value $h_f^* = 1$ is attained, the parameter f adapted to alterations is designated as an output. In case h_f^* equals 0, it pertains to an input.

$$
\begin{aligned}
& Min \quad \theta \\
& s.t. \quad p\left\{\sum_{d=1}^{D} \lambda_d \tilde{e}_{ad} \le \theta \sum_{d=1}^{D} \tilde{e}_{ad}\right\} \ge 1-\alpha, a = 1, 2, ..., A, \\
& \qquad p\left\{\sum_{d=1}^{D} \lambda_d \tilde{g}_{bd} \ge \sum_{d=1}^{D} \tilde{g}_{bd}\right\} \ge 1-\alpha, b = 1, 2, ..., B, \\
& either \\
& \qquad p\left\{\sum_{d=1}^{D} \lambda_d \tilde{l}_{fd} \le \theta \sum_{d=1}^{D} \tilde{l}_{fd}\right\} \ge 1-\alpha, f = 1, 2, ..., F, \\
& or \\
& \qquad p\left\{\sum_{d=1}^{D} \lambda_d \tilde{l}_{fd} \ge \sum_{d=1}^{D} \tilde{l}_{fd}\right\} \ge 1-\alpha, f = 1, 2, ..., F, \\
& \qquad \lambda_d \ge 0, d = 1, ...D.
\end{aligned} \tag{14}
$$

In the similar way of the aforementioned approach, model (14) can be substituted with models (15) and (16).

$$
\begin{aligned}
& Min \quad \theta \\
& s.t. \quad \sum_{d=1}^{D} \lambda_d e_{ad} - \theta \sum_{d=1}^{D} e_{ad} \le \Phi^{-1}(\alpha)\sigma_a^o(\lambda_d, \theta), a = 1, 2, ..., A, \\
& \qquad \sum_{d=1}^{D} g_{bd} - \sum_{d=1}^{D} \lambda_d g_{bd} \le \Phi^{-1}(\alpha)\sigma_b^o(\lambda_d), b = 1, 2, ..., B, \\
& either \\
& \qquad \sum_{d=1}^{D} \lambda_d l_{fd} - \theta \sum_{d=1}^{D} l_{fd} \le \Phi^{-1}(\alpha)\sigma_f^o(\lambda_d, \theta), f = 1, 2, ..., F, \\
& or \\
& \qquad \sum_{d=1}^{D} l_{fd} - \sum_{d=1}^{D} \lambda_d l_{fd} \le \Phi^{-1}(\alpha)\sigma_f^o(\lambda_d), f = 1, 2, ..., F, \\
& \qquad \lambda_d \ge 0, d = 1, ..., D.
\end{aligned} \tag{15}
$$

$$
\begin{aligned}
& Min \ \ \theta \\
& s.t. \ \ -\Phi^{-1}(\alpha)\left(\sum_{d=1}^{D}\lambda_d m_{ad} - \theta\sum_{d=1}^{D} m_{ad}\right) \le \theta\sum_{d=1}^{D} e_{ad} - \sum_{d=1}^{D}\lambda_d e_{ad}, a = 1, 2, ...A, \\
& -\Phi^{-1}(\alpha)\left(\sum_{d=1}^{D}\lambda_d m_{ad} - \theta\sum_{d=1}^{D} m_{ad}\right) \ge \sum_{d=1}^{D}\lambda_d e_{ad} - \theta\sum_{d=1}^{D} e_{ad}, a = 1, 2, ..., A, \\
& -\Phi^{-1}(\alpha)\left(\sum_{d=1}^{D}\lambda_d n_{bd} - \sum_{d=1}^{D} n_{bd}\right) \le \sum_{d=1}^{D}\lambda_d g_{bd} - \sum_{d=1}^{D} g_{bd}, b = 1, 2, ..., B, \\
& -\Phi^{-1}(\alpha)\left(\sum_{d=1}^{D}\lambda_d n_{bd} - \sum_{d=1}^{D} n_{bd}\right) \ge \sum_{d=1}^{D} g_{bd} - \sum_{d=1}^{D}\lambda_d g_{bd}, b = 1, 2, ..., B, \\
& -\Phi^{-1}(\alpha)\left(\sum_{d=1}^{D}\lambda_d s_{fd} - \theta\sum_{d=1}^{D} s_{fd}\right) \le \theta\sum_{d=1}^{D} l_{fd} - \sum_{d=1}^{D}\lambda_d l_{fd} + Mh_f, f = 1, 2, ..., F, \\
& -\Phi^{-1}(\alpha)\left(\sum_{d=1}^{D}\lambda_d s_{fd} - \theta\sum_{d=1}^{D} s_{fd}\right) \ge \sum_{d=1}^{D}\lambda_d l_{fd} - \theta\sum_{d=1}^{D} l_{fd} - Mh_f, f = 1, 2, ..., F, \\
& -\Phi^{-1}(\alpha)\left(\sum_{d=1}^{D}\lambda_d s_{fd} - \sum_{d=1}^{D} s_{fd}\right) \le \sum_{d=1}^{D}\lambda_d l_{fd} - \sum_{d=1}^{D} l_{fd} + M(1 - h_f), f = 1, 2, ..., F, \\
& -\Phi^{-1}(\alpha)\left(\sum_{d=1}^{D}\lambda_d s_{fd} - \sum_{d=1}^{D} s_{fd}\right) \ge \sum_{d=1}^{D} l_{fd} - \sum_{d=1}^{D}\lambda_d l_{fd} - M(1 - h_f), f = 1, 2, ..., F, \\
& \lambda_d \ge 0, d = 1, ..., D, h_f \in \{0,1\}.
\end{aligned}
\tag{16}
$$

In the following, non-radial chance-constrained DEA models are presented from the perspectives of the individual DMU and aggregate efficiency.

3.1.3 Non-oriented Flexible Chance-Constrained DEA Model

Presently, the proposed methodologies for addressing systems characterized by flexible measures involve the utilization of a non-oriented stochastic efficiency measure. This measure accounts for the reduction of inputs and flexible parameters, which are handled as inputs, as well as the augment of outputs and flexible parameters, which are treated as outputs, in a simultaneous manner. The subsequent model presented in this work is an expansion of Tohidi and Matroud's strategy (Tohidi & Matroud, 2017).

3.1.4 Individual DMU Perspective

The non-radial chance-constrained DEA approach from the perspective of individual DMU and its equivalent deterministic form can be expressed as models (17) and (18), respectively:

$$\begin{aligned}
& Min\ \frac{\pi}{\eta} \\
& s.t.\ p\left\{\sum_{d=1}^{D}\lambda_d\tilde{e}_{ad}\le\pi\tilde{e}_{ao}\right\}\ge 1-\alpha, a=1,2,\dots,A, \\
& p\left\{\sum_{d=1}^{D}\lambda_d\tilde{g}_{bd}\ge\eta\tilde{g}_{bo}\right\}\ge 1-\alpha, b=1,2,\dots,B, \\
& either \\
& p\left\{\sum_{d=1}^{D}\lambda_d\tilde{l}_{fd}\le\pi\tilde{l}_{fo}\right\}\ge 1-\alpha, f=1,2,\dots,F, \\
& or \\
& p\left\{\sum_{d=1}^{D}\lambda_d\tilde{l}_{fd}\ge\eta\tilde{l}_{fo}\right\}\ge 1-\alpha, f=1,2,\dots,F, \\
& \sum_{d=1}^{D}\lambda_d=1, \\
& \lambda_d\ge 0, d=1,\dots,D, \pi,\eta\ge 0,
\end{aligned} \tag{17}$$

And

$$\begin{aligned}
& Min\ \frac{\pi}{\eta} \\
& s.t.\ -\Phi^{-1}(\alpha)\left(\sum_{d=1}^{D}\lambda_d m_{ad}-\pi m_{ao}\right)\le\pi e_{ao}-\sum_{d=1}^{D}\lambda_d e_{ad}, a=1,2,\dots,A, \\
& -\Phi^{-1}(\alpha)\left(\sum_{d=1}^{D}\lambda_j m_{ad}-\pi m_{ao}\right)\ge\sum_{d=1}^{D}\lambda_d e_{ad}-\pi e_{ao}, a=1,2,\dots,A, \\
& -\Phi^{-1}(\alpha)\left(\sum_{d=1}^{D}\lambda_d n_{bd}-\eta n_{bo}\right)\le\sum_{d=1}^{D}\lambda_d g_{bd}-\eta g_{bo}, b=1,2,\dots,B, \\
& -\Phi^{-1}(\alpha)\left(\sum_{d=1}^{D}\lambda_d n_{bd}-\eta n_{bo}\right)\ge\eta g_{bo}-\sum_{d=1}^{D}\lambda_d g_{bd}, b=1,2,\dots,B, \\
& -\Phi^{-1}(\alpha)\left(\sum_{d=1}^{D}\lambda_d s_{fd}-\pi s_{fo}\right)\le\pi l_{fo}-\sum_{d=1}^{D}\lambda_d l_{fd}+Mh_f, f=1,2,\dots,F, \\
& -\Phi^{-1}(\alpha)\left(\sum_{d=1}^{D}\lambda_d s_{fd}-\pi s_{fo}\right)\ge\sum_{d=1}^{D}\lambda_j l_{fd}-\pi l_{fo}-Mh_f, f=1,2,\dots,F, \\
& -\Phi^{-1}(\alpha)\left(\sum_{d=1}^{D}\lambda_d s_{fd}-\eta s_{fo}\right)\le\sum_{d=1}^{D}\lambda_d l_{fd}-\eta l_{fo}+M(1-h_f), f=1,2,\dots,F, \\
& -\Phi^{-1}(\alpha)\left(\sum_{d=1}^{D}\lambda_d s_{fd}-\eta s_{fo}\right)\ge\eta l_{fo}-\sum_{d=1}^{D}\lambda_d l_{fd}-M(1-h_f), f=1,2,\dots,F, \\
& \sum_{d=1}^{D}\lambda_d=1, \\
& \lambda_d\ge 0, d=1,\dots,D, \pi,\eta\ge 0, h_f\in\{0,1\}.
\end{aligned} \tag{18}$$

Definition 2. The model (18) is deemed to be efficient as long as the optimum value $\frac{\pi^*}{\eta^*}$ is equivalent to the value 1. Furthermore, the model (18) produces suboptimal objective values below unity, indicating the inefficiency of DMU_o. To determine the function of flexible parameters, the paradigm of majority rule is utilized. As a demonstration, the identification of the position of the flexible parameter is achieved by considering the principle of majority rule. Moreover, Toloo (2012) indicated that there has been a failure to account for alternative measures in the determination of the flexible measure's role.

3.1.5 Aggregate Perspective

The equivalent deterministic form of the non-radial chance-constrained DEA model from the perspective of aggregate efficiency can be expressed as follows:

$$\begin{aligned}
&Min\ \frac{\pi}{\eta}\\
&s.t.\ -\Phi^{-1}(\alpha)\left(\sum_{d=1}^{D}\lambda_d m_{ad}-\pi\sum_{d=1}^{D}m_{ad}\right)\le \pi\sum_{d=1}^{D}e_{ad}-\sum_{j=1}^{n}\lambda_d e_{ad},\ a=1,2,\dots,A,\\
&-\Phi^{-1}(\alpha)\left(\sum_{d=1}^{D}\lambda_d m_{ad}-\pi\sum_{d=1}^{D}m_{ad}\right)\ge \sum_{d=1}^{D}\lambda_d e_{ad}-\pi\sum_{d=1}^{D}e_{ad},\ a=1,2,\dots,A,\\
&-\Phi^{-1}(\alpha)\left(\sum_{d=1}^{D}\lambda_d n_{bd}-\eta\sum_{d=1}^{D}n_{bd}\right)\le \sum_{d=1}^{D}\lambda_d g_{bd}-\eta\sum_{d=1}^{D}g_{bd},\ b=1,2,\dots,B,\\
&-\Phi^{-1}(\alpha)\left(\sum_{d=1}^{D}\lambda_d n_{bd}-\eta\sum_{d=1}^{D}n_{bd}\right)\ge \eta\sum_{d=1}^{D}g_{bd}-\sum_{d=1}^{D}\lambda_d g_{bd},\ b=1,2,\dots B,\\
&-\Phi^{-1}(\alpha)\left(\sum_{d=1}^{D}\lambda_d s_{fd}-\pi\sum_{d=1}^{D}s_{fd}\right)\le \pi\sum_{d=1}^{D}l_{fd}-\sum_{d=1}^{D}\lambda_d l_{fd}+Mh_f,f=1,2,\dots,F,\\
&-\Phi^{-1}(\alpha)\left(\sum_{d=1}^{D}\lambda_d s_{fd}-\pi\sum_{d=1}^{D}s_{fd}\right)\ge \sum_{d=1}^{D}\lambda_d l_{fd}-\pi\sum_{d=1}^{D}l_{fd}-Mh_f,f=1,2,\dots,F,\\
&-\Phi^{-1}(\alpha)\left(\sum_{d=1}^{D}\lambda_d s_{fd}-\eta\sum_{d=1}^{D}s_{fd}\right)\le \sum_{d=1}^{D}\lambda_d l_{fd}-\eta\sum_{d=1}^{D}l_{fd}+M(1-h_f),f=1,2,\dots,F,\\
&-\Phi^{-1}(\alpha)\left(\sum_{d=1}^{D}\lambda_d s_{fd}-\eta\sum_{d=1}^{D}s_{fd}\right)\ge \eta\sum_{d=1}^{D}l_{fd}-\sum_{d=1}^{D}\lambda_d l_{fd}-M(1-h_f),f=1,2,\dots,F,\\
&\sum_{d=1}^{D}\lambda_d=1,\\
&\lambda_d\ge 0,d=1,\dots,D,\pi,\eta\ge 0,h_f\in\{0,1\}.
\end{aligned}\tag{19}$$

4 Empirical Analysis

In this area, a case study of the banking industry in Iran is applied to clarify the suggested idea in this research. There are 20 branches corresponding to the degree 2 in an Iraninan bank that have been examined. Two factors, capital expenses and operating expenses are considered as random inputs. Loans and interest incomes are deemed as random outputs. Deposits are treated as flexible random measures. To illustrate, according to Cook and Zhu (2007), bank deposits may be regarded as an outcome in view of their generation of revenue. Conversely, the allocation of staff resources towards facilitating deposit transactions could be more effectively utilized for promoting higher-margin products, thereby classifying such efforts as input. The estimated mean values and standard deviations are presented in Table 1. It is considered all stochastic variables are normally distributed. To analyze the efficiency and the function of the flexible factor, the proposed oriented and non-oriented chance-constrained DEA models are computed from two standpoints, individual DMU and aggregate efficiency. The outcomes are given in Table 2 for the risk levels 0.1, 0.2, 0.3, 0.4 and 0.5. As can be seen, the efficiency scores non-increasing when the risk levels increase. Furthermore, in conformity with the majority aspect, the function of deposits is determined in the form of the input from the individual DMU aspect for the different levels of risk. Moreover, the outcomes of performance values and the role of deposit from an aggregate perspective for the risk levels of 0.1, 0.2, 0.3, 0.4 and 0.5 are displayed in the last five rows of Table 2. The present analysis reveals a negative correlation between the level of risk and aggregate efficiency scores. Specifically, as the level of risk increases, the performance subsequently does not experience an upward trend. Also, the role of deposit is determined as output from the aggregate aspect. Cook and Zhu (2007) postulated that the difference in outcomes between the two approaches could be attributed to the possibility that the preference for the preferred status input, as evaluated by the model with individual DMU aspect, may not have been as pronounced as the preference for output as opposed to input in other circumstances. Moreover, there is the acknowledgment that the aggregate methodology may face criticism for exhibiting excessive sensitivity towards extreme points or those that are considered to be comparatively larger.

In order to conduct a comparative analysis between the planned techniques and existing ones, the solution for models (2) and (3) with respect to the tested mean values is determined. The discovery is presented in the last column of Table 2. It is evident that the outcomes are comparable to the suggested methodologies concerning the risk level of 0. 5.

Therefore, the proposed approaches can be used by managers and policy-makers to analyze the efficacy of entities and classify flexible random measures in a stochastic environment.

Table 1 Average values (AV) and standard deviations (SD) of branches

Branch	Capital expenses		Operating expenses		Deposits		Loans		Interest Incomes	
	AV	SD	AV	SD	AV	SD	AV	SD	AV	SD
1	3,632	4.50E + 09	587	15.55635	2,350,953	116,409	788,291	17,854	3,364	22,774,547,196
2	2,660	3.33E + 09	482.5	23.33452	1,810,247	69,205	911,252	10,189	11,690	18,162,158,462
3	3,029	3.71E + 09	457	26.87006	3,157,583	135,361	1,016,639	21,303	946	36,412,772,484
4	3,298	4.37E + 09	446.5	26.16295	2,094,351	85,049	731,101	11,408	4,268	21,099,360,180
5	3,797	4.74E + 09	385	19.79899	2,147,664	43,010	732,528	2,665	6,068	20,803,485,285
6	3,562	4.60E + 09	306.5	19.09188	1,872,368	73,093	479,098	11,716	4,090	24,281,041,988
7	2,384	2.87E + 09	359.5	26.16295	1,625,894	167,674	470,589	4,781	909	14,171,344,326
8	2,931	3.83E + 09	355	19.79899	1,805,289	42,552	906,804	7,326	11,709	18,169,672,534
9	3,157	4.08E + 09	434	15.55635	1,545,846	48,259	846,271	13,871	11,812	15,645,318,789
10	2,615	3.49E + 09	367	41.01219	1,912,165	166,027	415,714	4,915	4,521	23,081,637,724
11	2,279	2.89E + 09	272.5	33.23402	1,518,972	19,301	522,964	16,203	3,337	18,272,575,079
12	2,260	2.96E + 09	346	42.42641	1,351,660	62,756	772,859	11,259	11,556	13,517,100,281
13	3,753	4.98E + 09	545	43.84062	1,492,406	57,481	618,934	4,401	4,213	15,928,119,789
14	2,980	3.67E + 09	263.5	20.5061	1,862,083	33,355	464,802	5,246	3,234	21,018,967,625
15	3,662	4.61E + 09	366	28.28427	1,444,455	20,042	958,012	343	16,723	15,570,613,347
16	2,554	3.41E + 09	169	42.42641	1,104,037	10,761	714,563	54	11,835	12,377,237,172
17	2,953	3.46E + 09	125	43.84062	1,813,807	85,921	807,377	39,691	8,249	19,094,763,680
18	2,549	3.13E + 09	372	33.94113	1,661,553	211,928	934,691	251,025	12,764	14,122,676,800
19	2,031	2.67E + 09	56	42.42641	1,249,594	289,212	2,493,099	50,194	78,435	11,069,326,989
20	1,948	2.59E + 09	675	36.76955	1,065,695	104,868	723,270	52,030	20,203	7,763,729,774

Table 2 Results

Branch	Efficiency scores and h^*										
	$\alpha =$ 0.1	h^*	$\alpha =$ 0.2	h^*	$\alpha =$ 0.3	h^*	$\alpha =$ 0.4	h^*	$\alpha =$ 0.5	h^*	Models (2) and (3)
1	0.805	0	0.805	0	0.805	0	0.804	0	0.177	0	0.177
2	0.883	0	0.879	0	0.876	0	0.869	0	0.279	0	0.279
3	1	0 or 1	1	0 or 1	1	0 or 1	1	0 or 1	0.273	0	0.273
4	0.883	0	0.874	0	0.866	0	0.858	0	0.181	0	0.181
5	0.814	0	0.806	0	0.799	0	0.792	0	0.171	0	0.171
6	0.903	1	0.881	1	0.867	1	0.855	1	0.128	0	0.128
7	0.752	0	0.75	0	0.746	0	0.737	0	0.161	0	0.161
8	0.908	0	0.894	0	0.879	0	0.866	0	0.252	0	0.252
9	0.768	1	0.754	1	0.732	1	0.684	1	0.274	0	0.274
10	1	0 or 1	1	0 or 1	1	0 or 1	1	0 or 1	0.13	0	0.13
11	0.847	1	0.82	1	0.818	1	0.817	1	0.187	0	0.187
12	0.898	0	0.889	0	0.879	0	0.869	0	0.287	0	0.287
13	0.637	1	0.624	1	0.614	1	0.605	1	0.208	0	0.208
14	0.931	1	0.852	1	0.823	1	0.814	1	0.127	0	0.127
15	0.636	1	0.589	1	0.527	1	0.485	1	0.332	0	0.332
16	1	0 or 1	1	0 or 1	1	0 or 1	1	0 or 1	0.324	0	0.324
17	1	0 or 1	1	0 or 1	1	0 or 1	1	0 or 1	0.223	0	0.223
18	0.786	0	0.779	0	0.773	0	0.762	0	0.299	0	0.299
19	1	0 or 1	1	0 or 1	1	0 or 1	1	0 or 1	1	0 or 1	1
20	0.759	0	0.759	0	0.759	0	0.759	0	0.34	0	0.34
α	Aggregate efficiency										h^*
0.1					0.812						1
0.2					0.811						1
0.3					0.802						1
0.4					0.764						1
0.5					0.626						1

5 Conclusions

Conducting an efficiency analysis of frameworks would hold utmost importance for supervisors with the aim of making informed decisions. Furthermore, it is crucial to determine the status of input and output components in order to accurately ascertain their efficiency. Across various studies, it has been observed that flexible random measures encompassing input and output roles are prevalent. The purpose of the current investigation is to ascertain the placement of flexible parameters and evaluate the comparative efficacy metrics of frameworks featuring flexible, stochastic parameters. The utilization of DEA methodologies has been proposed as a means of calculating the operational efficiencies of organizations that employ flexible stochastic measures. In order to provide a more comprehensive demonstration, various models geared towards the individual DMU perspective, including both oriented and non-oriented approaches, have been suggested with the aim of effectively addressing this matter. Moreover, the utilization of the majority rule has been implemented to ascertain the function of flexible variables. The suggested methodology involves using aggregate approaches to assess the appropriate placement of random flexible parameters with regards to optimizing overall efficiency. In order to scrutinize effectiveness as well as the significance of flexible measures, adaptable chance-constrained DEA methodologies have been devised. A dataset has been proffered to explicate and illustrate the proposed methodologies. The findings garnered from the suggested methodologies have demonstrated that the integration of flexible stochastic measures significantly impacts the efficacy of frameworks.

References

Amirteimoori, A., & Emrouznejad, A. (2011). Flexible measures in production process: A DEA-based approach. *RAIRO-Oper. Res., 45*(1), 63–74. https://doi.org/10.1051/ro/2011103

Amirteimoori, A., Emrouznejad, A., & Khoshandam, L. (2013). Classifying flexible measures in data envelopment analysis: A slack-based measure. *Measurement, 46*(10), 4100–4107. https://doi.org/10.1016/j.measurement.2013.08.019.

Boďa, M. (2020). Classifying flexible measures in data envelopment analysis: A slacks-based measure – A comment. *Measurement, 150*, 107045. https://doi.org/10.1016/j.measurement.2019.107045.

Charnes, A., & Cooper, W. W. (1959). Chance-constrained programming. *Management Science, 6*(1), 73–79. https://doi.org/10.1287/mnsc.6.1.73

Cook, W. D., & Zhu, J. (2007). Classifying inputs and outputs in data envelopment analysis. *European Journal of Operational Research, 180*(2), 692–699. https://doi.org/10.1016/j.ejor.2006.03.048.

Cooper, W. W., Deng, H., Huang, Z., & Li, S. X. (2002). Chance constrained programming approaches to technical efficiencies and inefficiencies in stochastic data envelopment analysis. *Journal of the Operational Research Society, 53*(12), 1347–1356.

Cooper, W. W., Deng, H., Huang, Z., & Li, S. X. (2004). Chance constrained programming approaches to congestion in stochastic data envelopment analysis. *European Journal of Operational Research, 155*(2), 487–501.

Ghiyasi, M., & Cook, W. D. (2020). Classifying dual role variables in DEA: The case of VRS. *Journal of the Operational Research Society, 1–8*,. https://doi.org/10.1080/01605682.2020.1790309

Hosseini Monfared, S. N., Hosseinzadeh Lotfi, F. H., Mozaffari, M. R., & Malkhalifeh, M. R. (2021a). Radial models for classifying flexible measures in two-stage network DEA. In Progress in Intelligent Decision Science: Proceeding of IDS 2020 (pp. 483–500). Advances in Intelligent Systems and Computing, *1301*. Springer, Cham. https://doi.org/10.1007/978-3-030-66501-2_38.

Hosseini Monfared, S. N., Hosseinzadeh Lotfi, F., Mozaffari, M. R., & Rostamy Malkhalifeh, M. (2021b). Classifying flexible and integer data in two-stage network data envelopment analysis. *Journal of applied research on industrial engineering*, *8*(3), 270–289. https://doi.org/10.22105/jarie.2021.261652.1231.

Hosseini Monfared, S. N., Mozaffari, M. R., & Rostamy Malkhalifeh, M. (2022). Classifying Flexible Measures in Two-Stage Network DEA. *International Journal of Industrial Mathematics*, *14*(3), 305–318. https://doi.org/10.30495/ijim.2022.19684.

Huang, Z., & Li, S. X. (2001). Stochastic DEA models with different types of input-output disturbances. *Journal of Productivity Analysis, 15*, 95–113. https://doi.org/10.1023/A:1007874304917

Joulaei, M., Mirbolouki, M., & Bagherzadeh-Valami, H. (2019). Classifying fuzzy flexible measures in data envelopment analysis. *Journal of Intelligent & Fuzzy Systems, 36*(4), 3791–3800. https://doi.org/10.3233/JIFS-18698

Kordrostami, S., & Noveiri, M. J. S. (2012). Evaluating the efficiency of decision making units in the presence of flexible and negative data. *Indian Journal of Science and Technology*, *5*(12), 3776–3782. https://doi.org/10.17485/ijst/2012/v5i12.20.

Kordrostami, S., Farajpour, G., & Jahani Sayyad Noveiri, M. (2014). Evaluating the efficiency and classifying the fuzzy data: A DEA based approach. *International Journal of Industrial Mathematics*, *6*(4), 321–327. http://ijim.srbiau.ac.ir/article_4836_991280d1e4d3b379ff0af4d6a82e4339.pdf.

Kordrostami, S., Amirteimoori, A., & Jahani Sayyad Noveiri, M. (2019). Inputs and outputs classification in integer-valued data envelopment analysis. *Measurement*, *139*, 317–325. https://doi.org/10.1016/j.measurement.2019.02.087.

Kordrostami, S., & Jahani Sayyad Noveiri, M. (2021). Performance analysis in the presence of bounded, discrete and flexible measures. *Operations Research and Decisions*, *31*. https://doi.org/10.37190/ord210303.

Kordrostami, S., & Noveiri, M. J. S. (2014). Evaluating the performance and classifying the interval data in data envelopment analysis. *International Journal of Management Science and Engineering Management*, *9*(4), 243–248. https://doi.org/10.1080/17509653.2014.900655

Land, K. C., Lovell, C. K., & Thore, S. (1993). Chance-constrained data envelopment analysis. *Managerial and Decision Economics, 14*(6), 541–554. https://doi.org/10.1002/mde.4090140607

Li, D., Li, Y., Gong, Y., & Yang, J. (2021). Estimation of bank performance from multiple perspectives: An alternative solution to the deposit dilemma. *Journal of Productivity Analysis, 56*, 151–170. https://doi.org/10.1007/s11123-021-00614-z

Jahani Sayyad Noveiri, M., & Kordrostami, S. (2023). Estimating sustainability dimensions using fuzzy inverse directional distance model with flexible measures: a health sector application. *Soft Computing*, 1-17. https://doi.org/10.1007/s00500-023-08666-z.

Jahani Sayyad Noveiri, M., Kordrostami, S., & Ghiyasi, M. (2023). Inverse data envelopment analysis optimization approaches with flexible measures, *Journal of Modelling in Management.* https://doi.org/10.1108/JM2-06-2022-0138.

Jahani Sayyad Noveiri, M., Kordrostami, S., & Amirteimoori, A. (2023). Multi-period efficiency analysis with flexible measures: Oriented and non-oriented approaches. *Iranian Journal of Management Studies,* 16(3), 627–645. https://doi.org/10.22059/ijms.2022.339606.674988.

Olesen, O. B., & Petersen, N. C. (2016). Stochastic data envelopment analysis—A review. *European Journal of Operational Research, 251*(1), 2–21. https://doi.org/10.1016/j.ejor.2015.07.058

Sharifi, M., Tohidi, G., Daneshian, B., & Modarres Khiyabani, F. (2021). A new stochastic model for classifying flexible measures in data envelopment analysis. *Journal of the Operations Research Society of China, 9*(3), 569–592. https://doi.org/10.1007/s40305-020-00318-5

Tavana, M., Izadikhah, M., Toloo, M., & Roostaee, R. (2020). A new non-radial directional distance model for data envelopment analysis problems with negative and flexible measures. *Omega*, 102355. https://doi.org/10.1016/j.omega.2020.102355.

Tohidi, G., & Matroud, F. (2017). A new non-oriented model for classifying flexible measures in DEA. *Journal of the Operational Research Society, 68*(9), 1019–1029. https://doi.org/10.1057/s41274-017-0207-6

Toloo, M., Allahyar, M., & Hančlová, J. (2018). A non-radial directional distance method on classifying inputs and outputs in DEA: Application to banking industry. *Expert Systems with Applications, 92*, 495–506. https://doi.org/10.1016/j.eswa.2017.09.034.

Toloo, M., Keshavarz, E., & Hatami-Marbini, A. (2018). Dual-role factors for imprecise data envelopment analysis. *Omega, 77*, 15–31. https://doi.org/10.1016/j.omega.2017.05.005.

Toloo, M., Ebrahimi, B., & Amin, G. R. (2020). New data envelopment analysis models for classifying flexible measures: The role of non-Archimedean epsilon. *European Journal of Operational Research*. https://doi.org/10.1016/j.ejor.2020.11.029.

Toloo, M. (2012). Alternative solutions for classifying inputs and outputs in data envelopment analysis. *Computers & Mathematics with Applications, 63*(6), 1104–1110. https://doi.org/10.1016/j.camwa.2011.12.016.

Zarrin, M. (2023). A mixed-integer slacks-based measure data envelopment analysis for efficiency measuring of German university hospitals. *Health Care Management Science, 26*(1), 138–160. https://doi.org/10.1007/s10729-022-09620-5

Performance Evaluation of Indian Banking Financial Sector by Using DEA Approach

R. Venugopal, C. Veeramani, V. T. Dhanaraj, and E. Kungumaraj

Abstract New approaches that give data beyond what can be obtained from a formal analysis of financial statements are needed to measure and evaluate the effectiveness of the bank's operations. A mathematical programming approach called Data Envelopment Analysis (DEA) identifies inefficient banks while considering the breadth of the services offered and the resources required to supply these banking services. Based on cross-sectional data from the top 10 nationalized banks for the period of April 2018–April 2022, this study aims to evaluate intra-sector performance in the Indian banking system. This study uses a DEA method to assess the relative effectiveness of a group of Indian banks in the real world. Finally, the bank is ranked using CRS and VRS models based on input and output financial ratio values. The investigation will highlight the banks that function effectively, areas where bank efficiency is not up to par, and probable causes of inefficiency.

Keywords Data envelopment analysis (DEA) · Banks efficiency · Financial ratio analysis

---

R. Venugopal · C. Veeramani (✉)
Department of Applied Science (Mathematics), PSG College of Technology, Coimbatore, Tamilnadu 641 004, India
e-mail: veerasworld@yahoo.com

V. T. Dhanaraj
Department of Commerce, Rathinam College of Arts and Science, Coimbatore, Tamilnadu 641 021, India

E. Kungumaraj
Sakthi Institute of Information and Management Studies, Coimbatore, Pollachi, Tamilnadu 642 001, India

© The Author(s), under exclusive license to Springer Nature Singapore Pte Ltd. 2024
S. A. Edalatpanah et al. (eds.), *Analytical Decision Making and Data Envelopment Analysis*, Infosys Science Foundation Series in Mathematical Sciences,
https://doi.org/10.1007/978-981-97-6972-8_6

1 Introduction

The banking system plays a crucial role in mobilizing financial resources and allocating them to ventures that offer higher expected returns for a given level of risk. This aids in promoting economic growth by directing funds to productive sectors. Additionally, banks provide essential payment and transaction services, improving the efficiency of economic activities. Since the initiation of financial sector deregulation in India in 1992, significant regulatory reforms have been implemented to strengthen the banking sector. At the macro level, these reforms included the deregulation of the previously controlled interest rate structure and the reduction of penalties on bank deposits. Micro-level measures focused on introducing more competition, enhancing transparency through improved disclosure practices in bank balance sheets, and implementing various prudential regulations. These measures encompassed exposure standards, income recognition, asset categorization, provisioning processes, capital adequacy, and investment values. The ongoing financial sector reforms aim to enhance the economic efficiency of resources by fostering operational flexibility, improving economic feasibility, and strengthening institutional capacity. The ultimate objective is to create a diversified, efficient, and competitive financial system. It is expected that the banking sector will expand in terms of higher productivity, increased profitability, reduced intermediation costs, and improved customer service.

The evolution of the banking system's structure will depend on factors such as the size and efficiency of the product mix that banks can pursue within the new opportunities created by the reforms. To take advantage of cost benefits, banks need to prioritize factors like profitability, sound management practices, and adequate capitalization to absorb potential negative shocks arising from both identified and unidentified risks. By selecting the most cost-effective size and product mix while managing portfolio risk, banks can position themselves favorably to achieve relative cost advantages. The importance of bank efficiency in this environment, particularly at the time of financial deregulation in a rising country like India, can hardly be ignored. Marjanovi et al. (2018), Kumar et al. (2016). It is commonly believed that inefficiency plays a significant role in the cost of the Indian banking industry. High spreads are a direct result of low productivity due to inefficient resource utilization. But assessing efficiency is tough since it's difficult to measure bank outputs. And maybe more significantly, banks might not generate the same kinds of outcomes consistently. While there have been several attempts to look into the topic of bank efficiency in industrialized nations, there hasn't been much research looking into bank efficiency in emerging nations.

In order to create a suitable model for efficiency evaluation, it is necessary to regularly analyse the bank's activities as well as the entire competitive market Managers' ability to make decisions may be substantially aided by a thorough investigation of the operations of banks and the identification of variables that contribute to inefficiency. Analysis based on financial indicators is frequently utilised in practise, although under current circumstances, this method does not yield sufficient information. Two-stage Data envelopment analysis (DEA) was used by Azad et al. (2017) to look at Malaysian bank efficiency. In their study of Taiwanese commercial banks, Kao and Liu (2016) analyse internal efficiency using a parallel production boundaries technique. The findings show that from 2008 to 2013, these institutions' efficiency increased.

The effectiveness of Serbian banks' operations from 2014 to 2016 will be evaluated using the DEA analysis, as mentioned by Marjanovi et al. (2018). Altuntas and Dereli (2015) introduced an innovative method combining the DEMATEL technique and patent citation analysis for ranking investment project portfolios. This approach, embodying the government's viewpoint, uniquely considers the impact on foreign trade deficit reduction and the potential to attract new investments. Akhtar, Alam, and Ansari (2021) utilized DEA to assess the efficiency of India's commercial banks from 2009 to 2018. Their analysis reveals inefficiencies in how these banks manage resources, with public sector banks outperforming private and foreign banks in efficiency scores. This study, marking a novel application of the Data Envelopment Window Analysis (DEWA) in evaluating the Indian banking sector over time, offers critical insights for policymakers on improving bank performance through managerial and operational enhancements. The study by Goyal et al. (2019) was conducted to assess the efficiency within the Indian banking sector, distinguishing among public, private, and foreign banks through a meta-frontier directional distance function DEA approach. Utilizing data from 66 banks for the fiscal year 2015–16, the analysis revealed a sector-wide efficiency of 73.44%, with efficiency variances across different ownership types. Foreign banks were found to be the most efficient, closely aligning with the meta-frontier, while public sector banks were identified as the least efficient, supporting the consolidation recommendations by the Reserve Bank of India and the Ministry of Finance. Ray and Das (2010) employed a non-parametric DEA approach to estimate the cost and profit efficiency of Indian banks during the post-reform period. Their findings revealed significant variations in the average levels of profit efficiency among different bank ownership groups. Alqahtani et al. (2017) utilized DEA and Stochastic Frontier Analysis to assess the effectiveness of Islamic and conventional banks in the GCC area, both during and after the global financial crisis; see also (Montazeri, 2020; Mozaffari & Ostovan, 2021). Venugopal and Veeramani (2021) discussed the application of DEA in stock market company rankings. The study uses DEA models, including CCR, CCR-Aggressive, and CCR-Benvelovent, to rank 24 NASDAQ-listed companies based on derived input and output measures; see (Bazargan et al., 2023; Ekram Nosratian & Taghavi Fard, 2023; Imeni et al., 2021; Maghbouli & Yekta, 2023; Sıcakyuz, 2023). Rasoulzadeh et al. (2022) discussed these tools and proposed a new combined Markowitz and cross DEA model using the returns of intuitionistic fuzzy numbers; see (Akram et al., 2023; El-Demerdash et al., 2023; Rasoulzadeh & Fallah, 2020; Ucal Sari & Ak, 2022). Wanke et al. (2016) identified efficiency-related elements in OECD banks, evaluating a sample of 128 banks from different OECD nations between 2004 and 2013 using financial criteria aligned with the CAMELS rating methodology and a robust TOPSIS approach; see also (Jing et al., 2023; Rasinojehdehi & Najafi, 2023; Sinha & Edalatpanah, 2023). Mihailovi (2016) employed one parametric approach (I-distance) and one non-parametric method (DEA) to assess and rank Serbian banks according to their effectiveness. Frontier analysis, as utilized by Berger and Humphrey (1997), provides a comprehensive empirical assessment and rating of enterprises that would not be possible otherwise. DEA is one of the most widely used non-parametric frontier approaches for assessing bank effectiveness. The primary objective of this article is to analyze the efficiency dynamics of Indian banks from April 2018 to April 2022. The investigation aims to identify banks with efficient operations and those with inefficiencies, as well as the potential root causes. The historical data for the period April 2018 to April 2022 were gathered from the website (http://www.https://finance.yahoo.com/). The CCR (DEA) Model is utilized to assess the relative performance ranking of the financial ratios input and output. The best DMU performance evaluation by using the CRS and VRS Model. The paper is structured into the following sections: (1) Proposed DEA Model, (2) Case study of the Indian bank, (3) Results and Discussion, and (4) Conclusion.

2 DEA Framework

DEA models are commonly used to estimate the effectiveness, capability, or productivity of homogeneous decision-making units. These models provide results that represent the outputs of the decision-making units, as referred to in the literature by Halkos and Salamouris (2004). Several DEA models have been described in the literature, but the two most commonly employed ones are the CCR model (developed by Charnes, Cooper and Rhodes (1978)) and the BCC model (Banker et al., 1984). The efficiency metric for the decision-making units (DMUs) (Jemric & Vujcic, 2002) is determined by solving the following linear programming problem:

$$\max_{l} z_0 = \sum_{r=1}^{s} l_r y_{r0} \tag{1}$$

Subject to

$$\sum_{r=1}^{s} l_r y_{rj} - \sum_{i=1}^{m} d_j x_{ij} x_{ij} \leq 0, j = 1,2, 3, \ldots, n \tag{2}$$

$$\sum\nolimits_{i=1}^{m} d_i x_{i0} = 1 \tag{3}$$

$$l_r \geq 0, r = 1,2, \ldots, s \tag{4}$$

$$d_i \geq 0, i = 1,2, \ldots, m \tag{5}$$

where x_{ij} is input of the *ith* type of the *jth* DMU and y_{rj} is output of the *ith* type of *jth* DMU. The dual of the above model is

$$min_{\psi} z_0 = \omega \tag{6}$$

Subject to

$$\sum_{j=1}^{n} \psi_j y_{rj} \geq y_{r0}, r = 1,2, \ldots, s \tag{7}$$

$$\omega x_{i0} - \sum_{j=1}^{n} \psi_j x_{rj} \geq 0, i = 1,2, \ldots, m \tag{8}$$

$$\psi_j \geq 0, j = 1,2, \ldots, n \tag{9}$$

The ideal solution ω for the particular DMU is represented by the efficiency score given by either the primal or dual model. DMUs are seen as being comparatively efficient when $\omega = 1$ but they are regarded as being relatively inefficient when omega is less than 1. By including a convexity requirement for X, or by including one more constraint in the previous model, variable returns-to-scale can be included in the model.

$$\sum \psi_{j=1}^{n} = 1 \tag{10}$$

The BCC model is the next iteration of the DEA model. It is possible to explicitly express the input-oriented BCC model for the DAMs as (Jemric & Vujcic, 2002).

$$min_{\psi} z_0 = \omega \tag{11}$$

Subject to

$$\sum_{j=1}^{n} \psi_j y_{rj} \geq y_{r0}, r = 1,2, \ldots, s \tag{12}$$

$$\omega x_{i0} - \sum_{j=1}^{n} \psi_j x_{rj} \geq 0, i = 1,2, \ldots, m \tag{13}$$

Title Suppressed Due to Excessive Length

$$\sum \psi_{j=1}^{n} = 1 \tag{14}$$

$$\psi_j \geq 0, j = 1,2, \ldots, n \tag{15}$$

The effectiveness scores generated using a model that accounts for variable returns-to-scale, as described by Jemric and Vujcic (2002), are commonly referred to as "pure technical efficiency scores". These scores provide an assessment of the efficiency of each decision-making unit (DMU) without considering the scale aspect. It is important to note that for each DMU, the CCR efficiency value should not exceed the corresponding BCC efficiency value. This implies that the CCR model assumes constant returns-to-scale, while the BCC model allows for variable returns-to-scale.

2.1 Case Study in the Indian Banking Sector

In this study, the CCR approach of the DMU is used efficiently under Indian banking financial sector environment. The proposed method is explained with a case study example as follows:

1. The variables for the input-oriented CRS/VRS models are calculated from the income statements and balance sheets form the period April 2018 to April 2022 of the top 10 nationalized banks in India. The Select the top 10 potential efficient banks such as State Bank of India (SBI), Canara Bank Ltd (CB), Indian Bank (IB), Indian Overseas Bank (IOB), Bank of India (BOI), Bank of Baroda (BOB), Bank of Maharashtra (BOM), Central Bank of India (CBI), Punjab National Bank (PNB), Union Bank of India (UBI). The variables had been used for calculating the input and output financial ratio.
2. The input-based seven financial ratios such Capital adequacy ratio $D1$, Debt Equity Ratio $D2$, Net NPA'S to total advances $D3$, Total investments to total assets ratio $D4$, the Percentage change in NPAs $D5$, Total advances to total deposits ratio $D6$, Return on assets ratio $D7$, and output based financial ratios such: Net profit to average assets $D8$, Spread ratio $D9$, Government securities to total assets $D10$, Liquid assets to total assets $D11$, Liquid assets to total deposits $D12$, Profit per employee $D13$,Return on net worth D 14. The input and output criteria are explained and shown in Appendix. Moreover, the input and output variables are calculated to make a decision matrix as shown in Table 1.

2.2 Result and Discussion

It is possible to infer from Table 2, under the CRS model's premise, that 8 banks ran continuously and effectively. The findings showed that just two banks had inefficient operations during the study period. Scale scores are also examined. The ratio of technical efficiency (CRS) to pure technical efficiency is used to compute scale scores (VRS). According to Thanassoulis (2001), scale efficiency is 1 if a DMU's technical efficiency (CRS) and pure technical efficiency (VRS) are equal. There is no evidence that scale size has a negative impact on DMU production. On the other

Table 1 Decision matrix input and output variable

DMU	C1	C2	C3	C4	C5	C6	C7	C8	C9	C10	C11	C12	C13	C14
SBI	9.13	477.38	1.02	0.30	2.27	0.67	15.84	11.48	2.59	24.71	2.74	2.74	1.49	14.50
CB	0.010	467.58	1.50	0.30	3.37	0.67	14.99	12.82	2.97	22.61	2.86	2.86	1.62	14.32
IB	0.012	352.57	2.23	0.26	3.13	0.72	13.00	9.33	3.00	23.72	2.13	2.13	0.89	14.00
IOB	0.12	451.58	3.00	0.26	4	0.75	13.00	7.00	3.00	23.34	1.24	1.24	0.01	10.00
BOI	0.14	405.78	6.00	0.31	4	0.71	12.00	7.01	3.00	22.66	1.20	1.20	0.96	9.00
BOB	0.04	365.38	2.65	0.26	2.65	0.74	13.84	14.44	4.10	36.42	0.2.63	2.63	2.39	14.52
BOM	0.12	332.58	3.82	0.28	3.58	0.73	14.81	11.96	3.52	40.24	2.20	2.20	1.05	12.56
CBI	0.14	210.57	4.22	0.26	5.44	0.73	11.72	10.00	2.85	39.98	1.38	1.38	1.14	13.00
PNB	0.14	319.12	5.00	0.23	10.81	0.73	10.00	11.00	1.98	37.89	2.42	2.42	2.19	12.00
UBI	0.12	282.78	7.00	0.28	15	0.72	9.04	10.00	2.00	31.46	2.56	2.56	2.32	11.50

Table 2 Year wise efficiency scores form 2018–2022

2018					2019			
DMU	CRS	VRS	SE	RTS	CRS	VRS	SE	RTS
SBI	1	1	1	Constant	1	1	1	Constant
CB	1	1	1	Constant	1	1	1	Constant
IB	1	1	1	Constant	1	1	1	Constant
IOB	1	1	1	Constant	1	1	1	Constant
BOI	1	1	1	Constant	0.68	0.95	0.72	Increasing
BOB	1	1	1	Constant	1	1	1	Constant
BOM	1	1	1	Constant	1	1	1	Constant
CBI	1	1	1	Constant	1	1	1	Constant
PNB	1	1	1	Constant	1	1	1	Constant
UBI	1	1	1	Constant	1	1	1	Constant

hand, the DMU's scale efficiency will be less than 1 if its VRS efficiency scores are larger than its CRS efficiency scores. This leads to the conclusion that scale operation has an impact on the DMU's effectiveness. The lower scale efficiency value that results from the bigger difference between the CRS and VRS efficiency ratings would further exacerbate the detrimental effects of scale size on production.

2020					2021			
DMU	CRS	VRS	SE	RTS	CRS	VRS	SE	RTS
SBI	1	1	1	Constant	1	1	1	Constant
CB	1	1	1	Constant	1	1	1	Constant
IB	0.99	1	0.99	Increasing	1	1	1	Constant
IOB	0.74	0.97	0.76	Increasing	1	1	1	Constant
BOI	1	1	1	Constant	0.79	0.99	0.80	Increasing
BOB	1	1	1	Constant	1	1	1	Constant
BOM	1	1	1	Constant	1	1	1	Constant
CBI	1	1	1	Constant	1	1	1	Constant
PNB	1	1	1	Constant	1	1	1	Constant
UBI	1	1	1	Constant	1	1	1	Constant

2022				
DMU	CRS	VRS	SE	RTS
SBI	1	1	1	Constant
CB	1	1	1	Constant
IB	1	1	1	Constant

(continued)

(continued)

2022				
DMU	CRS	VRS	SE	RTS
IOB	0.72	0.97	0.74	Increasing
BOI	0.96	1	0.96	Increasing
BOB	1	1	1	Constant
BOM	1	1	1	Constant
CBI	1	1	1	Constant
PNB	1	1	1	Constant
UBI	1	1	1	Constant

From Table 3 results, VRS model-based all the banks secured high-scale efficiency (above 0.9). It clearly indicates that all the banks are well efficient. Moreover, VRS model-based IOB and BI secured (less than 0.85) these two banks clearly indicate inefficiently. From Table 3 the outcome of the results in the year 2018 is well efficient because all the bank RTS scale is secured (above 0.9). Moreover, the Bank of India and Indian overseas bank have RTS scale secured (less than 0.85). It is clearly indicated that these two banks were only inefficient during the period 2019 to 2022 and another bank was well efficient. From Table 3 results, we conclude that the Bank of India and Indian Overseas Bank are inefficient. In the future, this inefficiency could lead to challenges for these two banks, while other banks are expected to operate more efficiently.

Table 3 Efficiency scores overall period form 2018 to 2022

S.NO	DMU	CRS	VRS	SE	RTS
1	SBI	1	1	1	Constant
2	CB	1	1	1	Constant
3	IB	1	1	1	Constant
4	IOB	0.7790	0.9882	0.7883	Decreasing
5	BOI	0.8439	1	0.8439	Decreasing
6	BOB	1	1	1	Constant
7	BOM	1	1	1	Constant
8	CBI	1	1	1	Constant
9	PNB	1	1	1	Constant
10	UBI	1	1	1	Constant

3 Conclusion and Future Work

The performance of the financial sector plays a crucial role in driving a nation's overall economic growth. As a result, evaluating the efficiency of banks has become increasingly important in today's context. Conducting a thorough review of efficiency can provide decision-makers in inefficient businesses with valuable information that can help them better manage their resources and improve their overall performance. In this particular study, the researchers employed the Data Envelopment Analysis (DEA) technique to compare the relative effectiveness of nationalized banks in the Indian banking industry over the period from April 2018 to 2022. DEA is considered one of the alternative methods for assessing bank performance and offers several advantages over the conventional approach that relies solely on financial indicators to gauge efficiency. DEA provides several benefits compared to traditional financial analysis, which tends to focus on financial ratios. The primary advantage of DEA is that it provides a comprehensive and objective numerical evaluation of each bank's efficiency. It goes beyond simple ratios and provides a thorough assessment of a bank's performance relative to its peers. DEA ranks each inefficient unit, highlighting those banks that are not operating at their maximum potential. Moreover, DEA also suggests strategies and areas for improvement, enabling decision-makers to take concrete steps towards enhancing efficiency. The results of the study indicate that approximately two banks in the sample ran inefficiently during the observation period. Inefficiency in these banks can be attributed to various factors such as ineffective operations, suboptimal management practices, or unfavorable circumstances. By identifying the root causes of inefficiency, decision-makers can gain insights into the areas that require improvement and can take appropriate actions to enhance the bank's overall efficiency.

Overall, this study contributes to the existing empirical literature on bank efficiency evaluation, shedding light on the relative effectiveness of nationalized banks in the Indian banking industry. It emphasizes the significance of conducting efficiency assessments in the financial sector and highlights the benefits of using DEA as an analytical tool. Going forward, further research could explore additional performance measures and consider different DEA models within a fuzzy environment to enhance the understanding of bank efficiency and facilitate continuous improvement in the industry.

Appendix: The Input and Output Criteria Detailed Explained as Follows

1. Capital adequacy ratio

The capital adequacy ratio (CAR) is a assess the how much capital a bank has available, reported as a percentage of a bank's risk-weighted credit exposures. The capital adequacy ratio helps measure the financial strength or the ability of financial institutions to meet their obligations using their assets and capital.

Capital Adequacy Ratio Formula = (Tier 1 Capital + Tier 2 Capital) / Risk-Weighted Assets

2. Debt-to-equity (D/E) Ratio

Debt-to-equity (D/E) ratio is used to assess the bank financial leverage and is calculated by dividing a bank's total liabilities by its shareholder equity. D/E ratio is an important metric in bank finance. The calculation of Debt/Equity = Total Shareholders'/ Equity Total Liabilities

3. Net NPA to advances

Net NPA to Advances bank loans, it is used for a measure of the overall quality of the bank's loan book. Provision Coverage Ratio = Total provisions / Gross NPAs.

4. Total investments to total assets ratio

This ratio evaluates the liquid assets being held by an individual against the total assets accumulated. Investments in different stocks, mutual funds or other such investments which can be converted to cash easily are considered as liquid assets.

5. Percentage change in NPAs

NPAs are not favorable for banks as they are non-performing. A high number of NPAs means that too many loans have turn into non-functional or are not generating any interest income for the bank **Net non-performing assets = NPAs – Provisions** is the formula for calculating Non Performing Assets (NPA).

6. Total advances to total deposits ratio

Total advances to total deposits ratio is used to assess a bank's liquidity by comparing a bank's total loans to its total deposits for the same period.

7. Return on assets ratio

Return on assets provides how much profit a company can generate from its assets and the higher the number, the more efficient a company's management is at managing its balance sheet to generate profits. The return on total assets ratio is calculated by dividing a company's earnings after tax by its total assets.

8. Net profit to average assets

Return on average assets ROAA is an indicator used to assess the profitability of a firm's assets, and it is most often used by banks as a means to gauge financial performance.

9. Spread ratio

Spread ratio refers to the difference between the interest earning and Interest Paid

10. Government securities to total assets

This ratio indicate that the measures the risk associated with the assets held with the bank The financial stability of banks and the overall banking system is among the most important.

11. Liquid assets to total assets

A liquid asset is an asset that can easily be converted into cash in a short amount of time. It can be concerned with tracking liquid assets as a portion of their net worth.

12. Liquid assets to total deposits

A liquid asset is explicit as the responsibility of commercial banks to maintain a fixed percentage of total deposits and certain other liabilities in the form of liquid assets.

13. Profit per employee

Profit per employee, referred to net income per employee (NIPE), is a metric that you can use to calculate your business's net income divided by the total number of employees. Is a show that much profit each of your employees brings in over the course of period

14. Return on net worth

Return on Net worth (RONW) is used in finance as a measure of a bank's profitability. It reveals how much profit a company generates with the money that the equity shareholders have invested.

References

Akhtar, S., Alam, M. & Ansari, M. S. (2021). Measuring the performance of the Indian banking industry: data envelopment window analysis approach. *Benchmarking: An International Journal, 29*(9), 2842–2857.

Akram, M., Shah, S. M. U., Al-Shamiri, M. M. A., & Edalatpanah, S. A. (2023). Extended DEA method for solving multi-objective transportation problem with Fermatean fuzzy sets. *Aims Math, 8*, 924–961.

Alqahtani, F., Mayes, D. G., & Brown, K. (2017). Islamic bank efficiency compared to conventional banks during the global crisis in the GCC region. *Journal of International Financial Markets, Institutions and Money, 51*, 58–74.

Altuntas, S., & Dereli, T. (2015). A novel approach based on DEMATEL method and patent citation analysis for prioritizing a portfolio of investment projects. *Expert Systems with Applications, 42*(3), 1003–1012.

Azad, M. A. K., Munisamy, S., Masum, A. K. M., Saona, P., & Wanke, P. (2017). Bank efficiency in Malaysia: A use of malmquist meta-frontier analysis. *Eurasian Business Review, 7*, 287–311.

Banker, R. D., Charnes, A., & Cooper, W. W. (1984). Some models for estimating technical and scale inefficiencies in data envelopment analysis. *Management Science, 30*(9), 1078–1092.

Bazargan, A., Najafi, S. E., Lotfi, F. H., Fallah, M., & Edalatpanah, S. A. (2023). Presenting a productivity analysis model for Iran oil industries using Malmquist network analysis. *Decision Making: Applications in Management and Engineering, 6*(2), 251–292.

Berger, A. N., & Humphrey, D. B. (1997). Efficiency of financial institutions: International survey and directions for future research. *European Journal of Operational Research, 98*(2), 175–212.

Charnes, A., Cooper, W. W., & Rhodes, E. (1978). Measuring the efficiency of decision making units. *European Journal of Operational Research, 2*(6), 429–444.

Ekram Nosratian, N., & Taghavi Fard, M. T. (2023). A proposed model for the assessment of supply chain management using DEA and knowledge management. *Computational Algorithms and Numerical Dimensions, 2*(3), 136–147.

El-Demerdash, B. E., Edalatpanah, S. A., & Khalifa, H. A. E. W. (2023). On treating input oriented data envelopment analysis model under neutrosophic environment. *Neutrosophic Sets and Systems, 60*(1), 213–226.

Goyal, J., Singh, M., Singh, R., & Aggarwal, A. (2019). Efficiency and technology gaps in Indian banking sector: Application of meta-frontier directional distance function DEA approach. *The Journal of Finance and Data Science, 5*(3), 156–172.

Halkos, G. E., & Salamouris, D. S. (2004). Efficiency measurement of the Greek commercial banks with the use of financial ratios: A data envelopment analysis approach. *Management Accounting Research, 15*(2), 201–224.

Imeni, M., Fallah, M., & Edalatpanah, S. A. (2021). The effect of managerial ability on earnings classification shifting and agency cost of Iranian listed companies. *Discrete Dynamics in Nature and Society, 2021*, 1–10.

Jemric, I., & Vujcic, B. (2002). Efficiency of banks in Croatia: A DEA approach. *Comparative Economic Studies, 44*, 169–193.

Jing, D., Imeni, M., Edalatpanah, S. A., Alburaikan, A., & Khalifa, H. A. E. W. (2023). Optimal selection of stock portfolios using multi-criteria decision-making methods. *Mathematics, 11*(2), 415.

Kao, C., & Liu, S. T. (2016). A parallel production frontiers approach for intertemporal efficiency analysis: The case of Taiwanese commercial banks. *European Journal of Operational Research, 255*(2), 411–421.

Kumar, M., Charles, V., & Mishra, C. S. (2016). Evaluating the performance of Indian banking sector using DEA during post-reform and global financial crisis. *Journal of Business Economics and Management, 17*(1), 156–172.

Maghbouli, M., & Yekta, A. P. (2023). Undesirable input in production process: A DEA-based approach. *J. Oper. Strateg Anal., 1*(2), 46–54.

Marjanović, I., Stanković, J. J., & Popović, Ž. (2018). Efficiency estimation of commercial banks based on financial performance: Input oriented DEA CRS/VRS models. *Economic Themes, 56*(2), 239–252.

Mihailović, N. (2016). Ranking of banks in Serbia. *Yugoslav Journal of Operations Research, 19*(2), 323–334.

Montazeri, F. Z. (2020). An overview of data envelopment analysis models in fuzzy stochastic environments. *Journal of Fuzzy Extension and Applications, 1*(4), 272–278.

Mozaffari, M. R., & Ostovan, S. (2021). Finding projection in the two-stage supply chain in DEA-R with random data using (CRA) model. *Big Data and Computing Visions, 1*(3), 146–155. https://doi.org/10.22105/bdcv.2021.142083

Rasinojehdehi, R., & Najafi, S. (2023). Integrating PCA and DEA techniques for strategic assessment of network security. *Computational Algorithms and Numerical Dimensions, 2*(1), 23–34.

Rasoulzadeh, M., & Fallah, M. (2020). An overview of portfolio optimization using fuzzy data envelopment analysis models. *Journal of Fuzzy Extension and Applications, 1*(3), 180–188.

Rasoulzadeh, M., Edalatpanah, S. A., Fallah, M., & Najafi, S. E. (2022). A multi-objective approach based on Markowitz and DEA cross-efficiency models for the intuitionistic fuzzy portfolio selection problem. *Decision Making: Applications in Management and Engineering, 5*(2), 241–259.

Ray, S. C., & Das, A. (2010). Distribution of cost and profit efficiency: Evidence from Indian banking. *European Journal of Operational Research, 201*(1), 297–307.

Sıcakyuz, C. (2023). Bibliometric analysis of data envelopment analysis in supply chain management. *J. Oper. Strateg Anal., 1*(1), 14–24.

Sinha, R. P., & Edalatpanah, S. A. (2023). Efficiency and fiscal performance of Indian states: An empirical analysis using network DEA. *J. Oper. Strateg Anal., 1*(1), 1–7.

Thanassoulis, E. (2001). *Introduction to the theory and application of data envelopment analysis*. Kluwer Academic Publishers.

Ucal Sari, I., & Ak, U. (2022). Machine efficiency measurement in industry 4.0 using fuzzy data envelopment analysis. *Journal of Fuzzy Extension and Applications, 3*(2), 177–191

Venugopal, R., & Veeramani, C. (2021, December). Data envelopment analysis and the implementation of their applications in Python. In Proceedings of the First International Conference on Combinatorial and Optimization, ICCAP 2021, December 7–8 2021, Chennai, India.

Wanke, P., Azad, M. A. K., & Barros, C. P. (2016). Efficiency factors in OECD banks: A ten-year analysis. *Expert Systems with Applications, 64*, 208–227.

Application of Data Envelopment Analysis in Decision Making of Civil Engineering Problems

Sanaz Razmyan and Azad Yazdani

Abstract Data envelopment analysis (DEA) can convert fractional linear efficiency into a linear programming model for decision analysis. DEA evaluates decision-making units (DMUs) using a nonparametric method. It is a mathematical programming method for assessing DMU performance. This method does not identify general relationships between all units. DEA is a frontier-based statistical regression method. In this chapter, two examples of DEA applications in civil engineering are provided. Two of the applications relate to structural design engineering and earthquake engineering, respectively.

1 Introduction

Externally bonding reinforcement (EBR) with fiber-reinforced polymer (FRP) laminates is a common technique for repairing and strengthening reinforced concrete (RC) structures. Premature debonding complicates the estimation of FRP-to-concrete bond capacity. Premature debonding shows the importance of estimating FRP-to-concrete bond capacity. To evaluate the performance of FRP-to-concrete bonds, a large number of lap shear tests have been conducted. Numerous bond capacity estimation models resulted from these experiments and theoretical research. This study evaluated bond capacity models' accuracy and performance using various criteria. To achieve this, 31 bond capacity prediction models were chosen.

A database of 345 test specimens not utilized in any of the models was compiled. The models were initially evaluated utilizing log-likelihood, Euclidean distance ranking, Bayesian factor, and variance reduction. Using the technique of data envelopment analysis (DEA), the final ranking was determined by applying the results of these methods to a multi-criteria decision-making procedure.

S. Razmyan
Department of Mathematics, Firoozkooh Branch, Islamic Azad University, Firoozkooh, Iran

A. Yazdani (✉)
Department of Civil Engineering, University of Kurdistan, Sanandaj, Iran
e-mail: a.yazdani@uok.ac.ir

© The Author(s), under exclusive license to Springer Nature Singapore Pte Ltd. 2024

S. A. Edalatpanah et al. (eds.), *Analytical Decision Making and Data Envelopment Analysis*, Infosys Science Foundation Series in Mathematical Sciences,
https://doi.org/10.1007/978-981-97-6972-8_7

In probabilistic seismic-hazard analysis (PSHA), ground motion prediction equations (GMPEs) are essential. Most logic tree frameworks use multiple GMPEs to address epistemic uncertainty. Experts choose the GMPEs and assign weights, usually based on gut feeling. Recent statistical criteria based on goodness-of-fit measures reduce subjectivity in GMPE selection. Therefore, we use DEA as a multi-criteria efficiency evaluation framework to rank different criteria. The DEA method can assess each GMPE's efficiency. The DEA methodology can also rank multiple target intensity measures like spectral amplitude in different structural periods. Using DEA, the Central Iran seismotectonic province is studied as an example. The results show that the DEA can assess GMPE efficiency and supplement ranking procedures.

2 Selecting Appropriate FRP-To-Concrete Bond Strength Models

For the external reinforcement of reinforced concrete (RC) structures, structural engineers have focused on using fiber-reinforced polymer (FRP) composites (Kotynia et al., 2008). FRP composites are widely used due to their high tensile strength, lightweight, corrosion resistance, and ability to maintain element dimensions (Pham & Al-Mahaidi, 2004). Externally bonded reinforcement (EBR) is one of the most widely used techniques for strengthening FRP. FRP-concrete bond examination is essential for accurate strengthening design. Recent lap shear tests have examined FRP-to-concrete bonds (Yao et al., 2005). Concrete, FRP composite, and test-dependent parameters affected bond capacity. FRP composites affect strip thickness, width, elastic modulus, bond length, shear modulus, and adhesive materials thickness (Pellegrino 2008). Shear stress distribution is affected by the ratio of FRP strip width to concrete specimen width, resulting in a width ratio factor. The results showed that bond length above a certain value did not increase bond capacity. The effective bond length included this length (Carloni & Focacci, 2016). Early bond strength models ignored effective bond length. However, more experimental and analytical studies incorporated this parameter into more contemporary models (Yazdani et al., 2021a). In models in which the bond length was shorter than the effective bond length, a reduction factor was applied to the bond strength equation (Wu et al., 2009). Other models incorporate the effective bond length directly (Chen & Teng, 2001).

Three categories of models are proposed. Empirical models are first. The second category consists of analytical models derived from stress analysis or fracture mechanics (Yazdani et al., 2021a). The third group consists of numerical models (Zhou et al., 2020). Strengthening provisions include FRP-to-concrete bond strength models. These provisions either suggest an independent model or accept and recommend existing models. ACI 440.2R-17 (ACI 2017) accepted Chen and Teng's (2001) model, whereas HB 305 (HB 2008) accepted Chen and Teng's (2001) model as well as Seracino's (2007) model. CNR-DR 200 (CNR-DT 2013) and *fib* Bulletin 90 (*fib* 2019) present distinct model specifications.

Model extraction procedure varies by study in approach, methods, and parameters. Thus, bond capacity models may vary in accuracy. Engineers can design more accurate retrofits by understanding model accuracy and performance. Thus, it is necessary to accurately predict FRP-to-concrete bond models. Literature employs a variety of statistical methods to test model compatibility with experimental data. Classical statistical analyses include the Pearson's correlation coefficient, variance reduction, Nash–Sutcliffe efficiency coefficient, and Kolmogorov–Smirnov test. These traditional methods based on residual analysis remain the most widely used technique for assessing model predictions. Model bias is determined through the analysis of mean residuals and the fitting of straight lines to residual components. Due to a lack of useful model definitions and step-by-step documentation, however, the traditional statistical method of model selection may be subjective and non-transparent. Scherbaum et al. (2004) found inconsistent results when ranking and selecting candidate models using observed data. Thus, a reliable method for selecting the best model objectively is required.

Ranking methods were used to objectively choose models from a suite of available data. Predicting experimental data scores for each model. Recent research proposes statistically objective and robust criteria for enhancing model selection (Yazdani et al., 2021b). Different methods use different logic to rank the model's accuracy. Thus, choosing a ranking method may affect the final result.

Data envelopment analysis (DEA) is an objective, multi-criteria decision-making technique that assesses decision-making units (DMUs) without seeking general relationships between them. This study uses the DEA for selection and ranking. To assess FRP-to-concrete bond capacity prediction models. The data-driven criteria reduce decision-making subjectivity. 31 literature-based FRP bond-strength models are chosen. Each model's bond strength prediction is assessed using a large lap shear tests database. The DEA is then utilized to rank the models according to four distinct ranking strategies. The top ten models include strengthening provisions and fracture mechanics models.

2.1 Bond Strength Models

There are numerous FRP-to-concrete bond capacity models in the literature. Empirical or theoretical bond capacity models exist. Fracture mechanics or stress analysis generates theoretical models. Bond capacity is often estimated using fracture mechanics (Carloni et al., 2015). Fracture mechanics-based bond capacity models use bond fracture energy G_f as a key parameter. 31 bond strength models, M1-M31, are evaluated in this study. Yazdani et al. (2023) provided a comprehensive description of the used models.

The M_1, M_3, M_6, M_{10}, and M_{14} models are first-type empirical methods that disregard effective bond length. Regression methods extract these models from average shear stress values. The M_7, M_8, and M_{13} models are the second category of empirical models. These models are comparable to the first type, but the effective bond length is taken into account. The M_2, M_4, M_5, M_9, M_{11}, M_{12}, M_{19}, M_{23}, M_{25}, M_{29}, and M_{30} models are fracture mechanics-based models. These models' coefficient calibrations were determined using regression on experimental data. Stress analysis extracts models like M_{17}, M_{18}, M_{22}, M_{26}, and M_{27}. The Monti et al. (2003) model uses stress analysis and finite element modeling. The model of Lu et al. (2005) is acknowledged as a mesoscale finite element method. The failure plane effect is taken into account in the shear stress-slip relationship only by the M_{27} model, which is used in HB 305 (HB 2008). Additionally, the model developed by Chen and Tang (2001) used in ACI 440.2R-17 (ACI 2017) is recommended by HB 305 (HB 2008). As the most recent model, *fib* Bulletin 90 (*fib* 2019) was derived by considering a bi-linear relationship between shear stress and slip behavior.

The variety of bond strength models may make selecting one for analysis and design confusing. Thus, each model's prediction quality must be understood. These 31 models are evaluated based on a variety of criteria using a large database of experimental test results from the scientific literature. The database was filtered and all tests used to develop the 31 selected FRP bond strength models were removed to fairly evaluate their accuracy and performance. Thus, it was determined that none of the 345 tests from 36 studies were ever used in model extractions. Yazdani et al. (2023) provided a comprehensive description of the data used.

2.2 *Evaluation of Goodness-Of-Fit*

Several methods can be used to evaluate the prediction of experimental data by a physical model. These methods typically use residual distribution tests or data-model prediction pairs. Residuals are the difference between model predictions and data. Parameters are used to calculate FRP-to-concrete bond capacity model. It is practical to categorize these approaches as either classical or recently developed.

The mean and variance test p-value are classical methods for testing center and variance tendencies. The normalized residual distribution shape can be examined using the t-test, the Chi-square Misfit, the Wilcoxon rank sum test, and the Kolmogorov–Smirnov test. The variance reduction technique is often used to evaluate a model's goodness-of-fit (Scherbaum et al., 2004). This method normalizes residuals by data values:

$$\Delta\sigma^2 = \left(1 - \frac{[d - g(m)]^T.C_d^{-1}.[d - g(m)]}{d^T.C_d^{-1}.d}\right).100\% \tag{1}$$

where d is a vector of data, $g(m)$ is the model prediction, and C_d^{-1} is the data weighting inverse of the data covariance matrix. Equation (1) normalized by N is useful in practice. A better fit has a lower value of $\Delta\sigma^2$. In the past decade, various researchers have developed and employed robust goodness-of-fit measures to evaluate the data fit of various models. These methods attempt to present a single score as a criterion so that the decision maker can conveniently evaluate the quality of each model's prediction of a dataset. Listed below are descriptions of some well-known techniques:

2.2.1 Log-Likelihood Approach

Log-likelihood (LLH) is a technique for selecting models based on the information theory. A log-likelihood approach is used to calculate the distance between two continuous probability density functions, $f(x)$ and $g(x)$ (Scherbaum et al., 2009). $f(x)$ represents the probability distribution of an experimental database data point. The median and standard deviation of the FRP-to-concrete bond capacity model are assumed to be the probability distribution $g(x)$ for estimating the data point. Since $f(x)$ is unknown, it is assumed that it has the same characteristics as $g(x)$. As shown in Eq. (2), the LLH is estimated as the average log-likelihood of the model under the assumption of experimental data:

$$\text{LLH}(g, x) = -\frac{1}{N}\sum_{i=1}^{N} log_2(g(x_i)) \tag{2}$$

N represents the total number of data in Eq. (2), while x_i represents the experimental data for $i = 1, \ldots, N$, where N is the total number of experimental data. A lower value of LLH indicates that the model produces more accurate data. This attribute enables the LLH to be used for model selection.

2.2.2 Euclidean Distance Ranking

Recent model selection and ranking methods include Euclidean distance ranking (EDR) (Kale & Akkar, 2013). This method added model prediction uncertainty and the trend between experimental data and median model estimations to the Euclidean distance (ED). Smaller EDR values also indicate a more accurate physical model description of the experimental dataset in this method. The EDR index is the result of combining model uncertainty with data-model trend. Nevertheless, if necessary, the two factors can be analyzed independently:

$$\text{EDR} = \sqrt{\kappa.\frac{1}{N}.\sum_{i=1}^{N} MDE_i^2} \tag{3}$$

where MDE represents model uncertainty in model performance evaluation using an N-dataset. This factor resembles residual analysis. The κ factor in Eq. (3) shows the data-median model estimation trend.

In an ideal case, κ factor is equal to 1, the median model prediction matches the observed data perfectly. Deviations of κ from 1 indicate that the median prediction of models is biased. The MDE values are normalized by the total number of data to produce an index independent of the size of the dataset.

2.2.3 Bayesian Factor Analysis

Based on Bayesian theory, the Bayesian factor (BF) technique compares model and data in order to calculate the probability that the data and model are compatible (Shahidzadeh et al., 2020). Bayesian weights indicate each model's database contribution in the BF method. Greater BF weights indicate more accurate model estimation. In contrast to the EDR method, the BF method considers the correlation of data within the dataset. Combining expert knowledge of model performance with experimental database information is an additional advantage of the BF method. This is useful in situation where data scarcity and correlation render decision based solely on data unreliable. The BF definition is given by Eq. (4):

$$\mathrm{BF}_i = \frac{P(M_i|D)}{\sum_j P(M_j|D)} = \frac{L(M_i|D)\,\Pr(M_i)}{\sum_j L(M_j|D)\,\Pr(M_j)} \tag{4}$$

where $L(M_i|D)$ is the probability that the model M_i corresponds to the observed data D. $P(M_i)$ represents the prior probability that the model M_i is independent of data D. The likelihood is a multi-dimensional normal distribution and is defined as a function of σ_i for each model M_i given data D (Arroyo et al. 2014):

$$\begin{aligned} L(M_i, \sigma_i|D) &= P(D|M_i, \sigma_i) \\ &= (2\pi)^{-n/2}\left(\sigma_i^2\right)^{-n/2}|\Phi_i|^{-1/2}\exp\left(\frac{-1}{2\sigma_i^2}(Y - Y_i)^T\Phi_i^{-1}(Y - Y_i)\right) \end{aligned} \tag{5}$$

where n is the total number of experimental data Y and Y_i are the *ith* model's median prediction. For model M_i, the variance of median model output Y_i is $\sigma_i{}^2$, while the correlation between observed data values is an n by n block diagonal symmetric matrix Φ_I. It is an unreliable predictor. The model likelihood $L(M_i|D)$ can be calculated:

$$L(M_i|D) = \int L(M_i, \sigma_i|D)\,\Pr(\sigma_i)d\sigma_i \tag{6}$$

where $P(\sigma_i)$ is a probability distribution function for model prediction uncertainty σ_i when dataset D is predicted by model M_i.

2.3 *Data Envelopment Analysis -SBM*

Data envelopment analysis (DEA) utilizing linear programming can transform the fractional linear measure of efficiency in decision analysis. A group of comparable organizations, known as decision-making units (DMUs), is evaluated using DEA as a nonparametric technique. This method (Cooper et al., 2007) does not emphasize the identification of general relationships between all the evaluated units. DMU is any operation performed as part of input- and output-based decision-making. There is no need to assign a weight to each criterion prior to evaluating the efficacy of DMUs in this procedure. Numerous industries, including manufacturing, banking, educational systems, healthcare, refineries, and powerhouses, can be evaluated using empirical applications of DEA usages (Aldamak & Zolfaghari, 2017; Muniz et al.., 2022; Rasoulzadeh et al., 2023; Maghbouli & Yekta, 2023). The DEA method is used to estimate efficiency, but it can also be used to rank DMUs (Adler et al., 2002). Different models are used by DEA to rank DMUs. They all have benefits and drawbacks (Charnes et al., 2013; Shermeh al., 2018; Sinha & Edalatpanah, 2023; Sıcakyüz, 2023). In the current study, a method based on a slacks-based measure (SBM) of efficiency, which considers both input and output variables at once, is used (Tone, 2002).

The DEA's main goal is to measure DMU efficiency using scalar measures (Yazdani et al., 2015). The worst efficiency is 0 and the best is 1 on this scalar. Let's assume that DEA analyzes the n DMUs that generate s outputs from m inputs. The production possibility set P is defined by the input and output matrices $\boldsymbol{X} = (x_{ij}) \varepsilon R^{m\times n}$ and $\boldsymbol{Y} = (y_{ij}) \varepsilon \boldsymbol{R}^{s\times n}$ as:

$$P = \{(x, y)|x \geq \boldsymbol{X}\lambda, y \leq \boldsymbol{Y}\lambda, \lambda \geq 0\} \tag{7}$$

where λ is a non-negative vector. An index ρ is defined by the slacks s^- and s^+, which get for the excess of input and shortfall of output, respectively:

$$\rho = \frac{1 - \frac{1}{m}\sum_{i=1}^{m} s_i^- / x_{i0}}{1 + \frac{1}{s}\sum_{r=1}^{s} s_r^+ / y_{r0}} \tag{8}$$

where the index ρ is a number between 0 and 1. The fractional program below is written using the SBM method to determine the efficiency of (x_0,y_0):

$$\begin{aligned} \min \quad & \rho \\ & x_0 = X\lambda + s^-, \\ \text{subject to } & y_0 = Y\lambda - s^+, \\ & \lambda \geq 0,\ s^- \geq 0,\ s^+ \geq 0. \end{aligned} \tag{9}$$

Transformation allows SBM to be converted into a linear program (Cooper et al., 2007). A DMU (x_0, y_0) is considered to be SBM-efficient if an optimal ρ is equal to 1.0. On the basis of this presumption, the super-efficiency score is defined. The result is the definition of a set of production scenarios that are encompassed by $(\boldsymbol{X}, \boldsymbol{Y})$ and do not include (x_0, y_0). The equation for the super-efficiency of the value of the ideal objective function, (x_0, y_0), is as follows:

$$\min \delta* = \min \delta = \frac{\frac{1}{m}\sum_{i=1}^{m} \overline{x}_i / x_{i0}}{\frac{1}{s}\sum_{r=1}^{s} \overline{y}_r / y_{r0}}$$

$$subject\ to \quad \begin{aligned} &\overline{x} \geq \sum_{j=1,\neq 0}^{n} \lambda_j x_j, \\ &\overline{y} \leq \sum_{j=1,\neq 0}^{n} \lambda_j y_j, \\ &\overline{x} \geq x_0, \overline{y} \leq y_0, \overline{y} \geq 0, \lambda \geq 0 \end{aligned} \tag{10}$$

If the units used to measure inputs and outputs are the same for each DMU, the super-efficiency score δ^* is unaffected by these differences. The main benefit of this method is that all DMUs can be fully ranked. The efficiency of different models of FRP-to-concrete bond capacity can be evaluated using the aforementioned method. In addition, this method is advantageous when the analyst wishes to rank and select models according to multiple criteria.

2.4 Evaluation of Available FRP-Concrete Bond Strength Models

In this section, a variety of selection criteria are used to choose the best FRP-concrete bond strength models based on experimental data. Typically, a classic residual analysis is used to assess the predictive power of existing FRP-concrete bond strength models. The extensive experimental dataset compiled from the scientific literature is used in this study to calculate model scores by the LLH, EDR, and BF methods. Each method ranks models differently as a result of the different underlying principles on which the scoring systems are based. The DEA is then employed to reach a conclusion regarding model performance based on the results of the variance reduction, the LLH, the EDR, and the BF methods. The final decision therefore takes into account the logic of all methods. The BF method necessitates a prior assumption about the performance of the model that is not supported by data. Here, all models had uniform prior or equal weights. This is a non-informative prior, strictly speaking. Non-uniform weights may be used as an informative prior if the expertise of the experts reveals a preference for specific models. The likelihood function and the BF score are directly proportional when the weights are equal. It was discovered that the BF score produced significantly higher numbers during the DEA process than the EDR and LLH scores. In order to normalize the input data, the negative logarithm of the likelihood function was used rather than the BF score.

An easy way to assess model precision is to visually compare model predictions to experimental data. The residual scatter and distribution are displayed in Fig. 1. Ideal lognormal residuals have a mean of 1. An accurate model of the bond strength between FRP and concrete has a lower bound standard deviation of residuals of 0.25, indicating model uncertainty due to input parameter variability (Yazdani et al.,

2021a). The plots demonstrate that M1, M11, M22, M23, and M24 do not accurately predict the first 50 data points. At 70, 100, and 135 data points, some models reach their peaks. The mean and standard deviation of the residual distribution, which are displayed on the right side of each plot, will change as a result of these departures from the center. A mean close to 1.0 and a standard deviation (s) close to 0.25 indicate a model's dataset prediction is reliable. Table 1 suggests M_{20}, M_{28}, and M_{31} are good models. M_3, M_6, and M_{13} fail to predict the experimental dataset. Model bias has an impact on how well a model predicts. Model bias is the difference between the experimental data and the model estimation. Model bias is depicted in Fig. 2 as a departure from the bisector line of the plot between model predictions and experimental data. Models M3 and M6 have a significant model bias and are far from the bisector line, as shown in Fig. 2. Low biases exist in M22, M28, and M31, and a fitted line is located close to one.

A tool that compiles all the data into a single score is preferable to visualizing the residuals for data prediction analysis. Results will be complicated by data and models. As a result, current ranking techniques use residuals to order models based on the prediction of experimental data. Models can be ranked by experimental dataset prediction using the LLH, EDR, BF, and variance reduction. They all employ residual analysis to score models and rank them by performance. However, because each method assesses model performance using a different logic, it is best to reach a decision that takes into account the logic of all methods. Model bias is the κ factor in EDR. In order to quantify model performance, ranking methods can be used as DEA inputs or outputs. In the DEA's multi-criteria decision-making process, the four methods are ranked in order of importance. Models of FRP-to-concrete bond strength are ranked using the logic of all four approaches. The experimental dataset DEA rankings are displayed in Table 2.

Score variability must be taken into account in the final decision. When using a ranking method, each model is given a score based on data that is insufficient to fully describe a physical process. We can now understand the phenomenon better thanks to new experiments and their new data. The model's score will change as a result of the same method. Scores are random. To determine if the models are distinct, consider score variability. It is impractical to wait for new experiments to evaluate model performance variability because thorough and well-planned experiments are expensive and uncommon. Resampling should therefore be used to study the variability of random variables (Shahidzadeh et al., 2020). Score variability is considered using cluster bootstrap. To maintain the data hierarchy, the cluster bootstrap chooses an experiment and uses data from the sampled event. The original dataset and the sampled number of experiments are identical. Cluster data are permuted using randomized cluster bootstraps (Field & Welsh, 2007). The four ranking methods were used to calculate model scores 100 times from 100 samples from the collected dataset. Each score set was used in the DEA model rankings. Model rankings are shown in Fig. 3. Figure 3 demonstrates that score variability gives each model a range rather than a rank. High-overlapping ranks may predict experimental data similarly.

The shear stress-slip behavior was a key consideration in the development of the M20 model. In the M20 model, the width ratio factor was also changed. The

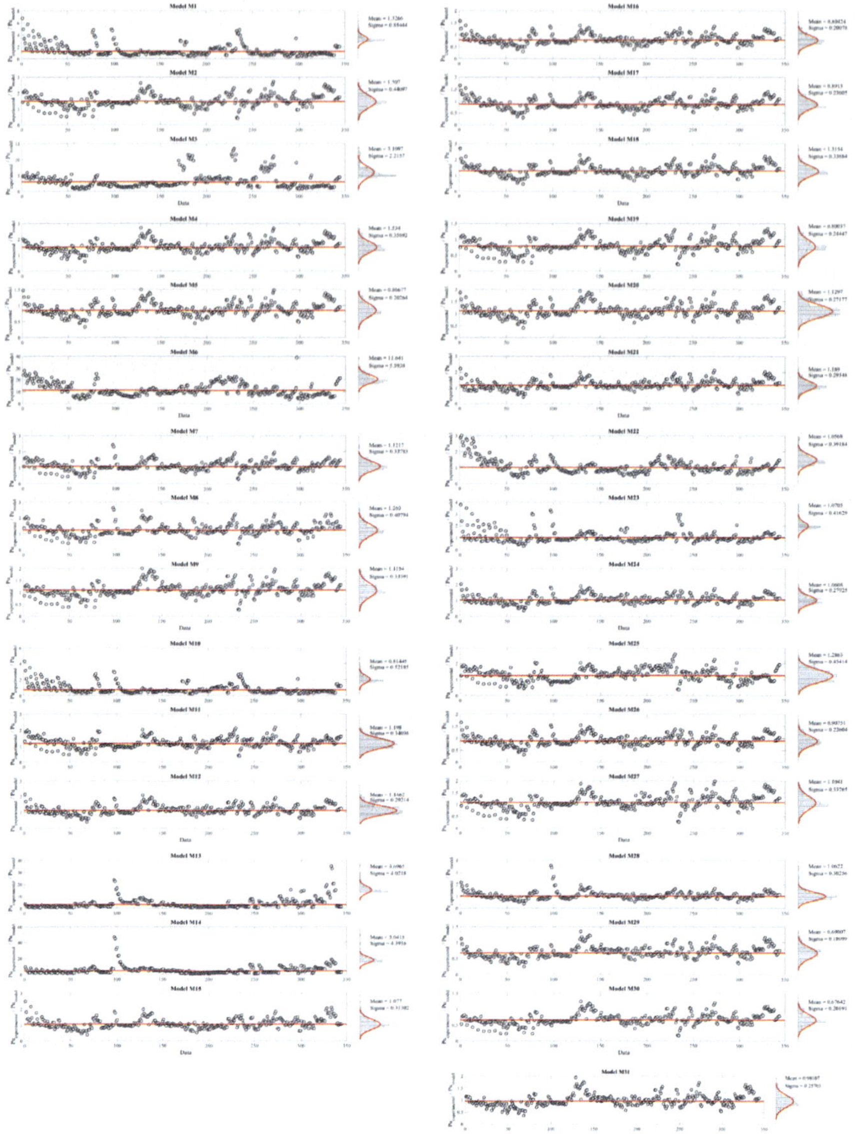

Fig. 1 Distribution of model residuals with respect to each FRP-to-concrete bond strength model

effective bond length expression of the M31 model is very different from other models. This model extracted, calibrated, and estimated precise values for effective bond length from a large database. As a result, the bond capacity is predicted with greater accuracy. In contrast to the other models, the M28 is unique. In addition, only the M28 model incorporates the two different FRP bond types—pre-cured and wet lay-up FRP—to estimate fracture energy. The effective bond length expression

Table 1 Statistical properties of residuals for highly and poorly performing models

Performance quality	Model	Mean	Standard deviation (σ)
High	M_{20}	1.013	0.27
	M_{28}	1.06	0.31
	M_{31}	0.98	0.26
Poor	M_3	2.11	2.32
	M_6	11.64	5.6
	M_{13}	3.7	4.02

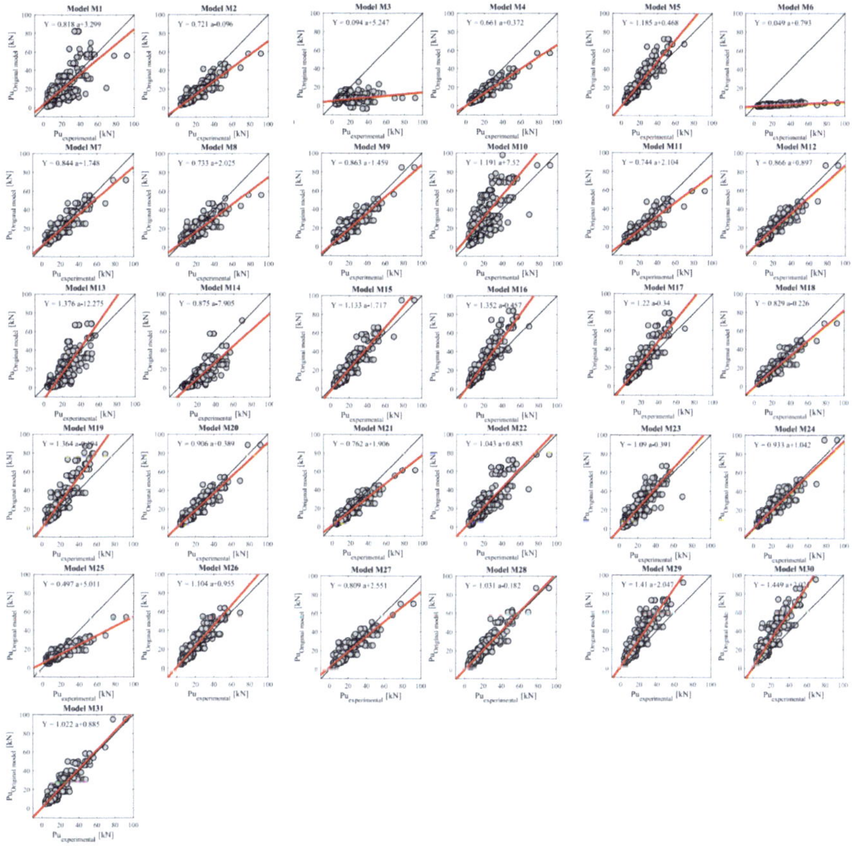

Fig. 2 Scatter plots of experimental data versus their model estimations

Table 2 Ranking of different bond strength models

ID of model	Model	Rank
M_1	Van Gemert (1980)	27
M_2	Holzenkampfer (1994)	18
M_3	Tanaka (1996)	29
M_4	Niedermeier (1996)	17
M_5	Neubauer and Rostasy (1997)	10
M_6	Hiroyuki and Wu (1997)	31
M_7	Maeda et al. (1997)	15
M_8	Khalifa et al. (1998)	13
M_9	Yuan et al. (2001)	11
M_{10}	Adhikary and Mutsuyoshi (2001)	30
M_{11}	Yang et al. (2001)	9
M_{12}	Chen and Teng (2001)	6
M_{13}	Sato (2003)	28
M_{14}	Izumo (2003)	25
M_{15}	Iso (2003)	8
M_{16}	Monti et al. (2003)	19
M_{17}	Kanakubo et al. (2003)	16
M_{18}	Ulaga et al. (2003)	12
M_{19}	Dai et al. (2005)	23
M_{20}	Lu et al. (2005)	2
M_{21}	Seracino et al. (2007)	7
M_{22}	Camli and Binici (2007)	20
M_{23}	Wu et al. (2009)	21
M_{24}	Zhou (2009)	5
M_{25}	Wu et al. (2010)	22
M_{26}	Wu and Jiang (2013)	14
M_{27}	Serbescu et al. (2013)	1
M_{28}	CNR-DT 200 R1 (2013)	4
M_{29}	Li et al. (2015)	24
M_{30}	Yuan et al. (2019a)	26
M_{31}	*fib* Bulletin 90 (2019)	3

is specific to the M31 model. The effective bond length in this model is determined by the width ratio factor.

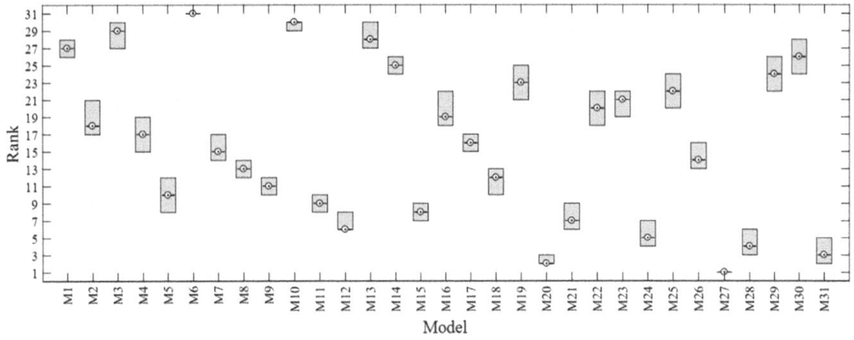

Fig. 3 Ranking of FRP-concrete bond strength models considering score variability

3 Selection and Ranking of Ground Motion Prediction Equations

Earthquakes damage buildings and kill people. Thus, pre-earthquake seismic demand prediction is essential. The most popular technique for assessing seismic hazards is called probabilistic seismic-hazard analysis (PSHA) (Cornell, 1968). The PSHA helps verify, design, and assess engineering structures and lifelines. Seismic wave propagation and interference can be simulated using a variety of simulation models that are based on the physics of earthquake ground motion (Boore, 2003). Parameter uncertainty makes such models unsuitable for PSHA. Additionally, several input variables that cannot have known values are required for physically based models. These models need in-depth knowledge of the wave path and the source of the upcoming earthquake. PSHA cannot use such models. This problem is addressed by statistically based simplified ground motion prediction equations (GMPEs) (Douglas, 2018). These equations explain the relationship between seismic parameters such as earthquake magnitude, distance from the epicenter, site effects, peak ground acceleration (PGA), and 5% damped pseudo absolute response spectral acceleration.

It is practical to model uncertainties as aleatory or epistemic. Aleatory uncertainty comes from natural variability, like empirical model scatter, while epistemic uncertainty comes from ignorance. Due to the PSHA procedure's integration over the distribution of ground motion amplitudes around the median (Bommer et al., 2005), the results exhibit aleatory uncertainties. GMPE epistemic uncertainties strongly influence PSHA results (Yazdani et al., 2016). GMPEs reflect a wide range of functional forms and dataset selections. Thus, GMPE selection is PSHA's biggest epistemic uncertainty. Since the exact GMPE is unknown, a logic tree framework is used to take into account a number of GMPEs with weights (Atkinson et al., 2014). The selected GMPEs and their weights are usually chosen subjectively by experts. Researchers have proposed statistical objective criteria for selecting and weighting GMPEs. Data-driven PSHA criteria aim to reduce subjectivity. To evaluate GMPE reliability, Scherbaum et al. (2004) proposed a straightforward likelihood-based (LH) goodness-of-fit measure. To enhance the LH method, Scherbaum et al. (2009) created the information theoretic log-likelihood (LLH) criteria. Euclidean distance ranking (EDR), which was proposed by Kale and Akkar (2013), attempts to explain the trend between observed and estimated data.

Even though the LLH and EDR are currently the most popular data-driven criteria, under certain conditions they might yield very different results. However, these criteria may result in different ranking orders when analyzing various target ground motion intensity measures. This study presents a reliable DEA-based method for scoring the GMPEs to address these complexities. DEA is a nonparametric operation research procedure that takes into account the use of analytical techniques to produce better decisions. Group DMUs can be divided into efficient and inefficient sets using DEA, and the efficient DMUs can then be sorted according to their efficiency scores. In this study, the DEA method is used to assess various GMPEs of horizontal response spectra in the seismotectonic province of Central Iran. The appropriate GMPEs are selected in accordance with their DEA efficiency scores. Additionally, the relevant GMPEs are ranked and weighted using the efficiency scores.

3.1 Statistical Criteria Applied to Rank GMPEs

To more accurately predict seismic hazards worldwide, a variety of GMPEs have been developed over the past few decades (Douglas, 2018). The best prediction models are selected in practical applications for evaluating seismic risk in a specific area. In general, given a set of recorded ground motion data, goodness-of-fit measures can be used to assess the candidate GMPE's predictive efficacy. The goodness-of-fit metrics set the appropriate models apart from the rest. Choosing a weighting procedure comes next after choosing the appropriate GMPEs. It is standard procedure in this regard to subjectively assign weight to each chosen GMPE based on the judgment of experts. In order to lessen subjectivity in PSHA, earlier studies (Roselli et al., 2016) developed objective procedures based on goodness-of-fit measures. In LLH and EDR, the suitability of a GMPE is assessed by using residuals to examine the discrepancy between observed and predicted data.

The data-driven model-selection techniques aim to quantitatively assess the candidate GMPEs given a set of ground motion data collected in a specific area. The general form that GMPEs follow is:

$$z = f(\boldsymbol{m}, \boldsymbol{\beta}) + \varepsilon\sigma \tag{11}$$

where $\boldsymbol{m}$ is a vector of independent variables, including the magnitude and distance of the earthquake, and z denotes the logarithmic ground motion intensity measure, in this case, pseudo-spectral acceleration at period T. $\boldsymbol{\beta}$ denotes the parameters of the GMPE. $f(\boldsymbol{m}, \boldsymbol{\beta})$ is deterministic term. The terms σ and ε stand for the data's standard deviation and the Gaussian error term, which is symbolized by zero mean and unit standard deviation, respectively. A truncated Gaussian probability distribution can therefore be used to describe each predicted value of z.

$$g(z) = \frac{1}{\sigma\sqrt{2\pi}} e^{-\frac{(z-f)^2}{2\sigma^2}};\ (z \leq z_0) \tag{12}$$

where z_0 is the truncation point. An assortment of ground motion observations $z_i = z_1, z_2, \ldots, z_N$ are given. Therefore, GMPEs for PSHA are scored using several criteria. Thus, it seeks multiple scoring criteria for GMPE selection. In this study, GMPEs are scored and ranked using multiple criteria.

3.2 Data Envelopment Analysis-CCR

A mathematical programming technique called DEA can be used to assess the effectiveness of a collection of DMUs (Charnes et al., 2013). DEA is a statistical regression technique that focuses on frontier rather than central tendencies (Cooper et al., 2007). Therefore, the DEA is particularly adept at uncovering relationships that are not revealed by other methods. Efficiency is achieved in DEA without the requirement of explicitly stated assumptions and variation with regression models (Charnes et al., 2013; Cooper et al., 2011).

Let an evaluation of n DMUs take place. Several units each use m inputs to generate s outputs. In this case, DMU_j provides the quantity y_{rj} of output r while taking into account the quantity x_{ij} of input i. Relative efficiency is defined as the ratio of total weighted output to total weighted input to assess the level of efficiency of a DMU (Charnes et al. 1978), named CCR ratio model. The efficiency measure for $DMU_j = DMU_o$ is defined as follows:

$$\begin{aligned} &\max\ h_o(u, v) = \frac{\sum_{r=1}^{s} u_r y_{ro}}{\sum_{i=1}^{m} v_i x_{io}} \\ &\text{subject to} \\ &\frac{\sum_{r=1}^{s} u_r y_{rj}}{\sum_{i=1}^{m} v_i x_{ij}} \leq 1\, for\, j = 1, \ldots, n \\ &u_r, v_i \geq 0 \text{ for all } i \text{ and } r \end{aligned} \tag{13}$$

where the weight vector for the input and output, respectively, are represented by the non-negative values u_r and v_i. For each DMU, Eq. (13) is equivalent to n linear programs. A scalar measure with a value between zero and one can be used to calculate the efficiency (θ^*) of an LP model through a dual theorem, and the weights assigned to each linear aggregation are the results of the corresponding LP model (Cooper et al., 2007),

$$\theta^* = \min\theta$$

subject to

$$\sum_{j=1}^{n} x_{ij}\lambda_j \leq \theta x_{io} i = 1,2,\ldots,m$$

$$\sum_{j=1}^{n} y_{rj}\lambda_j \geq y_{ro} r = 1,2,\ldots,s$$

$$\lambda_j \geq 0 j = 1,2,\ldots,n \tag{14}$$

Equation (14), θ^*, has a solution that yields an efficiency score for a particular DMU. A real variable θ and a vector $\boldsymbol{\lambda}$ of non-negative variables are used to express the dual problem of the LP. If the DMU_j's efficiency ratio score is lower than 1, it is considered inefficient. Equation (14) gives all efficient DMUs the same value, super-efficiency scores allow for different ranking of efficient units (Anderson et al., 2002). Major DMUs with high efficiency can obtain a score greater than one using this procedure. This model's vector form is as follows:

$$\theta_S^* = \min\theta - \varepsilon e s^+$$

subject to

$$\theta x_{i0} = \sum_{j=1,\neq 0}^{n} \lambda_j x_{ij} + s_i^-$$

$$y_{r0} = \sum_{j=1,\neq 0}^{n} \lambda_j y_{rj} - s_r^+ \tag{15}$$

where ε is positive and all s^- and s^+ components are non-negative. $\boldsymbol{e}$ is a row unit vector as well. The s^- and s^+ variables are slack variables that are used to create equivalent equations from the inequalities in Eq. (14). All DMUs can be completely ranked using this approach. With this method, inaccurate weight results might be avoided (Anderson et al., 2002). The efficiency of different GMPEs can be assessed using this methodology in order to determine which ones are best for PSHA. In addition, GMPEs can be ranked and weighted using the findings of DEA analysis. The DEA method can also be used when there are multiple target intensity measures that need to be taken into account as different criteria during the ranking process, such as S_a at various structural periods.

3.3 Dataset and Candidate GMPEs; Use of DEA in Ranking GMPEs

To show how well the DEA procedure can find efficient GMPEs, it is used in a seismotectonic region in Iran. Iran is prone to devastating earthquakes that kill many and damage much (Yazdani & Kowsari, 2013). Arabia and Eurasia compress the Central Iran seismotectonic province. The last century saw many devastating earthquakes in Central Iran. Selecting the best GMPEs and determining their logic tree weights improves PSHA results. This study evaluates LLH, EDR, and residuals at different structural periods. Equation (14) estimates GMPE using efficiency score. Equation (15) estimates efficient GMPE weights in this seismotectonic province. Eftekhari et al. (2020) have provided extensive detail about the utilized data and candidate GMPEs. Candidate GMPEs are listed in Table 3 along with the dominant area, magnitude, distance, and period ranges.

3.4 Results and Discussions

This section lists and ranks the best GMPEs for the Central Iran area based on a variety of criteria. The main goal is to show how the DEA application works with real data. The findings may reveal GMPEs' seismic hazard assessment performance.

GMPEs are determined by spectral accelerations with periods of 0.1, 0.2, 0.3, 0.5, 0.7, 1, 1.5, and 2 s. For each of the considered periods, LLH and EDR values were determined using Eqs. (2) and (3). GMPE models for rock sites are ranked in Fig. 4 according to LLH and EDR values during the considered periods. Figure 4 shows different ranking orders at different structural periods. It's possible that the ranking for EDR and LLH will differ greatly. These findings suggest that selecting regional ground motion GMPEs is difficult. Thus, GMPE selection requires a processor that considers multiple criteria.

DEA can rank candidate GMPEs using multi-criteria efficiency evaluation. This procedure uses period-specific LLH and EDR values. Since ground motion model data can be skewed by observed data, as was already mentioned, LLH metric ranking analysis may yield erroneous results. DEA uses residual values to eliminate this error. Table 4 show DEA-based ranking results. The DEA efficiency and super-efficiency results from Eqs. (14) and (15) are displayed in this table for each DMU. Getal09a, Setal12, Aetal14, Ketal16, Zetal18, and SP17 are six rock site GMPEs with efficiency scores of one. 15 additional models are inefficient GMPEs with relative efficiency scores under one. Getal09a, the simplest candidate GMPE, performs well in the DEA ranking process. It demonstrated that a complex model with more parameters is not always preferable.

Even though efficient GMPEs have unity efficiency scores, super-efficiency scores can still rank them. The observations and predictions match better when θ^*_s is larger. Table 4 shows θ^*_s values for different DMUs. The best model at rock sites in the

Table 3 Candidate ground motion prediction equations

GMPE	Acronym	Dominant region	Magnitude range	Distance metric*	Period range (sec)
Akkar and Bommer (2010) [37]	AB10	Europe and Middle East	5.0–7.6	R_{jb}	0.0–3.0
Akkar et al. (2014) [38], [39]	Aetal14	Europe and Middle East	4.0–7.6	R_{jb}, R_{epi}	0.0–4.0
Ambraseys et al. (1996) [40]	Aetal96	Europe and Middle East	4.0–7.9	R_{jb}, R_{epi}	0.1–2.0
Ambraseys et al. (2005) [41]	Aetal05	Europe and Middle East	5.0–7.6	R_{jb}, R_{epi}	0.0–2.5
Ameri et al. (2017) [42]	Aetal17	Europe and Middle East	3.0–7.6	R_{jb}, R_{epi}	0.0–3.0
Bindi et al. (2014) [43], [44]	Betal14	Europe and Middle East	4.0–7.6	R_{jb}	0.0–3.0
Bommer et al. (2003) [45]	Betal03	Europe and Middle East	4.0–7.9	R_{jb}, R_{epi}	0.0–2.0
Farajpour et al. (2019) [46]	Fetal19	Iran	4.8–7.5	R_{rup}	0.0–4.0
Ghasemi et al. (2009) [47]	Getal09a	Iran- West Eurasia	5.0–7.4	R_{rup}, R_{hyp}	0.05–3
GhodratiAmiri et al. (2009) [48]	Getal09b	Iran	4.0–7.7	R_{hyp}	0.1–4.0
Hamzehloo and Mahood (2012) [49]	HM12	Central Iran	4.9–7.4	R_{jb}	0.0–5.0
Kale et al. (2015) [50]	Ketal15	Turkey & Iran	4.0–7.6	R_{jb}	0.0–4.0
Kotha et al. (2016) [51], [52]	Ketal16	Europe and Middle East	4.0–7.6	R_{jb}, R_{epi}	0.0–4.0
Kuehn and Scherbaum (2015) [53]	KS15	Europe and Middle East	4.0–7.6	R_{jb}	0.0–4.0
Saffari et al. (2012) [54]	Setal12	Iran	5.0–7.4	R_{rup}, R_{hyp}	0.0–5.0
Sedaghati and Pezashk (2017) [55]	SP17	Iran	4.7–7.4	R_{jb}	0.0–4.0
Segou and Voulgaris (2013) [56]	SV13	Europe and Middle East	4.1–6.6	R_{epi}	0.0–2.0
Shahidzadeh and Yazdani (2017) [57]	SY17	Iran	5.0–7.4	R_{jb}, R_{epi}	0.0–2.5

(continued)

Table 3 (continued)

GMPE	Acronym	Dominant region	Magnitude range	Distance metric*	Period range (sec)
Shoushtari et al. (2016) [58]	Setal16	Malaysia, Japan, Iran	5.0–7.7	R_{hyp}	0.0–5.0
Sigbjornsson and Elnashai (2006) [59]	SE06	Europe and Middle East	4.0–7.9	R_{jb}, R_{epi}	0.0–4.0
Zafarani et al. (2018) [60]	Zetal18	Iran	4.0–7.3	R_{jb}, R_{epi}	0.0–4.0

* R_{jb}, Joyner-Boore distance; R_{epi}, epicentral distance; R_{rup}, closest distance to fault plane; R_{hyp}, hypocentral distance

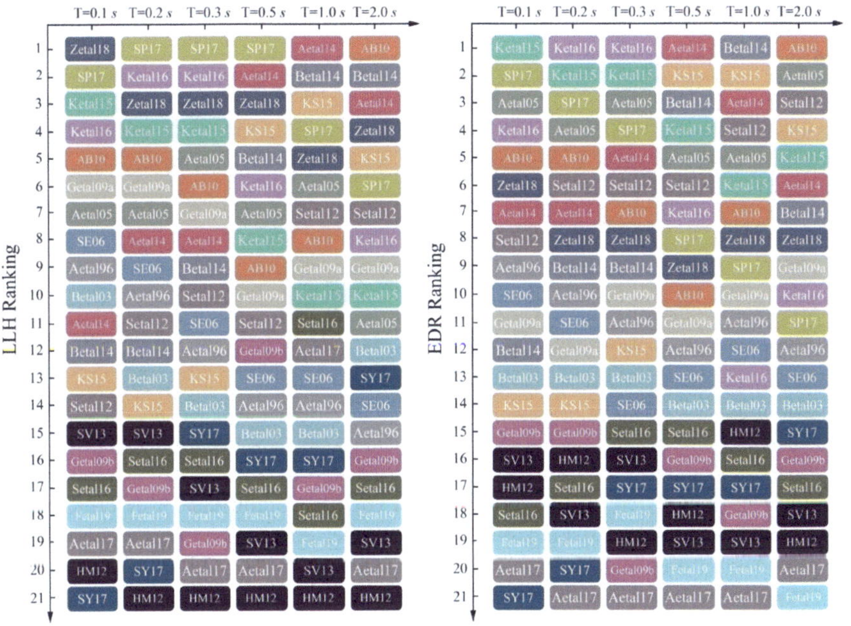

Fig. 4 Ranking of GMPEs based on LLH and EDR methods for rock sites at the Central Iran seismotectonic region

study region, according to the super-efficiency scores, is SP17, which is followed by Aetal14, Getal09a, Ketal16, Setal12, and Zetal18. The most accurate models for estimating ground motion spectral amplitudes at soil sites are Setal12, AB10, Ketal16, and Getal09a. The findings demonstrate that the site class affects how effective GMPE is.

Expert judgment is PSHA's main weighting method. To lessen subjectivity, the PSHA weight of suitable GMPEs can be estimated using the super-efficiency score,

Table 4 DEA analysis for Central Iran seismotectonic region

GMPE	Rock		Soil	
	θ^*	θ^*_s	θ^*	θ^*_s
AB10	0.68	–	1.00	1.19
Aetal14	1.00	0.57	0.28	–
Aetal96	0.18	–	0.32	–
Aetal05	0.33	–	0.33	–
Aetal17	0.04	–	0.04	–
Betal14	0.90	–	0.45	–
Betal03	0.14	–	0.22	–
Fetal19	0.79	–	0.16	–
Getal09a	1.00	0.89	1.00	0.71
Getal09b	0.81	–	0.50	–
HM12	0.21	–	0.54	–
Ketal15	0.96	–	0.98	–
Ketal16	1.00	0.36	1.00	0.66
KS15	0.43	–	0.29	–
Setal12	1.00	0.51	1.00	1.37
SP17	1.00	1.10	0.83	–
SV13	0.11	–	0.16	–
SY17	0.12	–	0.23	–
Setal16	0.44	–	0.76	–
SE06	0.19	–	0.32	–
Zetal18	1.00	0.42	0.82	–

θ^*_s, that was calculated for efficient GMPEs. GMPE weights can be determined by the scores estimated by Eq. (15). Normalizing super-efficiency scores yields GMPE weights. Models that match observed data are weighted higher. Table 5 shows Central Iran block DEA-based estimated weights. Expert opinion and these objective weights can determine GMPE weights.

4 Conclusions

In this study, the predictive accuracy of FRP-to-concrete bond capacity models was ranked. 31 models of the FRP-to-concrete bond capacity were selected. A non-model extraction database ranked these models.

Variance reduction, Euclidean distance, log-likelihood, and Bayesian factor were used to score and rank the models. Using multi-criteria decision-making, the DEA finalized the rankings. The top ten models included FRP strengthening provision

Table 5 Estimated weights based on DEA analysis

GMPE	Rock	Soil
AB10	–	0.30
Aetal14	0.15	–
Getal09a	0.23	0.18
Ketal16	0.09	0.17
Setal12	0.13	0.35
SP17	0.29	–
Zetal18	0.11	–

models. Fracture mechanics-derived models rank 1st to 10th in the ranking table. Stress analysis models ranked 11–20th. Most empirical models were 21–31. The number of model extraction tests affected their ranks. Coefficient calibration required at least 253 test specimens for models ranked 1–4. The models in the 23rd through 30th positions, however, used a maximum of 60 test specimens. Model parameters significantly affected model ranking. The compressive or tensile strength of concrete is included in all models from 1 to 14. The 1st–26th models have FRP stiffness. The first seven models have a stiffness power of 0.50. Models of bond capacity that take into account effective bond length values directly perform better than those that use a reduction factor.

This study presents a number of problems and restrictions with the current statistical frameworks used to choose the appropriate GMPEs in PSHA. In particular, it is demonstrated that traditional ranking techniques cannot specify results set that contains all scenarios when multiple target ground motion parameters are desired to be taken into account in the selection and ranking procedure. As a result, we offer a reliable method for choosing and ranking GMPEs that is based on DEA. This procedure takes multiple criteria for fit into account. In addition, this process is flexible enough to take into account multiple target ground motion parameters in the ranking analysis. The efficiency or inefficiency of each GMPE can be assessed using the DEA technique. The weight of GMPEs in PSHA can also be estimated using this method. The final ranking of 21 candidate GMPEs is determined using the DEA procedure. The values of LLH, EDR, and residuals at different structural periods are taken into consideration as ranking criteria. Finally, based on the DEA efficiency scores, the efficient GMPEs for each scenario are identified. Additionally, the efficient GMPEs are ranked and given weight based on the DEA super-efficiency scores. This study shows how well the method works in identifying the appropriate GMPEs for PSHA. The epistemic uncertainty connected to the choice of GMPEs can be lessened by using this strategy.

References

ACI (American Concrete Institute). (2017). Guide for the design and construction of externally bonded FRP systems for strengthening concrete structures. ACI 440.2R-17. Farmington Hills, MI: ACI.

Adhikary, B. B., Mutsuyoshi, H. (2001). Study on the bond between concrete and externally bonded CFRP sheet. In FRPRCS-5: *Fibre-reinforced plastics for reinforced concrete structures Volume 1: Proceedings of the fifth international conference on fibre-reinforced plastics for reinforced concrete structures*, pp. 371–378. Cambridge, UK: Thomas Telford Publishing.

Adler, N., Friedman, L., & Sinuany-Stern, Z. (2002). Review of ranking methods in the data envelopment analysis context. *Eur. J. Operat. Resear., 140*(2), 249–265.

Aldamak, A., & Zolfaghari, S. (2017). Review of efficiency ranking methods in data envelopment analysis. *Measur., 106*, 161–172.

Anderson, T. R., Hollingsworth, K., & Inman, L. (2002). The fixed weighting nature of a cross-evaluation model. *Journal of Productivity Analysis., 17*(3), 249–255.

Atkinson, G. M., Bommer, J. J., & Abrahamson, N. A. (2014). Alternative approaches to modeling epistemic uncertainty in ground motions in probabilistic seismic-hazard analysis. *Seismological Research Letters., 85*, 1141–1144.

Bommer, J. J., Scherbaum, F., Bungum, H., Cotton, F., Sabetta, F., & Abrahamson, N. A. (2005). On the use of logic trees for ground-motion prediction equations in seismic-hazard analysis. *Bulletin of the Seismological Society of America., 95*(2), 377–389.

Boore, D. M. (2003). Simulation of ground motion using the stochastic method. *Pure and Applied Geophysics 160*(3–4), 635–676.

Camli, U. S., & Binici, B. (2007). Strength of carbon fiber reinforced polymers bonded to concrete and masonry. *Construction and Building Materials, 21*(7), 1431–1446.

Carloni, C., & Focacci, F. (2016). FRP-masonry interfacial debonding: An energy balance approach to determine the influence of the mortar joints. *Eur. J. Mechanics-A/Solids, 55*, 122–133.

Carloni, C., D'Antino, T., Sneed, L. H., & Pellegrino, C. (2015). Role of the matrix layers in the stress-transfer mechanism of FRCM composites bonded to a concrete substrate. *Journal of Engineering Mechanics, 141*(6), 04014165.

Charnes, A., Cooper, W. W., & Rhodes, E. (1978). Measuring the efficiencies of DMUs. *European Journal of Operational Research., 2*, 429–444.

Charnes, A., Cooper, W. W., Lewin, A. Y., & Seiford, L. M. (Eds.). (2013). *Data envelopment analysis: Theory, methodology, and applications*. Springer Science & Business Media.

Chen, J. F., & Teng, J. G. (2001). Anchorage strength models for FRP and steel plates bonded to concrete. *Journal of the Structural Engineering. American Society of Civil Engineers, 127*(7), 784–791. https://doi.org/10.1061/(ASCE)0733-9445(2001)127:7(784)

CNR (Italian National Research Council). (2013). Guide for the design and construction of externally bonded FRP systems for strengthening existing structures. *CNR-DT 200 R1/2013*, Rome.

Cooper, W. W., Seiford, L. M., & Zhu, J. (2011). *Handbook on data envelopment analysis (Vol. 164)*. Springer Science & Business Media.

Cooper, W. W., Seiford, L. M., Tone, K. (2007) Data envelopment analysis–A Comprehensive Text with Models, Applications, References and DEA –Solver Software. *Kluwer Academic Publishers, Second edition.*

Cornell, C. A. (1968). Engineering seismic risk analysis. *Bullet. Seismolog. Society Am., 58*(5), 1583–1606.

Dai, J., Ueda, T., & Sato, Y. (2005). Development of the nonlinear bond stress–slip model of fiber reinforced plastics sheet–concrete interfaces with a simple method. *Journal of Composites for Construction, 9*(1), 52–62. https://doi.org/10.1061/(ASCE)1090-0268(2005)9:1(52)

Douglas, J. (2018). Ground motion prediction equations 1964–2018. Department of Civil and Environmental Engineering, University of Strathclyde, pp. 624.

Ebrahimzadeh Shermeh, H., Alavidoost, M. H., & Darvishinia, R. (2018). Evaluating the efficiency of power companies using data envelopment analysis based on SBM models: A case study in power industry of Iran. *Journal of Applied Research on Industrial Engineering, 5*(4), 286–295.

Eftekhari, N., Yazdani, A., Razmyan, S., & Shamohammadi, A. (2020). Data envelopment analysis based procedure for selection and ranking of ground motion prediction equations. *Soil Dynamics and Earthquake Engineering, 137*, 106303. https://doi.org/10.1016/j.soildyn.2020.106303

fib (International Federation for Structural Concrete). 2019. *Externally applied FRP reinforcement for concrete structures.* fib Bulletin 90. Lausanne, Switzerland: fib.

Field, C. A., & Welsh, A.H. (2007). Bootstrapping clustered data. *J. Roy. Statist. Soci.: Series B (Statistical Methodology), 69*(3), 369–390.

HB (NSW: Standards Australia). (2008). "*Design handbook for RC structures retrofitted with FRP and metal plates: beams and slabs.*" HB 305, Sydney.

Hiroyuki, Y. (1997). "Analysis of debonding fracture properties of CFS strengthened RC member subject to tension." In *Non-Metallic (FRP) Reinforcement for Concrete Structures, Proc. 3rd Intern. Symp,* pp. 287–294. The Japan Concrete Institute.

Izumo, K., Saeki, N., Fukao, M., & Horiguchi, T. (2000). Bond behavior and strength between fiber sheets and concrete. *Trans. Japan Concr. Instit., 21*, 423–430.

Kale, Ö., & Akkar, S. (2013). A new procedure for selecting and ranking ground-motion prediction equations (GMPEs): The Euclidean distance-based ranking (EDR) method. *Bulletin of the Seismological Society of America, 103*(2A), 1069–1084.

Kanakubo, T., Furuta, T, Fukuyama, H. (2003). Bond strength between fiber-reinforced polymer laminates and concrete. Proc 6th Int Symp on Fibre-Reinforced Polymer Reinforcement for Concrete Structures, pp. 133–142. Singapore: World Scientific Publications.

Khalifa, A., Gold, W. J., Nanni, A., Mi, A. A. (1998). Contribution of externally bonded FRP to shear capacity of RC flexural members. *J. Compos. Constr., 2*(4), 195-202. https://doi.org/10.1061/(ASCE)1090-0268(1998)2:4(195).

Kotynia, R., Abdel Baky, H., Neale, K. W., & Ebead, U. A. (2008). Flexural strengthening of RC beams with externally bonded CFRP systems: Test results and 3D nonlinear FE analysis. *Journal of Composites for Construction, 12*(2), 190–201. https://doi.org/10.1061/(ASCE)1090-0268(2008)12:2(190)

Li, W., Li, J., Ren, X., Leung, C. K., & Xing, F. (2015). Coupling effect of concrete strength and bonding length on bond behaviors of fiber reinforced polymer–concrete interface. *Journal of Reinforced Plastics and Composites, 34*(5), 421–432.

Lu, X. Z., Teng, J. G., Ye, L. P., & Jiang, J. J. (2005). Bond–slip models for FRP sheets/plates bonded to concrete. *Engineering Structures, 27*(6), 920–937.

Maeda T., Asano, Y., Sato, Y., Ueda, T., & Kakuta, Y. (1997). A study on bond mechanism of carbon fiber sheet. *Proc 3rd Int Symp on Non-Metallic (FRP) Reinforcement for Concr Struct* 1:279–285.

Maghbouli, M., & Yekta, A. P. (2023). Undesirable input in production process: A DEA-based approach. *J. Oper. Strateg Anal, 1*(2), 46–54.

Monti, G., Renzelli, M., Luciani, P. (2003). FRP adhesion in uncracked and cracked concrete zones. *Proc 6th Int Symp on Fibre-Reinforced Polymer Reinforcement for Concrete Structures*, pp. 183–192. Singapore: World Scientific Publications.

Muniz, R. D. F., Andriola, W. B., Muniz, S. M., & Thomaz, A. C. F. (2022). The use of data envelopment analysis to estimate the educational efficiency of Brazilian schools. Journal of applied research on industrial engineering, pp. 374–383.

Neubauer, U., & Rostasy, F. S. (1997). Design aspects of concrete structures strengthened with externally bonded CFRP-plates. In *Proc., 7th Int. Conf. on Structural Faults and Repair,* pp. 109–118. Edinburgh, Scotland: ECS Publications.

Niedermeier, R. (1996). Stellungnahme zur richtlinie für das verkleben von betonbau- teilen durch ankleben von stahllaschen-entwurf märz 1996. Schreiben Nr. 1390 vom 30.10.1996 des Lehrstuhls für Massivbau, TU München.

Pellegrino, C., Tinazzi, D., & Modena, C. (2008). Experimental study on bond behavior between concrete and FRP reinforcement. *Journal of Composites for Construction, 12*(2), 180–189. https://doi.org/10.1061/(ASCE)1090-0268(2008)12:2(180)

Pham, H., & Al-Mahaidi, R. (2004). Experimental investigation into flexural retrofitting of reinforced concrete bridge beams using FRP composites. *Composite Structures, 66*, 617–625.

Rasoulzadeh, M., Edalatpanah, S. A., Fallah, M., & Najafi, S. E. (2022). A multi-objective approach based on Markowitz and DEA cross-efficiency models for the intuitionistic fuzzy portfolio selection problem. *Decision Making: Applications in Management and Engineering, 5*(2), 241–259.

Roselli, P., Marzocchi, W., & Faenza, L. (2016). Toward a new probabilistic framework to score and merge ground-motion prediction equations: The case of the Italian region. *Bulletin of the Seismological Society of America., 106*(2), 720–733.

Sato, Y., Asano, Y., & Ueda, T. (2000). Fundamental study on bond mechanism of carbon fiber sheet. *J. Mater., Concr. Struct. Pavem., JSCE, 47* (648), 71–87.

Scherbaum, F, Schmedes, J., & Cotton, F. (On the conversion of source-to-site distance measures for extended earthquake source models). *Bulletin of the Seismological Society of America, 94*(3), 1053–1069.

Scherbaum, F., Delavaud, E., & Riggelsen, C. (2009). Model selection in seismic hazard analysis: An information-theoretic perspective. *Bulletin of the Seismological Society of America, 99*(6), 3234–3247.

Scherbaum, F., Cotton, F., & Smit, P. (2004). On the use of response spectral-reference data for the selection and ranking of ground-motion models for seismic-hazard analysis in regions of moderate seismicity: The case of rock motion. *Bulletin of the Seismological Society of America, 94*(6), 2164–2185.

Seracino, R., Raizal Saifulnaz, M. R., & Oehlers, D. J. (2007). Generic debonding resistance of EB and NSM plate-to-concrete joints. *Journal of Composites for Construction, 11*(1), 62–70. https://doi.org/10.1061/(ASCE)1090-0268(2007)11:1(62)

Serbescu, A., Guadagnini, M., & Pilakoutas, K. (2013). Standardised double-shear test for determining bond of FRP to concrete and corresponding model development. *Composites, Part B: Engineering, 55*, 277–297.

Shahidzadeh, M. S., Yazdani, A., & Eftekhari, S. N. (2020). Multivariate Bayesian hypothesis testing for ground motion model selection. *J. Seism., 24*(3), 511–529.

Sıcakyüz, C. (2023). Bibliometric analysis of data envelopment analysis in supply chain management. *Journal of Operational and Strategic Analytics, 1*(1), 14–24.

Sinha, R. P., & Edalatpanah, S. A. (2023). Efficiency and fiscal performance of Indian states: An empirical analysis using network DEA. *J. Oper. Strateg Anal, 1*(1), 1–7.

Stewart, J. P., Douglas, J., Javanbarg, M., Bozorgnia, Y., Abrahamson, N. A., Boore, D. M., Campbell, K. W., Delavaud, E., Erdik, M., & Stafford, P. J. (2015). Selection of ground motion prediction equations for the Global Earthquake Model. *Earthquake Spectra., 31*, 19–45.

Tanaka, T. (1996). Shear resisting mechanism of reinforced concrete beams with CFS as shear reinforcement. Graduation Thesis, Hokkaido University, Japan.

Tone, K. (2002). A slacks-based measure of super-efficiency in data envelopment analysis. *Eur. J. Operat. Resea., 143*(1), 32–41.

Ulaga, T., Vogel, T., & Meier, U. (2003). Bilinear stress-slip bond model: Theoretical background and significance. *Proc 6th Int Symp on Fibre-Reinforced Polymer Reinforcement for Concrete Structures*, pp. 153–162. Singapore: World Scientific Publications.

Van Gemert, D. (1980). Force transfer in epoxy-bonded steel/concrete joints. *I. J. Adhes. Adhes., 1*(2), 67–72.

Wu, Y., Zhou, Z., Yang, Q., & Chen, W. (2010). On shear bond strength of FRP-concrete structures. *Engineering Structures, 32*(3), 897–905.

Wu, Y. F., & Jiang, C. (2013). Quantification of bond-slip relationship for externally bonded FRP-to-concrete joints. *Journal of Composites for Construction, 17*(5), 673–686. https://doi.org/10.1061/(ASCE)CC.1943-5614.0000375

Wu, Z., Islam, S. M., & Said, H. (2009). A three-parameter bond strength model for FRP-concrete interface. *Journal of Reinforced Plastics and Composites, 28*(19), 2309–2323.

Yang, Y. X., Yue, Q. R., & Hu, Y. C. (2001). Experimental study on bond performance between carbon fiber sheets and concrete. *J. Build. Struct., 3*, 36–41. [in Chainese].

Yao, J., Teng, J. G., & Chen, J. F. (2005). Experimental study on FRP-to-concrete bonded joints. *Composites, Part B: Engineering, 36*(2), 99–113.

Yazdani, A., Nicknam, A., Eftekhari, S. N., & Yousefi Dadras, E. (2016). Sensitivity of near-fault PSHA results to input variables based on information theory. *Bulletin of the Seismological Society of America., 106*(4), 1858–1866.

Yazdani, A., & Kowsari, M. (2013). Earthquake ground-motion prediction equations for northern Iran. *Natural Hazards., 69*(3), 1877–1894.

Yazdani, A., Sanginabadi, K., Shahidzadeh, M. S., Salimi, M. R., & Shamohammadi, A. (2021a). Consideration of data correlation to estimate FRP-to-concrete bond capacity models. *Construction and Building Materials, 308*, 125106.

Yazdani, A., Sanginabadi, K., Shahidzadeh, M.-S., Razmyan, S., Salimi, M.-R., & MostofinejadJ, D. (2023). Evaluation of existing FRP-to-concrete bond strength models using data envelopment analysis. *Compos. Constr., 27*(3), 04023026.

Yazdani, A., Shahidzadeh, M. S., & Takada, T. (2021b). Merging data and experts' knowledge-based weights for ranking GMPEs. *Earthq. Spectr., 37*(2), 857–875.

Yazdani, A., Razmyan, S., & Baharmast Hossainabadi, H. (2015). Approximate incremental dynamic analysis using reduction of ground motion records. *Inter. J. Eng., 28*(2), 190–197.

Yuan, C., Chen, W., Pham, T. M., & Hao, H. (2019). Effect of aggregate size on bond behaviour between basalt fibre-reinforced polymer sheets and concrete. *Composites, Part B: Engineering, 158*, 459–474.

Yuan, H., Wu, Z., & Yoshizawa, H. (2001). Theoretical solutions on interfacial stress transfer of externally bonded steel/composite laminates. *Doboku Gakkai Ronbunshu, 2001*(675), 27–39.

Zhou, Y., Zheng, S., Huang, Z., Sui, L., & Chen, Y. (2020). Explicit neural network model for predicting FRP-concrete interfacial bond strength based on a large database. *Composite Structures, 240*, 111998.

A Robust Optimization Approach for Estimating the Most Productive Scale Size in Uncertain Data Envelopment Analysis

Pejman Peykani, Farhad Hamidzadeh, Mir Saman Pishvaee, Elaheh Memar-Masjed, and Armin Jabbarzadeh

Abstract Productivity measurement, ranking, performance assessment, and benchmarking of homogeneous decision-making units (DMUs), as well as estimating the most productive scale size (MPSS) and returns to scale (RTS), are among the most significant challenges faced by managers and decision-makers (DMs) in various real-world situations and problems. Data envelopment analysis (DEA), a widely used and powerful approach, can be applied to address all of these challenges. It is important to note that, in the presence of uncertain and ambiguous data, traditional DEA approaches cannot be utilized effectively. Therefore, this research presents a novel method for estimating the most productive scale size in DEA within a deep uncertainty environment. Notably, the robust optimization (RO) method, recognized for its effectiveness and practicality in uncertain programming, is employed to propose the robust most productive scale size (RMPSS) model. The implementation of the developed robust MPSS method is demonstrated through a numerical example and a real-life case study from the Iranian healthcare system. Furthermore, the results

P. Peykani (✉)
Department of Industrial Engineering, Faculty of Engineering, Khatam University, Tehran, Iran
e-mail: p.peykani@khatam.ac.ir; pejman.peykani@yahoo.com

F. Hamidzadeh · M. S. Pishvaee
School of Industrial Engineering, Iran University of Science and Technology, Tehran, Iran
e-mail: farhad.hamidzadeh@gmail.com

M. S. Pishvaee
e-mail: pishvaee@iust.ac.ir

E. Memar-Masjed
Department of Industrial Engineering, Faculty of Engineering, Ferdowsi University of Mashhad, Mashhad, Iran
e-mail: e.memarmasjed@gmail.com

A. Jabbarzadeh
Department of Systems Engineering, École de Technologie Supérieure (ETS), University of Quebec, Montreal, Canada
e-mail: armin.jabbarzadeh@etsmtl.ca

© The Author(s), under exclusive license to Springer Nature Singapore Pte Ltd. 2024
S. A. Edalatpanah et al. (eds.), *Analytical Decision Making and Data Envelopment Analysis*, Infosys Science Foundation Series in Mathematical Sciences,
https://doi.org/10.1007/978-981-97-6972-8_8

indicate the effectiveness and efficacy of the proposed approach in estimating MPSS within uncertain DEA.

Keywords Most productive scale size estimation · Data envelopment analysis · Hospital performance measurement · Robust optimization · Uncertain data

1 Introduction

One of the data-driven methods for assessing the decision-making units (DMUs) performance is data envelopment analysis (DEA). Furthermore, DEA is a non-parametric method that assesses the DMUs' efficiency without requiring a production function (Cooper et al., 2011). Charnes et al. (1978) developed a DEA model for evaluating the efficiencies of DMUs, assuming constant returns to scale (CRS), considering Farrell's (1957). Banker et al. (1984) subsequently described an approach to evaluate efficiencies under variable returns to scale (VRS) presumption. DEA is also a broadly utilized and well-known method that utilizes multiple inputs to generate multiple outputs (Liu et al., 2016; Emrouznejad et al., 2008, 2022; 2023; Cooper et al., 2007). Nowadays, DEA models can be used in a variety of real-life situations. The use of the DEA technique has been observed in a broad variety of different subjects, encompassing healthcare, banking, agriculture, education, transportation, finance, insurance, and regional competitiveness (Emrouznejad & Yang, 2018; Hamidzadeh & Pishvaee, 2023; Liu et al., 2013a, b; Nepomuceno et al., 2023; Peykani et al., 2021, 2022a).

DEA facilitates the analyzed units in enhancing their operations while identifying long- and short-term policy choices; performance evaluation also acts as a policy mechanism in this swiftly changing economic climate that businesses should endure. Enhancing operations of a unit, like reducing inventory and minimizing transportation time and lead, reduces production costs and increases service (Emrouznejad et al., 2023a, b). The utilization of the DEA technique is significant due to its applicability across different fields, such as organizations and production processes. By considering several inputs and outputs, the DEA technique enables the extraction of unit efficiency. By incorporating a more detailed illustration of the transformation procedure, a more accurate depiction of the actual operations performed can be achieved, resulting in a more realistic performance score. Undoubtedly, DEA has attracted significant attention from researchers and professionals since its establishment, as indicated by the considerable volume of publications focused on its methodologies and practical applications (Emrouznejad & Yang, 2018; Emrouznejad et al., 2023a, b; Omrani et al., 2023; Sari et al., 2018).

DEA provides a significant emphasis on the topic of the most productive scale size (MPSS), which is connected to returns-to-scale (RTS) (Eslami & Khoveyni, 2014; Moghaddas & Vaez-Ghasemi, 2014; Roozbeh et al., 2015). Banker (1984) demonstrated the MPSS principle for the first time in DEA. Subsequently, Cooper et al. (1996) developed a fractional function of an objective approach to identify the

MPSS, while an input–output orientation approach considering a linear objective function to estimate the MPSS has been utilized by Jahanshahloo and Khodabakhshi (2003). The evolution of MPSS as a component of the RTS paradigm was investigated by Banker et al. (2004). Furthermore, Khodabakhshi (2009) delved into the MPSS estimation when stochastic data is gained. Determining the RTS for each DMU within the VRS production possibility set is a crucial consideration in efficiency improvement, as highlighted by Banker and Thrall (1992). The type of RTS indicates the necessary rescaling direction. When a DMU demonstrates a growing return to scale (IRS), expansion is recommended, while a reducing return to scale (DRS) suggests contraction within efficiency optimization. In cases where the DMU displays CRS, it is assumed that the DMU operates at its MPSS (Peykani et al., 2018; Sari et al., 2018; Sarkar, 2015).

The MPSS concept also has considerable significance in the economics and management fields, particularly among managers and decision-makers. The estimation of MPSS enables managers to achieve a maximum ratio of overall outputs to overall inputs, which could result in several benefits, such as the conservation of natural resources during production, reduced costs, and increased revenues and profits. Additionally, MPSS units serve as benchmarks for other firms for enhancing their performance. Therefore, decision-makers strive to attain optimal scales. Although closely related, it should be considered that the MPSS and efficiency are not interchangeable concepts. Although each MPSS can function as an efficient DMU, the reverse is not always true. When an efficient DMU reaches the efficient frontier parts with decreasing or increasing RTS, it cannot be considered as an MPSS (Esfandiar et al., 2023; Mottaghi et al., 2017).

Some DEA-based approaches for identifying MPSS firms were developed earlier. For example, Banker (1984) presented a DEA-based approach utilizing the CRS efficient frontier to identify the units of MPSS. Thus, he presented an MPSS pattern for the evaluated DMU. Nevertheless, those units of MPSS described by Banker (1984) might not be MPSS. Then, Cooper et al. (1996) pointed out that Banker's (1984) method could not accurately identify MPSS units, so the method was adapted to include slack variables for determining the MPSS units. In addition, Banker et al. (1996) developed a customized DEA method for determining the MPSS units when multiple optimal solutions exist. Nevertheless, the approach they use could lead to various optimal solutions when evaluating a particular DMU, making it impossible to identify the target uniquely.

Appa and Yue (1999) described multiple linear methods that aim to obtain a target characterized by a specific scale tied to either the largest MPSS or the smallest MPSS. Furthermore, Zhu (2000) developed an alternate approach for target setting based on the largest or smallest MPSS. In addition, none of the largest and smallest units of MPSS provided by Zhu (2000) were obviously the units of MPSS closest to the DMU being evaluated, and these units of MPSS may not fall within the existing unit of MPSS discovered in the technological advances. These concerns demonstrate the limitations of Zhu's (2000) approach. Considering that it is simpler for decision-makers of the evaluated DMUs for accessing the closest identified units of MPSS rather than the non-observed ones, they are more likely to select one of the closest identified units of MPSS as a reference to improve the DMUs' performance. This leads to increased enthusiasm for utilizing the closest discovered units of MPSS as benchmarks for enhancing DMU performance. An integrated DEA-based approach was developed by Amin and Toloo (2007) for identifying the most effective DMU among the extant effective DMUs. However, Amin (2009) showed that their integrated approach may yield multiple DMUs with the highest efficiency. Consequently, he presented an enhanced integrated approach for identifying the most efficient DMU.

Fukuyama (2003) described a measurement of scale elasticity by defining the MPSS approach as originally established by Banker (1984) and compared it to the conventional scale elasticity measure. Jahanshahloo and Khodabakhshi (2003) developed a linear input–output oriented DEA approach to address the nonlinearity of Cooper et al.'s (1996) and Banker's (1984) DEA models, which was then extended to stochastic data by Khodabakhshi (2009). Wang and Lan (2013) and Eslami et al. (2012) employed various approaches for estimating the MPSS: an imprecise-chance constrained DEA approach and a double frontiers approach, respectively. Additionally, Davoodi et al. (2015) presented the closest MPSS pattern paradigm, demonstrating that the unit of MPSS proposed by Banker (1984) represents the closest MPSS pattern for a given DMU. On the other side, Banker et al.'s (1996) and Banker's (1984) MPSS unit may not adhere to the characteristics of an actual MPSS unit within the technology. This highlights limitations within their methods, as well as those presented by Davoodi et al. (2015). Lee (2016) developed a multi-objective DEA approach that examines the balance between the fulfillment of the demand benchmark and the MPSS unit. Similarly, a novel DEA-based technique for identifying units of MPSS in the existence of both nonnegative and negative data was developed by Sahoo et al. (2016). Additionally, a system of MPSS within two-stage network procedures taking a series structure into consideration was investigated by Assani et al. (2018). Note that in all DEA approaches, data needs to be crisp and definite. This means that traditional DEA approaches cannot be utilized when uncertain data are involved (Emrouznejad et al., 2014; Olesen & Petersen, 2016; Peykani et al., 2020a, b). Consequently, the primary goal of this research is to develop a new method to estimate the most productive scale size through uncertainty. The proposed approach involves specifying a MPSS set units according to the Jahanshahloo and Khodabakhshi (2003) approach. Notably, the robust optimization approach is utilized to eliminate uncertainty concerns in the MPSS method. Nowadays, the robust optimization method is among the most popular techniques for coping with uncertainty. (Dehnokhalaji et al., 2022; Omrani et al., 2023; Peykani et al., 2022b, 2024; Toloo et al., 2022).

The remainder of this study is organized as follows. The research background will be introduced in Sect. 2. Then, the novel method for estimating MPSS under uncertainty of data using robust optimization will be presented in Sect. 3. The execution of the developed robust MPSS model is exemplified by a numerical example and a real data set in Sect. 4. Ultimately, Sect. 5 concludes with suggestions and conclusions for future research.

2 Research Background

Consider that there are n peer DMUs that each $DMU_j (j = 1, ..., n)$ utilizes multiple inputs $x_{ij}(x_{1j}, ..., x_{mj})$ to generate multiple outputs $y_{rj}(y_{1j}, ..., y_{sj})$ and p is the evaluation index for DMU. As mentioned before, for the first time, Banker (1984) proposed the most productive scale size concept. Model (1) is the classical DEA approach for estimating MPSS.

$$Max\ \Psi = \frac{\omega}{\xi} \tag{1-1}$$

$$S.t.\ \sum_{j=1}^{n} \lambda_j x_{ij} \leq \xi x_{ip}, \forall i \tag{1-2}$$

$$\sum_{j=1}^{n} \lambda_j y_{rj} \geq \omega y_{rp}, \forall r \tag{1-3}$$

$$\sum_{j=1}^{n} \lambda_j = 1 \tag{1-4}$$

$$\omega, \xi \geq 0 \tag{1-5}$$

$$\lambda_j \geq 0, \forall j \tag{1-6}$$

Cooper et al. (1996) developed Model (1) for MPSS estimation. It should be noted that if $\Psi^* = 1$, DMU_p is MPSS. The objective is fractional, as demonstrated by the Model (1). An input–output orientation approach for estimating MPSS was developed by Jahanshahloo and Khodabakhshi (2003). Model (2) utilized a linear objective function in its concept. Regarding the Model (2) if $\Omega^* = 0$, DMU_p is MPSS.

$$\text{Max}\Omega = \omega - \xi \tag{2-1}$$

$$\text{S.t.} \sum_{j=1}^{n} \lambda_j x_{ij} \leq \xi x_{ip}, \forall i \tag{2-2}$$

$$\sum_{j=1}^{n} \lambda_j y_{rj} \geq \omega y_{rp}, \forall r \tag{2-3}$$

$$\sum_{j=1}^{n} \lambda_j = 1 \tag{2-4}$$

$$\omega, \xi \geq 0 \tag{2-5}$$

$$\lambda_j \geq 0, \forall j \tag{2-6}$$

Jahanshahloo et al. (2004) are the leading investigators who work upon estimating RTS and MPSS under uncertainty. Then, Khodabakhshi (2009) and Eslami et al. (2012) proposed a new method for MPSS estimation in the presence of stochastic data in DEA, and they applied their approach in the software and banking industries, respectively. Further, Khodabakhshi et al. (2017) determined the MPSS of Iran's provinces in the employment field using intervals of data. Finally, regarding the possibility-probability constraints, Kheirollahi et al. (2022) described the fuzzy stochastic DEA approach for evaluating the MPSS of DMUs that generate multiple fuzzy randomized outputs from multiple fuzzy randomized inputs. Table 1 summarizes the main characteristics of research that work on estimating MPSS in the existence of uncertain data. In the final row of Table 1, related characteristics of the current research have been proposed.

As demonstrated in Table 1, the robust optimization approach has not been used for estimating MPSS under uncertainty. Notably, according to Table 1, this field of DEA has potential directions for future research directions.

Table 1 A review of most productive scale size estimation under uncertainty

Author(s) (publication year)	Interval optimization	Stochastic optimization	Fuzzy optimization	Robust optimization
Jahanshahloo et al. (2004)	✓			
Malekmohammadi et al. (2009)	✓			
Khodabakhshi (2009)		✓		
Khodabakhshi et al. (2010)			✓	
Eslami et al. (2012)		✓		
Khodabakhshi et al. (2017)	✓			
Dibachi (2018)		✓		
Jahani Sayyad Noveiri et al. (2021)		✓		
Meng and Liu (2021)			✓	
Kheirollahi et al. (2022)		✓	✓	
This study				✓

3 The Proposed Approach

The methods for modeling uncertainty include a wide range of methodologies, including probabilistic, possibilistic, probabilistic-possibilistic hybrid, and robust methods. It should be considered that the primary purpose of utilizing such methods relates to determine how much an uncertain input parameter will affect the system's output parameters and consequences. However, the main distinction between these systems is the use of alternative methods for defining the ambiguity of input parameters (Salimian & Mousavi, 2022). Probabilistic approaches utilize the probability density function, as utilized by Oaksford and Chater (2001) and Yancheshmeh and Adeli (2023). These approaches presume that the probability density function input values have been known. Dantzig (1955) provided an early example of the application of this concept in the field of stochastic programming. A membership function is utilized by fuzzy possibilistic programming to model input parameters, according to Zadeh (1996). Robust optimization is another method for handling uncertainty that defines sets to specify the input values uncertainty. By using this approach, optimal computation decisions can be made under worst-case scenarios for a given set with vague parameters, as demonstrated by Mousavi and Vahdani (2017).

Robust programming is a subfield of optimization theory that provides risk-averse solutions to the challenges of coping with uncertainty in optimization-related situations. Soyster (1973) pioneered this field by developing a worst-case robust programming technique to deal with imprecise linear programming conditions. It should be mentioned that authors have given a variety of robust programming methodologies for real-world uses, like supply chain network design (Arabsheybani & Arshadi Khasmeh, 2021; Baghalian et al., 2013; Mousazadeh et al., 2015; Nayeri et al., 2020), closed-loop supply chain network design (Hosseini Dehshiri et al., 2023; Jabbarzadeh et al., 2018; Nayeri et al., 2020; Yavari & Geraeli, 2019), open innovation (Rahmanzadeh et al., 2023), power systems (Conejo & Wu, 2022; Malcolm & Zenios, 2017), portfolio optimization (Kara et al., 2019; Sehgal & Jagadesh, 2023; Zymler et al., 2011), inventory management (Bertsimas & Thiele, 2006; Lim & Wang, 2017; Mamani et al., 2017), environmental management (Cunha, 2023; Li et al., 2008), healthcare systems (Ash et al., 2022; He et al., 2019; Karamyar et al., 2018; Meng et al., 2015; Wang et al., 2021) in the past few years.

In the context of optimization problems, a solution is deemed robust when it possesses both optimality and feasibility robustness. It should be considered that the concept of feasibility robustness relates to the solution's ability to stay feasible throughout a wide range of uncertain parameter values. Additionally, optimality robustness relates to the ability of a solution to maintain closeness objective function optimal value or to deviate minimally from this value across a wide range of possible uncertain parameter values for uncertain parameters.

Robust optimization methods could be divided up into the following three categories: realistic robust programming (Leung et al., 2007; Mulvey et al., 1995; Pan & Nagi, 2010), soft worst-case robust programming (Bertsimas & Sim, 2004; Kasperski & Kulej, 2009; Nie et al., 2007), and hard worst-case robust programming

(Ben-Tal & Nemirovski, 1998; El Ghaoui et al., 1998; Greenberg & Morrison, 2008). Realistic robust programming seeks to balance the trade-off between robustness cost, robustness, and other goals like improving the performance of the system. Soft worst-case robust programming minimizes the worst possible objective function value without reaching constraints in their severe worst-case scenario. Maximum immunity or safety against uncertainty is provided by hard worst-case robust programming utilizing immunizing solutions from being infeasible for all uncertain parameter values. By using this method, the goal function is guaranteed never to violate towards the optimal result gained by implementing the relevant mathematical programming approach. Despite allowing constraint violations, realistic methods seek a relatively robust solution consisting of DM's preferences or total interests that are close to optimal and feasible for the most possible uncertain parameter values. For a wide range of uncertain parameters, the solution obtained is both feasible and nearly optimal.

Ben-Tal et al. (2009) described that the hard worst-case-oriented method might be more effective than soft methods because it does not acquire any knowledge regarding the uncertain parameters' distribution possibility or probability, nor does it leave decisions vulnerable to uncertainty. Furthermore, they argue that the conservative nature of this approach is an advantage as it ensures safety in all potential scenarios. The worst-case robust programming method is criticized by Bertsimas and Sim (2004) for being excessively conservative since it assumes all uncertain parameters will simultaneously attain their worst-case value. The repercussions of this presumption can lead to high costs for decision-makers. They also indicate that it is often unfavorable to examine the objective worst-case value function because doing so can lead to excessive expenses for stakeholders, and this is why the robustness of optimality is important.

Pishvaee et al. (2012) indicate that the hard worst-case method seems suitable to decision-makers who are risk-averse and fully conservative. This approach is particularly relevant in instances where just a small deviation from the expected system functionality may lead to catastrophic outcomes, such as in military and emergency contexts. On the other side, the soft worst-case method is conservative. However, it allows for some degree of flexibility within the framework of worst-case scenarios. The realistic robust programming method, which includes a range between average cases and worst while controlling feasibility and optimality robustness, is better suited to profit-seeking and flexible decision-makers. This approach has broad applicability in business contexts, and it could be demonstrated that one of the specific cases of realistic robust programming is the hard worst-case method.

This section focuses on a new methodology for determining MPSS when uncertain data exists. As mentioned earlier, to deal with uncertainty in the MPSS model, robust optimization is utilized. Note that Bertsimas, Ben-Tal and Nemirovski (2000) and Sim (2004), and Soyster (1973) developed widespread and main robust optimization approaches. In terms of the robust counterpart linearity in the robust method of Bertsimas and Sim (2004), this methodology is going to be utilized in this research to present a robust MPSS approach as Model (3).

$$\text{Max}\Theta = \omega - \xi \tag{3-1}$$

$$\text{S.t.} \sum_{j=1}^{n} \lambda_j x_{ij} - \xi x_{ip} + Z_i^x \Gamma_i^x + \sum_{j=1}^{n} \alpha_{ij} + \alpha_{ip} \le 0, \forall i \tag{3-2}$$

$$Z_i^x + \alpha_{ij} \ge \varepsilon x_{ij} \lambda_j, \forall i, j \tag{3-3}$$

$$Z_i^x + \alpha_{ip} \ge \varepsilon x_{ip} \xi, \forall i \tag{3-4}$$

$$\sum_{j=1}^{n} \lambda_j y_{rj} - \omega y_{rp} - Z_r^y \Gamma_r^y - \sum_{j=1}^{n} \beta_{rj} + \beta_{rp} \ge 0, \forall r \tag{3-5}$$

$$Z_r^y + \beta_{rj} \ge \varepsilon y_{rj} \lambda_j, \forall r, j \tag{3-6}$$

$$Z_r^y + \beta_{rp} \ge \varepsilon y_{rp} \omega, \forall r \tag{3-7}$$

$$\sum_{j=1}^{n} \lambda_j = 1 \tag{3-8}$$

$$Z_i^x, Z_r^y \ge 0, \forall i, r \tag{3-9}$$

$$\alpha_{ij}, \alpha_{ip} \ge 0, \forall i, j \tag{3-10}$$

$$\beta_{rj}, \beta_{rp} \ge 0, \forall r, j \tag{3-11}$$

$$\omega, \xi \ge 0 \tag{3-12}$$

$$\lambda_j \ge 0, \forall j \tag{3-13}$$

It should be explained the parameters Γ^x and Γ^y adjust the conservative level of the robust MPSS model. According to Model (3), DMU_p is MPSS if and only if $\Theta^* \le 0$. It should be noted that if this condition is met for several DMUs, the most negative DMU will be MPSS.

4 Numerical and Experimental Results

Within this particular section, the efficacy and robust MPSS model applicability are demonstrated by utilizing a numerical example and real-world case application from the healthcare area.

4.1 Numerical Example

Table 2 indicates that the numerical illustration is associated within one uncertain input and one uncertain output considering five DMUs.

Now, the robust MPSS model has been solved for different perturbation values, including 0, 1, 5, and 10%. The findings gained from Model (3) are introduced in Table 3.

As demonstrated in Table 3, DMU B is MPSS under certainty and all uncertainty conditions. Notably, in the field of production technology, the MPSS unit that is located most directly close to the DMU. Being evaluated, whether it is observed or not, is considered the closest observed (non-observed) MPSS unit.

4.2 Healthcare Application

In this subsection, the implementation of the developed robust MPSS model using real-world data from the Iranian healthcare system is examined. It should be explained that the input variables include the number of beds (NOBE) and the number of staff

Table 2 Data set for five DMUs

Data	DMU_{01}	DMU_{02}	DMU_{03}	DMU_{04}	DMU_{05}
Input	1	2	3	4	2
Output	1	3	4.5	5	2.75

Table 3 Findings for DMUs

DMUs	Perturbation values							
	0%		1%		5%		10%	
DMU-01	1.50		1.35		0.76		0.02	
DMU-02	0.00	MPSS	–0.04	MPSS	–0.20	MPSS	–0.34	MPSS
DMU-03	0.00	MPSS	–0.03		–0.13		–0.23	
DMU-04	0.15		0.12		–0.01		–0.12	
DMU-05	0.14		0.07		–0.12		–0.31	

(NOST). Also, the output variables include the number of surgeries (NOSU) and the number of patients (NOPA). Summary of real-world data for 15 Iranian hospitals are introduced in Table 4.

Now, the proposed robust MPSS model has been solved for different perturbation values, including 0, 1, 5, and 10%. The findings gained from Model (3) are presented in Table 5.

According to the Table 5, Hospital 02, Hospital 05, and Hospital 07 are MPSS under certainty and all uncertainty conditions. Notably, by identifying MPSS hospitals, the manager or decision-maker can utilize these hospitals as a reference point for their hospital. This enables them to achieve optimal size in order to enhance efficiency scores, increasing profits and decreasing costs for their hospital in an easily accessible manner. Additionally, recognition of the closest discovered MPSS unit could be utilized just like a measure for reference units of MPSS ranking in production technology when evaluating a DMU.

It is important to highlight that in production technology that is not MPSS, every existing DMU, regardless of how efficiently it operates or how inefficiently it operates, can have its closest MPSS unit identified. Additionally, it is crucial to realize that the closest units of MPSS for distinguished DMUs under consideration may not be identical. Therefore, in production technology, it is possible to have multiple DMUs being evaluated with distinct closest MPSS units.

Table 4 A real data set for 15 Iranian hospitals

Hospitals	Inputs		Outputs	
	NOBE	NOST	NOSU	NOPA
H-01	94	175	1155	97,932
H-02	24	100	432	78,954
H-03	120	356	1867	58,734
H-04	125	315	4223	78,278
H-05	73	107	2062	85,139
H-06	141	333	3218	76,489
H-07	20	76	85	60,628
H-08	30	95	630	46,196
H-09	452	878	19,321	420,434
H-10	285	399	3080	146,468
H-11	122	362	555	142,352
H-12	175	320	5837	136,582
H-13	78	212	2185	96,451
H-14	89	223	1752	108,205
H-15	76	186	1800	48,854

Table 5 Findings for hospitals

Hospitals	Perturbation values							
	0%		1%		5%		10%	
H-01	0.25		0.22		0.11		–0.03	
H-02	0.00	MPSS	–0.04	MPSS	–0.20	MPSS	–0.40	MPSS
H-03	3.39		3.17		2.31		1.25	
H-04	0.96		0.80		0.14		–0.20	
H-05	0.00	MPSS	–0.04	MPSS	–0.20	MPSS	–0.40	MPSS
H-06	2.29		2.12		1.43		0.60	
H-07	0.00	MPSS	–0.04	MPSS	–0.20	MPSS	–0.40	MPSS
H-08	0.60		0.53		0.25		–0.10	
H-09	0.00	MPSS	–0.04	MPSS	–0.06		–0.08	
H-10	0.67		0.57		0.23		0.15	
H-11	0.29		0.27		0.20		0.12	
H-12	0.33		0.24		–0.04		–0.18	
H-13	0.27		0.23		0.05		–0.17	
H-14	0.28		0.25		0.14		–0.01	
H-15	2.66		2.37		1.21		0.48	

5 Conclusions and Future Research Directions

Estimating the most productive scale size is one of the most important applications of data envelopment analysis techniques. This work, in the existence of uncertain data, aims to develop a novel approach to estimate the most productive size scale, where their lower and upper bounds are the only evaluation parts that are known. In order to accomplish this objective, an uncertainty set-based convex robust optimization technique is being applied for the purpose of providing a robust counterpart of the traditional most productive scale size approach while taking into account the impact of uncertainty. Ultimately, a numerical example is utilized to show the developed robust most productive size scale model usefulness by utilizing uncertain input and output. Notably, for future researches, the neutrosophic theory (Abdelfattah, 2019; Edalatpanah, 2018, 2020; Tapia, 2021; Yang et al., 2020) and the uncertainty theory (Jiang et al., 2018; Mohmmad Nejad & Ghaffari-Hadigheh, 2018; Peykani et al., 2022a, b, c, 2024; Pourmahmoud & Bagheri, 2023; Wen et al., 2017) could be applied for coping with data ambiguity and uncertainty.

References

Abdelfattah, W. (2019). Data envelopment analysis with neutrosophic inputs and outputs. *Expert Systems, 36*(6), e12453.
Amin, G. R. (2009). Comments on finding the most efficient DMUs in DEA: An improved integrated model. *Computers & Industrial Engineering, 56*(4), 1701–1702.
Amin, G. R., & Toloo, M. (2007). Finding the most efficient DMUs in DEA: An improved integrated model. *Computers & Industrial Engineering, 52*(1), 71–77.
Appa, G., & Yue, M. (1999). On setting scale efficient targets in DEA. *Journal of the Operational Research Society, 50*(1), 60–69.
Arabsheybani, A., & Arshadi Khasmeh, A. (2021). Robust and resilient supply chain network design considering risks in food industry: Flavour industry in Iran. *International Journal of Management Science and Engineering Management, 16*(3), 197–208.
Ash, C., Diallo, C., Venkatadri, U., & VanBerkel, P. (2022). Distributionally robust optimization of a Canadian healthcare supply chain to enhance resilience during the COVID-19 pandemic. *Computers & Industrial Engineering, 168*, 108051.
Assani, S., Jiang, J., Cao, R., & Yang, F. (2018). Most productive scale size decomposition for multi-stage systems in data envelopment analysis. *Computers & Industrial Engineering, 120*, 279–287.
Baghalian, A., Rezapour, S., & Farahani, R. Z. (2013). Robust supply chain network design with service level against disruptions and demand uncertainties: A real-life case. *European Journal of Operational Research, 227*(1), 199–215.
Banker, R. D. (1984). Estimating most productive scale size using data envelopment analysis. *European Journal of Operational Research, 17*(1), 35–44.
Banker, R. D., & Thrall, R. M. (1992). Estimation of returns to scale using data envelopment analysis. *European Journal of Operational Research, 62*(1), 74–84.
Banker, R. D., Chang, H., & Cooper, W. W. (1996). Equivalence and implementation of alternative methods for determining returns to scale in data envelopment analysis. *European Journal of Operational Research, 89*(3), 473–481.
Banker, R. D., Charnes, A., & Cooper, W. W. (1984). Some models for estimating technical and scale inefficiencies in data envelopment analysis. *Management Science, 30*(9), 1078–1092.
Banker, R. D., Cooper, W. W., Seiford, L. M., Thrall, R. M., & Zhu, J. (2004). Returns to scale in different DEA models. *European Journal of Operational Research, 154*(2), 345–362.
Ben-Tal, A., & Nemirovski, A. (1998). Robust convex optimization. *Mathematics of Operations Research, 23*(4), 769–805.
Ben-Tal, A., & Nemirovski, A. (2000). Robust solutions of linear programming problems contaminated with uncertain data. *Mathematical Programming, 88*(3), 411–424.
Ben-Tal, A., El Ghaoui, L., & Nemirovski, A. (2009). *Robust optimization*. Princeton University Press.
Bertsimas, D., & Sim, M. (2004). The price of robustness. *Operations Research, 52*(1), 35–53.
Bertsimas, D., & Thiele, A. (2006). A robust optimization approach to inventory theory. *Operations Research, 54*(1), 150–168.
Charnes, A., Cooper, W. W., & Rhodes, E. (1978). Measuring the efficiency of decision making units. *European Journal of Operational Research, 2*(6), 429–444.
Charnes, A., Cooper, W., Lewin, A. Y., & Seiford, L. M. (1997). Data envelopment analysis theory, methodology and applications. *Journal of the Operational Research Society, 48*(3), 332–333.
Conejo, A. J., & Wu, X. (2022). Robust optimization in power systems: A tutorial overview. *Optimization and Engineering, 23*(4), 2051–2073.
Cooper, W. W., Seiford, L. M., & Tone, K. (2007). *Data Envelopment Analysis: A Comprehensive Text with Models, Applications, References and DEA-Solver Software*. Springer, New York, NY.
Cooper, W. W., Seiford, L. M., & Zhu, J. (2011). *Handbook on data envelopment analysis*. Springer.
Cooper, W. W., Thompson, R. G., & Thrall, R. M. (1996). Extensions and new developments in DEA. *Annals of Operations Research, 66*, 3–45.

Cunha, M. D. C. (2023). Water and environmental systems management under uncertainty: From scenario construction to robust solutions and adaptation. *Water Resources Management, 37*(6), 2271–2285.

Dantzig, G. B. (1955). Linear programming under uncertainty. *Management Science, 1*(3–4), 197–206.

Davoodi, A., Zarepisheh, M., & Rezai, H. Z. (2015). The nearest MPSS pattern in data envelopment analysis. *Annals of Operations Research, 226*, 163–176.

Dehnokhalaji, A., Khezri, S., & Emrouznejad, A. (2022). A box-uncertainty in DEA: A robust performance measurement framework. *Expert Systems with Applications, 187*, 115855.

Dibachi, H. (2018). Stochastic multiplicative DEA for estimating most productive scale size. *Theory of Approximation and Applications, 12*(1), 93–115.

Edalatpanah, S. A. (2018). Neutrosophic perspective on DEA. *Journal of Applied Research on Industrial Engineering, 5*(4), 339–345.

Emrouznejad, A., Petridis, K., & Charles, V. (2023). Data envelopment analysis with GAMS: A handbook on productivity analysis and performance measurement.

Edalatpanah, S. A. (2020). Data envelopment analysis based on triangular neutrosophic numbers. *CAAI Transactions on Intelligence Technology, 5*(2), 94–98.

El Ghaoui, L., Oustry, F., & Lebret, H. (1998). Robust solutions to uncertain semidefinite programs. *SIAM Journal on Optimization, 9*(1), 33–52.

Emrouznejad, A., & Yang, G. L. (2018). A survey and analysis of the first 40 years of scholarly literature in DEA: 1978–2016. *Socio-Economic Planning Sciences, 61*, 4–8.

Emrouznejad, A., Amin, G. R., Ghiyasi, M., & Michali, M. (2023). A review of inverse data envelopment analysis: origins, development, and future directions. *IMA Journal of Management Mathematics*, dpad006.

Emrouznejad, A., Parker, B. R., & Tavares, G. (2008). Evaluation of research in efficiency and productivity: A survey and analysis of the first 30 years of scholarly literature in DEA. *Socio-Economic Planning Sciences, 42*(3), 151–157.

Emrouznejad, A., Tavana, M., & Hatami-Marbini, A. (2014). The state of the art in fuzzy data envelopment analysis. *Performance Measurement with Fuzzy Data Envelopment Analysis*, pp. 1–45. Springer, Berlin, Heidelberg.

Emrouznejad, A., Yang, G. L., Khoveyni, M., & Michali, M. (2022). Data envelopment analysis: Recent developments and challenges. *The Palgrave Handbook of Operations Research*, pp. 307–350.

Esfandiar, E., Eslami, R., Khoveyni, M., & Gilani, A. (2023). Identifying the closest most productive scale size unit in data envelopment analysis. *Or Spectrum, 45*, 623–660.

Eslami, R., & Khoveyni, M. (2014). New insights on estimating most productive scale size in DEA. *Recent Developments in Data Envelopment Analysis and Its Applications.*

Eslami, R., Khodabakhshi, M., Jahanshahloo, G. R., Hosseinzadeh Lotfi, F., & Khoveyni, M. (2012). Estimating most productive scale size with imprecise-chance constrained input–output orientation model in data envelopment analysis. *Computers & Industrial Engineering, 63*(1), 254–261.

Farrell, M. J. (1957). The measurement of productive efficiency. *Journal of the Royal Statistical Society. Series A (General), 120*(3), 253.

Fukuyama, H. (2003). Scale characterizations in a DEA directional technology distance function framework. *European Journal of Operational Research, 144*(1), 108–127.

Greenberg, H. J., & Morrison, T. (2008). Robust optimization. *Operations Research and Management Science Handbook*, 1–33. CRC Press, Boca Raton, Florida.

Hamidzadeh, F., & Pishvaee, M. S. (2023). A data envelopment analysis approach to evaluate efficiencies in organ allocation problem: A case study. *Journal of Industrial and Systems Engineering, 14*(4), 138–157.

He, S., Sim, M., & Zhang, M. (2019). Data-driven patient scheduling in emergency departments: A hybrid robust-stochastic approach. *Management Science, 65*(9), 4123–4140.

Hosseini Dehshiri, S. J., Amiri, M., Olfat, L., & Pishvaee, M. S. (2023). A robust fuzzy stochastic multi-objective model for stone paper closed-loop supply chain design considering the flexibility of soft constraints based on Me measure. *Applied Soft Computing*, p. 134.

Jabbarzadeh, A., Haughton, M., & Khosrojerdi, A. (2018). Closed-loop supply chain network design under disruption risks: A robust approach with real world application. *Computers & Industrial Engineering, 116*, 178–191.

Jahani Sayyad Noveiri, M., Kordrostami, S., & Amirteimoori, A. (2021). Sustainability assessment and most productive scale size: A stochastic DEA approach with dual frontiers. *Environmental Modeling & Assessment, 26*(5), 723-735.

Jahanshahloo, G. R., & Khodabakhshi, M. (2003). Using input–output orientation model for determining most productive scale size in DEA. *Applied Mathematics and Computation, 146*(2–3), 849–855.

Jahanshahloo, G. R., Kazemi-Matin, R., & Vencheh, A. H. (2004). On return to scale of fully efficient DMUs in data envelopment analysis under interval data. *Applied Mathematics and Computation, 154*(1), 31–40.

Jiang, B., Lio, W., & Li, X. (2018). An uncertain DEA model for scale efficiency evaluation. *IEEE Transactions on Fuzzy Systems, 27*(8), 1616–1624.

Kara, G., Özmen, A., & Weber, G. W. (2019). Stability advances in robust portfolio optimization under parallelepiped uncertainty. *Central European Journal of Operations Research, 27*(1), 241–261.

Karamyar, F., Sadeghi, J., & Yazdi, M. M. (2018). A Benders decomposition for the location-allocation and scheduling model in a healthcare system regarding robust optimization. *Neural Computing and Applications, 29*(10), 873–886.

Kasperski, A., & Kulej, M. (2009). Choosing robust solutions in discrete optimization problems with fuzzy costs. *Fuzzy Sets and Systems, 160*(5), 667–682.

Kheirollahi, H., Rostamzadeh, M., & Marzang, S. (2022). Assessing most productive scale size with fuzzy stochastic data envelopment analysis. *Journal of Intelligent & Fuzzy Systems, 43*(3), 2231–2241.

Khodabakhshi, M. (2009). Estimating most productive scale size with stochastic data in data envelopment analysis. *Economic Modelling, 26*(5), 968–973.

Khodabakhshi, M., Gholami, Y., & Kheirollahi, H. (2010). An additive model approach for estimating returns to scale in imprecise data envelopment analysis. *Applied Mathematical Modelling, 34*(5), 1247–1257.

Khodabakhshi, M., Papi, S., Fallahnejad, R., & Yazdanpanah Maryaki, M. (2017). Estimating most productive scale size of the provinces of Iran in the employment sector using interval data in imprecise data envelopment analysis (IDEA). *International Journal of Data Envelopment Analysis, 5*(4), 1399–1410.

Lee, C. Y. (2016). Most productive scale size versus demand fulfillment: A solution to the capacity dilemma. *European Journal of Operational Research, 248*(3), 954–962.

Leung, S. C. H., Tsang, S. O. S., Ng, W. L., & Wu, Y. (2007). A robust optimization model for multi-site production planning problem in an uncertain environment. *European Journal of Operational Research, 181*(1), 224–238.

Li, Y. P., Huang, G. H., Nie, X. H., & Nie, S. L. (2008). A two-stage fuzzy robust integer programming approach for capacity planning of environmental management systems. *European Journal of Operational Research, 189*(2), 399–420.

Lim, Y. F., & Wang, C. (2017). Inventory management based on target-oriented robust optimization. *Management Science, 63*(12), 4409–4427.

Liu, J. S., Lu, L. Y., & Lu, W. M. (2016). Research fronts in data envelopment analysis. *Omega, 58*, 33–45.

Liu, J. S., Lu, L. Y., Lu, W. M., & Lin, B. J. (2013a). A survey of DEA applications. *Omega, 41*(5), 893–902.

Liu, J. S., Lu, L. Y., Lu, W. M., & Lin, B. J. (2013b). Data envelopment analysis 1978–2010: A citation-based literature survey. *Omega, 41*(1), 3–15.

Malcolm, S. A., & Zenios, S. A. (1994). Robust optimization for power systems capacity expansion under uncertainty. *Journal of the Operational Research Society, 45*(9), 1040–1049.
Malekmohammadi, N., Hosseinzadeh Lotfi, F., & Jaafar, A. B. (2009). Centralized resource allocation in DEA with interval data: An application to commercial banks in Malaysia. *International Journal of Mathematical Analysis, 3*(13–16), 757–764.
Mamani, H., Nassiri, S., & Wagner, M. R. (2017). Closed-form solutions for robust inventory management. *Management Science, 63*(5), 1625–1643.
Meng, F., Qi, J., Zhang, M., Ang, J., Chu, S., & Sim, M. (2015). A robust optimization model for managing elective admission in a public hospital. *Operations Research, 63*(6), 1452–1467.
Meng, M., & Liu, L. (2021). An input-output orientation model for estimating most productive scale size in fuzzy data envelopment analysis. *Advances in Natural Computation, Fuzzy Systems and Knowledge Discovery*, pp. 750–760. Springer, Cham.
Moghaddas, Z., & Vaez-Ghasemi, M. (2014). Estimating most productive scale size in DEA with real and integer value data. *International Journal of Industrial Mathematics, 6*(2), 107–114.
Mohmmad Nejad, Z., & Ghaffari-Hadigheh, A. (2018). A novel DEA model based on uncertainty theory. *Annals of Operations Research, 264*, 367–389.
Mohseni, S., & Pishvaee, M. S. (2016). A robust programming approach towards design and optimization of microalgae-based biofuel supply chain. *Computers and Industrial Engineering, 100*, 58–71.
Mottaghi, A., Ezzati, R., & Khorram, E. (2017). Resource allocation based on DEA for distance improvement to MPSS points considering environmental factors. *International Journal of Data Envelopment Analysis, 5*(2), 1207–1230.
Mousavi, S. M., & Vahdani, B. (2017). A robust approach to multiple vehicle location-routing problems with time windows for optimization of cross-docking under uncertainty. *Journal of Intelligent and Fuzzy Systems, 32*(1), 49–62.
Mousazadeh, M., Torabi, S. A., & Zahiri, B. (2015). A robust possibilistic programming approach for pharmaceutical supply chain network design. *Computers & Chemical Engineering, 82*, 115–128.
Mulvey, J. M., Vanderbei, R. J., & Zenios, S. A. (1995). Robust optimization of large-scale systems. *Operations Research, 43*(2), 264–281.
Nayeri, S., Paydar, M. M., Asadi-Gangraj, E., & Emami, S. (2020). Multi-objective fuzzy robust optimization approach to sustainable closed-loop supply chain network design. *Computers & Industrial Engineering, 148*, 106716.
Nepomuceno, T. C. C., Costa, A. P. C. S., & Daraio, C. (2023). Theoretical and empirical advances in the assessment of productive efficiency since the introduction of DEA: A bibliometric analysis. *International Journal of Operational Research, 46*(4), 505–549.
Nie, X. H., Huang, G. H., Li, Y. P., & Liu, L. (2007). IFRP: A hybrid interval-parameter fuzzy robust programming approach for waste management planning under uncertainty. *Journal of Environmental Management, 84*(1), 1–11.
Oaksford, M., & Chater, N. (2001). The probabilistic approach to human reasoning. *Trends in Cognitive Sciences, 5*(8), 349–357. Elsevier Current Trends.
Olesen, O. B., & Petersen, N. C. (2016). Stochastic data envelopment analysis—A review. *European Journal of Operational Research, 251*(1), 2–21.
Omrani, H., Shamsi, M., Emrouznejad, A., & Teplova, T. (2023). A robust DEA model under discrete scenarios for assessing bank branches. *Expert Systems with Applications, 219*, 119694.
Pan, F., & Nagi, R. (2010). Robust supply chain design under uncertain demand in agile manufacturing. *Computers and Operations Research, 37*(4), 668–683.
Peykani, P., Hosseinzadeh Lotfi, F., Sadjadi, S. J., Ebrahimnejad, A., & Mohammadi, E. (2022a). Fuzzy chance-constrained data envelopment analysis: A structured literature review, current trends, and future directions. *Fuzzy Optimization and Decision Making, 21*(2), 197–261.
Peykani, P., Gheidar-Kheljani, J., Farzipoor Saen, R., & Mohammadi, E. (2022b). Generalized robust window data envelopment analysis approach for dynamic performance measurement under uncertain panel data. *Operational Research, 22*(5), 5529–5567.

Peykani, P., Gheidar-Kheljani, J., Rahmani, D., Karimi Gavareshki, M. H., & Jabbarzadeh, A. (2022c). Uncertain super-efficiency data envelopment analysis. *Advances in Econometrics, Operational Research, Data Science and Actuarial Studies: Techniques and Theories*, pp. 311–320. Springer, Cham.

Peykani, P., Emrouznejad, A., Mohammadi, E., & Gheidar-Kheljani, J. (2024). A novel robust network data envelopment analysis approach for performance assessment of mutual funds under uncertainty. *Annals of Operations Research, 339*(3), 1149–1175.

Peykani, P., Farzipoor Saen, R., Seyed Esmaeili, F. S., & Gheidar-Kheljani, J. (2021). Window data envelopment analysis approach: A review and bibliometric analysis. *Expert Systems, 38*(7), e12721.

Peykani, P., Mohammadi, E., & Seyed Esmaeili, F. S. (2018). Measuring performance, estimating most productive scale size, and benchmarking of hospitals using DEA approach: A case study in Iran. *International Journal of Hospital Research, 7*(2), 21–41.

Peykani, P., Mohammadi, E., Farzipoor Saen, R., Sadjadi, S. J., & Rostamy-Malkhalifeh, M. (2020a). Data envelopment analysis and robust optimization: A review. *Expert Systems, 37*(4), e12534.

Peykani, P., Mohammadi, E., Jabbarzadeh, A., Rostamy-Malkhalifeh, M., & Pishvaee, M. S. (2020b). A novel two-phase robust portfolio selection and optimization approach under uncertainty: A case study of Tehran stock exchange. *PLoS ONE, 15*(10), e0239810.

Pishvaee, M. S., Razmi, J., & Torabi, S. A. (2012). Robust possibilistic programming for socially responsible supply chain network design: A new approach. *Fuzzy Sets and Systems, 206*, 1–20.

Pourmahmoud, J., & Bagheri, N. (2023). Uncertain Malmquist productivity index: An application to evaluate healthcare systems during COVID-19 pandemic. *Socio-Economic Planning Sciences*, 101522.

Rahmanzadeh, S., Pishvaee, M. S., & Rasouli, M. R. (2023). A robust fuzzy-stochastic optimization model for managing open innovation uncertainty in the ambidextrous supply chain planning problem. *Soft Computing, 27*(10), 6345–6365.

Roozbeh, F., Eslami, R., & Ahadzadeh Namin, M. (2015). Estimating most productive scale size with double frontiers in data envelopment analysis using negative data. *International Journal of Data Envelopment Analysis, 3*(4), 867–873.

Sahoo, B. K., Khoveyni, M., Eslami, R., & Chaudhury, P. (2016). Returns to scale and most productive scale size in DEA with negative data. *European Journal of Operational Research, 255*(2), 545–558.

Salimian, S., & Mousavi, S. M. (2022). A robust possibilistic optimization model for organ transplantation network design considering climate change and organ quality. *Journal of Ambient Intelligence and Humanized Computing*, 1–24.

Sari, Y. D., Efendi, S., & Zarlis, M. (2018). Estimating most productive scale Size in data envelopment analysis with integer value data. *IOP Conference Series: Materials Science and Engineering, 300*(1), 012014. IOP Publishing.

Sarkar, S. (2015). Assessment of performance using MPSS based DEA. *Benchmarking: An International Journal, 22*(4), 624–642.

Sehgal, R., & Jagadesh, P. (2023). Data-driven robust portfolio optimization with semi mean absolute deviation via support vector clustering. *Expert Systems with Applications, 224*, 120000.

Shafiee, F., Kazemi, A., Jafarnejad Chaghooshi, A., Sazvar, Z., & Amoozad Mahdiraji, H. (2021). A robust multi-objective optimization model for inventory and production management with environmental and social consideration: A real case of dairy industry. *Journal of Cleaner Production, 294*, 126230.

Soyster, A. L. (1973). Convex programming with set-inclusive constraints and applications to inexact linear programming. *Operations Research, 21*(5), 1154–1157.

Tapia, J. F. D. (2021). Evaluating negative emissions technologies using neutrosophic data envelopment analysis. *Journal of Cleaner Production, 286*, 125494.

Toloo, M., Mensah, E. K., & Salahi, M. (2022). Robust optimization and its duality in data envelopment analysis. *Omega, 108*, 102583.

Wang, C., Liu, Y., Li, J., & Yang, G. (2021). A robust optimization model for a community healthcare service network design problem. *IFIP Advances in Information and Communication Technology, 633*, 568–573.

Wang, Y. M., & Lan, Y. X. (2013). Estimating most productive scale size with double frontiers data envelopment analysis. *Economic Modelling, 33*, 182–186.

Wen, M., Zhang, Q., Kang, R., & Yang, Y. (2017). Some new ranking criteria in data envelopment analysis under uncertain environment. *Computers & Industrial Engineering, 110*, 498–504.

Yancheshmeh, B. S., & Adeli, M. M. (2023). A probabilistic approach for seismic demand estimation of steel moment frames considering capacity uncertainty. *Asian Journal of Civil Engineering*, 1–23.

Yang, W., Cai, L., Edalatpanah, S. A., & Smarandache, F. (2020). Triangular single valued neutrosophic data envelopment analysis: Application to hospital performance measurement. *Symmetry, 12*(4), 588.

Yavari, M., & Geraeli, M. (2019). Heuristic method for robust optimization model for green closed-loop supply chain network design of perishable goods. *Journal of Cleaner Production, 226*, 282–305.

Zadeh, L. A., Klir, G. J., & Yuan, B. (1996). *Fuzzy sets, fuzzy logic, and fuzzy systems*. World Scientific.

Zhu, J. (2000). Setting scale efficient targets in DEA via returns to scale estimation method. *Journal of the Operational Research Society, 51*(3), 376–378.

Zymler, S., Rustem, B., & Kuhn, D. (2011). Robust portfolio optimization with derivative insurance guarantees. *European Journal of Operational Research, 210*(2), 410–424.

Goal Programming Method for Solving Tri-Level Data Envelopment Analysis

Morteza Shafiee and Hilda Saleh

Abstract Data Envelopment Analysis (DEA) is a methodical approach utilizing linear programming to assess the effectiveness and efficiency of Decision-Making Units (DMUs). It particularly focuses on scenarios where these DMUs possess multiple inputs and outputs. However, when dealing with practical situations, we often come across intricate and interconnected circumstances that operate within a hierarchical framework, with decisions being made in a decentralized manner. The traditional DEA models are not suitable for these hierarchical issues because they assume a single decision-making center with all decision-making power and do not consider the decentralized nature of the decision-making process. Recently, a group of scholars proposed an innovative bi-level programming data envelopment analysis approach to assess the entities within a hierarchical framework, wherein decentralized decision-making involves two tiers of decision-making centers. The bi-level programming DEA takes into account the two levels of decision-making centers and their interactions. It considers the decision-making process as a bi-level optimization problem, where the upper-level decision-making center aims to maximize the overall efficiency of the system, while the lower-level decision-making centers aim to optimize their own efficiencies. In this chapter, the DEA model is extended for units with tri-level structures and then to solve the model, a goal programming approach is applied. Finally, an illustrative example is presented to demonstrate the efficacy of this method.

Keywords Data envelopment analysis · Efficiency · Goal programming · Tri-level programming · Tri-level DEA

M. Shafiee
Industrial Management, Economic and Management Faculty, Shiraz Branch, Islamic Azad University, Shiraz, Iran

H. Saleh (✉)
Department of Mathematics, Faculty of Science, Central Tehran Branch, Islamic Azad University, Tehran, Iran
e-mail: hilda_saleh@yahoo.com

© The Author(s), under exclusive license to Springer Nature Singapore Pte Ltd. 2024
S. A. Edalatpanah et al. (eds.), *Analytical Decision Making and Data Envelopment Analysis*, Infosys Science Foundation Series in Mathematical Sciences,
https://doi.org/10.1007/978-981-97-6972-8_9

1 Introduction

As business competition grows fiercer, the evaluation of efficiency has emerged as a crucial concern for all types of organizations. It has now become a pivotal element for advancement and success. The organizations always seek to increase their efficiency in real-world decision-making situations. When seeking to improve performance, selecting an appropriate tool is very important. Thus, an appropriate efficiency evaluation tool should be designed to improve performance. Among the various methods of evaluation, DEA has gained extensive popularity for assessing the relative efficiency of a group of production processes known as Decision Making Units (DMUs). DEA models offer a unique advantage as they do not rely on precise knowledge of the production function involving multiple inputs and outputs (Hosseinzadeh Lotfi et al., 2023a, b). So this tool is gaining increased attention in use and matter of many researchers.

DEA determines the efficiencies of DMUs within a group and chose the most effective of them to construct the efficiency frontier that plays a benchmark role to other DMUs. DEA is a method based on linear programming to evaluate the efficiency of DMUs that handle numerous inputs and outputs. Unlike other techniques, DEA calculates efficiency based on the distance a DMU is from the frontier, which represents the performance of the efficient units within the system.

Real-life scenarios that require decision-making can frequently be represented using mathematical programming problems. However, these problems typically encompass several objectives that may contradict each other, necessitating simultaneous consideration. So because of these conflicting objectives and interactions, calculating efficiency becomes more complicated.

In the current study, we investigate the performance evaluation in a tri-level structure that consists of a leader (top-level), follower 1 (middle-level), and follower 2 (bottom-level) by use of the DEA models. In other words, we are trying to construct a model for decentralized decisions, consisting of the objective functions in three different decision levels with given constraints known as tri-level linear fractional programming (TLLFP). Additionally, we can assume that the leader's strategy is well-known to the followers, and that follower2 is aware of follower1's strategy. Moreover, it is important to recognize that upper-level decisions will have a significant impact on the lower-level decisions. As depicted in the illustration (Fig. 1), the hierarchical structure determines that the flow of decision-making progresses from the highest level to the lower levels.

Then by applying the GP approach to linear fractional programming, proposed by Baky (2009), we obtain the most satisfactory solution. In this method, solutions of each level are calculated individually. Then we define a satisfactory function to objective function and decision variables of upper levels and add these functions to lower levels constraints. This procedure will continue to the third level and obtaining of an overall satisfactory solution for all three levels. Also, to avoid deadlock during the decision-making process, some flexibility parameters have been considered in the modelling.

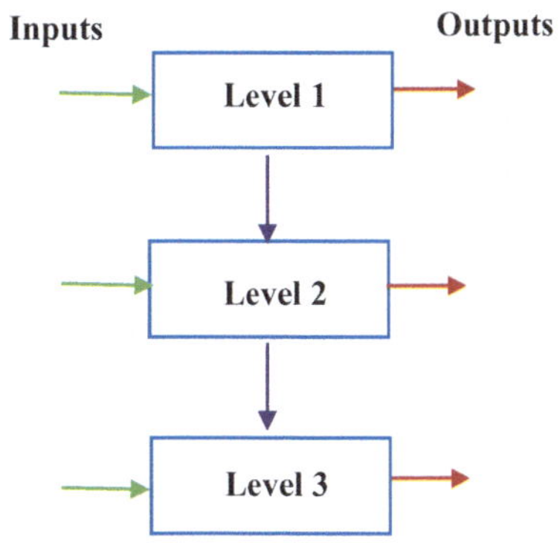

Fig. 1 A hierarchy tri-level structure

The results and discussions can be easily generalized into a multi-level structure where the number of levels is more than three, as well as Baky noted in (Baky, 2010). The primary benefit of the suggested method is that they avoid any complications arising from repeatedly reassessing the problem and modifying the criteria for achieving greater satisfaction. (Pramanik & Roy, 2007).

The arrangement of this chapter is as follows: Following the introduction presented in Sect. 1 and a concise analysis of relevant literature in Sect. 2, Sect. 3 introduces the construction of a Tri-level DEA model. This model utilizes a fractional objective function at each level of the hierarchy structure to assess efficiency. In order to address the identified issues in solving the proposed model and the conversion of the developed models into linear single-level programming models, Sect. 4 utilizes the GP method. To illustrate the characteristics of the proposed model and how to achieve the best possible solution, Sect. 5 presents a numerical example. Lastly, Sect. 6 outlines the conclusions drawn from the study and emphasizes the need for future research endeavors.

2 Literature Review

2.1 DEA Method

The DEA method that was initially proposed by Charnes et al. in 1978 and later expanded upon by Banker et al. in 1984, is a nonparametric approach utilized for assessing the relative efficiency of similar DMUs.

In the conventional DEA models, the focus has typically been on overlooking the internal workings of DMUs, treating them as “black box”. Put differently, a DMU is typically seen as a singular operation that converts inputs into outputs, disregarding any conflicting goals. So the network (Shi et al., 2021; Xiao et al., 2021; Michali et al., 2021; Zhu et al., 2021) and multi-level form of structures (Yao et al., 2020; Yang et al., 2021; Monge et al., 2023) is a matter of recent DEA researchers. Coelli (1998) first proposed a multi-stage methodology that evaluates the efficiencies of each subunit within a main DMU. Sexton and Lewis (2003) proposed a novel variation of the DEA model, where a DMU is constructed by integrating two interconnected sub-DMUs. Also, Tone and Tsutsui (2009) devised a network DEA framework to assess the efficiencies of DMUs, encompassing both divisional and overall performances. Cook et al. (2010) also, applied additive models for DMUs exhibiting a network framework. These researchers try to develop the use of DEA by considering the internal relation of DMUs to allow greater insight to identify organizational inefficiencies (Kao, 2009; Saleh & Rostamy, 2013; Saleh, 2011; Sahoo, 2021; Wang et al., 2020; Zhu, 2022).

2.2 *Multi-Level Programming Problem*

In practical scenarios, we frequently come across situations within hierarchical organizations where multiple decision-makers exist. These individuals engage in decision-making either sequentially or simultaneously, aiming to optimize their objectives. This type of problem is referred to as multi-level mathematical programming problems. Extensive exploration has been performed in the field of multi-level mathematical programming aimed at tackling organizational planning and decision-making challenges, as of late (Lachhwani et al., 2018; Liu et al., 2020; Wei et al., 2021; Fathollahi-Fard, 2022; Ma et al., 2022; Cheng et al., 2022). Most of the focus in research and practical implementations has revolved around bi-level programming problems. The bi-level non-linear programming was extensively examined in previous works such as Abo-Sinna (2001) and Abo-Sinna and Baky (2007). A different approach was introduced by Shi and Xia (1997) where they proposed an interactive algorithm specifically for bi-level multi-objective programming.

Three-level programming problem (TLPP) represents a distinct category of MLPPs, where there is a three decision center in the DMU structure. Hybrid extreme-point search algorithm (Bialas & Karwan, 1984; Desai et al., 2005), penalty function approach (Anandalingam, 1988; Lee & Shih, 2012), fuzzy sets [] Sakawa and Matsui (2012), Baky (2010), Osman et al. (2004), Mohamed (1997), Lee and Shih (2012), Kth-best algorithm (Zhang et al. 2010) and KKT transformation approach (Sinha & Sinha, 2002) are developed to solve the MLPPs. Baky (2010) proposed a fuzzy goal programming strategy for addressing multi-level multi-objective linear programming problems. This approach was applied within this chapter to solve tri-level DEA problems, thereby obtaining an optimal solution.

2.3 DEA in a Hierarchical Structure

Multi-level DEA is a kind of Multi-level mathematical programming problem. Multi-level mathematical programming pertains to mathematical problems that entail the involvement of various decision-makers within a multi-level or hierarchical organizational framework. Also, considering conflicting objectives and interactions between them, better insight into inefficiency and its causes are studied.

Wu (2012) introduced a new bi-level DEA approach to assess cost efficiency in a hierarchy structure. He believes that the bi-level DEA offers a means to unveil the inner workings of a 'black box' system, enabling a comprehensive assessment of subsystem performance. Shafiee (2016) considers bank branch as a bi-level system and evaluates them using bi-level DEA. Zhou (2018) evaluates bi-level systems with multiple followers.

Hajiagha et al. (2019) proposed a target-setting method for the efficiency of bi-level units. And also, Zhu et al. (2019) and Ding et al. (2019) suggested a new model for fixed cost allocation in a bi-level system. Despite much research on network DEA structure, DEA in multi-level structures has been less in the research subjects. For more information about the bi-level DEA model see (Hosseinzadeh Lotfi et al., 2023a, b). So based on the literature review, this issue is important that real modeling and solution for multi-level DEA problems need to be further developed.

3 Problem Formulation

Assume that a decision-making problem is a three levels problem in a hierarchy structure. In other words, the decision problem encompasses three optimization sub-problems occurring at distinct levels, involving interactive undertakings and internal consequences. To evaluate the efficiency of such a structure, the DEA method is applied. So model (1) for DMUo is formulated as:

$$
\begin{aligned}
&\max \frac{u^s y_o^s + w^s z_o^s}{v^s x_o^s}\\
&s.t\\
&\frac{u^s y_j^s + w^s z_j^s}{v^s x_j^s} \le 1, \quad j - 1, \ldots, n,\\
&u^s \ge 0, w^s \ge 0, v^s \ge 0,\\
&\max \frac{u^m y_o^m + w^m z_o^m}{v^m x_o^m + w^s z_o^s}\\
&\text{s.t}\\
&\frac{u^m y_j^m + w^m z_j^m}{v^m x_j^m + w^s z_j^s} \le 1, \qquad j = 1, \ldots, n,
\end{aligned}
$$

$$u^m \geq 0, w^m \geq 0, w^s \geq 0, v^m \geq 0,$$

$$\max \frac{u^d y_o^d}{v^d x_o^d + w^m z_o^m}$$

$$\text{s.t}$$

$$\frac{u^d y_j^d}{v^d x_j^d + w^m z_j^m} \leq 1, \quad j = 1, \ldots, n,$$

$$u^d \geq 0, w^m \geq 0, v^d \geq 0 \tag{1}$$

where $j = 1, \ldots, n$ is the DMUs number, (x^s, x^m, x^d) and (y^s, y^m, y^d) are input and output vectors in the first, second and third levels. (z^s, z^m) are intermediate variable vectors that play the output role in the upper level and the input role in the lower level. Increasing these variables is a pleasure to the upper level and decreasing them to lower levels and this issue make a conflict between levels that must be moderated by the decision-maker. Also, (v^s, v^m, v^d), (u^s, u^m, u^d) and (w^s, w^m) are the vector of input, output and intermediate relations weights, where must be optimized.

4 Solution Methodology

In order to address the aforementioned issue related to the fractional objective function, we adopt the suggested method introduced by Baky (2010). This methodology allows us to attain optimal solution for every DMU within a hierarchical structure consisting of three levels. So we need to define a goal for the objective function of all levels and decision variables of the upper levels (Baky, 2010).

Achieving a solution that meets the first level's acceptance criteria involves taking a single action, which subsequently provides decision variables and objectives to the second level, allowing for a degree of flexibility to attain a satisfactory outcome (Osman et al., 2004). Then the second level treats the same as the first level. In other words, each level strives to optimize its own aim while also ensuring that the overarching goals of the higher level are fulfilled.

Then a satisfaction function is built with attention to goals and tolerances by calculating individual maximum values (z_{jk}^+) and individual minimum values (z_{jk}^-) of all the objective functions for all levels under the given constraints. So that:

$$z_{jk}^+ = \max\{z_{jk} | k = s, m, d, j = 1, \ldots, n\} \tag{2}$$

and

$$z_{jk}^- = \min\{z_{jk} | k = s, m, d, j = 1, \ldots, n\} \tag{3}$$

Satisfaction function μ_z can be formulated as:

$$\mu_z = \begin{cases} 1 & z_{jk}(R_{jk}) \geq z_{jk}^+ \\ \frac{z_{jk}^+ - z_{jk}(R_{jk})}{z_{jk}^+ - z_{jk}^-} & z_{jk}^- < {}_{jk}(R_{jk}) < z_{jk}^+ \\ 0 & z_{jk}(R_{jk}) \leq z_{jk}^- \end{cases} \tag{4}$$

R_{jk} is k-level variables vector in DMU_j.

To increase the satisfaction level of the objective function of the first level, we obtain the optimal solution of the model (5).

$$\begin{aligned}
&\min w_{os}^+ d_{os}^+ \\
&s.t \\
&\frac{z_{os}^+ - \frac{u^s y_o^s + w^s z_o^s}{v^s x_o^s}}{z_{os}^+ - z_{os}^-} + d_{os}^- - d_{os}^+ = 1, \\
&u^s y_j^s + w^s z_j^s - v^s x_j^s \leq 0,\ j = 1, \ldots, n, \\
&u^m y_j^m + w^m z_j^m - v^m x_j^m - w^s z_j^s \leq 0,\ j = 1, \ldots, n, \\
&u^d y_j^d - v^d x_j^d - w^m z_j^m \leq 0,\ j = 1, \ldots, n, \\
&d_{o1}^- . d_{o1}^+ = 0, \\
&u^s \geq 0, u^d \geq 0, u^m \geq 0, v^s \geq 0, v^m \geq 0, v^d \geq 0, w^s \geq 0, w^m \geq 0, d_{os}^-, d_{os}^+ \geq 0
\end{aligned} \tag{5}$$

where, d_{os}^-, d_{os}^+ represent the vector of under and over deviations from the aspired levels in DMUo, w_{os}^+ represent the relative importance of the goals of each level of DMUo that are known as weights. To assign values of w_{os}^+ to each level, Mohamed (1997) proposed a unique weighting scheme which is determined as (6).

$$w_{jk}^+ = \frac{1}{z_{jk}^+ - z_{jk}^-},\ k = s, m, d, j = 1, \ldots, n \tag{6}$$

Model (5) is non-linear. To linearization process, using the change of the variable, if $L_{jk} = \frac{1}{z_{jk}^+ - z_{jk}^-}$ then $\frac{z_{jk}^+ - \frac{u^s y_j^s + w^s z_j^s}{v^s x_j^s}}{z_{jk}^+ - z_{jk}^-} + d_{jk}^- - d_{jk}^+ = 1$ is converted to (7).

$$L_{jk} z_{jk}^+ - L_{jk} \frac{u^s y_j^s + w^s z_j^s}{v^s x_j^s} + d_{jk}^- - d_{jk}^+ = 1 \tag{7}$$

As a result:

$$L_{jk} z_{jk}^+ v^s x_j^s - L_{jk}(u^s y_j^s + w^s z_j^s) + d_{jk}^- v^s x_j^s - d_{jk}^+ v^s x_j^s = v^s x_j^s, \tag{8}$$

So:

$$-\mathrm{L}_{jk}(u^s y_j^s + w^s z_j^s) + d_{jk}^- v^s x_j^s - d_{jk}^+ v^s x_j^s = v^s x_j^s[1 - \mathrm{L}_{jk} z_{jk}^+] \tag{9}$$

We define: $L_{jk} = 1 - L_{jk} z_{jk}^+$, So:

$$-\mathrm{L}_{jk}(u^s y_j^s + w^s z_j^s) - L_{jk} v^s x_j^s + d_{jk}^- v^s x_j^s - d_{jk}^+ v^s x_j^s = 0 \tag{10}$$

Finally, relation (10) becomes relation (11).

$$-c^s y_j^s + c^s z_j^s - b_{jk} x_j^s + D_{jk}^- - D_{jk}^+ = 0 \tag{11}$$

So that: $c^s = \mathrm{L}_{jk} u^s$, $c^s = -\mathrm{L}_{jk} w^s$, $b_{jk} = L'_{jk} v^s$, $D_{jk}^- = d_{jk}^- v^s x_j^s$ and $D_{jk}^+ = d_{jk}^+ v^s x_j^s$.

Also, in the decision-making process, minimizing d_{jk}^+ is equivalent to minimizing $d_{jk}^+ v^s x_j^s$, , which is a non-linear relation. It is important to mention that if full access is achieved to the level of satisfaction stated in (), the value of d_{jk}^+ equals zero, and if zero access is achieved, the value of d_{jk}^+ equals one. So constraint (12) is added to the model (5).

$$0 \le d_{jk}^+ \le 1 \Rightarrow \frac{D_{jk}^+}{v^s x_j^s} \le 1 \Rightarrow D_{jk}^+ - v^s x_j^s \le 0 \tag{12}$$

As a result, model (5) has been modified and is now referred to as model (13).

$$\begin{aligned}
&\min w_{os}^+ D_{os}^+ \\
&s.t \\
&c^s z_o^s - c^s y_o^s - b_{jk} x_o^s + D_{os}^- - D_{os}^+ = 0, \\
&D_{os}^+ - v^s x_o^s \le 0, \\
&u^s y_j^s + w^s z_j^s - v^s x_j^s \le 0, \quad j = 1, \ldots, n, \\
&u^m y_j^m + w^m z_j^m - v^m x_j^m - w^s z_j^s \le 0, \ j = 1, \ldots, n, \\
&u^d y_j^d - v^d x_j^d - w^m z_j^m \le 0, \quad j = 1, \ldots, n, \\
&D_{o1}^- . D_{o1}^+ = 0, \\
&u^s \ge 0, u^d \ge 0, u^m \ge 0, v^s \ge 0, v^m \ge 0, v^d \ge 0, w^s \ge 0, w^m \ge 0, D_{os}^-, D_{os}^+ \ge 0
\end{aligned} \tag{13}$$

After solving model (13), the explained process is repeated for the second level. But this issue may pose a problem to the upper level and change the first level optimal solution in the next step. To avoid this, by defining the tolerance variables to keep the previous solution, we must construct the satisfaction functions to decision variables.

Thus, we have:

$$\mu(R_{jk}) = \begin{cases} \frac{[R_{jk}^{*}+t_{jk}^{L}]-R_{jk}}{t_{jk}^{L}} & R_{jk}^{*} \le R_{jk} \le R_{jk}^{*} + t_{jk}^{R} \\ \frac{R_{jk}-[R_{jk}^{*}-t_{jk}^{L}]}{t_{jk}^{L}} & R_{jk}^{*} - t_{jk}^{L} \le R_{jk} \le R_{jk}^{*} \\ 0 & O.W \end{cases} \tag{14}$$

where R_{jk}, t_{jk}^{L} and t_{jk}^{R} are the decision variable vector, right and left tolerance at k-th level decision variable values in DMU_j, respectively.

$$R_{jk}^{*} - t_{jk}^{L} \le R_{jk} \le R_{jk}^{*}+t_{jk}^{R} \tag{15}$$

It is necessary to say that t_{jk}^{L} and t_{jk}^{R} are not necessarily the same (Pramanik & Roy, 2007). Here positive and negative tolerance values are so chosen that the satisfying solution is compelled towards the optimal solution to keep the previous upper-level solution. On the other hand, relation (15) leads to the decision variable being around the optimal decision variable R_{jk}^{*} with maximum left and right tolerances.

Also, it should be noted that the importance of the left and right tolerances is not necessarily the same. Therefore, to consider this difference, weights (relative importance) of t_{jk}^{L} and t_{jk}^{R} are defined using (16).

$$w_{jk}^{L} = \frac{1}{t_{jk}^{L}} \quad and \quad w_{jk}^{R} = \frac{1}{t_{jk}^{R}} \tag{16}$$

So the model (17) for the second level, by considering the relation between the first and second level, is represented as follows:

$$\begin{aligned} & \min w_{os}^{+}D_{os}^{+} + w_{om}^{+}D_{om}^{+} + w_{os}^{L}(d_{os}^{L+} + d_{os}^{L-}) + w_{os}^{R}(d_{os}^{R+} + d_{os}^{R-}) \\ & s.t \\ & - c_{o}^{s}z_{o}^{s} - c_{o}^{s}y_{o}^{s} - b_{o}^{s}x_{o}^{s} + D_{os}^{-} - D_{os}^{+} = 0, \\ & D_{os}^{+} - v^{s}x_{o}^{s} \le 0, \\ & c_{o}^{m}z_{o}^{m} - c_{o}^{m}y_{o}^{m} - b_{o}^{m}x_{o}^{m} - b_{o}^{m}z_{o}^{m} + D_{om}^{-} - D_{om}^{+} = 0, \\ & D_{om}^{+} - (v^{m}x_{o}^{m} + w^{m}z_{o}^{m}) \le 0, \end{aligned}$$

$$u^{s}y_{j}^{s} + w^{s}z_{j}^{s} - v^{s}x_{j}^{s} \le 0, \quad j = 1, \dots, n,$$

$$u^{m}y_{j}^{m} + w^{m}z_{j}^{m} - v^{m}x_{j}^{m} - w^{s}z_{j}^{s} \le 0, \quad j = 1, \dots, n,$$

$$u^{d}y_{j}^{d} - v^{d}x_{j}^{d} - w^{m}z_{j}^{m} \le 0, \quad j = 1, \dots, n,$$

$$\frac{R_{os} - [R_{os}^{*} - t_{os}^{L}]}{t_{os}^{L}} + d_{os}^{L-} - d_{os}^{L+} = 1,$$

$$\frac{[R_{os}^{*} + t_{os}^{R}] - R_{os}}{t_{os}^{R}} + d_{os}^{R-} - d_{os}^{R+} = 1,$$

$$D^-_{os}.D^+_{os}=0,$$
$$D^-_{om}.D^+_{om}=0,$$
$$u^s\geq 0, u^d\geq 0, u^m\geq 0, v^s\geq 0, v^m\geq 0, v^d\geq 0, w^s\geq 0, w^m\geq 0, D^-_{os}, D^+_{os}, D^-_{om}, D^+_{om}\geq 0 \tag{17}$$

So that: $R^*_{os}=(v^{s*}, w^{s*}, u^{s*})$ is obtained from model (13).

Finally, by a process similar to the first and second levels, model (17) was extended to the third level and the final model was constructed as (18):

$$\begin{aligned}
&\min w^+_{os}D^+_{os}+w^+_{om}D^+_{om}+w^+_{od}D^+_{od}+w^L_{os}(d^{L+}_{os}+d^{L-}_{os})+w^R_{os}(d^{R+}_{os}+d^{R-}_{os})\\
&+w^L_{om}(d^{L+}_{om}+d^{L-}_{om})+w^R_{om}(d^{R+}_{om}+d^{R-}_{om})\\
&s.t\\
&-c^s_oz^s_o-c^s_oy^s_o-b^s_ox^s_o+D^-_{os}-D^+_{os}=0,\\
&D^+_{os}-v^sx^s_o\leq 0,\\
&-c^m_oz^m_o-c^m_oy^m_o-b^m_ox^m_o-b^m_oz^m_o+D^-_{om}-D^+_{om}=0,\\
&D^+_{om}-v^mx^m_o-w^mz^m_o\leq 0,\\
&-c^d_oy^d_o-b^d_ox^d_o-b^d_oz^d_o+D^-_{od}-D^+_{od}=0,\\
&D^+_{od}-v^dx^d_o-w^dz^d_o\leq 0,\\
&u^sy^s_j+w^sz^s_j-v^sx^s_j\leq 0, && j=1,\ldots,n,\\
&u^my^m_j+w^mz^m_j-v^mx^m_j-w^sz^s_j\leq 0, && j=1,\ldots,n,\\
&u^dy^d_j-v^dx^d_j-w^mz^m_j\leq 0, && j=1,\ldots,n,
\end{aligned}$$

$$\begin{aligned}
&\frac{R_{os}-[R^*_{os}-t^L_{os}]}{t^L_{os}}+d^{L-}_{os}-d^{L+}_{os}=1,\\
&\frac{[R^*_{os}+t^R_{os}]-R_{os}}{t^R_{os}}+d^{R-}_{os}-d^{R+}_{os}=1,\\
&\frac{R_{om}-[R^*_{om}-t^L_{om}]}{t^L_{os}}+d^{L-}_{om}-d^{L+}_{om}=1,\\
&\frac{[R^*_{om}+t^R_{om}]-R_{om}}{t^R_{om}}+d^{R-}_{om}-d^{R+}_{om}=1,\\
&D^-_{os}.D^+_{os}=0,\\
&D^-_{om}.D^+_{om}=0,\\
&D^-_{od}.D^+_{od}=0,\\
&u^s\geq 0, u^d\geq 0, u^m\geq 0, v^s\geq 0, v^s\geq 0, v^d\geq 0, w^s\geq 0,\\
&w^m\geq 0, D^-_{os}, D^+_{os}, D^-_{om}, D^+_{om}, D^-_{od}, D^+_{od}\geq 0
\end{aligned} \tag{18}$$

Also, $R^*_{os} = (v^{s*}, w^{s*}, u^{s*})$ and $R^*_{om} = (v^{m*}, w^{m*}, u^{m*})$ are the optimal solution of models (13) and (17).

Model (18) provides the most satisfactory solution for the tri-level DEA problem. It should be mentioned that this technique has the potential to be applied to DEA problems that involve multiple levels.

5 Numerical Example

This section aims to demonstrate the suggested approach using a numerical example. Let's consider a group of five DMUs, each having distinct inputs and outputs as detailed in Table 1 and also represented in Fig. 2.

Table 1 Input, intermediate and output data

DMU	x_j^s	x_j^m	x_j^d	xd_j^s	xd_j^m	xd_j^d	z_j^s	z_j^m	y_j^s	y_j^m	y_j^d
1	2	4	6	3	4	5	6	5	3	4	6
2	4	3	4	2	4	4	4	3	4	3	7
3	3	5	3	3	3	3	3	4	3	2	5
4	2	3	5	4	3	5	2	3	4	4	3
5	3	2	2	4	4	4	4	5	5	5	5

Note that $x_j^k, k = s, m, d$ and $xd_j^k, k = s, m, d$ are the shared and direct inputs of each level, also, $y_j^k, k = s, m, d$ and $z_j^k, k = s, m$ are outputs and intermediate values of each level. A tri-level DEA model for the explained problem is as the model (19)

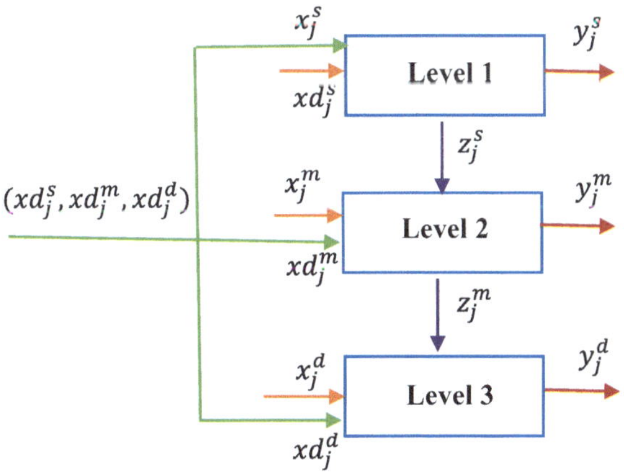

Fig. 2 A tri-level DMU

$$
\begin{aligned}
&\max z_{1s} = \frac{6w^s + 3u^s}{2v^s + 3p^s} \\
&s.t \\
&6w^s + 3u^s - 2v^s - 3p^s \le 0 \\
&4w^s + 4u^s - 4v^s - 2p^s \le 0 \\
&3w^s + 3u^s - 3v^s - 3p^s \le 0 \\
&2w^s + 4u^s - 2v^s - 4p^s \le 0 \\
&4w^s + 5u^s - 3v^s - 4p^s \le 0 \\
&u^s, v^s, p^s, w^s \ge 0 \\
&\max z_{1m} = \frac{5w^m + 4u^m}{4v^m + 4p^m + 6w^s} \\
&s.t \\
&5w^m + 4u^m - 4v^m - 4p^m - 6w^s \le 0 \\
&3w^m + 3u^m - 3v^m - 4p^m - 4w^s \le 0 \\
&4w^m + 2u^m - 5v^m - 3p^m - 3w^s \le 0 \\
&3w^m + 4u^m - 3v^m - 3p^m - 2w^s \le 0 \\
&5w^m + 5u^m - 2v^m - 4p^m - 4w^s \le 0 \\
&u^m, v^m, p^m, w^m, w^s \ge 0 \\
&\max z_{1d} = \frac{6u^d}{6v^d + 5p^d + 5w^m} \\
&s.t \\
&6u^d - 6v^d - 5p^d - 5w^m \le 0 \\
&7u^d - 4v^d - 4p^d - 3w^m \le 0 \\
&5u^d - 3v^d - 3p^d - 4w^m \le 0 \\
&3u^d - 5v^d - 5p^d - 3w^m \le 0 \\
&5u^d - 2v^d - 4p^d - 5w^m \le 0 \\
&u^d, v^d, p^d, w^m \ge 0
\end{aligned}
\tag{19}
$$

Minimum and maximum individual values, variable tolerances and also weights are summarized in Table 2.

Table 2 Minimum, maximum individual values, variable tolerances and weights

Level k	z_{1k}^{-}	z_{1k}^{+}	W_{1k}^{+}	t_{1k}^{R}	t_{1k}^{L}	W_{1k}^{R}	W_{1k}^{L}
1	–1	0	1	10	10	0.1	0.1
2	–0.975	0	1.026	10	10	0.1	0.1
3	–0.686	0	1.46	–	–	–	–

Finally, the optimal solution of the model (19) for the DMU1 according to the proposed methodology is summarized in Table 3.

In a similar procedure, the optimal objective function for all five DMU was obtained and the findings are documented in Table 4.

By considering Table 4, in the first and second levels, optimal objective function values ($Z_{is}^{opt.}$) are most close to their individual optimal objective function value ($Z_{is}^{ind.}$) than in the third level. On the other hand, e_{is} (difference between individual and optimal value) have less average value in upper levels than lower ones. Hence, these findings highlight the significance of prioritizing the objective functions of higher levels in a hierarchical structure over those of lower levels. Ultimately, to assess the efficiency of the system, we have the option to:

1. Utilize the average of the efficiency of different levels.
2. Use the convex combination of the efficiency of different levels.
3. Use a ratio of weighted outputs to weighted inputs of levels as system efficiency.

We believe that all of the above procedures give an efficiency score to the whole of the system but the exact quantity of system efficiency is ambiguous and uncertain. In other words, each of these procedures must be proven to be known in an accurate way that can be a matter of future studies.

Table 3 The optimal solution of the model (20) for the DMU1

v^s	v^m	v^d	p^s	p^s	p^d	w^s	w^m	u^s	u^m	u^d u^d
2.3350	2.665	1.54611	19.56	16.2179	25.52733	10.556	11.365220	14.014	16.18423	14.63632
Z_1	Z_2	Z_3								
1	0.974	0.685								

Table 4 The optimal objective function and the individual objective function

DMU_i	$Z_{is}^{ind.}$	$Z_{is}^{opt.}$	e_{is}	$Z_{im}^{ind.}$	$Z_{im}^{opt.}$	e_{im}	$Z_{id}^{ind.}$	$Z_{id}^{opt.}$	e_{id}
1	1	1	0	0.975	0.974	0.001	0.686	0.685	0.001
2	1	1	0	0.6	0.6	0	1	1	0
3	0.730	0.73	0	1	1	0	0.9524	0.589	0.363
4	1	1	0	1	1	0	0.4286	0.428	0.0006
5	1	1	0	1	1	0	1	1	0

6 Conclusion

In this chapter, the goal programming approach to get a satisfactory solution to the tri-level DEA problem is used. The approach is based on the satisfaction degree of objective function and variables. In each level to obtain the solution, previous level objective function and decision variable values are kept with some flexibility and this issue is shown by adding some constraints to the model.

In short, the steps to solve the proposed tri-level DEA model are as follows:

1. Calculate the individual maximum values (z_{jk}^{+}) and individual minimum values (z_{jk}^{-}) of all the objective functions for all levels under the given constraints.
2. Calculate the weights of the objective functions (w_{jk}^{+}) using the relation (6).
3. Satisfaction function (μ_z) is formulated by the relation (4).
4. Obtain the optimal solution of the model (13).
5. Consider the positive and negative tolerance values (t_{os}^{R} and t_{os}^{L}) for the decision variable vector of the first level.
6. Compute weights (relative importance) of the positive and negative tolerance values (w_{os}^{R} and w_{os}^{L}) using the relation (16).
7. Solve the model (17) for the second level, by considering the relation between the first and second levels.
8. Define t_{om}^{L} and t_{om}^{R} for the decision variable vector of the second level.
9. Compute the weights of the positive and negative tolerance values (w_{om}^{R} and w_{om}^{L}) using the relation (16).
10. Solve the model (18) for the third level to provide the most satisfactory solution for the tri-level DEA problem.

References

Abo-Sinna, M. A. (2001). A bi-level non-linear multi-objective decision-making under fuzziness. *Opsearch, 38*, 484–495.

Abo-Sinna, M. A., & Baky, I. A. (2007). Interactive balance space approach for solving multi-level multi-objective programming problems. *Information Sciences, 177*(16), 3397–3410.

Anandalingam, G. (1988). A mathematical programming model of decentralized multi-level systems. *Journal of the Operational Research Society, 39*(11), 1021–1033.

Baky, I. A. (2009). Fuzzy goal programming algorithm for solving decentralized bi-level multi-objective programming problems. *Fuzzy Sets and Systems, 160*(18), 2701–2713.

Baky, I. A. (2010). Solving multi-level multi-objective linear programming problems through fuzzy goal programming approach. *Applied Mathematical Modelling, 34*(9), 2377–2387.

Banker, D., Charnes, A., & Cooper, W. W. (1984). Some models for estimating technical and scale inefficiencies in data envelopment analysis. *Management Science, 30*, 1078–1092.

Bialas, W. F., & Karwan, M. H. (1984). Two-level linear programming. *Management Science, 30*(8), 1004–1020.

Charnes, A., Cooper, W. W., & Rhodes, E. (1979). Measuring the efficiency of decision-making units. *European Journal of Operational Research, 3*(4), 339.

Cheng, Q., Chen, Y., & Liu, Z. (2022). A bi-level programming model for the optimal lane reservation problem. *Expert Systems with Applications, 189*, 116147.

Coelli, T. (1998). A multi-stage methodology for the solution of orientated DEA models. *Operations Research Letters, 23*(3–5), 143–149.

Cook, W. D., Zhu, J., Bi, G., & Yang, F. (2010). Network DEA: Additive efficiency decomposition. *European Journal of Operational Research, 207*(2), 1122–1129.

Desai, A., Ratick, S. J., & Schinnar, A. P. (2005). Data envelopment analysis with stochastic variations in data. *Socio-Economic Planning Sciences, 39*(2), 147–164.

Ding, T., Zhu, Q., Zhang, B., & Liang, L. (2019). Centralized fixed cost allocation for generalized two-stage network DEA. *INFOR: Information Systems and Operational Research, 57*(2), 123–140.

Fathollahi-Fard, A. M., Hajiaghaei-Keshteli, M., Tavakkoli-Moghaddam, R., & Smith, N. R. (2022). Bi-level programming for home health care supply chain considering outsourcing. *Journal of Industrial Information Integration, 25*, 100246.

Hajiagha, S. H. R., Mahdiraji, H. A., & Tavana, M. (2019). A new bi-level data envelopment analysis model for efficiency measurement and target setting. *Measurement, 147*, 106877.

Hosseinzadeh Lotfi, F., Allahviranloo, T., Shafiee, M., & Saleh, H. (2023a). Performance evaluation of supply chains by bi-level DEA. *Supply chain performance evaluation: Application of data envelopment analysis* (pp. 419–442). Springer International Publishing.

Hosseinzadeh Lotfi, F., Allahviranloo, T., Shafiee, M., & Saleh, H. (2023b). Data envelopment analysis. *Supply chain performance evaluation: Application of data envelopment analysis* (pp. 179–241). Springer International Publishing.

Kao, C. (2009). Efficiency decomposition in network data envelopment analysis: A relational model. *European Journal of Operational Research, 192*(3), 949–962.

Lachhwani, K., & Dwivedi, A. (2018). Bi-level and multi-level programming problems: Taxonomy of literature review and research issues. *Archives of Computational Methods in Engineering, 25*, 847–877.

Lee, E. S., & Shih, H. S. (2012). *Fuzzy and multi-level decision making: an interactive computational approach*. Springer Science & Business Media.

Lewis, H. F., & Sexton, T. R. (2004). Network DEA: Efficiency analysis of organizations with complex internal structure. *Computers & Operations Research, 31*(9), 1365–1410.

Liu, R., Mu, P., Yuan, X., Zeng, S., & Zhang, J. (2020, November). A generic first-order algorithmic framework for bi-level programming beyond lower-level singleton. In *International Conference on Machine Learning* (pp. 6305–6315). PMLR.

Ma, M., Huang, H., Song, X., Peña-Mora, F., Zhang, Z., & Chen, J. (2022). Optimal sizing and operations of shared energy storage systems in distribution networks: A bi-level programming approach. *Applied Energy, 307*, 118170.

Michali, M., Emrouznejad, A., Dehnokhalaji, A., & Clegg, B. (2021). Noise-pollution efficiency analysis of European railways: A network DEA model. *Transportation Research Part D: Transport and Environment, 98*, 102980.

Mohamed, R. H. (1997). The relationship between goal programming and fuzzy programming. *Fuzzy Sets and Systems, 89*(2), 215–222.

Monge, J. F., & Ruiz, J. L. (2023). Setting closer targets based on non-dominated convex combinations of Pareto-efficient units: A bi-level linear programming approach in data envelopment analysis. *European Journal of Operational Research., 311*(3), 1084–1096.

Osman, M. S., Abo-Sinna, M. A., Amer, A. H., & Emam, O. (2004). A multi-level non-linear multi-objective decision-making under fuzziness. *Applied Mathematics and Computation, 153*(1), 239–252.

Pramanik, S., & Roy, T. K. (2007). Fuzzy goal programming approach to multilevel programming problems. *European Journal of Operational Research, 176*(2), 1151–1166.

Sakawa, M., & Matsui, T. (2012). Stackelberg solutions for random fuzzy two-level linear programming through possibility-based probability model. *Expert Systems with Applications, 39*(12), 10898–10903.

Saleh, H., & Rostamy, M. M. (2013). Performance evaluation in bank branch with two-stage DEA model.

Saleh, H., Hosseinzadeh Lotfi, F., Toloie Eshlaghy, A., & Shafiee, M. (2011). A new two-stage DEA model for bank branch performance evaluation. In *3rd National Conference on Data Envelopment Analysis, Islamic Azad University of Firoozkooh.*

Sexton, T. R., & Lewis, H. F. (2003). Two-stage DEA: An application to major league baseball. *Journal of Productivity Analysis, 19*, 227–249.

Shafiee, M., Lotfi, F. H., Saleh, H., & Ghaderi, M. (2016). A mixed integer bi-level DEA model for bank branch performance evaluation by Stackelberg approach. *Journal of Industrial Engineering International, 12*, 81–91.

Shi, X., & Xia, H. (1997). Interactive bilevel multi-objective decision making. *Journal of the Operational Research Society, 48*, 943–949.

Shi, X., Emrouznejad, A., & Yu, W. (2021). Overall efficiency of operational process with undesirable outputs containing both series and parallel processes: A SBM network DEA model. *Expert Systems with Applications, 178*, 115062.

Sinha, S., & Sinha, S. B. (2002). KKT transformation approach for multi-objective multi-level linear programming problems. *European Journal of Operational Research, 143*(1), 19–31.

Tone, K., & Tsutsui, M. (2009). Network DEA: A slacks-based measure approach. *European Journal of Operational Research, 197*(1), 243–252.

Wang, Y., Pan, J. F., Pei, R. M., Yi, B. W., & Yang, G. L. (2020). Assessing the technological innovation efficiency of China's high-tech industries with a two-stage network DEA approach. *Socio-Economic Planning Sciences, 71*, 100810.

Wei, J., Zhang, Y., Wang, J., & Wu, L. (2021). Distribution LMP-based demand management in industrial park via a bi-level programming approach. *IEEE Transactions on Sustainable Energy, 12*(3), 1695–1706.

Wu, D. D. (2010). Bilevel programming data envelopment analysis with constrained resources. *European Journal of Operational Research, 207*(2), 856–864.

Xiao, H., Wang, D., Qi, Y., Shao, S., Zhou, Y., & Shan, Y. (2021). The governance-production nexus of eco-efficiency in Chinese resource-based cities: A two-stage network DEA approach. *Energy Economics, 101*, 105408.

Yang, Z., Hui, L., & Chen, X. (2021). Efficiency evaluation of unattended convenience store based on bi-level DEA with multi-followers. In *E3S Web of Conferences* (Vol. 253, p. 03005). EDP Sciences.

Yao, L., Shuai, Y., & Chen, X. (2020). Regional water system vulnerability evaluation: A bi-level DEA with multi-followers approach. *Journal of Hydrology, 589*, 125160.

Zhang, G., Lu, J., Montero, J., & Zeng, Y. (2010). Model, solution concept, and Kth-best algorithm for linear trilevel programming. *Information Sciences, 180*(4), 481–492.

Zhou, X., Luo, R., Tu, Y., Lev, B., & Pedrycz, W. (2018). Data envelopment analysis for bi-level systems with multiple followers. *Omega, 77*, 180–188.

Zhu, J. (2022). DEA under big data: Data enabled analytics and network data envelopment analysis. *Annals of Operations Research, 309*(2), 761–783.

Zhu, W., Zhang, Q., & Wang, H. (2019). Fixed costs and shared resources allocation in two-stage network DEA. *Annals of Operations Research, 278*(1), 177–194.

Machine Learning Techniques and Efficiency Evaluation: A Survey of Methodological Contributions

Juan Aparicio, Miriam Esteve, and Qianying Jin

Abstract This chapter surveys the literature on two types of related contributions. The first group is made up of models devoted to adapting well-known machine learning techniques for estimating production frontiers, satisfying shape constraints (free disposability, convexity, ...). The second group consists in approaches that apply frontier estimators to classify observations under the classical framework of supervised machine learning with two or more classes. Thus, this survey represents a round-trip between two relatively unconnected fields to date: machine learning and frontier analysis. In particular, we conduct a review of the existing literature devoted to methodological aims.

Keywords Data envelopment analysis · Efficiency · Machine learning · Classification

---

J. Aparicio (✉)
Center of Operations Research (CIO), Miguel Hernandez University (UMH), Avda. de La Universidad S/N, 03202 Elche (Alicante), Spain
e-mail: j.aparicio@umh.es

Valencian Graduate School and Research Network of Artificial Intelligence (valgrAI), Valencia, Spain

M. Esteve
Center of Operations Research (CIO), Miguel Hernandez University, Elche, Spain
e-mail: miriam.estevec@umh.es

Q. Jin
College of Economics and Management, Nanjing University of Aeronautics and Astronautics, Nanjing, China
e-mail: qianying.jin@nuaa.edu.cn

© The Author(s), under exclusive license to Springer Nature Singapore Pte Ltd. 2024
S. A. Edalatpanah et al. (eds.), *Analytical Decision Making and Data Envelopment Analysis*, Infosys Science Foundation Series in Mathematical Sciences,
https://doi.org/10.1007/978-981-97-6972-8_10

1 Introduction

There is currently a growing interest in the literature, both economic and engineering, for the evaluation of the performance of all types of decision-making units, from companies to public institutions. In an environment of scarce resources, the search for efficiency is vital for the survival of the company or for the adequate provision of the services provided by the corresponding public body. In the context of production processes, technical efficiency is concerned with achieving maximum outputs with the least resources (inputs). Unfortunately, it is not always possible for the decision-making unit to produce goods and services complying with the efficiency criteria, in most cases due to poor internal management of the resources of the company or public body. It is in this case, when it becomes necessary to identify the degree of technical efficiency of the decision-making unit. In this regard, it is a very common in practice to resort to counterfactual evaluation methods, through which the behaviour of the evaluated unit is contrasted with respect to the operation of a set of homogeneous units belonging to the same sector of activity and whose results have also been observed. Within this line of work, we can highlight frontier-based methods as those most used in practice when determining the degree of technical efficiency of production units. These methods, from the observation of a data sample, i.e., inputs and outputs of a set of units belonging to the same sector, are capable of determining the estimate of the reference technology associated with the productive sector in question. This technology represents the current technological knowledge available to companies and, formally, is associated with the set of combinations of inputs and outputs that can be observed. That is why, in the specialized literature, technology is also known as the Production Possibilities Set (PPS). A certain subset of the technology frontier, which functions as a kind of edge of possibility, is associated with the combinations of inputs and outputs that perform best from a technical point of view. This subset is known as the efficient frontier of the technology and is used, in practice, to identify the technical inefficiency of units (firms, public organizations, ...), by calculating the distance of each observation to the subset. In the particular case of productive processes based on the generation of a single output, the concept of efficient frontier is equivalent to the concept of production function. This function indicates the largest quantity of output that it is possible to produce from a particular input profile.

There are many different ways to estimate the reference technology or, failing that, the efficient frontier (or production function in the single-output context) associated with the said technology from a sample of observations. It is usual to classify these methods into two large groups: parametric methods and non-parametric methods. Taking for granted the statistical approach of the frontier models of Daraio and Simar (2007), where a data generating process (DGP) gave rise to the data sample that was finally observed in reality, the fundamental difference between the parametric and non-parametric methods can be found in the way in which the mathematical expression of the (true and unknown to the observer) production function linked to the data generating process is identified from a very early phase of the estimation process. In the case of parametric methods, the production function is usually identified by means of a mathematical expression that relates the output to a series of coefficients to be estimated and the inputs of the productive process, in such a way that it is usually relatively simple, once certain values have been determined for these coefficients, even identifying the importance of the inputs in the production process through the value of its associated coefficient. On the other hand, non-parametric methods are much more flexible, which can be understood as a methodological advantage, since the user of the technique does not have to define in advance an expression of this type when estimating the true production function lying behind the generation of the observed data. In short, it could be said that non-parametric methods stand out above parametric ones due to their flexibility and other features.

In this chapter of the book, we will focus on the use of non-parametric methods for the estimation of efficient frontiers and the corresponding identification of technical inefficiency. In this regard, the techniques that clearly stand out in the literature due to the number of users who have resorted to them in recent decades are Data Envelopment Analysis (DEA) (Banker et al., 1984; Charnes et al., 1978) and Free Disposal Hull (FDH) (Deprins et al., 1984). DEA builds a splines-based estimator from the technology through the fulfilment of a series of properties. In particular, the DEA technology is the most reduced set (due to the minimal extrapolation principle) that meets free disposal (that is, it is always possible to do worse), convexity and that includes the observations of the data sample. In the case of FDH, the efficient frontier has a ladder structure and the technology is built assuming the same postulates that DEA assumes, except that of convexity. FDH and DEA share many characteristics with Machine Learning (ML) (see Efron, 2020).

Despite the similarities between DEA and machine learning techniques and the importance that ML-based methods are currently having within the field of data analysis, to date, there are few contributions in the specialized literature that have proposed methodological developments combining both worlds: estimation of production frontiers and machine learning. Indeed, there are many articles that apply some standard ML technique in some phase of data analysis associated with identifying technical efficiency. In this regard, a simple Google Scholar search for the word strings "Data Envelopment Analysis" and "Machine learning" produces more than 8,500 results. However, the vast majority of these correspond to articles in which a true adaptation of an ML technique is not produced so that an efficient frontier can be estimated appropriately or a frontier technique, such as DEA, can be adapted to facilitate its application for the same purpose as many of the well-known ML techniques, for example, to classify observations belonging to two different classes.

The objective of this chapter is not to review all the literature that connects ML techniques and frontier techniques, but rather to carry out a detailed survey of the existing contributions that in particular introduce methodological developments adapting techniques belonging to one of these two scientific fields to the other field. In particular, this chapter surveys the literature on two types of related contributions. The first group is made up of models devoted to adapting well-known machine learning techniques for estimating production frontiers, satisfying shape constraints (free disposability, convexity, ...). The second group comprises approaches that apply frontier estimators to classify observations under the classical framework of supervised machine learning with two or more classes. Thus, this survey represents a round-trip between two relatively unconnected fields to date: ML and frontier analysis. As we mentioned above, we conduct a review of the existing literature that concentrates on methodological aims.

The rest of the chapter is organized as follows. In Sect. 2, we review and discuss the main contributions existing in the literature that tailored standard Machine Learning techniques to be used for measuring technical efficiency, competing against FDH and DEA. Section 3 is devoted to detailing the key extant contributions that extended DEA to the field of classification rules within ML. Section 4 shows the main conclusions of the survey and states possible research avenues for the future.

2 A Review of Methodological Contributions that Adapt ML Techniques for Estimating Frontiers

In this part of the chapter, we review the main methodological contributions that can be classified as machine learning techniques created to determine technical efficiency. These methods compete against the standard DEA and FDH, depending on whether the postulate of convexity is or not assumed. This is the reason why we structure this section into two different subsections. The first one aims to introduce the models associated with the techniques that assume convexity, which is equivalent to the concavity of the production function in the single-output case. The second subsection is devoted to show the contributions that do not suppose the typical convexity axiom in microeconomics.

Regarding notation, we assume that we have observed n units, also called Decision Making Units (DMUs). These units (firms, organizations, etc.) consume $\boldsymbol{x}_i = (x_{1i}, \ldots, x_{mi}) \in R_+^m$ inputs (i.e., resources) to produce $\boldsymbol{y}_i = (y_{1i}, \ldots, y_{si}) \in R_+^s$ outputs (i.e., goods or services). Bold face letters, as $\boldsymbol{x}$, $\boldsymbol{y}$ or $\boldsymbol{\beta}$, will denote vectors throughout the manuscript. Furthermore, non-bold face letters, as λ, will denote scalars.

2.1 *Machine Learning Techniques that Assume Convexity*

Probably, the first methodological contribution that was made in the literature on the measurement of technical efficiency that can be related to the machine learning field is that by Kuosmanen and Johnson (2010). These authors introduced a new frontier estimator that resembles the DEA estimator because it is also based on splines (i.e., both are piece-wise linear frontier estimators). The paper by Kuosmanen and Johnson (2010) introduced the single-output multi-input model, while the paper Kuosmanen and Johnson (2017) extended the previous paper. Nevertheless, seeking simplicity, we show here the single-output approach, which can be useful to estimate production functions as well as cost and revenue functions. In the case of the production function, the response variable is the output (quantity) of a production process, while in the case of the cost and revenue functions, the response variables are the monetary cost and monetary revenue associated with the production process at market prices, respectively.

The technique introduced by Kuosmanen and Johnson (2010) is called as Corrected Concave Nonparametric Least Squares (C^2NLS). It is grounded on Concave Nonparametric Least Squares (CNLS), which is a nonparametric regression technique that does not require any prior assumption about the functional form of the target function to be estimated. The difference between CNLS and standard regression techniques is that CNLS is subjected to continuity, monotonicity, and concavity constraints. In particular, CNLS is based on the assumptions that the target function to be estimated belongs to the set of continuous, monotonic increasing and globally concave functions.

The C^2NLS technique consists of two steps. In the first one, the optimization model linked to CNLS must be solved. After that, once we have an optimal solution, the second stage aims to correct the residuals to get a final frontier estimate such that it envelops the data sample from above, as that happens in the case of the DEA frontier estimate. In this way, the final frontier estimator derived from C^2NLS will satisfy the same microeconomic postulates as DEA except minimal extrapolation. This axiom, clearly linked to Occam's razor or the principle of parsimony in Science and Philosophy, is the responsible of the overfitting problem noted in DEA (the DEA frontier is located as close as possible to the observations, implying a bad generalization power).

Next, we show the two steps that must be executed to get the frontier estimate linked to C^2NLS by Kuosmanen and Johnson (2010). First, we must solve the following optimization model based on quadratic programming:

$$\min_{\alpha,\beta,\varepsilon}\left\{\sum_{i=1}^{n}\varepsilon_i^2 : \begin{array}{ll} y_i = \alpha_i + \langle \boldsymbol{\beta}_i, \boldsymbol{x}_i\rangle + \varepsilon_i, & \forall i = 1,\ldots,n \\ \alpha_i + \langle \boldsymbol{\beta}_i, \boldsymbol{x}_i\rangle \le \alpha_h + \langle \boldsymbol{\beta}_h, \boldsymbol{x}_h\rangle, & \forall h,i = 1,\ldots,n \\ \boldsymbol{\beta}_i \ge 0, & \forall i = 1,\ldots,n \end{array}\right\}, \quad (1)$$

where $\langle .,. \rangle$ denotes the scalar product of two vectors.

Model (1) estimates n different regression lines (see the first constraint), as many as observations, rather than fitting the typical single regression line to the data cloud in Statistics. These n regression lines lead to a splines-based estimator. Due to the objective function, model (1) is similar to OLS (Ordinary Least Squares). The second restriction enforces concavity of the estimator by applying the system of Afriat's inequalities (Afriat, 1972). Note that the concavity of the production function is equivalent to convexity of the production possibility set that can be defined from that production function. The non-negativity constraints in model (1) impose monotonicity of the estimator (roughly speaking, more input implies more output or, at least, not less). There is a relationship between monotonicity of the production function and the axiom of free disposability for the technology. In some sense, they are the same property but restricted to different production scenarios, that is, only one output and multiple outputs, respectively.

However, model (1) does not try to capture (extreme) frontier patterns in the data but mean patterns. In this regard, it is worth mentioning that the residuals derived from model (1), $\varepsilon_i^*, i = 1, \ldots, n$, can be positive, negative or zero. This is the reason why, the second step of the algorithm linked to the C^{2}NLS technique, has as an objective to determine a frontier estimate by transforming $\varepsilon_i^*, i = 1, \ldots, n$, into non-positive residuals, that is, residuals associated with a surface that really represents a frontier because it envelops the data from above. Next, we show the two steps.

Step 1: Determine an optimal solution of model (1): ε_i^*, α_i^*, and $\boldsymbol{\beta}_i^*$, $i = 1, \ldots, n$.

Step 2: This is the stage to correct the values obtained in step 1. In particular, the residuals and the intercepts of each regression line must be modified as follows:

$$\hat{\varepsilon}_i^{C2NLS} = \varepsilon_i^* - \max_h \varepsilon_h^*. \tag{2}$$

$$\hat{\alpha}_i^{C2NLS} = \alpha_i^* + \max_h \varepsilon_h^*. \tag{3}$$

The contribution by Kuosmanen and Johnson (2010) has been extended in several ways in the last years (see, for example, Tsionas, 2022a).

Later, Parmeter and Racine (2013) proposed a class of smooth constrained nonparametric and semiparametric frontier estimators consistent with theoretical axioms of production. Smoothness (i.e., continuous differentiability) can be an appealing feature since many typical theoretical production functions in microeconomics satisfy this property (for example, the Cobb–Douglas production function). Probably, the most related approach from those introduced by Parmeter and Racine (2013) to the techniques listed in this chapter is the constrained nonparametric deterministic frontier estimator. Nevertheless, we want to point out that a constrained semiparametric stochastic frontier version was also introduced by these same authors, which relies on parametric structure for the composed error distribution (technical inefficiency plus random noise). The main idea behind these methods is the use of constrained kernel estimation techniques, imposing the satisfaction of shape restrictions from production theory, as concavity and monotonicity of the production function. In particular, as we mentioned above, concavity of the production function is related to the convexity of the corresponding technology.

In this same line of estimating convex technologies, Daouia et al. (2016) introduced a new technique based on using polynomial spline fitting. The method allows dealing with both monotonicity and concavity. Additionally, frontier smoothing is also considered. The method requires solving a convex programming problem with second-order conic constraints. Although the approach by Daouia et al. (2016) is limited to the production of only one output from an only input, it has been extended to the multi-input case in Selk et al. (2022).

Olesen and Ruggiero (2022) have recently adapted a technique known as Hinging Hyperplanes by Breiman (1993) as a flexible estimator of S-shaped production functions. Hinging hyperplanes is another spline-based technique in ML. In production theory, the law of diminishing returns says that in productive activities, after some optimal level of capacity is reached, augmenting the quantity of an input, while keeping all other inputs constant, will result in smaller increases in the quantity of output produced. Graphically, this situation corresponds to a S-shaped production function. If one wants to introduce this type of shape constraint in the econometric analysis, it is necessary to identify the point in the input space at which the target function to be estimated changes from convex to concave (a consequence of the S-shape). In their method, Olesen and Ruggiero assume that the output, since this approach has been only designed for the single output case, comes from a DGP in the following way: $y_i = F(g_{CORE}(\boldsymbol{x}_i)) + \varepsilon_i$, where $\varepsilon_i \in R$ is a mixture of technical inefficiency and statistical noise. Due to computational difficulties, the authors resort to a grid search over a set of preselected hinge locations.

Recently, Guerrero et al. (2022) have studied in depth how to deal with the structural error of a frontier model following the previous ideas exploited by the Support Vector Machines (SVM) (see Vapnik, 1998). The approach by Guerrero et al. minimizes the structural error of the frontier model while meeting shape restrictions (the enveloping property, free disposability and convexity). In this regard, the optimization program to be solved is as follows:

$$
\begin{aligned}
&\underset{v,u,\xi,\xi\prime,\boldsymbol{w},\beta,\delta}{Minimize}\; v + u + C\left(\sum_{i=1}^{n} \xi_i^2 + \sum_{i=1}^{n} \xi_i\prime^2\right)\\
&s.t.\\
&\qquad \|\boldsymbol{w}_i\|_1 \leq u && \forall i = 1,\ldots,n \quad (5.1)\\
&\qquad \beta_i \leq v && \forall i = 1,\ldots,n \quad (5.2)\\
&\qquad \delta_p y_i \leq \langle \boldsymbol{w}_p, \boldsymbol{x}_i\rangle + \beta_p && \forall i,p = 1,\ldots,n \; (5.3)\\
&\qquad \boldsymbol{w}_i, \delta_i \geq 0 && \forall i = 1,\ldots,n \quad (5.4)\\
&\qquad \langle \boldsymbol{w}_i, \boldsymbol{x}_i\rangle + \beta_i - \delta_i y_i \leq \varepsilon + \xi_i && \forall i = 1,\ldots,n \quad (5.5)\\
&\qquad \delta_i y_i - \langle \boldsymbol{w}_i, \boldsymbol{x}_i\rangle - \beta_i \leq \varepsilon + \xi_i\prime && \forall i = 1,\ldots,n \quad (5.6)\\
&\qquad \xi_i, \xi_i\prime \geq 0 && \forall i = 1,\ldots,n \quad (5.7)\\
&\qquad \|(\boldsymbol{w}_i, \delta_i)\|_1 = 1 && \forall i = 1,\ldots,n \quad (5.8)\\
&\qquad \langle \boldsymbol{w}_i, \boldsymbol{x}_i\rangle + \beta_i - \delta_i y_i \leq \langle \boldsymbol{w}_p, \boldsymbol{x}_i\rangle + \beta_p - \delta_p y_i && \forall i,p = 1,\ldots,n \; (5.9)
\end{aligned}
\tag{4}
$$

DEAM determines a maximum of n different hyperplanes $\langle \boldsymbol{w}_p^*, \boldsymbol{x}\rangle + \beta_p^* - \delta_p^* y \geq 0, p = 1,\ldots,n$. In the case of DEAM, the estimate of the technology coincides with the intersection of the half-spaces associated to the n hyperplanes and the non-negative orthant of the input–output space.

Finally, we end up this subsection by mentioning a very recent contribution, Aparicio and Esteve (2023), which combines the training/test paradigm of ML techniques and the estimation of technical efficiency. This technique, called Cross-Validated DEA (CVDEA), is based on 'peeling' the standard DEA frontier by removing supporting hyperplanes of the efficient frontier. The way of finding out which hyperplanes should be removed, and in what order, is considering a learning sample to fit the model and a test sample to score each possible combination of hyperplanes to be eliminated. The scoring rule is grounded on the prediction error.

2.2 Machine Learning Techniques that Do not Assume Convexity

Deprins et al. (1984) introduced the alternative technique known as Free Disposal Hull (FDH), which relies only on free disposability and minimal extrapolation in contrast to DEA, which assumes free disposability, convexity and minimal extrapolation. FDH, which yields stepwise efficient frontiers, may yield the DEA technology. Indeed, the convex hull of the FDH technology generates the DEA production possibility set. Recently, FDH has been highlighted in the literature as an appealing technique, even in comparison with DEA, due to its flexibility in not having to assume convexity (see the recent papers by Kerstens and Van de Woestyne, 2021, Ang et al., 2023; Kerstens et al., 2022). This is the reason why we focus our attention on this type of technique in this subsection.

A recent technique related to stepwise functions for estimating efficient frontiers is Efficiency Analysis Trees (EAT). Efficiency Analysis Trees use the same grounds as Classification and Regression Trees (CART) by Breiman et al. (1984). In particular, Efficiency Analysis Trees build technologies that satisfy the same production axioms as FDH with the exception of minimal extrapolation, that is, the technology contains all the observations and satisfies free disposability in inputs and outputs. From a computational perspective, Efficiency Analysis Trees is undoubtedly more complicated than Free Disposal Hull, being grounded on a recursive algorithm. Additionally, Efficiency Analysis Trees grant a non-overfitted estimate of the unknown Data Generating Process that produced the data cloud. This point contrast to what happens in the case of the Free Disposal Hull approach, where the principle of minimal extrapolation implies overfitting data. However, both EAT and FDH build stepwise surfaces as estimates of production functions. Figure 1 shows a toy example of FDH and EAT.

After applying the EAT algorithm, we get a tree structure that is too 'deep', using the terminology utilized in regression trees. In other words, the model only 'describes' the set of observations. Something similar happens in the case of the Free Disposal Hull approach. The deep tree suffers from overfitting. In the case of FDH, there is not a simple solution to overcome this drawback. However, for Efficiency Analysis Trees, due to their natural tree structure, it is possible to implement a solution based on pruning (see Breiman et al., 1984). In this sense, let $T(\aleph)$ be the final tree structure after applying the pruning process. Also, given the tree $T(\aleph)$, let $\boldsymbol{d}^{T(\aleph)}(\boldsymbol{x})$ be the

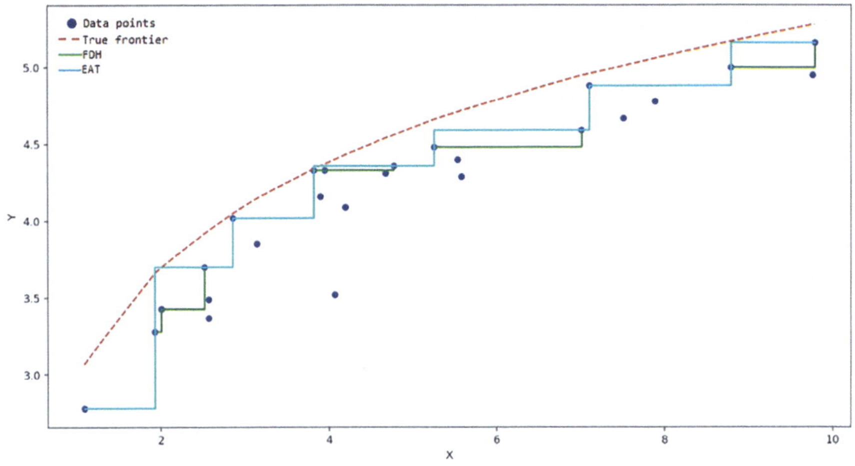

Fig. 1 Graphical illustration of EAT and FDH for a single input and a single output

output estimator: $d_r^{T(\aleph)}(\boldsymbol{x}) = \sum_{t \in \tilde{T}(\aleph)} y_r(t) I(\boldsymbol{x} \in t)$, $r = 1, \ldots, s$, where $y_r(t)$ denotes the output estimation of the r-th output at terminal node t and $I(\cdot)$ is the indication function. Then, the estimator of the technology linked to EAT is as follows:

$$\hat{\Psi}_{T(\aleph)} = \left\{ (\boldsymbol{x}, \boldsymbol{y}) \in R_+^{m+s} : \boldsymbol{y} \leq \boldsymbol{d}^{T(\aleph)}(\boldsymbol{x}) \right\} \tag{5}$$

As Esteve et al. (2020) proved, $\hat{\Psi}_{T(\aleph)}$ contains all the observations and satisfies free disposability. Additionally, $\hat{\Psi}_{T(\aleph)}$ contains, as a subset, the technology generated by FDH. Moreover, the efficient frontier provided by EAT has a staggered shape. All these features made the authors of the EAT technique to claim that Efficiency Analysis Trees can be seen as a 'pruned' version of FDH, which avoids overfitting, or as a FDH-type out-of-sample estimator of the underlying technology, using a terminology that belongs to the ML field.

In the case of EAT, if we want to determine the output-oriented measure to gauge technical inefficiency of point $(\boldsymbol{x}_k, \boldsymbol{y}_k)$, we must obtain an optimal solution of the following linear program:

$$\begin{aligned} \phi^{EAT}(\boldsymbol{x}_k, \boldsymbol{y}_k) = \max\ & \phi \\ s.t.\ & \\ & \sum_{t \in \tilde{T}(\aleph)} \lambda_t a_{jt} \leq \phi x_{ik}, \quad j = 1, \ldots, m \\ & \sum_{t \in \tilde{T}(\aleph)} \lambda_t d_r^{T(\aleph)}(\boldsymbol{a}_t) \geq y_{rk}, \quad r = 1, \ldots, s \\ & \sum_{t \in \tilde{T}(\aleph)} \lambda_t = 1, \\ & \lambda_t \in \{0, 1\}, \quad t \in \tilde{T}(\aleph) \end{aligned} \tag{6}$$

The difference between model (6) and the typical optimization model linked to FDH (enveloping form) is the left-hand side of the first two groups of constraints. Instead of directly using the information of the observed inputs, the EAT model resorts to the points $\boldsymbol{a}_t$ associated with the support of each node $t \in \tilde{T}(\aleph)$, which denotes the set of leaves of the final tree (see the details in Esteve et al., 2020). Additionally, outputs are substituted with their estimations. To see the optimizations programs that must be solved in the case of other technical efficiency measures, please see Aparicio et al. (2021).

More recently, Tsionas (2022b) have adapted probabilistic regression trees to provide a smooth approximation to a production function in microeconomics. This contribution is in the same line as the methodology introduced by Esteve et al. (2020). However, Tsionas (2022b) also deals with panel data. While in usual regression trees the estimator has the form $\hat{f}(\boldsymbol{x}) = \sum_{t \in T(\aleph)} \hat{y}(t) I(\boldsymbol{x} \in t)$, in probabilistic regression trees the estimator is $\hat{f}(\boldsymbol{x}) = \sum_{t \in T(\aleph)} \hat{y}(t) P_t(\boldsymbol{x})$, where $P_t(\boldsymbol{x})$ denotes a probability, with $P_t(\boldsymbol{x}) \geq 0$ and $\sum_{t \in T(\aleph)} P_t(\boldsymbol{x}) = 1$. In his algorithm, Tsionas (2022b) resorts to probabilistic node splitting, which ensures smoothness of the expected value of the output. Additionally, different Cobb–Douglas functions are fitted at each node rather than a constant. Given that the estimator is the sum of weighted Cobb–Douglas functions, which are monotone non-decreasing and concave functions, the final estimator is monotone non-decreasing and concave as well. We mention this contribution in this subsection due to its clear relationship with Efficiency Analysis Trees. However, by nature, Tsionas' approach should appear in the previous subsection since it generates convex technologies.

Unfortunately, it is well-known that the estimators linked to regression trees usually have small bias, what is a good feature, but large variance, which yields negative effects on the confidence of the value of the corresponding estimate. One of the typical strategies to solve this problem is based on determining more than one tree and aggregating all the created information in a final estimator of the target function. This same line was followed by Esteve et al. (2023), who resorted to the technique known as Random Forest, and Guillen et al. (2023), who adapted Gradient Tree Boosting to estimate efficient frontiers. Both methodologies, Random Forest and Gradient Tree Boosting, are grounded on the generation of several tree structures rather than only one and used as a base the EAT algorithm, but they are different because the main idea behind each one is clearly different. Under Random Forest, hundreds of trees are fitted from random subsamples of observations and, additionally, when the splitting procedure is applied, a different random subset of inputs is used. Finally, the information of each tree, which is created by invoking the original EAT algorithm, is combined through the average. Regarding the approach based on Gradient Tree Boosting, a recursive algorithm is applied where, at each stage, the EAT algorithm is executed on the original data sample using the original set of inputs but using as outputs the residuals determined for each output variable at a previous stage. Next, we show the steps that must be taken to apply the adaptations of these two well-known ML techniques: Random Forest and Gradient Tree Boosting.

Algorithm 1. RF+EAT

Inputs of the algorithm:

p, number of trees

$\aleph$, original data with m inputs and s outputs

$mtry$, number of inputs to selected for each split

n_{min}, max number of observations in leaf nodes

Outputs of the algorithm:

$RF^{EAT} := \{ T^{EAT}(\aleph_q) : q = 1, \ldots, p \}$, Random Forest + EAT model

$\{ \aleph_q : q = 1, \ldots, p \}$

```
RF^EAT := {}
FOR q: = 1 TO p
    ℵ_q := Bootstrap sample of ℵ
    T^EAT(ℵ_q) := { t_0 : t_0 = root node }
    FOR EACH t in T^EAT(ℵ_q) : t is a leaf node ⇔ n(t) ≤ n_min
        Randomly selects mtry (≤ m) of the original inputs
        Select the best input among the mtry inputs for t and split the data in t_L and t_R nodes
        T^EAT(ℵ_q) := T^EAT(ℵ_q) ∪ { t_L , t_R }
    END FOR
    RF^EAT := RF^EAT ∪ { T^EAT(ℵ_q) }
END FOR
```

Algorithm 1. RF + EAT algorithm, the adaptation of Random Forest to determine technical inefficiency

In Algorithm 1, we show the main steps of the so-called RF + EAT algorithm. After executing the algorithm, we obtain p different tree structures (usually 500 or 1,000, depending of the power of the computer), denoted as $T^{EAT}(\aleph_1), \ldots, T^{EAT}(\aleph_p)$, where $\aleph_1, \ldots, \aleph_p$ denote bootstrap subsamples. Given an input profile $\boldsymbol{x} \in R_+^m$, the output bundle estimated from $T^{EAT}(\aleph_q)$ is indicated as $\boldsymbol{d}_{T^{EAT}(\aleph_q)}(\boldsymbol{x})$. To determine a final output estimation from the RF + EAT algorithm, we average the p trees as follows:

$$\boldsymbol{y}^{RF+EAT(\aleph)}(\boldsymbol{x}) := \frac{1}{p}\sum_{q=1}^{p} \boldsymbol{d}_{T^{EAT}(\aleph_q)}(\boldsymbol{x}). \tag{7}$$

Given $\boldsymbol{y}^{RF+EAT(\aleph)}(\boldsymbol{x})$, Esteve et al. (2023) defined a possible estimation of the production possibility set as:

$$\hat{\Psi}_{RF+EAT} = \left\{(\boldsymbol{x}, \boldsymbol{y}) \in R_+^{m+s} : \boldsymbol{y} \leq \boldsymbol{y}^{RF+EAT(\aleph)}(\boldsymbol{x})\right\}. \tag{8}$$

Let $(\boldsymbol{x}_k, \boldsymbol{y}_k)$ be the point to be assessed. Esteve et al. (2023) proved that the way of calculating the output-oriented radial measure would be as follows: $\phi^{RF+EAT}(\boldsymbol{x}_k, \boldsymbol{y}_k) = \min_{r=1,\ldots,s}\left\{\frac{y_r^{RF+EAT(\aleph)}(\boldsymbol{x}_k)}{y_{rk}}\right\}$. Put in words, the score corresponds to the minimum calculated over the ratios between the estimation of each output and its corresponding observed value. However, how to determine other types of technical efficiency measures (distances to the efficient frontier of the technology) through the RF + EAT algorithm is a challenge that has not been solved so far.

A different proposal to define a frontier estimator based upon a tree structure with relatively low bias and also low variance is that grounded on Boosting. Boosting is a class of ML technique based on the ensemble of several models (Hastie et al., 2009). In comparison with typical ML methods, where an individual "strong" predictive model is tuned, boosting merges several "weak" predictive models with the objective of obtaining a stronger estimator of the target function. In contrast to Random Forest, the boosting algorithm is grounded on a greedy stagewise strategy (that is, the model is sequentially enhanced). In the case of EATBoosting by Guillen et al. (2023), the base model used at each iteration of the algorithm corresponds to an EAT model where the number of terminal nodes has been limited. This is the way of working with a weak predictive model.

The steps to be followed with respect to the EATBoosting algorithm are shown in Algorithm 2. The estimation provided by this algorithm can be understood as a valid frontier estimation because, as Guillen et al. (2023) proved, it is able to generate a technology that satisfies the enveloping property and free disposability in inputs and outputs but fails the minimal extrapolation principles. Also, the efficient frontier is estimated by stepwise functions, since the method is based on the EAT technique. In this sense, the outcome of the EATBoosting algorithm can be seen as a possible competitor of the standard FDH when estimating technical efficiency is the goal.

Algorithm 2: EATBoosting

1. Set $\boldsymbol{f}_0(\boldsymbol{x}) = \left(\max_{i=1,\ldots,n}\{y_{1i}\}, \ldots, \max_{i=1,\ldots,n}\{y_{si}\}\right)$
2. For $q = 1$ to Q:
    a. For $i = 1, 2, \ldots, n$ calculate $\boldsymbol{e}_{iq} = \boldsymbol{y}_i - \boldsymbol{f}_{q-1}(\boldsymbol{x}_i)$
    b. Fit a deep EAT to the targets $\boldsymbol{e}_{iq}$ given terminal regions R_{hq}, $h = 1, 2, \ldots, J_q$
    c. For $h = 1, 2, \ldots, J_q$ calculate $\gamma_{hq} = \boldsymbol{d}^{T^{EAT}(\aleph_q)}(R_{hq})$
    d. Update $\boldsymbol{f}_q(\boldsymbol{x}) = \boldsymbol{f}_{q-1}(\boldsymbol{x}) + v\sum_{h=1}^{J_q} \gamma_{hq} I(\boldsymbol{x} \in R_{hq})$
3. Final estimation: $\hat{\boldsymbol{f}}(\boldsymbol{x}) = \boldsymbol{f}_Q(\boldsymbol{x})$

Algorithm 2. The steps of the EATBoosting algorithm

The starting point of the method consists in defining the initial estimation as a vector with the maximum observed output for each component. In each generic step 2, the algorithm first determines the so-called pseudo-residual for each observation, as the difference between the observed output and the output estimation for the corresponding input bundle. After that, an EAT model (without pruning) must be fitted to a new database where the outputs are substituted with the values of the pseudo-residuals and the inputs are exactly the same as in the original data sample. An important point in this process is that the number of terminal nodes J_q is a user-defined parameter to be tuned. Moreover, pruning is no longer necessary because variance reduction is achieved, thanks to the assembling process of many fitted models. The EAT algorithm yields J_q terminal nodes and their corresponding supports in the input space (the regions R_{hq}, $h = 1, \ldots, J_q$, in the q-th step of the algorithm). Then, the vector $\boldsymbol{\gamma}_{hq}$ is determined. Each component of this vector is the output estimation for any input bundle that belongs to the region R_{hq} (recall that any input profile that belongs to the same support has the same output estimate). The next step says how to update the estimation of the outputs given an input vector $\boldsymbol{x}$. To do that, we must use the previous estimation and add $\boldsymbol{\gamma}_{hq}$. The indication function activates the part linked to the region that contains $\boldsymbol{x}$. Additionally, a learning rate ν corrects the estimation provided by the updating. In the final step of the algorithm, the output estimation produced by EATBoosting is defined as the output estimation generated from the last model (after iteration Q). Finally, an estimator of the production technology is $\hat{\Psi}_B = \left\{(\boldsymbol{x}, \boldsymbol{y}) \in R_+^{m+s} : \boldsymbol{y} \leq \hat{\boldsymbol{f}}(\boldsymbol{x})\right\}$.

The EATBoosting algorithm has three parameters to be tuned: ν, the learning rate, Q, the total number of iterations, and J_q, the number of terminal nodes of each tree. These parameters must be tuned by resorting to cross-validation. Nevertheless, it is worth mentioning that it is usual to set $J_q = J, \forall q$ with $4 \leq J \leq 10$ (Hastie et al., 2009). Moreover, $\nu \leq 0.1$ in practice.

Resorting to an elaborated simulation study, Guillen et al. (2023) proved that the frontier estimator provided by the EATBoosting algorithm is clearly better than that associated with the FDH technique, both regarding the bias and mean squared error as performance criteria. In this sense, EATBoosting is able to overcome the overfitting problems suffered by the standard FDH. Some extensions of the EATBoosting algorithm and its use can be found in Guillen et al. (2022).

Another possible method based on the adaptation of a well-known ML technique to estimate efficient frontiers and technical efficiency as a by-product is Support Vector Frontiers (SVF) (see Valero-Carreras et al., 2021). This method tailors SVM (Support Vector Machines) to estimate target functions that envelop the data cloud from above and also satisfy monotonicity. Before going on, let us introduce some relevant notation. Given a set of knots $T_j = \left\{t_{jl_j} : l_j = 1, \ldots, k_j\right\}, j, j = 1, \ldots, m$, a grid G is introduced as follows: $C_{1\ldots1}, \ldots, C_{k_1\ldots k_m}$ (called cells) such that $C_{l_1\ldots l_m} := \left\{\boldsymbol{x} \in \mathbb{R}_+^m / t_{jl_j} \leq x_j < t_{jl_j+1}, j = 1, \ldots, m\right\}$, $l_1 \in \{1, \ldots, k_1\}, \ldots, l_m \in \{1, \ldots, k_m\}$ with $t_{jk_j+1} := \infty, \forall j = 1, \ldots, m$. Furthermore, each cell can be rewritten in vectorial format as $C_{l_1\ldots l_m} = \left\{\boldsymbol{x} \in \mathbb{R}_+^m : \boldsymbol{a}_{l_1\ldots l_m} \leq \boldsymbol{x} < \boldsymbol{b}_{l_1\ldots l_m}, j = 1, \ldots, m\right\}$ with $\boldsymbol{a}_{l_1\ldots l_m} = \left(t_{l_1}^{(1)}, \ldots, t_{l_m}^{(m)}\right)$ and $\boldsymbol{b}_{l_1\ldots l_m} = \left(t_{l_1+1}^{(1)}, \ldots, t_{l_m+1}^{(m)}\right)$. Moreover, it is necessary to define the notion of the activation function for each cell $C_{l_1 \ldots l_m}$ as $L_{l_1 \ldots l_m}(\boldsymbol{x}) = \prod_{j=1}^{m} B\left(x_j - t_{jl_j}\right)$, where

$$B\left(x_j - t_{jl_j}\right) = \begin{cases} 1, \text{ if } x_j - t_{jl_j} \geq 0 \\ 0, \text{ if } x_j - t_{jl_j} < 0 \end{cases}, \forall l_j = 1, \ldots, k_j, \forall j = 1, \ldots, m.$$

For any $\boldsymbol{x}$ and G, $\phi_{SVF}^{G}(\boldsymbol{x})$ can be defined as:

$$\phi_{SVF}^{G}(\boldsymbol{x}) = \begin{pmatrix} L_{11\ldots11}(\boldsymbol{x}), L_{11\ldots12}(\boldsymbol{x}), \ldots, L_{11\ldots1k_m}(\boldsymbol{x}), L_{11\ldots21}(\boldsymbol{x}), L_{11\ldots22}(\boldsymbol{x}), \ldots, \\ L_{11\ldots2k_m}(\boldsymbol{x}), \ldots, L_{k_1 k_2 \ldots k_m}(\boldsymbol{x}) \end{pmatrix} \tag{9}$$

$\phi_{SVF}^{G}(\boldsymbol{x})$ is the transformation function used by SVF as we show next. SVF builds an estimation function by minimizing a combination of two types of errors: the empirical error and the generalization error. This fact contrasts to FDH or DEA, which only minimizes the empirical error. To minimize these two types of errors, SVF tries to find a balance between both: the regularization term $\|\boldsymbol{w}\|$ and the empirical error $\sum_{i=1}^{n} \xi_i$ through a parameter C in the objective function of the corresponding optimization program (see (10)). Due to the nature of the transformation function, SVF yields stepwise production functions as $f_{SVF}(\boldsymbol{x}) = \left\langle \boldsymbol{w}^*, \phi_{SVF}^{G}(\boldsymbol{x}) \right\rangle$, with $\boldsymbol{w}^* \in \mathbb{R}^q$ being an optimal solution of model (10). In the model, ε, which is the so-called margin, is a parameter associated with the robustness of the outcomes. In practice, C and ε are determined by some type of statistical validation.

$$\begin{array}{llll} \underset{\boldsymbol{w},\xi_i}{Min} & \|\boldsymbol{w}\|_1 + C\sum_{i=1}^{n} \xi_i & & (10.0) \\ s.t. & y_i - \left\langle \boldsymbol{w}, \phi_{SVF}^{G}(\boldsymbol{x}_i) \right\rangle \leq 0, & i = 1, \ldots, n & (10.1) \\ & \left\langle \boldsymbol{w}, \phi_{SVF}^{G}(\boldsymbol{x}_i) \right\rangle - y_i \leq \varepsilon + \xi_i, & i = 1, \ldots, n & (10.2)' \\ & W_{l_1 l_2 \ldots s_j \ldots l_m} \leq W_{l_1 l_2 \ldots l_m}, & \forall j = 1, \ldots, m, \forall l_1, \ldots, l_m, \forall s_j = l_j - 1 & (10.3) \\ & \xi_i \geq 0, & i = 1, \ldots, n & (10.4) \end{array} \tag{10}$$

where $W_{l_1 \ldots l_m} := \sum_{\substack{s_1 = 1, \ldots, l_1 \\ \vdots \\ s_m = 1, \ldots, l_m}} w_{s_1 \ldots s_m}$.

In model (10), restriction (17.1) ensures that the observations are enveloped from above. Constrain (17.2) states a margin of value ε around the estimation function linked to the robustness of the technique. Restriction (17.3) guarantees that the estimation function is a monotone non-decreasing function. Finally, constraint (17.4) states the non-negativity of the individual empirical error (ξ_i).

Next, we show graphically how the Support Vector Frontiers work with respect to the traditional Free Disposal Hull through Fig. 2.

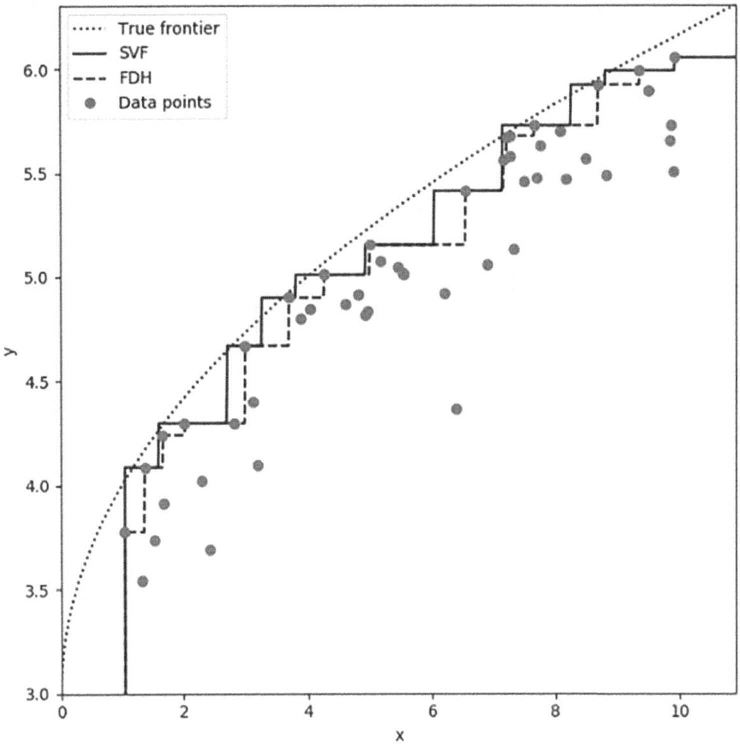

Fig. 2 Example of SVF in comparison with FDH

Additionally, the parameter ε is related to robustness, stating a region of size ε above and below the estimation of the frontier (see Fig. 3). In this way, the technique yields an upper bound (adding epsilon) and a lower bound (subtracting epsilon) of the estimation. Within this region, the observations have $\xi_i = 0$, i.e., an empirical error of zero, which allows introducing a robust notion of technical efficiency. In this regard, a DMU will be considered ε-insensitive technically efficient if $f_{SVF}(\boldsymbol{x}_i) - \varepsilon \leq y_i \leq f_{SVF}(\boldsymbol{x}_i) + \varepsilon$. Other definitions of robustness can be found in stochastic DEA, for example, resorting to chance-constrained programming and its application to DEA models (e.g., Olesen & Petersen, 1995), and in fuzzy DEA, for example, this is the case of the α-level based approach by Kao and Liu (2000).

Finally, see Valero-Carreras et al. (2021, 2022) to find a multi-output version of SVF.

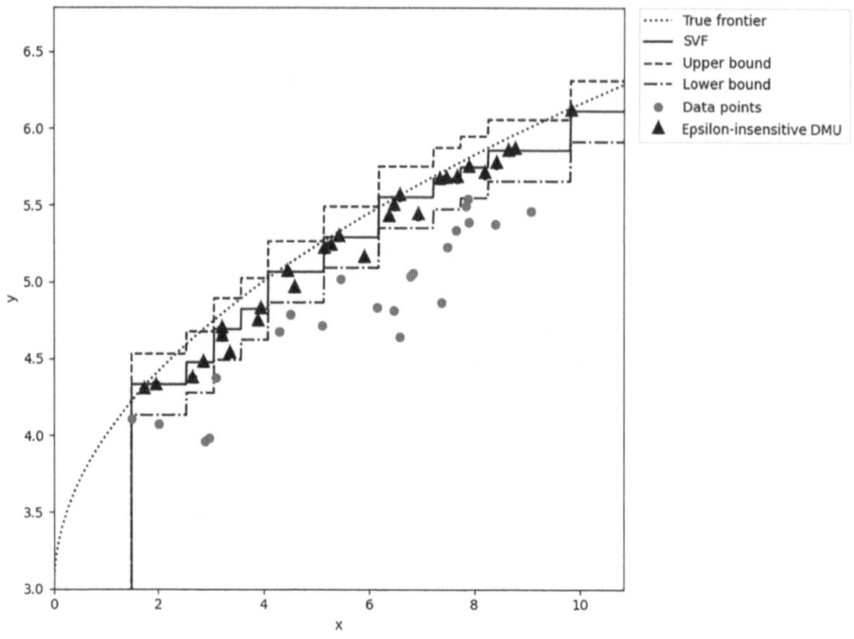

Fig. 3 Illustration of the concept of robustness in the case of SVF

3 A Review of Methodological Contributions that Adapt Frontier Techniques for Classifying

Supervised Machine Learning (ML) refers to the process of modeling the correlation between several characteristics of data and several labels. The determined model is then applied to new unknown data for predicting the corresponding label. In supervised ML, classification may be seen as one of the most important spotlights. The goal is to build a classifier via learning from labeled observations, which are characterized by a number of characteristics. The resulted classifier is then used to predict the class label of a new observation whose class label is unknown. The classification problem is important and quite common in practical applications. Examples of this problem include but are not limited to costumer churn (e.g., De Caigny et al., 2020), bankruptcy prediction (e.g., De Bock, 2017), credit scoring (e.g., Lessmann et al., 2015), etc.

In this part of the chapter, we review the main methodological contributions that apply the nonparametric frontier methods to provide a classification. The main categories of the nonparametric frontier methods include DEA and FDH, depending on whether the axiom of convexity is retained or not. DEA methods have been applied for classification problems from three different perspectives. However, to the best of our knowledge, the only attempt that applies the FDH for classification is Jin et al. (2024) where nonconvex frontier-based classification methods are proposed. Thus, this section is structured based on the different perspectives of DEA applications in classification. The first perspective is categorized as the DEA efficiency-based classification methods where a certain DEA efficiency is used as a cut-off value to classify the groups of observations. The second perspective is known as the DEA-Discriminant Analysis (DEA-DA) methods proposed by Sueyoshi (1999). The DEA-DA methods attempt to incorporate the advantage of the DEA methods into the traditional DA methods. The third perspective is categorized as the frontier-based classification methods. The frontier of a certain group of observations is used as a separating hypersurface to differentiate the groups of observations. Only in this perspective, both convex and nonconvex frontier estimators have been applied for classification.

3.1 DEA Efficiency-Based Classification Methods

While incorporating the DEA method into classification, a straightforward idea would be using efficiency scores. In this case, the classification is accomplished by comparing the calculated efficiency with a pre-determined cut-off efficiency. Yeh (1996) is among the first to use the DEA efficiency as an indicator of potential bankruptcy. Along with financial ratios, the DEA efficiency helps identify the poorly performed banks. Afterwards, the DEA efficiency is generally acknowledged as a key contributor to reveal a company's bankrupt.

In the DEA efficiency-based classifier, an observation is assigned a membership by comparing to a cut-off efficiency. Assume that there are n observations, and each observation is characterized by L factors. Specifically, observation i $(i = 1, \ldots, n)$ is represented by $\mathrm{z}_i = (\mathrm{x}_i, \mathrm{y}_i) = (x_{1i}, \ldots, x_{ji}, \ldots, x_{mi}, y_{1i}, \ldots, y_{ri}, \ldots, y_{si})$, where $m + s = L$. The observation z_k is then evaluated with model (11).

$$
\begin{aligned}
&\min \theta \\
&s.t.\ \sum_i \lambda_i x_{ji} \le \theta x_{jk} \quad j = 1, \ldots, m \\
&\sum_i \lambda_i y_{ri} \ge y_{rk} \quad r = 1, \ldots, s \\
&\sum_i \lambda_i = 1 \\
&\lambda_i \ge 0 \qquad\qquad i = 1, \ldots, n
\end{aligned} \tag{11}
$$

For the n observations, those with DEA efficiencies (θ) over a cut-off efficiency are classified into the good group. Correspondingly, the observations with DEA efficiencies below the cut-off efficiency are classified into the bad group.

Obviously, the choice of cut-off efficiency determines, to some extent, the performance of efficiency-based classifiers. Thus, various methods have been proposed for determining a proper cut-off efficiency. However, no consensus on the choice of the cut-off efficiency has been reached. Some researchers prefer a cut-off efficiency determined in a subjective manner by experts (Emel et al. 2003; Malhotra and Tsetsekos 2016). Based on the distribution of the DEA efficiencies, a cut-off efficiency can also be a certain statistic value. For the credit scoring of manufacturing firms in Min and Lee (2008), the median of DEA efficiencies is selected as the cut-off efficiency due to their skewed distribution. Among the statistics, the mean value is most commonly selected (see Lu et al. (2012)). In an objective manner, Paradi and Yang (2014) proposes to choose a cut-off efficiency that reaches the highest classification accuracy in the test sample.

Besides the choice of the cut-off efficiency, the literature also works on applying various DEA models to improve the classification performance. Instead of using a best-practice frontier, Premachandra et al. (2009) build a worst-practice frontier. All firms on the frontier are identified as bankruptcy. While those inefficient firms with respect to the worst-practice frontier are identified as non-bankruptcy. To formulate the worst practice frontier, model (11) turns to model (12) by having an opposite preference for the input-like and output-like factors.

$$\begin{aligned} \min\ & \varphi \\ s.t.\ & \sum_i \lambda_i x_{ji} \geq \varphi x_{jk}\ j = 1, \ldots, m \\ & \sum_i \lambda_i y_{ri} \leq y_{rk} \quad r = 1, \ldots, s \\ & \sum_i \lambda_i = 1 \\ & \lambda_i \geq 0 \qquad\qquad i = 1, \ldots, n \end{aligned} \tag{12}$$

Following Premachandra et al. (2009), Premachandra et al. (2011) define a discriminant index by combining the best-practice and worst-practice frontiers. From the perspective of evaluation measures, the original DEA efficiency-based classifier uses the radial measure, while the subsequent work uses the additive measure, slacks-based measure, etc. (Premachandra et al. 2009; Premachandra et al. 2011; Paradi and Yang 2014).

In the empirical analysis, the DEA efficiency-based classifiers are examined to outperform some classical classification methods, e.g., the linear discriminant analysis (Malhotra and Tsetsekos 2016), the logistic regression (Premachandra et al. 2009; Premachandra et al. 2011). Not only empirically, the DEA efficiency-based classifiers are also methodologically competitive in comparison with the above classification methods. The linear discriminant analysis, as all MP-based discriminant analysis does, restricts the form of the discriminant function. The logistic regression, like most statistical classification methods do, have specific restriction on the distribution of the data. Both restrictions do not apply while applying the DEA efficiency-based classifiers.

3.2 DEA-DA Methods

During the same period when the DEA efficiency-based classifier emerged, a mathematical programming (MP) classification method, known as the Data Envelopment Analysis- Discriminant Analysis (DEA-DA), is proposed by Sueyoshi (1999). The DEA-DA classifier is expected to be able to overcome the weakness of the MP-based classifiers. Intuitively, the MP-based classifiers generate one or multiple hypersurfaces which provide an optimal separation between groups of observations (Mangasarian 1965; Freed and Glover 1981; Stam and Joachimsthaler 1989). However, the shape of the separating hypersurfaces is predetermined by assuming an explicit form of the discriminant function. This is not impossible, but very difficult to prescribe a functional form to fit for real applications. To fix this weakness, the proposed DEA-DA classifier is expected to generate a piecewise linear hypersurface whose shape is decided by the data.

In the view of goal programming, Sueyoshi and Kirihara (1998) directs the research towards another type of DEA application, which is membership classification. Although the differences and similarities between the ratio DEA and DA have been discussed in Retzlaff-Roberts (1996) and Retzlaff-Roberts and Puelz (1996), Sueyoshi (1999) showed that the additive DEA share more similarities with the MP-based DA. Based on the minimization of the sum of deviations (MSD) DA method, Sueyoshi (1999) restricts the sum of weights to be 1. This avoids a trivial but common solution where all weights are zero.

Similar notations are adopted to formulate the basic DEA-DA model proposed by Sueyoshi (1999). Specifically, there are n observations that constitute the observation set G. Each observation is characterized by L factors. These factors are not differentiated as input-like or output-like factors. Thus, observation i $(i = 1, \dots, n)$ is now represented by $z_i = (z_{1i}, \dots, z_{Li})$. In the classification, prior knowledge is given in a manner that all observations can be classified into either Group 1 (G_1) or Group 2 (G_2), such that $G_1 \cup G_2 = G$. The basic DEA-DA model is formulated with two stages.

The first stage aims at identifying the overlap with model (13).

$$
\begin{aligned}
\min\ & \sum_{i \in G_1} S_{1i}^- + \sum_{i \in G_2} S_{2i}^+ \\
s.t.\ & \sum_l \alpha_l z_{li} + S_{1i}^+ - S_{1i}^- = d - \eta \quad \forall i \in G_1 \\
& \sum_l \beta_l z_{li} + S_{2i}^+ - S_{2i}^- = d \qquad \forall i \in G_2 \\
& \sum_l \alpha_l = 1 \\
& \sum_l \beta_l = 1 \\
& \alpha_l \geq 0, \beta_l \geq 0, \text{all slacks} \geq 0 \\
& d \text{ free}
\end{aligned}
\tag{13}
$$

By solving mode (13), two separating lines are generated. They are represented by $\sum_l \alpha_l^* z_{li} = d^*$ and $\sum_l \beta_l^* z_{li} = d^*$, respectively. If an observation is located below both lines, then it belongs to Group 1. If an observation is located above both lines, then it belongs to Group 2. For those observations that are located on different sides of the two lines, they are in the overlap. Accordingly, three sets are defined.

$$R_1 = \{i \in G | \sum_l \alpha_l^* z_{li} < d^*, \sum_l \beta_l^* z_{li} < d^*\} \tag{14}$$

$$R_2 = \{i \in G | \sum_l \alpha_l^* z_{li} \geq d^*, \sum_l \beta_l^* z_{li} \geq d^*\} \tag{15}$$

$$R_0 = \left\{ i \in G \left| \begin{array}{l} \sum_l \alpha_l^* z_{li} \leq d^* < \sum_l \beta_l^* z_{li} \\ \text{or } \sum_l \alpha_l^* z_{li} \geq d^* > \sum_l \beta_l^* z_{li} \end{array} \right. \right\} \tag{16}$$

The set R_0 represents the overlap. If it is empty, then the observations are linearly separable. Otherwise, there exists overlap and the second stage is needed to further classify the observations in the overlap.

$$\begin{array}{ll} \min & \sum_{i \in G_1} S_{1i}^- + \sum_{i \in G_2} S_{2i}^+ \\ s.t. & \sum_l \gamma_l z_{li} + S_{1i}^+ - S_{1i}^- = c - \eta \quad \forall i \in G_1 \\ & \sum_l \gamma_l z_{li} + S_{2i}^+ - S_{2i}^- = c \qquad \forall i \in G_2 \\ & \sum_l \gamma_l = 1 \\ & \gamma_l \geq 0, \text{ all slacks} \geq 0 \\ & c \text{ free} \end{array} \tag{17}$$

By solving model (17), the third separating line represented by $\sum_l \gamma_l^* z_{li} = c^*$ is generated. For the observation in the overlap, if it is located below this line, then it belongs to Group 1, otherwise Group 2. Accordingly, the observations in R_0 are classified by the following rules:

$$R_{01} = \{i \in R_0 | \sum_l \gamma_l^* z_{li} < c^*\} \tag{18}$$

$$R_{02} = \{i \in R_0 | \sum_l \gamma_l^* z_{li} \geq c^*\} \tag{19}$$

Figure 4 is a graphical illustration of the basic DEA-DA method (Sueyoshi 1999). In Fig. 4, the red asterisks represent the observations belonging to G_1 and the blue circles represent the observations belonging to G_2. In Fig. 4a, two crossed lines are

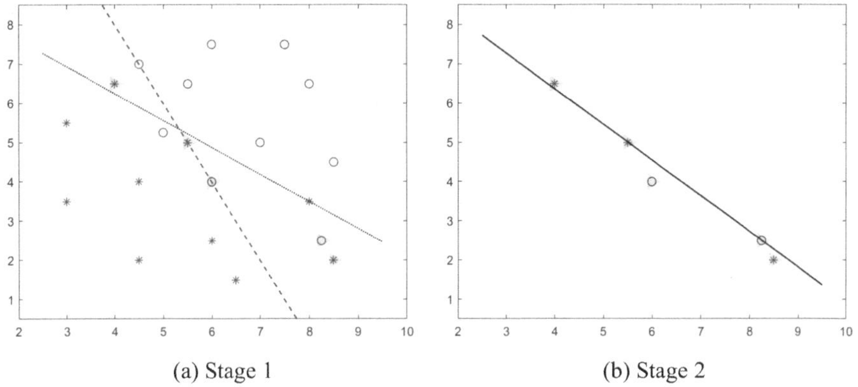

Fig. 4 Illustration of the basic DEA-DA method

generated from the solving model (13). The red dashed line represents $\sum_l \alpha_l^* z_{li} = d^*$ and the blue dotted line represents $\sum_l \beta_l^* z_{li} = d^*$. In stage 1, five observations marked by shaded triangles are observed to be located in the overlap. Thus, the second stage is needed and shown in Fig. 4b. The black solid line is generated from the second stage and represents $\sum_l \gamma_l^* z_{li} = c^*$. The five observations in the overlap are classified by this third separating line.

To classify a new observation, more than one separating line are needed in the basic DEA-DA method. First, it is classified by the two separating lines generated from model (13). If it is located in the overlap, then it is further classified by the third separating line generated from model (17).

The basic DEA-DA method in Sueyoshi (1999) cannot deal with negative data and assumes that all factors are positively related with the classification decision. To overcome these shortcomings, the basic DEA-DA model is extended by Sueyoshi (2001), and then further modified by introducing a different objective function in Sueyoshi (2004). To improve the discriminant capability, the objective function is changed to minimize the total number of misclassifications. Thus, the DEA-DA model in Sueyoshi (2004) becomes a mixed integer programming (MIP) problem. The MIP DEA-DA method also involves two stages. The first stage aims at identifying the overlap.

$$
\begin{aligned}
&\min s \\
&s.t. \sum_l (\lambda_l^+ - \lambda_l^-) z_{li} \le d + s \qquad \forall i \in G_1 \\
&\sum_l (\lambda_l^+ - \lambda_l^-) z_{li} \ge d - s \qquad \forall i \in G_2 \\
&\sum_l (\lambda_l^+ + \lambda_l^-) = 1 \\
&\varepsilon \zeta_l^+ \le \lambda_l^+ \le \zeta_l^+ \\
&\varepsilon \zeta_l^- \le \lambda_l^- \le \zeta_l^- \\
&\zeta_l^+ + \zeta_l^- \le 1 \\
&\sum_l (\zeta_l^+ + \zeta_l^-) = l \\
&\zeta_l^+ \in \{0, 1\}, \zeta_l^- \in \{0, 1\} \\
&s \text{ and } d \text{ free}
\end{aligned}
\tag{20}
$$

By solving model (20), two parallel separating lines are generated. They are represented by $\sum_l (\lambda_l^{+*} - \lambda_l^{-*}) z_{li} = d^* + s^*$ and $\sum_l (\lambda_l^{+*} - \lambda_l^{-*}) z_{li} = d^* - s^*$, respectively. If an observation is located below $\sum_l (\lambda_l^{+*} - \lambda_l^{-*}) z_{li} = d^* - s^*$, then it belongs to Group 1. If an observation is located above $\sum_l (\lambda_l^{+*} - \lambda_l^{-*}) z_{li} = d^* + s^*$, then it belongs to Group 2. For those observations that are located between these two separating lines, they are located in the overlap. Accordingly, three sets are defined.

$$
R_1 = \{i \in G | \sum_l (\lambda_l^{+*} - \lambda_l^{-*}) z_{li} \le d^* - s^*\} \tag{21}
$$

$$
R_2 = \{i \in G | \sum_l (\lambda_l^{+*} - \lambda_l^{-*}) z_{li} \ge d^* + s^*\} \tag{22}
$$

$$
R_0 = \left\{ i \in G \middle| d^* - s^* < \sum_l (\lambda_l^{+*} - \lambda_l^{-*}) z_{li} < d^* + s^* \right\} \tag{23}
$$

The set R_0 represents the overlap. If it is empty, then the observations are linearly separable. Otherwise, there exists overlap. Note that not all observations in R_1 are correctly classified. There may exist misclassifications in this stage. The sets $C_1 = R_1 \cap G_1$ and $C_2 = R_2 \cap G_2$ depict the observations that are correctly classified in the first stage. The sets $D_1 = G_1 - C_1$ and $D_2 = G_2 - C_2$ depict the observations that are not correctly classified in this stage. Thus, the second stage is used to classify the observations in $D_1 \cup D_2$ which are misclassified or unclassified in the first stage.

$$
\begin{aligned}
\min\ & \sum_{i \in D_1} y_i + \sum_{i \in D_2} y_i \\
s.t.\ & \sum_l (\lambda_l^+ - \lambda_l^-) z_{li} - M y_i \leq c - \eta \qquad \forall i \in D_1 \\
& \sum_l (\lambda_l^+ - \lambda_l^-) z_{li} + M y_i \geq c \qquad \forall i \in D_2 \\
& \sum_l (\lambda_l^+ + \lambda_l^-) = 1 \\
& \varepsilon \zeta_l^+ \leq \lambda_l^+ \leq \zeta_l^+ \\
& \varepsilon \zeta_l^- \leq \lambda_l^- \leq \zeta_l^- \\
& \zeta_l^+ + \zeta_l^- \leq 1 \\
& \sum_l (\zeta_l^+ + \zeta_l^-) = l \\
& \zeta_l^+ \in \{0, 1\}, \zeta_l^- \in \{0, 1\}, y_i \in \{0, 1\} \\
& c : \text{unconstrained}
\end{aligned}
\tag{24}
$$

where M is a given large number.

By solving model (24), a separating line represented by $\sum_l (\lambda_l^{+*} - \lambda_l^{-*}) z_{li} = c^*$ is generated. The observations in the overlap are then separated as follows.

$$R_{01} = \{i \in R_0 | \sum_l (\lambda_l^{+*} - \lambda_l^{-*}) z_{li} \leq c^*\} \tag{25}$$

$$R_{02} = \{i \in R_0 | \sum_l (\lambda_l^{+*} - \lambda_l^{-*}) z_{li} > c^*\} \tag{26}$$

Figure 5 is a graphical illustration of the MIP DEA-DA method (Sueyoshi 2004). In Fig. 5(a), two parallel separating lines are generated from solving model (20). The observations, marked by shaded triangles, are located in the overlap. Thus, the second stage is executed and is shown in Fig. 5b. The black solid line is generated from model (24) and represents $\sum_l (\lambda_l^{+*} - \lambda_l^{-*}) z_{li} = c^*$.

To classify a new observation, it is compared to the two separating lines generated from model (20). If it is located in the overlap, then it is further classified by the third separating line generated from model (24).

The DEA-DA classifier is claimed to incorporate a methodological strength of DEA into the DA formulation, thereby a piecewise linear classification frontier is expected. However, one should note that the eventual classification function of the DEA-DA method remains to be linear. Rather than using an assumption-free frontier, a linear hyperplane is generated from the DEA-DA methods to separate two groups of observations. Thus, it is retainable to claim that the assumption-free strength of DEA is well adapted to the DEA-DA classifier.

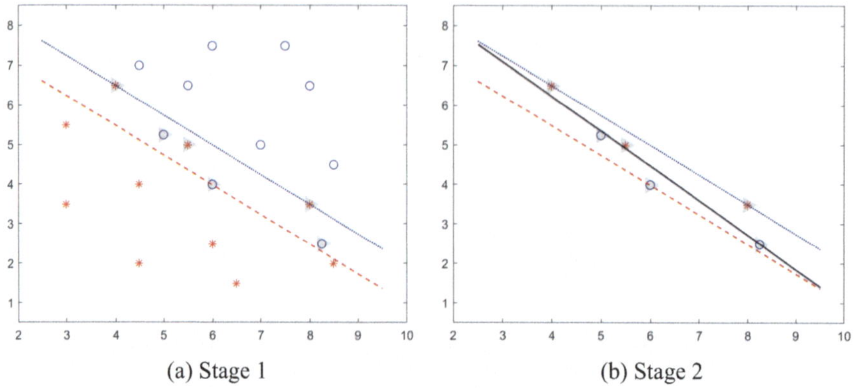

Fig. 5 Illustration of the extended DEA-DA classifier

3.3 Frontier-Based Classification Methods

In line with the general idea of locating a separating hypersurface, Troutt et al. (1996) first propose to use the index DEA model to generate an acceptability frontier for the credit applicant acceptance systems. Seiford and Zhu (1998) modify the method in Troutt et al. (1996) by proposing an alternative objective function. Thus, Seiford and Zhu (1998) determine both the acceptability of a new case and the relative distance of it to the frontier. Different groups of observations are expected to be well located on the opposite sides of the DEA frontier. Moreover, the shape of the frontier based on Data Envelopment Analysis is calculated from the observations instead of being pre-determined.

Similar notations are adopted to formulate the DEA frontier-based model. Specifically, there are n observations that constitute the observation set G. Each observation is characterized by L factors. An observation i ($i = 1, \ldots, n$) is represented by $z_i = (z_{1i}, \ldots, z_{Li})$. In the classification, prior knowledge is given in a manner that all observations can be classified into either Group 1 (G_1) or Group 2 (G_2). The two groups have n_1 and n_2 observations, respectively, such that $n_1 + n_2 = n$. Based on the observations in G_2, a classic DEA model is formulated.

$$
\begin{aligned}
& \min \theta \\
& s.t. \sum_{i \in G_2} \lambda_i z_{li} \leq \theta z_{lk} \qquad l = 1, \ldots, L \\
& \qquad \sum_{i \in G_2} \lambda_i = 1 \\
& \qquad \lambda_i \geq 0 \qquad i = 1, \ldots, n_2
\end{aligned}
\tag{27}
$$

To determine the membership of a new observation z_k, model (27) is applied. If it is feasible, then the new observation z_k is classified into Group 2, otherwise Group 1.

Figure 6 is a graphical illustration of DEA frontier-based classifier. In Fig. 6, the red asterisks denote the observations of Group 1 and the blue circles denote the observations of Group 2. By solving model (27), a piece-wise linear DEA frontier is generated to separate two groups. If an observation is feasible with respect to model (27), then it is located within the frontier. In Fig. 6, it is therefore located above the blue dotted frontier 2. Thus, the observations within the frontier are classified into Group 2. Otherwise, if an observation is located beyond the frontier (below the frontier 2), then it is classified into Group 1.

Ever since the first application of the DEA frontier in classification proposed by Troutt et al. (1996), the idea of employing a DEA frontier as the separating hypersurface has been well adapted in several ways. Both Seiford and Zhu (1998) and Troutt et al. (1996) restrict the characteristic variables to be discretionary and equally important. In Leon and Palacios (2009), the DEA frontier method is extended to the cases with non-discretionary characteristic variables. As for the variations in the importance of characteristic variables, Yan and Wei (2011) handled this by introducing a preference cone to the DEA model. Moreover, the DEA frontier-based classifier can solve the inverse classification problem (Pendharkar 2002).

In these DEA frontier-based classifiers, only one separating frontier is trained from a certain group of observations, and then used to differentiate between two groups of observations. It works well when the two groups of observations can be clearly separated. However, groups of observations in most applications are found to have overlaps.

In order to capture the overlap, Chang and Kuo (2008) proposes to adopt a pair of DEA frontiers for classification, where each frontier describes a group of

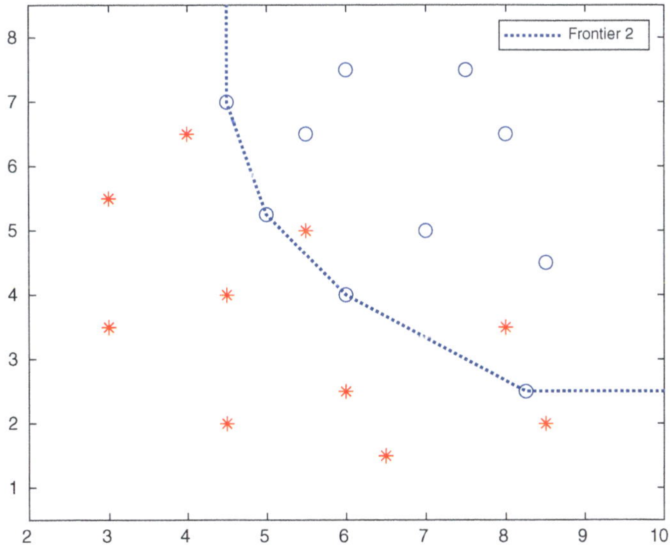

Fig. 6 Illustration of the DEA frontier-based classifier with one frontier

observations. The intersection of these two frontiers is defined as the data-based overlap.

In the model of Chang and Kuo (2008), one frontier is generated from model (27) based on the observations from G_2, the other is derived from the observations in G_1 with model (28).

$$\begin{aligned} \min\ & \phi \\ s.t.\ & \sum_{i \in G_1} \lambda_i z_{li} \geq \phi z_{lk} \qquad l = 1, \ldots, L \\ & \sum_{i \in G_1} \lambda_i = 1 \\ & \lambda_i \geq 0 \qquad i = 1, \ldots, n_1 \end{aligned} \tag{28}$$

To determine the membership of a new observation z_k, both models (27) and (28) are applied. If it is feasible with model (27) but infeasible with model (28), then it belongs to Group 2. If it is feasible with model (28) but infeasible with model (27), then it belongs to Group 1. If it is feasible with both models, then it is located in the overlap.

Figure 7 is a graphical illustration of the DEA frontier-based classifier with two frontiers. In Fig. 7, frontier 1, represented by the red dashed polyline, is generated from model (28). Frontier 2, represented by the blue dotted polyline, is generated from model (28). If an observation is located within frontier 1 and beyond frontier 2, then it belongs to Group 1. On the contrary, if an observation is located within frontier 2 and beyond frontier 1, then it belongs to Group 2. Lastly, if an observation is located within both frontiers, then it is located in the overlap.

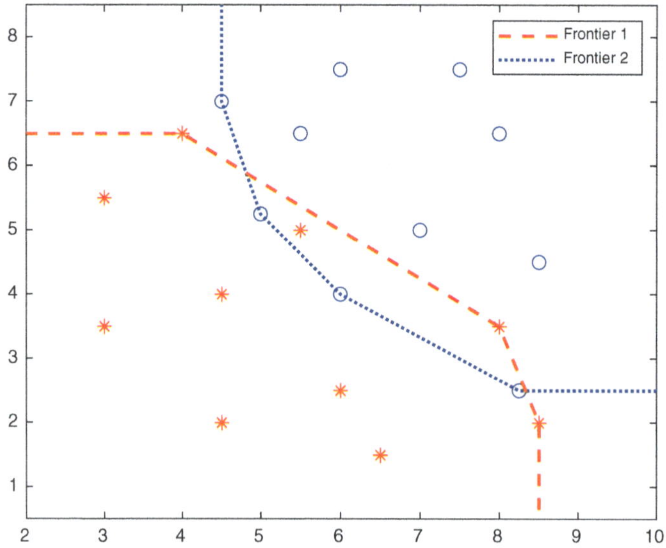

Fig. 7 Illustration of the DEA frontier-based classifier with two frontiers

In classification, the overlap region is the main source of misclassifications, which worsens the classification performance. To improve the classification performance, it is prominent to minimize the overlap in the training process. Thus, Chang and Kuo (2008) applies the stratified DEA method to shift the frontiers inwards layer by layer until there is no overlap existed for the observations. To further account for the uneven misclassification costs, an asymmetric-stratified DEA method is proposed in Kuo (2013), so that the number of layers removed from two groups could be different and is determined by achieving the minimal total misclassification cost.

Except for minimizing the overlap in the training process, classification performance depends mostly on how well the discriminant rule can classify the observations in the overlap (McLachlan 1992, p. 16). Along this alternative line to improve the classification performance, Pendharkar and his coauthors have proposed several options to further classify the observations in the overlap. In Pendharkar (2011) and Pendharkar (2012), the nearest neighborhood approach is applied to determine the class of an example in the overlap. The neighborhood is measured by the Euclidean distance of the example to the corresponding frontier projections. In Pendharkar and Troutt (2014), the popular MP-based minimize sum of deviations (MSD) model is applied to further classify the observations in the overlap. In all of these work, the overlap region is retained as the original intersection of two DEA frontiers without any treatment to minimize the overlap.

In addition to focusing on the overlap, the double frontier-based classifiers are extended in several other directions. Yan and Wei (2011) describe the DEA frontier by an intersection of several linear inequalities, and introduces the preference cone to reflect the different importance of the characteristics. In Pendharkar and Troutt (2011), the DEA-frontier based method is extended to solve a 3-group classification problem. Pendharkar (2018) extends the frontier-based classifier to include negative characteristics.

The classification performance of the frontier-based classifier has been examined and compared to other classifiers with empirical analysis. With the data set of breast cancer, the DEA frontier-based classifier is shown to outperform the linear discriminant analysis method. Moreover, the DEA frontier-based classifier, in general, performs as well as or better than competing classifiers, e.g., the artificial neural networks (Pendharkar et al. 1999), the learning Bayesian networks (Pendharkar et al. 2000), the feed forward neural network using error backpropagation learning algorithm (Pendharkar 2011), and the probabilistic neural network (Pendharkar 2011). For cases where the neural networks outperform the DEA frontier-based classifier, one of the reasons could be that DEA assumes the convexity of the acceptable cases and neural networks relax this assumption (Pendharkar et al. 1999; Pendharkar 2011).

Following the paper by Troutt et al. (1996), a lot of attempts has been made to improve the classification capacity of the DEA frontier-based classification methods. One common thing in the literature is that the convexity assumption is always retained, although the real shape of the separating boundary is unknown. Recently, Jin et al. (2024) proposes a nonconvex frontier-based classification method by using the FDH methods. Instead of restricting the factors to be all inputs or all outputs, the L factors can be differentiated into input-type and output-type factors depending on its monotonicity relation. Moreover, a directional distance function measure is introduced rather than the commonly used radial measure, so that the programming problem is always feasible, see (29).

$$\begin{aligned} & \max\ \theta \\ & s.t.\ \sum_{i\in G_2} \lambda_i x_{ji} \geq x_{jk} + \theta\left|x_{jk}\right| \quad j = 1, \ldots, m \\ & \sum_{i\in G_2} \lambda_i y_{ri} \leq y_{rk} - \theta\left|y_{rk}\right| \quad r = 1, \ldots, s \\ & \sum_{i\in G_2} \lambda_i = 1 \\ & \lambda_i \in \{0, 1\} \qquad i = 1, \ldots, n_2 \end{aligned} \tag{29}$$

To determine the membership of a new observation z_k, model (29) is applied. If the optimized θ^* is non-negative, then the new observation z_k is classified into Group 2. If θ^* is negative, then it should be classified into Group 1.

Figure 8 is a graphical illustration of DEA frontier-based classifier where a nonconvex staircase frontier is generated to separate two groups. If an observation has a positive θ^* with respect to model (29), then it is located within the frontier. In Fig. 8, it is therefore located above the blue dotted frontier. Thus, the observations within the frontier are classified into Group 2. Otherwise, if an observation is located beyond the frontier (below the frontier), then it is classified into Group 1. The two groups of observations are correctly classified with the nonconvex frontier, while two observations from Group 1 are misclassified with the convex frontier in Fig. 6. That is, the nonconvex frontier generates a more compact boundary which may differentiate the observations better.

4 Discussions and Directions for Future Research

This chapter provides a summary of the main methodological contributions devoted to both the adaptation of machine learning techniques for estimating production frontiers and the modification of frontier approaches to be used to classify observations within the machine learning field. There is currently a growing interest in the scientific literature for the application of the power of machine learning techniques to any analysis where a data sample has been observed from an unknown Data Generating Process. In this regard, many contributions have been made in the line of combining technical efficiency measurement and machine learning in the last years. Nevertheless, most of them independently apply each method in different stages of the analysis rather than adapting one of the techniques to be used into the other field (see, for example, the contributions in Charles et al., 2020). In contrast, to the best of our knowledge, this chapter represents the first attempt to gather the main approaches that actually combine these two fields, i.e., machine learning and frontier analysis, from a methodological point of view. These new links could be seen as the

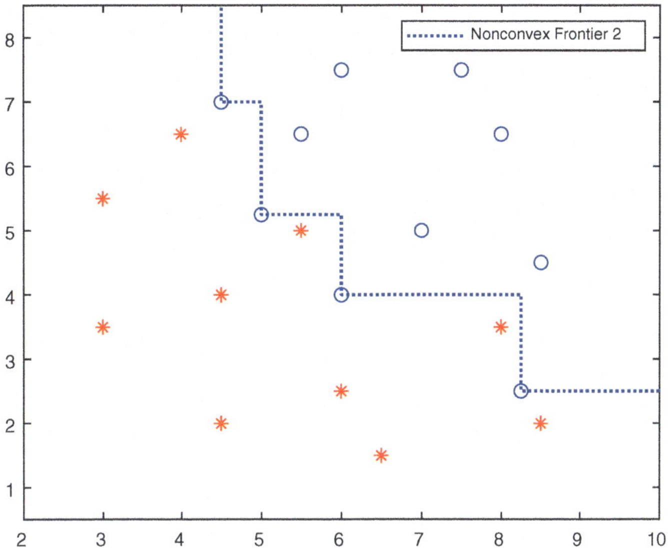

Fig. 8 Illustration of the nonconvex frontier-based classification method

starting point of a new research line. The main objective of this chapter, therefore, is to bring this new research line closer to potentially interested researchers. A way to build on this is to know the state of the art and identify possible gaps in the existing contributions.

In a natural way, the chapter was split into two parts. The first part surveyed the models devoted to adapting well-known machine learning techniques for estimating production frontiers, satisfying shape constraints (free disposability, convexity, …). The second part of the chapter consists in approaches that apply frontier estimators to classify observations under the classical framework of supervised machine learning with two or more classes.

Regarding the first group of approaches, we showed that many well-known machine learning techniques have already been tailored to estimate production frontiers and technical efficiency, as local kernel methods, splines, regression trees, boosting, random forest, support vector machines, etc. However, at this moment, we are not able to claim which technique is the best one regarding accuracy when the objective is to determine a suitable estimation of technical efficiency. Therefore, a comparison of all the existing techniques, or at least most of them, is one possible research avenue for the future. Other possible research line is the adaptation of alternative machine learning techniques, e.g., neural networks, to be used for the estimation of production frontiers and technical efficiency. Additionally, a gap of the literature is that some existing techniques do not apply a cross-validation process and/or do not deal with the multi-output production framework. A consequence of this fact is that they could suffer from overfitting and may not cope with the more general production scenario (the multi-input multi-output case). Another interesting research line could be adapting machine learning techniques to estimate S-shaped production functions following the law of diminishing returns (see, for example, Olesen & Ruggiero, 2022).

As for the second group of approaches, we review the main methodological contributions that apply the frontier estimators to get a classification of observations. Based on the existing work, we identify several research directions that future studies could explore to further improve classification using these frontier estimators. To further enhance the classification capacity of the nonparametric frontier techniques, one prominent direction is to relax the convexity assumption. In its traditional application area, production, the argument on convexity is already a hot topic. In the context of classification, Pendharkar et al. (1999, p. 231) have already highlighted this issue as a potential weakness of methods based on DEA in comparison with, for example, neural networks. The convex nonparametric frontier techniques, commonly known as the DEA methods, have been explored in three different directions to solve the classification problems. For all these three perspectives, it is worthwhile to explore the relaxation of the convexity assumption and to investigate to which extent the classification capacity can be improved. Besides the convexity assumption, another assumption inherited from production theory is the monotonicity. In classification problems, factors and classification labels are not necessarily always monotonically related. Therefore, it is of interest to explore whether the strongly monotonicity assumption can be properly relaxed. By relaxing the monotonicity assumption, the nonparametric frontier techniques are expected to be able to solve classification problems without the monotonicity constraints. Concerning the relaxation of the monotonicity assumption, see Briec et al. (2016, 2018). Except for improving the classification capacity of the nonparametric frontier techniques, improving its interpretability is crucial for their adoption in practice. In real applications, decision makers often prefer the linear discriminant analysis models and other statistical classification methods than complex machine learning algorithms although the latter has better classification capacity. This is due to the strong interpretability of the linear discriminant analysis models and other statistical classification methods. In the literature, the theoretical foundation of applying the nonparametric frontier techniques to classification has not been well explored yet. Thus, it is an important topic to explore so that the nonparametric frontier techniques can be better accepted in real applications.

Finally, it is worth noting that the first group of approaches was structured into two subsets, depending on whether the postulate of convexity is or not assumed for the building of the underlying technology. If convexity is assumed, the described approaches compete against DEA. Otherwise, they compete against FDH. In all the cases considered, the new approaches overcome the standard ones regarding the mean squared error and bias. Recently, Kerstens et al. (2022), Ang et al. (2023) and Kerstens and Van de Woestyne (2021) have illustrated that convexity is an unnecessary and very strong microeconomic postulate. Consequently, we can claim that, among the alternative approaches described in the first part of the chapter, those that do not assume convexity can be considered more appealing than the techniques that force convexity, due to their flexibility in building a production frontier estimate. However, we could not organize the second group of approaches of this chapter in the same way as we did in the case of the first set of methods, that is, considering or not the assumption of convexity. The reason was that, as far as we are aware, the only attempt that applies the nonconvex frontier estimators for classification is Jin et al. (2024) where the nonconvex frontier-based classification method also shows superior performance in comparison with the convex frontier-based classification method.

Acknowledgements J. Aparicio thanks the grant PID2022-136383NB-I00 funded by MICIU/ AEI/ 10.13039/501100011033 and by ERDF/EU. Additionally, J. Aparicio thanks the grant PROMETEO/2021/063 funded by the Valencian Community (Spain).

References

Afriat, S. N. (1972). Efficiency estimation of production functions. *International Economic Review*, 568–598.

Ang, F., Kerstens, K., & Sadeghi, J. (2023). Energy productivity and greenhouse gas emission intensity in Dutch dairy farms: A Hicks–Moorsteen by-production approach under non-convexity and convexity with equivalence results. *Journal of Agricultural Economics, 74*(2), 492–509.

Aparicio, J., & Esteve, M. (2023). How to peel a data envelopment analysis frontier: A cross-validation-based approach. *Journal of the Operational Research Society, 74*(12), 2558–2572.

Aparicio, J., Esteve, M., Rodriguez-Sala, J. J., & Zofio, J. L. (2021). The estimation of productive efficiency through machine learning techniques: efficiency analysis trees. In *Data-enabled analytics* (pp. 51–92). Springer, Cham.

Banker, R. D., Charnes, A., & Cooper, W. W. (1984). Some models for estimating technical and scale inefficiencies in data envelopment analysis. *Management Science, 30*(9), 1078–1092.

Breiman, L. (1993). Hinging hyperplanes for regression, classification, and function approximation. *IEEE Transactions on Information Theory, 39*(3), 999–1013.

Breiman, L., Friedman, J., Olshen, R., & Stone, C. (1984). *Classification and regression trees*. Taylor & Francis.

Briec, W., Kerstens, K., & Van de Woestyne, I. (2016). Congestion in production correspondences. *Journal of Economics, 119*(1), 65–90.

Briec, W., Kerstens, K., & Van de Woestyne, I. (2018). Hypercongestion in production correspondences: An empirical exploration. *Applied Economics, 50*(27), 2938–2956.

Chang, D., & Kuo, Y. (2008). An approach for the two-group discriminant analysis: An application of DEA. *Mathematical and Computer Modelling, 47*(9–10), 970–981.

Charles, V., Aparicio, J., & Zhu, J. (2020). *Data science and productivity analytics*. Springer.

Charnes, A., Cooper, W. W., & Rhodes, E. (1978). Measuring the efficiency of decision making units. *European Journal of Operational Research, 2*(6), 429–444.

Daouia, A., Noh, H., & Park, B. U. (2016). Data envelope fitting with constrained polynomial splines. *Journal of the Royal Statistical Society: Series B (statistical Methodology), 78*(1), 3–30.

Daraio, C., & Simar, L. (2005). Introducing environmental variables in nonparametric frontier models: A probabilistic approach. *Journal of Productivity Analysis, 24*(1), 93–121.

Daraio, C., & Simar, L. (2007). Conditional nonparametric frontier models for convex and nonconvex technologies: A unifying approach. *Journal of Productivity Analysis, 28*(1), 13–32.

De Bock, K. W. (2017). The best of two worlds: Balancing model strength and comprehensibility in business failure prediction using spline-rule ensembles. *Expert Systems with Applications, 90*, 23–39.

De Caigny, A., Coussement, K., De Bock, K. W., & Lessmann, S. (2020). Incorporating textual information in customer churn prediction models based on a convolutional neural network. *International Journal of Forecasting, 36*(4), 1563–1578.

Deprins, D., Simar, L., & Tulkens, H. (1984). Measuring labor inefficiency in post offices. In M. Marchand, P. Pestieau, & H. Tulkens (Eds.), *The performance of public enterprises: Concepts and measurements* (pp. 243–267). North Holland: Amsterdam.

Efron, B. (2020). Prediction, estimation, and attribution. *International Statistical Review, 88*, S28–S59.

Emel, A. B., Oral, M., Reisman, A., & Yolalan, R. (2003). A credit scoring approach for the commercial banking sector. *Socio-Economic Planning Sciences, 37*(2), 103–123.

Esteve, M., Aparicio, J., Rabasa, A., & Rodriguez-Sala, J. J. (2020). Efficiency analysis trees: A new methodology for estimating production frontiers through decision trees. *Expert Systems with Applications, 162*, 113783.

Esteve, M., Aparicio, J., Rodriguez-Sala, J. J., & Zhu, J. (2023). Random forests and the measurement of super-efficiency in the context of free disposal hull. *European Journal of Operational Research, 304*(2), 729–744.

Freed, N., & Glover, F. (1981). Simple but powerful goal programming models for discriminant problems. *European Journal of Operational Research, 7*(1), 44–60.

Guerrero, N. M., Aparicio, J., & Valero-Carreras, D. (2022). Combining data envelopment analysis and machine learning. *Mathematics, 10*(6), 909.

Guillen, M. D., Aparicio, J., & Esteve, M. (2022). Performance evaluation of decision making units through boosting methods in the context of free disposal hull: Some exact and heuristic algorithms. *International Journal of Information Technology & Decision Making (in Press)*. https://doi.org/10.1142/S0219622023500050

Guillen, M. D., Aparicio, J., & Esteve, M. (2023). Gradient tree boosting and the estimation of production frontiers. *Expert Systems with Applications, 214*, 119134.

Hastie, T., Tibshirani, R., Friedman, J. H., & Friedman, J. H. (2009). *The elements of statistical learning: data mining, inference, and prediction* (Vol. 2, pp. 1–758). New York: Springer.

Jin, Q., Kerstens, K. & Van de Woestyne, I. (2024) Convex and nonconvex nonparametric frontier-based classification methods for anomaly detection. OR Spectrum. https://doi.org/10.1007/s00291-024-00751-5

Kao, C., & Liu, S. T. (2000). Fuzzy efficiency measures in data envelopment analysis. *Fuzzy Sets and Systems, 113*(3), 427–437.

Kerstens, K., & Van de Woestyne, I. (2021). Cost functions are nonconvex in the outputs when the technology is nonconvex: Convexification is not harmless. *Annals of Operations Research, 305*(1), 81–106.

Kerstens, K., Mazza, P., Ren, T., & Van de Woestyne, I. (2022). Multi-time and multi-moment nonparametric frontier-based fund rating: Proposal and buy-and-hold backtesting strategy. *Omega, 113*, 102718.

Kuo, Y.-C. (2013). Consideration of uneven misclassification cost and group size for bankruptcy prediction. *American Journal of Industrial and Business Management, 3*(08), 708.

Kuosmanen, T., & Johnson, A. (2017). Modeling joint production of multiple outputs in StoNED: Directional distance function approach. *European Journal of Operational Research, 262*(2), 792–801.

Kuosmanen, T., & Johnson, A. L. (2010). Data envelopment analysis as nonparametric leastsquares regression. *Operations Research, 58*(1), 149–160.

Leon, C. F., & Palacios, F. (2009). Evaluation of rejected cases in an acceptance system with data envelopment analysis and goal programming. *Journal of the Operational Research Society, 60*(10), 1411–1420.

Lessmann, S., Baesens, B., Seow, H.-V., & Thomas, L. C. (2015). Benchmarking state-of-the-art classification algorithms for credit scoring: An update of research. *European Journal of Operational Research, 247*(1), 124–136.

Lu, S. L., Lee, K. J., & Zou, M. L. (2012). How to gauge credit risk: An investigation based on Data envelopment analysis and the Markov chain model. *Applied Financial Economics, 22*(11), 887–897.

Malhotra, R., & Tsetsekos, G. (2016). Evaluating loans using variable benchmark data envelopment analysis. *International Journal of Business Intelligence and Systems Engineering, 1*(1), 77–98.

Mangasarian, O. L. (1965). Linear and nonlinear separation of patterns by linear programming. *Operations Research, 13*(3), 444–452.

Mclachlan, G. J. (1992). Discriminant analysis and statistical pattern recognition. In *Wiley series in probability and mathematical statistics*. New York: Wiley.

Min, J. H., & Lee, Y. C. (2008). A practical approach to credit scoring. *Expert Systems with Applications, 35*(4), 1762–1770.

Olesen, O. B., & Petersen, N. C. (1995). Chance constrained efficiency evaluation. *Management Science, 41*(3), 442–457.

Olesen, O. B., & Ruggiero, J. (2022). The hinging hyperplanes: An alternative nonparametric representation of a production function. *European Journal of Operational Research, 296*(1), 254–266.

Paradi, J., & Yang, X. (2014). Data envelopment analysis of corporate failure for non-manufacturing firms using a slacks-based measure. *Journal of Service Science and Management, 7*(04), 277.

Parmeter, C. F., & Racine, J. S. (2013). Smooth constrained frontier analysis. In *Recent advances and future directions in causality, prediction, and specification analysis* (pp. 463–488). Springer, New York, NY.

Pastor, J. T., Lovell, C. A., & Aparicio, J. (2012). Families of linear efficiency programs based on Debreu's loss function. *Journal of Productivity Analysis, 38*(2), 109–120.

Pendharkar, P. (2012). Fuzzy classification using the data envelopment analysis. *Knowledge-Based Systems, 31*, 183–192.

Pendharkar, P. (2018). Data envelopment analysis models for probabilistic classification. *Computers & Industrial Engineering, 119*, 181–192.

Pendharkar, P. C. (2002). A potential use of data envelopment analysis for the inverse classification problem. *Omega, 30*(3), 243–248.

Pendharkar, P. C. (2011). A hybrid radial basis function and data envelopment analysis neural network for classification. *Computers & Operations Research, 38*(1), 256–266.

Pendharkar, P. C., & Troutt, M. D. (2011). DEA based dimensionality reduction for classification problems satisfying strict non-satiety assumption. *European Journal of Operational Research, 212*(1), 155–163.

Pendharkar, P. C., & Troutt, M. D. (2014). Interactive classification using data envelopment analysis. *Annals of Operations Research, 214*(1), 125–141.

Pendharkar, P., Khosrowpour, M., & Rodger, J. (2000). Application of Bayesian network classifiers and data envelopment analysis for mining breast cancer patterns. *Journal of Computer Information Systems, 40*(4), 127–132.

Pendharkar, P., Rodger, J., & Yaverbaum, G. (1999). Association, statistical, mathematical and neural approaches for mining breast cancer patterns. *Expert Systems with Applications, 17*(3), 223–232.

Premachandra, I., Bhabra, G., & Sueyoshi, T. (2009). DEA as a tool for bankruptcy assessment: A comparative study with logistic regression technique. *European Journal of Operational Research, 193*(2), 412–424.

Premachandra, I., Chen, Y., & Watson, J. (2011). DEA as a tool for predicting corporate failure and success: A case of bankruptcy assessment. *Omega, 39*(6), 620–626.

Retzlaff-Roberts, D. L. (1996). Relating discriminant analysis and data envelopment analysis to one another. *Computers & Operations Research, 23*(4), 311–322.

Retzlaff-Roberts, D., & Puelz, R. (1996). Classification in automobile insurance using a DEA and discriminant analysis hybrid. *Journal of Productivity Analysis, 7*(4), 417–427.

Seiford, L., & Zhu, J. (1998). An acceptance system decision rule with data envelopment analysis. *Computers & Operations Research, 25*(4), 329–332.

Selk, L., Tillier, C., & Marigliano, O. (2022). Multivariate boundary regression models. *Scandinavian Journal of Statistics, 49*(1), 400–426.

Stam, A., & Joachimsthaler, E. A. (1989). Solving the classification problem in discriminant analysis via linear and nonlinear programming methods. *Decision Sciences, 20*(2), 285–293.

Sueyoshi, T. (1999). DEA-discriminant analysis in the view of goal programming. *European Journal of Operational Research, 115*(3), 564–582.

Sueyoshi, T. (2001). Extended DEA-discriminant analysis. *European Journal of Operational Research, 131*(2), 324–351.

Sueyoshi, T. (2004). Mixed integer programming approach of extended DEA-discriminant Analysis. *European Journal of Operational Research, 152*(1), 45–55.

Sueyoshi, T., & Kirihara, Y. (1998). Efficiency measurement and strategic classification of Japanese banking institutions. *International Journal of Systems Science, 29*(11), 1249–1263.

Troutt, M. D., Rai, A., & Zhang, A. (1996). The potential use of DEA for credit applicant acceptance systems. *Computers & Operations Research, 23*(4), 405–408.

Tsionas, M. G. (2022a). Convex non-parametric least squares, causal structures and productivity. *European Journal of Operational Research.*

Tsionas, M. G. (2022b). Efficiency estimation using probabilistic regression trees with an application to Chilean manufacturing industries. *International Journal of Production Economics*, 108492.

Valero-Carreras, D., Aparicio, J., & Guerrero, N. M. (2021). Support vector frontiers: A new approach for estimating production functions through support vector machines. *Omega, 104*, 102490.

Valero-Carreras, D., Aparicio, J., & Guerrero, N. M. (2022). Multi-output support vector frontiers. *Computers & Operations Research, 143*, 105765.

Vapnik, V. (1998). The support vector method of function estimation. In *Nonlinear modeling* (pp. 55–85). Springer, Boston, MA.

Wu, J., An, Q., & Liang, L. (2011). A modified super-efficiency DEA approach for solving multi-groups classification problems. *International Journal of Computational Intelligence Systems, 4*(4), 606–618.

Yan, H., & Wei, Q. (2011). Data envelopment analysis classification machine. *Information Sciences, 181*(22), 5029–5041.

Yeh, Q.-J. (1996). The application of data envelopment analysis in conjunction with financial ratios for bank performance evaluation. *Journal of the Operational Research Society, 47*(8), 980–988.

A Literature Review for Nonparametric Frontier Methods Applied to Portfolio Analysis

Tiantian Ren, Helu Xiao, and Zhongbao Zhou

Abstract This chapter systematically summarizes previous research on nonparametric frontier methods employed for portfolio performance evaluation and benchmarking, including the diversified and nondiversified frontier models. The former is based on the diversified portfolio frontier, which explicitly considers the diversification effect when combining portfolios, while the latter directly derived from the production involves the envelope of the convex or nonconvex combinations of observed portfolios. Both mainstream methods are reviewed and discussed in single-horizon and multi-horizon portfolio analysis frameworks, respectively, covering the latest developments in this field, existing opportunities, and potential directions for future research. Additionally, we provide a generic production possibility set (PPS) formula for each class of methods to analytically clarify their modeling ideas. This literature study, along with a comprehensive summary of conceptual, methodological, and empirical developments, serves as a reference and guideline for future investigative work on the applications of nonparametric frontier methods in portfolio performance assessment.

Keywords Portfolio efficiency · Diversified portfolio · Data envelopment analysis · Free disposal hull

---

T. Ren
School of Business, Xiangtan University, Xiangtan 411105, China
e-mail: tiantianren@xtu.edu.cn

H. Xiao
School of Business, Hunan Normal University, Changsha 410081, China
e-mail: xiaohelu1986@163.com

Z. Zhou (✉)
School of Business Administration, Hunan University, Changsha 410082, China
e-mail: z.b.zhou@163.com

© The Author(s), under exclusive license to Springer Nature Singapore Pte Ltd. 2024
S. A. Edalatpanah et al. (eds.), *Analytical Decision Making and Data Envelopment Analysis*, Infosys Science Foundation Series in Mathematical Sciences,
https://doi.org/10.1007/978-981-97-6972-8_11

1 Introduction

As the burgeoning development of global financial markets, there has been a remarkable increase in the number and diversity of portfolios available to investors, including hedge funds, bond funds, exchange-traded funds, and social responsibility funds, among others. In this background, both individual and institutional investors heavily rely on risk-adjusted return (i.e., "performance") measures to recognize and construct portfolios that are worth investing in.

Consequently, the performance appraisal of funds based on explicit performance measures has gained increasing attention. An effective portfolio evaluation method can offer valuable support not only in screening funds for investors but also in benchmarking investments for portfolio managers to enhance the performance of their managed portfolios. The pioneering work of Markowitz (1952) on modern portfolio mean–variance (MV) theory introduces the concept of portfolio efficiency, defined as the ability of a set of assets to maximize returns for a given level of risk or minimize risk for a given expected return. However, the classical MV theory is hindered by strong assumptions on probability distributions of assets and Von Neumann-Morgenstern utility functions of investors, leading to various theoretical challenges (Harvey et al., 2010; Jondeau & Rockinger, 2003; Martellini & Ziemann, 2010). Despite the existence of numerous methods in the existing literature for gauging portfolio performance, none of them has achieved universal approval.

Recently, the nonparametric frontier methods have gained significant popularity as effective tools for portfolio assessment and benchmarking. The fundamental idea of the nonparametric frontier portfolio gauging can be intuitively summarized as follows: With the help of available efficiency measures, these frontier methods assess portfolio efficiency through estimating the gap between the portfolio under evaluation and its projection portfolio on nonparametric estimators of the portfolio efficient frontier, where the projection portfolio corresponding to nonparametric frontier provides a benchmark for the inefficient portfolio. To the best of our knowledge, research on portfolio performance appraisal by applying the nonparametric frontier can be mainly divided into two categories, that is, the diversified and nondiversified nonparametric frontier portfolio evaluation methods. The former is based on the diversified nonparametric frontier that considers the diversification effect of portfolios and thus is also referred to as diversification-consistent data envelopment analysis (DC-DEA) in the literature of Lamb and Tee (2012a). The latter, derived from production theory, is introduced in the finance field as an alternative approach for assessing portfolio performance, which includes convex (known as data envelopment analysis, DEA) and nonconvex nonparametric frontier models (known as free disposal hull, FDH). In this case, the nondiversified frontier specifications are used to approximately estimate the portfolio frontier or the diversified nonparametric frontier (Liu et al., 2015). Moreover, several studies provide an extensive discussion on the properties of the convex and nonconvex frontier models in the context of approximating the nonconvex portfolio frontiers (Kerstens et al., 2011; Nalpas et al., 2017; Xiao et al., 2022a).

In this chapter, we summarize previous research works on diversified and nondiversified nonparametric frontier methods applied to portfolio performance gauging by paying attention to its methodological and empirical developments. It needs to highlight that the intention of this chapter is not to advocate for one nonparametric frontier model or technique over others. Instead, the primary objective of our work is to provide a comprehensive discussion regarding the application of nonparametric frontier in portfolio analysis. More specifically, the purposes of our work are threefold: (i) classify and identify the main results of the related studies; (ii) discuss and explore the most recent developments related to the key topics of our research theme; (iii) highlight and present potential directions for future work on these topics.

With the aforementioned purposes in mind, the remainder of this chapter is structured as follows: Section 2 provides an introduction to the generic diversified models and presents a comprehensive literature review, including a classification of relevant studies. Section 3 delves into previous studies on the application of nondiversified models for estimating portfolio efficiency. Section 4 concludes the study by summarizing the key findings and highlighting potential directions for future research.

2 Portfolio Evaluation Based on the Diversified Frontier: Methodologies and Reviews

The portfolio evaluation models based on the diversified frontier are principally inspired by the typical idea of portfolio diversification in Markowitz's work, where the portfolio frontier is estimated by considering the diversification effects of portfolios. Numerous scholars have contributed to the development of a wide range of single- and multi-horizon diversified nonparametric frontier models for gauging portfolio efficiency.

2.1 *Single-Horizon Diversified Framework*

Consider that there are N portfolios under evaluation in the financial market and the return series of the j-th portfolio is denoted as a random variable r_j ($j = 1, \ldots, N$). In accordance with the investment objectives (or investment criteria) of decision makers, we select m input-like variables and s output-like variables to capture the characteristics of portfolios, which can be denoted as $x(r_j) = (x_1(r_j), \ldots, x_m(r_j))$ and $y(r_j) = (y_1(r_j), \ldots, y_s(r_j))$. In most literature on the diversified portfolio frontier, the risk measures (e.g., expected return) and return measures (e.g., standard deviation or variance) are regarded as the input-like and output-like variables of portfolios, respectively.

If strong free disposability and variable returns to scale (VRS) are assumed, an algebraic representation of single-horizon production possibility sets (PPSs) in the diversified framework for a sample of N portfolios can be expressed in a general form as follows:

$$P_{Div} = \left\{ (x, y) \in \mathrm{R}^m \times \mathrm{R}^s \left| \begin{array}{l} \forall i \in \{1, \ldots, m\} : x_i \geq x_i(\sum_{j=1}^{N} \mathrm{w}_j r_j) \\ \forall r \in \{1, \ldots, s\} : y_r \leq y_r(\sum_{j=1}^{N} \mathrm{w}_j r_j) \\ \forall j \in \{1, \ldots, N\} : \mathrm{w}_j \geq 0, \\ \sum_{j=1}^{N} \mathrm{w}_j = 1. \end{array} \right. \right\} \quad (1)$$

In P_{Div}, $\mathrm{w} = (\mathrm{w}_1, \ldots, \mathrm{w}_N)$ represents the vector of portfolio strategy on these samples of the portfolio. The condition $w_j \geq 0$ is imposed whenever short sales are excluded. Several studies use the inequality constraint $\sum_{j=1}^{N} \mathrm{w}_j \leq 1$ based on the nonincreasing returns to scale (NIRS) assumption instead of the equality constraint $\sum_{j=1}^{N} \mathrm{w}_j = 1$, allowing ones to opt for a partial non-investment in their portfolios. (Lamb & Tee, 2012a; Tarnaud & Leleu, 2018). The boundary of P_{Div} is identified as the diversified frontier (also called the diversified portfolio frontier).

For an observed portfolio $z_o = (x_o, y_o) \in \mathrm{R}^m \times \mathrm{R}^s$ ($o \in \{1, \ldots N\}$), if there exists a portfolio with $\sum_{j=1}^{N} \mathrm{w}_j r_j$ in P_{Div} (i.e., $\left(x\left(\sum_{j=1}^{N} \mathrm{w}_j r_j\right), y\left(\sum_{j=1}^{N} \mathrm{w}_j r_j\right)\right) \in P_{Div}$) whose input-like and output-like variables dominate in these considered variables of the observed portfolio, then z_o is inefficient. Conversely, if there is no such a portfolio in P_{Div}, this observed portfolio is efficient and located at the diversified portfolio frontier.

As one can see, the above basic PPS in the diversified framework primarily concentrates on the portfolio performance within a single time horizon. In reviewing the literature on single-horizon portfolio performance gauging in the diversified framework, several major research concerns emerge.

(1) MV portfolio performance evaluation

For MV portfolio performance appraisals, Briec et al. (2004) propose the use of the shortage function (Luenberger, 1995) for assessing portfolio efficiency. This approach allows investors to simultaneously reduce variance and increase expected return, providing a comprehensive measure of portfolio efficiency. Moreover, their work establishes a connection between portfolio theory and developments in production theory. Their fundamental idea for gauging portfolio performance involves the application of the shortage function. This enables the measurement of portfolio efficiency by evaluating the distance between a given portfolio and the diversified MV frontier. Inspired by this work, Kerstens et al. (2012) systematically discuss the impacts of different direction vectors of the generalized shortage function on the relative efficiency and ranking of MV portfolios. In a similar vein, Xiao et al. (2021)

extend the diversified models by incorporating the uncertainty of portfolio parameters, and then construct bi-level diversified models accordingly. Their models enable the derivation of lower and upper bounds for portfolio efficiency in the MV context.

Different from the previous work that uses the risk and expected return to construct a portfolio input–output process, Zhou et al. (2019) and Xiao et al. (2022b) develop a novel portfolio input–output process for portfolio management that aligns with the actual investment practices. By emphasizing the initial wealth as the input and the terminal wealth as the output, their work aims to capture the essence of the actual investment process. Under this input–output process, they propose a series of diversified frontier to calculate the MV portfolio efficiency based on various assumptions for the portfolio returns. These developments are intriguing due to their utilization of inputs and outputs derived directly from real investment processes. It partly offers a theoretical foundation for incorporating efficiency measures from production theory into portfolio evaluation. By aligning the evaluation framework with actual investment practices, these efforts provide additional evidence for the application of the efficiency measures in real-world investments.

(2) Alternative risk measures

Given several limitations of the traditional MV approach (Alexander & Baptista, 2002; Jondeau & Rockinger, 2006), a significant portion of modern portfolio theory proceeds with variations on these bi-objective MV evaluation criteria. The recent portfolio evaluation literature offers a wide range of alternative risk measures, including expected shortfall, semi-variance, system risk, and various forms of Value-at-Risk (VaR), etc. Lozano and Gutiérrez (2008a) integrate the second-order stochastic dominance (SSD) criteria into the diversified frontier models, and present six models with the mean return or above target mean return as output and various risk measures or safety measures as input, allowing for an efficiency measure of portfolio performance that is aligned with SSD efficiency. Zhao et al. (2011) incorporate the information of both system and non-system risk of portfolios and provide two diversified models for portfolio evaluation based on endogenous benchmarks. Lamb and Tee (2012a) provided a diversified frontier model that incorporated multiple return measures and coherent risk measures. They systematically explore the connections between diversification, coherent risk measures, and stochastic dominance. In a subsequent study, the work of Branda (2013) extends the work of Lamb and Tee (2012a) by incorporating the general deviation measure instead of the coherent risk measure.

More literature of related discussion includes, e.g., Lamb and Tee (2012b); Branda (2015); Branda (2016); Banihashemi and Navidi (2017); Choi and Min (2017); Lin and Li (2020); Adam and Branda (2021); Bilbao Terol et al. (2021), among others.

(3) Higher-order moments

Another important concern is the incorporation of multiple moments in portfolio evaluation. In effect, while the Mean–Variance (MV) portfolio evaluation methods are widely used by practitioners and researchers, they are consistent only with the quadratic utility function of investors. However, for utility functions that describe mixed risk aversion, it is necessary to incorporate higher-order moments to accurately assess the performance of portfolios aligned with the general investor preference (Trautmann and van de Kuilen, 2018). Consequently, expanding the classical framework with multi-moment diversified models presents a potentially interesting improvement for the field of finance.

Joro and Na (2006) provide a diversified frontier model within the MVS framework to study the effect of skewness on portfolio efficiency. Briec et al. (2007) introduce a general distance function, also known as a shortage function, to identify improvements in portfolio efficiency within the MVS framework. Their approach involves seeking simultaneous improvements in mean return and positive skewness while reducing risk. In a more general case, Briec and Kerstens (2010) extend the work to assess portfolio performance in the context of general moments, allowing to seek enhancements of odd moments and decreases of even moments simultaneously. More applications regarding this diversified multi-moment evaluation method can be found in Lozano and Gutiérrez (2008b); Bacmann and Benedetti (2009); Jurczenko et al. (2012); Branda and Kopa (2014); Khemchandani and Chandra (2014); Massol and Banal-Estañol (2014); Krüger (2021), among others.

2.2 *Multi-Horizon Diversified Framework*

Several studies have examined the influence of time dimensions on portfolio performance evaluation. In practice, the multi-horizon performance of portfolios available to investors is likely to provide significant additional information compared to assessing performance over a single time horizon. Three types of literature employ various approaches to investigate the multi-horizon performance of portfolios, all of which are based on the diversified frontier models.

(1) Temporal diversified models

To the best of our knowledge, Morey and Morey (1999) pioneer the idea of developing the MV portfolio performance assessment in a multi-horizon or temporal setting, which gauge and incorporate the relative performance of a given portfolio over various time horizons, such as 1 year, 3 years, 5 years, and 10 years. In essence, the basic purpose of their work is to propose an alternative weighting scheme for evaluating portfolio performance across multiple time horizons, employing objective weights instead of subjective weights utilized by certain commercial rating services (e.g., Morningstar and Lipper). Their approach involves establishing two temporal efficiency measures under risk and return orientations based on the diversified nonparametric frontier within a standard MV framework. The first efficiency measure focuses on minimizing all risk dimensions with no decrease in any return dimensions, while the second efficiency measure aims to maximize all return dimensions without increasing any risk dimensions.

Briec and Kerstens (2009) build upon the previous work of Morey and Morey (1999) by incorporating a multi-horizon perspective. They extend the analysis and introduce benchmark portfolios that take into account both risk contraction and mean return expansions by utilizing the temporal shortage function, as described in detail by Briec et al. (2006). Moreover, the portfolio weights are set to be constant over the given time horizon in the modeling of Morey and Morey (1999), essentially following a long-term investment perspective, whereas the study of Briec and Kerstens (2009) allows for the variation of benchmark weights over time, aiming to find a periodically rebalanced benchmark across different time horizons from a short-run investment perspective. An empirical application can be found in Ren et al. (2021), arguing the importance of considering multiple time horizons in portfolio performance assessment.

Based on the modeling idea in the above literature, this charter proposes a basic methodology on the temporal diversified frontier methods in a general setting. Suppose that there are N portfolios under evaluation, and decision makers have access to the return series of these portfolios from time 0 to time t, where $t = 1, \ldots, T$. This feature enables decision makers to analyze portfolio returns across various time horizons, facilitating a comprehensive evaluation of performance. Regarding the j-th portfolio, the return series from time 0 to time t is considered as a random variable $r_j^{0,t}$, where $j = 1, \cdots, N$ and $t = 1, \cdots, T$. Furthermore, one can define the notion of temporal (or multi-horizon) path of input-like and output-like variables as $(x_j^T, y_j^T) = (x(r_j^{0,t}), y(r_j^{0,t}))_{t=1}^T$ for the portfolio j, where $x(r_j^{0,t}) = (x_1(r_j^{0,t}), \ldots, x_m(r_j^{0,t}))$ and $y(r_j^{0,t}) = (y_1(r_j^{0,t}), \ldots, y_s(r_j^{0,t}))$ represent m input-like variables and s output-like variables from time 0 to time t, respectively. Supposing VRS for all time $t \in \{1, \ldots, T\}$ and strong free disposability of all input-like and out-like variables, an algebraic representation of temporal PPS in the diversified framework for a sample of N portfolios can be expressed as:

$$P_{Div}^T = \left\{ (x^T, y^T) \subset \mathbb{R}^{m\times T} \times \mathbb{R}^{s\times T} \middle| \begin{array}{l} \forall i \in \{1, \ldots, m\} : x_i^T \geq x_i\left[\sum_{j=1}^N (\mathrm{w}_j^1 r_j^{0,1}, \ldots, \mathrm{w}_j^T r_j^{0,T})\right] \\ \forall r \in \{1, \ldots, s\} : y_r^T \leq y_r\left[\sum_{j=1}^N (\mathrm{w}_j^1 r_j^{0,1}, \ldots, \mathrm{w}_j^T r_j^{0,T})\right] \\ \forall j \in \{1, \ldots, N\}, \forall t \in \{1, \ldots, T\} : \mathrm{w}_j^t \geq 0, \sum_{j=1}^N \mathrm{w}_j^t = 1. \end{array} \right\} \quad (2)$$

In the above P_{Div}^T, $\mathrm{w}^t = (\mathrm{w}_1^t, \ldots, \mathrm{w}_N^t)$ represents the vector of portfolio strategy on these samples of portfolios from time 0 to time t ($t \in \{1, \ldots, T\}$). Note that the portfolio weights are constant over time (i.e., $\mathrm{w}^1 = \mathrm{w}^2 = \cdots = \mathrm{w}^T$) in Morey and Morey (1999).

From the general PPS of temporal diversified models, one can clearly understand the modeling idea of the above literature. These temporal efficiency measurements focus on the portfolio performances over multiple periods from a given initial time and explicitly offer a weighting scheme to provide an inclusive assessment of portfolio performance for a given initial investment over different time horizons. Consequently, their dynamic nature is limited to some extent.

(2) Dynamic network diversified models

Differing from the idea of temporal diversified models above mentioned, Lin et al. (2017) introduce a network diversified frontier model that uses the net asset value (NAV) as the linkage of portfolio between adjacent periods, where the overall efficiency of a portfolio across the entire investment horizon is deconstructed into efficiencies calculated for individual periods. Their work is concerned with the information encompassed within the complete investment process of portfolios, with a strong emphasis on measuring the portfolio's performance efficiency throughout the entire process using a stringent and dynamic approach. By taking diversification into the multi-period network DEA model (Tone & Tsutsui, 2014), the proposed diversified method explores the potential of these network DEA models in the financial evaluation field. Following the idea of Lin et al. (2017), Xiao et al. (2022c) propose a dynamic diversified model that assesses the multi-horizon performance of socially responsible investment (SRI) by incorporating the social responsibility score (SRS) and NAV as intermediate linkages between adjacent periods. This model takes into account both financial and SRI criteria to provide a comprehensive evaluation of SRI performance.

In analogy, to introduce their modeling ideas explicitly, we provide a general methodology on the dynamic network diversified models. Based on the notions and definitions employed in temporal diversified models above, we consider the return series from time $t-1$ to time t for the j-th portfolio as a random variable $r_j^{t-1,t}$, where $j = 1, \cdots, N$ and $t = 1, \cdots, T$. Similarly, we can define the notion of a dynamic path of input-like and output-like variables as $(\hat{x}_j^T, \hat{y}_j^T) = (x(r_j^{t-1,t}), y(r_j^{t-1,t}))_{t=1}^T$, in which $x(r_j^{t-1,t}) = (x_1(r_j^{t-1,t}), \ldots, x_m(r_j^{t-1,t}))$ and $y(r_j^{t-1,t}) = (y_1(r_j^{t-1,t}), \ldots, y_s(r_j^{t-1,t}))$ represent m input-like variables and s output-like variables for time $t-1$ to time t, respectively. One can clearly see that the multi-horizon path $(\hat{x}_j^T, \hat{y}_j^T) = (x(r_j^{t-1,t}), y(r_j^{t-1,t}))_{t=1}^T$ contains input-like and output-like variables of portfolio j for all adjacent time periods within T.

Additionally, let $z_j^t = (z_{1j}^t, \ldots, z_{fj}^t)$ denote f intermediate variables of the portfolio j within the whole time period T: z_j^0 and z_j^T are treated as input-like variables for the first period and output-like variables for the last period, respectively, and all other z_j^t $(t \in \{1, \ldots, T-1\})$ are not only the output-like variables for time t, but also the input-like variables for time $t+1$. Similar to P_{Div}^T in Eq. (2), suppose VRS assumption for these time $t \in \{1, \ldots, T\}$ and strong free disposability for input-like and out-like variables, an algebraic representation of dynamic PPS in the diversified framework for a sample of N portfolios can be written as:

$$\hat{P}_{Div}^{T} = \left\{ (\hat{x}^{T}, \hat{y}^{T}) \in R^{m\times T} \times R^{s\times T} \left| \begin{array}{l} \forall i \in \{1,\dots,m\} : \hat{x}_i^{T} \geq x_i\left[\sum_{j=1}^{N} (\hat{w}_j^1 r_j^{0,1}, \dots, \hat{w}_j^T r_j^{0,T})\right] \\ \forall r \in \{1,\dots,s\} : \hat{y}_r^{T} \leq y_r\left[\sum_{j=1}^{N} (\hat{w}_j^1 r_j^{0,1}, \dots, \hat{w}_j^T r_j^{0,T})\right] \\ \forall d \in \{1,\dots,f\}, \forall t \in \{1,\dots,T-1\} : \sum_{j=1}^{N} \hat{w}_j^t z_{dj}^t = \sum_{j=1}^{N} \hat{w}_j^{t+1} z_{dj}^t \\ \forall d \in \{1,\dots,f\} : z_d^0 \geq \sum_{j=1}^{N} \hat{w}_j^1 z_{dj}^0,\ z_d^T \leq \sum_{j=1}^{N} \hat{w}_j^T z_{dj}^T \\ \forall j \in \{1,\dots,N\}, \forall t \in \{1,\dots,T\} : \hat{w}_j^t \geq 0,\ \sum_{j=1}^{N} \hat{w}_j^t = 1. \end{array} \right. \right\} \quad (3)$$

In $\hat{P}_{Div}^{T}$, $\hat{w}^t = (\hat{w}_1^t, \dots, \hat{w}_N^t)$ represents the vector of portfolio strategy on these samples of portfolio for time $t-1$ to time t ($t \in \{1, \dots, T\}$). The construction of linking conditions for two adjacent periods is a widely employed technique in dynamic network DEA models derived from production theory. This approach can be intuitively elucidated as follows: the constraint $\sum_{j=1}^{N} \hat{w}_j^t z_{dj}^t = \sum_{j=1}^{N} \hat{w}_j^{t+1} z_{dj}^t$ ensures that the value of the intermediate variables for time t ($t \in \{1, \dots, T-1\}$), which is recognized as the output-like variable, is equivalent to the value of the intermediate variable for time $t+1$, which is recognized as the input-like variable (Lin et al., 2017).

(3) Portfolio Productivity Indicators

The last type of method in the diversified framework for multi-horizon performance evaluation is to employ some extensions of diversified models combined with the productivity indicator from production theory (Chambers, 2002; Chambers et al., 1996). Brandouy et al. (2010) proposed an innovative approach to track changes in portfolio performance over time by integrating the shortage function, which is based on the combination of the diversified MV portfolio frontier and the Luenberger productivity indicator. The portfolio productivity indicator, in this case, is divided into two distinct components: efficiency change and frontier change. The efficiency change component evaluates the portfolio manager's ability by estimating efficiency changes over time, while the frontier change component captures shifts in the efficient frontier caused by market volatility.

Their research marks a significant contribution in establishing a connection between indicator theory and the evaluation framework for portfolio performance and sheds light on the potential of the portfolio productivity indicator and its decomposition as a valuable measurement tool for appraising fund performance in discrete time. This effort highlights the importance of considering the indicator theory within the dynamic context of portfolio performance evaluation, providing valuable insights for future research in this area.

3 Portfolio Evaluation Based on the Nondiversified Frontier: Review and Classification

In most cases, the diversified frontier models above introduced often rely on nonlinear programming techniques. However, their potential complexity and computational burden pose a challenge, rendering these models unsuitable for large-scale evaluations (Kerstens et al., 2022; Liu et al., 2015). Relatively recently, portfolio performance assessment has witnessed a gradual and partial transposition of successful nondiversified nonparametric frontier estimation methodologies, originally derived from production theory. Intuitively, these nondiversified frontiers estimate the efficient frontier based upon the convex or nonconvex combinations of observations and use an efficiency measure to position each observation relative to the convex or nonconvex nonparametric frontier (i.e., DEA or FDH frontier). This chapter also summarizes articles on the nondiversified models for portfolio performance assessment in single- and multi-horizon contexts.

3.1 Single-Horizon Nondiversified Methods

We briefly introduce the basic definitions and properties of nondiversified models that have been applied in portfolio evaluation literature. In analogy, suppose that there exist portfolios being evaluated, where return series are recorded as a random variable $r_1, \ldots, r_N$. The portfolio j is described by m input-like variables and s output-like variables, which are also denoted as $x(r_j) = (x_1(r_j), \ldots, x_m(r_j))$ and $y(r_j) = (y_1(r_j), \ldots, y_s(r_j))$. Based on the assumption of VRS and strong disposability for all inputs and outputs, a unified algebraic representation of convex and nonconvex PPS for this sample of N portfolios is:

$$P_{D/F} = \left\{ (x, y) \in \mathrm{R}^m \times \mathrm{R}^s \;\middle|\; \begin{array}{l} \forall i \in \{1, \ldots, m\} : x_i \geq \sum_{j=1}^{N} \lambda_j x_i(r_j) \\ \forall r \in \{1, \ldots, s\} : y_r \leq \sum_{j=1}^{N} \lambda_j y_r(r_j) \\ \lambda \in \Lambda. \end{array} \right\} \quad (4)$$

where:

$\Lambda \equiv \Lambda_C = \{\lambda \in \mathrm{R}^N | \sum_{j=1}^{N} \lambda_j = 1 \text{ and } \forall j \in \{1, \ldots, N\} : \lambda_j \geq 0\}$ if convexity is assumed, and

$\Lambda \equiv \Lambda_{NC} = \{\lambda \in \mathrm{R}^N | \sum_{j=1}^{N} \lambda_j = 1 \text{ and } \forall j \in \{1, \ldots, N\} : \lambda_j \in \{0, 1\}\}$ if nonconvexity is assumed.

The existence of an input–output combination $\left(\sum_{j=1}^{N} \lambda_j x(r_j), \sum_{j=1}^{N} \lambda_j y(r_j)\right) \in P_{D/F}$ that requires fewer inputs and produces more outputs than the observed portfolio indicates inefficiency. Portfolios are efficient when no further improved input–output combinations can be identified, which are located on the boundary of $P_{D/F}$, known as the convex or nonconvex nonparametric frontier. Comparing the P_{Div} in Eq. (1) with the above $P_{D/F}$, it is clear that these nondiversified frontier models can be computed by the linear (or binary mixed integer) programming since the diversification effects of portfolios are excluded.

The work of Murthi et al. (1997) makes a significant contribution by applying convex nonparametric frontier methods to calculate portfolio efficiency. Subsequently, these nondiversified frontier performance evaluation methods have been amply extended across directions. Hereafter, this chapter summarizes the previous efforts of nondiversified frontier models that are applied to single-horizon portfolio performance evaluation. The literature can be provided from the following four interesting concerns.

(1) Multiple options of inputs and outputs

One concern of these extensions on the basic nondiversified models involves establishing and enriching the portfolio assessment indicators (i.e., multi-dimensional inputs and outputs) used to construct the nondiversified models. By allowing for multiple inputs and outputs, these researchers apply several basic nondiversified frontier-based models to gauge portfolio performance. For instance, Basso and Funari (2001) develop a nondiversified frontier model to evaluate the efficiency of Italian funds. Their approach involved considering various risk indicators of a portfolio as inputs and the expected return and stochastic dominance indicators as outputs, aiming to provide a comprehensive evaluation of the funds' efficiency while accounting for multiple factors. Gregoriou et al. (2005) employ a total of six variables in a risk-return framework corresponding to the hedge funds, and assess the single-horizon performance of hedge funds based on the nondiversified frontier models. More importantly, their empirical results argue that the performance measure derived from the nondiversified frontier plays a significant role in effectively identifying superior-performing funds, whereas the use of traditional risk-measurement tools may lead to misleading conclusions.

More examples of the alternative options on inputs and outputs of portfolios can be found in McMullen and Strong (1998); Basso and Funari (2003); Barros and Garcia (2006); Eling (2006); Eling and Schuhmacher (2007); Belu (2009); Kumar et al. (2010); Pérez Gladish et al. (2013); Goel and Mani (2018); Valadkhani and Moradi-Motlagh (2023), among others.

(2) Modeling specification issues

The second main concern is to discuss the variety of model specification issues regarding the application of nondiversified frontier when gauging the portfolio performance, such as the returns to scale (RTS) issue and the assumption of convexity.

One of the key issues that has been discussed in the nondiversified frontier literature gauging portfolio performance is the RTS assumption of the underlying "technology". These studies mainly involve specifying VRS, constant returns to scale (CRS) and constant returns to scale (CRS), and non-increasing returns to scale (NIRS) for the nondiversified nonparametric frontier. If CRS is imposed into the corresponding model, then the condition on set Λ to the above $P_{D/F}$ (Eq. (4)) should be changed as: $\Lambda \equiv \Lambda_C = \{\lambda \in \mathrm{R}^N \mid \forall j \in \{1, \ldots, N\} : \lambda_j \geq 0\}$ and $\Lambda \equiv \Lambda_{NC} = \{\lambda \in \mathrm{R}^N | \forall j \in \{1, \ldots, N\} : \lambda_j \in \{0, 1\}\}$ (Alexakis & Tsolas, 2011; Hu & Chang, 2008). If the NIRS assumption is imposed, then this condition on this set Λ needs to be changed into: $\Lambda \equiv \Lambda_C = \{\lambda \in \mathrm{R}^N \mid \sum_{j=1}^{N} \lambda_j \leq 1 \text{ and } \forall j \in \{1, \ldots, N\} : \lambda_j \geq 0\}$ and $\Lambda \equiv \Lambda_{NC} = \{\lambda \in \mathrm{R}^N \mid \sum_{j=1}^{N} \lambda_j \leq 1 \text{ and } \forall j \in \{1, \ldots, N\} : \lambda_j \in \{0, 1\}\}$ (Xiao et al., 2022a). The important article of Kerstens et al. (2011) propose a systematical discussion and empirical examples on the RTS issues of nondiversified models. Subsequently, a relevant discussion also can be found in Basso and Funari (2014). Xiao et al. (2022a) focus on exploring the potential of the NIRS assumption for estimating the portfolio efficiency where the self-financing constraint is allowed (i.e., $\sum_{j=1}^{N} \lambda_j \leq 1$.).

Another main specification issue is whether to impose the convexity assumption on the nondiversified models. The majority of nondiversified frontier studies that evaluate portfolio performance typically rely on the traditional convexity assumption (Anderson et al., 2004; Haslem, 2003; McMullen & Strong, 1998; Shahrour, 2022). For this specification issue, Kerstens et al. (2011) also indicate that a standard convexity assumption is questionable from both portfolio theory and hedonic price function perspectives: nonconvexity emerges as a more conservative hypothesis to maintain within nondiversified nonparametric models. More discussions regarding the convexity and nonconvexity issues for nonparametric modeling are found in Daraio and Simar (2006); Matallín-Sáez et al. (2014); Abdelsalam et al. (2014a); Abdelsalam et al. (2014b); Brandouy et al. (2015); Nalpas et al. (2017).

(3) Adaptions of models

The third intriguing concern is to emphasize the adaptation of the nondiversified nonparametric models or their integration with other methods. The basic nondiversified nonparametric frontier models have already found their means in various other literatures: The first example is their extensions to the super-efficiency context for fully identifying and discriminating the best-performing portfolios among the efficient ties (Gregoriou, 2006; Tsolas, 2022).

Another example focuses on the two-stage process of the portfolio management process for providing a comprehensive portfolio performance analysis. Premachandra et al. (2012) introduce a two-stage DEA that aims to evaluate the performance of mutual fund families, where the overall efficiency is decomposed into two distinct components: operational efficiency and portfolio efficiency. This approach allows for a detailed analysis of the factors contributing to a fund's overall efficiency and offers insights into areas for potential improvement within the operational and portfolio aspects of the activities of mutual fund families. A general two-stage portfolio analysis framework is shown in Fig. 1. More recent proposals on the two-stage nondiversified models for portfolio performance assessment are found in Galagedera et al. (2016); Sánchez-González et al. (2017); Galagedera et al. (2018); Tavana et al. (2018); Galagedera (2019); Galagedera et al. (2020); Hsieh et al. (2020); Tsolas (2020); Lin et al. (2021); Kazemi and Galagedera (2022); Koronakos et al. (2022); Peykani et al. (2022), among others.

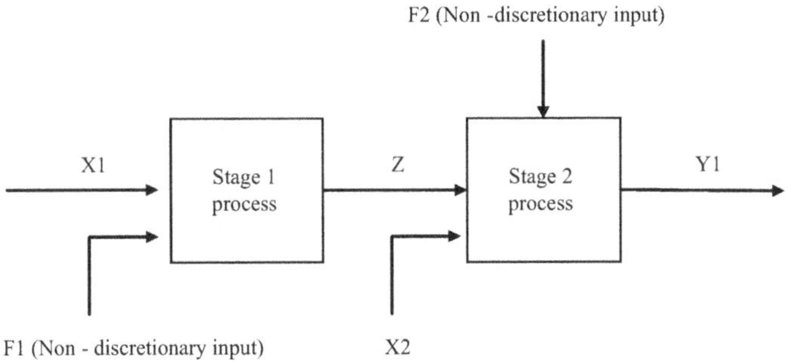

Fig. 1 A generic two-stage framework for the whole mutual fund management process

A final example is the integration of nondiversified nonparametric frontier models with other methods (e.g., metafrontier technology, regression analysis, and portfolio optimization) to make ample use of portfolio efficiency measures. For instance, Makni et al. (2015) combine the metafrontier approach with the traditional DEA model to compare the efficiency of Islamic equity funds. Moreover, many studies make efforts to analyze the impacts on portfolio efficiency by incorporating the nondiversified frontier models with several regression models (Allevi et al., 2019; Basso & Funari, 2017; Galagedera & Silvapulle, 2002; Galagedera & Watson, 2015; Hassan et al., 2020; Hsu & Lin, 2007; Tsolas, 2014; Tsolas & Charles, 2015; Tuzcu & Ertugay, 2020). In the meantime, the nondiversified frontier approach has also been integrated with the typical portfolio optimization models to realize improvements in portfolio efficiency (Chen et al., 2020; Deng & Fang, 2019; Edirisinghe & Zhang, 2007; Gardijan & Škrinjarić, 2015; Huang et al., 2015; Lim et al., 2014; Mashayekhi & Omrani, 2016; Pätäri et al., 2012; Rotela Junior et al., 2015; Zamani et al., 2014; Zhou et al., 2018a, 2018b, 2021).

(4) Theoretical properties

The final direction of the theoretical properties of these nondiversified frontier portfolio evaluation models (Ding et al., 2014; Liu et al., 2015; Zhou et al., 2018b). Among these, the key work of Liu et al. (2015) remark that when the real portfolio frontier exhibits concavity (such as having concave return measures and convex risk measures), the convex nonparametric frontier, also known as the DEA frontier, converges to the real efficient frontier in probability. This finding establishes the validity and applicability of the convex nonparametric frontier in analyzing and estimating portfolio efficiency. As evident from their contribution, a fundamental principle is that nondiversified nonparametric frontier specifications are ideally expected to underestimate the eventual performance of a diversified portfolio model.

However, in the case of the nonconvex diversified portfolio models, it is clear that the nonconvex frontier specifications already provide a conservative underestimation, while the convex nonparametric frontier specification may lead to an overestimation of the performance of the corresponding diversified portfolio model (Kerstens et al.,

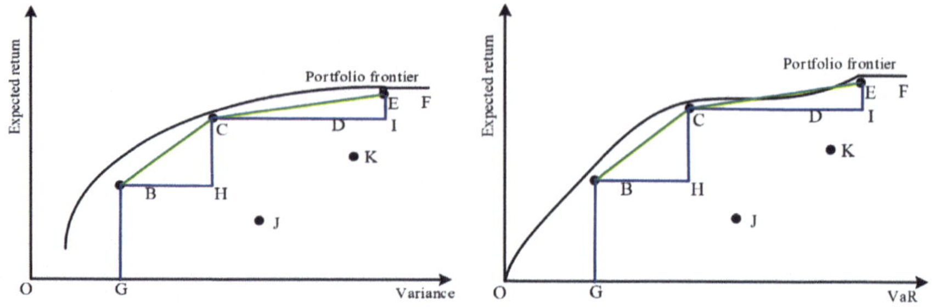

(a) MV frontier compared with convex and nonconvex VRS frontiers

(b) Mean-VaR frontier compared with convex and nonconvex VRS frontiers

Fig. 2 Comparison of different frontiers generated by various nondiversified models

2011, 2022; Xiao et al., 2022a). An intuitive explanation of the above elaboration in the literature is shown in Fig. 2.

3.2 Multi-Horizon Nondiversified Methods

In effect, the portfolio evaluation models discussed above, which are based on the nondiversified nonparametric frontier, belong to the category of single-horizon performance evaluation. Regarding research on the nondiversified models for measuring the multi-horizon performance of portfolios, these can be summarized into three categories similar to the multi-horizon diversified methods.

(1) Temporal nondiversified models

One research direction of multi-horizon nondiversified modeling is to transpose the basic idea of Morey and Morey (1999) and Briec and Kerstens (2009) into the context of the nondiversified frontier. Kerstens et al. (2022) propose a range of nondiversified convex and nonconvex frontier models with the help of the temporal shortage function, which can deal with multiple moments and multiple times simultaneously. More importantly, their work empirically tests the potential advantages of the proposed models in selecting promising funds through a backtesting analysis.

Similarly, this charter provides a general PPS formula in the nondiversified framework for clarifying the modeling idea of temporal nondiversified models in Kerstens et al. (2022). Based on the notations defined for temporal diversified models (see point (1) subsection 2.2), we also assume VRS for all time $t \in \{1, \ldots, T\}$ and strong free disposability of input-like and output-like variables, an algebraic representation of temporal PPS in the diversified framework for a sample of N portfolios can be expressed as:

$$P^T_{D/F} = \left\{ (x^T, y^T) \in R^{m\times T} \times R^{s\times T} \left| \begin{array}{l} \forall i \in \{1,\ldots,m\} : x_i^T \geq \sum_{j=1}^{N} [\lambda_j^1 x_i(r_j^{0,1}),\ldots,\lambda_j^T x_i(r_j^{0,T})] \\ \forall r \in \{1,\ldots,s\} : y_r^T \leq \sum_{j=1}^{N} [\lambda_j^1 y_r(r_j^{0,1}),\ldots,\lambda_j^T y_r(r_j^{0,T})] \\ \forall\, t \in \{1,\ldots,T\} : \lambda^t \in \Lambda^t. \end{array} \right. \right\} \quad (5)$$

where:

$\Lambda^t \equiv \Lambda^t_C = \{\lambda^t \in R^N | \sum_{j=1}^{N} \lambda_j^t = 1 \text{ and } \forall j \in \{1,\ldots,N\} : \lambda_j^t \geq 0\}$ if convexity is assumed, and $\Lambda^t \equiv \Lambda^t_{NC} = \{\lambda^t \in R^N | \sum_{j=1}^{N} \lambda_j^t = 1 \text{ and } \forall j \in \{1,\ldots,N\} : \lambda_j^t \in \{0,1\}\}$ if nonconvexity is assumed.

In $P^T_{D/F}$, $\hat{w}^t = (\hat{w}_1^t,\ldots,\hat{w}_N^t)$ represents the vector of portfolio strategy on these samples of portfolio from time $t-1$ to time t ($t \in \{1,\ldots,T\}$). From the above $P^T_{D/F}$, one can find that the modeling idea is to enable each portfolio to expand its multiple outputs while reducing its multiple inputs across all time horizons, starting from a specific initial time to catch the boundary of $P^T_{D/F}$. As a result, there are no temporal connections or interdependencies among the evaluations of portfolio performance at each individual time horizon.

(2) Dynamic network nondiversified models

Another direction is the application of dynamic network DEA models considering the carryover activities between adjacent periods. Chang et al. (2021) propose nested dynamic network models to evaluate the dynamic performance of portfolios by considering the carry-over activities of portfolios between adjacent periods. A variety of extensions on the dynamic network nondiversified models within portfolio performance appraisal can also be found in Lin and Liu (2021); Lu et al. (2021).

In a similar vein, this chapter provides a general PPS for introducing the fundamental modeling of the dynamic network nondiversified models. Based on the notations and assumptions given in dynamic network diversified models (see point (2) in subsection 2.2), we can define algebraic representation of dynamic PPS in the nondiversified framework for a sample of N portfolios as follows:

$$\hat{P}^T_{D/F} = \left\{ (\hat{x}^T, \hat{y}^T) \in R^{m\times T} \times R^{s\times T} \left| \begin{array}{l} \forall i \in \{1,\ldots,m\} : \hat{x}_i^T \geq \sum_{j=1}^{N} \left[\hat{\lambda}_j^1 x_i(r_j^{0,1}),\ldots,\hat{\lambda}_j^T x_i(r_j^{0,T})\right] \\ \forall r \in \{1,\ldots,s\} : \hat{y}_r^T \leq \sum_{j=1}^{N} \left[\hat{\lambda}_j^1 y_r\left(r_j^{0,1}\right),\ldots,\hat{\lambda}_j^T y_r(r_j^{0,T})\right] \\ \forall d \in \{1,\ldots,f\}, \forall t \in \{1,\ldots,T-1\} : \sum_{j=1}^{N} \hat{\lambda}_j^t z_{dj}^t = \sum_{j=1}^{N} \hat{\lambda}_j^{t+1} z_{dj}^t \\ \forall d \in \{1,\ldots,f\} : z_d^0 \geq \sum_{j=1}^{N} \hat{\lambda}_j^1 z_{dj}^0,\ z_d^T \leq \sum_{j=1}^{N} \hat{\lambda}_j^T z_{dj}^T \\ \forall\, t \in \{1,\ldots,T\} : \hat{\lambda}^t \in \Lambda^t. \end{array} \right. \right\} \quad (6)$$

where:

$\Lambda^t = \Lambda^t_C = \{\hat{\lambda}^t \in R^N | \sum_{j=1}^{N} \hat{\lambda}_j^t = 1 \text{ and } \forall j \in \{1,\ldots,N\} : \hat{\lambda}_j^t \geq 0\}$ if convexity is assumed, and $\Lambda^t \equiv \Lambda^t_{NC} = \{\hat{\lambda}^t \in R^N | \sum_{j=1}^{N} \hat{\lambda}_j^t = 1 \text{ and } \forall j \in \{1,\ldots,N\} : \hat{\lambda}_j^t \in \{0,1\}\}$ if nonconvexity is assumed.

Differing from the $P^T_{D/F}$ (see Eq. (5)), the dynamic network nondiversified models constructed based on $\hat{P}^T_{D/F}$ are regarded as strictly dynamic evaluation methods, which not only consider inputs and outputs for each individual period but also account for the carry-overs between adjacent periods for portfolios.

(3) Productivity indicator and window analysis

The final direction regarding the multi-horizon nondiversified approaches is to combine the basic nondiversified models with the productivity indicator analysis or window analysis that are commonly employed to calculate the performance evolution of an observation. For instance, Babalos et al. (2012) applied the Malmquist index driven by DEA to measure the efficiency change of Greek equity funds over time. In addition, their work investigates the relationship between the size of funds and the obtained efficiency by employing a panel logit model. More recently, Djaghballou et al. (2018) examine the efficiency and productivity performance of zakat funds by combining DEA models with the Malmquist productivity index. Zhang and Chen (2018) offer a comprehensive evaluation framework for dynamic performance assessment of energy investment portfolios by combining window analysis with the directional distance function.

4 Conclusion and Future Research

Probably in light of the extensive criticisms surrounding traditional financial performance measures, a substantially growing number have focused on nonparametric frontier methods of evaluating, analyzing, and improving portfolio efficiency, which has garnered a wide attention from both academia and industry. This chapter reviews previous research efforts that applied the nonparametric frontier methods to portfolio performance appraisal and benchmarking issues. All the previous works are classified into the diversified and nondiversified nonparametric methods, along with the research trend and recent developments within the basic classification framework. In this review, we highlight the primary features of publications pertaining to nonparametric frontier methods in portfolio analysis. Moreover, we also provide a generic PPS formula for each class of methods to clarify their fundamental modeling ideas, covering the diversified frontier models and nondiversified frontier models in single- and multi-horizon frameworks. The main contributions of the chapter are that it summarizes recent research popularity regarding the various classes of nonparametric frontier evaluation methods, and it provides a clear picture regarding on modeling ideas of each class of methods.

As mentioned above, the nonparametric frontier method is considered a promising approach for assessing portfolio performance. Nevertheless, it is essential to acknowledge that this methodology has its limitations. Consequently, an additional contribution of this chapter is to provide a valuable insight and future directions to enhance the effective utilization of nonparametric frontier models in the domain of portfolio efficiency.

First, the nonparametric frontier approaches can be combined with portfolio optimization. To our knowledge, a complete portfolio process involves two important steps, one is the selection of investment assets and the other is the determination of investment weights. The former requires the evaluation of the investment value of the assets, while the latter optimizes the portfolio weighing of selected assets. The nonparametric frontier approaches are not only able to measure and rate the value of the assets to be selected, but the resulting efficiency values can also be used as a reference for the asset portfolio.

Second, a promising avenue for future research is to investigate the impacts of different projection directions on the performance measure for portfolios in both diversified and nondiversified nonparametric frontier models. So far, most nonparametric frontier contributions measuring the portfolio performance assume that the projection direction of the observation under evaluation is exogenous. Several literatures in production assessment challenge the validity of the assumption on the exogenous projection direction (Wang et al., 2019). It is clear that the selection of projection direction vectors is a critical factor in portfolio evaluation using shortage functions or distance functions. Testing the impact of different directions determined by various direction-selecting techniques is an interesting topic, especially to develop these nonparametric frontier methods with the use of the endogenous direction models for searching optimized directions, such as direction towards the closest benchmark (Baek & Lee, 2009), or indicating the largest potential for efficiency improvement (Hampf & Krüger, 2015).

Third, the data sources of indicators for portfolio evaluation can be increased. Most studies on portfolio evaluation have used their trading data to construct return and risk measures, but the trading data do not always fully describe the portfolio performance, making it difficult for investors to assess the true investment value of portfolios. To our knowledge, some textual big data (e.g., social media and news data) can make up for the shortage of traditional trading data. Therefore, constructing multi-source data-driven nonparametric frontier portfolio evaluation methods are also the direction that can be expanded by subsequent researchers.

References

Abdelsalam, O., Duygun, M., Matallín-Sáez, J. C., & Tortosa-Ausina, E. (2014a). Do ethics imply persistence? The case of Islamic and socially responsible funds. *Journal of Banking & Finance, 40*, 182–194.

Abdelsalam, O., Fethi, M. D., Matallín, J. C., & Tortosa-Ausina, E. (2014b). On the comparative performance of socially responsible and Islamic mutual funds. *Journal of Economic Behavior & Organization, 103*, 108–128.

Adam, L., & Branda, M. (2021). Risk-aversion in data envelopment analysis models with diversification. *Omega, 102*, 102338.

Alexakis, P., & Tsolas, I. E. (2011). Appraisal of mutual equity fund performance using data envelopment analysis. *Multinational Finance Journal, 15*(3/4), 273–296.

Alexander, G. J., & Baptista, A. M. (2002). Economic implications of using a mean-VaR model for portfolio selection: A comparison with mean-variance analysis. *Journal of Economic Dynamics and Control, 26*(7–8), 1159–1193.

Allevi, E., Basso, A., Bonenti, F., Oggioni, G., & Riccardi, R. (2019). Measuring the environmental performance of green SRI funds: A DEA approach. *Energy Economics, 79*, 32–44.

Anderson, R. I., Brockman, C. M., Giannikos, C., & McLeod, R. W. (2004). A non-parametric examination of real estate mutual fund efficiency. *International Journal of Business and Economics, 3*, 225–238.

Babalos, V., Caporale, G. M., & Philippas, N. (2012). Efficiency evaluation of Greek equity funds. *Research in International Business and Finance, 26*(2), 317–333.

Bacmann, J., & Benedetti, S. M. (2009). Optimal Bayesian portfolios of hedge funds. *International Journal of Risk Assessment and Management, 11*(1–2), 39–58.

Baek, C., & Lee, J. (2009). The relevance of DEA benchmarking information and the least-distance measure. *Mathematical and Computer Modelling, 49*(1–2), 265–275.

Banihashemi, S., & Navidi, S. (2017). Portfolio performance evaluation in Mean-CVaR framework: A comparison with non-parametric methods value at risk in Mean-VaR analysis. *Operations Research Perspectives, 4*, 21–28.

Barros, C. P., & Garcia, M. T. M. (2006). Performance evaluation of pension funds management companies with data envelopment analysis. *Risk Management and Insurance Review, 9*(2), 165–188.

Basso, A., & Funari, S. (2001). A data envelopment analysis approach to measure the mutual fund performance. *European Journal of Operational Research, 135*(3), 477–492.

Basso, A., & Funari, S. (2003). Measuring the performance of ethical mutual funds: A DEA approach. *Journal of the Operational Research Society, 54*(5), 521–531.

Basso, A., & Funari, S. (2014). Constant and variable returns to scale DEA models for socially responsible investment funds. *European Journal of Operational Research, 235*(3), 775–783.

Basso, A., & Funari, S. (2017). The role of fund size in the performance of mutual funds assessed with DEA models. *The European Journal of Finance, 23*(6), 457–473.

Belu, C. (2009). Ranking corporations based on sustainable and socially responsible practices. A data envelopment analysis (DEA) approach. *Sustainable Development, 17*(4), 257–268.

Bilbao Terol, A., Arenas Parra, M. and Bilbao Terol, C. (2021). Measuring the overall efficiency of SRI and conventional mutual funds by a diversification-consistent DEA model. International Transactions in Operational Research, https://doi.org/10.1111/itor.12974.

Branda, M. (2013). Diversification-consistent data envelopment analysis with general deviation measures. *European Journal of Operational Research, 226*(3), 626–635.

Branda, M. (2015). Diversification-consistent data envelopment analysis based on directional-distance measures. *Omega, 52*, 65–76.

Branda, M. (2016). Mean-value at risk portfolio efficiency: approaches based on data envelopment analysis models with negative data and their empirical behaviour. *4OR, 14*(1), 77–99.

Branda, M., & Kopa, M. (2014). On relations between DEA-risk models and stochastic dominance efficiency tests. *Central European Journal of Operations Research, 22*, 13–35.

Brandouy, O., Briec, W., Kerstens, K., & Van de Woestyne, I. (2010). Portfolio performance gauging in discrete time using a Luenberger productivity indicator. *Journal of Banking & Finance, 34*(8), 1899–1910.

Brandouy, O., Kerstens, K. & Van de Woestyne, I. (2015). Frontier-based versus traditional mutual fund ratings: A first backtesting analysis. *European Journal of Operational Research, 242* (1), 332–342.

Briec, W., & Kerstens, K. (2009). Multi-horizon Markowitz portfolio performance appraisals: A general approach. *Omega, 37*(1), 50–62.

Briec, W., & Kerstens, K. (2010). Portfolio selection in multidimensional general and partial moment space. *Journal of Economic Dynamics and Control, 34*(4), 636–656.

Briec, W., Comes, C., & Kerstens, K. (2006). Temporal technical and profit efficiency measurement: Definitions, duality and aggregation results. *International Journal of Production Economics, 103*(1), 48–63.
Briec, W., Kerstens, K., & Jokung, O. (2007). Mean-variance-skewness portfolio performance gauging: A general shortage function and dual approach. *Management Science, 53*(1), 135–149.
Briec, W., Kerstens, K., & Lesourd, J. (2004). Single-period Markowitz portfolio selection, performance gauging, and duality: A variation on the Luenberger shortage function. *Journal of Optimization Theory and Applications, 120*(1), 1–27.
Chambers, R. G. (2002). Exact nonradial input, output, and productivity measurement. *Economic Theory*, 751–765.
Chambers, R. G., Fāure, R., & Grosskopf, S. (1996). Productivity growth in APEC countries. *Pacific Economic Review, 1*(3), 181–190.
Chang, T., Tone, K., & Wu, C. (2021). Nested dynamic network data envelopment analysis models with infinitely many decision making units for portfolio evaluation. *European Journal of Operational Research, 291*(2), 766–781.
Chen, W., Li, S., Zhang, J., & Mehlawat, M. K. (2020). A comprehensive model for fuzzy multi-objective portfolio selection based on DEA cross-efficiency model. *Soft Computing, 24*, 2515–2526.
Choi, H., & Min, D. (2017). Efficiency of well-diversified portfolios: Evidence from data envelopment analysis. *Omega, 73*, 104–113.
Daraio, C., & Simar, L. (2006). A robust nonparametric approach to evaluate and explain the performance of mutual funds. *European Journal of Operational Research, 175*(1), 516–542.
Deng, X., & Fang, W. (2019). A novel mean-variance-maverick DEA prospect cross-efficiency approach for fuzzy portfolio selection. *Journal of Intelligent & Fuzzy Systems, 37*(6), 8113–8130.
Ding, H., Zhou, Z., Xiao, H., Ma, C. & Liu, W. (2014). Performance evaluation of portfolios with margin requirements. *Mathematical Problems in Engineering*, 2014.
Djaghballou, C., Djaghballou, M., Larbani, M., & Mohamad, A. (2018). Efficiency and productivity performance of zakat funds in Algeria. *International Journal of Islamic and Middle Eastern Finance and Management, 11*(3), 474–494.
Edirisinghe, N. C., & Zhang, X. (2007). Generalized DEA model of fundamental analysis and its application to portfolio optimization. *Journal of Banking & Finance, 31*(11), 3311–3335.
Eling, M. (2006). Performance measurement of hedge funds using data envelopment analysis. *Financial Markets and Portfolio Management, 20*, 442–471.
Eling, M., & Schuhmacher, F. (2007). Does the choice of performance measure influence the evaluation of hedge funds? *Journal of Banking & Finance, 31*(9), 2632–2647.
Galagedera, D. U. (2019). Modelling social responsibility in mutual fund performance appraisal: A two-stage data envelopment analysis model with non-discretionary first stage output. *European Journal of Operational Research, 273*(1), 376–389.
Galagedera, D. U., & Silvapulle, P. (2002). Australian mutual fund performance appraisal using data envelopment analysis. *Managerial Finance, 28*(9), 60–73.
Galagedera, D. U., & Watson, J. (2015). Benchmarking superannuation funds based on relative performance. *Applied Economics, 47*(28), 2959–2973.
Galagedera, D. U., Fukuyama, H., Watson, J., & Tan, E. K. (2020). Do mutual fund managers earn their fees? New measures for performance appraisal. *European Journal of Operational Research, 287*(2), 653–667.
Galagedera, D. U., Roshdi, I., Fukuyama, H., & Zhu, J. (2018). A new network DEA model for mutual fund performance appraisal: An application to US equity mutual funds. *Omega, 77*, 168–179.
Galagedera, D. U., Watson, J., Premachandra, I. M., & Chen, Y. (2016). Modeling leakage in two-stage DEA models: An application to US mutual fund families. *Omega, 61*, 62–77.
Gardijan, M., & Škrinjarić, T. (2015). Equity portfolio optimization: A DEA based methodology applied to the Zagreb stock exchange. *Croatian Operational Research Review, 6*(2), 405–417.

Goel, S., & Mani, M. (2018). Efficiency measurement of open-ended mutual fund schemes with respect to Indian mutual fund industry. *International Journal of Financial Services Management, 9*(2), 140–167.

Gregoriou, G. N. (2006). Optimisation of the largest US mutual funds using data envelopment analysis. *Journal of Asset Management, 6*(6), 445–455.

Gregoriou, G. N., Sedzro, K., & Zhu, J. (2005). Hedge fund performance appraisal using data envelopment analysis. *European Journal of Operational Research, 164*(2), 555–571.

Hampf, B., & Krüger, J. J. (2015). Optimal directions for directional distance functions: An exploration of potential reductions of greenhouse gases. *American Journal of Agricultural Economics, 97*(3), 920–938.

Harvey, C. R., Liechty, J. C., Liechty, M. W., & Müller, P. (2010). Portfolio selection with higher moments. *Quantitative Finance, 10*(5), 469–485.

Haslem, J. (2003). *Mutual funds: Risk and performance analysis for decision making*. Blackwell.

Hassan, A., Chachi, A. & Munshi, M. R. (2020). Performance measurement of Islamic mutual funds using DEA method. *Journal of Islamic Accounting and Business Research.*

Hsieh, H. P., Tebourbi, I., Lu, W. M., & Liu, N. Y. (2020). Mutual fund performance: The decision quality and capital magnet efficiencies. *Managerial and Decision Economics, 41*(5), 861–872.

Hsu, C., & Lin, J. (2007). Mutual fund performance and persistence in Taiwan: A non-parametric approach. *The Service Industries Journal, 27*(5), 509–523.

Hu, J., & Chang, T. (2008). Decomposition of mutual fund underperformance. *Applied Financial Economics Letters, 4*(5), 363–367.

Huang, C., Chiou, C., Wu, T., & Yang, S. (2015). An integrated DEA-MODM methodology for portfolio optimization. *Operational Research, 15*, 115–136.

Jondeau, E., & Rockinger, M. (2003). Conditional volatility, skewness, and kurtosis: Existence, persistence, and comovements. *Journal of Economic Dynamics and Control, 27*(10), 1699–1737.

Jondeau, E., & Rockinger, M. (2006). Optimal portfolio allocation under higher moments. *European Financial Management, 12*(1), 29–55.

Joro, T., & Na, P. (2006). Portfolio performance evaluation in a mean–variance–skewness framework. *European Journal of Operational Research, 175*(1), 446–461.

Jurczenko, E., Maillet, B. & Merlin, P. (2012). Hedge fund portfolio selection with higher–order moments: a nonparametric mean–variance–skewness–kurtosis efficient frontier. *Multi–Moment Asset Allocation and Pricing Models*, 51–66.

Kazemi, A. & Galagedera, D. U. (2022). An inverse DEA model for intermediate and output target setting in serially linked general two-stage processes. *IMA Journal of Management Mathematics.*

Kerstens, K., Mazza, P., Ren, T., & Van de Woestyne, I. (2022). Multi-time and multi-moment nonparametric frontier-based fund rating: proposal and buy-and-hold backtesting strategy. *Omega, 113*, 102718.

Kerstens, K., Mounir, A., & Van de Woestyne, I. (2011). Non-parametric frontier estimates of mutual fund performance using C-and L-moments: Some specification tests. *Journal of Banking & Finance, 35*(5), 1190–1201.

Kerstens, K., Mounir, A., & Van de Woestyne, I. (2012). Benchmarking mean-variance portfolios using a shortage function: The choice of direction vector affects rankings! *Journal of the Operational Research Society, 63*(9), 1199–1212.

Khemchandani, R., & Chandra, S. (2014). Efficient trading frontier: A shortage function approach. *Optimization, 63*(10), 1533–1548.

Koronakos, G., Sotiros, D., Despotis, D. K., & Kritikos, M. N. (2022). Fair efficiency decomposition in network DEA: A compromise programming approach. *Socio-Economic Planning Sciences, 79*, 101100.

Krüger, J. J. (2021). Nonparametric portfolio efficiency measurement with higher moments. *Empirical Economics, 61*(3), 1435–1459.

Kumar, U. D., Roy, A. B., Saranga, H., & Singal, K. (2010). Analysis of hedge fund strategies using slack-based DEA models. *Journal of the Operational Research Society, 61*, 1746–1760.

Lamb, J. D., & Tee, K. (2012a). Data envelopment analysis models of investment funds. *European Journal of Operational Research, 216*(3), 687–696.
Lamb, J. D., & Tee, K. (2012b). Resampling DEA estimates of investment fund performance. *European Journal of Operational Research, 223*(3), 834–841.
Lim, S., Oh, K. W., & Zhu, J. (2014). Use of DEA cross-efficiency evaluation in portfolio selection: An application to Korean stock market. *European Journal of Operational Research, 236*(1), 361–368.
Lin, R., & Li, Z. (2020). Directional distance based diversification super-efficiency DEA models for mutual funds. *Omega, 97*, 102096.
Lin, R., & Liu, Q. (2021). Multiplier dynamic data envelopment analysis based on directional distance function: An application to mutual funds. *European Journal of Operational Research, 293*(3), 1043–1057.
Lin, R., Chen, Z., Hu, Q., & Li, Z. (2017). Dynamic network DEA approach with diversification to multi-period performance evaluation of funds. *Or Spectrum, 39*(3), 821–860.
Lin, S., Lu, W., & Lin, F. (2021). Entrusting decisions to the public service pension fund: An integrated predictive model with additive network DEA approach. *Journal of the Operational Research Society, 72*(5), 1015–1032.
Liu, W., Zhou, Z., Liu, D., & Xiao, H. (2015). Estimation of portfolio efficiency via DEA. *Omega, 52*, 107–118.
Lozano, S., & Gutiérrez, E. (2008a). Data envelopment analysis of mutual funds based on second-order stochastic dominance. *European Journal of Operational Research, 189*(1), 230–244.
Lozano, S., & Gutiérrez, E. (2008b). TSD-consistent performance assessment of mutual funds. *Journal of the Operational Research Society, 59*(10), 1352–1362.
Lu, W., Kweh, Q. L., & Wang, C. (2021). Integration and application of rough sets and data envelopment analysis for assessments of the investment trusts industry. *Annals of Operations Research, 296*(1), 163–194.
Luenberger, D. G. (1995). *Microeconomic theory*. Mcgraw-Hill College.
Makni, R., Benouda, O., & Delhoumi, E. (2015). Large scale analysis of Islamic equity funds using a meta-frontier approach with data envelopment analysis. *Research in International Business and Finance, 34*, 324–337.
Markowitz, H. M. (1952). Portfolio selection. *Journal of Finance, 7*(1), 77–91.
Martellini, L., & Ziemann, V. (2010). Improved estimates of higher order comoments and implications for portfolio selection. *The Review of Financial Studies, 23*(4), 1467–1502.
Mashayekhi, Z., & Omrani, H. (2016). An integrated multi-objective Markowitz–DEA cross-efficiency model with fuzzy returns for portfolio selection problem. *Applied Soft Computing, 38*, 1–9.
Massol, O., & Banal-Estañol, A. (2014). Export diversification through resource-based industrialization: The case of natural gas. *European Journal of Operational Research, 237*(3), 1067–1082.
Matallín-Sáez, J. C., Soler-Domínguez, A., & Tortosa-Ausina, E. (2014). On the informativeness of persistence for evaluating mutual fund performance using partial frontiers. *Omega, 42*(1), 47–64.
McMullen, P. R., & Strong, R. A. (1998). Selection of mutual funds using data envelopment analysis. *The Journal of Business and Economic Studies, 4*, 1–12.
Morey, M. R., & Morey, R. C. (1999). Mutual fund performance appraisals: A multi-horizon perspective with endogenous benchmarking. *Omega, 27*(2), 241–258.
Murthi, B., Choi, Y. K., & Desai, P. (1997). Efficiency of mutual funds and portfolio performance measurement: A non-parametric approach. *European Journal of Operational Research, 98*(2), 408–418.
Nalpas, N., Simar, L., & Vanhems, A. (2017). Portfolio selection in a multi-moment setting: A simple Monte-Carlo-FDH algorithm. *European Journal of Operational Research, 263*(1), 308–320.
Pätäri, E., Leivo, T., & Honkapuro, S. (2012). Enhancement of equity portfolio performance using data envelopment analysis. *European Journal of Operational Research, 220*(3), 786–797.

Pérez Gladish, B., Rodríguez, P. M., M'Zali, B., & Lang, P. (2013). Mutual funds efficiency measurement under financial and social responsibility criteria. *Journal of Multi-Criteria Decision Analysis, 20*(3–4), 109–125.

Peykani, P., Emrouznejad, A., Mohammadi, E. and Gheidar-Kheljani, J. (2022). A novel robust network data envelopment analysis approach for performance assessment of mutual funds under uncertainty. *Annals of Operations Research*, 1–27.

Premachandra, I. M., Zhu, J., Watson, J., & Galagedera, D. U. (2012). Best-performing US mutual fund families from 1993 to 2008: Evidence from a novel two-stage DEA model for efficiency decomposition. *Journal of Banking & Finance, 36*(12), 3302–3317.

Ren, T., Zhou, Z., & Xiao, H. (2021). Estimation of portfolio efficiency considering social responsibility: Evidence from the multi-horizon diversification DEA. *RAIRO-Operations Research, 55*(2), 611–637.

Rotela Junior, P., Pamplona, E. D. O., Rocha, L. C. S., Valerio, V. E. D. M., & Paiva, A. P. (2015). Stochastic portfolio optimization using efficiency evaluation. *Management Decision, 53*(8), 1698–1713.

Sánchez-González, C., Sarto, J. L., & Vicente, L. (2017). The efficiency of mutual fund companies: Evidence from an innovative network SBM approach. *Omega, 71*, 114–128.

Shahrour, M. H. (2022). Measuring the financial and social performance of French mutual funds: A data envelopment analysis approach. *Business Ethics, the Environment & Responsibility, 31*(2), 398–418.

Tarnaud, A. C., & Leleu, H. (2018). Portfolio analysis with DEA: Prior to choosing a model. *Omega, 75*, 57–76.

Tavana, M., Khalili-Damghani, K., Arteaga, F. J. S., Mahmoudi, R., & Hafezalkotob, A. (2018). Efficiency decomposition and measurement in two-stage fuzzy DEA models using a bargaining game approach. *Computers & Industrial Engineering, 118*, 394–408.

Tone, K., & Tsutsui, M. (2014). Dynamic DEA with network structure: A slacks-based measure approach. *Omega, 42*(1), 124–131.

Trautmann, S. T., & van de Kuilen, G. (2018). Higher order risk attitudes: A review of experimental evidence. *European Economic Review, 103*, 108–124.

Tsolas, I. E. (2014). Precious metal mutual fund performance appraisal using DEA modeling. *Resources Policy, 39*, 54–60.

Tsolas, I. E. (2020). Precious metal mutual fund performance evaluation: A series two-stage DEA modeling approach. *Journal of Risk and Financial Management, 13*(5), 87.

Tsolas, I. E. (2022). Performance evaluation of utility exchange-traded funds: a super-efficiency approach. *Journal of Risk and Financial Management, 15*(7), 318.

Tsolas, I. E., & Charles, V. (2015). Green exchange-traded fund performance appraisal using slacks-based DEA models. *Operational Research, 15*, 51–77.

Tuzcu, S. E., & Ertugay, E. (2020). Is size an input in the mutual fund performance evaluation with DEA? *Eurasian Economic Review, 10*(4), 635–659.

Valadkhani, A. and Moradi-Motlagh, A. (2023). An empirical analysis of exchange-traded funds in the US. Economic Analysis and Policy.

Wang, K., Xian, Y., Lee, C., Wei, Y., & Huang, Z. (2019). On selecting directions for directional distance functions in a non-parametric framework: A review. *Annals of Operations Research, 278*, 43–76.

Xiao, H., Liu, X., Ren, T., & Zhou, Z. (2022a). Estimation of portfolio efficiency via stochastic DEA. *RAIRO-Operations Research, 56*(4), 2367–2387.

Xiao, H., Liu, X., Ren, T. & Zhou, Z. (2022c). Measuring the dynamic efficiency of socially responsible investment funds: evidence from dynamic network DEA with diversification. *INFOR: Information Systems and Operational Research, 60*(4), 531–557.

Xiao, H., Ren, T., Zhou, Z., & Liu, W. (2021). Parameter uncertainty in estimation of portfolio efficiency: Evidence from an interval diversification-consistent DEA approach. *Omega, 103*, 102357.

Xiao, H., Zhou, Z., Ren, T., & Liu, W. (2022c). Estimation of portfolio efficiency in nonconvex settings: A free disposal hull estimator with non-increasing returns to scale. *Omega, 111*, 102672.

Zamani, L., Beegam, R., & Borzoian, S. (2014). Portfolio selection using Data Envelopment Analysis (DEA): A case of select Indian investment companies. *International Journal of Current Research and Academic Review, 2*(4), 50–55.

Zhang, Y., & Chen, M. (2018). Evaluating the dynamic performance of energy portfolios: Empirical evidence from the DEA directional distance function. *European Journal of Operational Research, 269*(1), 64–78.

Zhao, X., Wang, S., & Lai, K. K. (2011). Mutual funds performance evaluation based on endogenous benchmarks. *Expert Systems with Applications, 38*(4), 3663–3670.

Zhou, Z., Chen, E., Xiao, H., Ren, T., & Jin, Q. (2019). Performance evaluation of portfolios with fuzzy returns. *RAIRO-Operations Research, 53*(5), 1581–1600.

Zhou, Z., Gao, M., Xiao, H., Wang, R., & Liu, W. (2021). Big data and portfolio optimization: A novel approach integrating DEA with multiple data sources. *Omega, 104*, 102479.

Zhou, Z., Jin, Q., Xiao, H., Wu, Q., & Liu, W. (2018a). Estimation of cardinality constrained portfolio efficiency via segmented DEA. *Omega, 76*, 28–37.

Zhou, Z., Xiao, H., Jin, Q., & Liu, W. (2018b). DEA frontier improvement and portfolio rebalancing: An application of China mutual funds on considering sustainability information disclosure. *European Journal of Operational Research, 269*(1), 111–131.

An Optimization Algorithm to Solve Imprecisely Defined Unconstrainted Optimization Problem

Paresh Kumar Panigrahi and Sukanta Nayak

Abstract Many optimal solution driven engineering problems are operated through various parameters which are uncertain in nature. Therefore, for better understanding of the system and estimation of the field variables, the problem can be considered with epistemic type of uncertainties. Here, Trapezoidal Fuzzy Number is considered to visualize the epistemic constants and coefficients. A parametric concept is adopted here to model the governing imprecise algebraic equations to a fuzzy unconstrainted optimization problem. Then a search algorithm is implemented to handle the fuzzy unconstrained minimization problem. Moreover, to quantify the uncertainty, the algorithm with fuzzy theory is discussed in various cases. The different cases are discussed in details through couple of test electrical network problems. Finally, a comparative study of the present approach with others is presented.

Keywords Fuzzy number · Trapezoidal fuzzy number · Unconstrained optimization problem · Direct search optimization algorithm

1 Introduction

Many decision-making problems play an important role in linear and/or nonlinear systems of equations. Due to the complexity of the problem in real practice often numerical methods are adopted to study the field variables. But there are various difficulties and complications to handle the nonlinear system of equations. In this regard, the optimization strategy is one of the tools to solve the nonlinear system of equations. Then, the same can apply to convert system of equations to unconstrained minimization problems. As such, the steepest descent optimization method, conjugate gradient method, newton method, and quasi-newton method, etc. are employed to solve the unconstrained optimization problem are discussed in Deb (2004), Rao

P. K. Panigrahi · S. Nayak (✉)
Department of Mathematics, School of Advanced Sciences, VIT-AP University, Beside AP Secretariat, Inavolu, Amaravati, AP, India
e-mail: sukantgacr@gmail.com

© The Author(s), under exclusive license to Springer Nature Singapore Pte Ltd. 2024

S. A. Edalatpanah et al. (eds.), *Analytical Decision Making and Data Envelopment Analysis*, Infosys Science Foundation Series in Mathematical Sciences,
https://doi.org/10.1007/978-981-97-6972-8_12

(1995), Nayak (2020). Generally, for the gradient-based method, we need to calculate the gradient and Hessian matrix to solve the unconstrained minimization problem. We conclude that the uncertainties are arising in the systems. Furthermore, the presence of uncertainties makes the system challenging to solve. The uncertainties caused due to experimental errors, lack of knowledge, and partial information. As such, systems parameters and field variable are taken as fuzzy to handle the uncertain system. In this context, Zadeh (1965) introduced the concept of fuzzy set theory and their computation through fuzzy and/or interval arithmetic.

In this regard, many researchers presented different analytical approaches to solve fuzzy equations. Buckley and Qu (1990, 1991) introduced an analytical approach to solve fuzzy linear and quadratic equations. Jafari and Yu (2017) presented a fuzzy model of uncertain nonlinear equations with fuzzy equations. Shokri (2008) developed a two-step iterative method to solve fuzzy nonlinear equations. In this context, Abbasbandy and Asady (2004) used Newton's method to investigate fuzzy nonlinear equations. Further, Abbasbandy and Ezzati (2006) have proposed Newton's optimization method for a fuzzy nonlinear system of equations. Nayak and Chakraverty (2015) have developed Newton's method for solving the interval system of a nonlinear equation. Moreover, the fuzzy system can be analyzed as only a fuzzy and fully fuzzy system depending on the usage of fuzziness. Jafari et al. (2018) used a computational iterative approach to solve fully fuzzy nonlinear systems. Whereas, Kajani et al. (2005) extended fuzzy to a dual fuzzy nonlinear system of equations, and an iterative algorithm is adapted to find the solution of the system. As such, Adak and Kumar (2022) used TOPSIS method to solve multiple criteria decision analysis problems in a Pythagorean fuzzy environment.

The above literature review reveals that the uncertain system is more challenging to understand and solve using gradient-based techniques. Because, in gradient search, we need to compute the gradient of the objective function with fuzzy theory. Therefore, one of the best ideas is direct search algorithms can be implemented for easy understanding and solving the same. In light of this, the direct search optimization techniques are based on the direct line search approach and can be easily introduced to obtain the solution to the fuzzy unconstrained optimization problem. Moreover, various researchers proposed optimization techniques for the fuzzy system. Jafarian and Jafari (2019) developed a computational approach for fuzzy nonlinear programming problems and fuzzy nonlinear systems of equations. A revised hybrid direct search technique for studied convex quadratic programming problems was developed by Bibi et al. (2020). Mekawy (2022) has introduced a unique approach to solving the multi-objective linear fractional programming problem in uncertain environment. Whereas, Nayak and Chakraverty (2013) have developed a limit approach and fuzzy arithmetic combined to handle the fuzzy system of linear equations. Nayak and Pooja (2021) have proposed an IODS optimization direct search algorithm to handle interval nonlinear systems with the bounded parameter. Recently Stanimirovic et al. (2022) has developed a descent direction method to solve unconstrainted optimization problem involved neutrosophy concept. Panigrahi and Nayak (2023) have proposed a direct search technique to solve uncertain nonlinear unconstrained optimization problem. Hence, lack of direct search optimization techniques has been used to solve fuzzy unconstrained optimization problems from fuzzy systems.

Most of the investigations in a fuzzy nonlinear system of equations have been done by dealing with analytical, numerical method and gradient-based optimization methods. Then, the fuzzy system can be converted into a fuzzy unconstrained optimization problem with case-wise. Therefore, we have proposed a direct search optimization algorithm to handle the converted fuzzy unconstrainted optimization problem. In this algorithm, there are two computational processes i.e., exploratory search and pattern search. The exploratory and pattern search can break into two-step calculations that is inner and outer computation. Then, the obtained solution can assemble using the regularity principle to get the final solution. Using two example problems with the application of an electric circuit problem can examine the effectiveness of the present algorithm. To better understand the comparisons of the present algorithm and existing Vertex method, Krawczyk method, Newton's method, and IODS method are discussed here. Then, the graphical representation of the final solution, its width, and objective function also represent graphical convergence. Finally, it is seen that there is a good agreement of the uncertain solution with the special case (membership value is 1).

This chapter is structured in the following manner. Section 2 includes the preliminaries of fuzzy numbers and arithmetic operations using fuzzy numbers. Section 3 describes the organization of the fuzzy system of equation with different cases. Whereas, Sect. 4 presents the proposed algorithm in a fuzzy environment. In Sect. 5, two example problems are demonstrated through algorithms and graphical representations.

2 Preliminaries

This section includes the fundamentals of fuzzy numbers and its arithmetic (Zimmermann, 2001).

2.1 Definition 1

A fuzzy number $\tilde{\mathcal{X}}$ is a convex normalized piecewise continuous fuzzy set $\tilde{\mathcal{X}}$ on the real line R with the membership function $\mu_{\tilde{\mathcal{X}}}(x) : R \rightarrow [0,1], \forall x \in R$.

2.2 Definition 2

A fuzzy number $\widetilde{\mathcal{X}} = [x_1, x_2, x_3, x_4]$ is said to be a trapezoidal fuzzy number (TrFN) if the membership values are defined as

$$\mu_{\tilde{\mathcal{X}}}(x) = \begin{cases} \frac{x-x_1}{x_2-x_1}, & x_1 \le x \le x_2 \\ 1, & x_2 \le x \le x_3 \\ \frac{x_4-x}{x_4-x_3}, & x \le x_4 \\ 0, & otherwise \end{cases} \tag{1}$$

For the computational utility, an arbitrary TrFN $\widetilde{\mathcal{X}} = [x_1, x_2, x_3, x_4]$ can be transformed into an interval from

By taking α-cuts approach (Leandry et al., 2022) the TrFN can be rewritten as

$$\widetilde{\mathcal{X}} = [x_1, x_2, x_3, x_4] \approx [\xi_L, \xi_R] \tag{2}$$

where,

$$\widetilde{\mathcal{X}}_L = x_1 + \alpha(x_2 - x_1) \text{ and } \widetilde{\mathcal{X}}_R = x_4 + \alpha(x_3 - x_4);\ \alpha \in [0, 1]$$

where, $\widetilde{\mathcal{X}}_L$ is the left monotonically non-decreasing function and $\widetilde{\mathcal{X}}_R$ is the right monotonically non-increasing function. The crisp representation of TrFN $\widetilde{\mathcal{X}}$ become $\widetilde{\mathcal{X}}_L - \beta\left(\widetilde{\mathcal{X}}_L - \widetilde{\mathcal{X}}_R\right), \beta \in [0,1]$.

2.3 Definition 3

Suppose that $\widetilde{\mathcal{X}} = [\underline{\mathcal{X}}(\alpha), \overline{\mathcal{X}}(\alpha)]$ and $\widetilde{\mathcal{Y}} = [\underline{\mathcal{Y}}(\alpha), \overline{\mathcal{Y}}(\alpha)]$ are fuzzy numbers, then their arithmetic is similar to interval arithmetic. The interval arithmetic is defined as

Addition:

$$\tilde{\mathcal{X}} + \tilde{\mathcal{Y}} = \left[\underline{\mathcal{X}}(\alpha) + \underline{\mathcal{Y}}(\alpha),\ \bar{\mathcal{X}}(\alpha) + \bar{\mathcal{Y}}(\alpha)\right].$$

Subtraction:

$$\tilde{\mathcal{X}} - \tilde{\mathcal{Y}} = \left[\underline{\mathcal{X}}(\alpha) - \bar{\mathcal{Y}}(\alpha), \bar{\mathcal{X}}(\alpha) - \underline{\mathcal{Y}}(\alpha)\right].$$

Multiplication:

$$\tilde{\mathcal{X}} \times \tilde{\mathcal{Y}} = \left[\min\{\underline{\mathcal{X}}(\alpha) \times \underline{\mathcal{Y}}(\alpha), \underline{\mathcal{X}}(\alpha) \times \overline{\mathcal{Y}}(\alpha), \overline{\mathcal{X}}(\alpha) \times \underline{\mathcal{Y}}(\alpha), \overline{\mathcal{X}}(\alpha) \times \overline{\mathcal{Y}}(\alpha)\},\right.$$
$$\left.\max\left\{\underline{\mathcal{X}}(\alpha) \times \underline{\mathcal{Y}}(\alpha), \underline{\mathcal{X}}(\alpha) \times \overline{\mathcal{Y}}(\alpha), \overline{\mathcal{X}}(\alpha) \times \underline{\mathcal{Y}}(\alpha), \overline{\mathcal{X}}(\alpha) \times \overline{\mathcal{Y}}(\alpha)\right\}\right]$$

Division:

$$\tilde{\mathcal{X}} \div \tilde{\mathcal{Y}} = \left[\min\cdot\left\{\underline{\mathcal{X}}(\alpha) \div \underline{\mathcal{Y}}(\alpha), \underline{\mathcal{X}}(\alpha) \div \overline{\mathcal{Y}}(\alpha), \overline{\mathcal{X}}(\alpha) \div \underline{\mathcal{Y}}(\alpha), \overline{\mathcal{X}}(\alpha) \div \overline{\mathcal{Y}}(\alpha)\right\},\right.$$
$$\left.\max\left\{\underline{\mathcal{X}}(\alpha) \div \underline{\mathcal{Y}}(\alpha), \underline{\mathcal{X}}(\alpha) \div \overline{\mathcal{Y}}(\alpha), \overline{\mathcal{X}}(\alpha) \div \underline{\mathcal{Y}}(\alpha), \overline{\mathcal{X}}(\alpha) \div \overline{\mathcal{Y}}(\alpha)\right\}\right]$$

where $\mathcal{Y}(\alpha) \neq 0$ and $\overline{\mathcal{Y}}(\alpha) \neq 0$.

As $\bar{\text{T}}$rFN is a union of the intervals that is for each membership value $\alpha \in [0, 1]$, one gets an interval and the union of all these intervals give the same TrFN. Hence, we may conclude that while computation, the operation takes place pointwise. Therefore, one needs to construct a function using the variable α and then compute the TrFNs. (Chakraborty & Guha, 2010). In the next section, we will study how to solve the fuzzy system of equations using the mentioned arithmetic operations.

3 Fuzzy System of Equations

The matrix form of the system of equations can be written as,

$$\tilde{\mathcal{M}}\tilde{x} = \tilde{\mathcal{B}} \tag{3}$$

In Eq. (3), the coefficient matrix $\underset{\sim}{\mathcal{M}} = [\tilde{m}_{ij}]$ is of crisp $n \times n$ matrix, $\underset{\sim}{\mathcal{B}} = [\tilde{b}_1, \tilde{b}_2, \ldots, \tilde{b}_n]^T$ right-side vector is a crisp $n \times n$ matrix.

The fuzzy system can be modelled by executing the fuzzy number in both left hand side matrix and right-side vector of the above crisp system. By using the single parametric form, the fuzzy systems can be converted into an interval system. Then, the fully fuzzy system may be represented as

$$\begin{bmatrix} \left[\tilde{m}^{\alpha}_{L_{11}}, \tilde{m}^{\alpha}_{R_{11}}\right]\left[\tilde{x}^{\alpha}_{L_1}, \tilde{x}^{\alpha}_{R_1}\right] & \left[\tilde{m}^{\alpha}_{L_{12}}, \tilde{m}^{\alpha}_{R_{12}}\right]\left[\tilde{x}^{\alpha}_{L_2}, \tilde{x}^{\alpha}_{R_2}\right] & \cdots & \left[\tilde{m}^{\alpha}_{L_{1n}}, \tilde{m}^{\alpha}_{R_{1n}}\right]\left[\tilde{x}^{\alpha}_{L_n}, \tilde{x}^{\alpha}_{R_n}\right] \\ \left[\tilde{m}^{\alpha}_{L_{21}}, \tilde{m}^{\alpha}_{R_{21}}\right]\left[\tilde{x}^{\alpha}_{L_1}, \tilde{x}^{\alpha}_{R_1}\right] & \left[\tilde{m}^{\alpha}_{L_{22}}, \tilde{m}^{\alpha}_{R_{22}}\right]\left[\tilde{x}^{\alpha}_{L_2}, \tilde{x}^{\alpha}_{R_2}\right] & \cdots & \left[\tilde{m}^{\alpha}_{L_{2n}}, \tilde{m}^{\alpha}_{R_{2n}}\right]\left[\tilde{x}^{\alpha}_{L_n}, \tilde{x}^{\alpha}_{R_n}\right] \\ \vdots & \vdots & \ddots & \vdots \\ \left[\tilde{m}^{\alpha}_{L_{n1}}, \tilde{m}^{\alpha}_{R_{n1}}\right]\left[\tilde{x}^{\alpha}_{L_1}, \tilde{x}^{\alpha}_{R_1}\right] & \left[\tilde{m}^{\alpha}_{L_{n2}}, \tilde{m}^{\alpha}_{R_{n2}}\right]\left[\tilde{x}^{\alpha}_{L_2}, \tilde{x}^{\alpha}_{R_2}\right] & \cdots & \left[\tilde{m}^{\alpha}_{L_{nn}}, \tilde{m}^{\alpha}_{R_{nn}}\right]\left[\tilde{x}^{\alpha}_{L_n}, \tilde{x}^{\alpha}_{R_n}\right] \end{bmatrix} = \begin{bmatrix} \left[\tilde{b}^{\alpha}_{L_1}, \tilde{b}^{\alpha}_{R_1}\right] \\ \left[\tilde{b}^{\alpha}_{L_2}, \tilde{b}^{\alpha}_{R_2}\right] \\ \vdots \\ \left[\tilde{b}^{\alpha}_{L_n}, \tilde{b}^{\alpha}_{R_n}\right] \end{bmatrix} \tag{4}$$

The above-mentioned system is written as follow,

$$\sum_{i,j=1}^{n}\left[\tilde{m}^{\alpha}_{L_{ij}},\tilde{m}^{\alpha}_{R_{ij}}\right]\left[\tilde{x}^{\alpha}_{L_j},\tilde{x}^{\alpha}_{R_j}\right]=\left[\tilde{b}^{\alpha}_{L_j},\tilde{b}^{\alpha}_{R_j}\right] \tag{5}$$

Equation (5) can equivalently be written as the following two equation

$$F_L=\sum_{i,j=1}^{n}\tilde{m}^{\alpha}_{L_{ij}}\tilde{x}^{\alpha}_{L_j}=\tilde{b}^{\alpha}_{L_j} \tag{6}$$

$$F_R=\sum_{i,j=1}^{n}\tilde{m}^{\alpha}_{R_{ij}}\tilde{x}^{\alpha}_{R_j}=\tilde{b}^{\alpha}_{R_j} \tag{7}$$

In the above equation case-wise discussion of the proposed algorithm for solving the fuzzy unconstrainted optimization problem is performed.

3.1 Case 1

In Eq. (5), the entries of the coefficient matrix are TrFNs. The entry $\tilde{a}_{ij}$ is defined as $[a_{L_{ij}}, a_{N_{1ij}}, a_{N_{2ij}}, a_{R_{ij}}]$ and the right-side vector is b_j (crisp).

3.2 Case 2

In Eq. (5), the right-side vector is $\tilde{b}_j$ TrFNs. The right-side vector of $\tilde{b}_j$ is defined as $[b_{L_j}, b_{N_{1j}}, b_{N_{2j}}, b_{R_j}]$. The coefficient of the left side $\tilde{a}_{ij}$ is (crisp).

The above cases will be discussed and solved through example problems in the coming sections. The next section deals with a direct search optimization algorithm in a fuzzy environment.

4 Direct Search Optimization Algorithm in Fuzzy Environment

In this section, the basic idea is the fuzzy system can be converted into a fuzzy unconstrained minimization problem. Then, the proposed fuzzy direct search optimization algorithm is applied to solve the same. In the fuzzy environment, the field variable is taken as a fuzzy parameter. However, fuzzy systems can be found in many engineering problems and data analysis. Therefore, the uncertain analysis can examine by using the proposed algorithm.

For the sake of understanding, we have considered a fuzzy unconstrainted optimization problem

$$\text{Min } F_k(X) = 0 \tag{8}$$

Equation (8) can be transformed into the interval parametric form

$$F_k(X) = \left[F_{L_k}, F_{R_k}\right] \text{ where } X = x_1, x_2, \ldots, x_n \tag{9}$$

where, F_{L_k} and F_{R_k} are found in Eqs. (6) and (7). Here, $k = 1, 2, \ldots n$,

In the above two interval system the solution x_1 and x_2 defined by applying the developed algorithm in terms of α and β. Then, Eqs. (6) and (7) substitute the in Eq. (9). We get

$$F_1(X) = \sum_{j=1}^{n} \tilde{m}^{\alpha}_{L_{kj}} \tilde{x}^{\alpha}_{L_j} - \tilde{b}^{\alpha}_{L_k}, \sum_{j=1}^{n} \tilde{m}^{\alpha}_{R_{kj}} \tilde{x}^{\alpha}_{R_j} - \tilde{b}^{\alpha}_{R_k} \tag{10}$$

$$F_2(X) = \sum_{j=1}^{n} \tilde{m}^{\alpha}_{L_{kj}} \tilde{x}^{\alpha}_{L_j} - \tilde{b}^{\alpha}_{L_k}, \sum_{j=1}^{n} \tilde{m}^{\alpha}_{R_{kj}} \tilde{x}^{\alpha}_{R_j} - \tilde{b}^{\alpha}_{R_k} \tag{11}$$

Then, the objective function can be represented as

$$F(X) = \left(\sum_{j=1}^{n} \tilde{m}^{\alpha}_{L_{kj}} \tilde{x}^{\alpha}_{L_j} - \tilde{b}^{\alpha}_{L_k}, \sum_{j=1}^{n} \tilde{m}^{\alpha}_{R_{kj}} \tilde{x}^{\alpha}_{R_j} - \tilde{b}^{\alpha}_{R_k}\right)^2 + \left(\sum_{j=1}^{n} \tilde{m}^{\alpha}_{L_{kj}} \tilde{x}^{\alpha}_{L_j} - \tilde{b}^{\alpha}_{L_k}, \sum_{j=1}^{n} \tilde{m}^{\alpha}_{R_{kj}} \tilde{x}^{\alpha}_{R_j} - \tilde{b}^{\alpha}_{R_k}\right)^2 \tag{12}$$

To minimize the objective function $F(X) : R^n \rightarrow R$, we need to assume the starting point x^0 and choose the step size (Δ) and stopping condition (ϵ). In this method, the procedure consists of two types of searches viz. exploratory move and pattern search. Firstly, it required explaining exploratory searches. In exploratory search, we have to move forward and backward direction.

For the sake of understanding, we have to take two variables fuzzy unconstrainted optimization problem

$$\text{Min } F(X), \text{ where } X = \tilde{x}_1, \tilde{x}_2$$

Then, we find the backward and forward direction

$$\left(\tilde{x}_1^{(0)} - \Delta, x_2^{(0)}\right), \left(\tilde{x}_1^{(0)} + \Delta, x_2^{(0)}\right)$$

Further, we can apply the value in a given objective function. Such as

$$F^{-}\left(\tilde{x}_1^{(0)} - \Delta, x_2^{(0)}\right), F\left(\tilde{x}_1^{(0)}, x_2^{(0)}\right), F^{+}\left(\tilde{x}_1^{(0)} + \Delta, x_2^{(0)}\right)$$

Then, find $F_{\min} = \min\left\{F^{-}\left(\tilde{x}_1^{(0)} - \Delta, x_2^{(0)}\right), F\left(\tilde{x}_1^{(0)}, x_2^{(0)}\right), \ F^{+}\left(\tilde{x}_1^{(0)} + \Delta, x_2^{(0)}\right)\right\}$ as well as we have to find corresponding $x_{1\,min}$.

Suppose $\left(x_{1\,min}, x_2^{(0)}\right)$, is our minimum point of functional value. Similarly, we can find another point by using the backward and forward direction

$$\left(X_{1\,min}, x_2^{(0)} - \Delta\right), \left(X_{1\,min}, x_2^{(0)} + \Delta\right)$$

Further, we can apply the value in a given objective function. Such as

$$F^{-}\left(X_{1\,min}, x_2^{(0)} - \Delta\right), F\left(X_{1\,min}, x_2^{(0)}\right), F^{+}\left(X_{1\,min}, x_2^{(0)} + \Delta\right)$$

Then, find $F_{min} = min\{F^{-}(X_{1\,min}, x_2^{(0)} - \Delta), F(X_{1\,min}, x_2^{(0)}), F^{+}(X_{1\,min}, x_2^{(0)} + \Delta)\}$ as well as we have to find corresponding x_{2min}. Similarly, every iteration exploratory search will perform in the same manner.

Moreover, we have to search pattern search

$$x_p^{(k+1)} = x^{(k)} + \left(x^{(k)} - x^{(k-1)}\right).$$

where $x_p^{(k+1)}$ is the new point and $x^{(k)}$ is obtain the current point by using exploratory search and $x^{(k-1)}$ is the previous point. If the current point is equal to a new point, then we will reduce the step size parameter. This process will be maintained till the stopping criteria. The search to get the minimum objective function is controlled by different computations that are inner and outer computations. For inner-outer computation refer to the following algorithm.

4.1 Fuzzy Direct Search Optimization Algorithm

In the algorithm given in Fig. 1, one needs to solve fuzzy unconstrained optimization problems. Out of these three are solved by outer computations viz. left, center, and right solution of the fuzzy unconstrained optimization problem. The other four are investigated by inner computation when initial conditions are incorporated with the values $\alpha, \beta = \{0, 1\}$. The solution vector for the same is written as $\tilde{x}_{\alpha,\beta}^k$. Here, k is the number of variables ($k = 1, 2, 3, \ldots, n$). The next section included two example problems viz. circuit problem derived with the proposed algorithm.

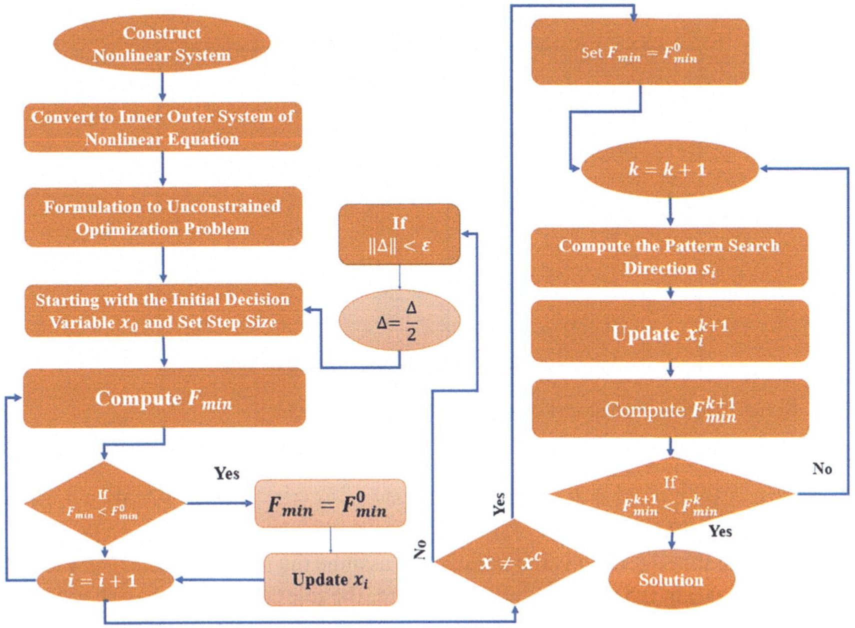

Fig. 1 Flow chart of fuzzy direct search optimization algorithm

5 Numerical Example

In this section, we represent two numerical examples to test the effectiveness of the proposed algorithm. Example 1 represents a case study of the proposed algorithm. Then, the proposed algorithm is applied to solve the modelled unconstrained optimization problem. Further, the comparative study of the present algorithm with previously existing methods is reported in Example 2.

5.1 Example 1

An electrical circuit problem is taken for study which is shown in Fig. 2. By using Kirchhoff's Law and Ohm's Law the circuit are modeled as a system of equation by using Fig. 2. Then, the developed algorithm is applied to solve the same.

The obtained a fuzzy system of equations

$$\tilde{a}_{11}\tilde{x}_1 + \tilde{a}_{12}\tilde{x}_2 = \tilde{\chi}_1$$

$$\tilde{a}_{21}\tilde{x}_1 + \tilde{a}_{22}\tilde{x}_2 = \tilde{\chi}_2 \tag{13}$$

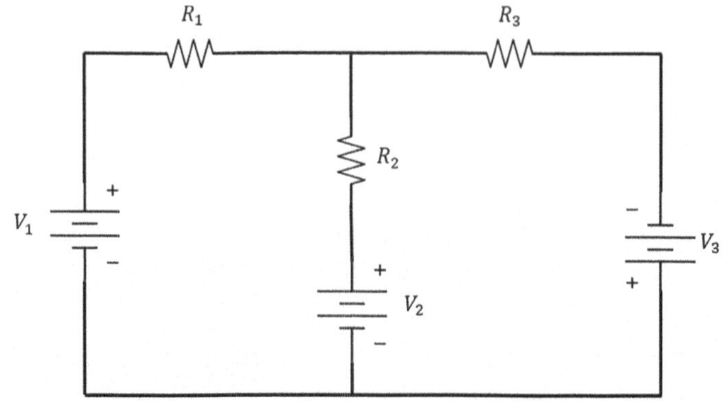

Fig. 2 Sketch diagram of an electrical circuit with fuzzy parameter

where, $\tilde{a}_{11} = [8 + \alpha, 11 - \alpha]$, $\tilde{a}_{12} = [-6 + \alpha, -3 - \alpha]$, $\tilde{a}_{21} = [-6 + \alpha, -3 - \alpha]$, $\tilde{a}_{22} = [14 + \alpha, 17 - \alpha]$, $\tilde{\chi}_1 = [26 + \alpha, 31 - 3\alpha]$ and $\tilde{\chi}_2 = [34 + \alpha, 38 - 2\alpha]$. After applying the $\alpha \in [0,1]$ value in Eq. (13), assume the initial value $x^{(0)} = (1,1)^T$, step size $\Delta = (0.5, 0.5)^T$, and $\epsilon = 10^{-4}$. Here, the tolerance value is ϵ. It is noted that the iterations are terminated if the step size becomes less than the tolerance value. Initially, the system is to construct the fuzzy outer system and then Eq. (13) convert into a fuzzy unconstrained minimization problem. The transformed fuzzy unconstrained minimization problem is formulated as

$$F(x) = (\tilde{a}_{11}\tilde{x}_1 + \tilde{a}_{12}\tilde{x}_2 - \tilde{\chi}_1)^2 + (\tilde{a}_{21}\tilde{x}_1 + \tilde{a}_{22}\tilde{x}_2 - \tilde{\chi}_2)^2 \tag{14}$$

After 13 iterations, the desired solution of the present algorithm is obtained by using MATLAB. The width solution of TrFN can be computed through inner and outer solutions. Case 1 represents the fuzzy system of equations where only the coefficient matrix is fuzzy. Case 2 possesses only right-side vector fuzzy. The aim of discussing two cases is to get a complete idea of the propagation of fuzzy uncertainties in a fuzzy system. Then, the case-wise solution and their graphical representation are shown below. Applying the proposed algorithm, the final TrFN solution and width solution is represented in Figs. 3, 4, 5 and 6 with case-wise.

Case 1

Here, we have taken the coefficient matrix as fuzzy. By applying the present algorithm, the TrFN solution of $\tilde{x}_1 = [2.989, 3.5073, 4.1935, 5.1384]$ and $\tilde{x}_2 = [1.6263, 1.7683, 1.9489, 2.1848]$ are graphically described in Figs. 3, 4, 5 and 6.

Case 2

Here, we have taken the right-side vector as fuzzy. By applying the proposed algorithm, the TrFN solution of $\tilde{x}_1 = [3.2866, 3.3971, 3.5073, 3.8303]$ and

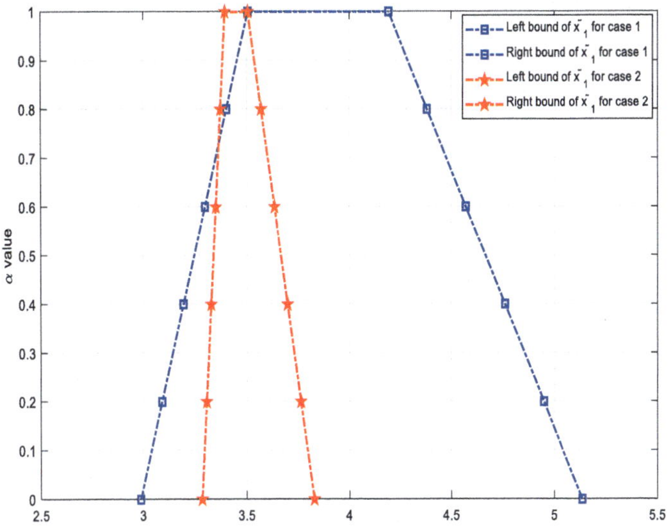

Fig. 3 TrFN solution of $\tilde{x}_1$ for case 1 and case 2 of Example 1

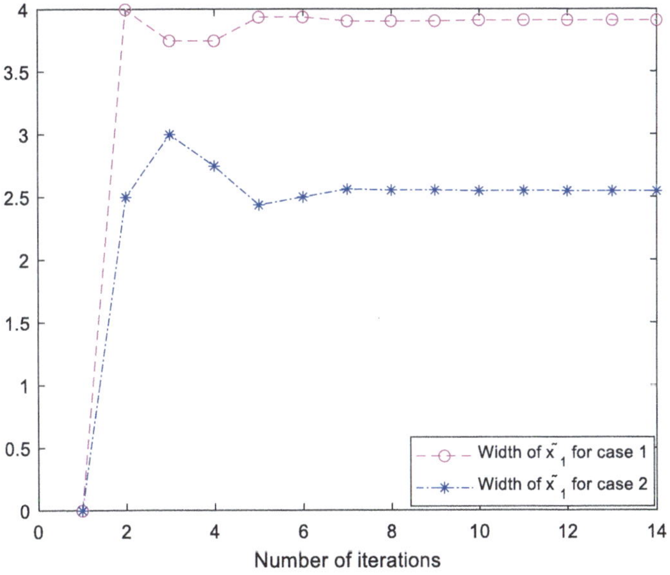

Fig. 4 Width for $\tilde{x}_1$ of case 1 and case 2 of Example 1

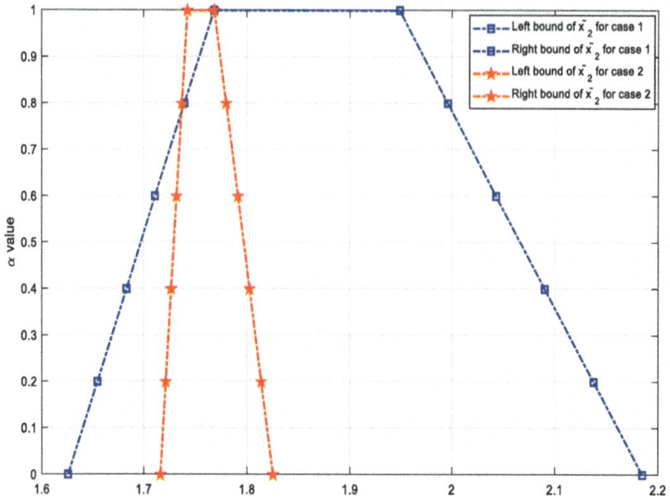

Fig. 5 TrFN solution of $\tilde{x}_2$ for case 1 and case 2 of Example 1

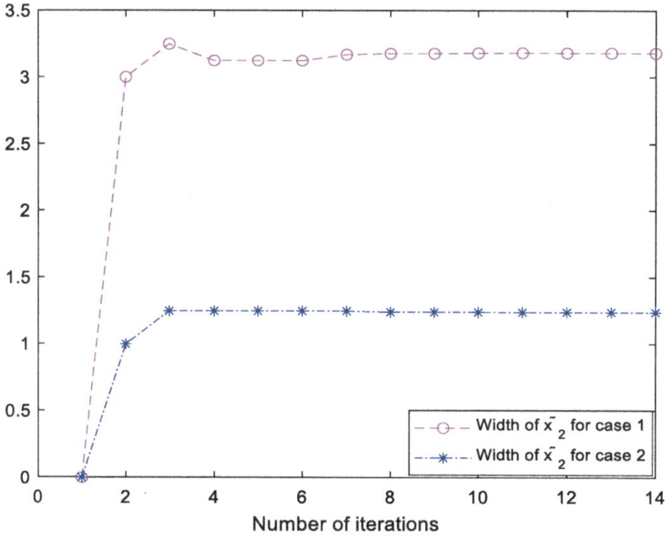

Fig. 6 Width for $\tilde{x}_2$ of case 1 and case 2 of Example 1

$\tilde{x}_2 = [1.7166, 1.7427, 1.7683, 1.8256]$ and are graphically represented in Figs. 3, 4, 5 and 6.

To quantify uncertainty, different α-cut value of $\tilde{x}_1$ and $\tilde{x}_2$ for case 1 and case 2 of the circuit problem are depicted in Table 1. In Fig. 3, after 13 iterations the TrFN solution components of $\tilde{x}_1$ of case 1 and case 2 gives graphically. It is observed that

Table 1 Different α-cut value of $\tilde{x}_1$ and $\tilde{x}_2$ for case 1 and case 2 of the circuit problem

α-cut	Case 1				Case 2			
	$\tilde{x}_{L1}$	$\tilde{x}_{R1}$	$\tilde{x}_{L2}$	$\tilde{x}_{R2}$	$\tilde{x}_{L1}$	$\tilde{x}_{R1}$	$\tilde{x}_{L2}$	$\tilde{x}_{R2}$
0	2.989	5.1384	1.6263	2.1848	3.2866	3.8303	1.7166	1.8256
0.2	3.09266	4.94942	1.6547	2.13762	3.3087	3.7657	1.72182	1.81414
0.4	3.19632	4.76044	1.6831	2.09044	3.3308	3.7011	1.72704	1.80268
0.6	3.29998	4.57146	1.7115	2.04326	3.3529	3.6365	1.73226	1.79122
0.8	3.40364	4.38248	1.7399	1.99608	3.375	3.5719	1.73748	1.77976
1	3.5073	4.1935	1.7683	1.9489	3.3971	3.5073	1.7427	1.7683

the case 2 TrFN solution is close to the crisp solution. The width-wise solution $\tilde{x}_1$ of case 1 and case 2 are represented in Fig. 4.

In Fig. 5, after 13 iterations the TrFN solution components of $\tilde{x}_1$ of case 1 and case 2 gives graphically. It is observed that the case 2 TrFN solution is close to the crisp solution. The width-wise solution $\tilde{x}_1$ of case 1 and case 2 are represented in Fig. 6.

In Fig. 7, after 13 iterations the TrFN solution components of the objective function of case 1 and case 2 gives graphically. It is observed that after 13 iterations the objective function of TrFNs converges. Width-wise iterative fuzzy solution of objective functions of the case study also convergence is shown in Fig. 8. From the above case study, we conclude that the current gives the best result and is close to the exact solution in case 2.

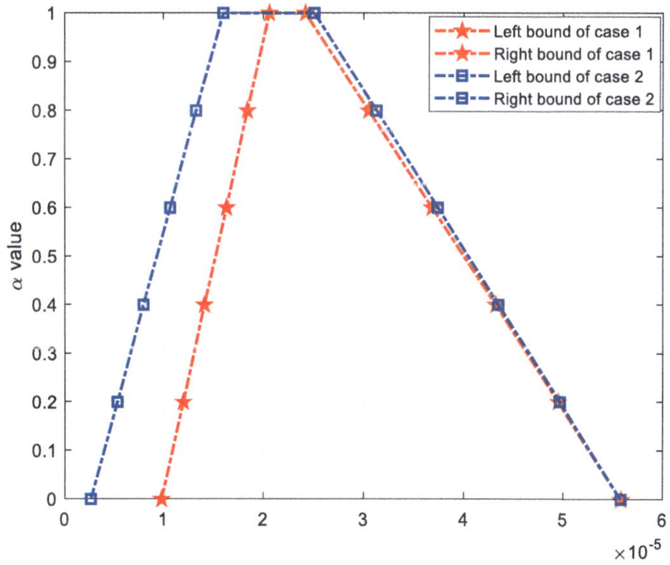

Fig. 7 TrFN objective function for case 1 and case 2 of Example 1

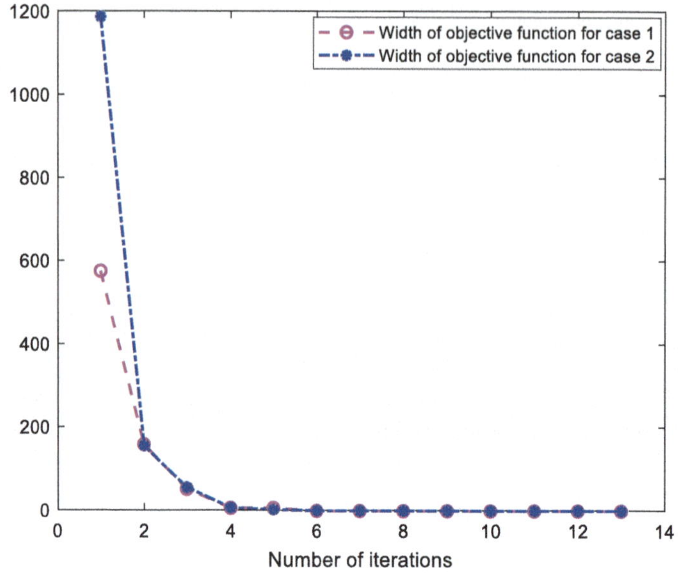

Fig. 8 Width for the objective function of case 1 and case 2 of Example 1

5.2 *Example 2*

Take a fuzzy system of equations from Sukanta and Pooja (2021)

$$\tilde{a}_{11}x_1^2 + \tilde{a}_{12}x_2 = \tilde{\chi}_1$$

$$\tilde{a}_{21}x_1 + \tilde{a}_{22}x_2^2 = \tilde{\chi}_2 \tag{15}$$

where, $\tilde{a}_{11} = [0.8 + 0.1\alpha, 1.4 - 0.4\alpha]$, $\tilde{a}_{12} = [0.75 + 0.05\alpha, 1.6 - 0.6\alpha]$, $\tilde{a}_{21} = [0.6 + 0.25\alpha, 1.1 - 0.1\alpha]$, $\tilde{a}_{22} = [0.5 + 0.25\alpha, 1.2 - 0.2\alpha]$, $\tilde{\chi}_1 = [10.9 + 0.05\alpha, 11.1 - 0.1\alpha]$ and $\tilde{\chi}_2 = [6.9 + 0.05, 7.1 - 0.1\alpha]$. After applying the $\alpha \in [0,1]$ value in Eq. (15), assume the initial value $x^{(0)} = (1,1)^T$, step size $\Delta = (0.5, 0.5)^T$, and $\epsilon = 10^{-4}$. Here, the tolerance value is ϵ. It is noted that the iterations are terminated if the step size becomes less than the tolerance value.

The initial step is to establish the fuzzy outer system and then the Eq. (15) converted into a fuzzy unconstrained minimization problem. The transformed fuzzy unconstrained minimization problem is formulated as

$$F(x) = \left(\tilde{a}_{11}x_1^2 + \tilde{a}_{12}x_2 - \tilde{\chi}_1\right)^2 + \left(\tilde{a}_{21}x_1 + \tilde{a}_{22}x_2^2 - \tilde{\chi}_2\right)^2 \tag{16}$$

After 13 iterations, the desired solution of the developed algorithm is obtained by using MATLAB. The width solution of TrFN can be computed through the inner

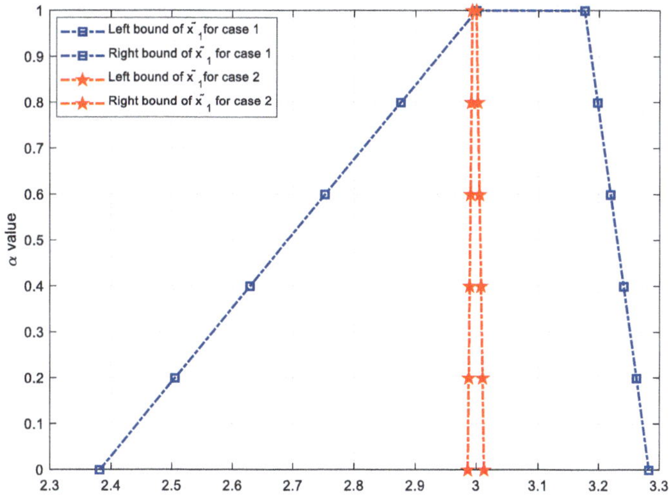

Fig. 9 TrFN solution of $\tilde{x}_1$ for case 1 and case 2 of Example 2

and outer solutions. Case 1 represents the fuzzy system of equations where only the coefficient matrix is fuzzy. Case 2 possesses only right-side vector fuzzy. The aim of discussing two cases is to get a complete idea of the propagation of fuzzy uncertainties in a fuzzy system. Then, the case-wise solution and their graphical representation are shown below. Applying the proposed algorithm, the final TrFN solution and width solution is represented in Figs. 9, 10, 11 and 12 case-wise.

Case 1

Here, we have taken the coefficient matrix as fuzzy. By applying the present algorithm, the TrFN solution of $\tilde{x}_1 = [2.382, 3, 3.1771, 3.2827]$ and $\tilde{x}_2 = [1.9105, 2, 2.3943, 3.1719]$ are graphically described in Figs. 9, 10, 11 and 12.

Case 2

Here, we have taken the right-side vector as fuzzy. By applying the current algorithm, the TrFN solution of $\tilde{x}_1 = [2.9869, 2.9934, 3, 3.0131]$ and $\tilde{x}_2 = [1.9781, 1.9891, 2, 2.0216]$ and are graphically represented in Figs. 9, 10, 11 and 12. Further, to the effectiveness of the proposed algorithm, the obtained TrFN solutions are compared with the very known Vertex Method, Krawczyk Method, and Newton's method (Nayak & Chakraverty, 2015) are presented in Table 2. To quantify uncertainty, different α-cut value of $\tilde{x}_1$ and $\tilde{x}_2$ for case 1 and case 2 of the circuit problem are depicted in Tables 2 and 3.

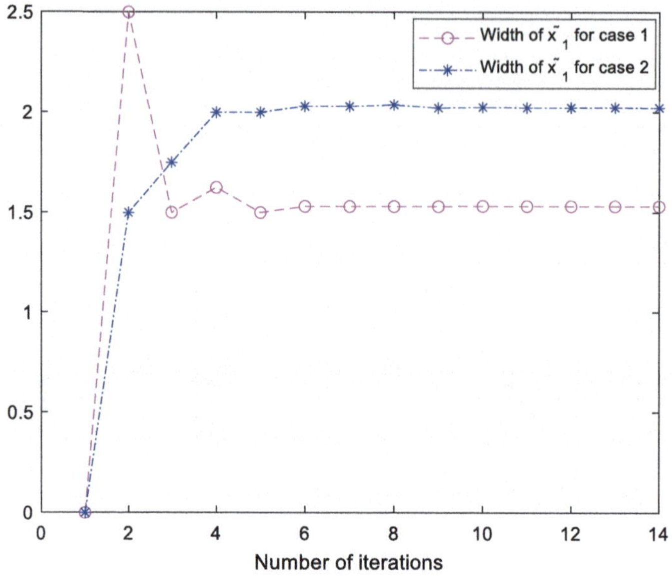

Fig. 10 Width for $\tilde{x}_1$ of case 1 and case 2 of Example 2

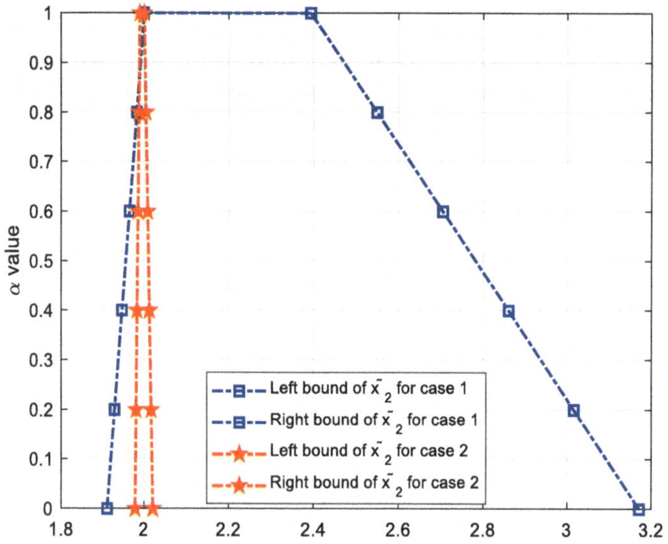

Fig. 11 TrFN solution of $\tilde{x}_2$ for case 1 and case 2 of Example 2

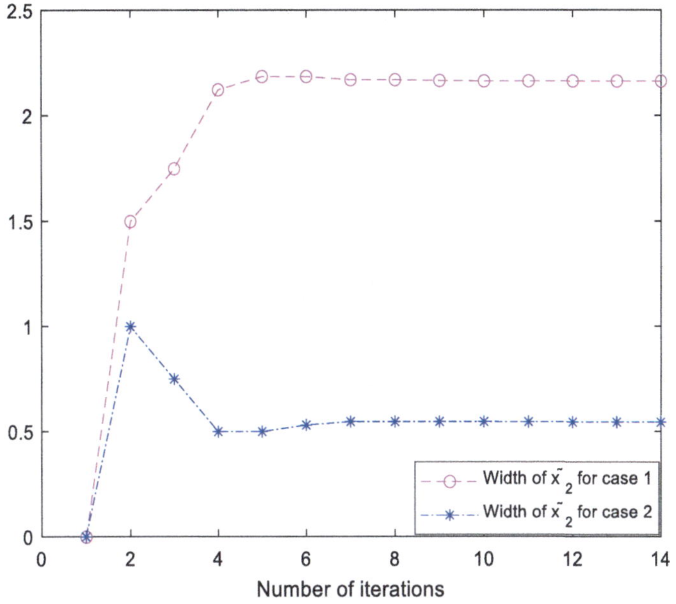

Fig. 12 Width for $\tilde{x}_2$ of case 1 and case 2 of Example 2

In Fig. 9, after 13 iterations the TrFN solution components of $\tilde{x}_1$ of case 1 and case 2 gives graphically. It is observed that the case 2 the TrFN solution is close to crisp solution. The width wise solution $\tilde{x}_1$ of case 1 and case 2 are represent in Fig. 10.

In Fig. 11, after 13 iterations the TrFN solution components of $\tilde{x}_1$ of case 1 and case 2 gives graphically. It is observed that the case 2 the TrFN solution is close to the crisp solution. The width-wise solution $\tilde{x}_1$ of case 1 and case 2 are represented in Fig. 12.

In Fig. 13, after 13 iterations the TrFN solution components of the objective function of case 1 and case 2 gives graphically. It is observed that after 13 iterations the objective function of TrFNs converges. Width-wise iterative fuzzy solution of objective functions of the case study also convergence is shown in Fig. 14.

From the above two example problem applying the developed algorithm is to solve the fuzzy unconstrainted optimization problem, it is observed that the present algorithm is one of the direct search algorithms so no need to find any gradient and Hessian matrix. The present algorithm is simpler to solve uncertain unconstrained optimization problems and reduced to computational complexity.

Table 2 Comparison solution of $\tilde{x}_1$ and $\tilde{x}_2$ of example 2 with the existing method (Nayak & Pooja, 2021)

Variable	Vertex method	Krawczyk method	Nayak and Chakraverty (2015)	Interval IODS method Nayak and Pooja (2021)	Present method
$\tilde{x}_1$	[2.9782, 3.0217]	[2.744592, 3.255408]	[2.9782, 3.0217]	[2.9160, 3.0137]	[2.9869, 3.0131]
$\tilde{x}_2$	[1.9693, 2.0302]	[1.603804, 2.396196]	[1.9693, 2.0302]	[1.8555, 2.0215]	[1.9781, 2.0216]

Table 3 Different α-cut value of $\tilde{x}_1$ and $\tilde{x}_2$ for case 1 and case 2 of Example 2

α-cut	Case 1				Case 2			
	$\tilde{x}_{L1}$	$\tilde{x}_{R1}$	$\tilde{x}_{L2}$	$\tilde{x}_{R2}$	$\tilde{x}_{L1}$	$\tilde{x}_{R1}$	$\tilde{x}_{L2}$	$\tilde{x}_{R2}$
0	2.382	3.2827	1.9105	3.1719	2.9869	3.0131	1.9781	2.0216
0.2	2.5056	3.26158	1.9284	3.01638	2.9882	3.01048	1.9803	2.01728
0.4	2.6292	3.24046	1.9463	2.86086	2.9895	3.00786	1.9825	2.01296
0.6	2.7528	3.21934	1.9642	2.70534	2.9908	3.00524	1.9847	2.00864
0.8	2.8764	3.19822	1.9821	2.54982	2.9921	3.00262	1.9869	2.00432
1	3	3.1771	2	2.3943	2.9934	3	1.9891	2

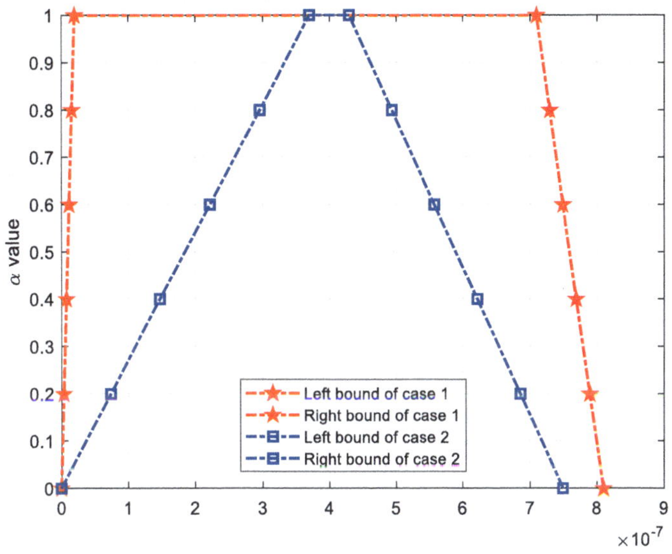

Fig. 13 TrFN objective function of case 1 and case 2 of Example 2

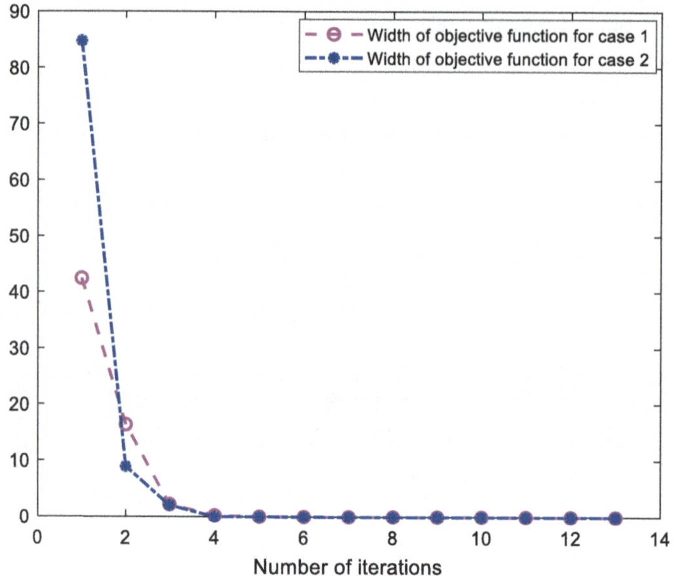

Fig. 14 Width value of the objective function for case 1 and case 2 of Example 2

6 Conclusion

This chapter explains a direct search optimization approach in fuzzy environment to solve the fuzzy unconstrained optimization problem as well as the application of the same. As such, a newly developed fuzzy direct search optimization algorithm is present here. The algorithm is implemented for two electrical network problems that was first modeled and then converted into fuzzy unconstrained optimization problem. Considering the fuzziness of the involved parameters problems are investigated with fuzzy coefficient matrix and fuzzy right-hand vector. Then, the solution of current algorithm is compared with other existing methods viz. Vertex method, Krawczyk method, Newton's method, and IODS method. Further, it is observed that the proposed algorithm is easy to handle uncertain linear and nonlinear systems as well as due to the derivative-free approach it decreases the computational complexity and time cost. Finally, the authors believes that the present method may be used for complex engineering problems, viz. structural dynamics, fluid flow and mass transfer etc. with uncertainty and it may be extended to other fuzzy numbers e.g., Gaussian fuzzy numbers, pseudo fuzzy numbers, and Pythagorean fuzzy numbers, etc.

References

Abbasbandy, S., & Asady, B. (2004). Newton's method for solving fuzzy nonlinear equations. *Applied Mathematics and Computation, 159*(2), 349–356.

Abbasbandy, S., & Ezzati, R. (2006). Newton's method for solving a system of fuzzy nonlinear equations. *Applied Mathematics and Computation, 175*(2), 1189–1199.

Adak, A. K., & Kumar, G. (2022). Spherical distance measurement method for solving MCDM problems under pythagorean fuzzy environment. *Journal of Fuzzy Extension and Applications, 4*(1), 28–39.

Bibi, M. O., Ikheneche, N., & Bentobache, M. (2020). A hybrid direction algorithm for solving a convex quadratic problem. *International Journal of Mathematics in Operational Research, 16*(2), 159–178.

Buckley, J. J., & Qu, Y. (1990). Solving linear and quadratic fuzzy equations. *Fuzzy Sets and Systems, 38*(1), 43–59.

Buckley, J. J., & Qu, Y. (1991). Solving fuzzy equations: A new solution concept. *Fuzzy Sets and Systems, 39*(3), 291–301.

Chakraborty, D., & Guha, D. (2010). Addition of two generalized fuzzy numbers. *International Journal of Industrial Mathematics, 2*(1), 9–20.

Deb, K. (2004). *Optimization for engineering design algorithms and examples*. Prentice Hall of India

Jafari, R., Razvarz, S., Gegov, A. (2018). A new computational method for solving fully fuzzy nonlinear systems. In *Computational collective intelligence*. Cham

Jafari, R., & Yu, W. (2017). Fuzzy modeling for uncertainty nonlinear systems with fuzzy equations. *Mathematical Problems in Engineering, 2017*, 10.

Jafarian, A., & Jafari, R. (2019). A new computational method for solving fully fuzzy nonlinear matrix equations. *International Journal of Fuzzy Computation and Modelling, 2*(4), 275–285.

Kajani, M. T., Asady, B., & Vencheh, A. H. (2005). An iterative method for solving dual fuzzy nonlinear equations. *Applied Mathematics and Computation, 167*(1), 316–323.

Leandry, L., Sosoma, I., & Koloseni, D. (2022). Basic fuzzy arithmetic operations using α–cut for the Gaussian membership function. *Journal of Fuzzy Extension and Applications, 3*(4), 337–348.

Mekawy, I. M. (2022). A novel method for solving multi-objective linear fractional programming problem under uncertainty. *Journal of Fuzzy Extension and Applications, 3*(2), 169–176.

Nayak, S. (2020). *Fundamentals of optimization techniques with algorithms*. Academic Press

Nayak, S., & Chakraverty, S. (2015). Numerical solution of interval nonlinear system of equations. In *2015 International conference on computational intelligence and networks*

Nayak, S., & Pooja, J. (2021). Numerical optimization technique to solve imprecisely defined nonlinear system of equations with bounded parameters. *International Journal of Mathematics in Operational Research*

Nayak, S., & Chakraverty, S. (2013). A New approach to solve fuzzy system of linear equations. *Journal of Mathematics and Computer Science, 7*(3), 205–212.

Panigrahi, P. K., & Nayak, S. (2023). Numerical investigation of non-probabilistic systems using Inner Outer Direct Search optimization technique. *AIMS Mathematics, 8*(9), 21329–21358.

Rao, S. S. (1995). *Optimization theory and applications*. New Age International (P) Limited Publishers.

Shokri, J. (2008). On systems of fuzzy nonlinear equations. *Applied Mathematical Sciences, 2*(25), 1205–1217.

Stanimirović, P.S., Ivanov, B., Stanujkić, D., Katsikis. V. N., Mourtas, S. D., Kazakovtsev, L. A., & Edalatpanah, S. A. (2022). Improvement of unconstrained optimization methods based on symmetry involved in neutrosophy. *Symmetry, 15*(1)

Zadeh, L. A. (1965). Fuzzy sets. *Information and Control, 8*(3), 338–353.

Zimmermann, H. J. (2001). *Fuzzy set theory—and its applications*. Springer, Dordrecht.

Examining Dimensions and Critical Success Factors of Supply Chains Based on the Blockchain and Internet of Things (B-IoT)

Esmaeil Najafi and Hamed Nozari

Abstract The technological revolution in the field of logistics and supply chain brings a large volume of innovations and new challenges. Using today's powerful and high-speed digital technologies, customers expect faster and on-time ordering and delivery of goods. As a result, organizations are always looking to implement today's new and transformative technologies to provide services faster and more efficiently. "Internet of Things" and "Blockchain" are expected innovations that will transform the complex supply chain into an integrated and empowered process. IoT innovations such as sensor data and RFID (radio identification technology) provide information to equip us with features such as real-time tracking and alerts to improve decision-making. Blockchain can also increase data security and transparency through decentralized data management. Such data can be turned into critical information to help improve business operations and processes. Therefore, the successful implementation of a supply chain based on these two valuable technologies can be an effective way to improve supply chain processes and help business growth in all supply chain processes. In this research, it has tried to identify and evaluate the most important critical success factors for the implementation of this smart supply chain. Correct understanding and prioritization of these factors can be an effective guide for the powerful implementation of a smart supply chain based on the Internet of Things and Blockchain.

Keywords IoT-based supply chain · Smart supply chain · Critical success factors · Blockchain technology

E. Najafi
Department of Industrial Engineering, Islamic Azad University, Science and Research Unit, Tehran, Iran

H. Nozari (✉)
Department of Industrial Engineering, Iran University of Science and Technology, Tehran, Iran
e-mail: ham.nozari.eng@iauctb.ac.ir

© The Author(s), under exclusive license to Springer Nature Singapore Pte Ltd. 2024

S. A. Edalatpanah et al. (eds.), *Analytical Decision Making and Data Envelopment Analysis*, Infosys Science Foundation Series in Mathematical Sciences,
https://doi.org/10.1007/978-981-97-6972-8_13

1 Introduction

Solutions based on the IoT can significantly help to optimize supply chain management and logistics processes and have more transparency in this field. The Internet of Things can bring more transparency and accuracy in the supply chain. Because logistics operators can receive real-time data about the location and status of each of the organization's assets. Using this data, they can modify and optimize the entire delivery route if changes are needed. The expansion of the Internet of Things has already started a change for the better. But still, the use of this technology is progressing very slowly. In the existing competitive market, economic and production enterprises, in addition to dealing with the organization and internal resources, have found themselves in need of managing and monitoring resources and elements related to outside the organization. Therefore, today supply chain management is considered as one of the infrastructural foundations of e-business implementation in the world. Today, managers' attitude towards the supply chain has changed and the use of information technology in this field is increasing. On the other hand, one of the most effective achievements of information technology is the improvement of business intelligence. Therefore, the use of intelligent software agents in supply chain management can improve management in this field. For example, the user can measure and remotely control many variables such as temperature, humidity, pressure, light exposure and even the GPS location of a package. This technology is very important in recording a good shopping experience for the customer (Nozari et al., 2021).

Traditional approaches in business create a lot of costs due to the inability to provide complex and diverse products. But new approaches seek to provide the services and products needed to the changing global markets. It is possible based on the combination of traditional business networks and communication and work interactions with the help of information and communication technology. For example, some cargoes require a certain temperature and humidity to maintain health and freshness during transportation. In the case of suitable sensors, they can inform customers or transport agents of any fluctuations in temperature and humidity during transportation, so that necessary and corrective measures can be taken to save the cargo at the right time.

The task of supply chain management is to manage and coordinate various flows within it. One of the important management challenges in this field is related to coordinating the flow of materials between several organizations and within each organization. Achieving this goal requires the use of technologies and tools to track materials along the path from origin to destination and record information at each stage (Nozari et al., 2019).

Due to the ineffectiveness of information transmission in the supply chain, a lot of money is lost, and this issue is more important in industries whose products are damaged and spoiled. The use of transparent and advanced blockchain technology helps companies to identify high-cost items and use cost-saving methods in those items. Blockchain can also eliminate the cost of money transfer fees through banks and other money transfer methods. The cost of these fees is included in the calculation of the final price and profit of the products, and removing them will increase the profit and lower the final cost for the customer. Block chain technology (of its permission-based type) allows different organizations and individuals to access or block access to view, register, maintain data, etc. Therefore, by granting access to the database, a tax organization can be empowered to collect VAT correctly by observing the correct flow of goods entering and leaving a company (Oudani et al., 2023).

An IoT network can process data transactions through multiple devices owned and managed by different organizations, making it difficult to accurately identify any data publisher in the event of an attack by cybercriminals. In addition, IoT generates a large amount of data, and with multiple stakeholders involved, data ownership is not clear. The main thing that enables blockchain technology to make the supply chain transparent is nothing but the ability to transfer ownership (Van Nguyen et al., 2023).

It is important to consider the simultaneous presence of these technologies in supply chain processes in the fourth industrial generation. In order to effectively implement smart supply chains, we need to understand the critical success factors in these supply chains. For this reason, in this research, it was tried to extract and evaluate the most important critical indicators of success by reviewing the literature. In the following sections, these indicators and their effects have been examined.

2 IoT Based Supply Chain

Supply chain management is a multi-stage process in which different groups often operate and each of them can somehow benefit from the role of the Internet of Things in supply chain management The Internet of Things can bring more transparency and accuracy in the supply chain. Because logistics operators can receive real-time data about the location and status of each of the organization's assets. Using this data, they can modify and optimize the entire delivery route if changes are needed. IoT-based solutions also help to manage the supply chain of cold products, and by detecting problems along the way, they can keep perishable materials safe to a large extent. Since the main mission of the Internet of Things is to establish communication between machines and between machines and humans, collect information and analyze them, it can be said that it is an innovative and transformative technology that before it there was no separate technology that has these functions specifically (Nozari et al., 2022).

Manufacturers, more than companies operating in other industries, need heavy machinery to produce their products and therefore, have a great interest in knowing about the performance of these machines. Manufacturing organizations have many opportunities in front of them. From computer imaging of devices to managing and tracking the shipment of goods, which are connected to systems developed with artificial intelligence that can predict and even correct events before they happen, it shows the wide range of applications of the Internet of Things in this sector (Jayashri et al.,

2023). Many manufacturing facilities rely on smart sensors and machine learning for on-line adaptation. The obtained data and the performed analyzes increase the efficiency and quality significantly. Collected information is used in predicting machine downtime and thus increasing machine performance and lifespan with predictive maintenance. The use of IoT in the manufacturing industry is not limited to maintenance. The production of electrical devices and tools is also affected by these technologies. Using different codes makes it difficult to guarantee cooperation and communication between devices and tools (Aliahmadi & Nozari, 2022).

Supply chain management in today's industrial environment is a new management method that has a direct impact on the success of organizations in today's highly competitive business environment. In recent years, supply chain management, with its new approach to management issues, has been able to bring about a change in the reduction of implementation costs and the correct implementation of management issues and the production of quality products in organizations. But the implementation of supply chain management can be useful in organizations when it can show itself well in interaction with the goals and components of the organization. On the other hand, with the advent of the Internet of Things, the world has changed drastically. With the help of the Internet of Things, different programs and devices can communicate with each other through the Internet connection. Internet of things is a valuable tool to optimize all assets in supply chain processes. Physical assets such as fleets and vehicles can be optimized with improved connectivity, such as the Internet of Things. Smarter routes can be planned, as can asset delivery delays due to traffic or being stuck in earlier stages of work. With the obtained data, the organization can monitor and analyze asset performance, and optimize the process by scheduling the maximum number of tasks for each asset. All these things boost the business as the delivered goods can be easily managed (Liang et al., 2023).

A strong supply chain not only helps to solve many logistics issues; it also works in providing the best customer service. Because managers can easily access information through mobile devices and apps to track complete trip details and real-time reports; it becomes easy to identify issues, contact customers to manage expectations or make necessary arrangements. The customer also has full control and visibility, which increases the entire supply chain transaction (Guo et al., 2022).

The Internet of Things promises us a lot, but the implementation of these promises is still in the early stages of the supply chain. The steps taken by organizations will surely reap the benefits of the Internet of Things in the near future with the advancement of technology. Cold storage logistics companies have developed intelligent applications that work based on the principles of the Internet of Things, in such a way that they create instant alerts after each milestone, which informs the customer of the location of the shipment slow. These facilities provide complete transparency and control to the client, to make the right business decisions based on the program reports. Figure 1 shows the applications of IoT in the supply chain (Ghahremani-Nahr et al., 2022).

Some of the most important advantages of using the Internet of Things in the supply chain are:

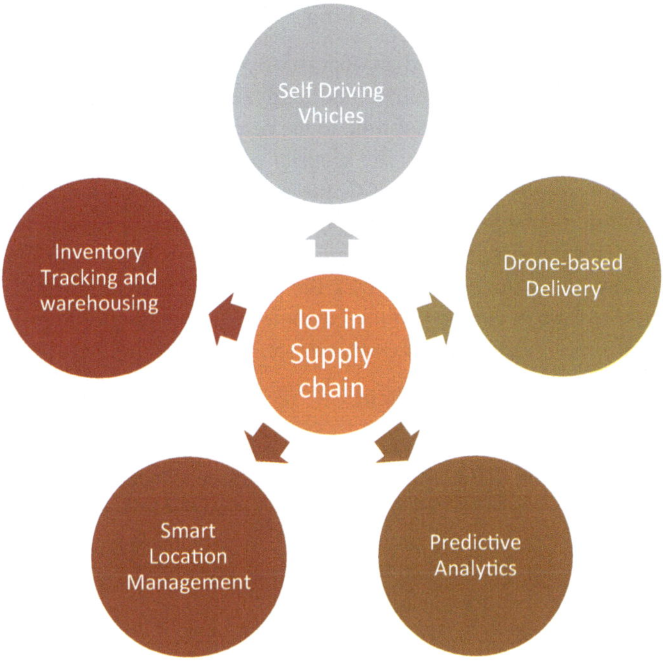

Fig. 1 Applications of the Internet of Things in supply chain and logistics

- **Better cooperation**

The Internet of Things provides an overview of how supply chains affect a business, which can be key, especially in more complex supply chains. Providing an overview in this area can align different parts of an organization with each other and allow them to work together to prevent problems from occurring. (Gharaibeh et al., 2022)

- **Provide better service to customers**

A supply chain in which the Internet of Things is also used can help provide better services to customers. Managers can access the information they need through mobile applications and predict the delivery time with high accuracy. This issue can solve the problems related to the speed of product delivery and meet the customer's expectations (Tano et al., 2022).

- **Improve the accuracy of forecasting**

By automatically collecting data, IoT-based systems and supply chains eliminate human error in data collection and help improve customer demand forecasting. Supply chain managers can forecast demand based on both historical and real-time data. Another important point is that supply chain data can be collected non-stop or at regular intervals. Either way, it allows businesses to tap into data that might be difficult or even impossible to collect manually (Lv et al., 2022).

- **Product shipment control and tracking**

Now, IOT technology has provided an opportunity for vehicles to be equipped with cameras and sensors that can evaluate and analyze the driver's physical and even mental state. This data is sent in real-time to the responsible people to better manage the shipping processes. In addition, the security of the cargo is also ensured in this way more reliably. With the help of IOT, the geographical location of the product, the arrival time of the cargo, the stopping time, the weather conditions of the transportation route and the distance traveled can be tracked with great accuracy. Another advantage of the IoT is the ability to track the process of providing goods from the warehouse to the time of delivery to the customer, which often leads to an increase in the speed of service delivery and customer satisfaction (Hrouga et al., 2022).

- **Warehouse inventory management**

Most of the supply chain processes depend on receiving real-time information from the warehouse inventory. This issue is especially important in large businesses. In these companies, the slightest delay may lead to irreparable losses. In this regard, the use of technologies such as the Internet of Things and big data analysis helps to know the stock status of the warehouse in real-time without the need to employ workers in different parts of the warehouse.

Figure 2 schematically shows a supply chain based on the IoT technology.

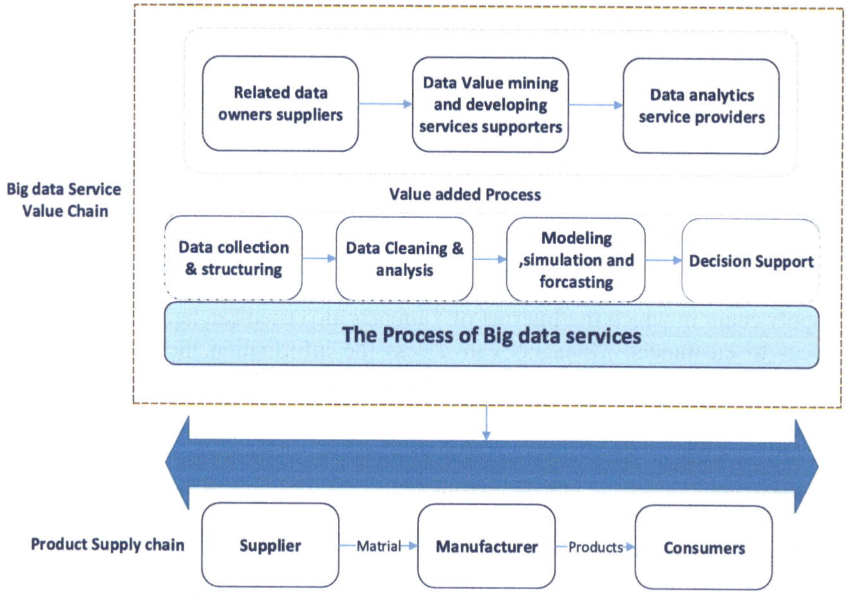

Fig. 2 IoT based on supply chain (He et al., 2020)

Smart decisions in the physical world with the help of Internet of Things equipment provide the possibility of value creation in supply chains. This value creation allows customers to have maximum satisfaction from purchasing various products.

3 Blockchain and IoT-Based Supply Chain Management

These days' supply chains around the world have become complex processes with many parties involved. For this reason, supply chain companies intend to improve their business operations using technologies such as the Blockchain and IoT in order to accurately monitor assets.

Internet of Things sensors are used to collect information related to environmental conditions, verifying how long the cargo stays in a certain truck or a certain port, and whether there have been any violations or problems with the cargo or not. This information provides us with reassuring evidence that can be used in case of any invoice discrepancies. Companies can use this information to optimize their supply chain operations to increase their business productivity (Kaur et al., 2022).

The Internet of Things is nothing but receiving and transmitting a huge amount of data. For this reason, the main issue is the security of that data. Data must flow through various devices and the facilities embedded in them, including data analytics, IoT devices, and related platforms. On the other hand, this data must pass through many implementation areas, each of which has its own policies. All this makes the issue of ensuring data security a bit complicated. Apart from security, ensuring that data is delivered securely at the right time, form and place are also quite important to address. Because blockchain is a decentralized distributed ledger, there is no central authority or specific executive organization to record data and transactions (Jiang et al., 2022). Blockchain technology is designed on the basis of cryptographic algorithms so that it can be used to ensure data security and immutability. Each block in the blockchain network has a hash of the previous block, which shows that none of the blocks can be changed or replaced. The integration of IoT with blockchain helps logistics companies deliver shipments more quickly and easily and optimize the operational costs of various applications. IoT, along with the Blockchain, can be extremely useful for protection of all types of digital things, and its use in the supply chain brings many benefits. Some of these applications include (Júnior et al., 2022):

- **Transparent information recording**

Supply chain members can see the status of resources and products during their transfer from one company to another, and since information cannot be manipulated in the blockchain, no one is to blame if a mistake occurs.

- **Cost Reduction**

Due to the ineffectiveness of data transmission in the supply chain, a lot of money is lost, and this issue is more important in industries whose products are damaged and spoiled. The use of transparent and advanced blockchain technology helps companies identify high-cost items and take advantage of ways to save on those items. Blockchain can also eliminate the cost of money transfer fees through banks and other money transfer methods. The cost of these fees is included in the calculation of the final price and profit of the products, and removing them will increase the profit and lower the final cost for the customer.

- **Interactive information production**

One of the most fundamental problems of the current supply chain is the inability to integrate and align information for all elements and parts of the chain. Blockchains are designed as a distributed system that provides a transparent and private repository for information. Each node (member of the chain) adds new information to the blockchain and verifies its validity. This means that all players in the supply chain in all companies and stores have access to the information and can confirm its validity and correctness at any stage.

- **An alternative to electronic information exchange**

Many companies use the Electronic Information Interchange system to send business information to each other, so this information is delayed and does not reach the companies at the same time as the products are sent. If product shipments are experiencing problems or prices are constantly changing, supply chain members receive this information in subsequent electronic information exchange packets. By using blockchain, the information is continuously updated and can be transferred to the companies in the supply chain at any time.

- **Digital agreements and document sharing**

It is important to have only one true copy for sharing supply chain documents. Necessary documents and contracts can be made available to people with blockchain and digital signature system; therefore, as a result of this action, all partners have access to the original and original version of the contract and documents. Blockchain ensures the immutability of the contract and agreements, and only if all partners reach a collective agreement, the terms of the contract can be changed.

Figure 3 shows the supply chain based on transformative technologies and Blockchain.

Blockchain creates integrity and there will be no disputes about transactions in the chain because all the factors that affect the chain have the same shared copy of this digital ledger. In the blockchain, everyone can see the chain of ownership of an asset in the entire chain. Records in the blockchain cannot be erased and this is very important for the transparency of a supply chain. By using this technology, supply chain management becomes easier and losses in this chain are reduced (Mangla et al., 2022).

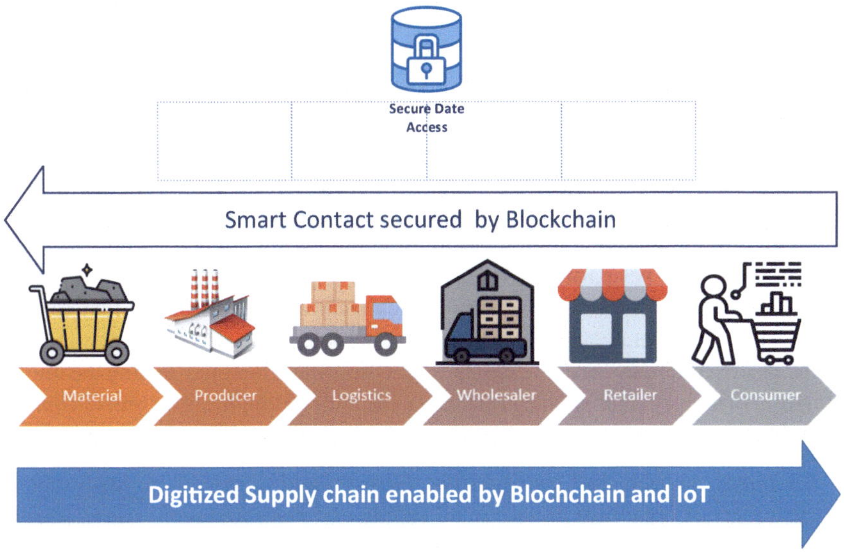

Fig. 3 Blockchani and IoT based supply chain

4 Critical Success Factors for Supply Chain Based on Blockchain and IoT

One of the advantages of blockchain and Internet of Things technologies is to minimize paperwork and administrative work, so it is very important to use integrated information devices such as Internet of Things technology in the field of supply chain as correctly as possible. These technologies deal with the challenges in automatic identification devices by using information tools, intelligent equipment such as RFIDs, wireless sensor networks, etc., middleware, web-based software platforms and relying on cloud computing. This results in generating a huge amount of data to be stored, processed and presented (Kayikci et al., 2022).

As innovation drives measurable change across multiple domains, the tripod of strategic thinking, including connected communities, holistic decision-making, and intelligent automation, can help shape the way goods move in the future. It is one of the biggest obstacles in the global movement of goods. The lack of proper connectivity between service providers, transport services, and end customers makes coordination difficult and ultimately leads to systemic inefficiency. Meeting growing demand and customer expectations requires ecosystem players and supply chain partners to rethink the way they work together to create an efficient network. Enabling technologies are key to unifying fragmented ecosystems as they facilitate advanced connectivity across the transportation network. This is also evident in reality, as strategic investments in connecting network components are becoming a mainstream technology.

When it comes to data (in a historically data-poor industry), increased digitization and greater connectivity seem to create new value in the business operations of transportation organizations. Functions such as sales, marketing, and customer relationship management (CRM) are particularly important for retail, where data sharing with supply chain partners is common and often centers around customer data. Evidence shows that creating connectivity will also improve coordination in the supply chain. As supply chain transformation in the coming years focuses on advanced technologies, global logistics players are expected to take a collaborative approach with their key partners to create innovation. There is no evidence of collaborative innovation, especially in technologies such as cyber security that require teamwork (Kayikci et al., 2022).

The results of researchers' studies show that the critical factors affecting the implementation of supply chain management systems with an emphasis on transformative technologies can be presented in 4 categories, which are:

1. ***Customer service and satisfaction***: Growth and increase of trust among customers of organizations and in all supply and distribution processes, growth and increase of loyalty of all customers and reduction of challenges in communication with customers of the organization.
2. **Growth and innovation**: Growth and increase of on-time delivery capabilities in distribution and supply systems, development and increase of competent suppliers and growth of government and private order systems (delay reduction, timely delivery of goods and services and elimination of possible errors).
3. **Financial performance**: Providing specific references for the smart and electronic supply chain, predicting the types of demand at the point of sale and improving inventory management and reducing the costs of distribution and delivery of goods.
4. **Internal performance of the organization**: Support of senior managers, coordination in logistics processes, use of up-to-date technology, information sharing with supply chain members, high flexibility in the production system, focus on strengths, and long-term vision for survival and growth.

In general, the most important critical factors of success for supply chains based on the Blockchain and the Internet of Things are shown in Fig. 4.

Creating collaborative operating models is critical to the industry, as the development of real-time communication in the ecosystem can help create new collaborative, transparent, technology-based ways of doing business. The effects of a connected society go beyond improving processes. Currently, the initial applications of this trend in asset and talent management represent changes in some operating models. Asset management, digital maturity, and ecosystem connectivity are strong examples of concepts such as asset sharing (i.e., a company's passive assets can be used by others). Figure 5 shows the framework of the presence of critical factors of success for the effective implementation of a smart supply chain based on the Blockchain and IoT. Overall, by connecting supply chain networks through a decentralized system, blockchain has the potential to enable frictionless movement between suppliers and manufacturers (Elhidaoui et al., 2022).

Fig. 4 Critical factors of success of smart IoT and Blockchain based supply chains (Singh et al., 2023)

The real-time and continuous tracking of products in the supply chain has created a series of auditable data, and thus businesses can make decisions with high confidence regarding the accuracy of information and the quality of their products. The distributed nature of this technology allows for greater monitoring and control, and in addition, real-time monitoring with the help of smart contracts allows stakeholders to make more efficient use of their resources by making diverse decisions and reduce the amount of non-productive working capital.

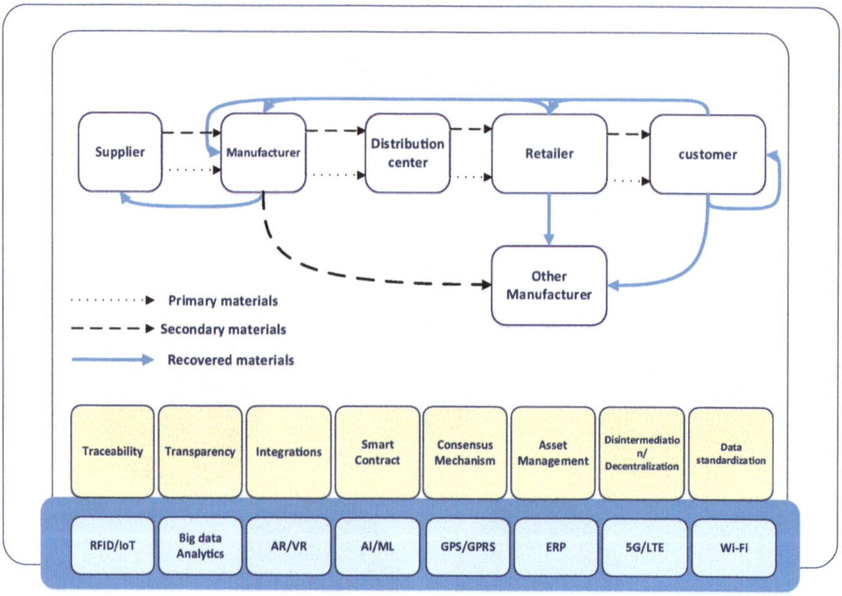

Fig. 5 The conceptual framework of the presence of critical factors of success in the smart supply chain based on the Blockchain and IoT

5 Conclusion

In general, with the development of technology and new technologies, different industries, whether they like it or not, are forced to use them to compete with competitors. The supply chain industry has also undergone many changes with recent developments and rapid growth in production. The development of artificial intelligence has encouraged companies active in the supply chain to use this technology to improve the quality control system. Further, with the development of Internet of Things technology, this technology was accompanied by the production of Internet of Things (IoT) devices and drones, which now play an important role in monitoring and maintaining goods. Before the penetration of blockchain technology in the supply chain, various technologies have revolutionized supply chains. With the emergence of this technology and its use by the largest companies, it has been able to create many developments in maintaining security, privacy, etc. Although the use of the Internet of Things and artificial intelligence technologies in the supply chain has been associated with high costs, blockchain, and its infrastructure are associated with cost reduction for companies active in this field while being highly efficient.

Creating a common market with the help of blockchain technology enables users to access various information such as the volume of warehouses, the amount of existing demand and other things in real-time and transparently, and smart contracts can produce very accurate and valuable analysis reports. Beneficiaries also benefit from the benefits of better control over warehouses, management of financial flows and leadership of all available processes and data of the supply chain, and they manage compliance with standards and discover points of delays more efficiently. With the help of smart contracts, they can facilitate and speed up the compliance of their current processes with measured work standards and supply chain management. In the event of any breach or fraud in the supply chain, comprehensive records recorded on the blockchain enable organizations to easily pinpoint the source of the problem. The Internet of Things equipment records the detailed information received and how the information flows and records the information flow and puts it on the blockchain platform. This information can only be viewed and retrieved by beneficiaries who have permission to access the information. Blockchain efficiency combined with IoT technology will make global supply chains more efficient by allowing companies to complete and confirm transactions directly. Integrated payment solutions reduce the time between order and payment processing and ensure proper and timely movement of products. Also, every step in the supply chain is securely recorded, meaning logistics issues can be easily traced back to their source. The same applies to the supply of parts or raw materials, which can be traced with the help of blockchain, increasing accountability and transparency, and reducing illegal activities are also other solutions that blockchain does in the supply chain for the prosperity of this industry.

All these cases show the importance of implementing smart supply chains based on these transformative technologies. In order to implement effectively, it is very necessary to extract the critical Success Factors in these supply chains and examine their place in the supply chain processes. Critical Success Factors (CSF) may sound complicated, but it is actually a very simple concept. A CSF is a high-level objective that is essential to the success of supply chain processes. In this research, it was tried to fully extract and examine the dimensions, components and types of critical success factors in supply chains based on the Internet of Things and Blockchain. At the end, a framework was presented to show the position of these factors. A proper understanding of these factors can be a valuable solution for the effective implementation of these digital supply chains. It can also contribute to the success of smarter supply chains.

References

Aliahmadi, A., & Nozari, H. (2022). Evaluation of security metrics in AIoT and blockchain-based supply chain by Neutrosophic decision-making method. In *Supply Chain Forum: An International Journal* (pp. 1–12). Taylor & Francis.

Elhidaoui, S., Benhida, K., El Fezazi, S., Kota, S., & Lamalem, A. (2022). Critical success factors of blockchain adoption ingreen supply chain management: contribution through an interpretive structural model. *Production & Manufacturing Research, 10*(1), 1–23.

Ghahremani-Nahr, J., Aliahmadi, A., & Nozari, H. (2022). An IoT-based sustainable supply chain framework and blockchain. *International Journal of Innovation in Engineering, 2*(1), 12–21.

Gharaibeh, L., Eriksson, K. M., Lantz, B., Matarneh, S., & Elghaish, F. (2022). Toward digital construction supply chain-based Industry 4.0 solutions: Scientometric-thematic analysis. *Smart and Sustainable Built Environment.*

Guo, L., Chen, J., Li, S., Li, Y., & Lu, J. (2022). A blockchain and IoT based lightweight framework for enabling information transparency in supply chain finance. *Digital Communications and Networks.*

He, L., Xue, M., & Gu, B. (2020). Internet-of-things enabled supply chain planning and coordination with big data services: Certain theoretic implications. *Journal of Management Science and Engineering, 5*(1), 1–22.

Hrouga, M., Sbihi, A., & Chavallard, M. (2022). The potentials of combining Blockchain technology and Internet of Things for digital reverse supply chain: A case study. *Journal of Cleaner Production, 337*, 130609.

Jayashri, N., Rampur, V., Gangodkar, D., Abirami, M., Balarengadurai, C., & Kumar, A. (2023). Improved block chain system for high secured IoT integrated supply chain. *Measurement: Sensors, 25*, 100633.

Jiang, R., Kang, Y., Liu, Y., Liang, Z., Duan, Y., Sun, Y., & Liu, J. (2022). A trust transitivity model of small and medium-sized manufacturing enterprises under blockchain-based supply chain finance. *International Journal of Production Economics, 247*, 108469.

Júnior, C. A. R., Sanseverino, E. R., Gallo, P., Koch, D., Schweiger, H. G., & Zanin, H. (2022). Blockchain review for battery supply chain monitoring and battery trading. *Renewable and Sustainable Energy Reviews, 157*, 112078.

Kaur, A., Singh, G., Kukreja, V., Sharma, S., Singh, S., & Yoon, B. (2022). Adaptation of IoT with blockchain in Food Supply Chain Management: An analysis-based review in development, benefits and potential applications. *Sensors, 22*(21), 8174.

Kayikci, Y., Gozacan-Chase, N., Rejeb, A., & Mathiyazhagan, K. (2022). Critical success factors for implementing blockchain-based circular supply chain. *Business Strategy and the Environment.*

Liang, W., Zhang, L., & Kadoch, M. (2023). 6G IoT tracking-and machine learning-enhanced blockchained supply chain management. *Electronics, 12*(1), 40.

Lv, M., Li, J., Niu, X., & Wang, J. (2022). Novel deterministic and probabilistic combined system based on deep learning and self-improved optimization algorithm for wind speed forecasting. *Sustainable Energy Technologies and Assessments, 52*, 102186.

Mangla, S. K., Kazançoğlu, Y., Yıldızbaşı, A., Öztürk, C., & Çalık, A. (2022). A conceptual framework for blockchain-based sustainable supply chain and evaluating implementation barriers: A case of the tea supply chain. *Business Strategy and the Environment.*

Nozari, H., Najafi, E., Fallah, M., & Hosseinzadeh Lotfi, F. (2019). Quantitative analysis of key performance indicators of green supply chain in FMCG industries using non-linear fuzzy method. *Mathematics, 7*(11), 1020.

Nozari, H., Szmelter-Jarosz, A., & Ghahremani-Nahr, J. (2022). Analysis of the challenges of Artificial Intelligence of Things (AIoT) for the smart supply chain (Case Study: FMCG Industries). *Sensors, 22*(8), 2931.

Nozari, H., Fallah, M., Kazemipoor, H., & Najafi, S. E. (2021). Big data analysis of IoT-based supply chain management considering FMCG industries. *Бизнес-информатика, 15*(1 (eng)), 78–96.

Oudani, M., Sebbar, A., Zkik, K., El Harraki, I., & Belhadi, A. (2023). Green Blockchain based IoT for secured supply chain of hazardous materials. *Computers & Industrial Engineering, 175*, 108814.

Singh, R., Khan, S., Dsilva, J., & Centobelli, P. (2023). Blockchain Integrated IoT for Food Supply Chain: A Grey Based Delphi-DEMATEL Approach. *Applied Sciences, 13*(2), 1079.

Tan, W. C., & Sidhu, M. S. (2022). Review of RFID and IoT integration in supply chain management. *Operations Research Perspectives*, 100229.

Van Nguyen, T., Cong Pham, H., Nhat Nguyen, M., Zhou, L., & Akbari, M. (2023). Data-driven review of blockchain applications in supply chain management: key research themes and future directions. *International Journal of Production Research*, 1–23.

Leveraging Data Mining Techniques to Render Unprecedented Opportunities for Business Organizations to Survive and Thrive in the Course of COVID-19

Pooja Bhakuni and Amrit Das

Abstract Big data in the face of saddling to anticipate, comprehend and react to future occasions becomes an interesting and well-designated platform for the research community associated with some administrative decisions. During a critical situation like the COVID-19 pandemic, to drive the researchers to make different administrative decisions following the different protocols, the existence of a comprehensive review of different data mining techniques to tackle the situation is very lean. In this paper or the methodology corner, we present an audit of methodological advancements of a variety of techniques utilized for mining data which can further render help in analyzing the contemporary issue of industries. We provide insight into how various descriptive and predictive methods of data mining can be leveraged to help different industries to increase their revenue even during these black swan events such as COVID-19.

Keywords Data mining techniques · Market basket analysis · Descriptive techniques · Predictive techniques · Apriori

1 Introduction

Calling out the impact of COVID-19 as one of the mightiest catastrophes to the world economy will be nothing but a euphemism. It is not just the millions of naive lives lost but also the lethal virus that has put a strain on almost all sectors of the world economy; the sectors perniciously affected by the novel virus range from tourism, electronics, and automobile to food and beverages (Barua, 2020). To have a bird's eye view of the tremendous impact of the deadly virus COVID-19 on different industries, let us peak into some examples, considering the companies providing various technology services that have shut down their offices along with the stores and have further put a check on the travel of their executives or the employees in certain affected areas

P. Bhakuni · A. Das (✉)
Department of Mathematics, School of Advanced Sciences, VIT University, Vellore, India
e-mail: das.amrit12@gmail.com; amrit.das@vit.ac.in

© The Author(s), under exclusive license to Springer Nature Singapore Pte Ltd. 2024

S. A. Edalatpanah et al. (eds.), *Analytical Decision Making and Data Envelopment Analysis*, Infosys Science Foundation Series in Mathematical Sciences,
https://doi.org/10.1007/978-981-97-6972-8_14

leading to a very adverse impact on supply chains. China, the leading technology provider in the world, is deeply affected (Fang et al., 2021; Jia et al., 2021). As the leading cause of the boom in COVID-19 cases is huge public gatherings thus, some of the biggest entertainment or theme parks across the globe, like Universal studios and Disney Park, are shut down (Yasharoff & Woodyward, 2020). The highly famed national basketball association (NBA), which consists of around 30 basketball teams from the USA & Canada, was made to suspend its season soon after one of the players tested positive for the virus (Aschburner, 2020). Similarly, the famous football club based out of London, Arsenal football club, asked the players to be in self-isolation and postponed many matches because of the outbreak of the virus (Ames, 2020). The cinema industry was badly impacted as most of the theatres were shut down across the country (Nhamo et al., 2020). One of the worst shakedowns amid the outbreak was experienced by the tourism industry (Kumar & Nafi, 2020; Ntounis et al., 2022). The report from International Air Transport Association (IATA) states that around $113 billion will be lost by the global airlines if the spread follows the same trend (Amankwah-Amoah et al., 2021). Figure 1 shows the global economic impact of COVID-19.

The deadly plight of COVID-19 has spread from developed to developing nations. The maestros from organizations such as United Nations development program and the world health organization have concluded that the situation of all the developing countries will be worrisome (WHO Director-General's opening remarks at the media briefing on, 2020). The non-industrial nations majorly depend on essential area jobs like farming and mining, jobs that involve the exploitation of natural resources; these are some of the jobs that cannot be carried out from home, and these jobs are highly affected by the adverse impact on supply chain and if the interest from their product decreases. These nation faces a huge crisis when their richer trading partner shut their

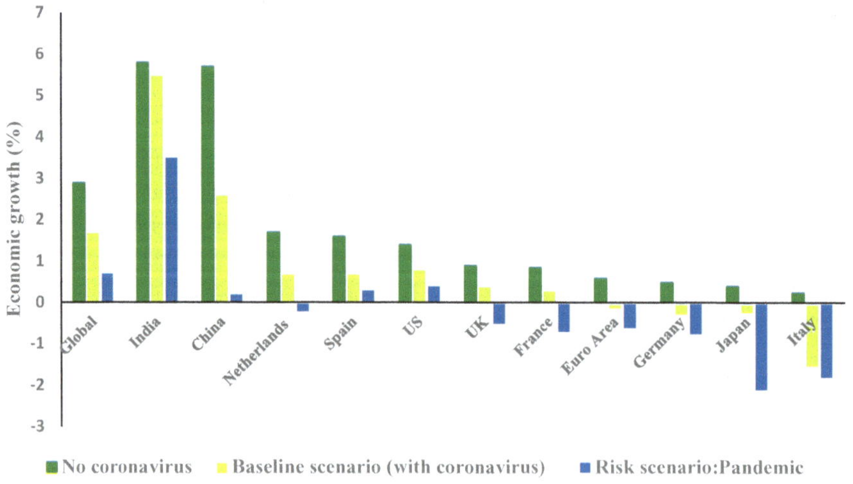

Fig. 1 Global economic impact of COVID-19 (Khandelwal et al., 2020)

borders since the global pandemic hit (Gupta et al., 2022; Vitenu-Sackey & Barfi, 2021). Figure 2 shows the impact of COVID-19 on various economic sectors. For a business to endure and thrive through this tough time, it needs to resort to the latest tools and techniques of data mining, web scraping, and data analysis. The only thing that hasn't abated even after the annexation of COVID-19 is the humongous amount of data. Organizations have seized much more data now than in the past. However, drawing meaning out of the colossal dimensions of ordered and unordered data can be a tedious task if the idea is to implement growth across the organization. If the data is not used judiciously, it can prune the assistance to be provided by the data.

To avail the benefit of the humongous amount of data available, we need to resort to data mining techniques. Data Mining is the technique used by various organizations to look in large bank of information to detect patterns, hidden insights from the data using series of techniques and algorithms (Mosa et al., 2022; Weir, 2021). The algorithms are developed using different branch of mathematics say linear algebra, real analysis, calculus & statistics. Machine learning plays a requisite role in development of techniques, and data base management system renders help in managing the huge data (Brownlee et al., 2022).

Although there exists variety of data mining technique but the one technique that we will deep dive into in this paper is the market basket analysis (MBA) technique. MBA is a salient method utilized by enormous retailers in order to reveal relationship across things. All in all, it permits retailers to recognize the connection in the middle of things that are often purchased together. It can build deals and consumer loyalty.

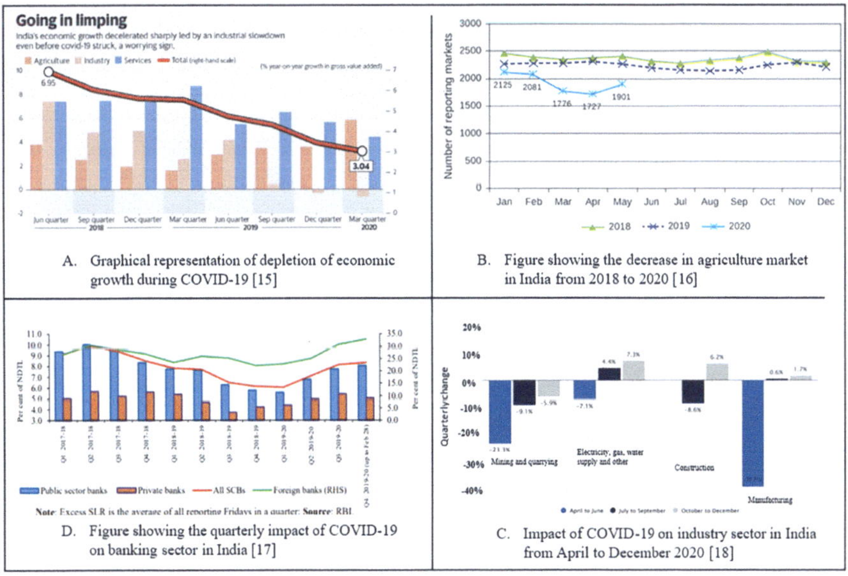

A. Graphical representation of depletion of economic growth during COVID-19 [15]

B. Figure showing the decrease in agriculture market in India from 2018 to 2020 [16]

D. Figure showing the quarterly impact of COVID-19 on banking sector in India [17]

C. Impact of COVID-19 on industry sector in India from April to December 2020 [18]

Fig. 2 Impact of COVID-19 on Indian economy through diverse lenses including agriculture, banking, and industry

Utilizing information to discover that items are regularly bought together, retailers can improve item arrangement, offer extraordinary arrangements, and make new item packages to support further deals of these mixes (Patwary et al., 2021; Ünvan, 2021).

The serious issue that we will address in this paper and will attempt to give an answer to utilizing diverse data mining procedures are as per the following:

- Manufacturing: predictive analysis of equipment failure
- Customer Behavior: correlating procurement of customers with socio-economic data and demographic
- Departmental store: positioning of products in store designs
- Geo tagging and facial recognition framework

The rest of the paper is assembled as follows. Section 2 deep dives into the literature review of data mining techniques, the impact of COVID-19 on business organizations, and the use of data mining techniques in reducing the impact of COVID-19. Section 3 throws light on data mining and its relevance in the knowledge discovery process (KDP) and explains all the steps of the KDP in detail. Descriptive and predictive data mining techniques are explained in this section. Section 4 introduces MBA along with its core concept and varied classification of this technique. Section 5 provides insight into various algorithms used for MBA with their pros and cons; at the same time, it suggests the best technique to apply MBA. Section 6 explains the Apriori algorithm used to implement MBA, along with the application methodology and variations. Section 7 explains the application of data mining techniques, especially MBA, in reducing the impact of COVID-19 on the different business models. Section 8 mentions the limitations of current research work. Section 9 states the conclusion and future work.

2 Literature Review

Data mining is maneuvered to extricate admissible patterns from huge data repositories, and it is one of the most crucial phases in the KDP in any database. Data mining has gained significant attention in the previous twenty years due to its relevance in decision-making and has evolved into a vital tool for a range of organizational processes (Leung, 2022). The literature review done here is broadly divided into three categories, as discussed.

2.1 Data Mining Techniques

Researchers have investigated a wide range of techniques for mining data in the past which include neural networks, genetic algorithms, visualization techniques, and machine learning (Chen et al., 1996; Gheware et al., 2014; Han et al., 2006). The kinds of trends or information to be found throughout the data mining can indeed be outlined using data mining operations or jobs. Summarization, discrimination, clustering, classification, characterization, outlier analysis, association, regression, and trend analysis are a few of the key data mining tasks (Hariri et al., 2019).

Classification algorithms use the approach of classifying new data entries in a data set based on the predetermined class (Han et al., 2006). Multiple classification algorithms have been proposed by researchers in the past (Sen et al., 2020). Some of the classification techniques are mentioned in detail in Table 1.

Apart from that, there are other classifiers brought forward by many researchers, such as classifiers established on predictor features (Kotsiantis et al., 2007) and classifications established on the grounds of properties (Craw et al., 2006). Clustering is another vital data mining technique; it works by segmenting data into clusters. Apart from data mining, clustering is employed in bioinformatics, image segmentation, and pattern recognition. In the last two decades, many clustering algorithms are already proposed and implemented by many researchers (Ezugwu et al., 2022; Fan et al., 2012; Jalal & Ali, 2021). Table 2 provide a brief description of some of the clustering technique; apart from that, some other clustering techniques are also proposed by researchers that include parameter exempted method that avails minimum description length (Mampaey & Vreeken, 2013). Density-based clustering was introduced by Campello et al. (2015), and initializing clusters was proposed by Khandare et al. to enhance the clustering algorithm (Khandare & Alvi, 2017). Next, we have association mining. Association analysis detects attribute values that may be realized jointly by-passing minimal acceptance and reliability criteria and finds relationships or linkages between datasets. In association mining, every frequently occurring item set is identified, and then secure association rules are generated (Khandare & Alvi, 2017; Shahin et al., 2021; Telikani et al., 2020). The MBA is performed mainly using association analysis. The Apriori algorithm is primarily availed for association rules (Ceglar & Roddick, 2006). Data mining extricates uninspiring and irrelevant patterns from the data; thus, pattern evaluation plays a paramount role in segregating only the relevant information (Liou et al., 2021).

Table 1 Classification algorithms and its basic conceptualization

Algorithm nomenclature	Type of classifiers	Basic conceptualization
Naïve Bayesian classifier	Statistics based Bayesian classifier	Baye's theorem
Support vector machine	Support vector machine classifier	Linear optimal separation hyperplane
Back propagation	Neural network-based classification using back propagation	Multilayer FF ANN
K-nearest neighbor	Lazy learners machine learning based	Analogy and Euclidian distance

Table 2 Clustering algorithms and its basic conceptualization

Algorithm nomenclature	Categorization based on type of clustering	Basic conceptualization
K-means and clustering large applications	Categorized based on partitioning	Centroid
Probabilistic hierarchical clustering	Categorized based on hierarchy	Probabilistic model
Clustering in quest	Categorized based on grid	Detection of packed cells' monotonicity in regard to dimensionality
Density based clustering	Categorized based on density	Density distribution function

2.2 *Impact of COVID-19 on Business Organization*

Due to COVID-19's quick proliferation, the entire world was forced to fight not just the illness but also the severe economic effects of the response measures enacted in less than three months. Governments in virtually all nations were compelled to restrict people's mobility rights both domestically and abroad, which effectively stopped the business in its tracks (Nicola et al., 2020). Businesses are confronted with a distinct issue. Their ability to survive relies on the use of organizational techniques that will help them deal with the influx of expenses that results not solely from rent, labor, and taxes, as well as those related to the increase in the rate of building ingredients given the dramatic fall in suppliers (Wang et al., 2020). This domain of study has quickly developed in an effort to identify possible approaches and to make it easier for businesses to convert to adapt to the recent reality, assuring their sustainability under the ideal circumstances (Sjödin et al., 2020). In order to assist merchants in coping with both the interruptions brought spawned by the outbreak in the long run and short run, a study was done to compile the difficulties they confront (Kirk & Rifkin, 2020; Wang et al., 2020). Organizations should utilize the position and momentum as a chance to implement social responsibility, customer values, and a marketing strategy. This would make it possible for businesses and customers to use more enticing tactics (Fairlie & Fossen, 2022; Sun et al., 2021). Apart from this, there were many other research studies that analyzed the impact of COVID-19 on business organizations. Table 3 summarize some of the article that shows impact of COVID-19 on business organizations.

2.3 *Use of Data Mining Technique in Reducing the Impact of COVID-19*

Governments around the world and medical organizations have heavily depended on simulation skills to make critical decisions in controlling COVID-19 epidemics and

Table 3 Summary of articles on impact of COVID-19 on business organizations

Article	Objective	Important conclusion
Donthu and Gustafsson (2020)	To evaluate and analyse the impact of COVID-19 on business and research	Since the COVID-19 epidemic, people have grown more cautious and guarded Foods, technology, and medications are all being stored by nations, or plans are being made to create them natively
He and Harris (2020)	Consider the impact of the COVID-19 epidemic on the evolution of CSR, customer morals, and philosophy of marketing	Whichever the modifications, it seems quite probable that the methods advertising has traditionally functioned will need to shift in order to adapt to the brand-new reality
Pantano et al. (2020)	List the difficulties that stores are experiencing in the course of the COVID-19 situation from the viewpoints of both customers and management	Reinventing adaptive marketing, a new position for merchants in community, putting customers first, and online technology are the primary topics on which retailers must concentrate
Sheth et al. (2020)	Analyze how the COVID-19 epidemics has affected customer behavior	Present behaviors will change as a result of modern technology that makes work, education, and consuming more convenient

minimizing the financial and social repercussions on various communities, which are mostly controlled by epidemiological modelling techniques. Given the unprecedented shock caused by COVID-19, a "black swan catastrophe" is difficult to foresee (Sheng et al., 2021). Administrative managers will have the ability to anticipate the outcomes of specific people and groups by extracting inner electronic documents such as emails, conversations, and worker-generated content, along with intelligence from performance management systems and data through human resources platforms (Leonardi & Contractor, 2018). For many working professionals, working from home has been the default option since the COVID-19 epidemic. Workforce planning while promoting social connection is a serious difficulty for most firms, given the new norm of "working from home." By gathering and analyzing information on workers' requirements, living circumstances, responsibilities, and extra pressures, person analysis with descriptive and diagnostic methodologies may be utilized to stabilize present processes (Karl et al., 2022). Proceeding on to the reinstating stage, predictive analytics may assist in anticipating the mental shifts that the COVID-19 emergency would generate in personnel and subsequently aid planning for the comeback to the office (Haas et al., 2020). To create more an interactive environment with consumers during the pandemic some studies suggested creating an interactive environment using artificial intelligence and machine learning (Pantano et al., 2020). Giants like Amazon are one step ahead of their competitors in leveraging the latest data mining techniques to improvise their business models and have come up as winners during the course of COVID-19 (Shah et al., 2021). Apart from this, data mining techniques were used in other fields, like maintaining food security during COVID-19 in Indonesia. It was used to make sure that there was sufficient availability of nutritious and affordable food to sustain a happy and productive life during the course of the pandemic (Elsi et al., 2020).

After a deep analysis of the literature review, it is very evident that there is an enormous amount of literature on data mining techniques; also, there is no scarcity of research material available on the impact of COVID-19. However, there is a shortage of literature available on how the data mining techniques like MBA can be availed by retailers to improvise their business model. At the same time, this research work deep dives into a comparison of different MBA implementation techniques and provides the best option.

3 Data Mining and Knowledge Discovery Process

Various researchers have mentioned quite a few machine learning algorithms to overcome the impact of COVID-19 on different business models, but the least discussed is the data mining technique, so we choose this procedure to be discussed in detail so that they can avail its benefit to improve their revenue count. Data mining is one of the quintessential processes of discovering knowledge in a database. This process encompasses steps which involve the collection of data and eventually lead to attaining some relevant information (Dogra & Wala, 2015). It depicts the absolute approach of tracking down utilitarian learning hailing from data. It comprises the assessment and feasible elucidation of the motif to decide what qualifies to be considered as knowledge and what doesn't. KDP provides the facility of encoding schemes for preprocessing and sampling so that the data can be projected to the data mining step. The mining of data has a variety of differences as compared to KDP, as we only deal with pattern extraction in data mining, whereas KDP has many other additional steps. Figure 3 states the primary steps of KDP.

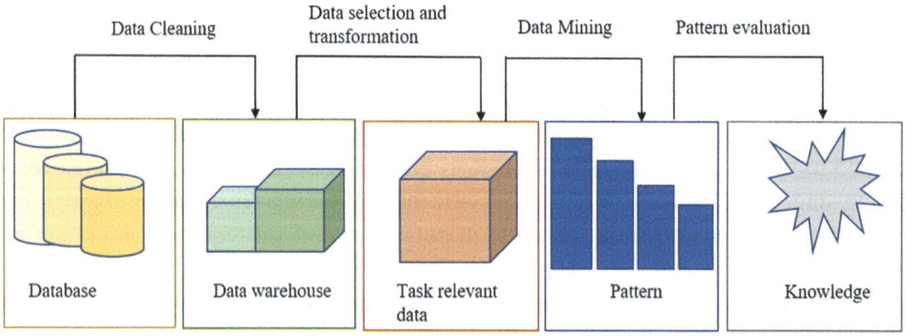

Fig. 3 Data mining in KDP process (Diwate & Sahu, 2014)

3.1 *Brief Elucidation of Each Step of KDP in the Database Process is as Follows*

i. Data Cleaning: It is the technique of abolition of boisterous and extraneous data from the complete data in order to have a finer idea of data. Data cleaning majorly contains the following steps:

   - Cleaning the values that are missing
   - Cleaning random data or the variance error, which is often referred to as noise or the noisy data
   - Cleansing is often carried out by the method, namely: data discrepancy detection and data transformation tools.

ii. Data Integration: It is the process of amalgamating heterogeneous data from diverse sources and further collecting it into a common source referred to as a data Warehouse; this is done in order to have all the relevant data in one place. Data integration is performed using the following tools and processes:

   - Tools for data migration
   - Tools for synchronization of data
   - Extract-load-transformation (ETL) process.

iii. Data Selection: It is the process where data pertaining to the exploration is spotted and fetched from the database. Data selection is performed using the following tools and techniques:

   - Neural network
   - Decision trees
   - Naive bayes
   - Clustering
   - Regression, etc.

iv. Data Transformation: It is the technique of transforming data into the pertinent form, which is a prerequisite for the procedure of mining.

v. Data Transformation is effectuated using duet steps:

   - Mapping of data: In this step, data is stipulated from the source to its destination with the aim of encapsulating transformations
   - Generation of code: In this, we write the original codes to accomplish the desired transformation.

vi. Data Mining: It is a set of erudite techniques implemented to draw out patterns which are potentially advantageous for data analysis. Data mining is performed by following these steps

   - Data is transformed into a pattern grouping the relevant data together
   - Use the techniques of classification and characterization to identify the aim of the model.

vii. Pattern Evaluation: It is the method to dig the patterns in data that delineate information. The process is carried out using the following steps:

- Look for an appealing score of every pattern
- Use visualization techniques over summarized data to make it easier to understand for the user.

viii. Knowledge representation: In this, we wisely use visualization tools to portray data mining results. It is accomplished using the following methods:

- Report generations
- Classification rules
- Table generation
- Generation of discriminate rules.

3.2 *Classification of Data Mining Techniques*

Data mining techniques are primarily classified into descriptive and predictive techniques, which are further divided into various techniques based on the process they follow. Refer to the Fig. 4 for detailed classification of data mining techniques. Descriptive mining techniques are used to find correlations, similarities and patterns in already existing data. This approach takes into consideration the models and uses the technique which distributes data based on probabilistic techniques, in this data is usually divided into models and groups based on similarity and the relations between the variables are evaluated (Han et al., 2022).

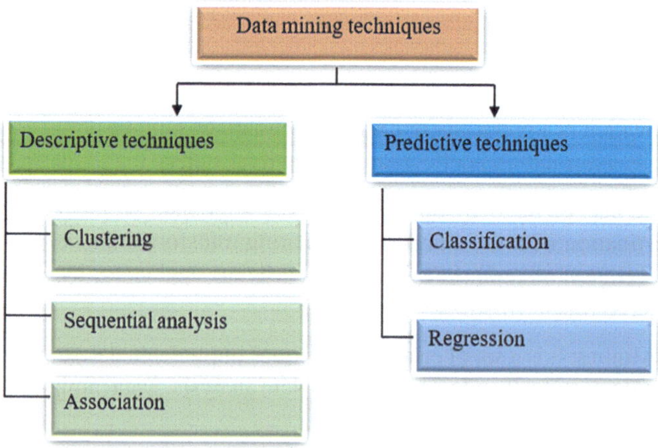

Fig. 4 Classification of data mining techniques

The main aim of the predictive approach for data mining is to predict the numbers of future from already existing data; it basically uses supervised learning algorithms to predict the target value attributes.

This paper will throw light majorly on the MBA method that falls under the association technique of descriptive mining, but before that, we can have a fair idea about the other techniques as well.

i. Predictive technique

Predictive technique profoundly talks about forecasting future results; it doesn't communicate much about the contemporary department of the data. It avails different modelling techniques to prophesy unknown variables of the future using known data from the present and past. Predictive techniques are broadly classified into two subcategories mentioned:

- Classification: These methods deal with the models that fabricate function which maps the discrete info factors to a label or category. It can have both discrete and real value variables that are arranged into at least one class. The most frequently used classification algorithms are random forest classifier, decision tree classifier, and k-nearest neighbor classifier.
- Regression: These algorithms anticipate a continuous value dependent on the information factors, which is the input variable. The fundamental objective of the regression algorithm is to gauge a mapping function based on input and output factors. It fundamentally finds the relationship between the dependent and independent variables. Here, the goal is to find the best-fit line that predicts the output variable more accurately. It is mostly used to predict weather and housing prices and for solving other business problems. It is broadly classified into two main categories linear and non-linear regression. Some of the algorithms frequently used to solve regression problems are simple linear regression, multiple linear regression, support vector machine decision tree, and random forest regression.

ii. Descriptive technique

Descriptive techniques do not predict the target value like predictive techniques, but they center more on the inborn structure, relations, and interconnectedness of the information. One of the significant applications of the descriptive technique is to identify and enthrall subgroups in a significant part of the data. It centers on the synopsis and transformation of the data into meaningful information for reporting and observing. The significant techniques under descriptive analysis are clustering, summarization, and association. A short depiction of every one of the sub-classes is as per the following:

- Clustering: It is a strategy valuable for investigating data. It comes as salvage when there is no regular grouping in the data. The aim of the clustering algorithm is to recognize acceptable quality clusters in data. A good quality cluster is one that has depressed inter-cluster similarity and intra-cluster similarity exceedingly high, which indicates the member of an identical cluster should be alike, and the member from different clusters should differ (Lee & Siau, 2001). The predominantly used methods for clustering methods are density-based clustering, fuzzy clustering, hierarchical clustering, partitioning method, and model-based clustering.

- Sequential analysis: The point of the sequential analysis technique is to discover the pattern in successive structures; it principally centers around the information that occurs in different transactions, whereas the association analysis which will be discussed further, spotlights data in the same transaction.
- Association rule mining: The aspiration of this method is to uncover the enthralling coalition and correlation relationship among the colossal size of the dataset. As the enumeration of data is proliferating every increasing day, almost every industry wants to explore the data mining technique to have a better perspective of their data. Some distinguished applications of the association rule mining technique are catalogue designing cross-marketing, planning shelf display, and loss-leader analysis. This paper will discuss a gripping example of this technique which is called MBA.

4 Market Basket Analysis: An Overview

MBA at some time is also referred to as association rule mining and is even alluded to as affinity analysis; this procedure is utilized in diverse fields such as bioinformatics, education, and nuclear science (Kaur & Kang, 2016). It fundamentally recognizes the connection of one item with another item in a single transaction and finds a pattern in customer purchasing conduct, as shown in Fig. 5. The recognizable proof of such affiliations can help retailers extend promoting methodologies by picking up an understanding of which things are, much of the time, bought by clients. It assists in increasing sales. During this difficult stretch of attack of the novel infection of COVID-19, this strategy can be utilized to expand deals as well as to keep up persistent interest and gracefully for the inventories. Utilizing this procedure, retailers can recognize the shortage of comparative items and can put a request for the things lying in the single bin at a time so that they don't confront a lack of the items and none of the things which is regularly purchased together leaves stock. The fundamental premise of MBA follows that the co-occurrence of any two or even more goods in most bundles indicates that such products are complementary in the sense that buying one will result in buying the others. Three item rules are the subject of this investigation.

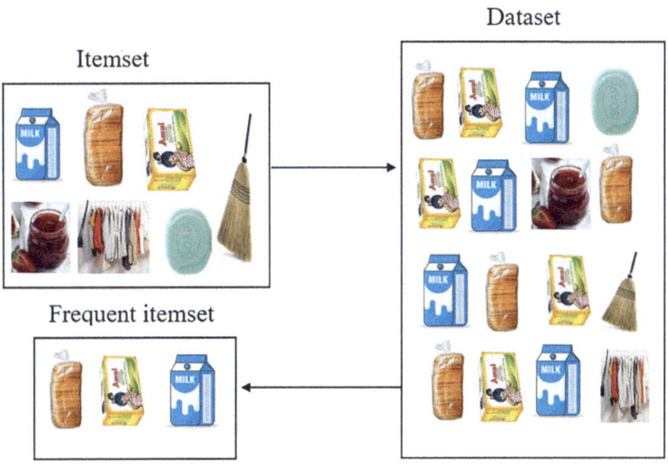

Fig. 5 Application of MBA in a departmental store

4.1 Core Concepts of MBA

To see all the significant phrasings MBA, we must comprehend the rationale or the calculation behind the process.

- Parameters used for MBA

$$T = Transaction$$

$$Itemset = Listofitems\{i_{1,}i_{2,}i_3 i_4, \ldots i_m\}$$

- Assumptions
  Consider the two transactions *Trans* 1 and *Trans* 2, such that

$$Trans\,1 \subset Itemset,\ Trans\,2 \subset Itemset,\ and\ Trans\,1 \cap Trans\,2 = \phi.$$

  Association rule is denoted by $Trans\,1 \Rightarrow Trans\,2$ and $T \subseteq Itemset$

- Key matrices of MBA
  (a) Support: It is the combined percentage of two item set i.e., if $Trans\,1 \Rightarrow Trans\,2$ clasps in a set of transactions *D* then support *s* refers to the percentage of transaction in D that contain $Trans\,1 \cup Trans\,2$, it can be calculated as:

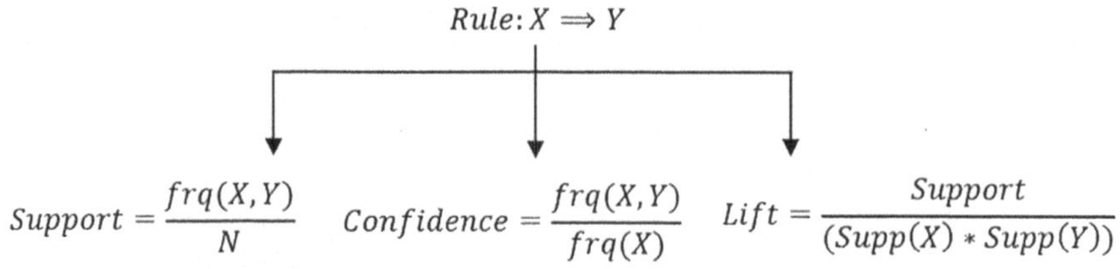

Fig. 6 Mathematical formula for key matrices of MBA

$$Support(Trans\,1 \Rightarrow Trans\,2) = Probability\{Trans\,1 \cup Trans\,2\}$$

(b) Confidence: The confidence c of the rule $Trans\,1 \Rightarrow Trans\,2$ is the ratio of transactions taken from D that accommodates $Trans\,1$ which also carries $Trans\,2$, it is calculated as:

$$Confidence(Trans\,1 \Rightarrow Trans\,2) = Probability\{Trans\,2|Trans\,1\}$$

(c) Lift: It states the relationship between two transactions irrespective of its direction.

$$Lift(Trans\,1 \Rightarrow Trans\,2) = Lift(Trans\,2 \Rightarrow Trans\,1)$$

Note: $Lift\,1 = 1$ means that there exists no association between $Trans\,1$ and $Trans\,2$. $Lift > 1$ means that there is a positive association between $Trans\,1$ and $Trans\,2$ that implies $Trans\,1$ and $Trans\,2$ happen more regularly than they happen arbitrarily. $Lift < 1$ means that there is a pessimistic association between $Trans\,1$and $Trans\,2$ that implies $Trans\,1$ and $Trans\,2$ infers they happen together less frequently than they happen haphazardly.

(d) Conviction: It is deciphered just as proportion of the anticipated frequency that Trans 1 happens without Trans 2 this implies the frequency that the rule makes a mistaken forecasting i.e., if Trans 1 and Trans 2 are freely partitioned by the detected frequency of inaccurate forecast. An illustration of all key matrices via an example is shown in Figs. 6 and 7.

4.2 Classification of MBA Based on the Varied Classes of Association Rule Mining

Based on the distinct classes of association rule mining that includes data type, dimension of data, abstraction level rules, and characteristic of association, the MBA can be performed under different classes.

Rule	Support	Confidence	Lift
$A \Rightarrow D$	2/5	2/3	10/9
$C \Rightarrow A$	2/5	2/4	5/6
$A \Rightarrow C$	2/5	2/3	5/6
$B \& C \Rightarrow D$	1/5	1/3	5/9

Fig. 7 Illustration of the calculation of vital matrices of MBA

- Established on the data type: If a rule concerns a coalition between the presence and non-attendance of things, it is named the rule of Boolean association. The other one is the rule of quantitative association, which states the relation between quantifiable attributes.
- Established on the dimension of data: There exist single and multi-dimension rules of association for the attributes that refer to just one dimension and at least two dimensions, respectively. For multi-dimension some of the examples that attributes consider of dimensions are time at which transactions are made, quantity or measurement of purchase, or the category to which customers belong.
- Established on abstraction level rules: In the event that the principles inside a given set don't reference things or properties at various degrees of deliberation, at that point, the set accommodates single-level association rules. In the event that the things purchased are referred to at various degrees of reflection, at that point, the standard set mined as comprising of multi-level rules.
- Established on the characteristics of the association: It is often elongated to correlation analysis in which the non-attendance or presence of corresponded things is usually recognized.

5 Algorithms Used to Perform MBA

There are various algorithms used to implement the MBA. Under this section, each of these techniques is highlighted with their advantages and disadvantages. The best possible technique is suggested for performing MBA.

5.1 AIS Algorithm

The working of the AIS algorithm starts with scanning of entire database manifold times. Every iteration involves scrutinizing the whole database. It decides whether things are significant or common in the collection by counting the response for each one individually in the initial run. In order to create the candidate itemset, the enormous of the large itemset from each iteration is expanded. Itemset that are identical to old and new iterations are identified. It concentrated on improvising databases availing the features required to handle decision support query processing. The primary objective of this particular algorithm is to find the qualitative rule.

- Advantage
  - It helps and aims to find any relevant association among the various department based on the purchasing pattern of consumers
- Disadvantage
  - One of the major drawbacks is the generation of lot of candidates which turns small at later stage
  - Lack of specific data structures in order to maintain

5.2 SETM Algorithm

The SETM algorithm iterates across the dataset, much like the AIS algorithm does. It takes the decision whether things are significant or common in the dataset by counting the support for each one individually in the initial run. Then, it extends a huge itemset from the last pass to create the contender itemset. The SETM also keeps track of the TIDs of the transaction that generated the contender itemset. To create a contender itemset, utilize the relational merge-join procedure.

- Advantage
  - The major advantage of SETM is that it set aside the duplicate of contender itemset in conjunction with the sequentially generated TID of generating transactions
- Disadvantage
  - The requirement of excess storage is a major drawback as for every single contender; the TID must be saved along with the other necessary information

5.3 Apriori Algorithm

This is, so far, the best algorithm available for applying association rule techniques in MBA. The detailed description of the Apriori algorithm, along with the methodology and variation, is provided in Sect. 6.

6 The Apriori Algorithm

The main job of this algorithm is to dig out the frequently occurring sets of items. Its nomenclature is derived from the concept that it utilizes earlier information on incessant thing set properties. Apriori utilizes a recursive methodology referred to as a degree-wise pursuit, which avails n-item sets to investigate (n–1) sets of items. To begin with, the arrangement of incessant 1-itemsets is found. This set is denoted as is utilized to discover, the regular 2-itemsets, which is utilized to discover, and so on, until not any more continuous k-thing sets can be found. One complete sweep of the database is required to find each. To ameliorate the effects of the degree-wise initiation of incessant item sets, a significant property referred to as the Apriori property, introduced underneath, is utilized to diminish the hunt space. Figure 8 shows the flow of work of Apriori algorithm.

6.1 Two-Step Application Methodology of Apriori Algorithm

Under this algorithm, the frequently occurring itemset generated in the previous step (L_{n-1}) is used to discover the set of a frequent occurring itemset in the current step (L_n), It's a dual-step process that has dual activities mentioned as follows: join and prune activities.

- Assumption: The Apriori algorithm operates on the premise that almost any subset of a frequent itemset must also be frequent.
- The join step: here, join the set L_{n-1} to itself ($L_{n-1} \bowtie L_{n-1}$)in order to evaluate L_n, this will create a bunch of n-item sets. Denote the arrangement of these sets with C_n. The join is denoted as, $L_{n-1} \bowtie L_{n-1} = \{A \bowtie B | A, B \epsilon L_{n-1}, |A \cap B| = n-2\}$.
- The prune step: Consider C_n, a superset of L_n. A sweep of the data collection to regulate the collection of each contender in C_n ought to ensue in the calculation of L_n. C_n, nonetheless, might be tremendous, thus this perhaps include substantial calculation. To decrease the magnitude of C_n, , the property of Apriori is utilized. A set can be a (n–1) subset of recurrent n-itemset scarcely if that n-1 item set is not persistent. Thus, if any (n–1)-subset of a nominated n-item set is not in L_{n-1}, then it can't be persistent either and so can be eradicated from C_n. Hash tree of frequent itemset is maintained for this subset testing.

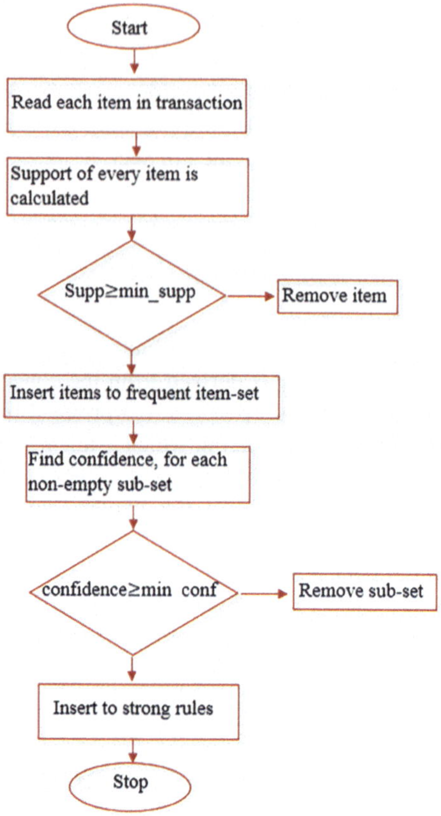

Fig. 8 Flowchart for methodology of Apriori algorithm

6.2 *Variations of Apriori Algorithms*

Numerous varieties of the Apriori calculation have been proposed. Some of these varieties are identified underneath.

- A hash-hinged approach: Hashing itemset tallies
- Scan pruning: Depleting the quantity of information base outputs
- Transaction pruning: Reducing the count of transactions that are scanned in future iterations
- Partitioning: Splitting the information to discover applicant item sets
- Sampling: Quarrying on a portion of the given information
- Dynamic itemset counting: Appending candidate itemset at contrasting extremities in the course of a scan
- Characteristic MBA: Unearthing itemset which is successive in a bunch of users characterized time spans
- Sequential patterns: Uncovering chronology of transactions related atop the long haul.

7 Application of Data Mining Techniques (Majorly MBA Under Association Rule Mining) to Reduce the Impact of COVID-19 on Various Business Models

i. MBA can be utilized by storekeepers to expand the offer of face covers and shields, hand sanitizers, careful evaluation materials, and gear, and other basic products, including goods, short-lived and durable food things by legitimate rack game plan.

ii. K-Apriori algorithm successfully produces exceptionally informative frequent itemset and association rules for the departmental Stores. Departmental stores generally utilized the MBA to deal with the position of products in their store design. Related items are put together in such a way that clients can intelligently discover things he/she may purchase, which builds consumer loyalty and consequently the benefit. Clients are sectioned, and affiliation rules are independently created to fulfil their requirements in a practical way utilizing some exceptional advancement for normal gatherings. MBA utilizing K-Apriori calculation for departmental stores improves its general income (Annie & Kumar, 2012).

iii. Data mining companies are assisting the public authority in constructing reconnaissance gadgets to contain the pandemic. The national health service is presently utilizing the administrations of giants like Microsoft, Amazon, and Palantir to follow clinical staff and assets to arrange the U.K.'s covid reaction; the U.S. Center for disease control and prevention model is taking assistance from Palantir. The companies like Alphabet, Facebook, and Amazon, along with data mining companies Clearview A.I. and tech monsters, are right now working for the white house to build up a scope of the following and reconnaissance advancements. They are working on techniques like geo-tagging of an individual based on the mobile phone. They also carry facial-identification architecture that can investigate snaps to decipher who perhaps have advanced into proximity with people who later tested positive for the virus (Tan et al., 2016).

iv. The quality and well-being unrest in different associations are simply because of the most recent data extraction methods through associated vehicle sensors, and GPS and text got from guarantee reports and conversion of call center speech conversation.

v. Information mining use in assembling encourages plan adherence, checking computerization, displaying for limit, and decrease of waste. The divisions are totally changed, and production lines become more astute by accomplishing full information straightforwardness.

vi. ABB, a colossal manufacturer, is utilizing measure mining for procurement-to-pay and production processes. ABB has benefitted a lot from data mining in attaining information about procurements, payments, and production processes. Using the mining technique at the backend, they get the direct report of all the necessary information that plots the earlier day's creation variations, throughput times, and the number of dismissals via email in the Hanau plant based out of

Germany. This was a tedious task earlier as they had multiple steps which were performed multiple times in a day, from importing relevant information to excel and rendering complex mathematical equations to dissect it. This technique has reduced manual work, thus improving the efficiency and accuracy (How data-mining companies are set to gain from the COVID-19 pandemic, 2020).

vii. The mining technique is rendered by the vehicle-producing industry as well, which is a billion-dollar industry. Using these mining techniques, they review the vehicles before they hit the market and may stop production in case any fault is identified. The items in this industry are moderately costly. For the customers and users of these vehicles and machines, early recognizable proof and preventive support regularly bring about more prominent uptime. In one of the cases from an organization, 28,000 vehicles were spared from review by the recognizable proof of an issue before vehicles hit the market.

8 Limitations of the Current Research

Some of the limitations of the current work are mentioned below. The first two limitations are based on the data mining technique implemented in the work, whereas the third limitation is regarding the practical implication based on real-time data to measure the impact of the study.

i. The Apriori algorithm has some drawbacks. It is a time taking process as it scrutinizes the database repeatedly. Each scan fabricates supplementary alternatives, thus surging the search task for the database. This leads to a scarcity of memory for supplementary data.
ii. Frequent item in the larger set length of the circumstances leads to a significant increase in computing time.
iii. The research work misses out on the implementation of the data mining technique discussed to execute MBA over real-time data in future that can be incorporated.

9 Conclusion and Future Work

In this research work, a brief elucidation of the data mining technique is presented that includes both descriptive and predictive techniques. The entire KDP is explained in detail with the steps. A special focus is laid on the impact of COVID-19 on the economy of the world. Various data mining techniques used to reduce the impact of COVID-19 are elaborated. However, there was a special focus provided to the MBA technique that falls under association rule mining to empower various business models by enriching their target and sales by increasing customer count in various ways mentioned below:

- Optimization of campaign and production
- Optimization of in-store operations
- Increasing the market share
- Analysis of customer behavior

The benefits and drawbacks of each potential MBA implementation strategy are examined. Apriori is ultimately determined to be the best method for implementing MBA currently available over AIS and SETM. A detailed flow is provided for Apriori's two-step application process. The application of this approach in real-world circumstances is briefly explained. By focusing on the bigger set length of frequent items, the computational time and memory consumption of Apriori may be decreased for future planning. The approach may subsequently be used to tackle other optimization problems, such as the solid transportation problem (Das et al., 2016; Sarma et al., 2020) and the multi-criteria decision-making problem where the need for quick rescue action in disaster-affected areas is predicted (Das et al., 2019).

References

Ames, N. (2020). Arsenal players in self-isolation as Manchester City game postponed due to coronavirus. https://www.theguardian.com/football/2020/mar/11/arsenal-self-isolation-postpone-game-manchester-city-premier-league-coronavirus-covid-19

Amankwah-Amoah, J., Khan, Z., & Osabutey, E. L. (2021). COVID-19 and business renewal: Lessons and insights from the global airline industry. *International Business Review, 30*(3), 101802.

Annie, L. C. M., & Kumar, A. D. (2012). Market basket analysis for a supermarket based on frequent itemset mining. *International Journal of Computer Science Issues (IJCSI), 9*(5), 257.

Aschburner, S. (2020). Coronavirus pandemic cause NBA to suspend season after player tests positive. https://www.nba.com/news/coronavirus-pandemic-causes-nba-suspend-season

Barua, S. (2020). *Understanding Coronanomics: The economic implications of the coronavirus (COVID-19) pandemic*. Available at SSRN 3566477.

Brownlee, J., Cristina, S. & Saeed, M. (2022). *Calculus for machine learning*. Machine Learning Mastery.

Ceglar, A. & Roddick, J.F. (2006). Association mining. *ACM Computing Surveys (CSUR), 38*(2), 5-es.

Chen, M. S., Han, J., & Yu, P. S. (1996). Data mining: An overview from a database perspective. *IEEE Transactions on Knowledge and Data Engineering, 8*(6), 866–883.

Campello, R. J., Moulavi, D., Zimek, A., & Sander, J. (2015). Hierarchical density estimates for data clustering, visualization, and outlier detection. *ACM Transactions on Knowledge Discovery from Data (TKDD), 10*(1), 1–51.

Craw, S., Wiratunga, N., & Rowe, R. C. (2006). Learning adaptation knowledge to improve case-based reasoning. *Artificial Intelligence, 170*(16–17), 1175–1192.

Das, A., Bera, U. K., & Maiti, M. (2016). A profit maximizing solid transportation model under a rough interval approach. *IEEE Transactions on Fuzzy Systems, 25*(3), 485–498.

Das, A., Bera, U. K., & Maiti, M. (2019). A solid transportation problem in uncertain environment involving type-2 fuzzy variable. *Neural Computing and Applications, 31*(9), 4903–4927.

Dev, S.M. & Sengupta, R. (2020). Covid-19: Impact on the Indian economy. *Indira Gandhi Institute of Development Research, Mumbai April.*

Diwate, R.B. & Sahu, A. (2014). Data mining techniques in association rule: A review. *International Journal of Computer Science and Information technology*, 227–229.

Donthu, N., & Gustafsson, A. (2020). Effects of COVID-19 on business and research. *Journal of Business Research, 117*, 284–289.

Dogra, A. K., & Wala, T. (2015). A review paper on data mining techniques and algorithms. *International Journal of Advanced Research in Computer Engineering & Technology (IJARCET), 4*(5), 1976–1979.

De Haas, M., Faber, R., & Hamersma, M. (2020). How COVID-19 and the Dutch 'intelligent lockdown 'change activities, work and travel behaviour: Evidence from longitudinal data in the Netherlands. *Transportation Research Interdisciplinary Perspectives, 6*, 100150.

Elsi, Z.R.S., Pratiwi, H., Efendi, Y., Rusdina, R., Alfah, R., Windarto, A.P. & Wiza, F. (2020). Utilization of data mining techniques in national food security during the Covid-19 pandemic in Indonesia. In *Journal of Physics: Conference Series* (Vol. 1594, No. 1, p. 012007). IOP Publishing.

Erken, Hugo. (2020). India: COVID-19 impact revisited https://economics.rabobank.com/publications/2020/april/india-covid-19-impact-revisited/

Estimated impact from the coronavirus (COVID-19) on the industry sector in India from April to December 2020, by type. (2020). https://www.statista.com/statistics/1229773/india-estimated-economic-impact-of-coronavirus-on-industry/

Ezugwu, A. E., Ikotun, A. M., Oyelade, O. O., Abualigah, L., Agushaka, J. O., Eke, C. I., & Akinyelu, A. A. (2022). A comprehensive survey of clustering algorithms: State-of-the-art machine learning applications, taxonomy, challenges, and future research prospects. *Engineering Applications of Artificial Intelligence, 110*, 104743.

Fang, J., Collins, A., & Yao, S. (2021). On the global COVID-19 pandemic and China's FDI. *Journal of Asian Economics, 74*, 101300.

Fan, C. Y., Fan, P. S., Chan, T. Y., & Chang, S. H. (2012). Using hybrid data mining and machine learning clustering analysis to predict the turnover rate for technology professionals. *Expert Systems with Applications, 39*(10), 8844–8851.

Fairlie, R., & Fossen, F. M. (2022). The early impacts of the COVID-19 pandemic on business sales. *Small Business Economics, 58*(4), 1853–1864.

Gheware, S.D., Kejkar, A.S. & Tondare, S.M. (2014). Data mining: Task, tools, techniques and applications. *International Journal of Advanced Research in Computer and Communication Engineering, 3*(10).

Gupta, V., Santosh, K. C., Arora, R., Ciano, T., Kalid, K. S., & Mohan, S. (2022). Socioeconomic impact due to COVID-19: An empirical assessment. *Information Processing & Management, 59*(2), 102810.

Hariri, R. H., Fredericks, E. M., & Bowers, K. M. (2019). Uncertainty in big data analytics: Survey, opportunities, and challenges. *Journal of Big Data, 6*(1), 1–16.

Han, J., Kamber, M. & Mining, D. (2006). Concepts and techniques. *Morgan Kaufmann, 340*, 94104-3205.

Han, J., Pei, J. & Tong, H. (2022). *Data mining: concepts and techniques*. Morgan kaufmann.

He, H., & Harris, L. (2020). The impact of Covid-19 pandemic on corporate social responsibility and marketing philosophy. *Journal of Business Research, 116*, 176–182.

How data-mining companies are set to gain from the COVID-19 pandemic. (2020). https://www.opendemocracy.net/en/can-europe-make-it/how-data-mining-companies-are-set-gain-covid-19-pandemic/

Jalal, A.A. & Ali, B.H. (2021). Text documents clustering using data mining techniques. *International Journal of Electrical & Computer Engineering (2088–8708), 11*(1).

Jia, Z., Wen, S., & Lin, B. (2021). The effects and reacts of COVID-19 pandemic and international oil price on energy, economy, and environment in China. *Applied Energy, 302*, 117612.

Kaur, M., & Kang, S. (2016). Market basket analysis: Identify the changing trends of market data using association rule mining. *Procedia Computer Science, 85*, 78–85.

Karl, K. A., Peluchette, J. V., & Aghakhani, N. (2022). Virtual work meetings during the COVID-19 pandemic: The good, bad, and ugly. *Small Group Research, 53*(3), 343–365.

Kirk, C. P., & Rifkin, L. S. (2020). I'll trade you diamonds for toilet paper: Consumer reacting, coping and adapting behaviors in the COVID-19 pandemic. *Journal of Business Research, 117*, 124–131.

Khandelwal, A., Agrawal, A., & Kumar, A. (2020). An outbreak of coronavirus (COVID-19) epidemic in India: Challenges and preventions. *J Infect Dis Ther, 8*(421), 2.

Khandare, A., & Alvi, A. S. (2017). Performance analysis of improved clustering algorithm on real and synthetic data. *International Journal of Computer Network and Information Security, 10*(10), 57.

Kotsiantis, S. B., Zaharakis, I., & Pintelas, P. (2007). Supervised machine learning: A review of classification techniques. *Emerging Artificial Intelligence Applications in Computer Engineering, 160*(1), 3–24.

Kumar, S. & Nafi, S.M. (2020). *Impact of COVID-19 pandemic on tourism: Perceptions from Bangladesh.* Available at SSRN 3632798

Leung, C.K. (2022). Big data analytics and mining for knowledge discovery. In *Research anthology on big data analytics, architectures, and applications* (pp. 708–721). IGI Global.

Lee, S.J. & Siau, K. (2001). A review of data mining techniques. *Industrial Management & Data Systems.*

Liou, J. J., Chang, M. H., Lo, H. W., & Hsu, M. H. (2021). Application of an MCDM model with data mining techniques for green supplier evaluation and selection. *Applied Soft Computing, 109*, 107534.

Leonardi, P., & Contractor, N. (2018). Better people analytics. *Harvard Business Review, 96*(6), 70–81.

Mampaey, M., & Vreeken, J. (2013). Summarizing categorical data by clustering attributes. *Data Mining and Knowledge Discovery, 26*(1), 130–173.

Mosa, M., Agami, N., Elkhayat, G. & Kholief, M. (2022). A novel hybrid segmentation approach for decision support: A case study in banking. *The Computer Journal.*

Nicola, M., Alsafi, Z., Sohrabi, C., Kerwan, A., Al-Jabir, A., Iosifidis, C., Agha, M., & Agha, R. (2020). The socio-economic implications of the coronavirus pandemic (COVID-19): A review. *International Journal of Surgery, 78*, 185–193.

Nhamo, G., Dube, K. & Chikodzi, D. (2020). Implications of COVID-19 on gaming, leisure and entertainment industry. In *Counting the cost of COVID-19 on the global tourism industry* (pp. 273–295). Springer, Cham.

Ntounis, N., Parker, C., Skinner, H., Steadman, C., & Warnaby, G. (2022). Tourism and hospitality industry resilience during the Covid-19 pandemic: Evidence from England. *Current Issues in Tourism, 25*(1), 46–59.

Pantano, E., Pizzi, G., Scarpi, D., & Dennis, C. (2020). Competing during a pandemic? Retailers' ups and downs during the COVID-19 outbreak. *Journal of Business Research, 116*, 209–213.

Patwary, A.H., Eshan, M.T., Debnath, P. and Sattar, A., 2021, July. Market Basket Analysis Approach to Machine Learning. In *2021 12th International Conference on Computing Communication and Networking Technologies (ICCCNT)* (pp. 1–9). IEEE.

Ramakumar, R. (2020). Agriculture and the Covid-19 pandemic: An analysis with special reference to India. *Review of Agrarian Studies, 10*(2369–2020–1856).

Sen, P.C., Hajra, M. & Ghosh, M. (2020). Supervised classification algorithms in machine learning: A survey and review. In *Emerging technology in modelling and graphics* (pp. 99–111). Springer, Singapore.

Shahin, M., Arakkal Peious, S., Sharma, R., Kaushik, M., Ben Yahia, S., Shah, S.A. & Draheim, D., 2021, January. Big data analytics in association rule mining: A systematic literature review. In *2021 the 3rd International Conference on Big Data Engineering and Technology (BDET)* (pp. 40–49).

Sheth, J. (2020). Impact of Covid-19 on consumer behavior: Will the old habits return or die? *Journal of Business Research, 117*, 280–283.

Sheng, J., Amankwah-Amoah, J., Khan, Z., & Wang, X. (2021). COVID-19 pandemic in the new era of big data analytics: Methodological innovations and future research directions. *British Journal of Management, 32*(4), 1164–1183.

Shah, B.K., Jaiswal, A.K., Shroff, A., Dixit, A.K., Kushwaha, O.N. & Shah, N.K. (2021). Sentiments detection for amazon product review. In *2021 International Conference on Computer Communication and Informatics (ICCCI)* (pp. 1–6). IEEE.

Sarma, D., Das, A., & Bera, U. K. (2020). Uncertain demand estimation with optimization of time and cost using Facebook disaster map in emergency relief operation. *Applied Soft Computing, 87*, 105992.

Sjödin, D., Parida, V., Kohtamäki, M., & Wincent, J. (2020). An agile co-creation process for digital servitization: A micro-service innovation approach. *Journal of Business Research, 112*, 478–491.

Sun, T., Zhang, W.W., Dinca, M.S. & Raza, M. (2021). Determining the impact of Covid-19 on the business norms and performance of SMEs in China. *Economic Research-Ekonomska Istraživanja*, 1–20.

Tan, P.N., Steinbach, M., & Kumar, V. (2016). *Introduction to data mining*. Pearson Education India.

Telikani, A., Gandomi, A. H., & Shahbahrami, A. (2020). A survey of evolutionary computation for association rule mining. *Information Sciences, 524*, 318–352.

Ünvan, Y. A. (2021). Market basket analysis with association rules. *Communications in Statistics-Theory and Methods, 50*(7), 1615–1628.

Vitenu-Sackey, P. A., & Barfi, R. (2021). The impact of Covid-19 pandemic on the global economy: Emphasis on poverty alleviation and economic growth. *The Economics and Finance Letters, 8*(1), 32–43.

Wang, Y., Hong, A., Li, X., & Gao, J. (2020). Marketing innovations during a global crisis: A study of China firms' response to COVID-19. *Journal of Business Research, 116*, 214–220.

Weir, J. (2021). Data mining: exploring the corporate asset. In *Data Management* (pp. 795–802). Auerbach Publications.

WHO Director-General's opening remarks at the media briefing on COVID-19 - 11 March 2020. (2020). https://www.who.int/director-general/speeches/detail/who-director-general-s-opening-remarks-at-the-media-briefing-on-covid-19---11-march-2020

Yasharoff, H., & Woodyward, C. (2020). Disneyland, Universal Studios Hollywood will temporarily close due to coronavirus. https://www.usatoday.com/story/travel/destinations/2020/03/12/coronavirus-disney-announces-closure/5030549002/

Optimizing Ecological Development Zone Selection: A Comparative Analysis of AHP and DEA-Modified VAHP Approaches in Geography

Mehdi Soltanifar and Saeid Kamyabi

Abstract This chapter delves into the practical application of decision science in geography, specifically focusing on the utilization of the Analytical Hierarchy Process (AHP) methodology. Acknowledging the limitations inherent in the conventional AHP method, a novel approach called Voting Analytical Hierarchy Process (VAHP) is proposed, which seamlessly integrates the principles of Data Envelopment Analysis (DEA). Emphasizing the significance of selecting appropriate ecological development zones, the chapter navigates through the challenges that arise in decision-making within this field. Additionally, the advantages and disadvantages of AHP and DEA are discussed, underscoring their respective roles in multi-criteria decision-making and performance evaluation. The VAHP approach emerges as a potent decision support tool, as it actively engages experts in the prioritization process, mitigating judgmental inconsistencies. Furthermore, the chapter presents a comprehensive comparative analysis of AHP and VAHP, executed through a case study within the realm of geography, thus providing valuable insights into their efficacy and reliability. The outcomes of this research contribute significantly to the advancement of decision science in geography and yield practical implications for promoting sustainable ecological development. As the chapter concludes, it offers insightful recommendations for researchers intending to employ AHP, DEA, and VAHP in analogous decision-making contexts. Overall, this chapter serves as a valuable resource, equipping both academics and practitioners in the field of geography with a comprehensive understanding of the application of AHP, DEA, and VAHP.

Keywords Analytical Hierarchy Process (AHP) · Data Envelopment Analysis (DEA) · Voting Analytical Hierarchy Process (VAHP) · Saffron cultivation · Zone selection

---

M. Soltanifar (✉)
Department of Mathematics, Semnan Branch, Islamic Azad University, Semnan, Iran
e-mail: soltanifar@khayam.ut.ac.ir

S. Kamyabi
Department of Geography, Semnan Branch, Islamic Azad University, Semnan, Iran
e-mail: S.Kamyabi@semnaniau.ac.ir

© The Author(s), under exclusive license to Springer Nature Singapore Pte Ltd. 2024

S. A. Edalatpanah et al. (eds.), *Analytical Decision Making and Data Envelopment Analysis*, Infosys Science Foundation Series in Mathematical Sciences,
https://doi.org/10.1007/978-981-97-6972-8_15

1 Introduction

The selection of suitable ecological development zones is a crucial task in geography, which requires a systematic and objective decision-making approach. In this chapter, we aim to present an application of decision science in the field of geography by investigating a case study and extracting valuable insights using the Analytical Hierarchy Process (AHP) methodology. Additionally, we propose a modified approach, namely Voting Analytical Hierarchy Process (VAHP), which integrates the principles of Data Envelopment Analysis (DEA) to address the limitations of the conventional AHP method, particularly in terms of expert judgment inconsistency (Natarajan et al., 2022; Thakkar, 2021; Lukinskiy and Lukinskiy, 2018; Zekhnini et al., 2021; Yi et al., 2020). The AHP is a widely adopted decision-making tool that enables the systematic analysis and prioritization of multiple criteria. It allows decision-makers to decompose complex problems into a hierarchical structure and facilitates pairwise comparisons to determine the relative importance of criteria and alternatives. While AHP offers several advantages, such as its ability to handle subjective judgments, it also has certain limitations, particularly in its interaction with experts (Amenta et al., 2020a, 2020b). One of the primary drawbacks of the AHP method is its vulnerability to inconsistency in expert judgments. As the number of criteria or alternatives increases, the likelihood of inconsistency in pairwise comparison matrices also grows, making it challenging to obtain reliable and consistent results. This inconsistency undermines the confidence and credibility of the decision-making process. To address this issue, various efforts have been made to reduce the number of judgments and increase the motivation of experts to engage in the decision-making process (Abastante et al. (2019). Some notable approaches that aim to mitigate the drawbacks of AHP include the BWM-AHP (Best Worst Method-Analytical Hierarchy Process) and AHP-express methods (Leal, 2020; Tavana et al., 2021). These approaches introduce the concept of best and worst alternatives or criteria, significantly reducing the number of pairwise comparisons required. By incorporating the notion of best and worst into the comparisons, these methods alleviate the burden on experts and enhance the reliability of the results. Overall, while AHP is a valuable method for multi-criteria decision-making, its limitations related to expert interaction and judgment inconsistency have prompted the development of alternative approaches. By considering these drawbacks and exploring innovative variations of AHP, researchers have strived to improve the reliability and effectiveness of the decision-making process in various fields, including geography.

DEA is a powerful non-parametric technique used for evaluating the relative efficiency of decision-making units. It has numerous advantages that make it a valuable tool in various domains. By drawing upon available scientific resources, we can highlight the benefits of DEA (Emrouznejad & Yang, 2018). First and foremost, DEA provides a comprehensive and flexible framework for performance evaluation. It allows for the assessment of multiple inputs and outputs simultaneously, enabling a holistic evaluation of decision-making units. This capability makes DEA well-suited for complex decision environments (Hosseinzadeh Lotfi et al., 2023). Furthermore,

DEA offers advantages such as its ability to handle multiple performance measures, accommodate different scales of measurement, and handle both quantitative and qualitative data. These features enhance the versatility and applicability of DEA in various contexts (Mardani et al., 2017). In addition to its application in performance evaluation, DEA has been widely utilized in resource allocation (Vretta et al., 2023), mergers and acquisitions (Chang et al., 2023), input and output estimation (Younesi et al., 2023), and other decision-making processes. DEA serves as a valuable tool for improving existing Multiple Attribute Decision-Making (MADM) methods and developing novel hybrid approaches. By integrating DEA into MADM, we can enhance the accuracy, robustness, and effectiveness of decision-making processes (Krmac & Mansouri Kaleibar, 2022). It is important, however, to acknowledge that DEA also presents certain challenges. These include the selection of appropriate inputs and outputs, the treatment of outliers and noise in the data, and the interpretation of efficiency scores. Researchers have devoted significant efforts to address these challenges and refine the DEA methodology, resulting in various extensions and enhancements. Overall, DEA offers a comprehensive approach to evaluating the relative efficiency of decision-making units and has the potential to improve existing MADM methods. By leveraging the strengths of DEA and addressing its limitations, researchers can continue to advance the field of decision-making and contribute to the development of innovative hybrid approaches in the future (Prevolšek et al., 2023).

To address the limitations of the conventional AHP method, the VAHP was developed by researchers, incorporating the DEA model within the AHP framework (Liu & Hai, 2005).

The VAHP approach offers numerous advantages that warrant its consideration. Firstly, it diverges from the traditional pairwise comparison matrices and instead involves experts in the prioritization of criteria and alternatives relative to each criterion. This approach significantly enhances the engagement and motivation of experts in the decision-making process. Secondly, the VAHP method does not rely on the calculation of inconsistency rates, as it inherently avoids judgment inconsistencies. This further reinforces the robustness and reliability of the approach. Consequently, VAHP serves as a more powerful tool for decision support compared to AHP (Soltanifar & Hosseinzadeh Lotfi, 2011). By combining the expertise of decision-makers with the quantitative efficiency measures derived from DEA, the VAHP approach provides a systematic and comprehensive evaluation. It enables a more objective and informed decision-making process, reducing the subjectivity associated with traditional AHP (Hadi-Vencheh & Niazi-Motlagh, 2011). In summary, the VAHP method, which integrates the DEA model into the AHP framework, overcomes the limitations of conventional AHP. Its unique characteristics, including the involvement of experts and the avoidance of judgment inconsistencies, make it a powerful tool for decision support. In our specific case study within the field of geography, we aim to apply the VAHP approach to obtain more reliable and insightful results (Pishchulov et al., 2019).

The use of optimization models in geography is crucial for addressing challenges in ecologically fragile regions, especially in rural areas facing underdeveloped social economies and poor natural conditions (Yin et al., 2023). Existing studies on rural settlement optimization have predominantly focused on regional ecological protection, neglecting the essential social-economic dimensions and their interaction with ecological factors. To bridge this gap, Yin et al. propose an analytical framework, the Voting Analytical Hierarchy Process (VAHP), which integrates Data Envelopment Analysis (DEA) principles, enabling spatial optimization of rural settlements from a social-ecological perspective. Through a case study in Kaitong Town, China, the authors assess the development capacity and ecosystem resilience in different villages, dividing the area into zones with distinct optimization directions. The VAHP approach provides a scientific basis for the layout of rural settlements in ecologically fragile regions and contributes to realizing sustainable development (Yin et al., 2023). Additionally, Fan et al. (2023) introduce an ecological network optimization strategy for urban-rural fringe regions. While the urban-rural fringe serves as a frontier zone for urban expansion and ecological improvement, few studies have addressed ecological network construction and optimization in this context. Utilizing the morphological spatial pattern analysis (MSPA) and minimum cumulative resistance model (MCR), the authors initially construct the ecological network and identify ecological security patterns in the study area. By proposing a new optimization strategy, they enhance the connectivity and accessibility of the ecological network, promoting overall ecological processes and achieving a balance between urban development and ecological protection (Fan et al., 2023). In a related study, Li et al. (2023) address the issue of ecological pollution in regions facing multi-source ecological risks. They propose an innovative method for constructing and optimizing the landscape pattern, using the Luojiang-Small Creek watershed as a case study. The authors assess the landscape ecological risk through a comprehensive evaluation of multiple factors and subsequently optimize the landscape pattern to improve watershed ecosystem services. The results provide valuable references for biodiversity conservation, green infrastructure planning, and sustainable development, contributing to ecological protection and planning in the study area (Li et al., 2023). The research conducted by Chuma et al. (2023) focuses on sustainable land resource management in rural areas. Through the assessment of land use suitability in the Itombwe Natural Reserve (RNI), they offer a decision-making framework for agroforestry, considering specific environmental and socio-economic factors. The study identifies different agroforestry suitability zones and provides a valuable resource for decision-makers in preserving the RNI from degradation related to inadequate anthropogenic practices (Chuma et al., 2023). In this book chapter, we present a comparative analysis of the AHP and VAHP approaches for ecological development zone selection in geography. By examining a case study and utilizing these decision-making methods, we aim to enhance the understanding of the strengths and weaknesses of each approach and identify the most suitable method for practical applications. The innovative integration of DEA into the AHP framework in the VAHP approach further enhances the decision-making process and addresses the limitations of the traditional AHP method. Overall, this research contributes to the advancement of decision science in geography and offers valuable insights for sustainable ecological development.

The remainder of the chapter is organized as follows: Section 2 presents a comprehensive literature review, which is divided into three subsections. The first subsection discusses the relevant literature on AHP, highlighting its applications and advancements. The second subsection explores the literature related to DEA and its role in enhancing MADM methods. The third subsection focuses on the VAHP and its integration with DEA, emphasizing the advantages and novel contributions of this hybrid approach. In Sect. 3, we delve into the practical application of these methods in the field of geography, elucidating the specific problem under study and its geographical context. We discuss the methodology and procedures employed to implement AHP and VAHP on the selected case study, providing insights into the decision-making process and the interpretation of results. The findings and comparative analysis of the application of AHP and VAHP on the case study are presented in Sect. 4. We examine the outcomes, discuss the similarities and differences, and evaluate the effectiveness and robustness of these methods in addressing the research problem. Furthermore, we highlight any noteworthy observations and implications derived from the comparison. Section 5 delves deeper into the discussions and managerial insights generated by the study. We analyze the implications of the findings, explore potential challenges and limitations, and suggest future research directions. This section provides a comprehensive understanding of the practical implications and strategic considerations associated with the use of AHP, DEA, and VAHP in the field of geography. Finally, Sect. 6 concludes the chapter by summarizing the main findings, emphasizing their significance, and offering concluding remarks. We also provide recommendations for practitioners and researchers interested in employing AHP, DEA, and VAHP in similar decision-making contexts. Overall, this chapter aims to contribute to the existing body of knowledge in the field of decision-making in geography, and to provide valuable insights for both academic and practical applications.

2 Literature Review

In this section of the chapter, we will briefly discuss the relevant literature, algorithms, and fundamental models required for the topic at hand.

2.1 AHP

AHP is a decision-making method that allows decision-makers to prioritize alternatives based on a hierarchical structure of criteria and sub-criteria. The algorithm for implementing AHP consists of the following steps (Saaty, 1980, 2006):

- Create a hierarchical structure: Initially, the decision problem is decomposed into a hierarchy of criteria, sub-criteria, and alternatives. This hierarchical structure helps organize the decision-making process and facilitates the analysis of complex problems.

- Form pairwise comparison matrices: Experts compare the elements within each level of the hierarchy in pairs. These comparisons are used to construct pairwise comparison matrices, where the elements' relative importance or preference is captured. The comparisons are typically done using a 9-point scale, allowing experts to express their judgments.
- Calculate the inconsistency rate: The pairwise comparison matrices are checked for consistency, as experts' judgments may introduce inconsistencies. Various methods can be employed to calculate the inconsistency rate, such as computing the consistency vector and the largest Eigenvalue of the pairwise comparison matrix. If the inconsistency ratio exceeds a certain threshold (e.g., 0.1), the judgments may need to be reviewed for potential revisions.
- Determine local priorities: Local priorities are calculated for each criterion and alternative relative to each criterion. Different weighting methods, such as the sum of rows, columns, arithmetic mean, geometric mean, eigenvector, ordinary least squares, and logarithmic least squares, can be used to assign weights to the elements.
- Calculate overall priorities: The overall priority of each alternative is obtained by summing the product of the local priority of the alternative and its corresponding weighted criterion. This step combines the local priorities to determine the relative importance of each alternative.
- Rank the alternatives: The alternatives are ranked based on their overall priorities. A higher overall priority indicates a better ranking position.

The strengths of the AHP method include:

(a) Structured approach: AHP provides a structured framework for decision-making by organizing the problem into a hierarchical structure. This helps decision-makers clarify their goals and systematically analyze the decision factors.
(b) Incorporation of subjective judgments: AHP allows decision-makers to incorporate their subjective feelings and judgments into the decision-making process. The use of pairwise comparisons helps capture and quantify these subjective preferences.
(c) Flexibility: AHP can accommodate a wide range of decision problems and criteria, making it applicable in various domains. It provides a versatile methodology that can be adapted to different decision contexts.

However, AHP also has some limitations:

(a) Expert dependency: AHP heavily relies on expert judgments, which can introduce biases and subjectivity. The accuracy and consistency of the pairwise comparisons depend on the expertise and experience of the decision-makers.
(b) Time and resource-intensive: Implementing AHP can be time-consuming, especially when dealing with complex decision problems or a large number of elements. Collecting and analyzing pairwise comparison data from multiple experts can require significant resources.

(c) Sensitivity to changes in the hierarchical structure: AHP requires the evaluation process to be repeated whenever there is a change in the hierarchical structure. Modifying the criteria or their relationships can impact the overall results, requiring additional effort and potential revisions.

A key weakness of the AHP method is its reliance on expert judgments, which can introduce biases and subjectivity into the decision-making process. This expert dependency becomes particularly critical when the desired level of consistency for pairwise comparison matrices or the hierarchical structure is not met. When experts encounter difficulties in making consistent judgments, it can lead to a decrease in their motivation to engage actively in the decision-making process and, ultimately, a decline in the accuracy and reliability of the results. The accuracy of the pairwise comparisons heavily relies on the expertise and experience of the decision-makers. If the experts have limited knowledge or insufficient understanding of the problem domain, it can negatively impact the quality of the judgments. Furthermore, even when experts are knowledgeable, inconsistencies may arise due to different interpretations, personal biases, or a lack of clear criteria for comparison. Inconsistencies in the pairwise comparison matrices can arise when the experts' judgments do not adhere to the principles of reciprocity and homogeneity. If the judgments are inconsistent, it may require the experts to revisit and revise their judgments, leading to additional effort and potential delays in the decision-making process. Similarly, changes in the hierarchical structure can also introduce challenges. Modifying the criteria or their relationships can affect the overall results and require experts to re-evaluate their judgments. This process of revising the hierarchical structure may lead to frustration and a loss of motivation for the experts, potentially compromising the accuracy and reliability of the decision outcomes. To mitigate the impact of expert dependency, it is crucial to ensure clear communication, provide adequate training, and foster a collaborative environment that encourages open discussions and the exchange of ideas among the experts. Furthermore, employing sensitivity analysis techniques can help assess the robustness of the results and identify the influence of varying expert judgments on the final outcomes. Overall, while AHP offers a structured approach and incorporates subjective judgments, it is essential to acknowledge and address the potential weaknesses associated with expert dependency. By understanding these limitations and implementing strategies to mitigate them, decision-makers can enhance the accuracy, objectivity, and reliability of the AHP method (Amenta et al., 2020a, 2020b; Tavana et al., 2021).

2.2 DEA

In this section, we provide an overview of DEA and its significance in decision-making processes. We delve into the theoretical foundations of DEA as a non-parametric approach for assessing the performance of decision-making units. Moreover, we explore the various models and methodologies employed in DEA, emphasizing their respective strengths and limitations. Notably, we highlight the noteworthy feature of the optimistic weight assignment policy in DEA. To introduce the foundational models in DEA, two approaches are commonly adopted. The first approach revolves around the concept of the Production Possibility Set (PPS), which encompasses fundamental principles governing its construction. This approach leads to the formulation of a non-parametric linear programming model known as the envelopment form of DEA. The acceptance or rejection of different principles in constructing the PPS gives rise to various types of envelopment models. The second approach involves the utilization of the concept of relative efficiency, leading us to the multiplicative form of DEA models. Importantly, the multiplicative form serves as the dual counterpart of the envelopment form. In this subsection, we exemplify the Constant Returns to Scale (CRS) multiplicative model to illustrate the concepts. The CRS model assumes a homogeneous set of decision-making units (DMUs) wherein each unit produces m outputs ($y_{1p}, y_{2p}, \ldots, y_{mp}$) while consuming s inputs ($x_{1p}, x_{2p}, \ldots, x_{sp}$) across n units ($p = 1, 2, \ldots, n$). We refer to the evaluation model for DMUp as model (1), which effectively captures the primary policy of DEA.

$$
\begin{aligned}
& Max \sum_{r=1}^{s} u_r y_{rp} \\
& s.t. \sum_{i=1}^{m} v_i x_{ip} = 1 \\
& \sum_{r=1}^{s} u_r y_{rj} - \sum_{i=1}^{m} v_i x_{ij} \leq 0, \ j = 1, \ldots, n \\
& u_i \geq 0, \ i = 1, \ldots, m \\
& v_r \geq 0, \ r = 1, \ldots, s
\end{aligned}
\tag{1}
$$

Through a comprehensive analysis of the literature, we aim to gain valuable insights into the practical application of DEA in MADM and explore potential synergies with other methods. By understanding the theoretical foundations and various DEA models, decision-makers can leverage this powerful technique to evaluate and benchmark the performance of DMUs in an objective and data-driven manner.

2.3 VAHP

Methods resulting from the combination of AHP and DEA are highly diverse and demonstrate significant effectiveness. Extensive research has been conducted to leverage the strengths of each method to address certain weaknesses of the other method (Tavana et al., 2023). In this section, we present VAHP, which is an intelligent combination of AHP and DEA models. By considering model (1), where all DMUs have a single input with a value of 1 and the output weights satisfy specific weight constraints, the model becomes suitable for evaluating the decision-making process among n candidates (model (2)). In this model, discrimination intensity functions ($d(.,\varepsilon)$) are obtained for the weight constraints after interacting with experts, allowing differentiation between the weight of each position and weights worse than itself. This model replaces pairwise comparisons in the AHP method, simplifying the interaction with experts and increasing their motivation. Additionally, the calculation of inconsistency ratios is no longer needed, as experts directly influence the prioritization of criteria, the prioritization of each option within a criterion, and the determination of discrimination intensity functions, which have a straightforward impact on the final results. As a result, VAHP becomes a more powerful tool for decision support, enhancing accuracy and improving expert interaction (Soltanifar & Hosseinzadeh Lotfi, 2011).

$$
\begin{aligned}
& Max \sum_{r=1}^{s} u_r y_{rp} \\
& s.t. \sum_{r=1}^{s} u_r y_{rj} \leq 1, j = 1, \ldots, n \\
& \quad u_r - u_{r+1} \geq d(r, \varepsilon), \quad r = 1, 2, \ldots, s-1 \\
& \quad u_s \geq d(s, \varepsilon)
\end{aligned}
$$

Using the VAHP method instead of AHP in real-world problems can make the group decision-making process more appealing due to its simpler interaction with experts, resulting in more desirable outcomes. VAHP eliminates the need for pairwise comparisons and instead incorporates experts' opinions directly into the prioritization of criteria, options within each criterion, and the determination of discrimination intensity functions. This streamlined interaction enhances the attractiveness of the decision-making process and ensures the desirability of the final results.

3 Practical Application in Geography

Saffron, known as a strategic product, has specific climatic requirements for successful cultivation. In the context of Khorasan Razavi Province in Iran, which is renowned for saffron production, identifying the favorable climatic conditions and determining the influential factors for cultivating this valuable crop is crucial. Khorasan Razavi Province, located in northeastern Iran, possesses favorable agro-climatic conditions for saffron cultivation. The region experiences a dry and continental climate, characterized by hot summers and cold winters. The optimal temperature range for saffron cultivation lies between 15 and 25 °C during the growing season. Moreover, the province benefits from a distinct diurnal temperature variation, which is essential for saffron production. Another vital climatic factor is rainfall. Saffron cultivation requires a specific pattern of rainfall distribution throughout the year. The ideal conditions entail a dry period during the growing season, with the majority of rainfall occurring in autumn and winter. Excessive rainfall during the flowering and corm development stages can negatively impact saffron yield and quality. Therefore, a well-defined pattern of precipitation is necessary to ensure successful saffron cultivation. Furthermore, sunlight plays a crucial role in the growth and development of saffron plants. Adequate exposure to sunlight enhances the production of carbohydrates and promotes the accumulation of valuable compounds, such as crocin and safranal, which contribute to the characteristic aroma, color, and flavor of saffron. Thus, regions with abundant sunshine hours are more suitable for saffron cultivation. In addition to climatic conditions, several other factors influence saffron cultivation. Soil quality is of paramount importance, with well-drained loamy or sandy soils being the most suitable. Adequate soil fertility, organic matter content, and appropriate pH levels (between 6 and 8) are also crucial for optimal saffron production. Considering the strategic importance of saffron as a high-value crop and the economic significance of its cultivation in Khorasan Razavi Province, prioritizing and identifying the influential factors for saffron cultivation becomes imperative. These factors encompass various aspects, including climate, soil conditions, irrigation techniques, pest and disease management, crop management practices, and post-harvest processing methods. Evaluating and understanding these factors through systematic research and expert opinions enable policymakers and farmers to make informed decisions and implement effective strategies to enhance saffron cultivation in the region. By determining the priority factors and understanding the climatic suitability, Khorasan Razavi Province can capitalize on its potential for saffron cultivation and further consolidate its position as a leading saffron producer globally. In order for saffron cultivation to thrive, favorable climatic conditions are typically required. In this section, we focus on Roshtkhar County in Khorasan Razavi Province, Iran, as a real-world case study for identifying the influential factors in saffron cultivation. Roshtkhar is situated in northeastern Iran, located at approximately 59° 37 mins and 30 seconds east longitude and 34° 58 mins and 23 seconds north latitude. The county has an elevation of around 1140 m above sea level and is approximately 200 kilometers away from the provincial capital, Mashhad. Roshtkhar encompasses 70

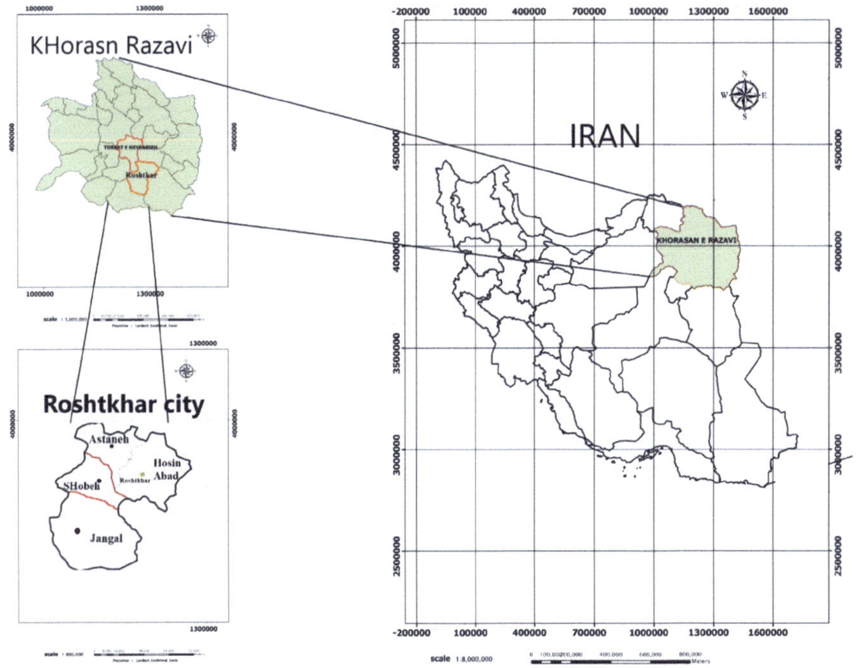

Fig. 1 The geographical location of Roshtkhar county

villages, farms, and settlements across two districts and four rural areas. Figure 1 illustrates the geographical location of Roshtkhar County.

4 Results Comparison and Analysis

In this study, the influential factors in saffron cultivation were initially identified through a questionnaire administered to a sample population of 60 individuals from Roshtkhar County, including 10 individuals from each subordinate district and 20 agricultural experts. The hierarchical tree structure for prioritizing the districts based on the factors influencing saffron cultivation is illustrated in Fig. 2.

The pairwise comparison matrices for this problem are presented in Table 1, which showcases the opinions of selected experts and farmers regarding the influential factors in saffron cultivation. These matrices are actually the geometric mean of the pairwise comparison matrices provided by the experts.

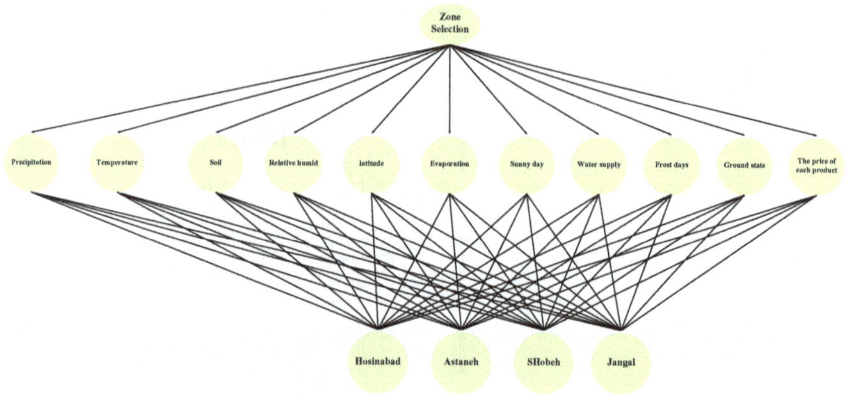

Fig. 2 The hierarchical tree

After calculating the inconsistency ratio for each pairwise comparison matrix and engaging with the experts to reach judgments with acceptable inconsistency ratios, as well as assessing the acceptability of the hierarchical inconsistency ratio, the final results are presented in Table 2. The AHP method was applied to derive these results.

In the following, we aim to modify the prioritization of criteria and alternatives based on expert interaction in this case study. We will create a decision matrix for criteria and alternatives, similar to Table 3.

In this interactive process, there is no need to calculate inconsistency rates, and the interaction with experts does not lead to time wastage or a decrease in their motivation. Subsequently, using the DEA model described in the previous section, also known as the Voting Model, we will calculate the relative weights. Finally, using the AHP method, we will determine the absolute weights and the final ranking, as presented in Table 4.

Additionally, we can assess the differences in prioritization positions through the use of discrimination intensity functions, which can be obtained by interacting with experts. This interaction with experts will greatly enhance the desirability of the final results.

Table 1 Opinions of experts and farmers on influential factors in saffron cultivation

Criteria	Precipitation	Temperature	Soil	Relative humid	latitude	Evaporation	Sunny day	Water supply	Frost days	Ground state	The price of each product			
Precipitation	1	3	4	5	7	6	8	8	4	8	6			
Temperature	1/3	1	3	4	6	5	7	7	3	7	5			
Soil	1/4	1/3	1	3	5	4	6	6	2	6	4			
Relative humid	1/5	1/4	1/3	1	4	3	5	5	2	5	3			
Latitude	1/7	1/6	1/5	1/4	1	2	4	4	2	4	2			
Evaporation	1/6	1/5	1/4	1/3	1/2	1	3	3	2	3	2			
Sunny day	1/8	1/7	1/6	1/5	1/4	1/4	1	2	2	2	2			
Water supply	1/8	1/7	1/6	1/5	1/4	1/4	1/3	1	2	2	2			
Frost days	¼	1/3	1/2	1/2	1/2	1/2	1/2	1/2	1	2	2			
Ground state	1/8	1/7	1/6	1/5	1/4	1/4	1/3	1/2	1/2	1	2			
The price of each product	1/6	1/5	1/4	1/3	1/2	1/2	1/2	1/2	1/2	1/2	1			
Precipitation	Hosinabad	Astaneh	SHobeh	Jangal	Temperature	Hosinabad	Astaneh	SHobeh	Jangal	Soil	Hosinabad	Astaneh	SHobeh	Jangal
Hosinabad	1	6	2	3	Hosinabad	1	5	2	3	Hosinabad	1	6/1	5/1	2/1
Astaneh	6/1	1	5	4	Astaneh	5/1	1	4	3	Astaneh	6	1	2	5
SHobeh	2/1	5/1	1	2	SHobeh	2/1	4/1	1	2	SHobeh	5	2/1	1	3
Jangal	3/1	4/1	2/1	1	Jangal	3/1	3/1	2/1	1	Jangal	2	5/1	3/1	1
Relative humid	Hosinabad	Astaneh	SHobeh	Jangal	latitude	Hosinabad	Astaneh	SHobeh	Jangal	Evaporation	Hosinabad	Astaneh	SHobeh	Jangal
Hosinabad	1	5/1	3/1	4/1	Hosinabad	1	3/1	2/1	7/1	Hosinabad	1	2	5	4

(continued)

Table 1 (continued)

Criteria	Precipitation	Temperature	Soil	Relative humid	latitude	Evaporation	Sunny day	Water supply	Frost days	Ground state	The price of each product			
Astaneh	5	1	4	3	Astaneh	3	1	2	6/1	Astaneh	2/1	1	4	3
SHobeh	3	4/1	1	2	SHobeh	2	2/1	1	5/1	SHobeh	5/1	4/1	1	2/1
Jangal	4	3/1	2/1	1	Jangal	7	6	5	1	Jangal	4/1	3/1	2	1
Sunny day	Hosinabad	Astaneh	SHobeh	Jangal	Water supply	Hosinabad	Astaneh	SHobeh	Jangal	Frost days	Hosinabad	Astaneh	SHobeh	Jangal
Hosinabad	1	4	2/1	5	Hosinabad	1	3/1	4/1	5	Hosinabad	1	3	2	6
Astaneh	4/1	1	3/1	6	Astaneh	3	1	2/1	4	Astaneh	3/1	1	2/1	4
SHobeh	2	3	1	7	SHobeh	4	2	1	6	SHobeh	2/1	2	1	5
Jangal	5/1	6/1	7/1	1	Jangal	5/1	4/1	6/1	1	Jangal	6/1	4/1	5/1	1
Ground state	Hosinabad	Astaneh	SHobeh	Jangal	The price of each product	Hosinabad	Astaneh	SHobeh	Jangal					
Hosinabad	1	5/1	3	4	Hosinabad	1	2/1	5	4					
Astaneh	5	1	5	6	Astaneh	2	1	6	5					
SHobeh	3/1	5/1	1	2	SHobeh	5/1	6/1	1	3/1					
Jangal	4/1	6/1	2/1	1	Jangal	4/1	5/1	3	1					

Table 2 Final results of the AHP method for prioritizing districts in saffron cultivation

Alternatives	Score	Rank
Hosinabad	0.360	1
Astaneh	0.329	2
SHobeh	0.187	3
Jangal	0.124	4

Based on these considerations and utilizing the AHP and VAHP methods, the ranking of lands in the Roshtkhar County for saffron cultivation based on climatic data will be presented using Geographic Information System (GIS), as depicted in Fig. 3.

5 Further Discussions and Managerial Insights

In this section, we highlight the significance of employing decision-making methods for ecological zone selection in geography. A prominent tool in this realm is the Analytic Hierarchy Process (AHP), which offers valuable insights into the decision-making process. However, it is essential to acknowledge the limitations of the AHP method, particularly when dealing with repeated interactions with experts and the potential inconsistency of their judgments. This management aspect should not be overlooked, as expert demotivation and insufficient precision in presenting results can undermine the credibility of the final outcomes. To enhance the AHP methodology, the incorporation of DEA brings notable advantages. Notably, the VAHP addresses the issues of expert demotivation. Through increased interaction with experts in determining discrimination intensity functions, VAHP ensures more desirable and reliable results. Moreover, we suggest exploring other hybrid approaches that combine DEA and AHP, as well as integrating DEA with other established MADM methods in the field of geography. These innovative methodologies offer promising avenues for further research and application, presenting opportunities to refine the decision-making process and enhance its effectiveness in geographical contexts. By including these insights and recommendations in the chapter book, readers will gain a comprehensive understanding of the significance of decision-making methods, the challenges associated with AHP, and the potential for leveraging DEA and hybrid approaches to improve decision-making in ecological zone selection.

Table 3 Expert voting for criteria and options prioritization

Criteria	1th	2th	3th	4th	5th	6th	7th	8th	9th	10th	11th			
Precipitation	5	0	3	1	5	1	0	0	0	0	0			
Temperature	6	7	0	0	1	0	0	1	0	0	0			
Soil	2	2	5	2	3	0	0	0	0	0	0			
Relative humid	0	0	0	0	0	0	2	7	1	2	3			
Latitude	0	4	1	1	0	1	1	2	3	2	0			
Evaporation	0	0	0	0	0	3	0	0	5	3	4			
Sunny day	0	0	3	2	0	0	0	2	1	2	5			
Water supply	0	1	0	0	2	1	2	2	3	4	0			
Frost days	1	1	0	6	2	1	2	1	1	0	0			
Ground state	0	0	2	0	0	3	5	0	1	1	3			
The price of each product	1	0	1	3	2	5	2	0	0	1	0			
Precipitation	1th	2th	3th	4th	Temperature	1th	2th	3th	4th	Soil	1th	2th	3th	4th
Hosinabad	9	2	1	3	Hosinabad	6	4	2	3	Hosinabad	6	1	1	7
Astaneh	2	7	3	3	Astaneh	4	6	3	2	Astaneh	1	6	7	1
SHobeh	1	3	10	1	SHobeh	4	1	7	3	SHobeh	5	3	5	2
Jangal	3	3	1	8	Jangal	1	4	3	7	Jangal	3	5	2	5
Relative humid	1th	2th	3th	4th	latitude	1th	2th	3th	4th	Evaporation	1th	2th	3th	4th
Hosinabad	1	7	0	7	Hosinabad	6	3	2	4	Hosinabad	6	6	0	3
Astaneh	9	3	3	0	Astaneh	3	8	4	0	Astaneh	5	7	2	1
SHobeh	0	3	10	2	SHobeh	2	4	8	1	SHobeh	1	2	11	1
Jangal	5	2	2	6	Jangal	4	0	1	10	Jangal	3	0	2	10
Sunny day	1th	2th	3th	4th	Water supply	1th	2th	3th	4th	Frost days	1th	2th	3th	4th

(continued)

Table 3 (continued)

Criteria	1th	2th	3th	4th	5th	6th	7th	8th	9th	10th	11th			
Hosinabad	1	2	5	7	Hosinabad	6	0	5	4	Hosinabad	9	0	3	3
Astaneh	0	2	8	5	Astaneh	0	11	1	3	Astaneh	0	11	3	1
SHobeh	5	8	2	0	SHobeh	6	3	1	5	SHobeh	2	4	8	1
Jangal	9	3	0	3	Jangal	3	1	8	3	Jangal	4	0	1	10
Ground state	1th	2th	3th	4th	The price of each product	1th	2th	3th	4th					
Hosinabad	10	5	0	0	Hosinabad	6	5	2	2					
Astaneh	5	10	0	0	Astaneh	5	6	2	2					
SHobeh	0	0	5	10	SHobeh	4	0	6	5					
Jangal	0	0	10	5	Jangal	0	4	5	6					

Table 4 Final ranking and absolute weights using VAHP method

Alternatives	Score	Rank
Hosinabad	0.280	1
Astaneh	0.273	2
SHobeh	0.239	3
Jangal	0.209	4

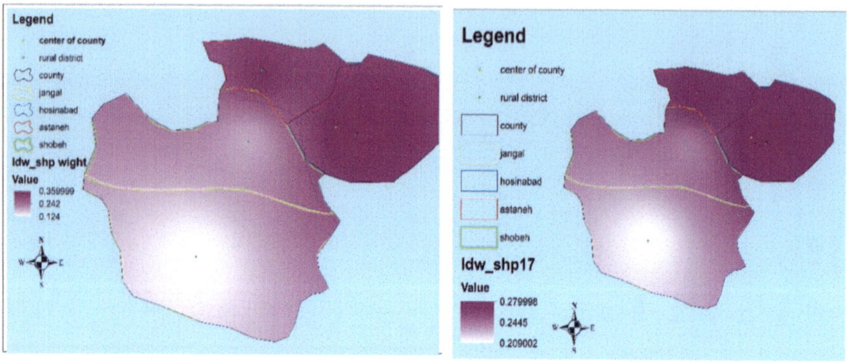

AHP **VAHP**

Fig. 3 Zone ranking using Geographic Information System (GIS)

6 Conclusion

In this book chapter, we have explored the prioritization of saffron cultivation districts in the Roshtkhar County, Khorasan Razavi Province, Iran, based on influential factors. We employed a comprehensive approach that involved expert opinions, pairwise comparison matrices, interaction with experts, and the utilization of decision-making methods such as AHP, VAHP, and DEA. Our findings revealed that the hierarchical tree constructed using expert opinions provided a valuable framework for prioritizing the districts. The AHP and VAHP methods facilitated the determination of relative weights and the final ranking of criteria and options. Moreover, the use of Geographic Information System (GIS) enhanced the analysis by incorporating spatial data and generating visual representations. We also addressed the limitations of the AHP method, particularly the repetitive consultation process with experts and the potential for loss of motivation and accuracy. To mitigate these issues, we highlighted the advantages of incorporating DEA and VAHP methods, which alleviate the concerns related to expert involvement and inconsistency in judgments. Furthermore, we discussed the managerial insights of employing decision-making methods in geographical selection processes. We emphasized the importance of considering ecological aspects and recommended the exploration of hybrid methods that combine

DEA and AHP, as well as other MADM approaches, to further enhance the decision-making process. In conclusion, this book chapter demonstrated the significance of employing a systematic and integrated approach for prioritizing saffron cultivation districts. The utilization of decision-making methods, along with GIS, offered valuable insights and informed decision-making in agricultural land selection processes. The presented methodologies and insights can serve as a valuable resource for researchers, practitioners, and policymakers involved in agricultural planning and decision-making processes.

References

Abastante, F., Corrente, S., Greco, S., Ishizaka, A., & Lami, I. M. (2019). A new parsimonious AHP methodology: Assigning priorities to many objects by comparing pairwise few reference objects. *Expert Systems with Applications*. https://doi.org/10.1016/j.eswa.2019.02.036

Amenta, P., Lucadamo, A., & Marcarelli, G. (2020a). On the transitivity and consistency approximated thresholds of some consistency indices for pairwise comparison matrices. *Information Sciences, 507*, 274–287.

Amenta, P., Lucadamo, A., & Marcarelli, G. (2020b). On the choice of weights for aggregating judgments in non-negotiable AHP group decision making. *European Journal of Operational Research., 288*(1), 294–301. https://doi.org/10.1016/j.ejor.2020.05.048

Chang, T. S., Lin, J. G., & Ouenniche, J. (2023). DEA-based Nash bargaining approach to merger target selection. *European Journal of Operational Research, 305*(2), 930–945.

Chuma, G. B., Cirezi, N. C., Mondo, J. M., Mugumaarhahama, Y., Ganza, D. M., Katcho, K., Mushagalusa, G. N., & Schmitz, S. (2023). Suitability for agroforestry implementation around Itombwe Natural Reserve (RNI), eastern DR Congo: Application of the Analytical Hierarchy Process (AHP) approach in geographic information system tool, *Trees. Forests and People, 6*, 100125.

Emrouznejad, A., & Yang, G. L. (2018). A survey and analysis of the first 40 years of scholarly literature in DEA: 1978–2016. *Socio-Economic Planning Sciences, 61*, 4–8.

Fan, J., Wang, Q., Ji, M., Sun, Y., Feng, Y., Yang, F., & Zhang, Z. (2023). Ecological network construction and gradient zoning optimization strategy in urban-rural fringe: A case study of Licheng District, Jinan City, China. *Ecological Indicators, 150*, 110251.

Hadi-Vencheh, A., & Niazi-Motlagh, M. (2011). An improved voting analytic hierarchy process–data envelopment analysis methodology for suppliers selection. *International Journal of Computer Integrated Manufacturing, 24*(3), 189–197.

Hosseinzadeh Lotfi, F., Allahviranloo, T., Shafiee, M., & Saleh, H. (2023). Data envelopment analysis. In *Supply chain performance evaluation. Studies in big data, vol. 122*. Springer, Cham. https://doi.org/10.1007/978-3-031-28247-8_6

Krmac, E., & Mansouri Kaleibar, M. A. (2022). Comprehensive review of data envelopment analysis (DEA) methodology in port efficiency evaluation. *Maritime Economics & Logistics*. https://doi.org/10.1057/s41278-022-00239-5

Leal, J. E. (2020). AHP-express: A simplified version of the analytical hierarchy process method. *MethodsX, 7*, 100748.

Li, S., He, W., Wang, L., Zhang, Z., Chen, X., Lei, T., Wang, S., & Wang, Z. (2023). Optimization of landscape pattern in China Luojiang Xiaoxi basin based on landscape ecological risk assessment. *Ecological Indicators, 146*, 109887.

Liu, F.-H.F., & Hai, H. L. (2005). The voting analytic hierarchy process method for selecting supplier. *International Journal of Production Economics, 97*(3), 308–317.

Lukinskiy, V., & Lukinskiy, V. (2018). The Analytic Hierarchy Process (AHP): Prospects for application in supply chain management. In: I. Kabashkin, I. Yatskiv, O. Prentkovskis, (eds.), *Reliability and statistics in transportation and communication. RelStat 2017. Lecture notes in networks and systems*, vol. 36. Springer, Cham. https://doi.org/10.1007/978-3-319-74454-4_27

Mardani, A., Zavadskas, E. K., Streimikiene, D., Jusoh, A., & Khoshnoudi, M. (2017). A comprehensive review of data envelopment analysis (DEA) approach in energy efficiency. *Renewable and Sustainable Energy Reviews, 70*, 1298–1322.

Natarajan, N., Vasudevan, M., Dineshkumar, S. K., & Anuja, R. (2022). Comparison of Analytic Hierarchy Process (AHP) and fuzzy analytic hierarchy process (f-AHP) for the sustainability assessment of a water supply project. *Journal of The Institution of Engineers (India): Series A*, 103, 1029–1039. https://doi.org/10.1007/s40030-022-00665-x

Pishchulov, G., Trautrims, A., Chesney, T., Gold, S., & Schwab, L. (2019). The voting analytic hierarchy process revisited: A revised method with application to sustainable supplier selection. *International Journal of Production Economics, 211*, 166–179. https://doi.org/10.1016/j.ijpe.2019.01.025

Prevolšek, B., Gačnik, M. B., & Rozman, Č. (2023). Applying integrated data envelopment analysis and analytic hierarchy process to measuring the efficiency of tourist farms: the case of Slovenia. *Sustainability, 15*(5), 4314.

Saaty, T. L. (1980). *The analytic hierarchy process, Mcgraw Hill* (p. 70). Agricultural Economics Review.

Saaty, T. L. (2006). *Fundamentals of decision making with the analytic hierarchy process.* RWS Publications.

Soltanifar, M., & Hosseinzadeh Lotfi, F. (2011). The voting analytic hierarchy process method for discriminating among efficient decision making units in data envelopment analysis. *Computers & Industrial Engineering, 60*(4), 585–592.

Tavana, M., Soltanifar, M., & Santos-Arteaga, F. J. (2021). Analytical hierarchy process: Revolution and evolution. *Annals of Operations Research.* https://doi.org/10.1007/s10479-021-04432-2

Tavana, M., Soltanifar, M., Santos-Arteaga, F. J., & Sharafi, H. (2023). Analytic hierarchy process and data envelopment analysis: A match made in heaven. *Expert Systems with Applications, 223*, 119902. https://doi.org/10.1016/j.eswa.2023.119902

Thakkar, J. J. (2021). Analytic Hierarchy Process (AHP). In *Multi-criteria decision making. Studies in systems, decision and control*, vol 336. Springer, Singapore. https://doi.org/10.1007/978-981-33-4745-8_3

Vretta, E.-M., Bitsis, K., Kaparis, K., Paltayian, G., & Georgiou, A. C. (2023). A stochastic bilevel DEA-based model for resource allocation. *Computer Sciences & Mathematics Forum, 7*(1), 40. https://doi.org/10.3390/IOCMA2023-14594

Yi, Z., Wei, W., Langfeng, M., Siqi, W., Fengyan, Z., & Li Lixin, L. (2020). Application of Analytic Hierarchy process (AHP) in the layout of jack-up drilling platform. *Chemistry and Technology of Fuels and Oils*, 56, 236–242. https://doi.org/10.1007/s10553-020-01134-6.

Yin, J., Wang, D., & Li, H. (2023). Spatial optimization of rural settlements in ecologically fragile regions: Insights from a social-ecological system. *Habitat International, 138*, 102854.

Younesi, A., Lotfi, F. H., & Arana-Jiménez, M. (2023). Using slacks-based model to solve inverse DEA with integer intervals for input estimation. *Fuzzy Optimization and Decision Making.* https://doi.org/10.1007/s10700-022-09403-1

Zekhnini, K., Cherrafi, A., Bouhaddou, I., & Benghabrit, Y. (2021). Analytic Hierarchy Process (AHP) for supply chain 4.0 risks management. In T. Masrour, A. Cherrafi, & I. El Hassani (eds.), *Artificial intelligence and industrial applications. a2ia 2020. advances in intelligent systems and computing*, vol. 1193. Springer, Cham. https://doi.org/10.1007/978-3-030-51186-9_7

A Multi-Objective Investment Selection Problem Using Fuzzy and Intuitionistic Fuzzy Approach

Prabjot Kaur, Nasreen Kausar, Salma Khan, and Dragan Pamucar

Abstract Investment refers to allocating funds in the expectation of some benefit in the future which in financial terms is the return. In the presence of various investment alternatives, the decision maker stands confused as to which option would offer him the highest return. Thus, the problem of appropriate investment selection can be treated as a multi-objective decision-making (MODM) problem that involves optimization of return on investment, time, risk, etc. However, the time, return, and risk involved in such problems cannot be defined in precise units and are fuzzy in nature. Amidst such a scenario in addition to fuzzy set (FS) theory, intuitionistic fuzzy sets (IFSs) which provide a mathematical framework to deal with imprecise information of the real world can be of much help. It can be seen as an alternative to describe a FS-in situation when the existing data is not enough to define a usual FS. Against this backdrop, this paper is an attempt to develop an IF multi-objective linear model (MOLM) for the investment selection problem where the coefficients of the objective functions (OFs) are represented by IF linear membership (MM) and non-membership (N-MM) functions. The constraints in the problem are treated as

P. Kaur (✉)
Department of Mathematics, Birla Institute of Technology, Mesra, Ranchi, Jharkhand, India
e-mail: prabjotkaur@bitmesra.ac.in

N. Kausar
Department of Mathematics, Faculty of Arts and Sciences, Yildiz Technical University, Esenler 34220 Istanbul, Turkey
e-mail: nkausar@yildiz.edu.tr

S. Khan
Department of Mathematics and Statistics, Hazara Universirty Mansehra, Khyber Pakhtinkhwa 21120, Pakistan
e-mail: 55312-f18@hu.edu.pk

D. Pamucar
Department of Operations Research and Statistics, Faculty of Organizational Sciences, University of Belgrade, Belgrade, Serbia

College of Engineering, Yuan Ze University, Taoyuan City, Taiwan

D. Pamucar
e-mail: dpamucar@gmail.com

© The Author(s), under exclusive license to Springer Nature Singapore Pte Ltd. 2024

S. A. Edalatpanah et al. (eds.), *Analytical Decision Making and Data Envelopment Analysis*, Infosys Science Foundation Series in Mathematical Sciences,
https://doi.org/10.1007/978-981-97-6972-8_16

crisp. The application of the methodology is explained with the help of a numerical example. Comparing the fuzzy and intuitionistic models it is seen that the IFO model gives optimal results in selection and order allocations to the investors. Also, a Pareto optimality test is performed to test the strength of the solution.

Keywords Multi-objective optimization · Investment alternatives · Fuzzy sets · Intuitionistic fuzzy sets

1 Introduction

Investors are increasingly inclined to invest in stocks and bonds instead of keeping their funds in banks, in search of higher returns. However, investment returns are not always favorable and carry inherent risks. Therefore, investors should thoroughly analyze their options before making investment decisions. The main challenge in this decision-making process stems from the inherent inaccuracy associated with various elements of the investment process. Investors prefer realistic representations rather than relying only on supposedly accurate models. To remedy the uncertainty, Zadeh (1965) introduced FSs as a powerful mathematical modelling tool. FS theory plays a crucial role in complex business decisions, finance and management systems. FSs reflect reality and serve as the basis for the development of theories capable of capturing the pervasive imprecision and uncertainty of the real world. Atanassov (1986, 1999) then extended FSs with the introduction of intuitionist fuzzy sets (IFSS), which include three components: MM, N-MM and hesitation.

The theme of IFSs has attracted considerable attention from researchers over the past two decades. Atanassov and Gargov (1999) presented the equivalence of IFSs and interval-valued FSs by introducing the notion of interval-valued IFSS (Zadeh, 1973). Coker (1997) contributed to the field by introducing various concepts related to IF topological spaces, such as fuzzy continuity, fuzzy compactness, fuzzy connectivity and Hausdorff fuzzy space. Bustince et al. (2000) initiated IF generators to verify the presence of equilibrium points and double points, defining characterization theorems and a method for initiating IF generators. Szmidt and Kacprzyk (2001) introduced a non-probabilistic entropy metric for IFSs. Park (2004) pointed out that intuitionist fuzzy metric spaces are a natural extension of fuzzy metric spaces. In addition, Szmidt and Kacprzyk (2000) explored the distance between intuitionist fuzzy sets.

Harry Markowitz is credited with developing the theory of optimal portfolio selection (PS) in the 1950s. His powerful work (Markowitz & Todd, 2000) formalized the concept of diversification as a key principle of PS, which earned him the Nobel Prize in Economics in 1990. Another research paper (Anderson, 1972) investigates the models used in the electricity supply industry to evaluate investments. The models propose exogenous quantities requested, input and output prices, and aim to identify the investments with the lowest costs over several periods. The decision-making variables analyzed include the choice of types of power plants, the location of the power plants, the directions of energy transmission, the timing of investments, replacement decisions and the optimal functioning of the system, including hydroelectric storage policies. These variables are studied using linear programming, nonlinear programming, dynamic programming and other optimization methods. The review covers both global models and approaches to optimizing subproblems within the system.

In (Yodmun & Witayakiattilerd, 2016), the authors sought to remedy the uncertainty inherent in financial markets by proposing an approach to solve the problem of financial asset selection in a non-linear and uncertain environment. They used fuzzy logic and genetic algorithms to optimize the profitability of investments. Another article from (Guo et al. 2012; Divya & Kumar, 2012) introduces an approach to stock selection that incorporates fuzzy procedures. The shares were classified into groups according to their business types, then classified using fuzzy quantitative analysis and the analytical hierarchy process (FAHP) to determine their investment weight. Presentation of a new framework designed by Bairagi (2023) in 2023, for the ecological selection of handling equipment in a fuzzy environment. Bozanic et al. (2020) developed multicriteria decision making model utilizing Z-numbers combining elements from FUCOM and MABAC model. Many researchers (Ejegwa & Onyeke, 2020; Eyo et al., 2021) used IF approaches in decision-making processes to predict COVID-19 time series and medical diagnosis on some selected patients. Mohan et al. (2020) developed a new technique for ranking IF number; for more fuzzy set extensions in this field, see (Edalatpanah et al., 2023; Kumar et al., 2019; Veeramani et al., 2021; Wang et al., 2021).

This study presents a multi-objective investment selection problem (MOISP), where the coefficients of the objective functions are supported by using the IF linear function. The constraints of the problem are treated as net. The multiple objectives (MO) of this problem involve maximizing the return on investment, minimizing the time and minimizing the risk associated with the investment. Section 2 gives an overview of the preliminaries on multi-objective optimization (MOO), while Sect. 3 formulates the investment selection problem using MOO techniques. To illustrate the procedure, a numerical example is presented in Sect. 4. Finally, Sect. 5 concludes the study and discusses the future directions of the research.

2 Preliminaries

2.1 Fuzzy Sets (Zadeh, 1965)

If we have a collection of objects presented by the variable x, a fuzzy set A in this collection, U can be defined as a set containing ordered pairs:

$$\tilde{A} = \{(\mathrm{x}, \mu_{\tilde{A}}(x)|x \in U\}\ , \mu_{\tilde{A}} : U \rightarrow [0, 1]\}$$

....

2.2 Intuitionistic Fuzzy Set (Atanassov, 1986)

Let X be a non-empty universal set. The mathematical structure of IFS in a universal set X is given as follow:

$$A = \{(x_i, \mu_A(x_i), \nu_A(x_i) : x_i \in X\}$$

where the functions $\mu_A : X \to [0, 1], x_i \in X \to \mu_A(x_i) \in [0,1]$
And $\nu_A : X \to [0,1], x_i \in X \to \nu_A(x_i) \in [0,1]$

where μ_A and ν_A represents degree of MM and N-MM respectively for all $x_i \in X$, such that

$$0 \le \mu_A(x_i) + \nu_A(x_i) \le 1$$

2.3 Multi Objective Linear Programming Problem (MOLPP) (Bharati & Singh, 2014)

Typically, a MOLPP consists of p objectives, q constraints, and n decision variables, and defined as follows:

$$\left.\begin{array}{c} maxQ_1(X), Q_2(X), Q_2(X) \\ such\ that \\ g_j(X) \le 0, j = 1, 2, \ldots, q \\ X = \{x_1, x_2, \ldots, x_n\} \\ x_i \ge 0, i = 1, 2, \ldots, n \end{array}\right\} \quad (1)$$

2.4 Efficient Solution of MOLP (Bharati & Singh, 2014)

An effective solution X^0 of a multi-objective linear program is represented as a feasible point where there is no other feasible point X, so that for a particular objective function, let's call it $f_i(X), f_i(X) < f_i(X^0)$, while for all other objective functions $f_j(X)$ is strictly less than $f_j(X^0)$, where j is between 1 and p.

3 Mathematical Formulation of Fuzzy Multi-Objective Linear Optimization Problem (FMOLOP)

The purpose of the model is a fuzzy approach to MO investment selection model is maximising return on investment, minimising time and minimising risk of investment. The MO functions are represented as fuzzy sets.

Zimmermann (1978) In his approach for solving FMOLPP used the following process:

Step 1: Solution of MOLPP is considering solution of one objective at a time. We obtained the maximum and minimum value for each objective function.

Step 2: Put $L_p = \min\{f_p(x_r)\}, p = 1,2,3; r = 1,2,\ldots,5$

$$U_p = \max\{f_p(x_r)\}, p = 1,2,3; r = 1,2,\ldots,5$$

Step 3: The MM function for each objective function is as follows:

$$\mu_{f_p}(x) = \left\{ \begin{matrix} 1, f_p(x) \leq L_p \\ \frac{U_p - f_p(x)}{U_p - L_p}, L_p \leq f_p(x) \leq U_p \\ 0, f_p(x) \geq L_p \end{matrix} \right\} \tag{2}$$

Step 4: The equivalent MOLPP into Single objective LPP is $max\lambda$ subject to

$$\left. \begin{matrix} \lambda(U_p - L_p) \leq U_p - f_p(X) \\ g_j(X) \leq b, j = 1,2,\ldots,q \\ X = \{x_1, x_2, \ldots, x_n\} \\ x_i \geq 0, i = 1,2,\ldots,n, \lambda\epsilon[0,1] \end{matrix} \right\} \tag{3}$$

4 Mathematical Formulation of Intuitionistic Fuzzy Multi-Objective Optimization Problem (Chakrabortty et al., 2011)

The objective of this model is to find out the problem of multi-objective investment selection (NOISE) in an IF environment. The MOFs involved in the problem are represented using the IFS. Depend on intuitionistic fuzzy optimization (IFO) and applying IFO, we use sharp transformation methods and describe the following solution procedure: In accordance with the theory of IFO our objective is to maximize the degree of MM of IF objectives and constraints while minimizing the degree of N-MM for the same IF objectives and constraints.

$$\left.\begin{array}{c}\max\{\mu_k(x)\};\\ \min\{v_k(x)\};\\ \mu_k(x), v_k(x) \geq 0;\\ \mu_k(x) \geq v_k(x)\\ g_j(X) \leq 0, j = 1,2,\ldots,q\\ 0 \leq \mu_k(x) + v_k(x) \leq 1\end{array}\right\} k = 1,2,\ldots,p+q \tag{4}$$

where $\mu_k(x)$ shows the degree of MM of x from the kth IFS and $v(x)$ denotes the degree of N-MM of x from the kth IFS.

4.1 Construction of MM and N-MM Functions (Bharati & Singh, 2014)

We Construct MM and N-MM Function for the OFs As

In IFO, the FOFs are defined by their linear MM and N-MM functions. For construction it is necessary to initially establish the lower and upper bounds of the MM function.

For MM Functions

$$\left.\begin{array}{l}U_p^{\mu} = \max(Q_r(x))\\ L_p^{\mu} = \min(Q_r(x))\end{array}\right\} \tag{5}$$

For N-MM Functions

$$\left.\begin{array}{l}U_p^{v} = U_p^{\mu} - \lambda\left(U_p^{\mu} - L_p^{\mu}\right)\\ L_p^{v} = L_p^{\mu} \ where\, 0 < \lambda < 1\end{array}\right\} \tag{6}$$

The formulation of MM and N-MM functions for the.
Objective functions are as follows:

$$\mu_p(Q_K(x)) = \begin{cases} 0 & if \quad Q_k \leq L_p^{\mu} \\ \frac{Q_k - L_p^{\mu}}{U_p^{\mu} - L_p^{\mu}} & if\ L_p^{\mu} < Q_p(x) < U_p^{\mu} \\ 1 & if \quad Q_k \geq U_p^{\mu} \end{cases} \tag{7}$$

$$v_p(Q_K(x)) = \begin{cases} 0 & if \quad Q_k \leq L_p^{v} \\ \frac{U_p^{v} - Q_k(x)}{U_p^{v} - L_p^{v}} & if\ L_p^{v} < Q_p(x) < U_p^{v} \\ 1 & if \quad Q_k \geq L_p^{v} \end{cases} \tag{8}$$

4.2 The LPP from IFO Technique for MOLP (Angelov, 1997)

$$\text{Maximize } (\alpha - \beta)$$

$$\left.\begin{array}{c} \mu_p(x) \geq \alpha, p = 1,2, \ldots, p+q \\ v_p(x) \leq \beta, p = 1,2, \ldots, p+q \\ \alpha + \beta \leq 1 \\ \alpha \geq \beta \\ \beta \geq 0, x \in X \end{array}\right\} \quad (9)$$

4.3 Pareto Optimal Solution

After obtaining an optimized solution of MOISP, Pareto-optimality test Sakawa (1983) is performed. Let x_1^*, x_2^*, x_3^* be the decision variables and optimum values obtained for objective functions are Q_1^*, Q_2^* and Q_3^* with these values the following problem is formulated for the model: $MaxV = \varepsilon_1 + \varepsilon_2 + \varepsilon_3$

Subject to:

$$\left.\begin{array}{c} Q_1 - \varepsilon_1 = Q_1^* \\ Q_2 + \varepsilon_2 = Q_2^* \\ Q_3 + \varepsilon_3 = Q_3^* \\ \alpha + \beta \leq 1 \\ \alpha \geq \beta \\ \alpha, \beta > 0 \\ \varepsilon_1, \varepsilon_2, \varepsilon_3 \geq 0 \end{array}\right\} \quad (10)$$

the optimal value of (9), say Q_1^{**}, Q_2^{**} and Q_3^{**} these values are called strong Pareto optimal solutions when the value of V is significantly small. However, if V exceeds a certain threshold, these solutions are instead classified as weak Pareto solutions.

5 Algorithm of Steps

1. Solve the MOP by treating it as a linear programming problem with a single objective. Determine the maximum and minimum values for each of the individual objective functions.
2. Develop the MM and N-MM functions for the different objective functions.
3. Turn the problem into a fuzzy linear programming (FLP) problem using Eq. (3).

4. Use Eq. (6) to convert the FLP problem into an intuitionistic fuzzy linear programming (IFLP) problem.
5. To check the results, get an optimal Pareto solution for the IFO problem.

6 Numerical Example

Imagine that Subodh Sharma is a person who has already been a government official, and has recently obtained retirement benefits, which include provisions such as provident fund, gratuity, and other relevant rights. He seeks broker's advice, takes his own experience and considers various investment alternatives to which he assigns corresponding expectations of yield (income or growth). The various investment alternatives are term deposit, Mutual Fund, Equity share, Growth Stock and Real Estate. The estimates of risk are based on subjective assessment. The data on the annual yield of investment, average term for which the fund will be blocked, and the judgemental risks involved are shown as follows:

Investment alternatives	Expected annual yields (in Rs)	Average term (in years)	Risk
Term deposit	6	15	1
Mutual fund	13	3	3
Equity share	10	5	2
Growth stock	20	6	5
Real estate	25	10	1

Subodh Sharma, a pensioner, is considering the optimal distribution of his funds between different investment alternatives to maximize his return on investment. He made it a condition that the funds should not remain immobilized for a period of more than 15 years. In order to achieve its capital expenditure, Subodh has established the following restrictions:

(i) The average period of investments should not exceed 15 years.
(ii) The average level of risk linked with investments should not exceed 4.
(iii) He would necessarily invest atmost25% in real estate.
(iv) The investment decision is to be limited to the five investment alternatives.

The investor's problem is to maximize his annual yield by satisfying the above-mentioned requirements.

Solution: In mathematical terms the above problem can be formulated as
Maximising return: $MaxQ_1 = 6x_1 + 13x_2 + 10x_3 + 20x_4 + 25x_5$
Minimising time: $MinQ_2 = 15x_1 + 3x_2 + 5x_3 + 6x_4 + 10x_5$
Minimizing risk: $MinQ_3 = x_1 + 3x_2 + 2x_3 + 5x_4 + x_5$

Subject to:

$$15x_1 + 3x_2 + 5x_3 + 6x_4 + 10x_5 \le 15x_1 + 3x_2 + 2x_3 + 5x_4 + x_5 \le 4x_5 \le 0.25$$

$$x_1 + x_2 + x_3 + x_4 + x_5 = 1$$

$$x_1, x_2, x_3, x_4, x_5 \ge 0$$

The solution of the above formulation by fuzzy and IFS approach is as follows.

Using fuzzy optimization techniques of Sect. 3, we obtain a formulation and its solution as:

$$max\lambda$$

Subject to:

$$15.25\lambda - 6x_1 - 13x_2 - 10x_3 - 20x_4 - 25x_5 \le 6$$

$$15.25\lambda - 6x_1 - 13x_2 - 10x_3 - 20x_4 - 25x_5 \le -6$$

$$12\lambda + 15x_1 + 3x_2 + 5x_3 + 6x_4 + 10x_5 \le 15$$

$$3\lambda + x_1 + 3x_2 + 2x_3 + 5x_4 + x_5 \le 4$$

$$x_1 + x_2 + x_3 + x_4 + x_5 = 1$$

$$15x_1 + 3x_2 + 5x_3 + 6x_4 + 10x_5 \le 15$$

$$x_1 + 3x_2 + 2x_3 + 5x_4 + x_5 \le 4$$

$$x_5 \le 0.25$$

$$x_i \ge 0, i = 1,2, 3,4, 5.\lambda \epsilon [0,1]$$

Using IFO formulation of Sect. 4, we obtain the following formulation

$$max(\alpha - \beta)$$

subject to:

$$15.25\alpha - 6x_1 - 13x_2 - 10x_3 - 20x_4 - 25x_5 \leq -6$$

$$12\alpha + 15x_1 + 3x_2 + 5x_3 + 6x_4 + 10x_5 \leq 15$$

$$3\alpha + x_1 + 3x_2 + 2x_3 + 5x_4 + x_5 \leq 4$$

$$7.78\beta + 6x_1 + 13x_2 + 10x_3 + 20x_4 + 25x_5 \geq 13.78$$

$$6.12\beta - 15x_1 - 3x_2 - 5x_3 - 6x_4 - 10x_5 \geq -3$$

$$1.53\beta - x_1 - 3x_2 - 2x_3 - 5x_4 - x_5 \geq -1$$

$$\alpha + \beta \leq 1$$

$$\alpha - \beta \geq 0$$

$$\alpha, \beta \geq 0$$

$$x_i \geq 0, i = 1{,}2, 3{,}4, 5.\lambda\epsilon[0{,}1]$$

Using formulation 8 we obtain the Pareto optimal solution in the Table 2.

7 Results and Discussion

In the optimal solution for Fuzzy multi-objective linear programming problem, we obtain value of degree of satisfaction $\lambda = .60$. The values of decision variables and objective functions as $x_1 = 0, x_2 = 0, x_3 = .60, x_4 = .15, x_5 = .25, Q1 = 15.25, Z2 = 6.4, Z3 = 8.95$. compared to IFO which gives value of degree of satisfaction and dissatisfaction as $\alpha = 0.62$ and $\beta = 0.38$,with decision variable values as $x_1 = 0, x_2 = 0.39, x_3 = 0, x_4 = 0, x_5 = .42$. The values of objective functions are $Z_1 = 15.57, Z_2 = 5.37.Z_3 = 1.59$. We observe that with IFO definitely values of objective functions are better. In IFO maximum allocation went to Real estate and then mutual fund. In fuzzy approach maximum went to equity share and minimum to term deposit and mutual fund. The results obtained by IFO techniques give better results than fuzzy approach (Table 1). The degree of satisfaction in IFO is better

Table1 Comparative chart for the two approaches

Fuzzy approach	IFO approach
The value of objective functions: $Q_1 = 15.25, Q_2 = 6.4, Q_3 = 8.95$	The value of objective functions: $Q1 = 15.57, Q2 = 5.37.Q3 = 1.59$
$\lambda = 0.60$	$\alpha = 0.62\, and\ \beta = 0.38$
$x_1 = 0, x_2 = 0, x_3 = 0.60, x_4 = .15, x_5 = 0.25$	$x_1 = 0, x_2 = 0.43, x_3 = 0, x_4 = 0, x_5 = 0.47$

Table 2 Pareto-optimal results

V	$\epsilon 1$	$\epsilon 2$	$\epsilon 3$	x1	x2	x3	x4	x5
0	0	0	0	0	0.43	0	0	0.47

than fuzzy approach. From Table 2 we observe that value of $V = 0$, indicating that Pareto-optimal solution are strong and can be accepted.

8 Conclusions

In this study a comparative analysis of a MOIS problem was done using fuzzy and IF approaches. The IF approach is found to be better than the fuzzy approach. The IFO approach satisfies the solution with a higher degree of NMM compared to fuzzy approach where degree of MM was lower. The disadvantage of fuzzy optimization approach is that it can handle either acceptance or rejection one at a time. For effective solution if degree of acceptance and rejection are taken simultaneously it handles optimization under uncertainty efficiently (Kabiraj et al., 2019). Thus, from an investor's perspective the model can help him take judicious decisions amidst uncertainty. However, it is just a demonstration of the real world, and the financial outcomes of these decisions will, in part; depend on the level of market growth achieved over the years. With the inclusion of more parameters and constraints, the model can further be extended for analysing more complex decision scenario.

References

Anderson, D. (1972). Models for determining least-cost investments in electricity supply. *The Bell Journal of Economics and Management Science., 1*, 267–299.

Angelov, P. P. (1997). Optimization in an intuitionistic fuzzy environment. *Fuzzy Sets and Systems. 86*(3), 299–306.

Atanassov, K. T. (1986). Intuitionistic fuzzy sets. *Fuzzy Sets and System, 20*, 87–96.

Atanassov, K. T. (1999). *Interval valued intuitionistic fuzzy sets. InIntuitionistic fuzzy sets 1999* (pp. 139–177). Physica, Heidelberg

Atanassov KT. Intuitionistic fuzzy sets. In *Intuitionistic fuzzy sets 1999* (pp. 1–137). Physica, Heidelberg.

Bairagi, B. (2023). A new framework for green selection of material handling equipment under fuzzy environment. *Decision Making: Applications in Management and Engineering., 6*(1), 57–69.

Bharati, S. K., & Singh, S. R. (2014). Intuitionistic fuzzy optimization technique in agricultural production planning: A small farm holder perspective. *International Journal of Computer Applications., 89*(6), 17–23.

Bozanic, D., Tešić, D., & Milić, A. (2020). Multicriteria decision making model with Z-numbers based on FUCOM and MABAC model. *Decision Making: Applications in Management and Engineering., 3*(2), 19–36.

Bustince, H., Kacprzyk, J., & Mohedano, V. (2000). Intuitionistic fuzzy generators application to intuitionistic fuzzy complementation. *Fuzzy Sets and Systems., 114*(3), 485–504.

Çoker, D. (1997). An introduction to intuitionistic fuzzy topological spaces. *Fuzzy Sets and Systems., 88*(1), 81–89.

Chakrabortty, S., Pal, M., & Nayak, P. K. (2011). Intuitionistic fuzzy optimization technique for the solution of an EOQ model. *Notes on Intuitionistic Fuzzy Sets., 17*(2), 52–64.

Divya, P., & Kumar, P. R. (2012). The investment portfolio selection using fuzzy logic genetic algorithm. *International Journal of Engineering Research and Applications., 2*(5), 2100–2105.

Edalatpanah, S. A., Pamučar, D., & Zhang, L. T. (2023). Preface to the special issue on numerical simulations and optimization under uncertainty. *Advances in Mechanical Engineering, 15*(3), 16878132231161484.

Ejegwa, P. A, Onyeke, I. C. (2020). Medical diagnostic analysis on some selected patients based on modified Thao et al.'s correlation coefficient of intuitionistic fuzzy sets via an algorithmic approach. *Journal of fuzzy extension and applications. 1*(2), 122–132.

Eyo, I., Eyoh, J., & Umoh, U. (2021). On the prediction of COVID-19 time series: An intuitionistic fuzzy logic approach. *Journal of Fuzzy Extension and Applications., 2*(2), 171–190.

Guo, H., Sun, B., Karimi, H. R., Ge, Y., & Jin, W. (2012). Fuzzy investment portfolio selection models based on interval analysis approach. *Mathematical Problems in Engineering., 1*, 2012.

Kabiraj, A., Nayak, P. K., & Raha, S. (2019). Solving intuitionistic fuzzy linear programming problem. *International Journal of Intelligence Science., 9*(1), 44–58.

Kumar, R., Edalatpanah, S. A., Jha, S., & Singh, R. (2019). A novel approach to solve gaussian valued neutrosophic shortest path problems. *International Journal of Engineering and Advanced Technology, 8*(3), 347–353.

Markowitz, H. M., & Todd, G.P. (2000). Mean-variance analysis in portfolio choice and capital markets. John Wiley & Sons

Mohan, S., Kannusamy, A. P., & Samiappan, V. (2020). A new approach for ranking of intuitionistic fuzzy numbers. *Journal of Fuzzy Extension and Applications., 1*(1), 15–26.

Park, J. H. (2004). Intuitionistic fuzzy metric spaces. *Chaos, Solitons & Fractals., 22*(5), 1039–1046.

Sakawa, M. (1983). Interactive computer programs for fuzzy linear programming with multiple objectives. *International Journal of Man-Machine Studies., 18*(5), 489–503.

Szmidt, E., & Kacprzyk, J. (2000). Distances between intuitionistic fuzzy sets. *Fuzzy Sets and Systems., 114*(3), 505–518.

Szmidt, E., & Kacprzyk, J. (2001). Entropy for intuitionistic fuzzy sets. *Fuzzy Sets and Systems., 118*(3), 467–477.

Veeramani, C., Edalatpanah, S. A., & Sharanya, S. (2021). Solving the multiobjective fractional transportation problem through the neutrosophic goal programming approach. *Discrete Dynamics in Nature and Society, 2021*, 1–17.

Wang, Q., Huang, Y., Kong, S., Ma, X., Liu, Y., Das, S. K., & Edalatpanah, S. A. (2021). A novel method for solving multiobjective linear programming problems with triangular neutrosophic numbers. *Journal of Mathematics, 2021*, 1–8.

Yodmun, S., & Witayakiattilerd, W. (2016). Stock selection into portfolio by fuzzy quantitative analysis and fuzzy multicriteria decision making. *Advances in Operations Research., 1*, 2016.

Zadeh, L. A. (1965). Fuzzy Sets. Information. *Control, 8*, 338–343.

Zadeh, L. A. (1973). Outline of a new approach to the analysis of complex systems and decision processes. *IEEE Transactions on Systems, Man, and Cybernetics.*, *1*, 28–44.

Zimmermann, H. J. (1978). Fuzzy programming and linear programming with several objective functions. *Fuzzy Sets and Systems.*, *1*(1), 45–55.

Revolutionizing Education: An Optimal MAGDM-Based e-Learning Approach for Curriculum Beyond the Classroom

Sumera Naz, Areej Fatima, Shariq Aziz But, and Arooj Ashiq

Abstract The rise of web applications in the form of e-learning websites has presented both opportunities and challenges for academic organizations and individuals involved in education. Many organizations have developed websites to provide education and enhance skills. However, the rapid growth of e-learning brings the challenge of evaluating and selecting the most suitable e-learning websites. One approach to address this challenge is through Multi-Attribute Group Decision-Making (MAGDM) problems. To select the best e-learning website, this study proposes an integrated model in a 2-tuple linguistic q-rung orthopair fuzzy (2TLq-R) set. The proposed model utilizes the 2TLq-R set, a robust mathematical framework capable of handling uncertainties and linguistic assessments in decision-making problems. To improve the model's effectiveness, new operators for 2TLq-R numbers are introduced, utilizing the Hamacher t-norm (TN) and t-conorm (TCN) operations. These operators enable efficient aggregation and comparison of linguistic evaluations, streamlining the selection process for the e-learning website. With the proposed approach, decision-makers can assess e-learning websites based on multiple attributes, including content quality, interactivity, user experience, and cost-effectiveness. This comprehensive evaluation allows decision-makers to make informed choices when selecting the most suitable e-learning platform. This paper investigates the properties and analyzes specific cases of 2TLq-R operators to understand their characteristics. Moreover, the study combines the Multi-Attributive Border Approximation Area Comparison (MABAC) method with the 2TLq-R operators to incorporate the decision-makers' psychological behavior. This integration leads to the development of a novel approach called 2TLq-R-MABAC, which effectively addresses real-world MAGDM problems. Additionally, the paper includes an illustrative example and a comparative evaluation to demonstrate the practicality and applicability of the proposed method for selecting the optimal e-learning website.

S. Naz (✉) · A. Fatima · A. Ashiq
Department of Mathematics, Division of Science and Technology, University of Education, Lahore, Pakistan
e-mail: sumera.naz@ue.edu.pk

S. Aziz But
Department of Computer Science, School of Systems and Technology, University of Management and Technology, Cantt, Lahore, Pakistan

© The Author(s), under exclusive license to Springer Nature Singapore Pte Ltd. 2024
S. A. Edalatpanah et al. (eds.), *Analytical Decision Making and Data Envelopment Analysis*, Infosys Science Foundation Series in Mathematical Sciences,
https://doi.org/10.1007/978-981-97-6972-8_17

Keywords Hamacher aggregation operators, 2TLq-RS, E-learning website, Multi-attribute group decision-making problem, MABAC method

1 Introduction

The swift advancements in technology for information and communication have led to the emergence of a modern approach to education known as e-learning. Unlike the traditional classroom setting, e-learning utilizes electronic media, particularly the Internet, to deliver education and knowledge to learners. The popularity of e-learning websites has grown significantly in recent decades due to the numerous advantages they offer, such as the flexibility to study at any time and from anywhere. Technological advancements have revolutionized the educational industry, aiming to enhance the teaching and learning processes. With the availability of e-learning, students now have the opportunity to learn a wide range of subjects from any location and at their preferred time. Many educational institutions have embraced e-learning to provide courses and academic degrees. Students can enroll in various programs and complete their exams online, eliminating the need to attend physical classrooms. This aspect is particularly beneficial for individuals who are working and have limited time to dedicate to traditional classes. In essence, e-learning is a combination of traditional teaching methods and Internet technology. It provides numerous advantages over traditional classroom education, including flexibility, adaptive learning, cost-effectiveness, and direct instructions. The widespread adoption of e-learning in academic institutions is a result of the rapid growth of Internet technology.

The transition from a conventional face-to-face education system to e-learning has prompted a comprehensive reevaluation of the entire educational landscape. E-learning, driven by technological advancements and digital platforms, has brought forth new opportunities and challenges in the realm of learning and teaching. A crucial aspect of this evaluation centers around the enhanced accessibility facilitated by e-learning. It has made education more readily available to a broader audience, transcending geographical limitations and enabling individuals from diverse backgrounds to engage in educational programs. This shift has opened doors for those who were previously constrained by factors such as physical disabilities, time constraints, or geographical remoteness. Moreover, e-learning has fundamentally transformed the pace of learning. Traditional classroom settings often adhere to a standardized curriculum and progress at a fixed tempo, which may not align with the individual learning styles and abilities of students. In contrast, e-learning offers flexible pacing, allowing learners to proceed at their own speed and revisit concepts whenever necessary. This personalized approach to learning cultivates a deeper comprehension and retention of knowledge. However, the increasing number of e-learning websites available poses a challenge for individuals seeking to choose the best option. Nevertheless, the assessment of the education system's transition to e-learning also sheds light on specific challenges. One prominent concern is the potential decline in social interaction and the absence of face-to-face communication. Classroom environments foster interactions between peers, collaboration, and the development of vital social skills. While e-learning platforms strive to replicate these aspects through online discussion forums and group projects, the lack of physical presence can still impede the extent of interpersonal connections.

Moreover, the digital divide presents a significant hurdle in the adoption of e-learning. Not all students have equal access to the necessary technology and Internet connectivity required for effective online education. This disparity in access can exacerbate existing educational inequalities, further marginalizing disadvantaged students. Another critical aspect of the evaluation revolves around the role of educators in the e-learning landscape. While e-learning platforms offer abundant resources and self-paced learning modules, the significance of skilled and dedicated teachers cannot be underestimated. Teachers play a crucial part in guiding and mentoring students, facilitating discussions, and providing personalized feedback. The challenge lies in adapting traditional teaching methodologies to the digital realm, ensuring that the instructional design is engaging, interactive, and effectively caters to the unique needs of online learners. These challenges can be approached as an MAGDM problem, where the evaluation of each alternative is performed by considering distinct attributes. The current study recognizes the ranking of e-learning websites as an MAGDM problem and emphasizes the need for a framework to assist decision-makers (DMs) in making informed choices. Several existing techniques, such as AHP, TOPSIS, VIKOR, and WDBA, have been used to address this problem. However, these methods have limitations, including long execution times and high complexity. Efficient selection of e-learning websites is crucial for the benefit of academics, administrators, and students alike. By developing an effective framework for evaluating and selecting e-learning websites, the study aims to provide significant advantages to all stakeholders involved in the educational process. Visual representation of evaluation of education system is presented in Fig. 1.

In the field of fuzzy set (FS) theory, Atanassov introduced the concept of intuitionistic FSs (IFSs) (Atanassov, 1986), which expand upon FSs (Zadeh, 1965). While FSs only consider membership degrees (MDs), IFSs incorporate both MDs and non-membership degrees (NMDs). The MD represents the degree of belongingness to the set, while the NMD represents the degree of non-belongingness. For an IFS, the sum of MD and NMD for every ordered pair must not exceed 1, reflecting uncertainty and hesitancy in decision-making. Based on this concept, Zhao et al. (2010) developed various aggregation operators (AOs) for IFSs, including IF weighted averaging, ordered weighted averaging, and hybrid average operators. These operators allow for the combination and aggregation of IFS information. Peykani et al. (2021) introduced a novel model for fuzzy multi-period multi-objective portfolio optimization. Their approach took into account three main objectives: wealth, risk, and liquidity. Additionally, Xu and Yager (2006) presented geometric AOs for IFSs which enable the representation of geometric interactions among IFS values. Xu and Yager demonstrated the application of the IFHWG operator in MAGDM scenarios using IFS information. These advancements in IFSs and the corresponding AOs provide valuable tools for handling uncertainty and ambiguity in decision-making processes, particularly in MAGDM contexts involving multiple attributes and decision-makers.

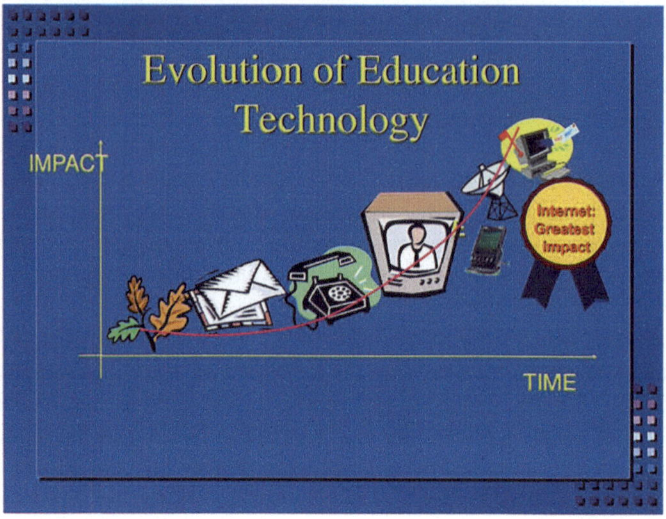

Fig. 1 Evaluation of education system

Adak and Kumar (2023) introduced a novel approach for measuring the distance between two Pythagorean fuzzy (PF) numbers. This spherical distance measurement plays a crucial role in the application of the PF TOPSIS method. It serves as a fundamental tool in determining distances for both the PF positive ideal solution and the PF negative ideal solution. Zadeh (1975) first proposed the notion of linguistic variables, wherein values are represented by words or sentences in natural languages. This concept has been proven valuable for addressing MAGDM problems with qualitative data. Sadeghi et al. (2021) put forward a novel method for assessing and prioritizing investment risks in advanced industries. Their approach involved employing the fuzzy TOPSIS technique, which relied on verbal variables, to achieve this objective. Consequently, there has been significant interest in MAGDM approaches concerning linguistic variables, as evidenced by the attention received in studies such as (Cid-Lopez et al., 2017; Liu et al., 2022; Naz et al., 2022; Garg et al., 2021; Akram et al., 2021; Zeng et al., 2019; Khan et al., 2019; Qiyas et al., 2019). Herrera and Martinez (2000) proposed a 2-tuple linguistic (2TL) model for computing with words to minimize data loss and decrease computational complexity expenses, one should strive to prevent information loss. Faizi et al. (2021) introduced the intuitionistic 2TL Hamacher weighted average and the intuitionistic 2TL Hamacher weighted geometric operators utilizing intuitionistic 2TL elements and Hamacher operations.

Due to the limitations of Pythagorean and IF sets, researchers have explored the q-RS as an alternative FS that overcomes the constraints encountered in MAGDM methods. q-RS enables the representation of complex uncertain information in real-world scenarios by allowing for a wider range of MDs and NMDs. Moreover, information systems with incomplete information play a crucial role in displaying the incompleteness inherent in MAGDM. Zhang et al. (2022) investigated a new MAGDM method based on multi-granulation probabilistic models, MULTIMOORA, and the precise order preference method in incomplete q-RS information systems. Rawat (2022) developed Muirhead mean operators, namely, the q-RS Hamacher Muirhead mean and q-RS Hamacher weighted Muirhead mean operators, utilizing Hamacher operations in a q-R environment, and demonstrated their desirable properties. Hasan et al. (2020) presented a set of picture fuzzy mean operators along with their decision-making properties, aiming to aggregate picture FSs. Aggregation operators serve as essential mathematical techniques employed to consolidate multiple inputs into a solitary output. The 2TLq-RS is a new innovation in FS theory introduced by Naz et al. (2022) for communicating data complexities. The 2TLq-RS integrates 2TL terms and q-RSs, expanding the set's validity and adaptability. The advantage of integrating the Hamacher operations with 2TLq-RS lies in their ability to assess both the interplay among multiple attributes and offer versatility in the aggregation procedure, owing to the inclusion of supplementary parameters. Wang et al. (2021) defined a novel interactive Hamacher operation and presented various PF interactive Hamacher power (PFIHP) AOs, such as PFIHP average, weighted average, ordered weighted average, PFIHP geometric, weighted geometric, and ordered geometric operators. Akram et al. (2021) presented some complex IF Hamacher weighted AOs. Garg et al. (2021) introduced multiple generalized Hamacher AOs that are weighted and ordered in nature. Hadi et al. (2021) introduced the concepts of Fermatean fuzzy Hamacher weighted averaging and geometric operators.

MAGDM plays a vital role in decision science by aiding in the selection of the best alternative from a limited set, taking into account various attributes. In MAGDM, two main categories of approaches are frequently utilized. The first category is information AOs, which consolidate a significant amount of data into a single consistent value. AOs commonly used in this category include weighted averaging, ordered weighted averaging, and power AOs. The second category is the MAGDM methods themselves, which encompass various techniques such as TOPSIS, VIKOR, TODIM, MOORA, and MABAC. Different decision-making procedures are applied in MAGDM situations based on specific requirements. However, each of these methods has its own limitations when it comes to selecting the optimal alternative from a given set of alternatives. The MABAC method is a decision-making approach specifically designed for addressing MAGDM problems. Its objective is to systematically evaluate and rank alternatives based on multiple criteria. The MABAC method utilizes the concept of border approximation areas to capture the preferences of DMs and the decision-making group. The process involves the following steps:

1. Criteria weight assignment: The decision-making group assigns weights to the criteria based on their relative importance. These weights reflect the significance of each criterion in the decision-making process.
2. Construction of border approximation areas: The MABAC method constructs border approximation areas for each alternative by considering the assigned weights. These areas define the boundaries within which the DM considers the alternatives to be acceptable.

3. Dominance and non-dominance assessment: The alternatives are compared pairwise to determine their dominance or non-dominance relationships. Dominance occurs when one alternative is preferred over another in all criteria, while non-dominance indicates a lack of clear preference.
4. Comparison of border approximation areas: The border approximation areas of the alternatives are compared to assess their relative performance. This comparison helps identify the alternatives with larger areas, indicating a higher preference.
5. Ranking of alternatives: Based on the comparison of border approximation areas, the alternatives are ranked from the highest to the lowest preference. This ranking provides a clear order of preference for decision-making.

The MABAC method offers a structured and intuitive approach for dealing with MAGDM problems. It takes into account the preferences of DMs and considers group dynamics. By systematically evaluating alternatives and considering multiple criteria simultaneously, the MABAC method assists DMs in making informed choices. Pamucar and Cirovic (2015) proposed the MABAC method to overcome these limitations and provide a viable solution for MAGDM problems. By employing the MABAC method, they effectively addressed challenges in transportation and processing resource selection at a logistics center. Their study showcased the method's efficacy by comparing it with alternative approaches such as SAW, COPRAS, TOPSIS, MOORA, and VIKOR. Pamucar et al. (2018) further improved the original MABAC method by incorporating interval-valued fuzzy-rough numbers. Liu and Wang (2022) suggested a modified MABAC method that incorporates two-dimensional uncertain linguistic variables to solve MAGDM situations where attribute weight information is unknown. Xu et al. (2021) presented MAGDM problems involving 2TL information using the Frank operator, the MABAC method, and the Best Worst Method. Jana (2021) developed an MAGDM technique based on a traditional MABAC model using bipolar fuzzy numbers by introducing two AOs. The continuous advancements and modifications to the MABAC method, along with its integration with other theories and techniques, reflect the ongoing research and development in the field of MAGDM. These efforts aim to improve the decision-making process in complex scenarios.

1.1 Motivation and Contributions

This paper aims to develop novel AOs for real-life MAGDM problems, offering flexibility and adaptability in the aggregation process. The introduction of the parameter q in the q-RS enables decision-makers (DMs) to expand their assessment decision range as needed. By combining operations of the Hamacher TN and Hamacher TCN with the MABAC method, the interdependency between numerous attributes is captured, allowing for flexible decision-making using additional parameters q and $\digamma$. The suggested AOs deliver a wide range of options by providing specific parameter values. The research focuses on developing an adaptive linguistic MAGDM model for 2TL scales, accommodating changes in both alternatives and attributes over time. The study recognizes the theoretical significance and practical benefits of considering language as attributes and exploring relationships between attributes in the MAGDM model. In MAGDM environments, AOs are extensively used and can be classified into average AOs and geometric AOs. However, these AOs fail to explain the interrelationships between attributes. To address this gap, the paper gives the concept of the 2TLq-RS-based Hamacher operators with the MABAC method. The main contributions of the paper are as follows:

1. Development of a family of Hamacher AOs for 2TLq-RSs, including the 2TLq-R Hamacher weighted average (2TLq-RHWA), 2TLq-R Hamacher ordered weighted average (2TLq-RHOWA), 2TLq-R Hamacher hybrid weighted average (2TLq-RHHWA), 2TLq-R Hamacher weighted geometric (2TLq-RHWG), 2TLq-R Hamacher ordered weighted geometric (2TLq-RHOWG), and 2TLq-R Hamacher hybrid weighted geometric (2TLq-RHHWG) operators. These AOs are designed specifically to address group decision-making problems.
2. Establishment of theorems, properties, and formal definitions for the proposed AOs under the given conditions. This ensures a solid theoretical foundation for their application in practice.
3. The 2TLq-R-MABAC technique is introduced as a means of ranking alternatives within the framework of MAGDM. This method combines the 2TLq-RHWA and 2TLq-RHWG operators and incorporates a novel MAGDM model to effectively capture the evaluation preferences of DMs. Through this approach, the 2TLq-R-MABAC method provides a comprehensive solution for ranking alternatives in MAGDM scenarios.
4. Illustration of the validity and credibility of the proposed 2TLq-R-MABAC method through an illustrative example. The example involves the selection of the best e-learning website, showcasing how the method can be applied to real-life decision-making scenarios.

By presenting these contributions, the paper advances the understanding and application of 2TLq-RSs, Hamacher AOs, and the 2TLq-R-MABAC method in the context of MAGDM.

1.2 Structure

This article adopts a structured framework to accomplish the cognitive approach, which can be outlined as follows:

In Sect. 2, essential concepts and definitions are introduced, including the term 2TL, q-RS, the Hamacher product $\otimes$, and Hamacher sum $\oplus$. Section 3 presents several novel 2TLq-RH AOs, such as the 2TLq-RHWA, the 2TLq-RHOWA, the 2TLq-RHHWA, the 2TLq-RHWG, the 2TLq-RHOWG, and the 2TLq-RHHWG operators. It also discusses their properties and provides specific instances. In Sect. 4, we propose an extended MABAC method for the MAGDM problem based on the 2TLq-RHWA and 2TLq-RHWG operators. Section 5 showcases the applicability and effectiveness of the proposed method through a case study focused on selecting the best e-learning website. Section 6 reports parameter and comparative assessments conducted to validate the superior performance of the proposed method. Finally, Sect. 7 summarizes the key findings and conclusions derived from this study.

This framework ensures a coherent progression of ideas and facilitates a comprehensive comprehension of the cognitive approach within the context of the article's subject matter.

2 Basic Definitions and Results

In this section, we provide a brief overview of some fundamental results associated with the 2TL term, q-RS, 2TLq-RS, score function, accuracy function, Hamacher product $\otimes$, and Hamacher sum $\oplus$.

Herrera and Martinez (2000) proposed a 2TL model for computing with words to avoid information loss in data processing.

Definition 1 Herrera and Martinez (2000) Let $\mathcal{S} = \{\xi_t | t = 0, 1, \ldots, \Theta\}$ represent an linguistic term set (LTS), and let $\digamma \in [0, \Theta]$ be a numerical value that represents the aggregation result of a linguistic symbolic. Then, a 2-tuple (ξ_t, υ) is capable of expressing information equivalent to $\digamma$. Furthermore, the function $\triangle$ can be used to obtain the 2-tuple as follows:

$$\triangle : [0, \Theta] \rightarrow \mathcal{S} \times [-1/2, 1/2),$$

$$\triangle(\digamma) = \begin{cases} \xi_t, t = \text{round}(\digamma) \\ \upsilon = \digamma - t, \ \upsilon \in [-1/2, 1/2). \end{cases} \tag{1}$$

Similarly, to convert the 2-tuple back to its equivalent numerical value $\digamma \in [0, \Theta] \subset \mathbb{R}$, there exists a function $\triangle^{-1}$ defined as follows:

$$\begin{aligned} \triangle^{-1} : \mathcal{S} \times [-1/2 = -0.5, 1/2 = 0.5) \rightarrow [0, \Theta], \\ \triangle^{-1}(\xi_t, \upsilon) = t + \upsilon = \digamma. \end{aligned} \tag{2}$$

Xu and Yager (2006) introduced the concept of the q-R set as an extension of IFS and PFS. The definition of a q-RS is given as follows:

Definition 2 Xu and Yager (2006) Consider a universal set denoted by U. A q-RS is defined by the set T such as:

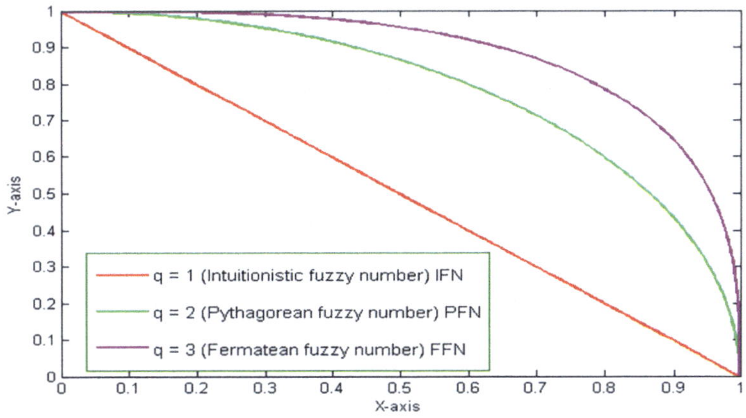

Fig. 2 Geometrical interpretation of IFN, PFN, and FFN

$$T = \{\langle u, j_T(u), l_T(u)\rangle | u \in U\},$$

and the real-valued functions $j_T(u) : U \to [0, 1]$ and $l_T(u) : U \to [0, 1]$ represent the MD and NMD of u, respectively. The conditions $0 \leq j^q(u) + l^q(u) \leq 1$ hold for a positive number $q \geq 1$. The refusal degree $r(u)$ is defined as $r(u) = \sqrt[q]{1 - (j^q(u) + l^q(u))}$. The pair (j, l) is referred to as a q-rung orthopair fuzzy number, which generalizes existing fuzzy frameworks. Figure 2 illustrates the relationship between these existing fuzzy frameworks and q-rung orthopair fuzzy numbers.

A novel concept of 2TLq-RS was introduced by Naz et al. (2022), drawing inspiration from the concepts of 2TL terms and q-RSs.

Definition 3 Naz et al. (2022) Let $\mathcal{S} = \{\xi_t | t = 0, 1, \ldots, \Theta\}$ be an LTS with an odd cardinality. If $(\xi_j(u), \mathcal{P}(u))$, $(\xi_l(u), \mathcal{Q}(u))$ is defined for $\xi_j(u), \xi_l(u) \in \mathcal{S}$, $\mathcal{P}(u)$, $\mathcal{Q}(u) \in [-0.5, 0.5)$, where $(\xi_j(u), \mathcal{P}(u))$ and $(\xi_l(u), \mathcal{Q}(u))$ represent the MD and NMD by 2TL terms, respectively. A 2TLq-RS is defined as follows:

$$\aleph = \{\langle (u), ((\xi_j(u), \mathcal{P}(u)), (\xi_l(u), \mathcal{Q}(u)))\rangle | (u) \in U\}, \tag{3}$$

where $0 \leq \Delta^{-1}(\xi_j(u), \mathcal{P}(u)) \leq \Theta, 0 \leq \Delta^{-1}(\xi_l(u), \mathcal{Q}(u)) \leq \Theta$, and $0 \leq (\Delta^{-1}(\xi_j(u), \mathcal{P}(u)))^q + (\Delta^{-1}(\xi_l(u), \mathcal{Q}(u)))^q \leq \Theta^q$.

In order to assess and differentiate between two 2TLq-RNs, their score function and accuracy function can be described in the following manner:

Definition 4 Naz et al. (2022) Let $\Re = ((\xi_j, \mathcal{P}), (\xi_l, \mathcal{Q}))$ be a 2TLq-RN. Then the score function SF of a 2TLq-RN $\Re$ can be represented as

$$SF(\Re) = \Delta\left(\frac{\Theta}{2}\left(1 + \left(\frac{\Delta^{-1}(\xi_j, \mathcal{P})}{\Theta}\right)^q - \left(\frac{\Delta^{-1}(\xi_l, \mathcal{Q})}{\Theta}\right)^q\right)\right),$$
$$\Delta^{-1}(SF(\Re)) \in [0, \Theta], \tag{4}$$

and its accuracy function AF is defined as

$$AF(\Re) = \Delta\left(\Theta\left(\left(\frac{\Delta^{-1}(\xi_j, \mathcal{P})}{\Theta}\right)^q + \left(\frac{\Delta^{-1}(\xi_l, \mathcal{Q})}{\Theta}\right)^q\right)\right), \; \Delta^{-1}(AF(\Re)) \in [0, \Theta]. \tag{5}$$

Definition 5 Naz et al. (2022) Let $\Re_1 = ((\xi_{j_1}, \mathcal{P}_1), (\xi_{l_1}, \mathcal{Q}_1))$ and $\Re_2 = ((\xi_{j_2}, \mathcal{P}_2), (\xi_{l_2}, \mathcal{Q}_2))$ be two 2TLq-RNs, they may be evaluated utilizing to the suggestions below:

(1) $SF(\Re_1) > SF(\Re_2) \Rightarrow \Re_1 > \Re_2$;
(2) $SF(\Re_1) = SF(\Re_2)$, we get:

- $AF(\Re_1) > AF(\Re_2) \Rightarrow \Re_1 > \Re_2$;
- $AF(\Re_1) = AF(\Re_2) \Rightarrow \Re_1 \sim \Re_2$.

Example 1 Let $\Re_1 = ((\xi_3, 0), (\xi_5, 0))$, $\Re_2 = ((\xi_6, 0), (\xi_2, 0))$, and $\Re_3 = ((\xi_7, 0), (\xi_1, 0))$ be three 2TLq-RNs which are derived from LTS $\mathcal{S} = \{\xi_t | t = 0, \ldots, 8\}$ and $q = 4$, then by utilizing Eq. (4), the scores of the given 2TLq-RNs can be calculated as

$$SF(\Re_1) = \Delta\left(\frac{8}{2}\left(1 + \left(\frac{\Delta^{-1}(\xi_3, 0)}{8}\right)^4 - \left(\frac{\Delta^{-1}(\xi_5, 0)}{8}\right)^4\right)\right),$$
$$= \Delta(3.4688) = (\xi_3, 0.4688).$$

$$SF(\Re_2) = \Delta\left(\frac{8}{2}\left(1 + \left(\frac{\Delta^{-1}(\xi_6, 0)}{8}\right)^4 - \left(\frac{\Delta^{-1}(\xi_2, 0)}{8}\right)^4\right)\right),$$
$$= \Delta(5.2500) = (\xi_5, 0.2500).$$

$$SF(\Re_3) = \Delta\left(\frac{8}{2}\left(1 + \left(\frac{\Delta^{-1}(\xi_7, 0)}{8}\right)^4 - \left(\frac{\Delta^{-1}(\xi_1, 0)}{8}\right)^4\right)\right),$$
$$= \Delta(6.3438) = (\xi_6, 0.3438).$$

According to Def. 5, the ranking of 2TLq-RNs can be obtained as

$$SF(\Re_3) > SF(\Re_2) > SF(\Re_1) \Rightarrow \Re_3 > \Re_2 > \Re_1.$$

However, there are instances where the scores of two or more 2TLq-RNs are equal. In such cases, the score function is unable to differentiate between the 2TLq-RNs. To address this scenario, the accuracy function is employed.

Definition 6 Naz et al. (2022) Let $\Re_1 = ((\xi_{j_1}, \mathcal{P}_1), (\xi_{l_1}, \mathcal{Q}_1))$ and $\Re_2 = ((\xi_{j_2}, \mathcal{P}_2), (\xi_{l_2}, \mathcal{Q}_2))$ be two 2TLq-RNs. We define the 2TLq-R normalized Hamming distance as

$$d(\Re_1, \Re_2) = \Delta\left(\frac{\Theta}{2}\left(\left|\left(\frac{\Delta^{-1}(\xi_{j_1}, \mathcal{P}_1)}{\Theta}\right)^q - \left(\frac{\Delta^{-1}(\xi_{j_2}, \mathcal{P}_2)}{\Theta}\right)^q\right| + \left|\left(\frac{\Delta^{-1}(\xi_{l_1}, \mathcal{Q}_1)}{\Theta}\right)^q - \left(\frac{\Delta^{-1}(\xi_{l_2}, \mathcal{Q}_2)}{\Theta}\right)^q\right|\right)\right). \quad (6)$$

The operational laws for 2TLq-RNs, which include addition, multiplication, scalar multiplication, and the power rule, are defined in the following manner:

Definition 7 Naz et al. (2022) Let $\Re = ((\xi_j, \mathcal{P}), (\xi_l, \mathcal{Q}))$, $\Re_1 = ((\xi_{j_1}, \mathcal{P}_1), (\xi_{l_1}, \mathcal{Q}_1))$, and $\Re_2 = ((\xi_{j_2}, \mathcal{P}_2), (\xi_{l_2}, \mathcal{Q}_2))$ be three 2TLq-RNs, $q \geq 1$, then

1. $\Re_1 \oplus \Re_2 = \left(\Delta\left(\Theta\sqrt[q]{1-\left(1-\left(\frac{\Delta^{-1}(\xi_{j_1},\mathcal{P}_1)}{\Theta}\right)^q\right)\left(1-\left(\frac{\Delta^{-1}(\xi_{j_2},\mathcal{P}_2)}{\Theta}\right)^q\right)}\right), \Delta\left(\Theta\left(\frac{\Delta^{-1}(\xi_{l_1},\mathcal{Q}_1)}{\Theta}\right)\left(\frac{\Delta^{-1}(\xi_{l_2},\mathcal{Q}_2)}{\Theta}\right)\right)\right);$
2. $\Re_1 \otimes \Re_2 = \left(\Delta\left(\Theta\left(\frac{\Delta^{-1}(\xi_{j_1},\mathcal{P}_1)}{\Theta}\right)\left(\frac{\Delta^{-1}(\xi_{j_2},\mathcal{P}_2)}{\Theta}\right)\right), \Delta\left(\Theta\sqrt[q]{1-\left(1-\left(\frac{\Delta^{-1}(\xi_{l_1},\mathcal{Q}_1)}{\Theta}\right)^q\right)\left(1-\left(\frac{\Delta^{-1}(\xi_{l_2},\mathcal{Q}_2)}{\Theta}\right)^q\right)}\right)\right);$
3. $\delta\Re = \left(\Delta\left(\Theta\sqrt[q]{1-\left(1-\left(\frac{\Delta^{-1}(\xi_j,\mathcal{P})}{\Theta}\right)^q\right)^\delta}\right), \Delta\left(\Theta\left(\frac{\Delta^{-1}(\xi_l,\mathcal{Q})}{\Theta}\right)^\delta\right)\right), \quad \delta > 0;$
4. $\Re^\delta = \left(\Delta\left(\Theta\left(\frac{\Delta^{-1}(\xi_j,\mathcal{P})}{\Theta}\right)^\delta\right), \Delta\left(\Theta\sqrt[q]{1-\left(1-\left(\frac{\Delta^{-1}(\xi_l,\mathcal{Q})}{\Theta}\right)^q\right)^\delta}\right)\right), \quad \delta > 0.$

Definition 8 Hamacher (1978) developed the Hamacher product TN and Hamacher sum TCN as expansions to the current Hamacher TN and Hamacher TCN operations. These novel operations are generalizations of Hamacher TNs and TCNs, respectively. Here are the formulations:

$$\mathfrak{T}_{\digamma}^{\mathfrak{H}}(\varepsilon, \varsigma) = \begin{cases} \frac{\varepsilon\varsigma}{\digamma + (1-\digamma)(\varepsilon+\varsigma-\varepsilon\varsigma)} & \text{if } \digamma > 0, \\ \frac{\varepsilon\varsigma}{\varepsilon+\varsigma-\varepsilon\varsigma} & \text{if } \digamma = 0, \end{cases}$$

$$(\mathfrak{T}^*)_{\digamma}^{\mathfrak{H}}(\varepsilon, \varsigma) = \begin{cases} \frac{\varepsilon+\varsigma-\varepsilon\varsigma-(1-\digamma)\varepsilon\varsigma}{1-(1-\digamma)\varepsilon\varsigma} & \text{if } \digamma > 0, \\ \frac{\varepsilon+\varsigma-2\varepsilon\varsigma}{1-\varepsilon\varsigma} & \text{if } \digamma = 0. \end{cases}$$

Clearly, when $\digamma = 1$, the algebraic TN and TCN can be derived from the Hamacher TN and Hamacher TCN as shown below:

$$\mathfrak{P}(\varepsilon, \varsigma) = \varepsilon\varsigma, \quad \mathfrak{P}^*(\varepsilon, \varsigma) = \varepsilon + \varsigma - \varepsilon\varsigma.$$

Furthermore, for $\digamma = 2$, the Hamacher TN and Hamacher TCN can be simplified to the Einstein TN and Einstein TCN Wang and Liu (2011) using the following approach:

$$\mathfrak{E}(\varepsilon, \varsigma) = \frac{\varepsilon\varsigma}{1 + (1-\varepsilon)(1-\varsigma)}, \quad \mathfrak{E}^*(\varepsilon, \varsigma) = \frac{\varepsilon + \varsigma}{1 + \varepsilon\varsigma}.$$

3 The 2TLq-R Hamacher Aos

In this section, we present a modified intersection and union operation for two 2TLq-RNs. These operations utilize the Hamacher product $\otimes$ and the Hamacher sum $\oplus$. The Hamacher operational laws for 2TLq-RNs are defined as follows:

Definition 9 Let $\mathfrak{R}_1 = ((\xi_{j_1}, \mathcal{P}_1), (\xi_{l_1}, \mathcal{Q}_1))$ and $\mathfrak{R}_2 = ((\xi_{j_2}, \mathcal{P}_2), (\xi_{l_2}, \mathcal{Q}_2))$ be two 2TLq-RNs, with $\digamma$ as a positive value. Now, let's define the basic Hamacher operations between $\mathfrak{R}_1$ and $\mathfrak{R}_2$ as follows:

1. $\mathfrak{R}_1 \oplus \mathfrak{R}_2$

$$= \left(\begin{array}{c} \Delta\left(\Theta\left(\sqrt[q]{\dfrac{\left(\frac{\Delta^{-1}(\xi_{j_1},\mathcal{P}_1)}{\Theta}\right)^q + \left(\frac{\Delta^{-1}(\xi_{j_2},\mathcal{P}_2)}{\Theta}\right)^q - \left(\frac{\Delta^{-1}(\xi_{j_1},\mathcal{P}_1)}{\Theta}\right)^q\left(\frac{\Delta^{-1}(\xi_{j_2},\mathcal{P}_2)}{\Theta}\right)^q - (1-\digamma)\left(\frac{\Delta^{-1}(\xi_{j_1},\mathcal{P}_1)}{\Theta}\right)^q\left(\frac{\Delta^{-1}(\xi_{j_2},\mathcal{P}_2)}{\Theta}\right)^q}{1-(1-\digamma)\left(\frac{\Delta^{-1}(\xi_{j_1},\mathcal{P}_1)}{\Theta}\right)^q\left(\frac{\Delta^{-1}(\xi_{j_2},\mathcal{P}_2)}{\Theta}\right)^q}}\right)\right), \\ \Delta\left(\Theta\left(\dfrac{\left(\frac{\Delta^{-1}(\xi_{l_1},\mathcal{Q}_1)}{\Theta}\right)\left(\frac{\Delta^{-1}(\xi_{l_2},\mathcal{Q}_2)}{\Theta}\right)}{\sqrt[q]{\digamma+(1-\digamma)\left(\left(\frac{\Delta^{-1}(\xi_{l_1},\mathcal{Q}_1)}{\Theta}\right)^q+\left(\frac{\Delta^{-1}(\xi_{l_2},\mathcal{Q}_2)}{\Theta}\right)^q-\left(\frac{\Delta^{-1}(\xi_{l_1},\mathcal{Q}_1)}{\Theta}\right)^q\left(\frac{\Delta^{-1}(\xi_{l_2},\mathcal{Q}_2)}{\Theta}\right)^q\right)}}\right)\right) \end{array} \right);$$

2. $\Re_1 \otimes \Re_2$

$$= \left(\begin{array}{c} \Delta\left(\Theta\left(\dfrac{\left(\frac{\Delta^{-1}(\xi_{j_1},\mathcal{P}_1)}{\Theta}\right)\left(\frac{\Delta^{-1}(\xi_{j_2},\mathcal{P}_2)}{\Theta}\right)}{\sqrt[q]{F+(1-F)\left(\left(\frac{\Delta^{-1}(\xi_{j_1},\mathcal{P}_1)}{\Theta}\right)^q+\left(\frac{\Delta^{-1}(\xi_{j_2},\mathcal{P}_2)}{\Theta}\right)^q-\left(\frac{\Delta^{-1}(\xi_{j_1},\mathcal{P}_1)}{\Theta}\right)^q\left(\frac{\Delta^{-1}(\xi_{j_2},\mathcal{P}_2)}{\Theta}\right)^q\right)}}\right)\right), \\ \Delta\left(\Theta\left(\sqrt[q]{\dfrac{\left(\frac{\Delta^{-1}(\xi_{l_1},\mathcal{Q}_1)}{\Theta}\right)^q+\left(\frac{\Delta^{-1}(\xi_{l_2},\mathcal{Q}_2)}{\Theta}\right)^q-\left(\frac{\Delta^{-1}(\xi_{l_1},\mathcal{Q}_1)}{\Theta}\right)^q\left(\frac{\Delta^{-1}(\xi_{l_2},\mathcal{Q}_2)}{\Theta}\right)^q-(1-F)\left(\frac{\Delta^{-1}(\xi_{l_1},\mathcal{Q}_1)}{\Theta}\right)^q\left(\frac{\Delta^{-1}(\xi_{l_2},\mathcal{Q}_2)}{\Theta}\right)^q}{1-(1-F)\left(\frac{\Delta^{-1}(\xi_{l_1},\mathcal{Q}_1)}{\Theta}\right)^q\left(\frac{\Delta^{-1}(\xi_{l_2},\mathcal{Q}_2)}{\Theta}\right)^q}}\right)\right) \end{array} \right);$$

3. $\delta\Re_1$

$$= \left(\begin{array}{c} \Delta\left(\Theta\left(\sqrt[q]{\dfrac{\left(1+(F-1)\left(\frac{\Delta^{-1}(\xi_{j_1},\mathcal{P}_1)}{\Theta}\right)^q\right)^\delta-\left(1-\left(\frac{\Delta^{-1}(\xi_{j_1},\mathcal{P}_1)}{\Theta}\right)^q\right)^\delta}{\left(1+(F-1)\left(\frac{\Delta^{-1}(\xi_{j_1},\mathcal{P}_1)}{\Theta}\right)^q\right)^\delta+(F-1)\left(1-\left(\frac{\Delta^{-1}(\xi_{j_1},\mathcal{P}_1)}{\Theta}\right)^q\right)^\delta}}\right)\right), \\ \Delta\left(\Theta\left(\dfrac{\sqrt[q]{F}\left(\frac{\Delta^{-1}(\xi_{l_1},\mathcal{Q}_1)}{\Theta}\right)^\delta}{\sqrt[q]{\left(1+(F-1)\left(1-\left(\frac{\Delta^{-1}(\xi_{l_1},\mathcal{Q}_1)}{\Theta}\right)^q\right)\right)^\delta+(F-1)\left(\frac{\Delta^{-1}(\xi_{l_1},\mathcal{Q}_1)}{\Theta}\right)^{q\delta}}}\right)\right) \end{array} \right), \delta > 0;$$

4. $\Re_1{}^\delta$

$$= \left(\begin{array}{c} \Delta\left(\Theta\left(\dfrac{\sqrt[q]{F}\left(\frac{\Delta^{-1}(\xi_{j_1},\mathcal{P}_1)}{\Theta}\right)^\delta}{\sqrt[q]{\left(1+(F-1)\left(1-\left(\frac{\Delta^{-1}(\xi_{j_1},\mathcal{P}_1)}{\Theta}\right)^q\right)\right)^\delta+(F-1)\left(\frac{\Delta^{-1}(\xi_{j_1},\mathcal{P}_1)}{\Theta}\right)^{q\delta}}}\right)\right), \\ \Delta\left(\Theta\left(\sqrt[q]{\dfrac{\left(1+(F-1)\left(\frac{\Delta^{-1}(\xi_{l_1},\mathcal{Q}_1)}{\Theta}\right)^q\right)^\delta-\left(1-\left(\frac{\Delta^{-1}(\xi_{l_1},\mathcal{Q}_1)}{\Theta}\right)^q\right)^\delta}{\left(1+(F-1)\left(\frac{\Delta^{-1}(\xi_{l_1},\mathcal{Q}_1)}{\Theta}\right)^q\right)^\delta+(F-1)\left(1-\left(\frac{\Delta^{-1}(\xi_{l_1},\mathcal{Q}_1)}{\Theta}\right)^q\right)^\delta}}\right)\right) \end{array} \right), \delta > 0.$$

Definition 10 Let $\Re_\rho = ((\xi_{j_\rho}, \mathcal{P}_\rho), (\xi_{l_\rho}, \mathcal{Q}_\rho))(\rho = 1, 2, \ldots, \imath)$ represent a collection of 2TLq-RNs. The 2TLq-RHWA operator is defined as follows:

$$2\text{TL}q\text{-RHWA}_{\varphi'}(\Re_1, \Re_2, \ldots, \Re_\iota) = \bigoplus_{\rho=1}^{\iota} \left(\varphi'_\rho \Re_\rho\right),$$

where $\varphi' = \left(\varphi'_1, \varphi'_2, \ldots, \varphi'_\iota\right)^T$ represents the weight vector of $\Re_\rho (\rho = 1, 2, \ldots, \iota)$, and $\varphi'_\rho > 0$, $\sum_{\rho=1}^{\iota} \varphi'_\rho = 1$.

We establish the following theorem by applying the 2TLq-RH operations based on Def. 10.

Theorem 1 *Let* $\Re_\rho = ((\xi_{j_\rho}, \mathcal{P}_\rho), (\xi_{l_\rho}, \mathcal{Q}_\rho))$ $(\rho = 1, 2, \ldots, \iota)$ *represent a collection of 2TLq-RNs, where* $F > 0$*. Then, for any non-negative q, employing the 2TLq-RHWA operator yields an aggregated value that is also a 2TLq-RN, and*

$$2TLq\text{-}RHWA_{\varphi'}(\Re_1, \Re_2, \ldots, \Re_\iota) = \bigoplus_{\rho=1}^{\iota} \left(\varphi'_\rho \Re_\rho\right)$$

$$= \left(\begin{array}{l} \Delta\left(\Theta\left(\sqrt[q]{\dfrac{\prod_{\rho=1}^{\iota}\left(1+(F-1)\left(\frac{\Delta^{-1}(\xi_{j_\rho},\mathcal{P}_\rho)}{\Theta}\right)^q\right)^{\varphi'_\rho} - \prod_{\rho=1}^{\iota}\left(1-\left(\frac{\Delta^{-1}(\xi_{j_\rho},\mathcal{P}_\rho)}{\Theta}\right)^q\right)^{\varphi'_\rho}}{\prod_{\rho=1}^{\iota}\left(1+(F-1)\left(\frac{\Delta^{-1}(\xi_{j_\rho},\mathcal{P}_\rho)}{\Theta}\right)^q\right)^{\varphi'_\rho} + (F-1)\prod_{\rho=1}^{\iota}\left(1-\left(\frac{\Delta^{-1}(\xi_{j_\rho},\mathcal{P}_\rho)}{\Theta}\right)^q\right)^{\varphi'_\rho}}}\right)\right), \\ \Delta\left(\Theta\left(\dfrac{\sqrt[q]{F}\prod_{\rho=1}^{\iota}\left(\frac{\Delta^{-1}(\xi_{l_\rho},\mathcal{Q}_\rho)}{\Theta}\right)^{\varphi'_\rho}}{\sqrt[q]{\prod_{\rho=1}^{\iota}\left(1+(F-1)\left(1-\left(\frac{\Delta^{-1}(\xi_{l_\rho},\mathcal{Q}_\rho)}{\Theta}\right)^q\right)\right)^{\varphi'_\rho} + (F-1)\prod_{\rho=1}^{\iota}\left(\frac{\Delta^{-1}(\xi_{l_\rho},\mathcal{Q}_\rho)}{\Theta}\right)^{q\varphi'_\rho}}}\right)\right) \end{array} \right). \tag{7}$$

Proof We establish the validity of Equation (7) by utilizing the technique of mathematical induction. For the base case $\iota = 2$, we utilize the operational laws (1) and (3) stated in Def. 9, which leads to the following outcome:

$$\varphi'_1\Re_1 \oplus \varphi'_2\Re_2$$

$$= \left(\begin{array}{l} \Delta\left(\Theta\left(\sqrt[q]{\dfrac{\left(1+(F-1)\left(\frac{\Delta^{-1}(\xi_{j_1},\mathcal{P}_1)}{\Theta}\right)^q\right)^{\varphi'_1} - \left(1-\left(\frac{\Delta^{-1}(\xi_{j_1},\mathcal{P}_1)}{\Theta}\right)^q\right)^{\varphi'_1}}{\left(1+(F-1)\left(\frac{\Delta^{-1}(\xi_{j_1},\mathcal{P}_1)}{\Theta}\right)^q\right)^{\varphi'_1} + (F-1)\left(1-\left(\frac{\Delta^{-1}(\xi_{j_1},\mathcal{P}_1)}{\Theta}\right)^q\right)^{\varphi'_1}}}\right)\right), \\ \Delta\left(\Theta\left(\dfrac{\sqrt[q]{F}\left(\frac{\Delta^{-1}(\xi_{l_1},\mathcal{Q}_1)}{\Theta}\right)^{\varphi'_1}}{\sqrt[q]{\left(1+(F-1)\left(1-\left(\frac{\Delta^{-1}(\xi_{l_1},\mathcal{Q}_1)}{\Theta}\right)^q\right)\right)^{\varphi'_1} + (F-1)\left(\frac{\Delta^{-1}(\xi_{l_1},\mathcal{Q}_1)}{\Theta}\right)^{q\varphi'_1}}}\right)\right) \end{array} \right)$$

$$\oplus\left(\begin{array}{c}\Delta\left(\Theta\left(\sqrt[q]{\dfrac{\left(1+(\mathcal{F}-1)\left(\frac{\Delta^{-1}\left(\xi_{j_2},\mathcal{P}_2\right)}{\Theta}\right)^{q}\right)^{\varphi_2'}-\left(1-\left(\frac{\Delta^{-1}\left(\xi_{j_2},\mathcal{P}_2\right)}{\Theta}\right)^{q}\right)^{\varphi_2'}}{\left(1+(\mathcal{F}-1)\left(\frac{\Delta^{-1}\left(\xi_{j_2},\mathcal{P}_2\right)}{\Theta}\right)^{q}\right)^{\varphi_2'}+(\mathcal{F}-1)\left(1-\left(\frac{\Delta^{-1}\left(\xi_{j_2},\mathcal{P}_2\right)}{\Theta}\right)^{q}\right)^{\varphi_2'}}}\right)\right),\\ \Delta\left(\Theta\left(\dfrac{\sqrt[q]{\mathcal{F}}\left(\frac{\Delta^{-1}\left(\xi_{l_2},\mathcal{Q}_2\right)}{\Theta}\right)^{\varphi_2'}}{\sqrt[q]{\left(1+(\mathcal{F}-1)\left(1-\left(\frac{\Delta^{-1}\left(\xi_{l_2},\mathcal{Q}_2\right)}{\Theta}\right)^{q}\right)\right)^{\varphi_2'}+(\mathcal{F}-1)\left(\frac{\Delta^{-1}\left(\xi_{l_2},\mathcal{Q}_2\right)}{\Theta}\right)^{q\varphi_2'}}}\right)\right)\end{array}\right)$$

$$=\left(\begin{array}{c}\Delta\left(\Theta\left(\sqrt[q]{\dfrac{\prod_{\rho=1}^{2}\left(1+(\mathcal{F}-1)\left(\frac{\Delta^{-1}\left(\xi_{j_\rho},\mathcal{P}_\rho\right)}{\Theta}\right)^{q}\right)^{\varphi_\rho'}-\prod_{\rho=1}^{2}\left(1-\left(\frac{\Delta^{-1}\left(\xi_{j_\rho},\mathcal{P}_\rho\right)}{\Theta}\right)^{q}\right)^{\varphi_\rho'}}{\prod_{\rho=1}^{2}\left(1+(\mathcal{F}-1)\left(\frac{\Delta^{-1}\left(\xi_{j_\rho},\mathcal{P}_\rho\right)}{\Theta}\right)^{q}\right)^{\varphi_\rho'}+(\mathcal{F}-1)\prod_{\rho=1}^{2}\left(1-\left(\frac{\Delta^{-1}\left(\xi_{j_\rho},\mathcal{P}_\rho\right)}{\Theta}\right)^{q}\right)^{\varphi_\rho'}}}\right)\right),\\ \Delta\left(\Theta\left(\dfrac{\sqrt[q]{\mathcal{F}}\prod_{\rho=1}^{2}\left(\frac{\Delta^{-1}\left(\xi_{l_\rho},\mathcal{Q}_\rho\right)}{\Theta}\right)^{\varphi_\rho'}}{\sqrt[q]{\prod_{\rho=1}^{2}\left(1+(\mathcal{F}-1)\left(1-\left(\frac{\Delta^{-1}\left(\xi_{l_\rho},\mathcal{Q}_\rho\right)}{\Theta}\right)^{q}\right)\right)^{\varphi_\rho'}+(\mathcal{F}-1)\prod_{\rho=1}^{2}\left(\frac{\Delta^{-1}\left(\xi_{l_\rho},\mathcal{Q}_\rho\right)}{\Theta}\right)^{q\varphi_\rho'}}}\right)\right)\end{array}\right).$$

We establish the validity of Eq. (7) for the case when $\iota = 2$. Assuming that the result holds true for $\iota = \mathcal{k}$, let us proceed with the next step.

$$\underset{\rho=1}{\overset{\mathcal{k}}{\oplus}}\left(\varphi_\rho'\Re_\rho\right)$$

$$=\left(\begin{array}{c}\Delta\left(\Theta\left(\sqrt[q]{\dfrac{\prod_{\rho=1}^{\mathcal{k}}\left(1+(\mathcal{F}-1)\left(\frac{\Delta^{-1}\left(\xi_{j_\rho},\mathcal{P}_\rho\right)}{\Theta}\right)^{q}\right)^{\varphi_\rho'}-\prod_{\rho=1}^{\mathcal{k}}\left(1-\left(\frac{\Delta^{-1}\left(\xi_{j_\rho},\mathcal{P}_\rho\right)}{\Theta}\right)^{q}\right)^{\varphi_\rho'}}{\prod_{\rho=1}^{\mathcal{k}}\left(1+(\mathcal{F}-1)\left(\frac{\Delta^{-1}\left(\xi_{j_\rho},\mathcal{P}_\rho\right)}{\Theta}\right)^{q}\right)^{\varphi_\rho'}+(\mathcal{F}-1)\prod_{\rho=1}^{\mathcal{k}}\left(1-\left(\frac{\Delta^{-1}\left(\xi_{j_\rho},\mathcal{P}_\rho\right)}{\Theta}\right)^{q}\right)^{\varphi_\rho'}}}\right)\right),\\ \Delta\left(\Theta\left(\dfrac{\sqrt[q]{\mathcal{F}}\prod_{\rho=1}^{\mathcal{k}}\left(\frac{\Delta^{-1}\left(\xi_{l_\rho},\mathcal{Q}_\rho\right)}{\Theta}\right)^{\varphi_\rho'}}{\sqrt[q]{\prod_{\rho=1}^{\mathcal{k}}\left(1+(\mathcal{F}-1)\left(1-\left(\frac{\Delta^{-1}\left(\xi_{l_\rho},\mathcal{Q}_\rho\right)}{\Theta}\right)^{q}\right)\right)^{\varphi_\rho'}+(\mathcal{F}-1)\prod_{\rho=1}^{\mathcal{k}}\left(\frac{\Delta^{-1}\left(\xi_{l_\rho},\mathcal{Q}_\rho\right)}{\Theta}\right)^{q\varphi_\rho'}}}\right)\right)\end{array}\right).$$

Next, we consider the case when $\iota = \mathcal{k} + 1$. By applying the operational laws described in Def. 9, we obtain the following expression:

$$\underset{\rho=1}{\overset{\mathcal{k}+1}{\oplus}}\left(\varphi_\rho'\Re_\rho\right)=\left(\underset{\rho=1}{\overset{\mathcal{k}}{\oplus}}\left(\varphi_\rho'\Re_\rho\right)\right)\oplus\left(\varphi_{\mathcal{k}+1}'\Re_{\mathcal{k}+1}\right)$$

$$
= \left(\begin{array}{c}
\Delta\left(\Theta\left(\sqrt[q]{\frac{\prod_{\rho=1}^{\mathscr{k}}\left(1+(\mathcal{F}-1)\left(\frac{\Delta^{-1}(\xi_{j_\rho},\mathcal{P}_\rho)}{\Theta}\right)^{q}\right)^{\varphi'_\rho}-\prod_{\rho=1}^{\mathscr{k}}\left(1-\left(\frac{\Delta^{-1}(\xi_{j_\rho},\mathcal{P}_\rho)}{\Theta}\right)^{q}\right)^{\varphi'_\rho}}{\prod_{\rho=1}^{\mathscr{k}}\left(1+(\mathcal{F}-1)\left(\frac{\Delta^{-1}(\xi_{j_\rho},\mathcal{P}_\rho)}{\Theta}\right)^{q}\right)^{\varphi'_\rho}+(\mathcal{F}-1)\prod_{\rho=1}^{\mathscr{k}}\left(1-\left(\frac{\Delta^{-1}(\xi_{j_\rho},\mathcal{P}_\rho)}{\Theta}\right)^{q}\right)^{\varphi'_\rho}}}\right)\right), \\
\Delta\left(\Theta\left(\frac{\sqrt[q]{\mathcal{F}}\prod_{\rho=1}^{\mathscr{k}}\left(\frac{\Delta^{-1}(\xi_{l_\rho},\mathcal{Q}_\rho)}{\Theta}\right)^{\varphi'_\rho}}{\sqrt[q]{\prod_{\rho=1}^{\mathscr{k}}\left(1+(\mathcal{F}-1)\left(1-\left(\frac{\Delta^{-1}(\xi_{l_\rho},\mathcal{Q}_\rho)}{\Theta}\right)^{q}\right)\right)^{\varphi'_\rho}+(\mathcal{F}-1)\prod_{\rho=1}^{\mathscr{k}}\left(\frac{\Delta^{-1}(\xi_{l_\rho},\mathcal{Q}_\rho)}{\Theta}\right)^{q\varphi'_\rho}}}\right)\right)
\end{array} \right)
$$

$$
\oplus \left(\begin{array}{c}
\Delta\left(\Theta\left(\sqrt[q]{\frac{\left(1+(\mathcal{F}-1)\left(\frac{\Delta^{-1}(\xi_{j_{\mathscr{k}+1}},\mathcal{P}_{\mathscr{k}+1})}{\Theta}\right)^{q}\right)^{\varphi'_{\mathscr{k}+1}}-\left(1-\left(\frac{\Delta^{-1}(\xi_{j_{\mathscr{k}+1}},\mathcal{P}_{\mathscr{k}+1})}{\Theta}\right)^{q}\right)^{\varphi'_{\mathscr{k}+1}}}{\left(1+(\mathcal{F}-1)\left(\frac{\Delta^{-1}(\xi_{j_{\mathscr{k}+1}},\mathcal{P}_{\mathscr{k}+1})}{\Theta}\right)^{q}\right)^{\varphi'_{\mathscr{k}+1}}+(\mathcal{F}-1)\left(1-\left(\frac{\Delta^{-1}(\xi_{j_{\mathscr{k}+1}},\mathcal{P}_{\mathscr{k}+1})}{\Theta}\right)^{q}\right)^{\varphi'_{\mathscr{k}+1}}}}\right)\right), \\
\Delta\left(\Theta\left(\frac{\sqrt[q]{\mathcal{F}}\left(\frac{\Delta^{-1}(\xi_{l_{\mathscr{k}+1}},\mathcal{Q}_{\mathscr{k}+1})}{\Theta}\right)^{\varphi'_{\mathscr{k}+1}}}{\sqrt[q]{\left(1+(\mathcal{F}-1)\left(1-\left(\frac{\Delta^{-1}(\xi_{l_{\mathscr{k}+1}},\mathcal{Q}_{\mathscr{k}+1})}{\Theta}\right)^{q}\right)\right)^{\varphi'_{\mathscr{k}+1}}+(\mathcal{F}-1)\left(\frac{\Delta^{-1}(\xi_{l_{\mathscr{k}+1}},\mathcal{Q}_{\mathscr{k}+1})}{\Theta}\right)^{q\varphi'_{\mathscr{k}+1}}}}\right)\right)
\end{array} \right)
$$

$$
= \left(\begin{array}{c}
\Delta\left(\Theta\left(\sqrt[q]{\frac{\prod_{\rho=1}^{\mathscr{k}+1}\left(1+(\mathcal{F}-1)\left(\frac{\Delta^{-1}(\xi_{j_\rho},\mathcal{P}_\rho)}{\Theta}\right)^{q}\right)^{\varphi'_\rho}-\prod_{\rho=1}^{\mathscr{k}+1}\left(1-\left(\frac{\Delta^{-1}(\xi_{j_\rho},\mathcal{P}_\rho)}{\Theta}\right)^{q}\right)^{\varphi'_\rho}}{\prod_{\rho=1}^{\mathscr{k}+1}\left(1+(\mathcal{F}-1)\left(\frac{\Delta^{-1}(\xi_{j_\rho},\mathcal{P}_\rho)}{\Theta}\right)^{q}\right)^{\varphi'_\rho}+(\mathcal{F}-1)\prod_{\rho=1}^{\mathscr{k}+1}\left(1-\left(\frac{\Delta^{-1}(\xi_{j_\rho},\mathcal{P}_\rho)}{\Theta}\right)^{q}\right)^{\varphi'_\rho}}}\right)\right), \\
\Delta\left(\Theta\left(\frac{\sqrt[q]{\mathcal{F}}\prod_{\rho=1}^{\mathscr{k}+1}\left(\frac{\Delta^{-1}(\xi_{l_\rho},\mathcal{Q}_\rho)}{\Theta}\right)^{\varphi'_\rho}}{\sqrt[q]{\prod_{\rho=1}^{\mathscr{k}+1}\left(1+(\mathcal{F}-1)\left(1-\left(\frac{\Delta^{-1}(\xi_{l_\rho},\mathcal{Q}_\rho)}{\Theta}\right)^{q}\right)\right)^{\varphi'_\rho}+(\mathcal{F}-1)\prod_{\rho=1}^{\mathscr{k}+1}\left(\frac{\Delta^{-1}(\xi_{l_\rho},\mathcal{Q}_\rho)}{\Theta}\right)^{q\varphi'_\rho}}}\right)\right)
\end{array} \right).
$$

Consequently, based on our assessment, we can conclude that Equation (7) is valid for $\iota = \mathscr{k} + 1$. By establishing its truth for both the base cases, where $\iota = 2$, and the induction step, where $\iota = \mathscr{k} + 1$, we can affirm that Equation (7) holds for all values of n.

In relation to the parameter $\mathcal{F}$, we can derive the following specific instances of Theorem 1:

Case 1 When $\digamma = 1$, the 2TLq-RHWA operator reduces to the 2TLq-R weighted average operator.

Case 2 When $\digamma = 2$, the 2TLq-RHWA operator simplifies to the 2TLq-R Einstein weighted average operator.

By considering different values of $\digamma$, we can observe the specialization of the 2TLq-RHWA operator to well-known operators within the 2TLq-R framework.

Example 2 Let $\Re_1 = ((\xi_3, 0), (\xi_5, 0))$, $\Re_2 = ((\xi_6, 0), (\xi_2, 0))$ and $\Re_3 = ((\xi_7, 0), (\xi_1, 0))$ be three 2TLq-RNs which are derived from LTS $\mathcal{S} = \{\xi_t | t = 0, \ldots, 8\}$. $\digamma = 3$, $q = 4$ and the weight vector is $\varphi' = (0.32, 0.25, 0.43)^T$, then

$$\prod_{\rho=1}^{\iota}\left(1+(\digamma-1)\left(\frac{\Delta^{-1}(\xi_{j_\rho}, \mathcal{P}_\rho)}{\Theta}\right)^q\right)^{\varphi'_\rho}$$
$$= \left(1+(3-1)\left(\frac{\Delta^{-1}(\xi_3,0)}{8}\right)^4\right)^{0.32} \times \left(1+(3-1)\left(\frac{\Delta^{-1}(\xi_6,0)}{8}\right)^4\right)^{0.25}$$
$$\times \left(1+(3-1)\left(\frac{\Delta^{-1}(\xi_7,0)}{8}\right)^4\right)^{0.43} = 1.5977$$

$$\prod_{\rho=1}^{\iota}\left(1-\left(\frac{\Delta^{-1}(\xi_{j_\rho}, \mathcal{P}_\rho)}{\Theta}\right)^q\right)^{\varphi'_\rho}$$
$$= \left(1-\left(\frac{\Delta^{-1}(\xi_3,0)}{8}\right)^4\right)^{0.32} \times \left(1-\left(\frac{\Delta^{-1}(\xi_6,0)}{8}\right)^4\right)^{0.25}$$
$$\times \left(1-\left(\frac{\Delta^{-1}(\xi_7,0)}{8}\right)^4\right)^{0.43} = 0.6182$$

$$\Delta\left(\Theta\left(\sqrt[q]{\frac{\prod_{\rho=1}^{\iota}\left(1+(\digamma-1)\left(\frac{\Delta^{-1}(\xi_{j_\rho},\mathcal{P}_\rho)}{\Theta}\right)^q\right)^{\varphi'_\rho} - \prod_{\rho=1}^{\iota}\left(1-\left(\frac{\Delta^{-1}(\xi_{j_\rho},\mathcal{P}_\rho)}{\Theta}\right)^q\right)^{\varphi'_\rho}}{\prod_{\rho=1}^{\iota}\left(1+(\digamma-1)\left(\frac{\Delta^{-1}(\xi_{j_\rho},\mathcal{P}_\rho)}{\Theta}\right)^q\right)^{\varphi'_\rho} + (\digamma-1)\prod_{\rho=1}^{\iota}\left(1-\left(\frac{\Delta^{-1}(\xi_{j_\rho},\mathcal{P}_\rho)}{\Theta}\right)^q\right)^{\varphi'_\rho}}}\right)\right)$$
$$= \Delta\left(8\left(\sqrt[4]{\frac{1.5977-0.6182}{1.5977+(3-1)1.5977}}\right)\right),$$
$$= \Delta\,(8\,(0.7667)) = (\xi_6, 0.1336).$$

Similarly,

$$\sqrt[q]{F}\prod_{\rho=1}^{\iota}\left(\frac{\Delta^{-1}(\xi_{l_\rho}, Q_\rho)}{\Theta}\right)^{\varphi'_\rho}$$

$$= \sqrt[4]{3}\left(\left(\frac{\Delta^{-1}(\xi_5, 0)}{8}\right)^{0.32} \times \left(\frac{\Delta^{-1}(\xi_2, 0)}{8}\right)^{0.25} \times \left(\frac{\Delta^{-1}(\xi_1, 0)}{8}\right)^{0.43}\right) = 0.3274$$

$$\prod_{\rho=1}^{\iota}\left(1+(F-1)\left(1-\left(\frac{\Delta^{-1}(\xi_{l_\rho}, Q_\rho)}{\Theta}\right)^{q}\right)\right)^{\varphi'_\rho}$$

$$= \left(1+2\left(1-\left(\frac{\Delta^{-1}(\xi_5, 0)}{8}\right)^{4}\right)\right)^{0.32} \times \left(1+2\left(1-\left(\frac{\Delta^{-1}(\xi_2, 0)}{8}\right)^{4}\right)\right)^{0.25}$$

$$\times \left(1+2\left(1-\left(\frac{\Delta^{-1}(\xi_1, 0)}{8}\right)^{4}\right)\right)^{0.43} = 2.8967$$

$$(F-1)\prod_{\rho=1}^{\iota}\left(\frac{\Delta^{-1}(\xi_{l_\rho}, Q_\rho)}{\Theta}\right)^{q\varphi'_\rho}$$

$$= (3-1)\left(\left(\frac{\Delta^{-1}(\xi_5, 0)}{8}\right)^{4\times0.32} \times \left(\frac{\Delta^{-1}(\xi_2, 0)}{8}\right)^{4\times0.25} \times \left(\frac{\Delta^{-1}(\xi_1, 0)}{8}\right)^{4\times0.43}\right) = 0.0077$$

$$\Delta\left(\Theta\left(\frac{\sqrt[q]{F}\prod_{\rho=1}^{\iota}\left(\frac{\Delta^{-1}(\xi_{l_\rho}, Q_\rho)}{\Theta}\right)^{\varphi'_\rho}}{\sqrt[q]{\prod_{\rho=1}^{\iota}\left(1+(F-1)\left(1-\left(\frac{\Delta^{-1}(\xi_{l_\rho}, Q_\rho)}{\Theta}\right)^{q}\right)\right)^{\varphi'_\rho} + (F-1)\prod_{\rho=1}^{\iota}\left(\frac{\Delta^{-1}(\xi_{l_\rho}, Q_\rho)}{\Theta}\right)^{q\varphi'_\rho}}}\right)\right)$$

$$= \Delta\left(8\left(\frac{0.3274}{\sqrt[4]{2.8967+0.0077}}\right)\right),$$

$$= \Delta(8(0.2508)) = (\xi_2, 0.0064).$$

Therefore,

$$2\text{TL}q\text{-RHWA}_{(0.32,0.25,0.43)}(\Re_1, \Re_2, \Re_3) = ((\xi_6, 0.1339), (\xi_2, 0.0064)).$$

Theorem 2 *Let* $\Re_\rho = ((\xi_{j_\rho}, \mathcal{P}_\rho), (\xi_{l_\rho}, Q_\rho))$ *and* $\Re'_\rho = ((\xi'_{j_\rho}, \mathcal{P}'_\rho), (\xi'_{l_\rho}, Q'_\rho))$ $(\rho = 1, 2, \ldots, \iota)$ *be two sets of 2TLq-RNs; then the 2TLq-RHWA operator has following properties:*

1. *(Idempotency). If all 2TLq-RNs* $\Re_\rho = ((\xi_{j_\rho}, \mathcal{P}_\rho), (\xi_{l_\rho}, Q_\rho))(\rho = 1, 2, \ldots, \iota)$ *are equal, i.e.,* $\Re_\rho = \Re = ((\xi_j, \mathcal{P}), (\xi_l, Q))$ *for all* ρ*, then*

$$2TLq\text{-}RHWA_{\varphi'}(\Re_1, \Re_2, \ldots, \Re_\iota) = \Re.$$

2. *(Boundedness). Let* $\Re_\rho$ $(\rho = 1, 2, \ldots, \iota)$ *be a collection of 2TLq-RNs, and let* $\Re^- = \min_\rho \Re_\rho$ *and* $\Re^+ = \max_\rho \Re_\rho$, *then*

$$\Re^- \leq 2TLq\text{-}RHWA_{\varphi'}(\Re_1, \Re_2, \ldots, \Re_\iota) \leq \Re^+.$$

3. *(Monotonicity). Let* $\Re_\rho$ *and* $\Re'_\rho$ $(\rho = 1, 2, \ldots, \iota)$ *be two collections of 2TLq-RNs, if* $\Re_\rho \leq \Re'_\rho$, *for all* ρ, *then*

$$2TLq\text{-}RHWA_{\varphi'}(\Re_1, \Re_2, \ldots, \Re_\iota) \leq 2TLq\text{-}RHWA_{\varphi'}\left(\Re'_1, \Re'_2, \ldots, \Re'_\iota\right).$$

4. *(Commutativity). If* $\Re'_\rho$ *is any permutation of* $\Re_\rho$ $(\rho = 1, 2, \ldots, \iota)$, *then*

$$2TLq\text{-}RHWA_{\varphi'}(\Re_1, \Re_2, \ldots, \Re_\iota) = 2TLq\text{-}RHWA_{\varphi'}\left(\Re'_1, \Re'_2, \ldots, \Re'_\iota\right).$$

Definition 11 Consider a collection of 2TLq-RNs $\Re_\rho = ((\xi_{j_\rho}, \mathcal{P}_\rho), (\xi_{l_\rho}, \mathcal{Q}_\rho))$ $(\rho = 1, 2, \ldots, \iota)$. The 2TL$q$-RHOWA operator is defined as follows:

$$2\text{TL}q\text{-RHOWA}_{\mathfrak{L}}(\Re_1, \Re_2, \ldots, \Re_\iota) = \bigoplus_{\rho=1}^{\iota} \left(\mathfrak{L}_\rho \Re_{\sigma(\rho)}\right).$$

Here, $(\sigma(1), \sigma(2), \ldots, \sigma(\iota))$ represents a permutation of $(1, 2, \ldots, \iota)$ such that $\Re_{\sigma(\rho-1)} \geq \Re_{\sigma(\rho)}$ for all $\rho = 2, \ldots, \iota$. Additionally, $\mathfrak{L} = (\mathfrak{L}_1, \mathfrak{L}_2, \ldots, \mathfrak{L}_\iota)^T$ is the vector of weights linked with the aggregation, satisfying $\mathfrak{L}_\rho \in [0, 1]$ and $\sum_{\rho=1}^{\iota} \mathfrak{L}_\rho = 1$. The parameter $\digamma > 0$.

Utilizing the Hamacher sum operation for 2TLq-R values as defined in Def. 9, we establish Theorem 3.

Theorem 3 *Let* $\Re_\rho = ((\xi_{j_\rho}, \mathcal{P}_\rho), (\xi_{l_\rho}, \mathcal{Q}_\rho))$ $(\rho = 1, 2, \ldots, \iota)$ *be a collection of 2TLq-RNs, where* $\digamma > 0$. *For any* $q \geq 0$, *we can demonstrate that the aggregated value obtained using the 2TLq-RHOWA operator remains a 2TLq-RN, and*

$$2TLq\text{-}RHOWA_{\mathfrak{L}}\left(\Re_1,\Re_2,\ldots,\Re_\iota\right)=\overset{\iota}{\underset{\rho=1}{\oplus}}\left(\mathfrak{L}_\rho \Re_{\sigma(\rho)}\right)$$

$$=\left(\begin{array}{c}\Delta\left(\Theta\left(\sqrt[q]{\dfrac{\prod_{\rho=1}^{\iota}\left(1+(F-1)\left(\frac{\Delta^{-1}\left(\xi_{j_{\sigma(\rho)}},\mathcal{P}_{\sigma(\rho)}\right)}{\Theta}\right)^q\right)^{\mathfrak{L}_\rho}-\prod_{\rho=1}^{\iota}\left(1-\left(\frac{\Delta^{-1}\left(\xi_{j_{\sigma(\rho)}},\mathcal{P}_{\sigma(\rho)}\right)}{\Theta}\right)^q\right)^{\mathfrak{L}_\rho}}{\prod_{\rho=1}^{\iota}\left(1+(F-1)\left(\frac{\Delta^{-1}\left(\xi_{j_{\sigma(\rho)}},\mathcal{P}_{\sigma(\rho)}\right)}{\Theta}\right)^q\right)^{\mathfrak{L}_\rho}+(F-1)\prod_{\rho=1}^{\iota}\left(1-\left(\frac{\Delta^{-1}\left(\xi_{j_{\sigma(\rho)}},\mathcal{P}_{\sigma(\rho)}\right)}{\Theta}\right)^q\right)^{\mathfrak{L}_\rho}}}\right)\right),\\ \Delta\left(\Theta\left(\dfrac{\sqrt[q]{F}\prod_{\rho=1}^{\iota}\left(\frac{\Delta^{-1}\left(\xi_{l_{\sigma(\rho)}},\mathcal{Q}_{\sigma(\rho)}\right)}{\Theta}\right)^{\mathfrak{L}_\rho}}{\sqrt[q]{\prod_{\rho=1}^{\iota}\left(1+(F-1)\left(1-\left(\frac{\Delta^{-1}\left(\xi_{l_{\sigma(\rho)}},\mathcal{Q}_{\sigma(\rho)}\right)}{\Theta}\right)^q\right)\right)^{\mathfrak{L}_\rho}+(F-1)\prod_{\rho=1}^{\iota}\left(\frac{\Delta^{-1}\left(\xi_{l_{\sigma(\rho)}},\mathcal{Q}_{\sigma(\rho)}\right)}{\Theta}\right)^{q\mathfrak{L}_\rho}}}\right)\right)\end{array}\right). \quad (8)$$

Definition 12 Let $\Re_\rho=((\xi_{j_\rho},\mathcal{P}_\rho),(\xi_{l_\rho},\mathcal{Q}_\rho))\,(\rho=1,2,\ldots,\iota)$ be a collection of 2TLq-RNs, where $\mathfrak{L}=(\mathfrak{L}_1,\mathfrak{L}_2,\ldots,\mathfrak{L}_\iota)^T$ is the linked weighting vector such that $\mathfrak{L}_\rho\in[0,1]$ and $\sum_{\rho=1}^{\iota}\mathfrak{L}_\rho=1$, and $\varphi'=\left(\varphi'_1,\varphi'_2,\ldots,\varphi'_\iota\right)^T$ is the weighted vector of 2TLq-RNs $\Re_\rho$ such that $\varphi'_\rho\in[0,1]$ and $\sum_{\rho=1}^{\iota}\varphi'_\rho=1$. Then, for any non-negative q, employing the 2TLq-RHHWA operator yields an aggregated value that is also a 2TLq-RN, given by

$$2\mathrm{TL}q\text{-RHHWA}_{\mathfrak{L},\varphi'}\left(\Re_1,\Re_2,\ldots,\Re_\iota\right)=\overset{\iota}{\underset{\rho=1}{\oplus}}\left(\mathfrak{L}_\rho\dot{\Re}_{\sigma(\rho)}\right),$$

where $\dot{\Re}_{\sigma(\rho)}$ is the ρth largest element of the 2TLq-RNs $\dot{\Re}_\rho\left(\dot{\Re}_\rho=\left(\iota\varphi'_\rho\right)\Re_\rho,\rho=1,2,\ldots,\iota\right)$, and $\sigma(\rho)$ is a permutation of $(1,2,\ldots,\iota)$ such that $\Re_{\sigma(\rho-1)}\geq\Re_{\sigma(\rho)}$ for all $\rho=2,\ldots,\iota$.

Theorem 4 *Let $\Re_\rho=((\xi_{j_\rho},\mathcal{P}_\rho),(\xi_{l_\rho},\mathcal{Q}_\rho))\,(\rho=1,2,\ldots,\iota)$ be a collection of 2TLq-RNs, where $F>0$. Then, for any non-negative q, employing the 2TLq-RHHWA operator yields an aggregated value that is also a 2TLq-RN, and*

$$2TLq\text{-}RHHWA_{\mathfrak{L},\varphi'}\left(\Re_1,\Re_2,\ldots,\Re_\iota\right)=\overset{\iota}{\underset{\rho=1}{\oplus}}\left(\mathfrak{L}_\rho \dot{\Re}_{\sigma(\rho)}\right)$$

$$=\left(\begin{array}{c}\Delta\left(\Theta\left(\sqrt[q]{\dfrac{\prod_{\rho=1}^{\iota}\left(1+(F-1)\left(\frac{\Delta^{-1}\left(\dot{\xi}_{j_{\sigma(\rho)}},\dot{\mathcal{P}}_{\sigma(\rho)}\right)}{\Theta}\right)^q\right)^{\mathfrak{L}_\rho}-\prod_{\rho=1}^{\iota}\left(1-\left(\frac{\Delta^{-1}\left(\dot{\xi}_{j_{\sigma(\rho)}},\dot{\mathcal{P}}_{\sigma(\rho)}\right)}{\Theta}\right)^q\right)^{\mathfrak{L}_\rho}}{\prod_{\rho=1}^{\iota}\left(1+(F-1)\left(\frac{\Delta^{-1}\left(\dot{\xi}_{j_{\sigma(\rho)}},\dot{\mathcal{P}}_{\sigma(\rho)}\right)}{\Theta}\right)^q\right)^{\mathfrak{L}_\rho}+(F-1)\prod_{\rho=1}^{\iota}\left(1-\left(\frac{\Delta^{-1}\left(\dot{\xi}_{j_{\sigma(\rho)}},\dot{\mathcal{P}}_{\sigma(\rho)}\right)}{\Theta}\right)^q\right)^{\mathfrak{L}_\rho}}}\right)\right),\\ \Delta\left(\Theta\left(\dfrac{\sqrt[q]{F}\prod_{\rho=1}^{\iota}\left(\frac{\Delta^{-1}\left(\dot{\xi}_{l_{\sigma(\rho)}},\dot{\mathcal{Q}}_{\sigma(\rho)}\right)}{\Theta}\right)^{\mathfrak{L}_\rho}}{\sqrt[q]{\prod_{\rho=1}^{\iota}\left(1+(F-1)\left(1-\left(\frac{\Delta^{-1}\left(\dot{\xi}_{l_{\sigma(\rho)}},\dot{\mathcal{Q}}_{\sigma(\rho)}\right)}{\Theta}\right)^q\right)\right)^{\mathfrak{L}_\rho}+(F-1)\prod_{\rho=1}^{\iota}\left(\frac{\Delta^{-1}\left(\dot{\xi}_{l_{\sigma(\rho)}},\dot{\mathcal{Q}}_{\sigma(\rho)}\right)}{\Theta}\right)^{q\mathfrak{L}_\rho}}}\right)\right)\end{array}\right). \quad (9)$$

Definition 13 Let $\Re_\rho$ be a collection of 2TLq-RNs, where $\Re_\rho = ((\xi_{j_\rho}, \mathcal{P}_\rho), (\xi_{l_\rho}, \mathcal{Q}_\rho))$ for $\rho = 1, 2, \ldots, \iota$. The 2TL$q$-RHWG operator is defined as

$$2\text{TL}q\text{-RHWG}_{\varphi'}(\Re 1, \Re_2, \ldots, \Re_\iota) = \bigotimes_{\rho=1}^{\iota} (\Re_\rho)^{\varphi'_\rho},$$

where $\varphi' = (\varphi'_1, \varphi'_2, \ldots, \varphi'_\iota)^T$ is the weight vector of $\Re_\rho$ for $\rho = 1, 2, \ldots, \iota$, and $\varphi'_\rho > 0$ with $\sum_{\rho=1}^{\iota} \varphi'_\rho = 1$.

From Def. 13, we deduce the following theorem using the 2TLq-RH operations.

Theorem 5 *Let $\Re_\rho = ((\xi_{j_\rho}, \mathcal{P}_\rho), (\xi_{l_\rho}, \mathcal{Q}_\rho))$ $(\rho = 1, 2, \ldots, \iota)$ be a collection of 2TLq-RNs, where $\digamma > 0$. Then, for any non-negative q, employing the 2TLq-RHWG operator yields an aggregated value that is also a 2TLq-RN, and*

$$2TLq\text{-}RHWG_{\varphi'}(\Re_1, \Re_2, \ldots, \Re_\iota) = \bigotimes_{\rho=1}^{\iota} (\Re_\rho)^{\varphi'_\rho}$$

$$= \left(\begin{array}{c} \Delta\left(\Theta\left(\dfrac{\sqrt[q]{\digamma}\prod_{\rho=1}^{\iota}\left(\frac{\Delta^{-1}(\xi_{j_\rho},\mathcal{P}_\rho)}{\Theta}\right)^{\varphi'_\rho}}{\sqrt[q]{\prod_{\rho=1}^{\iota}\left(1+(\digamma-1)\left(1-\left(\frac{\Delta^{-1}(\xi_{j_\rho},\mathcal{P}_\rho)}{\Theta}\right)^q\right)\right)^{\varphi'_\rho}+(\digamma-1)\prod_{\rho=1}^{\iota}\left(\frac{\Delta^{-1}(\xi_{j_\rho},\mathcal{P}_\rho)}{\Theta}\right)^{q\varphi'_\rho}}}\right)\right), \\ \Delta\left(\Theta\left(\sqrt[q]{\dfrac{\prod_{\rho=1}^{\iota}\left(1+(\digamma-1)\left(\frac{\Delta^{-1}(\xi_{l_\rho},\mathcal{Q}_\rho)}{\Theta}\right)^q\right)^{\varphi'_\rho}-\prod_{\rho=1}^{\iota}\left(1-\left(\frac{\Delta^{-1}(\xi_{l_\rho},\mathcal{Q}_\rho)}{\Theta}\right)^q\right)^{\varphi'_\rho}}{\prod_{\rho=1}^{\iota}\left(1+(\digamma-1)\left(\frac{\Delta^{-1}(\xi_{l_\rho},\mathcal{Q}_\rho)}{\Theta}\right)^q\right)^{\varphi'_\rho}+(\digamma-1)\prod_{\rho=1}^{\iota}\left(1-\left(\frac{\Delta^{-1}(\xi_{l_\rho},\mathcal{Q}_\rho)}{\Theta}\right)^q\right)^{\varphi'_\rho}}}\right)\right) \end{array} \right). \quad (10)$$

Based on the parameter $\digamma$, we can observe the following special cases of Theorem 5:

Case 3 When $\digamma = 1$, the 2TLq-RHWG operator simplifies to the 2TLq-R weighted geometric operator.

Case 4 When $\digamma = 2$, the 2TLq-RHWG operator simplifies to the 2TLq-R Einstein weighted geometric operator.

The 2TLq-RHWG operator exhibits the same properties as mentioned in Theorem 2.

Example 3 Let $\Re_1 = ((\xi_3, 0), (\xi_5, 0))$, $\Re_2 = ((\xi_6, 0), (\xi_2, 0))$ and $\Re_3 = ((\xi_7, 0), (\xi_1, 0))$ be three 2TLq-RNs which are derived from LTS $\mathcal{S} = \{\xi_t | t = 0, \ldots, 8\}$. $\digamma = 3$, $q = 4$ and the weight vector is $\varphi' = (0.32, 0.25, 0.43)^T$, then

$$\sqrt[q]{F}\prod_{\rho=1}^{\iota}\left(\frac{\Delta^{-1}\left(\xi_{j_\rho},\mathcal{P}_\rho\right)}{\Theta}\right)^{\varphi'_\rho}$$

$$=\sqrt[4]{3}\left(\left(\frac{\Delta^{-1}(\xi_3,0)}{8}\right)^{0.32}\times\left(\frac{\Delta^{-1}(\xi_6,0)}{8}\right)^{0.25}\times\left(\frac{\Delta^{-1}(\xi_7,0)}{8}\right)^{0.43}\right)=0.8449$$

$$\prod_{\rho=1}^{\iota}\left(1+(F-1)\left(1-\left(\frac{\Delta^{-1}\left(\xi_{j_\rho},\mathcal{P}_\rho\right)}{\Theta}\right)^q\right)\right)^{\varphi'_\rho}$$

$$=\left(1+2\left(1-\left(\frac{\Delta^{-1}(\xi_3,0)}{8}\right)^4\right)\right)^{0.32}\times\left(1+2\left(1-\left(\frac{\Delta^{-1}(\xi_6,0)}{8}\right)^4\right)\right)^{0.25}$$

$$\times\left(1+2\left(1-\left(\frac{\Delta^{-1}(\xi_7,0)}{8}\right)^4\right)\right)^{0.43}=2.2751$$

$$(F-1)\prod_{\rho=1}^{\iota}\left(\frac{\Delta^{-1}\left(\xi_{j_\rho},\mathcal{P}_\rho\right)}{\Theta}\right)^{q\varphi'_\rho}$$

$$=(3-1)\left(\left(\frac{\Delta^{-1}(\xi_3,0)}{8}\right)^{4\times0.32}\times\left(\frac{\Delta^{-1}(\xi_6,0)}{8}\right)^{4\times0.25}\times\left(\frac{\Delta^{-1}(\xi_7,0)}{8}\right)^{4\times0.43}\right)=0.3397$$

$$\Delta\left(\Theta\left(\frac{\sqrt[q]{F}\prod_{\rho=1}^{\iota}\left(\frac{\Delta^{-1}\left(\xi_{j_\rho},\mathcal{P}_\rho\right)}{\Theta}\right)^{\varphi'_\rho}}{\sqrt[q]{\prod_{\rho=1}^{\iota}\left(1+(F-1)\left(1-\left(\frac{\Delta^{-1}\left(\xi_{j_\rho},\mathcal{P}_\rho\right)}{\Theta}\right)^q\right)\right)^{\varphi'_\rho}+(F-1)\prod_{\rho=1}^{\iota}\left(\frac{\Delta^{-1}\left(\xi_{j_\rho},\mathcal{P}_\rho\right)}{\Theta}\right)^{q\varphi'_\rho}}}\right)\right)$$

$$=\Delta\left(8\left(\frac{0.8449}{\sqrt[4]{2.2751+0.3397}}\right)\right),$$
$$=\Delta(8(0.6644))=(\xi_5,0.3152).$$

Similarly,

$$\prod_{\rho=1}^{\iota}\left(1+(F-1)\left(\frac{\Delta^{-1}\left(\xi_{l_\rho},\mathcal{Q}_\rho\right)}{\Theta}\right)^q\right)^{\varphi'_\rho}$$

$$=\left(1+(3-1)\left(\frac{\Delta^{-1}(\xi_5,0)}{8}\right)^4\right)^{0.32}\times\left(1+(3-1)\left(\frac{\Delta^{-1}(\xi_2,0)}{8}\right)^4\right)^{0.25}$$

$$\times\left(1+(3-1)\left(\frac{\Delta^{-1}(\xi_1,0)}{8}\right)^4\right)^{0.43}=1.0913$$

$$\prod_{\rho=1}^{\iota}\left(1-\left(\frac{\Delta^{-1}\left(\xi_{l_\rho},\mathcal{Q}_\rho\right)}{\Theta}\right)^q\right)^{\varphi'_\rho}$$

$$=\left(1-\left(\frac{\Delta^{-1}(\xi_5,0)}{8}\right)^4\right)^{0.32}\times\left(1-\left(\frac{\Delta^{-1}(\xi_2,0)}{8}\right)^4\right)^{0.25}$$

$$\times\left(1-\left(\frac{\Delta^{-1}(\xi_1,0)}{8}\right)^4\right)^{0.43}=0.9474$$

$$\Delta\left(\Theta\left(\sqrt[q]{\frac{\prod_{\rho=1}^{\iota}\left(1+(F-1)\left(\frac{\Delta^{-1}(\xi_{l_\rho},Q_\rho)}{\Theta}\right)^q\right)^{\varphi'_\rho}-\prod_{\rho=1}^{\iota}\left(1-\left(\frac{\Delta^{-1}(\xi_{l_\rho},Q_\rho)}{\Theta}\right)^q\right)^{\varphi'_\rho}}{\prod_{\rho=1}^{\iota}\left(1+(F-1)\left(\frac{\Delta^{-1}(\xi_{l_\rho},Q_\rho)}{\Theta}\right)^q\right)^{\varphi'_\rho}+(F-1)\prod_{\rho=1}^{\iota}\left(1-\left(\frac{\Delta^{-1}(\xi_{l_\rho},Q_\rho)}{\Theta}\right)^q\right)^{\varphi'_\rho}}}\right)\right)$$
$$=\Delta\left(8\left(\sqrt[4]{\frac{1.0913-0.9474}{1.0913+(3-1)1.0913}}\right)\right),$$
$$=\Delta(8(0.4688))=(\xi_4,-0.2512).$$

Therefore,

$$\text{2TL}q\text{-RHWG}_{(0.32,0.25,0.43)}(\Re_1,\Re_2,\Re_3)=((\xi_5,0.3152),(\xi_4,-0.2512)).$$

Definition 14 Let $\Re_\rho=((\xi_{j_\rho},\mathcal{P}_\rho),(\xi_{l_\rho},Q_\rho))\ (\rho=1,2,\ldots,\iota)$ be a collection of 2TLq-RNs. The 2TLq-RHOWG operator is defined as

$$\text{2TL}q\text{-RHOWG}_{\mathfrak{L}}(\Re_1,\Re_2,\ldots,\Re_\iota)=\bigotimes_{\rho=1}^{\iota}\left(\Re_{\sigma(\rho)}\right)^{\mathfrak{L}_\rho},$$

where $(\sigma(1),\sigma(2),\ldots,\sigma(\iota))$ is a permutation of $(1,2,\ldots,\iota)$, such that $\Re\sigma(\rho-1)\geq\Re_{\sigma(\rho)}$ for all $\rho=2,\ldots,\iota$, and $\mathfrak{L}=(\mathfrak{L}_1,\mathfrak{L}_2,\ldots,\mathfrak{L}_\iota)^T$ is the aggregation-linked weight vector with $\mathfrak{L}_\rho\in[0,1]$ and $\sum_{\rho=1}^{\iota}\mathfrak{L}_\rho=1$.

Theorem 6 *Let* $\Re_\rho=((\xi_{j_\rho},\mathcal{P}_\rho),(\xi_{l_\rho},Q_\rho))\ (\rho=1,2,\ldots,\iota)$ *be a collection of 2TLq-RNs with* $F>0$. *Then, for any non-negative q, employing the 2TLq-RHOWG operator yields an aggregated value that is also a 2TLq-RN, and*

$$\text{2TL}q\text{-RHOWG}_{\mathfrak{L}}(\Re_1,\Re_2,\ldots,\Re_\iota)=\bigotimes_{\rho=1}^{\iota}\left(\Re_{\sigma(\rho)}\right)^{\mathfrak{L}_\rho}$$
$$=\left(\begin{array}{c}\Delta\left(\Theta\left(\dfrac{\sqrt[q]{F}\prod_{\rho=1}^{\iota}\left(\frac{\Delta^{-1}\left(\xi_{j_{\sigma(\rho)}},\mathcal{P}_{\sigma(\rho)}\right)}{\Theta}\right)^{\mathfrak{L}_\rho}}{\sqrt[q]{\prod_{\rho=1}^{\iota}\left(1+(F-1)\left(1-\left(\frac{\Delta^{-1}\left(\xi_{j_{\sigma(\rho)}},\mathcal{P}_{\sigma(\rho)}\right)}{\Theta}\right)^q\right)\right)^{\mathfrak{L}_\rho}+(F-1)\prod_{\rho=1}^{\iota}\left(\frac{\Delta^{-1}\left(\xi_{j_{\sigma(\rho)}},\mathcal{P}_{\sigma(\rho)}\right)}{\Theta}\right)^{q\mathfrak{L}_\rho}}}\right)\right),\\ \Delta\left(\Theta\left(\sqrt[q]{\dfrac{\prod_{\rho=1}^{\iota}\left(1+(F-1)\left(\frac{\Delta^{-1}\left(\xi_{l_{\sigma(\rho)}},Q_{\sigma(\rho)}\right)}{\Theta}\right)^q\right)^{\mathfrak{L}_\rho}-\prod_{\rho=1}^{\iota}\left(1-\left(\frac{\Delta^{-1}\left(\xi_{l_{\sigma(\rho)}},Q_{\sigma(\rho)}\right)}{\Theta}\right)^q\right)^{\mathfrak{L}_\rho}}{\prod_{\rho=1}^{\iota}\left(1+(F-1)\left(\frac{\Delta^{-1}\left(\xi_{l_{\sigma(\rho)}},Q_{\sigma(\rho)}\right)}{\Theta}\right)^q\right)^{\mathfrak{L}_\rho}+(F-1)\prod_{\rho=1}^{\iota}\left(1-\left(\frac{\Delta^{-1}(\xi_{l_\rho},Q_\rho)}{\Theta}\right)^q\right)^{\mathfrak{L}_\rho}}}\right)\right)\end{array}\right).\quad(11)$$

The 2TLq-RHOWG operator shares the same properties as stated in Theorem 2.

Definition 15 Let $\Re_\rho = ((\xi_{j_\rho}, \mathcal{P}_\rho), (\xi_{l_\rho}, \mathcal{Q}_\rho))\,(\rho = 1, 2, \ldots, \iota)$ be a collection of 2TLq-RNs. The 2TLq-RHHWG operator is defined as

$$\text{2TL}q\text{-RHHWG}_{\mathfrak{L},\varphi'}(\Re_1, \Re_2, \ldots, \Re_\iota) = \bigotimes_{\rho=1}^{\iota} \left(\dot{\Re}_{\sigma(\rho)}\right)^{\mathfrak{L}_\rho},$$

where $\mathfrak{L} = (\mathfrak{L}_1, \mathfrak{L}_2, \ldots, \mathfrak{L}_\iota)^T$ is the linked weighting vector, with $\mathfrak{L}_\rho \in [0, 1]$, $\sum_{\rho=1}^{\iota} \mathfrak{L}_\rho = 1$, and $\dot{\Re}_{\sigma(\rho)}$ is the ρth largest element of 2TLq-RNs $\dot{\Re}_\rho \left(\dot{\Re}_\rho = (\Re_\rho)^{n\varphi'_\rho}, \rho = 1, 2, \ldots, \iota\right)$, $\varphi' = \left(\varphi'_1, \varphi'_2, \ldots, \varphi'_\iota\right)$ is the weighted vector of 2TLq-RNs $\Re_\rho$, with $\varphi'_\rho \in [0, 1]$ and $\sum_{\rho=1}^{\iota} \varphi'_\rho = 1$, and n is the balancing coefficient, $\digamma > 0$. Especially, if $\mathfrak{L} = (1/\iota, 1/\iota, \ldots, 1/\iota)^T$, then 2TL$q$-RHHWG is reduced to the 2TLq-RHWG operator; if $\varphi' = (1/\iota, 1/\iota, \ldots, 1/\iota)$, then 2TL$q$-RHHWG is reduced to the 2TLq-RHOWG operator.

Using the Hamacher product operations defined in Def. 9 for the 2TLq-R values, we can establish Theorem 7.

Theorem 7 *Let $\Re_\rho = ((\xi_{j_\rho}, \mathcal{P}_\rho), (\xi_{l_\rho}, \mathcal{Q}_\rho))\,(\rho = 1, 2, \ldots, \iota)$ be a collection of 2TLq-RNs, where $\digamma > 0$. Then, for any non-negative q, employing the 2TLq-RHOWG operator yields an aggregated value that is also a 2TLq-RN, and*

$$\text{2TL}q\text{-RHHWG}_{\mathfrak{L},\varphi'}(\Re_1, \Re_2, \ldots, \Re_\iota) = \bigotimes_{\rho=1}^{\iota} \left(\dot{\Re}_{\sigma(\rho)}\right)^{\mathfrak{L}_\rho}$$

$$= \left(\begin{array}{c} \Delta\left(\Theta\left(\dfrac{\sqrt[q]{\digamma}\prod_{\rho=1}^{\iota}\left(\frac{\Delta^{-1}\left(\dot{\xi}_{j_{\sigma(\rho)}}, \dot{\mathcal{P}}_{\sigma(\rho)}\right)}{\Theta}\right)^{\mathfrak{L}_\rho}}{\sqrt[q]{\prod_{\rho=1}^{\iota}\left(1+(\digamma-1)\left(1-\left(\frac{\Delta^{-1}\left(\dot{\xi}_{j_{\sigma(\rho)}}, \dot{\mathcal{P}}_{\sigma(\rho)}\right)}{\Theta}\right)^q\right)\right)^{\mathfrak{L}_\rho} + (\digamma-1)\prod_{\rho=1}^{\iota}\left(\frac{\Delta^{-1}\left(\dot{\xi}_{j_{\sigma(\rho)}}, \dot{\mathcal{P}}_{\sigma(\rho)}\right)}{\Theta}\right)^{q\mathfrak{L}_\rho}}}\right)\right), \\ \Delta\left(\Theta\left(\sqrt[q]{\dfrac{\prod_{\rho=1}^{\iota}\left(1+(\digamma-1)\left(\frac{\Delta^{-1}\left(\dot{\xi}_{l_{\sigma(\rho)}}, \dot{\mathcal{Q}}_{\sigma(\rho)}\right)}{\Theta}\right)^q\right)^{\mathfrak{L}_\rho} - \prod_{\rho=1}^{\iota}\left(1-\left(\frac{\Delta^{-1}\left(\dot{\xi}_{l_{\sigma(\rho)}}, \dot{\mathcal{Q}}_{\sigma(\rho)}\right)}{\Theta}\right)^q\right)^{\mathfrak{L}_\rho}}{\prod_{\rho=1}^{\iota}\left(1+(\digamma-1)\left(\frac{\Delta^{-1}\left(\dot{\xi}_{l_{\sigma(\rho)}}, \dot{\mathcal{Q}}_{\sigma(\rho)}\right)}{\Theta}\right)^q\right)^{\mathfrak{L}_\rho} + (\digamma-1)\prod_{\rho=1}^{\iota}\left(1-\left(\frac{\Delta^{-1}\left(\dot{\xi}_{l_\rho}, \dot{\mathcal{Q}}_\rho\right)}{\Theta}\right)^q\right)^{\mathfrak{L}_\rho}}}\right)\right) \end{array} \right). \tag{12}$$

The 2TLq-RHHWG operator shares the same properties as Theorem 2.

4 The 2TLq-R-MABAC Method for MAGDM Based on the 2TLq-RHWA and 2TLq-RHWG Operators

To address group decision-making problems effectively, a new MABAC method is proposed. This necessitates the development of a 2TLq-R-MABAC model, which extends the MABAC method to incorporate linguistic assessment information using 2TLq-RNs. This section focuses on the development of the 2TLq-R-MABAC model, leveraging the 2TLq-RHWA and 2TLq-RHWG operators. The flexibility of 2TLq-RNs is taken into account during the development process.

Specifically, let's assume there exists a set of m alternatives $\beth = \{\beth_1, \beth_2, \ldots, \beth_\jmath\}$, a set of n attributes $\Phi = \{\Phi_1, \Phi_2, \ldots, \Phi_\imath\}$, and a set of h DMs $\varrho = \{\varrho_1, \varrho_2, \ldots, \varrho_h\}$, and let $\varphi' = (\varphi'_1, \varphi'_2, \ldots, \varphi'_\imath)^T$ and $\varphi = (\varphi_1, \varphi_2, \ldots, \varphi_h)^T$ represent the weighting vectors of the attributes and the DMs, respectively. They satisfy the conditions $\varphi'_\rho \in [0, 1]$, $\varphi_u \in [0, 1]$, $\sum_{\rho=1}^{\imath} \varphi'_\rho = 1$, and $\sum_{u=1}^{h} \varphi_u = 1$. The steps for implementing the 2TLq-R-MABAC technique are described as follows:

Step 1. Establish the 2TLq-R evaluation matrix $R^u = [\beth^u_{ß\rho}]_{\jmath\times\imath} = ((\xi_{j_{ß\rho}}, \mathcal{P}_{ß\rho})^u, (\xi_{l_{ß\rho}}, \mathcal{Q}_{ß\rho})^u)_{\jmath\times\imath}$ $(ß = 1, 2, \ldots, \jmath,\ \rho = 1, 2, \ldots, \imath,\ u = 1, 2, \ldots, h)$ of each DM as

$$R^u = [\beth^u_{ß\rho}]_{\jmath\times\imath} \tag{13}$$

$$= \begin{bmatrix} ((\xi_{j_{11}}, \mathcal{P}_{11})^u, (\xi_{l_{11}}, \mathcal{Q}_{11})^u) & ((\xi_{j_{12}}, \mathcal{P}_{12})^u, (\xi_{l_{12}}, \mathcal{Q}_{12})^u) & \cdots & ((\xi_{j_{1\imath}}, \mathcal{P}_{1\imath})^u, (\xi_{l_{1\imath}}, \mathcal{Q}_{1\imath})^u) \\ ((\xi_{j_{21}}, \mathcal{P}_{21})^u, (\xi_{l_{21}}, \mathcal{Q}_{21})^u) & ((\xi_{j_{22}}, \mathcal{P}_{22})^u, (\xi_{l_{22}}, \mathcal{Q}_{22})^u) & \cdots & ((\xi_{j_{2\imath}}, \mathcal{P}_{2\imath})^u, (\xi_{l_{2\imath}}, \mathcal{Q}_{2\imath})^u) \\ \vdots & \vdots & \ddots & \vdots \\ ((\xi_{j_{\jmath1}}, \mathcal{P}_{\jmath1})^u, (\xi_{l_{\jmath1}}, \mathcal{Q}_{\jmath1})^u) & ((\xi_{j_{\jmath2}}, \mathcal{P}_{\jmath2})^u, (\xi_{l_{\jmath2}}, \mathcal{Q}_{\jmath2})^u) & \cdots & ((\xi_{j_{\jmath\imath}}, \mathcal{P}_{\jmath\imath})^u, (\xi_{l_{\jmath\imath}}, \mathcal{Q}_{\jmath\imath})^u) \end{bmatrix},$$

where $\beth^u_{ß\rho} = ((\xi_{j_{ß\rho}}, \mathcal{P}_{ß\rho})^u, (\xi_{l_{ß\rho}}, \mathcal{Q}_{ß\rho})^u)(ß = 1, 2, \ldots, \jmath,\ \rho = 1, 2, \ldots, \imath)$ denotes the 2TLq-R information of alternatives $\beth_ß$ on attributes Φ_ρ by DM ϱ_u $(u = 1, 2, \ldots, h)$.

Step 2. Utilize the 2TLq-RHWA or 2TLq-RHWG operator from Eq. (7) or (10) to fuse overall $\beth^u_{ß\rho}$ to $\beth_{ß\rho}$, the fused 2TLq-RNs assessment matrix $R = [\beth_{ß\rho}]_{\jmath\times\imath}$ can be given as follows:

$$R = [\beth_{ß\rho}]_{\jmath\times\imath} \tag{14}$$

$$= \begin{bmatrix} ((\xi_{j_{11}}, \mathcal{P}_{11}), (\xi_{l_{11}}, \mathcal{Q}_{11})) & ((\xi_{j_{12}}, \mathcal{P}_{12}), (\xi_{l_{12}}, \mathcal{Q}_{12})) & \cdots & ((\xi_{j_{1\imath}}, \mathcal{P}_{1\imath}), (\xi_{l_{1\imath}}, \mathcal{Q}_{1\imath})) \\ ((\xi_{j_{21}}, \mathcal{P}_{21}), (\xi_{t_{21}}, \mathcal{Q}_{21})) & ((\xi_{j_{22}}, \mathcal{P}_{22}), (\xi_{l_{22}}, \mathcal{Q}_{22})) & \cdots & ((\xi_{j_{2\imath}}, \mathcal{P}_{2\imath}), (\xi_{l_{2\imath}}, \mathcal{Q}_{2\imath})) \\ \vdots & \vdots & \ddots & \vdots \\ ((\xi_{j_{\jmath1}}, \mathcal{P}_{\jmath1}), (\xi_{l_{\jmath1}}, \mathcal{Q}_{\jmath1})) & ((\xi_{j_{\jmath2}}, \mathcal{P}_{\jmath2}), (\xi_{l_{\jmath2}}, \mathcal{Q}_{\jmath2})) & \cdots & ((\xi_{j_{\jmath\imath}}, \mathcal{P}_{\jmath\imath}), (\xi_{l_{\jmath\imath}}, \mathcal{Q}_{\jmath\imath})) \end{bmatrix},$$

where $\beth_{ß\rho} = ((\xi_{j_{ß\rho}}, \mathcal{P}_{ß\rho}), (\xi_{l_{ß\rho}}, \mathcal{Q}_{ß\rho}))(ß = 1, 2, \ldots, \jmath,\ \ \rho = 1, 2, \ldots, \imath)$ represents the aggregated 2TLq-R information of alternative$\beth_ß$ on attribute Φ_ρ.

Step 3. To standardize the fused assessment matrix $R = [\beth_{ß\rho}]_{\jmath\times\imath}$, a formula is applied that is determined based on the nature of each attribute.

For benefit attributes:

$$N_{\text{ß}\rho} = \beth_{\text{ß}\rho} = ((\xi_{j_{\text{ß}\rho}}, \mathcal{P}_{\text{ß}\rho}), (\xi_{l_{\text{ß}\rho}}, \mathcal{Q}_{\text{ß}\rho})),\ \text{ß} = 1, 2, \ldots, \jmath,\ \rho = 1, 2, \ldots, \imath. \tag{15}$$

For cost attributes:

$$N_{\text{ß}\rho} = \beth^{c}_{\text{ß}\rho} = ((\xi_{l_{\text{ß}\rho}}, \mathcal{Q}_{\text{ß}\rho}), (\xi_{j_{\text{ß}\rho}}, \mathcal{P}_{\text{ß}\rho})),\ \text{ß} = 1, 2, \ldots, \jmath,\ \rho = 1, 2, \ldots, \imath. \tag{16}$$

Step 4. By utilizing the standardized matrix $N_{\text{ß}\rho} = ((\xi_{j_{\text{ß}\rho}}, \mathcal{P}_{\text{ß}\rho}), (\xi_{l_{\text{ß}\rho}}, \mathcal{Q}_{\text{ß}\rho}))$ and attribute's weights φ'_ρ, the 2TLq-R weighted standardized matrix $WN_{\text{ß}\rho} = ((\xi'_{j_{\text{ß}\rho}}, \mathcal{P}'_{\text{ß}\rho}), (\xi'_{l_{\text{ß}\rho}}, \mathcal{Q}_{\text{ß}\rho}))(\text{ß} = 1, 2, \ldots, \jmath,\quad \rho = 1, 2, \ldots, \imath)$ using the weighted average operator can be computed as

$$\begin{aligned} WN_{\text{ß}\rho} &= \varphi'_\rho \otimes N_{\text{ß}\rho} \\ &= \left(\Delta\left(\Theta\sqrt[q]{1-\left(1-\left(\frac{\Delta^{-1}(\xi_j, \mathcal{P})}{\Theta}\right)^q\right)^{\varphi'_\rho}}\right), \Delta\left(\Theta\left(\frac{\Delta^{-1}(\xi_l, \mathcal{Q})}{\Theta}\right)^{\varphi'_\rho}\right)\right). \end{aligned} \tag{17}$$

By utilizing the standardized matrix $N_{\text{ß}\rho} = ((\xi_{j_{\text{ß}\rho}}, \mathcal{P}_{\text{ß}\rho}), (\xi_{l_{\text{ß}\rho}}, \mathcal{Q}_{\text{ß}\rho}))(\text{ß} = 1, 2, \ldots, \jmath,\ \rho = 1, 2, \ldots, \imath)$ and attribute's weights φ'_ρ $(\rho = 1, 2, \ldots, \imath)$, the 2TL$q$-R weighted standardized matrix $WN_{\text{ß}\rho} = ((\xi'_{j_{\text{ß}\rho}}, \mathcal{P}'_{\text{ß}\rho}), (\xi'_{l_{\text{ß}\rho}}, \mathcal{Q}_{\text{ß}\rho}))$ $(\text{ß} = 1, 2, \ldots, \jmath,\ \rho = 1, 2, \ldots, \imath)$ using the weighted geometric operator can be computed as

$$\begin{aligned} WN_{\text{ß}\rho} &= \varphi'_\rho \otimes N_{\text{ß}\rho} \\ &= \left(\Delta\left(\Theta\left(\frac{\Delta^{-1}(\xi_j, \mathcal{P})}{\Theta}\right)^{\varphi'_\rho}\right), \Delta\left(\Theta\sqrt[q]{1-\left(1-\left(\frac{\Delta^{-1}(\xi_l, \mathcal{Q})}{\Theta}\right)^q\right)^{\varphi'_\rho}}\right)\right). \end{aligned} \tag{18}$$

Step 5. Determine the BAA matrix $G = [g_\rho]_{1\times\imath}$ $(\rho = 1, 2, \ldots, \imath)$ of attribute Φ_ρ. The element g_ρ can be computed by using weighted average operator:

$$\begin{aligned} g_\rho &= \left(\prod_{\text{ß}=1}^{\jmath} WN_{\text{ß}\rho}\right)^{1/\jmath} \\ &= \left(\Delta\left(\Theta\left(\prod_{\text{ß}=1}^{\jmath}\frac{\Delta^{-1}(\xi'_j, \mathcal{P}')}{\Theta}\right)^{\frac{1}{\jmath}}\right), \Delta\left(\Theta\sqrt[q]{1-\prod_{\text{ß}=1}^{\jmath}\left(1-\left(\frac{\Delta^{-1}(\xi'_l, \mathcal{Q}')}{\Theta}\right)^q\right)^{\frac{1}{\jmath}}}\right)\right). \end{aligned} \tag{19}$$

Determine the BAA matrix $G = [g_\rho]_{1\times\imath}$. The element g_ρ can be computed by using weighted geometric operator:

$$g_{\rho} = \left(\prod_{ß=1}^{J} WN_{ß\rho}\right)^{1/J}$$
$$= \left(\Delta\left(\Theta\sqrt[q]{1-\prod_{ß=1}^{J}\left(1-\left(\frac{\Delta^{-1}(\xi'_j,\mathcal{P}')}{\Theta}\right)^{q}\right)^{\frac{1}{J}}}\right), \Delta\left(\Theta\left(\prod_{ß=1}^{J}\frac{\Delta^{-1}(\xi'_l,\mathcal{Q}')}{\Theta}\right)^{\frac{1}{J}}\right)\right). \tag{20}$$

Step 6. Compute the distance utilizing Eq. 6 and the distance matrix $D = [d_{ß\rho}]_{J\times l}$ as follows:

$$d_{ß\rho} = \begin{cases} d(WN_{ß\rho}, g_{\rho}), & if \quad WN_{ß\rho} > g_{\rho}, \\ 0, & if \quad WN_{ß\rho} = g_{\rho}, \\ -d(WN_{ß\rho}, g_{\rho}), & if \quad WN_{ß\rho} < g_{\rho}. \end{cases} \tag{21}$$

In terms of the distances between alternatives $\beth_{ß}$ ($ß = 1, 2, \ldots, J$) and BAA denoted as $d_{ß\rho}$, as well as the distance between $WN_{ß\rho}$ and g_{ρ} represented as $d(WN_{ß\rho}, g_{\rho})$, we can obtain the following information based on the values of $d_{ß\rho}$.

(1) If $d_{ß\rho} > 0$, it indicates that the value of $d_{ß\rho}$ is greater than zero. In this case, the alternatives are classified as part of the upper approximation area (UAA) G^{+}. This suggests that these alternatives possess characteristics or attributes that place them in a higher position or superior level compared to other alternatives.
(2) If $d_{ß\rho} = 0$, it signifies that the value of $d_{ß\rho}$ is equal to zero. When this condition is met, the alternatives are considered as part of the border approximation area (BAA) G. In other words, these alternatives lie on the boundary or edge between the upper and lower approximation areas. They exhibit attributes that make them neither definitively superior nor inferior to other alternatives.
(3) If $d_{ß\rho} < 0$, it means that the value of $d_{ß\rho}$ is less than zero. In this scenario, the alternatives fall within the lower approximation area (LAA) G^{-}. These alternatives possess attributes or characteristics that position them at a lower level or inferior to other alternatives.

It is clear that the best alternatives belong to the set G^{+} (UAA), while the worst alternatives belong to the set G^{-} (LAA).

Step 7. Sum the values of each alternatives' $d_{ß\rho}$ as

$$S_{ß} = \sum_{\rho=1}^{l} d_{ß\rho}. \tag{22}$$

After completing the assessment and obtaining scores for all alternatives, the ranking of alternatives can be determined by arranging them in descending order based on their comprehensive assessment results. The alternative with

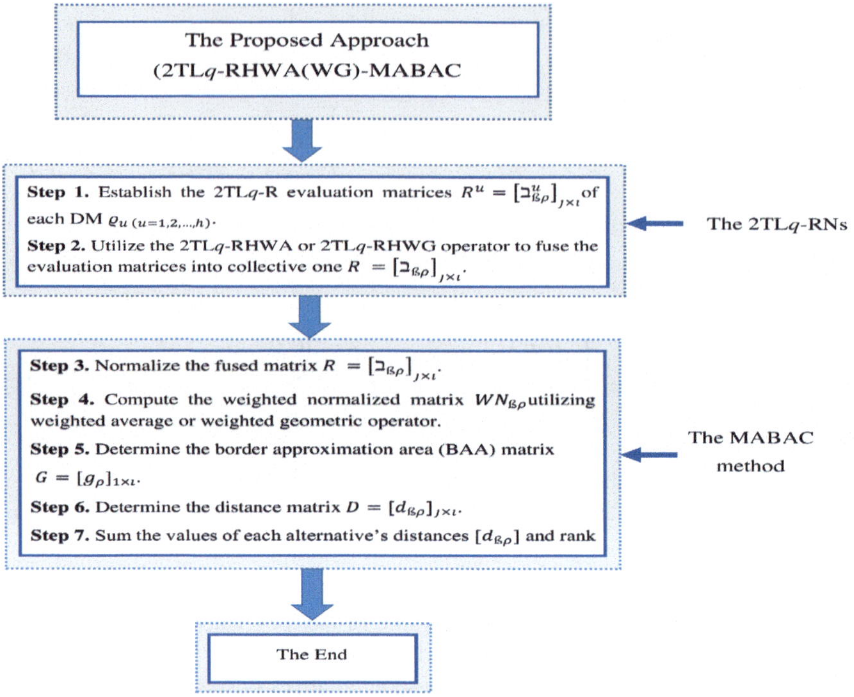

Fig. 3 Model of the 2TLq-R-MABAC method

the highest value of $S_ß$ is regarded as the most favorable or the best choice, while the alternative with the lowest $S_ß$ value is considered the least desirable.

The steps of the proposed approach are outlined in Fig. 3.

5 Application and Validation

In this subsection, we present an actual decision-making application that utilizes the 2TLq-R-MABAC model to choose the optimal alternative.

5.1 Evaluating e-Learning Websites

Assessing e-learning websites is crucial in today's digital era, where online education has gained immense popularity. When evaluating these platforms, several key factors should be taken into account. Firstly, content quality and relevance are fundamental aspects. An excellent e-learning website should offer well-structured and up-to-date courses that align with the learner's needs and objectives. The presence of comprehensive and engaging materials, such as videos, interactive quizzes, and supplementary resources, enhances the learning experience. Secondly, the user interface and overall design of the website play a significant role in its effectiveness. A visually appealing and user-friendly interface improves navigation and accessibility, enabling learners to easily locate and access desired content. Clear instructions, intuitive layout, and responsive design are vital for a positive user experience. Moreover, interactive features and communication tools foster active participation and collaboration among learners and instructors. Discussion forums, live chat, and virtual classrooms facilitate engagement, allowing learners to seek clarification, exchange ideas, and receive feedback. Timely and responsive support from instructors or customer service personnel is also crucial in ensuring a seamless learning process.

Furthermore, evaluating an e-learning website's credibility and reputation is essential. Accreditation from recognized educational institutions, endorsements from industry professionals, and positive reviews from previous learners serve as indicators of quality and reliability. Additionally, considering the website's track record in terms of successful outcomes and learner satisfaction is important. Lastly, assessing the accessibility and flexibility of the e-learning platform is a vital factor. Compatibility across various devices and operating systems, as well as support for multiple languages, enables learners from diverse backgrounds to conveniently access the content. Additionally, the availability of self-paced learning options and the ability to revisit course materials contribute to flexibility and adaptability. In conclusion, evaluating e-learning websites involves assessing factors such as content quality, user interface, interactivity, credibility, accessibility, and flexibility. By considering these aspects, learners can make informed decisions and select platforms that best meet their educational needs, thereby enhancing their overall e-learning experience. The quality of teaching procedures and the effectiveness of online access are both important factors in determining the objectives and expected outcomes of online teaching and learning. To achieve this, e-learning systems must be carefully designed and developed, particularly using a scientific approach that integrates established procedures and methodologies, in order to succeed, be effective, and provide a quality comparable to traditional educational learning systems. Websites serve as the primary interface for Internet users. In this context, it is necessary to delve deeper into the quality of e-learning websites.

E-learning enables greater adaptability, enhancing the teaching process. The effectiveness of delivering and acquiring knowledge through e-learning is remarkably high, as it simplifies comprehension and absorption of information. Audio-visual elements aid in retaining information for longer durations. Through e-learning, all students can access the same syllabus, study guides, materials, and training. E-learning helps save time, money, and travel expenses, making it more cost-effective compared to traditional learning. Consequently, the selection of e-learning websites is of paramount importance in the education sector. Therefore, there is a need to develop a framework that can significantly assist DMs in this selection process. This study has developed such a framework to aid DMs in choosing the best e-learning website from a pool of available options. To illustrate the applicability of the proposed methodology, a dataset comprising nine e-learning websites has been collected and evaluated using the seven outlined evaluation attributes. These nine e-learning websites are among the most popular and frequently utilized educational platforms by students. In today's fast-paced world, where time is of the essence, e-learning has emerged as a popular alternative to traditional classroom learning. With the advent of technology, it has become easier than ever to access knowledge from anywhere in the world. However, not all e-learning websites are created equal. Choosing the right website can make all the difference when it comes to effective learning. The importance of selecting the best e-learning website cannot be overstated. A well-designed website with high-quality content and interactive features can enhance the learning experience significantly. On the other hand, a poorly designed website with outdated information can lead to frustration and a waste of valuable time. Therefore, it is crucial to evaluate e-learning websites carefully before committing to one.

In this subsection, we offer a numerical illustration and assessment to demonstrate the practicality of our suggested approach. There is a set of nine alternatives $\daleth = \{\daleth_1, \daleth_2, \ldots, \daleth_9\}$, a set of seven attributes $\varPhi = \{\varPhi_1, \varPhi_2, \ldots, \varPhi_7\}$, and a set of four DMs $\varrho = \{\varrho_1, \varrho_2, \varrho_3, \varrho_4\}$. All attributes are of benefit type. The DMs subjectively assign the essential weights to the attributes as $\varphi' = (0.203, 0.022, 0.145, 0.179, 0.208, 0.039, 0.204)^T$ and $\varphi = (0.22, 0.32, 0.15, 0.31)^T$ be the weighting vector of the DMs. Each of the seven evaluation attributes has its own importance in the evaluation process. Each DM uses the 2TLq-RNs to assess each e-learning website for each attribute. Here are the details of nine e-learning websites that can be considered as alternatives:

1. Udemy: Udemy, an online marketplace, offers an extensive selection of courses taught by skilled instructors. The platform covers a diverse range of subjects, including business, personal development, programming, and more. Udemy courses are designed to be self-paced, allowing learners to progress at their own convenience. Additionally, these courses are often priced affordably, making education accessible to a wide audience (Fig. 4).

2. Coursera: Renowned for its extensive collection of courses from leading universities and institutions across the globe, Coursera stands as a prominent online learning platform. It offers a diverse range of subjects, encompassing fields such as business, technology, arts, and sciences. Coursera caters to both free and paid learners, granting them the opportunity to earn certificates and even pursue degree programs (Fig. 5).

3. edX: edX is renowned for being an open-source online learning platform that offers a wide range of courses from prestigious universities and organizations. It provides an extensive selection of courses covering various subjects including computer science, engineering, humanities, and more. Learners have the flexibility to choose between free or paid courses and can even obtain verified certificates upon completion (Fig. 6).

4. Khan Academy: Khan Academy, a non-profit organization, provides a wide array of free educational resources and courses. Their offerings encompass various subjects such as math, science, history, and more. The courses provided by Khan

Fig. 4 Udemy

Fig. 5 Coursera

Academy are designed to be self-paced and easily accessible, catering to learners of all age groups (Fig. 7).

5. LinkedIn Learning: LinkedIn Learning, previously known as Lynda.com, is an e-learning platform renowned for its wide range of courses and tutorials. This platform offers video-based instruction on diverse subjects such as business, technology, creative skills, and professional development. LinkedIn Learning follows a subscription-based model, providing learners with access to a vast library of courses and resources (Fig. 8).

6. Codecademy: Codecademy is a specialized platform for learning coding and programming languages. It offers interactive coding exercises, projects, and quizzes

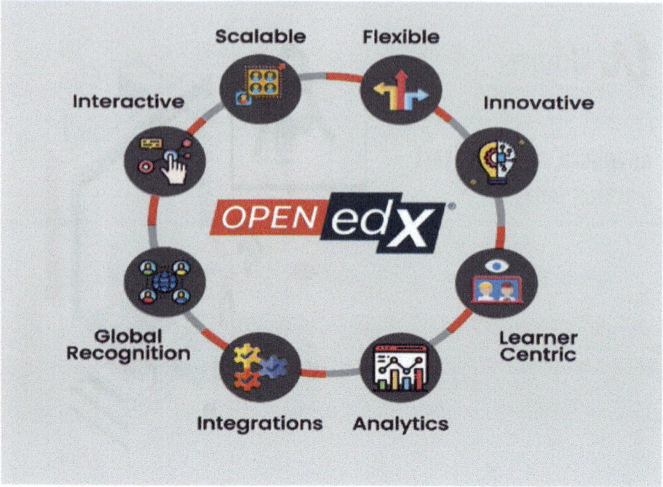

Fig. 6 edX

Fig. 7 Khan Academy

to help learners develop practical coding skills. Codecademy covers languages such as Python, JavaScript, HTML, CSS, and more (Fig. 9).

7. Skillshare: Skillshare is an online learning platform dedicated to fostering creativity and practical expertise. It offers a diverse array of classes taught by industry professionals, covering various subjects such as photography, design, writing, and entrepreneurship. By subscribing to Skillshare, learners gain access to a vast collection of courses, enabling them to acquire new skills and knowledge. The plat-

Fig. 8 LinkedIn Learning

Fig. 9 Codecademy

form operates on a subscription model, providing individuals with the opportunity to explore and learn from a wide range of educational content (Fig. 10).

8. FutureLearn: FutureLearn is a digital education platform that offers courses from reputable universities and institutions. It provides courses in various subjects, including health care, business, technology, and social sciences. FutureLearn offers both free and paid courses, with the option to earn certificates (Fig. 11).

9. Teachable: Teachable is a platform that empowers individuals to create and sell their own online courses. It provides tools for course creation, hosting, and

Fig. 10 Skillshare

Fig. 11 FutureLearn

marketing. Teachable is suitable for instructors, entrepreneurs, and professionals who aim to share their expertise and monetize their knowledge (Fig. 12).

These nine e-learning websites offer diverse educational content, varying course formats, and different pricing models. Learners can explore these alternatives and select the one that aligns best with their specific learning needs, preferences, and budget.

Tables 1 and 2 present the web addresses of the nine e-learning websites under consideration, along with the seven evaluation attributes. The linguistic variables

Fig. 12 Teachable

Table 1 Web addresses of nine e-learning websites

Alternative	Web address
$\beth_1$	https://www.udemy.com/
$\beth_2$	https://www.coursera.org/
$\beth_3$	https://www.edx.org/
$\beth_4$	https://www.khanacademy.org/
$\beth_5$	https://www.linkedin.com/learning/
$\beth_6$	https://www.codecademy.com/
$\beth_7$	https://www.skillshare.com/en/
$\beth_8$	https://www.futurelearn.com/
$\beth_9$	https://teachable.com/

associated with these attributes are listed in Table 3. Using these linguistic variables, the 2TLq-R evaluation matrix is constructed and presented in Table 4.

When evaluating e-learning websites, there are several attributes to consider. Here are seven key attributes that should be assessed.

By assessing these attributes, learners can make well-informed decisions and select e-learning platforms that align with their educational needs, thereby enhancing their overall learning experience.

Table 2 Description of seven evaluation attributes

Attribute	Description
Content quality (Φ_1)	This attribute focuses on the quality and relevance of the educational materials available on the website. It encompasses factors such as the accuracy, depth, and currency of the content, as well as the presence of interactive elements and supplementary resources
User interface and design (Φ_2)	This attribute pertains to the usability and visual appeal of the website. It involves evaluating the layout, navigation, and overall design aesthetics to ensure an intuitive and user-friendly experience
Interactivity (Φ_3)	This attribute assesses the level of engagement and interaction provided by the e-learning platform. It includes features like interactive quizzes, simulations, discussion forums, and collaborative tools that foster active participation and learner engagement
Credibility and reputation (Φ_4)	This attribute examines the credibility and reputation of the e-learning website. It involves considering factors such as accreditation from recognized institutions, endorsements from industry experts, and positive reviews or testimonials from previous learners
Accessibility (Φ_5)	This attribute focuses on the accessibility of the e-learning platform. It encompasses aspects like compatibility with different devices and operating systems, support for multiple languages, and compliance with accessibility standards to ensure inclusivity for learners with diverse backgrounds and needs
Flexibility (Φ_6)	This attribute evaluates the flexibility of the e-learning platform in terms of learning options and schedules. It includes features such as self-paced learning, the ability to revisit course materials, and the availability of alternative learning paths to accommodate different learning styles and preferences
Support and assistance (Φ_7)	This attribute considers the availability and quality of support and assistance provided to learners. It includes factors such as prompt and responsive customer support, access to instructors or subject matter experts for clarification, and the provision of feedback and guidance throughout the learning process

Table 3 Corresponding table between linguistic variables and 2TLq-RNs

Linguistic variables	2TLq-RNs	For convenience
Equally important (EI)	$((\xi_8, 0), (\xi_0, 0))$	(ξ_8, ξ_0)
Moderately important (MI)	$((\xi_7, 0), (\xi_1, 0))$	(ξ_7, ξ_1)
Moderately more important (MOMI)	$((\xi_6, 0), (\xi_2, 0))$	(ξ_6, ξ_2)
Moderately to definitely more important (MDMI)	$((\xi_5, 0), (\xi_3, 0))$	(ξ_5, ξ_3)
Much more important (MMI)	$((\xi_4, 0), (\xi_4, 0))$	(ξ_4, ξ_4)
Preferred to very much more important (PMMI)	$((\xi_3, 0), (\xi_5, 0))$	(ξ_3, ξ_5)
Very much more important (VMMI)	$((\xi_2, 0), (\xi_6, 0))$	(ξ_2, ξ_6)
Preferred to extremely important (PEXI)	$((\xi_1, 0), (\xi_7, 0))$	(ξ_1, ξ_7)
Extremely important (EXI)	$((\xi_0, 0), (\xi_8, 0))$	(ξ_0, ξ_8)

5.2 A Decision-making Approach Utilizing the 2TLq-RHWA Operator

In this subsection, we describe the evaluation procedure used for selecting the best alternative, employing the 2TLq-R-MABAC method with a specific emphasis on the 2TLq-RHWA operator. The evaluation process is based on the framework provided by the 2TLq-R-MABAC method. This method serves as the foundation for the evaluation, incorporating the essential role of the 2TLq-RHWA operator. The operator is responsible for aggregating the assessment information and determining the overall ranking of the alternatives. By utilizing the 2TLq-R-MABAC method and leveraging the capabilities of the 2TLq-RHWA operator, a comprehensive and systematic evaluation process is established to identify the best alternative among the available options.

The evaluation procedure involves several steps. These steps include

Step 1. We established a 2TLq-R evaluation matrix, $R^u = [\beth^u_{ß\rho}]_{9\times 7} = ((\xi_{j_{ß\rho}}, \mathcal{P}_{ß\rho})^u, (\xi_{l_{ß\rho}}, \mathcal{Q}_{ß\rho})^u)_{9\times 7}$ $(ß = 1, 2, \ldots, 9,\ \ \rho = 1, 2, \ldots, 7,\ \ u = 1, 2, 3, 4)$, representing the assessments of four DMs as shown in Table 5.

Step 2. Utilizing the 2TLq-RHWA AO, we fused overall $\beth^u_{ß\rho}$ to $\beth_{ß\rho}$, the fused 2TLq-RNs assessment matrix $R = [\beth_{ß\rho}]_{9\times 7}$ is shown in Table 6. (Suppose $q = 4$ and $F = 3$.)

Step 3. We utilized Eq. (15) because our all attributes are benefit type. Hence, the fused assessment matrix in Table 6 is our standardized one.

Step 4. According to the standardized matrix $N_{ß\rho} = ((\xi_{j_{ß\rho}}, \mathcal{P}_{ß\rho}), (\xi_{l_{ß\rho}}, \mathcal{Q}_{ß\rho}))$ and attribute weights φ'_ρ, the results of 2TLq-R weighted standardized matrix

Table 4 Linguistic variables assessment matrix by each DM

DMs	Alternatives	Attributes						
		Φ_1	Φ_2	Φ_3	Φ_4	Φ_5	Φ_6	Φ_7
ϱ_1	$\beth_1$	PMMI	EXI	MDMI	EI	MOMI	VMMI	MOMI
	$\beth_2$	EI	MOMI	PMMI	EXI	VMMI	MMI	MDMI
	$\beth_3$	VMMI	MI	PEXI	EI	MMI	EXI	MOMI
	$\beth_4$	MMI	VMMI	MI	PEXI	MDMI	VMMI	EXI
	$\beth_5$	MOMI	PMMI	EXI	MDMI	EI	MI	VMMI
	$\beth_6$	MI	PEXI	EI	MOMI	VMMI	MDMI	EXI
	$\beth_7$	EXI	MDMI	VMMI	PEXI	MI	MOMI	EI
	$\beth_8$	VMMI	MDMI	MI	PEXI	EI	EXI	MOMI
	$\beth_9$	EXI	MOMI	VMMI	EI	MDMI	MI	PEXI
ϱ_2	$\beth_1$	MDMI	VMMI	MI	MMI	MOMI	PEXI	EI
	$\beth_2$	MI	PEXI	EI	MOMI	PMMI	MDMI	EXI
	$\beth_3$	MOMI	PMMI	EXI	MDMI	PEXI	EI	VMMI
	$\beth_4$	PEXI	MMI	MOMI	PMMI	MI	EI	EXI
	$\beth_5$	VMMI	MI	PEXI	EI	EXI	MOMI	MMI
	$\beth_6$	MMI	MOMI	PMMI	EXI	PEXI	MI	EI
	$\beth_7$	EXI	MDMI	VMMI	MI	MOMI	PEXI	MMI
	$\beth_8$	MOMI	PMMI	EXI	MDMI	EI	MI	VMMI
	$\beth_9$	EI	MOMI	PMMI	EXI	VMMI	MMI	MDMI
ϱ_3	$\beth_1$	MI	PEXI	MDMI	EI	MDMI	PMMI	MOMI
	$\beth_2$	MOMI	EI	PEXI	PMMI	VMMI	MDMI	VMMI
	$\beth_3$	MDMI	VMMI	EXI	EI	PMMI	MOMI	MMI
	$\beth_4$	MMI	PMMI	VMMI	MDMI	MMI	MI	PEXI
	$\beth_5$	VMMI	MI	MMI	MOMI	PEXI	EI	PMMI
	$\beth_6$	MI	PEXI	EI	MMI	MOMI	MMI	VMMI
	$\beth_7$	EI	MMI	PMMI	PEXI	MI	MOMI	MDMI
	$\beth_8$	VMMI	MI	PEXI	EI	EXI	MOMI	MMI
	$\beth_9$	MDMI	VMMI	MI	MMI	MOMI	PEXI	EI
ϱ_4	$\beth_1$	MI	PEXI	MDMI	EI	VMMI	EI	PMMI
	$\beth_2$	PEXI	EXI	MMI	VMMI	EI	MDMI	MI
	$\beth_3$	MDMI	EI	VMMI	PEXI	PMMI	EXI	MOMI
	$\beth_4$	EI	VMMI	PMMI	MMI	EXI	MI	MDMI
	$\beth_5$	VMMI	MOMI	EXI	PMMI	MI	EI	MDMI
	$\beth_6$	PMMI	MI	EI	MOMI	PEXI	MDMI	EXI
	$\beth_7$	MMI	MDMI	PEXI	EXI	VMMI	MI	EI
	$\beth_8$	VMMI	MI	MMI	MOMI	PEXI	EI	PMMI
	$\beth_9$	MI	PEXI	MDMI	EI	MDMI	PMMI	MOMI

Table 5 2TLq-RNs assessment matrix by each DM

DMs	Alternatives	Attributes						
		Φ_1	Φ_2	Φ_3	Φ_4	Φ_5	Φ_6	Φ_7
ϱ_1	$\beth_1$	(ξ_3, ξ_5)	(ξ_0, ξ_8)	(ξ_5, ξ_3)	(ξ_8, ξ_0)	(ξ_6, ξ_2)	(ξ_2, ξ_6)	(ξ_6, ξ_2)
	$\beth_2$	(ξ_8, ξ_0)	(ξ_6, ξ_2)	(ξ_3, ξ_5)	(ξ_0, ξ_8)	(ξ_2, ξ_6)	(ξ_4, ξ_4)	(ξ_5, ξ_3)
	$\beth_3$	(ξ_2, ξ_6)	(ξ_7, ξ_1)	(ξ_1, ξ_7)	(ξ_8, ξ_0)	(ξ_4, ξ_4)	(ξ_0, ξ_8)	(ξ_6, ξ_2)
	$\beth_4$	(ξ_4, ξ_4)	(ξ_2, ξ_6)	(ξ_7, ξ_1)	(ξ_1, ξ_7)	(ξ_5, ξ_3)	(ξ_2, ξ_6)	(ξ_0, ξ_8)
	$\beth_5$	(ξ_6, ξ_2)	(ξ_3, ξ_5)	(ξ_0, ξ_8)	(ξ_5, ξ_3)	(ξ_8, ξ_0)	(ξ_7, ξ_1)	(ξ_2, ξ_6)
	$\beth_6$	(ξ_7, ξ_1)	(ξ_1, ξ_7)	(ξ_8, ξ_0)	(ξ_6, ξ_2)	(ξ_2, ξ_6)	(ξ_5, ξ_3)	(ξ_0, ξ_8)
	$\beth_7$	(ξ_5, ξ_3)	(ξ_2, ξ_6)	(ξ_0, ξ_8)	(ξ_1, ξ_7)	(ξ_7, ξ_1)	(ξ_6, ξ_2)	(ξ_8, ξ_0)
	$\beth_8$	(ξ_2, ξ_6)	(ξ_5, ξ_3)	(ξ_7, ξ_1)	(ξ_1, ξ_7)	(ξ_8, ξ_0)	(ξ_0, ξ_8)	(ξ_6, ξ_2)
	$\beth_9$	(ξ_0, ξ_8)	(ξ_6, ξ_2)	(ξ_2, ξ_6)	(ξ_8, ξ_0)	(ξ_5, ξ_3)	(ξ_7, ξ_1)	(ξ_1, ξ_7)
ϱ_2	$\beth_1$	(ξ_5, ξ_3)	(ξ_2, ξ_6)	(ξ_7, ξ_1)	(ξ_4, ξ_4)	(ξ_6, ξ_2)	(ξ_1, ξ_7)	(ξ_8, ξ_0)
	$\beth_2$	(ξ_7, ξ_1)	(ξ_1, ξ_7)	(ξ_8, ξ_0)	(ξ_6, ξ_2)	(ξ_3, ξ_5)	(ξ_5, ξ_3)	(ξ_0, ξ_8)
	$\beth_3$	(ξ_6, ξ_2)	(ξ_3, ξ_5)	(ξ_0, ξ_8)	(ξ_5, ξ_3)	(ξ_1, ξ_7)	(ξ_8, ξ_0)	(ξ_2, ξ_6)
	$\beth_4$	(ξ_1, ξ_7)	(ξ_4, ξ_4)	(ξ_6, ξ_2)	(ξ_3, ξ_5)	(ξ_7, ξ_1)	(ξ_8, ξ_0)	(ξ_0, ξ_8)
	$\beth_5$	(ξ_2, ξ_6)	(ξ_7, ξ_1)	(ξ_1, ξ_7)	(ξ_8, ξ_0)	(ξ_0, ξ_8)	(ξ_6, ξ_2)	(ξ_4, ξ_4)
	$\beth_6$	(ξ_4, ξ_4)	(ξ_6, ξ_2)	(ξ_3, ξ_5)	(ξ_0, ξ_8)	(ξ_1, ξ_7)	(ξ_7, ξ_1)	(ξ_8, ξ_0)
	$\beth_7$	(ξ_0, ξ_8)	(ξ_5, ξ_3)	(ξ_2, ξ_6)	(ξ_7, ξ_1)	(ξ_6, ξ_2)	(ξ_1, ξ_7)	(ξ_4, ξ_4)
	$\beth_8$	(ξ_6, ξ_2)	(ξ_3, ξ_5)	(ξ_0, ξ_8)	(ξ_5, ξ_3)	(ξ_8, ξ_0)	(ξ_7, ξ_1)	(ξ_2, ξ_6)
	$\beth_9$	(ξ_8, ξ_0)	(ξ_6, ξ_2)	(ξ_3, ξ_5)	(ξ_0, ξ_8)	(ξ_2, ξ_6)	(ξ_4, ξ_4)	(ξ_5, ξ_3)
ϱ_3	$\beth_1$	(ξ_7, ξ_1)	(ξ_1, ξ_7)	(ξ_5, ξ_3)	(ξ_8, ξ_0)	(ξ_5, ξ_3)	(ξ_3, ξ_5)	(ξ_6, ξ_2)
	$\beth_2$	(ξ_6, ξ_2)	(ξ_8, ξ_0)	(ξ_1, ξ_7)	(ξ_3, ξ_5)	(ξ_2, ξ_6)	(ξ_5, ξ_3)	(ξ_2, ξ_6)
	$\beth_3$	(ξ_5, ξ_3)	(ξ_2, ξ_6)	(ξ_0, ξ_8)	(ξ_8, ξ_0)	(ξ_3, ξ_5)	(ξ_6, ξ_2)	(ξ_4, ξ_4)
	$\beth_4$	(ξ_4, ξ_4)	(ξ_3, ξ_5)	(ξ_2, ξ_6)	(ξ_5, ξ_3)	(ξ_6, ξ_2)	(ξ_7, ξ_1)	(ξ_1, ξ_7)
	$\beth_5$	(ξ_2, ξ_6)	(ξ_7, ξ_1)	(ξ_4, ξ_4)	(ξ_6, ξ_2)	(ξ_1, ξ_7)	(ξ_8, ξ_0)	(ξ_3, ξ_5)
	$\beth_6$	(ξ_7, ξ_1)	(ξ_1, ξ_7)	(ξ_8, ξ_0)	(ξ_4, ξ_4)	(ξ_6, ξ_2)	(ξ_4, ξ_4)	(ξ_2, ξ_6)
	$\beth_7$	(ξ_8, ξ_0)	(ξ_4, ξ_4)	(ξ_3, ξ_5)	(ξ_1, ξ_7)	(ξ_7, ξ_1)	(ξ_6, ξ_2)	(ξ_5, ξ_3)
	$\beth_8$	(ξ_2, ξ_6)	(ξ_7, ξ_1)	(ξ_1, ξ_7)	(ξ_8, ξ_0)	(ξ_0, ξ_8)	(ξ_6, ξ_2)	(ξ_4, ξ_4)
	$\beth_9$	(ξ_5, ξ_3)	(ξ_2, ξ_6)	(ξ_7, ξ_1)	(ξ_4, ξ_4)	(ξ_6, ξ_2)	(ξ_1, ξ_7)	(ξ_8, ξ_0)
ϱ_4	$\beth_1$	(ξ_7, ξ_1)	(ξ_1, ξ_7)	(ξ_5, ξ_3)	(ξ_8, ξ_0)	(ξ_2, ξ_6)	(ξ_8, ξ_0)	(ξ_3, ξ_5)
	$\beth_2$	(ξ_1, ξ_7)	(ξ_0, ξ_8)	(ξ_4, ξ_4)	(ξ_2, ξ_6)	(ξ_8, ξ_0)	(ξ_5, ξ_3)	(ξ_7, ξ_1)
	$\beth_3$	(ξ_5, ξ_3)	(ξ_8, ξ_0)	(ξ_2, ξ_6)	(ξ_1, ξ_7)	(ξ_3, ξ_5)	(ξ_0, ξ_8)	(ξ_6, ξ_2)
	$\beth_4$	(ξ_8, ξ_0)	(ξ_2, ξ_6)	(ξ_3, ξ_5)	(ξ_4, ξ_4)	(ξ_0, ξ_8)	(ξ_7, ξ_1)	(ξ_5, ξ_3)
	$\beth_5$	(ξ_2, ξ_6)	(ξ_6, ξ_2)	(ξ_0, ξ_8)	(ξ_3, ξ_5)	(ξ_7, ξ_1)	(ξ_8, ξ_0)	(ξ_5, ξ_3)
	$\beth_6$	(ξ_3, ξ_5)	(ξ_7, ξ_1)	(ξ_8, ξ_0)	(ξ_6, ξ_2)	(ξ_1, ξ_7)	(ξ_5, ξ_3)	(ξ_0, ξ_8)
	$\beth_7$	(ξ_4, ξ_4)	(ξ_5, ξ_3)	(ξ_1, ξ_7)	(ξ_0, ξ_8)	(ξ_2, ξ_6)	(ξ_7, ξ_1)	(ξ_8, ξ_0)
	$\beth_8$	(ξ_2, ξ_6)	(ξ_7, ξ_1)	(ξ_4, ξ_4)	(ξ_6, ξ_2)	(ξ_1, ξ_7)	(ξ_8, ξ_0)	(ξ_3, ξ_5)
	$\beth_9$	(ξ_7, ξ_1)	(ξ_1, ξ_7)	(ξ_5, ξ_3)	(ξ_8, ξ_0)	(ξ_5, ξ_3)	(ξ_3, ξ_5)	(ξ_6, ξ_2)

Table 6 Fused assessment matrix by the 2TLq-RHWA operator

Alternatives	Φ_1	Φ_2	Φ_3	Φ_4
$\beth_1$	$((\xi_6, 0.0746), (\xi_2, 0.0379))$	$((\xi_2, -0.4635), (\xi_7, -0.0320))$	$((\xi_6, -0.0837), (\xi_2, 0.1139))$	(ξ_8, ξ_0)
$\beth_2$	$((\xi_8, 0)), (\xi_0, 0))$	(ξ_8, ξ_0)	(ξ_8, ξ_0)	$((\xi_5, -0.4876), (\xi_5, -0.3392))$
$\beth_3$	$((\xi_5, 0.1394), (\xi_3, 0.1028))$	(ξ_8, ξ_0)	$((\xi_2, -0.4918), (\xi_7, 0.271))$	(ξ_8, ξ_0)
$\beth_4$	(ξ_8, ξ_0)	$((\xi_3, 0.1729), (\xi_5, 0.1686))$	$((\xi_6, -0.4074), (\xi_3, -0.2691))$	$((\xi_4, -0.2594), (\xi_5, -0.2607))$
$\beth_5$	$((\xi_4, 0.0997), (\xi_5, -0.1772))$	$((\xi_6, 0.3092), (\xi_2, -0.2235))$	$((\xi_2, 0.4801), (\xi_7, 0.2068))$	(ξ_8, ξ_0)
$\beth_6$	$((\xi_6, -0.3497), (\xi_3, -0.4080))$	$((\xi_6, -0.1426), (\xi_3, -0.3202))$	(ξ_8, ξ_0)	$((\xi_5, 0.1642), (\xi_4, -0.2477))$
$\beth_7$	(ξ_8, ξ_0)	$((\xi_5, -0.4442), (\xi_4, -0.3183))$	$((\xi_2, 0.0451), (\xi_7, -0.3188))$	$((\xi_5, 0.2768), (\xi_4, 0.3929))$
$\beth_8$	$((\xi_4, 0.4942), (\xi_4, 0.3316))$	$((\xi_6, 0.0103), (\xi_2, 0.1494))$	$((\xi_5, -0.0319), (\xi_4, 0.3979))$	(ξ_8, ξ_0)
$\beth_9$	(ξ_8, ξ_0)	$((\xi_5, 0.1176), (\xi_4, -0.3787))$	$((\xi_5, -0.0864), (\xi_4, -0.4537))$	(ξ_8, ξ_0)
	Φ_5	Φ_6	Φ_7	
$\beth_1$	$((\xi_5, 0.2967), (\xi_3, 0.0352))$	(ξ_8, ξ_0)	(ξ_8, ξ_0)	
$\beth_2$	(ξ_8, ξ_0)	$((\xi_5, -0.1741), (\xi_3, 0.1980))$	$((\xi_5, 0.4735), (\xi_4, -0.4503))$	
$\beth_3$	$((\xi_3, 0.1054), (\xi_5, 0.3940))$	(ξ_8, ξ_0)	$((\xi_5, 0.1745), (\xi_3, 0.2067))$	
$\beth_4$	$((\xi_6, -0.2139), (\xi_3, -0.0750))$	(ξ_8, ξ_0)	$((\xi_4, -0.3028), (\xi_6, 0.3406))$	
$\beth_5$	(ξ_8, ξ_0)	(ξ_8, ξ_0)	$((\xi_4, 0.1151), (\xi_4, 0.1729))$	
$\beth_6$	$((\xi_4, -0.3053), (\xi_6, -0.1692))$	$((\xi_6, -0.1542), (\xi_2, 0.2091))$	(ξ_8, ξ_0)	
$\beth_7$	$((\xi_6, 0.0437), (\xi_2, 0.2141))$	$((\xi_6, -0.0615), (\xi_3, -0.4971))$	(ξ_8, ξ_0)	
$\beth_8$	(ξ_8, ξ_0)	(ξ_8, ξ_0)	$((\xi_4, 0.2969), (\xi_4, 0.2547))$	
$\beth_9$	$((\xi_5, -0.2205), (\xi_4, -0.4260))$	$((\xi_5, 0.0286), (\xi_4, -0.4802))$	(ξ_8, ξ_0)	

$WN_{ßρ} = ((\xi'_{j_{ßρ}}, \mathcal{P}'_{ßρ}), (\xi'_{l_{ßρ}}, \mathcal{Q}_{ßρ}))(ß = 1, 2, \ldots, 9, \quad ρ = 1, 2, \ldots, 7)$ are recorded in Table 7.

Step 5. Compute the BAA matrix $G = [g_ρ]_{1\times 7}$ $(ρ = 1, 2, \ldots, 7)$ of attribute $\Phi_ρ$.

$$g_1 = ((\xi_5, 0.0156), (\xi_6, 0.0472)),\ g_2 = ((\xi_2, 0.3784), (\xi_8, -0.2315)),\ g_3 = ((\xi_3, -0.0917), (\xi_7, 0.3850)),$$

$$g_4 = ((\xi_5, 0.2151), (\xi_6, 0.2585)),\ g_5 = ((\xi_4, 0.3434), (\xi_6, 0.4723)),\ g_6 = ((\xi_5, -0.2583), (\xi_7, -0.0431)),$$

$$g_7 = ((\xi_5, -0.3054), (\xi_6, 0.4443)).$$

Step 6. Compute the normalized Hamming distance $D = [d_{ßρ}]_{9\times 7}$ between alternatives and BAA utilizing Eq. (6) (see Table 8).

Step 7. Sum the values of each alternatives $d_{ßρ}$.

$$S_1 = \sum_{ρ=1}^{7} d_{1ρ} = 1.9975,\ S_2 = \sum_{ρ=1}^{7} d_{2ρ} = 2.5305,\ S_3 = \sum_{ρ=1}^{7} d_{3ρ} = 1.7625,$$

$$S_4 = \sum_{ρ=1}^{7} d_{4ρ} = 0.8622,\ S_5 = \sum_{ρ=1}^{7} d_{5ρ} = 1.5107,\ S_6 = \sum_{ρ=1}^{7} d_{6ρ} = 0.8458,$$

$$S_7 = \sum_{ρ=1}^{7} d_{7ρ} = 0.7670,\ S_8 = \sum_{ρ=1}^{7} d_{8ρ} = 1.6574,\ S_9 = \sum_{ρ=1}^{7} d_{9ρ} = 1.5807$$

The alternatives $\beth_ß(ß = 1, 2, \ldots, 9)$ can be ranked easily by utilizing the result of $S_ß$. The ranking is established by evaluating the values of $S_ß$, where the alternative with the highest $S_ß$ is considered the most favorable. The ranking of alternatives is presented below:

$$\beth_2 > \beth_1 > \beth_3 > \beth_8 > \beth_9 > \beth_5 > \beth_4 > \beth_6 > \beth_7.$$

Therefore, $\beth_2$ is the best e-learning website.

5.3 *A Decision-making Approach Utilizing the 2TLq-RHWG Operator*

This subsection provides an overview of the evaluation procedure used to select the best alternative, utilizing the 2TLq-R-MABAC method, with a specific emphasis on the 2TLq-RHWG operator. The 2TLq-R-MABAC method serves as the framework for the evaluation process, incorporating the 2TLq-RHWG operator, which plays

Table 7 The weighted standardized matrix $WN_{\text{ß}\rho}$

Alternatives	Φ_1	Φ_2	Φ_3	Φ_4
$\beth_1$	$((\xi_4, 0.2381), (\xi_6, 0.0607))$	$((\xi_1, -0.4081), (\xi_8, -0.0243))$	$((\xi_4, -0.2127), (\xi_7, -0.4040))$	(ξ_8, ξ_0)
$\beth_2$	(ξ_8, ξ_0)	(ξ_8, ξ_0)	(ξ_8, ξ_0)	$((\xi_3, -0.0330), (\xi_7, 0.2626))$
$\beth_3$	$((\xi_4, -0.4867), (\xi_7, -0.3993))$	(ξ_8, ξ_0)	$((\xi_1, -0.0692), (\xi_8, -0.1101))$	(ξ_8, ξ_0)
$\beth_4$	(ξ_8, ξ_0)	$((\xi_1, 0.2257), (\xi_8, -0.0765))$	$((\xi_4, -0.4494), (\xi_7, -0.1545))$	$((\xi_2, 0.4452), (\xi_7, 0.2843))$
$\beth_5$	$((\xi_3, -0.2286), (\xi_7, 0.2189))$	$((\xi_3, -0.4268), (\xi_8, -0.2605))$	$((\xi_2, -0.4681), (\xi_8, -0.1202))$	(ξ_8, ξ_0)
$\beth_6$	$((\xi_4, -0.1008), (\xi_6, 0.3640))$	$((\xi_2, 0.3484), (\xi_8, -0.1902))$	(ξ_8, ξ_0)	$((\xi_3, 0.4242), (\xi_7, -0.0139))$
$\beth_7$	(ξ_8, ξ_0)	$((\xi_2, -0.2217), (\xi_8, -0.1354))$	$((\xi_1, 0.2625), (\xi_8, -0.2063))$	$((\xi_4, -0.4946), (\xi_7, 0.1860))$
$\beth_8$	$((\xi_3, 0.0481), (\xi_7, 0.0632))$	$((\xi_2, 0.4222), (\xi_8, -0.2280))$	$((\xi_3, 0.1181), (\xi_7, 0.3352))$	(ξ_8, ξ_0)
$\beth_9$	(ξ_8, ξ_0)	$((\xi_2, 0.0149), (\xi_8, -0.1383))$	$((\xi_3, 0.0815), (\xi_7, 0.1098))$	(ξ_8, ξ_0)
	Φ_5	Φ_6	Φ_7	
$\beth_1$	$((\xi_4, -0.3483), (\xi_7, -0.4605))$	(ξ_8, ξ_0)	(ξ_8, ξ_0)	
$\beth_2$	(ξ_8, ξ_0)	$((\xi_2, 0.1810), (\xi_8, -0.2810))$	$((\xi_4, -0.2321), (\xi_7, -0.2221))$	
$\beth_3$	$((\xi_2, 0.1019), (\xi_7, 0.3703))$	(ξ_8, ξ_0)	$((\xi_4, -0.4565), (\xi_7, -0.3611))$	
$\beth_4$	$((\xi_4, 0.0291), (\xi_6, 0.4893))$	(ξ_8, ξ_0)	$((\xi_2, 0.4963), (\xi_8, -0.3705))$	
$\beth_5$	(ξ_8, ξ_0)	(ξ_8, ξ_0)	$((\xi_3, -0.2145), (\xi_7, 0.0053))$	
$\beth_6$	$((\xi_3, -0.4934), (\xi_7, 0.4906))$	$((\xi_3, -0.2984), (\xi_8, -0.3916))$	(ξ_8, ξ_0)	
$\beth_7$	$((\xi_4, 0.2373), (\xi_6, 0.1242))$	$((\xi_3, -0.2475), (\xi_8, -0.3544))$	(ξ_8, ξ_0)	
$\beth_8$	$((\xi_8, 0), (\xi_0, 0))$	(ξ_8, ξ_0)	$((\xi_3, -0.0874), (\xi_7, 0.0331))$	
$\beth_9$	$((\xi_3, 0.2710), (\xi_7, -0.2345))$	$((\xi_2, 0.2800), (\xi_8, -0.2521))$	(ξ_8, ξ_0)	

Table 8 The distance $d_{ß\rho}$ between alternatives and BAA

Alternatives	Φ_1	Φ_2	Φ_3	Φ_4	Φ_5	Φ_6	Φ_7
$\beth_1$	$d_{11} = -0.0393$	$d_{12} = -0.0533$	$d_{13} = 0.1484$	$d_{14} = 0.5970$	$d_{15} = -0.0308$	$d_{16} = 0.7242$	$d_{17} = 0.6512$
$\beth_2$	$d_{21} = 0.5860$	$d_{22} = 0.9407$	$d_{23} = 0.8544$	$d_{24} = -0.2332$	$d_{25} = 0.6708$	$d_{26} = -0.2064$	$d_{27} = -0.0818$
$\beth_3$	$d_{31} = -0.1271$	$d_{32} = 0.9407$	$d_{33} = -0.1186$	$d_{34} = 0.5970$	$d_{35} = -0.1871$	$d_{36} = 0.7242$	$d_{37} = -0.0666$
$\beth_4$	$d_{41} = 0.5860$	$d_{42} = -0.0402$	$d_{43} = 0.1057$	$d_{44} = -0.2423$	$d_{45} = -0.0135$	$d_{46} = 0.7242$	$d_{47} = -0.2576$
$\beth_5$	$d_{51} = -0.2383$	$d_{52} = 0.0081$	$d_{53} = -0.1156$	$d_{54} = 0.5970$	$d_{55} = 0.6708$	$d_{56} = 0.7242$	$d_{57} = -0.1354$
$\beth_6$	$d_{61} = -0.0860$	$d_{62} = -0.0097$	$d_{63} = 0.8544$	$d_{64} = -0.1770$	$d_{65} = -0.2087$	$d_{66} = -0.1783$	$d_{67} = 0.6512$
$\beth_7$	$d_{71} = 0.5860$	$d_{72} = -0.0251$	$d_{73} = -0.0957$	$d_{74} = -0.2101$	$d_{75} = 0.0466$	$d_{76} = -0.1859$	$d_{77} = 0.6512$
$\beth_8$	$d_{81} = -0.2073$	$d_{82} = -0.0011$	$d_{83} = 0.0125$	$d_{84} = 0.5970$	$d_{85} = 0.6708$	$d_{86} = 0.7242$	$d_{87} = -0.1387$
$\beth_9$	$d_{91} = 0.5860$	$d_{92} = -0.0236$	$d_{93} = 0.0534$	$d_{94} = 0.5970$	$d_{95} = -0.0710$	$d_{96} = -0.2124$	$d_{97} = 0.6512$

a vital role in aggregating the assessment information and determining the overall ranking. The evaluation procedure involves several steps. These steps include

Step 1. We established a 2TLq-R evaluation matrix $R^u = [\beth^u_{ß\rho}]_{9\times7} = ((\xi_{j_{ß\rho}}, \mathcal{P}_{ß\rho})^u, (\xi_{l_{ß\rho}}, \mathcal{Q}_{ß\rho})^u)_{9\times7}$ $(ß = 1, 2, \ldots, 9,\ \rho = 1, 2, \ldots, 7,\ u = 1, 2, 3, 4)$, which is describing the assessments of four DMs as shown in Table 5.

Step 2. Utilizing the 2TLq-RHWG AO, we fused overall $\beth^u_{ß\rho}$ to $\beth_{ß\rho}$, the fused 2TLq RNs assessment matrix $R = [\beth_{ß\rho}]_{9\times7}$ is shown in Table 9. (Suppose $q = 4$ and $F = 3$.)

Step 3. We utilized Eq. (15) because our all attributes are benefit type. Hence, the fused assessment matrix in Table 9 is our standardized one.

Step 4. According to the standardized matrix $N_{ß\rho} = ((\xi_{j_{ß\rho}}, \mathcal{P}_{ß\rho}), (\xi_{l_{ß\rho}}, \mathcal{Q}_{ß\rho}))$ and attribute weights φ'_ρ, the results of 2TLq-R weighted standardized matrix $WN_{ß\rho} = ((\xi'_{j_{ß\rho}}, \mathcal{P}'_{ß\rho}), (\xi'_{l_{ß\rho}}, \mathcal{Q}_{ß\rho}))(ß = 1, 2, \ldots, 9,\quad \rho = 1, 2, \ldots, 7)$ are recorded in Table 10.

Step 5. Compute the BAA matrix $G = [g_\rho]_{1\times7}$ $(\rho = 1, 2, \ldots, 7)$ of attribute Φ_ρ.

$$g_1 = ((\xi_7, -0.3242), (\xi_4, -0.0526)),\ g_2 = ((\xi_8, -0.2175), (\xi_2, 0.4983)),\ g_3 = ((\xi_7, -0.1008), (\xi_4, 0.1916)),$$

$$g_4 = ((\xi_7, -0.2620), (\xi_5, -0.4730)),\ g_5 = ((\xi_6, 0.2554), (\xi_5, -0.3660)),\ g_6 = ((\xi_8, -0.2561), (\xi_2, 0.3624)),$$

$$g_7 = ((\xi_7, -0.2548), (\xi_4, 0.0672)).$$

Table 9 Fused assessment matrix by the 2TLq-RHWG operator

Alternatives	Φ_1	Φ_2	Φ_3	Φ_4
$\beth_1$	$((\xi_5, 0.3744)(\xi_4, -0.4506))$	(ξ_0, ξ_8)	$((\xi_6, -0.3594), (\xi_3, -0.2738))$	$((\xi_7, -0.0948), (\xi_3, -0.0054))$
$\beth_2$	$((\xi_4, 0.2393), (\xi_5, 0.2378))$	$((\xi_0, 0)(\xi_8, 0))$	$((\xi_4, 0.1237), (\xi_5, -0.0982))$	(ξ_0, ξ_8)
$\beth_3$	$((\xi_4, 0.4012), (\xi_4, 0.2091))$	$((\xi_5, 0.0250), (\xi_4, 0.4211))$	(ξ_0, ξ_8)	$((\xi_4, -0.0088), (\xi_5, 0.2818))$
$\beth_4$	$((\xi_3, 0.4582), (\xi_5, 0.4435))$	$((\xi_3, -0.3409), (\xi_5, 0.4113))$	$((\xi_4, 0.3835), (\xi_4, 0.4187))$	$((\xi_3, -0.2028), (\xi_5, 0.3716))$
$\beth_5$	$((\xi_3, -0.4231), (\xi_6, -0.3676))$	$((\xi_6, -0.2932), (\xi_3, 0.4231))$	(ξ_0, ξ_8)	$((\xi_5, 0.4414), (\xi_4, -0.2041))$
$\beth_6$	$((\xi_5, -0.3595), (\xi_4, 0.0562))$	$((\xi_3, 0.4157), (\xi_5, 0.4891))$	$((\xi_6, 0.4806), (\xi_4, -0.2735))$	(ξ_0, ξ_8)
$\beth_7$	(ξ_0, ξ_8)	$((\xi_4, -0.0150), (\xi_4, 0.3647))$	(ξ_0, ξ_8)	(ξ_0, ξ_8)
$\beth_8$	$((\xi_3, -0.1100), (\xi_5, 0.4382))$	$((\xi_5, 0.1286), (\xi_4, -0.1853))$	(ξ_0, ξ_8)	$((\xi_4, 0.2098), (\xi_5, -0.1403))$
$\beth_9$	(ξ_0, ξ_8)	$((\xi_3, 0.0050), (\xi_6, -0.4349))$	$((\xi_4, -0.2752), (\xi_5, -0.2732))$	(ξ_0, ξ_8)
	Φ_5	Φ_6	Φ_7	
$\beth_1$	$((\xi_4, 0.2479), (\xi_4, 0.4880))$	$((\xi_3, -0.1565), (\xi_6, -0.1540))$	$((\xi_6, -0.3369), (\xi_4, -0.2735))$	
$\beth_2$	$((\xi_4, -0.2166), (\xi_5, 0.0840))$	$((\xi_5, -0.2333), (\xi_3, 0.3027))$	(ξ_0, ξ_8)	
$\beth_3$	$((\xi_2, 0.2550), (\xi_6, -0.1880))$	(ξ_0, ξ_8)	$((\xi_4, 0.0603), (\xi_5, -0.4050))$	
$\beth_4$	(ξ_0, ξ_8)	$((\xi_6, 0.0335), (\xi_4, 0.0528))$	(ξ_0, ξ_8)	
$\beth_5$	$((\xi_0, 0), (\xi_8, 0))$	$((\xi_7, 0.2510), (\xi_2, -0.4803))$	$((\xi_4, -0.4545), (\xi_5, -0.3277))$	
$\beth_6$	$((\xi_2, -0.4626), (\xi_7, -0.4499))$	$((\xi_5, 0.4721), (\xi_3, -0.0005))$	(ξ_0, ξ_8)	
$\beth_7$	$((\xi_5, -0.2785), (\xi_4, 0.4421))$	$((\xi_4, -0.2624), (\xi_5, 0.2878))$	$((\xi_6, 0.4191), (\xi_3, 0.1029))$	
$\beth_8$	(ξ_0, ξ_8)	(ξ_0, ξ_8)	$((\xi_3, 0.2409), (\xi_5, 0.0315))$	
$\beth_9$	$((\xi_4, -0.1138), (\xi_5, -0.4075))$	$((\xi_3, 0.4492), (\xi_5, 0.0276))$	$((\xi_4, 0.2098), (\xi_5, -0.1403))$	

Table 10 The weighted standardized matrix $W\mathcal{N}_{\beta\rho}$

Alternatives	Φ_1	Φ_2	Φ_3	Φ_4
$\beth_1$	$((\xi_7, 0.3794), (\xi_2, 0.3918))$	(ξ_0, ξ_8)	$((\xi_8, -0.3953), (\xi_2, -0.3153))$	$((\xi_8, -0.2080), (\xi_2, -0.0482))$
$\beth_2$	$((\xi_7, 0.0324), (\xi_4, -0.4139))$	(ξ_0, ξ_8)	$((\xi_7, 0.2670), (\xi_3, 0.0736))$	(ξ_0, ξ_8)
$\beth_3$	$((\xi_7, 0.0861), (\xi_3, -0.1523))$	$((\xi_8, -0.0814), (\xi_2, -0.2770))$	(ξ_0, ξ_8)	$((\xi_7, 0.0637), (\xi_4, -0.4909))$
$\beth_4$	$((\xi_7, -0.2524), (\xi_4, -0.2594))$	$((\xi_8, -0.1915), (\xi_2, 0.1435))$	$((\xi_7, 0.3317), (\xi_3, -0.2450))$	$((\xi_7, -0.3717), (\xi_4, -0.4255))$
$\beth_5$	$((\xi_6, 0.3565), (\xi_4, -0.1147))$	$((\xi_8, -0.0592), (\xi_1, 0.3238))$	(ξ_0, ξ_8)	$((\xi_7, 0.4667), (\xi_2, 0.4822))$
$\beth_6$	$((\xi_7, 0.1627), (\xi_3, -0.2589))$	$((\xi_8, -0.1484), (\xi_2, 0.1783))$	$((\xi_8, -0.2406), (\xi_2, 0.3114))$	(ξ_0, ξ_8)
$\beth_7$	(ξ_0, ξ_8)	$((\xi_8, -0.1217), (\xi_2, -0.3000))$	(ξ_0, ξ_8)	(ξ_0, ξ_8)
$\beth_8$	$((\xi_7, -0.4939), (\xi_4, -0.2634))$	$((\xi_8, -0.0779), (\xi_1, 0.4787))$	(ξ_0, ξ_8)	$((\xi_7, 0.1315), (\xi_3, 0.2081))$
$\beth_9$	(ξ_0, ξ_8)	$((\xi_8, -0.1705), (\xi_2, 0.2127))$	$((\xi_7, 0.1606), (\xi_3, -0.0429))$	(ξ_0, ξ_8)
	Φ_5	Φ_6	Φ_7	
$\beth_1$	$((\xi_7, 0.0131), (\xi_3, 0.0620))$	$((\xi_8, -0.3163), (\xi_3, -0.2984))$	$((\xi_7, 0.4556), (\xi_3, -0.4836))$	
$\beth_2$	$((\xi_7, -0.1539), (\xi_3, 0.4933))$	$((\xi_8, -0.1599), (\xi_1, 0.4729))$	(ξ_0, ξ_8)	
$\beth_3$	$((\xi_6, 0.1476), (\xi_4, 0.0497))$	(ξ_0, ξ_8)	$((\xi_7, -0.0336), (\xi_3, 0.1233))$	
$\beth_4$	(ξ_0, ξ_8)	$((\xi_8, -0.0875), (\xi_2, -0.1842))$	(ξ_0, ξ_8)	
$\beth_5$	(ξ_0, ξ_8)	$((\xi_8, -0.0306), (\xi_1, -0.3246))$	$((\xi_7, -0.2237), (\xi_3, 0.1785))$	
$\beth_6$	$((\xi_6, -0.3233), (\xi_5, -0.3239))$	$((\xi_8, -0.1176), (\xi_1, 0.3362))$	(ξ_0, ξ_8)	
$\beth_7$	$((\xi_7, 0.1690), (\xi_3, 0.0294))$	$((\xi_8, -0.2339), (\xi_2, 0.4093))$	$((\xi_8, -0.3514), (\xi_2, 0.0901))$	
$\beth_8$	(ξ_0, ξ_8)	(ξ_0, ξ_8)	$((\xi_7, -0.3467), (\xi_3, 0.4382))$	
$\beth_9$	$((\xi_7, -0.1156), (\xi_3, 0.1365))$	$((\xi_8, -0.2582), (\xi_2, 0.2795))$	$((\xi_7, 0.0179), (\xi_3, 0.3132))$	

Table 11 The distance $d_{ß\rho}$ between alternatives and BAA

Alternatives	Φ_1	Φ_2	Φ_3	Φ_4	Φ_5	Φ_6	Φ_7
$\beth_1$	$d_{11} = 0.1452$	$d_{12} = -0.9430$	$d_{13} = 0.1684$	$d_{14} = 0.2479$	$d_{15} = 0.1539$	$d_{16} = -0.0162$	$d_{17} = 0.1530$
$\beth_2$	$d_{21} = 0.0656$	$d_{22} = -0.9430$	$d_{23} = 0.0906$	$d_{24} = -0.7003$	$d_{25} = 0.1194$	$d_{26} = 0.0254$	$d_{27} = -0.7193$
$\beth_3$	$d_{31} = 0.0869$	$d_{32} = 0.0358$	$d_{33} = -0.7389$	$d_{34} = 0.0851$	$d_{35} = 0.0360$	$d_{36} = -0.9352$	$d_{37} = 0.0566$
$\beth_4$	$d_{41} = 0.0163$	$d_{42} = 0.0082$	$d_{43} = 0.1068$	$d_{44} = 0.0473$	$d_{45} = -0.6306$	$d_{46} = 0.0420$	$d_{47} = -0.7193$
$\beth_5$	$d_{51} = -0.0450$	$d_{52} = 0.0419$	$d_{53} = -0.7389$	$d_{54} = 0.1745$	$d_{55} = -0.6306$	$d_{56} = 0.0572$	$d_{57} = 0.0256$
$\beth_6$	$d_{61} = 0.1016$	$d_{62} = 0.0181$	$d_{63} = 0.2001$	$d_{64} = -0.7003$	$d_{65} = -0.0622$	$d_{66} = 0.0357$	$d_{67} = -0.7193$
$\beth_7$	$d_{71} = -0.7128$	$d_{72} = 0.0262$	$d_{73} = -0.7389$	$d_{74} = -0.7003$	$d_{75} = 0.1815$	$d_{76} = 0.0054$	$d_{77} = 0.1962$
$\beth_8$	$d_{81} = -0.0296$	$d_{82} = 0.0372$	$d_{83} = -0.7389$	$d_{84} = 0.1025$	$d_{85} = -0.6306$	$d_{86} = -0.9352$	$d_{87} = 0.0298$
$\beth_9$	$d_{91} = -0.7128$	$d_{92} = 0.0128$	$d_{93} = 0.0727$	$d_{94} = -0.7003$	$d_{95} = 0.1318$	$d_{96} = 0.0010$	$d_{97} = 0.0621$

Step 6. Compute the standardized Hamming distance $D = [d_{ß\rho}]_{9\times 7}$ between alternatives and BAA utilizing Eq. (6) (see Table 11).

Step 7. Sum the values of each alternatives $d_{ß\rho}$.

$$S_1 = \sum_{\rho=1}^{7} d_{1\rho} = -0.0908,\ S_2 = \sum_{\rho=1}^{7} d_{2\rho} = -2.0616,\ S_3 = \sum_{\rho=1}^{7} d_{3\rho} = -1.3736,$$

$$S_4 = \sum_{\rho=1}^{7} d_{4\rho} = -1.1293,\ S_5 = \sum_{\rho=1}^{7} d_{5\rho} = -1.1153,\ S_6 = \sum_{\rho=1}^{7} d_{6\rho} = -1.1263,$$

$$S_7 = \sum_{\rho=1}^{7} d_{7\rho} = -1.7428,\ S_8 = \sum_{\rho=1}^{7} d_{8\rho} = -2.1648,\ S_9 = \sum_{\rho=1}^{7} d_{9\rho} = -1.1328$$

The alternatives $\beth_ß (ß = 1, 2, \ldots, 9)$ can be ranked easily by utilizing the result of $S_ß$. The ranking is established by evaluating the values of $S_ß$, where the alternative with the highest $S_ß$ is considered the most favorable. The ranking of alternatives is presented below:

$$\beth_1 > \beth_5 > \beth_6 > \beth_9 > \beth_4 > \beth_3 > \beth_7 > \beth_2 > \beth_8.$$

Therefore, $\beth_1$ is the best e-learning website.

6 Parameter Assessment

The MADM approach developed in this study, specifically the 2TLq-RHWA and 2TLq-RHWG operators, underwent a parameter assessment to assess their impact on the results. The assessment involved varying the values of parameters q and $\digamma$. In the initial phase of the parameter assessment, the parameter q was systematically changed from 1 to 21, while the parameter $\digamma$ remained constant at a value of 3. The assessment focused on the sum of distances $S_{\text{ß}}$ (where $\text{ß} = 1, 2, \ldots, 9$) and the ranking results of the alternatives using the 2TLq-RHWA operator. The obtained results were summarized and presented in Table 12. The observed findings indicate that as the parameter q varies, the sum of distances also exhibits changes. This sensitivity of the 2TLq-RHWA operator to the parameter q is evident from the values in the table, providing insights into the magnitude and direction of these changes. Additionally, Table 13 presents the ranking results of the alternatives for different values of q in the 2TLq-RHWA operator. Minor variations in the ranks of alternatives are observed with different values of q, illustrating the influence of the parameter on the ranking outcomes. Based on the calculated results, larger values of the parameter q lead to smaller fused results by the 2TLq-RHWA operator. Moreover, these fused results tend to become more stable as q increases. This highlights that the parameter q not only affects the decision space but also impacts the final decision outcomes. In summary, the parameter assessment underscores the significance of selecting an appropriate value for q in the MADM approach utilizing the 2TLq-RHWA operator. The findings suggest that increasing values of q result in smaller fused results and increased stability in decision outcomes. It is important to note that without spe-

Table 12 Outcomes about 2TLq-RHWA operator and MABAC method ($\digamma = 3$)

Parameter	S_1	S_2	S_3	S_4	S_5	S_6	S_7	S_8	S_9	The highest sum
$q = 1$	1.9582	2.6343	1.7994	0.7644	1.6351	0.8178	0.7693	1.7022	1.6683	2.6343
$q = 3$	1.0038	1.0432	1.0025	0.5168	0.5464	0.5372	1.0039	1.0046	1.0062	1.0432
$q = 5$	1.0107	1.0258	1.0049	0.5066	0.5243	0.5164	1.0047	1.0020	1.0165	1.0258
$q = 7$	1.0114	1.0166	1.0041	0.5028	0.5146	0.5121	1.0042	1.0010	1.0159	1.0166
$q = 9$	1.0103	1.0114	1.0029	0.5020	0.5098	0.5091	1.0034	1.0006	1.0132	1.0114
$q = 11$	1.0089	1.0085	1.0019	0.5016	0.5072	0.5066	1.0031	1.0004	1.0103	1.0103
$q = 13$	1.0073	1.0063	1.0012	0.5013	0.5056	0.5047	1.0028	1.0004	1.0079	1.0079
$q = 15$	1.0058	1.0047	1.0007	0.5010	0.5043	0.5034	1.0023	1.0004	1.0060	1.0060
$q = 17$	1.0047	1.0035	1.0003	0.5008	0.5034	0.5025	1.0019	1.0004	1.0046	1.0047
$q = 19$	1.0036	1.0026	1.0002	0.5006	0.5026	0.5018	1.0015	1.0003	1.0035	1.0036
$q = 21$	1.0028	1.0020	1.0001	0.5005	0.5020	0.5013	1.0012	1.0002	1.0026	1.0028

Table 13 Ranking results of Table 12

Parameter	Ranking	The best alternative
$q = 1$	$\beth_2 > \beth_1 > \beth_3 > \beth_8 > \beth_9 > \beth_5 > \beth_6 > \beth_7 > \beth_4$	$\beth_2$
$q = 3$	$\beth_2 > \beth_9 > \beth_8 > \beth_7 > \beth_1 > \beth_3 > \beth_5 > \beth_6 > \beth_4$	$\beth_2$
$q = 5$	$\beth_2 > \beth_9 > \beth_1 > \beth_3 > \beth_7 > \beth_8 > \beth_5 > \beth_6 > \beth_4$	$\beth_2$
$q = 7$	$\beth_2 > \beth_9 > \beth_1 > \beth_7 > \beth_3 > \beth_8 > \beth_5 > \beth_6 > \beth_4$	$\beth_2$
$q = 9$	$\beth_2 > \beth_9 > \beth_1 > \beth_7 > \beth_3 > \beth_8 > \beth_5 > \beth_6 > \beth_4$	$\beth_2$
$q = 11$	$\beth_9 > \beth_1 > \beth_2 > \beth_7 > \beth_3 > \beth_8 > \beth_5 > \beth_6 > \beth_4$	$\beth_9$
$q = 13$	$\beth_9 > \beth_1 > \beth_2 > \beth_7 > \beth_3 > \beth_8 > \beth_5 > \beth_6 > \beth_4$	$\beth_9$
$q = 15$	$\beth_9 > \beth_1 > \beth_2 > \beth_7 > \beth_8 > \beth_3 > \beth_5 > \beth_6 > \beth_4$	$\beth_9$
$q = 17$	$\beth_1 > \beth_9 > \beth_2 > \beth_7 > \beth_8 > \beth_3 > \beth_5 > \beth_6 > \beth_4$	$\beth_1$
$q = 19$	$\beth_1 > \beth_9 > \beth_2 > \beth_7 > \beth_8 > \beth_3 > \beth_5 > \beth_6 > \beth_4$	$\beth_1$
$q = 21$	$\beth_1 > \beth_9 > \beth_2 > \beth_7 > \beth_8 > \beth_3 > \beth_5 > \beth_6 > \beth_4$	$\beth_1$

Table 14 Outcomes about 2TLq-RHWG operator and MABAC method ($\Gamma = 3$)

Parameter	S_1	S_2	S_3	S_4	S_5	S_6	S_7	S_8	S_9	The highest sum
$q = 1$	−0.1298	−2.1045	−1.3274	−1.1768	−1.1769	−1.2009	−1.9375	−2.2049	−1.1504	−0.1298
$q = 3$	0.0202	−0.4379	−0.9595	−0.4571	−0.4598	−0.4834	−0.4647	−0.4459	0.0385	0.0385
$q = 5$	0.0099	−0.4587	−0.9750	−0.4747	−0.4817	−0.4900	−0.4792	−0.4688	0.0197	0.0197
$q = 7$	0.0057	−0.4728	−0.9830	−0.4848	−0.4916	−0.4920	−0.4870	−0.4819	0.0108	0.0108
$q = 9$	0.0034	−0.4815	−0.9882	−0.4904	−0.4956	−0.4933	−0.4913	−0.4891	0.0063	0.0063
$q = 11$	0.0022	−0.4871	−0.9916	−0.4937	−0.4967	−0.4943	−0.4939	−0.4933	0.0038	0.0038
$q = 13$	0.0014	−0.4908	−0.9940	−0.4958	−0.4974	−0.4953	−0.4956	−0.4957	0.0024	0.0024
$q = 15$	0.0010	−0.4933	−0.9956	−0.4971	−0.4980	−0.4962	−0.4967	−0.4972	0.0016	0.0016
$q = 17$	0.0007	−0.4951	−0.9968	−0.4980	−0.4985	−0.4969	−0.4975	−0.4981	0.0011	0.0011
$q = 19$	0.0005	−0.4964	−0.9976	−0.4985	−0.4988	−0.4976	−0.4982	−0.4987	0.0007	0.0007
$q = 21$	0.0004	−0.4973	−0.9982	−0.4989	−0.4991	−0.4981	−0.4986	−0.4991	0.0005	0.0005

cific values and additional details from Tables 12 and 13, a more comprehensive assessment of the effects of parameter variations cannot be provided.

In the second phase of our study, we investigate the effect of varying the parameter q while keeping the other parameter Γ fixed at a value of 3. We explore different integer values of q ranging from 1 to 21. Specifically, we focus on the computation results obtained using the 2TLq-ROFHWG operator. The findings are summarized and presented in Table 14 for the sum of distances ($S_\text{ß}$ where $\text{ß} = 1, 2, \ldots, 9$) and in Table 15 for the ranking of alternatives. Upon analyzing the results from Tables 14 and 15, we observe slight variations in the ranking of alternatives with different values of the parameter q in the 2TLq-RHWA operator. However, as the parameter q increases, the fused results obtained using the 2TLq-RHWG operator become smaller. Additionally, these fused results demonstrate increased stability. This sug-

Table 15 Ranking results of Table 14

Parameter	Ranking	The best alternative
$q = 1$	$\beth_1 > \beth_9 > \beth_4 > \beth_5 > \beth_6 > \beth_3 > \beth_7 > \beth_2 > \beth_8$	$\beth_1$
$q = 3$	$\beth_9 > \beth_1 > \beth_2 > \beth_8 > \beth_4 > \beth_5 > \beth_7 > \beth_6 > \beth_3$	$\beth_9$
$q = 5$	$\beth_9 > \beth_1 > \beth_2 > \beth_8 > \beth_4 > \beth_7 > \beth_5 > \beth_6 > \beth_3$	$\beth_9$
$q = 7$	$\beth_9 > \beth_1 > \beth_2 > \beth_8 > \beth_4 > \beth_7 > \beth_5 > \beth_6 > \beth_3$	$\beth_9$
$q = 9$	$\beth_9 > \beth_1 > \beth_2 > \beth_8 > \beth_4 > \beth_7 > \beth_6 > \beth_5 > \beth_3$	$\beth_9$
$q = 11$	$\beth_9 > \beth_1 > \beth_2 > \beth_8 > \beth_4 > \beth_7 > \beth_6 > \beth_5 > \beth_3$	$\beth_9$
$q = 13$	$\beth_9 > \beth_1 > \beth_2 > \beth_6 > \beth_7 > \beth_8 > \beth_4 > \beth_5 > \beth_3$	$\beth_9$
$q = 15$	$\beth_9 > \beth_1 > \beth_2 > \beth_6 > \beth_7 > \beth_4 > \beth_8 > \beth_5 > \beth_3$	$\beth_9$
$q = 17$	$\beth_9 > \beth_1 > \beth_2 > \beth_6 > \beth_7 > \beth_4 > \beth_8 > \beth_5 > \beth_3$	$\beth_9$
$q = 19$	$\beth_9 > \beth_1 > \beth_2 > \beth_6 > \beth_7 > \beth_4 > \beth_8 > \beth_5 > \beth_3$	$\beth_9$
$q = 21$	$\beth_9 > \beth_1 > \beth_2 > \beth_6 > \beth_7 > \beth_4 > \beth_8 = \beth_5 > \beth_3$	$\beth_9$

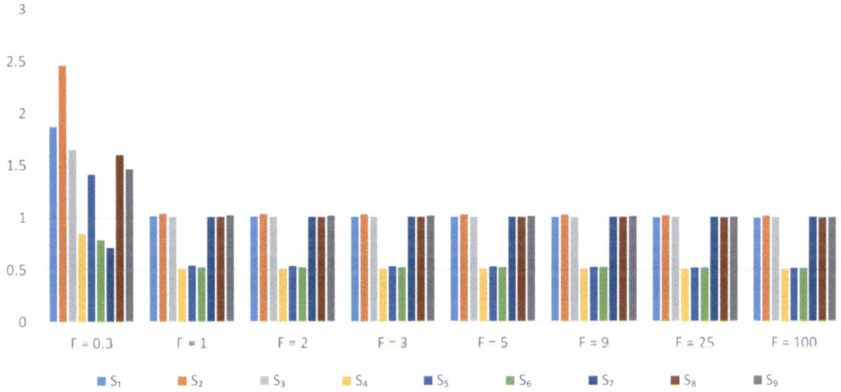

Fig. 13 Outcomes for different values of q utilizing Hamacher weighted average operator

gests that the parameter q not only expands the decision space but also influences the overall decision-making process. These findings shed light on the impact of the parameter q on the evaluation outcomes when employing the 2TLq-RHWA and 2TLq-RHWG operators, providing insights into the decision space and its influence on the final decision-making process (Figs. 13 and 14).

In the third phase of the assessment, the parameter Ϝ is varied within the range of [0.3, 25] using different values, while keeping the parameter q fixed at 4. The 2TLq-RHWA operator is employed to compute the results. The collected data is summarized in Tables 16 and 17. Upon analyzing the data presented, it becomes evident that altering the value of the parameter Ϝ leads to variations in the sum of distances $S_ß$ (where $ß = 1, 2, \ldots, 9$) and impacts the ranking order of the alternatives. Further examination of the results reveals that the rank of each alternative exhibits slight differences when different Ϝ values are employed with the 2TLq-RHWA

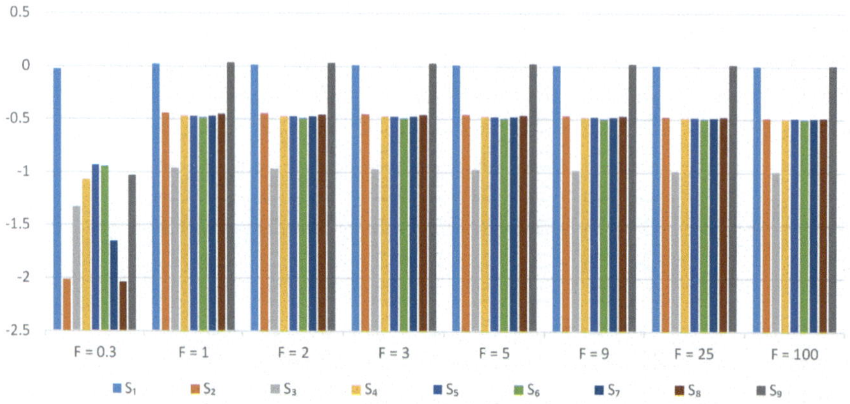

Fig. 14 Outcomes for different values of q utilizing Hamacher weighted geometric operator

Table 16 Outcomes about 2TLq-RHWA operator and MABAC method ($q = 4$)

Parameter	S_1	S_2	S_3	S_4	S_5	S_6	S_7	S_8	S_9	The highest sum
$\digamma = 0.3$	1.8743	2.4621	1.6532	0.8516	1.4141	0.7895	0.7115	1.5973	1.4633	2.4621
$\digamma = 1$	1.0141	1.0399	1.0071	0.5092	0.5405	0.5249	1.0061	1.0055	1.0211	1.0399
$\digamma = 2$	1.0105	1.0360	1.0055	0.5096	0.5360	0.5222	1.0052	1.0039	1.0169	1.0360
$\digamma = 3$	1.0084	1.0333	1.0045	0.5098	0.5331	0.5224	1.0047	1.0030	1.0140	1.0333
$\digamma = 5$	1.0057	1.0298	1.0031	0.5099	0.5294	0.5222	1.0042	1.0017	1.0104	1.0298
$\digamma = 9$	1.0027	1.0261	1.0016	0.5101	0.5253	0.5218	1.0038	1.0004	1.0066	1.0261
$\digamma = 25$	0.9985	1.0204	1.0003	0.5107	0.5194	0.5205	1.0037	0.9984	1.0012	1.0204
$\digamma = 100$	0.9952	1.0159	0.9996	0.5101	0.5135	0.5172	1.0040	0.9969	0.9968	1.0159

operator. As the parameter $\digamma$ increases, the fused results obtained through the 2TLq-RHWA operator become smaller, and the stability of these fused results gradually improves. This suggests that the parameter $\digamma$ plays a role in providing versatility to the aggregation procedure and influences the ultimate decision-making process.

In the fourth phase of the assessment, the parameter $\digamma$ is varied within the range of [0.3, 25] using different values, while the parameter q is held fixed at 4. The assessment focuses on the results obtained using the 2TLq-RHWG operator. Upon examining Tables 18 and 19, it is evident that both the sum of distances $S_ß$ (where $ß = 1, 2, \ldots, 9$) and the ranking order of alternatives exhibit changes as the parameter $\digamma$ varies. The computed results presented in these tables demonstrate slight variations in the ranking of alternatives when different $\digamma$ values are employed with the 2TLq-RHWG operator. Furthermore, it can be observed that as the parameter $\digamma$ increases, the fused results obtained through the 2TLq-RHWG operator become smaller and more stable. This suggests that the parameter $\digamma$ plays a role in the aggregation procedure, providing versatility, and also influences the decision-making process.

Table 17 Ranking results of Table 16

Parameter	Ranking	The best alternative
$\Gamma = 0.3$	$\daleth_2 > \daleth_1 > \daleth_3 > \daleth_8 > \daleth_9 > \daleth_5 > \daleth_4 > \daleth_6 > \daleth_7$	$\daleth_2$
$\Gamma = 1$	$\daleth_2 > \daleth_9 > \daleth_1 > \daleth_3 > \daleth_7 > \daleth_8 > \daleth_5 > \daleth_6 > \daleth_4$	$\daleth_2$
$\Gamma = 2$	$\daleth_2 > \daleth_9 > \daleth_1 > \daleth_3 > \daleth_7 > \daleth_8 > \daleth_5 > \daleth_6 > \daleth_4$	$\daleth_2$
$\Gamma = 3$	$\daleth_2 > \daleth_9 > \daleth_1 > \daleth_7 > \daleth_3 > \daleth_8 > \daleth_5 > \daleth_6 > \daleth_4$	$\daleth_2$
$\Gamma = 4$	$\daleth_2 > \daleth_9 > \daleth_1 > \daleth_7 > \daleth_3 > \daleth_8 > \daleth_5 > \daleth_6 > \daleth_4$	$\daleth_2$
$\Gamma = 5$	$\daleth_2 > \daleth_9 > \daleth_1 > \daleth_7 > \daleth_3 > \daleth_8 > \daleth_5 > \daleth_6 > \daleth_4$	$\daleth_2$
$\Gamma = 9$	$\daleth_2 > \daleth_9 > \daleth_7 > \daleth_3 > \daleth_1 > \daleth_8 > \daleth_6 > \daleth_5 > \daleth_4$	$\daleth_2$
$\Gamma = 25$	$\daleth_2 > \daleth_7 > \daleth_3 > \daleth_8 > \daleth_9 > \daleth_1 > \daleth_6 > \daleth_5 > \daleth_4$	$\daleth_2$
$\Gamma = 100$	$\daleth_2 > \daleth_7 > \daleth_3 > \daleth_8 > \daleth_9 > \daleth_1 > \daleth_6 > \daleth_5 > \daleth_4$	$\daleth_2$

Table 18 Outcomes about 2TLq-RHWG operator and MABAC method ($q = 4$)

Parameter	S_1	S_2	S_3	S_4	S_5	S_6	S_7	S_8	S_9	The highest sum
$\Gamma = 0.3$	−0.0267	−2.0140	−1.3230	−1.0664	−0.9318	−0.9424	−1.6527	−2.0390	−1.0295	−0.0267
$\Gamma = 1$	0.0188	−0.4392	−0.9581	−0.4630	−0.4699	−0.4803	−0.4692	−0.4530	0.0341	0.0341
$\Gamma = 2$	0.0143	−0.4440	−0.9651	−0.4643	−0.4721	−0.4857	−0.4710	−0.4560	0.0291	0.0291
$\Gamma = 3$	0.0136	−0.4482	−0.9692	−0.4661	−0.4734	−0.4883	−0.4727	−0.4584	0.0275	0.0275
$\Gamma = 5$	0.0125	−0.4552	−0.9737	−0.4702	−0.4748	−0.4908	−0.4756	−0.4628	0.0248	0.0248
$\Gamma = 9$	0.0111	−0.4630	−0.9786	−0.4748	−0.4772	−0.4934	−0.4790	−0.4681	0.0215	0.0215
$\Gamma = 25$	0.0084	−0.4741	−0.9859	−0.4820	−0.4824	−0.4935	−0.4844	−0.4770	0.0158	0.0158
$\Gamma = 100$	0.0051	−0.4849	−0.9926	−0.4894	−0.4891	−0.4950	−0.4904	−0.4866	0.0094	0.0094

Table 19 Ranking results of Table 18

Parameter	Ranking	The best alternative
$\Gamma = 0.3$	$\daleth_1 > \daleth_5 > \daleth_6 > \daleth_9 > \daleth_4 > \daleth_3 > \daleth_7 > \daleth_2 > \daleth_8$	$\daleth_1$
$\Gamma = 1$	$\daleth_9 > \daleth_1 > \daleth_2 > \daleth_8 > \daleth_4 > \daleth_7 > \daleth_5 > \daleth_6 > \daleth_3$	$\daleth_9$
$\Gamma = 2$	$\daleth_9 > \daleth_1 > \daleth_2 > \daleth_8 > \daleth_4 > \daleth_7 > \daleth_5 > \daleth_6 > \daleth_3$	$\daleth_9$
$\Gamma = 3$	$\daleth_9 > \daleth_1 > \daleth_2 > \daleth_8 > \daleth_4 > \daleth_7 > \daleth_5 > \daleth_6 > \daleth_3$	$\daleth_9$
$\Gamma = 4$	$\daleth_9 > \daleth_1 > \daleth_2 > \daleth_8 > \daleth_4 > \daleth_5 > \daleth_7 > \daleth_6 > \daleth_3$	$\daleth_9$
$\Gamma = 5$	$\daleth_9 > \daleth_1 > \daleth_2 > \daleth_8 > \daleth_4 > \daleth_5 > \daleth_7 > \daleth_6 > \daleth_3$	$\daleth_9$
$\Gamma = 9$	$\daleth_9 > \daleth_1 > \daleth_2 > \daleth_8 > \daleth_4 > \daleth_5 > \daleth_7 > \daleth_6 > \daleth_3$	$\daleth_9$
$\Gamma = 25$	$\daleth_9 > \daleth_1 > \daleth_2 > \daleth_8 > \daleth_5 > \daleth_4 > \daleth_7 > \daleth_6 > \daleth_3$	$\daleth_9$
$\Gamma = 100$	$\daleth_9 > \daleth_1 > \daleth_2 > \daleth_8 > \daleth_5 > \daleth_4 > \daleth_7 > \daleth_6 > \daleth_3$	$\daleth_9$

6.1 Comparative Assessment

In this subsection, we perform a comparative assessment of our developed MAGDM method with existing MAGDM methods to demonstrate the effectiveness of our approach. Specifically, we select the CODAS method Naz et al. (2022) and the TOPSIS method Naz et al. (2023) to address the problem of selecting the best e-learning website.

6.1.1 Comparison with the 2TLq-R-CODAS Method

Naz et al. Naz et al. (2022) introduced the 2TLq-R-CODAS method, which serves as an excellent approach for evaluating the efficacy of the proposed method (refer to Table 20). The calculation steps for this method are outlined as follows:

Step 1. Calculate the negative ideal solution (NS) by using 2TLq-RNs' score and accuracy functions:

$$NS = [NS_\rho]_{1\times\iota}; \quad NS_\rho = \min_{ß}(\beth_{ß\rho}).$$

Step 2. Calculate the weighted Euclidean distance $E_ß$ and Hamming distance $H_ß$ as follows:

Table 20 Comparative assessment according to the 2TLq-RHWA-CODAS method

CODAS method Naz et al. (2022)	Calculations
Negative ideal solution (NS)	$NS(\Phi_1) = 0.1757$, $NS(\Phi_2) = 0.0061$, $NS(\Phi_3) = 0.0270$, $NS(\Phi_4) = 0.1607$, $NS(\Phi_5) = 0.1205$, $NS(\Phi_6) = 0.0634$, $NS(\Phi_7) = 0.0911$
Hamming distance (H)	$H_1 = 3.3288$, $H_2 = 3.8628$, $H_3 = 3.0986$, $H_4 = 2.1935$, $H_5 = 2.8420$, $H_6 = 2.1771$, $H_7 = 2.0902$, $H_8 = 2.9894$, $H_9 = 2.9120$
Euclidean distance (E)	$E_1 = 3.6981$, $E_2 = 4.0189$, $E_3 = 3.3191$, $E_4 = 2.4587$, $E_5 = 3.0190$, $E_6 = 2.3226$, $E_7 = 2.3004$, $E_8 = 3.2425$, $E_9 = 3.1998$
Average solution (A)	$A_1 = 10.1690$, $A_2 = 17.8618$, $A_3 = 4.6858$, $A_4 = -11.2038$, $A_5 = -0.3240$, $A_6 = -12.5765$, $A_7 = -13.5581$, $A_8 = 3.0134$, $A_9 = 1.9325$
Ranking	$\beth_2 > \beth_1 > \beth_3 > \beth_8 > \beth_9 > \beth_5 > \beth_4 > \beth_6 > \beth_7$
The proposed method	$\beth_1 > \beth_9 > \beth_2 > \beth_3 > \beth_7 > \beth_8 > \beth_5 > \beth_6 > \beth_4$

$$E_{ß} = \sum_{\rho=1}^{\imath} E(t_{ß\rho}, NS_\rho); \quad H_{ß} = \sum_{\rho=1}^{\imath} H(t_{ß\rho}, NS_\rho), \quad t_{ß\rho} = \varphi'_\rho \otimes \beth_{ß\rho}.$$

Step 3. In the following equations, build the relative assessment matrix (R):

$$R = [h_{ßg}]_{J\times J}, \quad h_{ßg} = (E_{ß} - E_g) + (\mathfrak{s}(E_{ß} - E_g) \times (H_{ß} - H_g)),$$

where $g \in \{1, 2, \ldots, J\}$, and $\mathfrak{s}$ represents a significant function that has the potential to be designed as

$$\mathfrak{s}(\theta) = \begin{cases} 1 \; if \; |\theta| \geq \mathfrak{g} \\ 0 \; if \; |\theta| < \mathfrak{g} \end{cases},$$

where $\mathfrak{g} \in [0.01, 0.05]$ provided by DMs. In current study, $\mathfrak{g} = 0.02$.

Step 4. Obtain the average solution $A_{ß}$ using the following procedure:

$$A_{ß} = \sum_{g=1}^{J} h_{ßg}.$$

Step 5. Based on the computational performance of $A_{ß}$, it is possible to rank all the alternatives. The option with the highest ranking is considered the best.

6.1.2 Comparison with the 2TL*q*-R-TOPSIS Method

Naz et al. Naz et al. (2023) introduced the 2TLq R TOPSIS technique as a remarkable method for validating the efficacy of the proposed approach (refer to Table 21). The calculation steps for implementing this method are as follows:

Step 1. Determine the positive ideal solution (PS) and the NS by utilizing the score and accuracy values of 2TLq-RNs.

$$PS_\rho = \left[PS_\rho\right]_{1\times\imath}, \quad PS_\rho = \max_{ß}(\beth_{ß\rho});$$
$$NS_\rho = \left[NS_\rho\right]_{1\times\imath}, \quad NS_\rho = \min_{ß}(\beth_{ß\rho}).$$

Step 2. Compute the distances of each alternative from both the PS and the NS as P and N, respectively.

Step 3. Evaluate the relative closeness coefficient (R) of an alternative $\beth_\rho$ with respect to PS using the following formula:

$$R_\rho = \frac{N_\rho}{P_\rho + N_\rho}.$$

Table 21 Comparative assessment according to the 2TLq-RHWA-TOPSIS method

TOPSIS method Naz et al. (2023)	Calculations
The distance of alternatives from NS (N)	$N_1 = 3.6981,\ N_2 = 4.0189,\ N_3 = 3.3191,\ N_4 = 2.4587,\ N_5 = 3.0190,$ $N_6 = 2.3226,\ N_7 = 2.3004,\ N_8 = 3.2425,\ N_9 = 3.1998$
The distance of alternatives from PS (P)	$P_1 = 3.3952,\ P_2 = 2.6221,\ P_3 = 3.5038,\ P_4 = 4.4019,\ P_5 = 3.6309,$ $P_6 = 4.4051,\ P_7 = 4.4683,\ P_8 = 3.5231,\ P_9 = 3.5947$
Closeness coefficient C	$C_1 = -0.3747,\ C_2 = 0,\ C_3 = -0.5104,\ C_4 = -1.0670,\ C_5 = -0.6335,$ $C_6 = -1.1021,\ C_7 = -1.1317,\ C_8 = -0.5368,\ C_9 = -0.5747$
Ranking	$\beth_2 > \beth_1 > \beth_3 > \beth_8 > \beth_9 > \beth_5 > \beth_4 > \beth_6 > \beth_7$
The proposed method	$\beth_1 > \beth_9 > \beth_2 > \beth_3 > \beth_7 > \beth_8 > \beth_5 > \beth_6 > \beth_4$

Step 4. The R coefficient is frequently used to evaluate alternative rankings and determine the best option. However, Hadi Vencheh and Mirjaberi argued that the R coefficient may not consistently identify an optimal alternative that is simultaneously the closest to the PS and farthest from the NS. As a solution to this limitation, they introduced a revised closeness index, denoted as C:

$$C_\rho = \frac{N_\rho}{N_{\rho\,\max}} - \frac{P_\rho}{P_{\rho\,\min}}.$$

6.1.3 Comprehensive Comparison

Despite minor variations, all approaches consistently identify $\beth_1$ and $\beth_2$ as the optimal options, as shown in Table 22. The differences in the techniques employed may account for this discrepancy. The operator technique represents the fundamental approach in MAGDM. The 2TLq-RHWA operator focuses on the overall system evaluation, while the 2TLq-RHWG operator emphasizes individual assessments. Moreover, the 2TLq-R-CODAS and 2TLq-R-TOPSIS approaches evaluate the quality of e-learning websites by considering the Euclidean distance as the primary factor and the Hamming distance as the secondary factor, both computed based on the distance from the negative ideal point. The 2TLq-R-TOPSIS approach comprehensively examines all aspects of e-learning websites. Furthermore, the proposed 2TLq-R-MABAC technique takes into account the impact variables of DMs and the

Table 22 Outcomes from different approaches

Methods	Parameter	Ranking	The best alternative
2TLq-RHWA-CODAS Naz et al. (2022)		$\beth_2 > \beth_1 > \beth_3 > \beth_8 > \beth_9 > \beth_5 > \beth_4 > \beth_6 > \beth_7$	$\beth_2$
2TLq-RHWG-CODAS Naz et al. (2022)		$\beth_1 > \beth_5 > \beth_6 > \beth_9 > \beth_4 > \beth_3 > \beth_7 > \beth_2 > \beth_8$	$\beth_1$
2TLq-RHWA-TOPSIS Naz et al. (2023)		$\beth_2 > \beth_1 > \beth_3 > \beth_8 > \beth_9 > \beth_5 > \beth_4 > \beth_6 > \beth_7$	$\beth_2$
2TLq-RHWG-TOPSIS Naz et al. (2023)		$\beth_1 > \beth_6 > \beth_5 > \beth_9 > \beth_4 > \beth_3 > \beth_7 > \beth_2 > \beth_8$	$\beth_1$
2TLIFHWA-MABAC	$q = 1$	$\beth_2 > \beth_1 > \beth_3 > \beth_8 > \beth_9 > \beth_5 > \beth_4 > \beth_6 > \beth_7$	$\beth_2$
2TLIFHWG-MABAC		$\beth_1 > \beth_9 > \beth_4 > \beth_5 > \beth_6 > \beth_3 > \beth_7 > \beth_2 > \beth_8$	$\beth_1$
2TLPFHWA-MABAC	$q = 2$	$\beth_1 > \beth_9 > \beth_2 > \beth_3 > \beth_7 > \beth_8 > \beth_5 > \beth_6 > \beth_4$	$\beth_1$
2TLPFHWG-MABAC		$\beth_1 > \beth_9 > \beth_4 > \beth_6 > \beth_8 > \beth_7 > \beth_5 > \beth_2 > \beth_3$	$\beth_1$
2TLFFHWA-MABAC	$q = 3$	$\beth_1 > \beth_9 > \beth_2 > \beth_3 > \beth_7 > \beth_8 > \beth_5 > \beth_6 > \beth_4$	$\beth_1$
2TLFFHWG-MABAC		$\beth_1 > \beth_9 > \beth_4 > \beth_6 > \beth_8 > \beth_7 > \beth_5 > \beth_2 > \beth_3$	$\beth_1$
2TLq-RHWA-MABAC (The proposed)	$q = 4$	$\beth_1 > \beth_9 > \beth_2 > \beth_3 > \beth_7 > \beth_8 > \beth_5 > \beth_6 > \beth_4$	$\beth_1$
2TLq-RHWG-MABAC (The proposed)		$\beth_1 > \beth_9 > \beth_4 > \beth_6 > \beth_8 > \beth_5 > \beth_7 > \beth_2 > \beth_3$	$\beth_1$

ambiguity inherent in decision-making processes, resulting in more reliable evaluation outcomes.

When $q = 1, 2, 3$, the 2TLq-RNs degenerate into 2TLIF numbers, 2TLPF numbers, and 2TL Fermetean fuzzy (2TLFF) numbers, respectively. Therefore, 2TLIF-MABAC, 2TLPF-MABAC, and 2TLq-R-MABAC methods are used with HWA and HWG operators, respectively, to solve MAGDM problem of choosing the best e-learning website and the outcomes are shown in Table 22 and Figs. 15 and 16. When $q = 1$, the optimal alternative is $\beth_2$ for 2TLIFHWA-MABAC. When $q = 2, 3, 4$, the optimal alternative for all the methods is same which is $\beth_1$. This demonstrates how parameter q expands the range of uncertainty expression of DMs and provides more

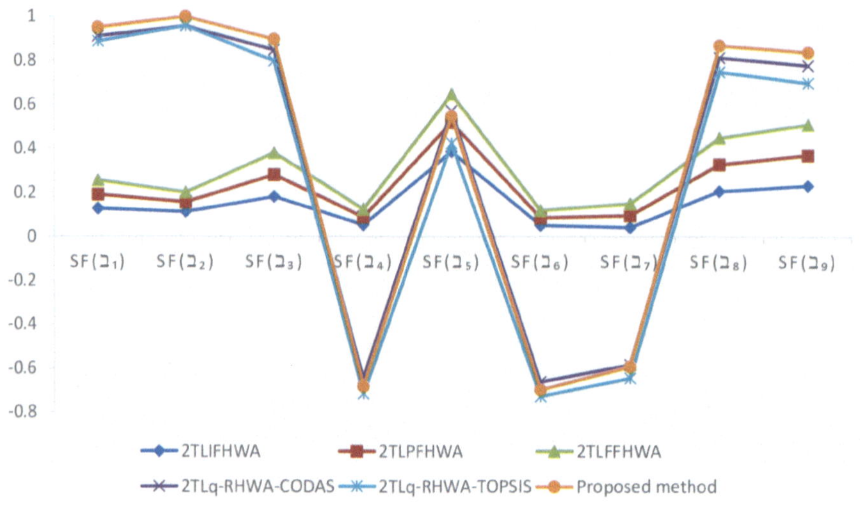

Fig. 15 Outcomes from different approaches utilizing Hamacher weighted average operator

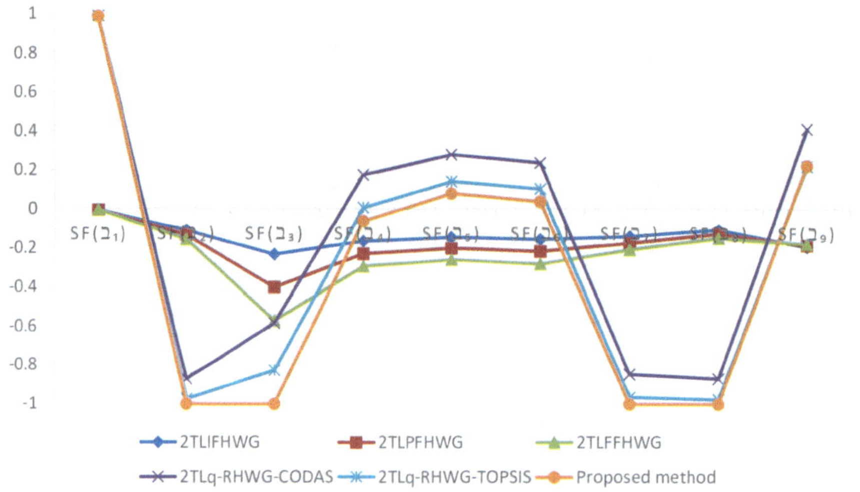

Fig. 16 Outcomes from different approaches utilizing Hamacher weighted geometric operator

comprehensive decision information for MAGDM. When $q > 4$, the information in the decision scope is sufficient to assist the DM in making the best choice among all alternatives. As a result, the 2TLq-RS is more dominating in MAGDM than 2TLIFS and 2TLPFS by changing q to select the best e-learning website that is most helpful to study at any time and from any location. Furthermore, it is observed that the scoring values of the e-learning websites change considerably under various evaluations. In summary, the three strategies can consistently and reliably identify the finest e-learning websites. And the outcomes of the comparison examination indicate the method's dependability once more. As a result, the new suggested 2TLq-R-MABAC technique is reliable.

7 Conclusions

The introduction of e-learning has transformed the way education is delivered and received, resulting in improved effectiveness and productivity. Utilizing advanced technology, educators can conveniently and efficiently deliver lessons to students. E-learning specifically refers to online courses that offer a flexible alternative to traditional classroom settings. In our study, we present a novel MAGDM technique aimed at identifying the top e-learning website using our unique approach. Our research paper introduces new AOs based on the Hamacher TN and Hamacher TCN. These AOs, named 2TLq-RHWA and 2TLq-RHWG AOs, are inspired by arithmetic operations conducted in a 2TLq-R environment. They provide flexibility and adaptability in the aggregation process by incorporating a parameter ($\digamma$). By employing the Hamacher TN- and Hamacher TCN-inspired operations in these AOs, we establish a correlation structure among the given arguments. This correlation structure offers valuable insights into the relationship and interplay between different factors, enabling a more comprehensive assessment and evaluation of the e-learning websites under consideration. In summary, the study draws the following conclusions:

1. The incorporation of the 2TL term enhances the representation of human perception, and the q-RS demonstrates increased reliability through the qth power of MD and NMD. To leverage these benefits, we introduce the concept of the 2TLq-RS, which combines the effects of q-RS and 2TL terms.
2. The weighted averaging and weighted geometric AOs are extended to the 2TLq-R environment by integrating the Hamacher operational laws. This leads to the proposal of six new operators: 2TLq-RHWA, 2TLq-RHOWA, 2TLq-RHHWA, 2TLq-RHWG, 2TLq-RHOWG, and 2TLq-RHOWG operators.
3. To address MAGDM problems in the 2TLq-R context, a novel decision-making method called the 2TLq-R-MABAC method is introduced, utilizing the Hamacher operator.
4. Finally, the newly developed MAGDM approach is applied to tackle the selection problem of an e-learning website. These findings contribute to the field by providing a comprehensive understanding of the 2TLq-R framework and its application in MAGDM, specifically in the context of selecting optimal e-learning websites.

Our developed model has the advantage of effectively representing fuzzy information and producing consistent computational results. Furthermore, this proposed method holds potential for application in more ambiguous decision fields in the future. The ability of 2TLq-R to describe the psychological state of DMs can help bridge gaps left by other methodologies. Additionally, we plan to explore the integration of

2TLq-RS with other decision-making methods. It is essential to acknowledge that the decision-making environment is becoming increasingly complex.

References

Adak, A. K., & Kumar, D. (2023). Spherical distance measurement method for solving MCDM problems under Pythagorean fuzzy environment. *Journal of Fuzzy Extension and Applications, 4*(1), 28–39.

Akram, M., Naz, S., Edalatpanah, S. A., & Mehreen, R. (2021). Group decision-making framework under linguistic q-rung orthopair fuzzy Einstein models. *Soft Computing, 25*(15), 10309–10334.

Akram, M., Peng, X., & Sattar, A. (2021). A new decision-making model using complex intuitionistic fuzzy Hamacher aggregation operators. *Soft Computing, 25*(10), 7059–7086.

Atanassov, K. T. (1986). Intuitionistic fuzzy sets. *Fuzzy Sets and Systems, 20*(1), 87–96.

Cid-Lopez, A., Hornos, M. J., Carrasco, R. A., Herrera-Viedma, E., & Chiclana, F. (2017). Linguistic multi-criteria decision-making model with output variable expressive richness. *Expert Systems with Applications, 83*, 350–362.

Faizi, S., Salabun, W., Nawaz, S., & ur Rehman, A., & W-trobski, J. (2021). Best-worst method and Hamacher aggregation operations for intuitionistic 2-tuple linguistic sets. *Expert Systems with Applications,181*, 115088.

Garg, H., Ali, Z., & Mahmood, T. (2021). Interval-valued picture uncertain linguistic generalized Hamacher aggregation operators and their application in multiple attribute decision-making process. *Arabian Journal for Science and Engineering, 46*(10), 10153–10170.

Garg, H., Naz, S., Ziaa, F., & Shoukat, Z. (2021). A ranking method based on Muirhead mean operator for group decision making with complex interval-valued q-rung orthopair fuzzy numbers. *Soft Computing, 25*(22), 14001–14027.

Hadi, A., Khan, W., & Khan, A. (2021). A novel approach to MADM problems using Fermatean fuzzy Hamacher aggregation operators. *International Journal of Intelligent Systems, 36*(7), 3464–3499.

Hamacher, H. (1978). Uber logische verknunpfungenn unssharferAussagen und deren Zugenhorige BewertungsfunktioneTrappl. *Progress in Cybernatics and Systems Research, 3*(1978), 276–288.

Hasan, M. K., Yasin Ali, M. D., Sultana, A., & Mitra, N. K. (2020). Some picture fuzzy mean operators and their applications in decision-making. *Journal of Fuzzy Extension and Applications, 3*(4), 349–361.

Herrera, F., & Martinez, L. (2000). A 2-tuple fuzzy linguistic representation model for computing with words. *IEEE Transactions on Fuzzy Systems, 8*(6), 746–752.

Jana, C. (2021). Multiple attribute group decision-making method based on extended bipolar fuzzy MABAC approach. *Computational and Applied Mathematics, 40*(6), 1–17.

Khan, A. A., Qiyas, M., Abdullah, S., Luo, J., & Bano, M. (2019). Analysis of robot selection based on 2-tuple picture fuzzy linguistic aggregation operators. *Mathematics, 7*(10), 1000.

Liu, P., Naz, S., Akram, M., & Muzammal, M. (2022). Group decision-making analysis based on linguistic q-rung orthopair fuzzy generalized point weighted aggregation operators. *International Journal of Machine Learning and Cybernetics, 13*(4), 883–906.

Liu, P., & Wang, D. (2022). A 2-dimensional uncertain linguistic MABAC method for multiattribute group decision-making problems. *Complex & Intelligent Systems, 8*(1), 349–360.

Naz, S., Akram, M., ul Hassan, M. M., & Fatima, A. (2023). A hybrid DEMATEL-TOPSIS approach using 2-tuple linguistic q-rung orthopair fuzzy information and its application in renewable energy resource selection. *International Journal of Information Technology & Decision Making, 1-44.*

Naz, S., Akram, M., Al-Shamiri, M. M. A., Khalaf, M. M., & Yousaf, G. (2022). A new MAGDM method with 2-tuple linguistic bipolar fuzzy Heronian mean operators. *Mathematical Biosciences and Engineering, 19*(4), 3843–3878.

Naz, S., Akram, M., Sattar, A., & Al-Shamiri, M. M. A. (2022). 2-Tuple linguistic q-rung orthopair fuzzy CODAS approach and its application in arc welding robot selection. *AIMS Mathematics, 7*(9), 17529–17569.

Pamucar, D., & Cirovic, G. (2015). The selection of transport and handling resources in logistics centers using multi-attributive border approximation area comparison (MABAC). *Expert Systems with Applications, 42*(6), 3016–3028.

Pamucar, D., Petrovic, I., & Cirovic, G. (2018). Modification of the best worst and MABAC methods: A novel approach based on interval-valued fuzzy-rough numbers. *Expert Systems with Applications, 91*, 89–106.

Peykani, P., Nouri, M., Eshghi, F., Khamechian, M., & Farrokhi-Asl, M. (2021). A novel mathematical approach for fuzzy multi-period multi-objective portfolio optimization problem under uncertain environment and practical constraints. *Journal of Fuzzy Extension and Application, 2*(3), 191–203.

Qiyas, M., Abdullah, S., Ashraf, S., Khan, S., & Khan, A. (2019). Triangular picture fuzzy linguistic induced ordered weighted aggregation operators and its application on decision making problems. *Mathematical Foundations of Computing, 2*(3), 183.

Rawat, S. S. (2022). Multiple attribute decision making based on q-rung orthopair fuzzy Hamacher Muirhead mean operators. *Soft Computing, 26*(5), 2465–2487.

Sadeghi, M. E., Nozari, H., Khajezadeh Dezfoli, H., & Khajezadeh Dezfoli, M. (2021). Ranking of different of investment risk in high-tech projects using TOPSIS method in fuzzy environment based on linguistic variables. *Journal of Fuzzy Extension and Application, 2*(3), 226–238.

Wang, L., Garg, H., & Li, N. (2021). Pythagorean fuzzy interactive Hamacher power aggregation operators for analysis of express service quality with entropy weight. *Soft Computing, 25*(2), 973–993.

Wang, W., & Liu, X. (2011). Intuitionistic fuzzy geometric aggregation operators based on Einstein operations. *International Journal of Intelligent Systems, 26*(11), 1049–1075.

Xu, L., Liu, Y., & Liu, F. (2021). Improved MABAC method based on single-valued neutrosophic 2-tuple linguistic sets and Frank aggregation operators for MAGDM. *Computational and Applied Mathematics, 40*(8), 1–32.

Xu, Z., & Yager, R. R. (2006). Some geometric Aos based on intuitionistic fuzzy sets. *International Journal of General Systems, 35*(4), 417–433.

Zadeh, L. A. (1965). Fuzzy sets. *Information and Control, 8*(3), 338–353.

Zadeh, L. A. (1975). The concept of a linguistic variable and its application to approximate reasoning-I. *Information Sciences, 8*(3), 199–249.

Zeng, S., Qiyas, M., Arif, M., & Mahmood, T. (2019). Extended version of linguistic picture fuzzy TOPSIS method and its applications in enterprise resource planning systems. *Mathematical Problems in Engineering.*

Zhang, C., Bai, W., Li, D., & Zhan, J. (2022). Multiple attribute group decision-making based on multigranulation probabilistic models, MULTIMOORA and TPOP in incomplete q-rung orthopair fuzzy information systems. *International Journal of Approximate Reasoning, 143*, 102–120.

Zhao, H., Xu, Z., Ni, M., & Liu, S. (2010). Generalized aggregation operators for intuitionistic fuzzy sets. *International Journal of Intelligent Systems, 25*(1), 1–30.

Balanced Neutrosophic Fermatean Graphs with Applications

Said Broumi, S. Sivasankar, Assia Bakali, and Mohamed Talea

Abstract In the context of ensuring timely and equitable healthcare access in a nation like India, the chapter investigates the concept of balanced neutrosophic fermatean graphs, a specialized form of graph theory that offers a means to establish evenly distributed network connectivity and balanced topologies. The exploration extends to self-complementary and strictly balanced neutrosophic fermatean graphs, showcasing their potential applications in addressing the critical challenge of providing timely medical care to underserved populations within Indian cities. This research not only contributes to the field of graph theory but also presents a structural framework for optimizing medical treatment delivery in government hospitals, with far-reaching implications for improving healthcare outcomes and reducing casualties.

Keywords Neutrosophic graphs · Fermatean sets · Fermatean neutrosophic graphs · Balanced network connectivity · Timely medical treatment

1 Introduction

In the realm of addressing the critical need for timely and equitable medical treatment across diverse demographic groups, the role of balanced networking is pivotal (Batista et al., 2022; Patel et al., 2014). Such networks can be effectively modeled

S. Broumi (✉) · M. Talea
Laboratory of Information Processing, Faculty of Science Ben M'Sik, University Hassan II, Casablanca, Morocco
e-mail: broumisaid78@gmail.com

S. Broumi
STIE team, Regional Center for the Professions of Education and Training(C.R.M.E.F), Casablanca -Settat, Morocco

S. Sivasankar
Department of Mathematics, RV Institute of Technology and Management, Bangalore, India

A. Bakali
Ecole Royale Navale-Boulevard Sour Jdid, Casablanca, Morocco

© The Author(s), under exclusive license to Springer Nature Singapore Pte Ltd. 2024

S. A. Edalatpanah et al. (eds.), *Analytical Decision Making and Data Envelopment Analysis*, Infosys Science Foundation Series in Mathematical Sciences,
https://doi.org/10.1007/978-981-97-6972-8_18

using the concept of Neutrosophic graphs, offering a framework for achieving even distribution of network connectivity and balanced topologies. Neutrosophic sets, introduced by Smarandache in the late 1990s, are an advanced mathematical concept designed to handle uncertainty, imprecision, vagueness, incompleteness, inconsistency, and indeterminacy (Smarandache, 1999). Characterized by three independent membership functions—truth, indeterminacy, and falsehood—neutrosophic sets allow membership values to range beyond the conventional [0, 1] interval, offering enhanced flexibility. This unique property makes them especially useful in diverse domains such as decision-making processes (Karaaslan, 2017; Liu & Wang, 2014; Martin & Edalatpanah, 2023; Saberhoseini et al., 2022; Veeramani et al., 2022; Ye, 2013; Zhan et al., 2019), Data Envelopment Analysis (Abdelfattah, 2019; Edalatpanah, 2018; Mao et al., 2020; Mohanta & Sharanappa, 2023; Tapia, 2021), shortest path problems (Broumi et al., 2019a; Kumar et al., 2019), optimization (Das & Edalatpanah, 2022; Edalatpanah, 2020a; Stanimirović et al., 2023; Veeramani et al., 2021; Wang et al., 2021), pure mathematics (Adebisi & Smarandache, 2023; Gayen et al., 2023; Mohan & Krishnaswamy, 2020; Smarandache, 2020), linear systems (Edalatpanah, 2020b, 2020c; Ye & Cui, 2018), statistical analysis (Debnath, 2021; Polymenis, 2021; Woodall et al., 2022), where they can accommodate inconsistent and incomplete information, and many other areas that require a sophisticated approach to uncertainty and vagueness. Neutrosophic graphs are an extension of traditional graph theory, incorporating the principles of neutrosophy to handle uncertain, imprecise, and indeterminate information. In a neutrosophic graph, each vertex and edge possesses three mentioned independent attributes (Broumi et al., 2016a, 2022a). This allows for a more comprehensive representation of real-world scenarios where relationships and entities might be ambiguous or uncertain. Their adaptability makes neutrosophic graphs valuable in areas like network design, decision-making processes, and systems analysis where conventional graphs might fall short in capturing the intricacies of uncertainty.

A Fermatean fuzzy set, an extension of the traditional fuzzy set, introduces a more nuanced representation of uncertainty by considering both the membership and non-membership degrees, but with an added twist inspired by Fermat's Last Theorem (Akram et al., 2022; Deng & Wang, 2022; Senapati & Yager, 2020). In this model, the sum of the powers of the membership and non-membership degrees is constrained to be less than or equal to one, with the power being an integer greater than 2 (Ejegwa & Zuakwagh, 2022). This unique characteristic provides a different mathematical perspective on fuzziness, enabling more intricate modeling of uncertainty in specific scenarios, and has potential applications in areas that require a refined approach to ambiguity and vagueness (Ejegwa & Zuakwagh, 2022; Rani et al., 2022). In this context, Fermatean neutrosophic graphs emerge as a powerful tool for representing and analyzing network structures. Neutrosophic graphs encompass a rich tapestry of concepts, including paths, walks, and circuits, which find application in diverse domains such as communication networks, medical complexity analysis, and traffic management.

The field of graph theory, with its extension into Fuzzy Graphs (FG) to handle uncertainty, has garnered widespread attention across various real-world applications and research domains. These range from networking and image segmentation to medical diagnosis, data collection, system grouping, artificial intelligence, and decision-making under conditions of incomplete information. Building upon the density factors outlined in previous research (Hobbs et al., 2010; Sivasankar & Broumi, 2022), this chapter introduces the notion of a Balanced Fermatean Neutrosophic network. The concept of balanced graphs has witnessed extensive exploration and application in fields spanning AI, robotics, network computing, visualization, and selection processes (Karunambigai et al., 2017; Ruciński & Vince, 1993; Shenggui et al., 2002). Within this landscape, the contributions of researchers like Al Hawary (2011), who discussed balanced fuzzy networks, and Karunambigai et al. (2015) who introduced and studied balanced intuitionistic fuzzy graphs, have been instrumental. Moreover, the properties of balanced neutrosophic graphs, as defined and investigated by Sivasankar and Broumi (2022) hold promise for addressing complex issues characterized by inconsistency and ambiguity, which are pervasive in real-world scenarios.

While fuzzy graphs have played a valuable role in handling uncertainty, neutrosophic graphs (NG) have emerged as a novel paradigm in network modeling. Neutosophic graphs (NG) have been proposed as a new level of graph network by Smarandache et al. (Broumi et al., 2019b; Kandasamy et al., 2015; Smarandache, 2006) as a generalization of the fuzzy network and the intuitionistic fuzzy network. In communication links where the link performance cannot be predicted, and single valued neutrosophic graphs (SVNG) are used Antony and Jansi introduced a new notion of Fermatean neutrosophic sets by fusing the ideas of Neutrosophic sets and Fermatean fuzzy sets. Broumi et al. (2016b, 2022b) developed and discussed the theoretical background and applications for Fermatean Neutrosophic graphs.

Balancing network structures presents an effective strategy for achieving equilibrium in high-edge density flow across the network. Inspired by the concept of balanced graphs and their extensions such as (Akram & Waseem, 2018; Akram et al., 2014; Mahapatra et al., 2019, 2020; Narayan & Sunitha, 2012; Parvathi & Karunambigai, 2006), this chapter specifically focuses on Fermatean Neutrosophic graphs. It introduces the concepts of balanced and strictly balanced networks and provides an in-depth exploration of the key characteristics of a balanced Fermatean Neutrosophic network. The subsequent sections delve into definitions, theorems, and characteristics of these networks, culminating in the modeling of a balanced Fermatean Neutrosophic network for delivering timely medical treatment in government hospitals in Indian cities.

This chapter explains a balanced fermatean neutrosophic network's key characteristics. Section 2 goes over the necessary definitions and theorems. In Sect. 3, the balanced fermatean neutrosophic graph and its characteristics are discussed. Several characteristics of balanced complementary and self-complementary fermatean neutrosophic graphs were also studied and in Sect. 4, a balanced fermatean neutrosophic graph is modeled for providing medical treatment in government hospitals of Indian cities, and Sect. 5 is used as the paper's conclusion.

2 Preliminaries

Definition 2.1 [69] An SVNG with node set X is defined to be a pair $G = (R, S)$ where

1. The functions $T_R : X \to [0, 1]$, $I_R : X \to [0, 1]$, and $F_R : X \to [0, 1]$, notate the membership degree of authentic, degree of ambiguous, and falsehood of the node $v_i \in X$, respectively, and $0 \le T_R(v_i) + I_R(v_i) + F_R(v_i) \le 3$ for all $v_i \in X$.
2. The functions $T_S : E \subseteq XxX \to [0, 1], I_s : E \subseteq XxX \to [0, 1]$, and $F_s : E \subseteq XxX \to [0, 1]$ are defined by $T_S(v_i, v_j) \le \min\{T_R(v_i), T_R(v_j)\} I_S(v_i, v_j) \ge \max\{I_R(v_i), I_R(v_j)\}$ and $F_S(v_i, v_j) \ge \max\{F_R(v_i), F_R(v_j)\}$ denotes the edge membership degree of authentic, ambiguous, and falsehood of all $(v_i, v_j) \in E$ respectively, where $0 \le T_S(v_i, v_j) + I_S(v_i, v_j) + F_S(v_i, v_j) \le 3$ for every $(v_i, v_j) \in E(i, j = 1, 2, \ldots, n)$. We call R the SVN node set of X, S the SVN edge set of E, respectively.

Definition 2.2 (Broumi et al., 2016b) A partially SVNG-subnetwork of SVNG $G = (R, S)$ is a SVNG $H = (V', E')$ such that $V' \subseteq V$, where $T'_R(v_i) \le T_R(v_i), I'_R(v_i) \ge I_R(v_i)$, and $F'_R(v_i) \ge F_R(v_i)$ for all $v_i \in V$ and $E' \subseteq E$, where $T'_S(v_i, v_j) \le T_S(v_i, v_j), I'_S(v_i, v_j) \ge I_S(v_i, v_j), F'_S(v_i, v_j) \ge F_S(v_i, v_j)$ for all $(v_i, v_j) \in E$.

Definition 2.3 (Huang et al., 2019) Let $P = (T_p, I_p, F_p)$ and $Q = (T_Q, I_Q, F_Q)$ be Fermatean Neutrosophic (FN) sets on X if Q is Fermatean Neutrosophic relation on X, then Q is called a Fermatean Neutrosophic relation on P if

$$T_Q(v_i, v_j) \le \min\{T_p(v_i), T_p(v_j)\}$$

$$I_Q(v_i, v_j) \ge \max\{I_p(v_i), I_p(v_j)\} And$$

$$F_Q(v_i, v_j) \ge \max\{F_p(v_i), F_p(v_j)\}$$

if $T_p(v_i), I_p(v_i)$ and $F_p(v_i) \in [0,1]$ for all$v_i, v_j \in X$.

Definition 2.3 (Huang et al., 2019) A Fermatean Neutrosophic graph (FNG) on a universal set X is a pair $G = (P, Q)$ where P is Fermatean Neutrosophic set on X and Q is a Fermatean Neutrosophic relation on X such that:

$$T_Q(v_i, v_j) \le \min\{T_p(v_i), T_p(v_j)\}$$

$$I_Q(v_i, v_j) \ge \max\{I_p(v_i), I_p(v_j)\}$$

$$F_Q(v_i, v_j) \ge \max\{F_p(v_i), F_p(v_j)\}$$

and $0 \leq T_Q^3(\mathrm{v}_i, \mathrm{v}_j) + I_Q^3(\mathrm{v}_i, \mathrm{v}_j) + F_Q^3(\mathrm{v}_i, \mathrm{v}_j) \leq 2$ for all $\mathrm{v}_i, \mathrm{v}_j \in X$, where $T_Q : X \times X \to [0, 1]$, $I_Q : X \times X \to [0, 1]$, and $F_Q : X \times X \to [0, 1]$, notate the edge membership degree of authentic, degree of ambiguous, and falsehood of Q respectively. Here P is the FN node set of G and Q is the FN edge set of G.

Definition 2.3 (Sivasankar & Broumi, 2022) Let $G = (P, Q)$ be a FNG. G is said to be a strong FNG if

$$T_{\mathrm{Q}}(u, v) = \min\{T_p(u), T_p(v)\},$$

$$I_{\mathrm{Q}}(u, v) = \max\{I_p(u), I_p(v)\} \ and$$

$$F_{\mathrm{Q}}(u, v) = \max\{F_p(u), F_p(v)\} \text{ for every} (u, v) \in Q.$$

Definition 2.4 (Sivasankar & Broumi, 2022) Let $G = (P, Q)$ be a FNG. G is said to be a complete FNG if

$$T_{\mathrm{Q}}(u, v) = \min\{T_p(u), T_p(v)\},$$

$$I_{\mathrm{Q}}(u, v) = \max\{I_p(u), I_p(v)\} \ and$$

$$F_{\mathrm{Q}}(u, v) = \max\{F_p(u), F_p(v)\}$$

for every$u, v \in P$.

Definition 2.5 (Sivasankar & Broumi, 2022) Let $G = (P, Q)$ be a FNG. $\overline{G} = (\overline{P}, \overline{Q})$ is the complement of a FNG if $\overline{P} = Pand\ \overline{Q}$ is computed as below

$$\overline{T_Q(u, v)} = \min\{T_p(u), T_p(v)\} - T_{\mathrm{Q}}(u, v),$$

$$I_Q(u, v) = \max\{I_p(u), I_p(v)\} - I_{\mathrm{Q}}(u, v)$$

and $\overline{F_Q(u, v)} = max\{F_p(u), F_p(v)\} - F_{\mathrm{Q}}(u, v)$ for every$(u, v) \in Q$.

Here, $\overline{T_Q(u, v)}$,$\overline{I_Q(u, v)}$ and $\overline{F_Q(u, v)}$ notate edge membership of the true, intermediate, and false degree for edge (u, v) of $\overline{G}$.

Definition 2.6 (Huang et al., 2019) Let $G = (A, B)$ be an SVNG. G is a regular neutrosophic graph if it satisfies the following conditions.

$$\sum_{u \neq v} T_{\mathrm{B}}(u, v) = \text{constant}, \sum_{u \neq v} I_{\mathrm{B}}(u, v) = \text{constant}, \text{ and } \sum_{u \neq v} F_{\mathrm{B}}(u, v) = \text{constant}.$$

Definition 2.7 (Huang et al., 2019) Let $G = (A, B)$ be an SVNG. G is a regularly strong NG if it satisfies the following conditions.

$$T_{\mathrm{B}}(u,v) = \min\{T_A(u), T_A(v)\} \text{ and } \sum_{u \neq v} T_{\mathrm{B}}(u,v) = \text{constant},$$

$$I_{\mathrm{B}}(u,v) = \max\{I_A(u), I_A(v)\} \text{ and } \sum_{u \neq v} I_{\mathrm{B}}(u,v) = \text{constant},$$

$$F_{\mathrm{B}}(u,v) = \max\{F_A(u), F_A(v)\} \text{ and } \sum_{u \neq v} F_{\mathrm{B}}(u,v) = \text{constant}.$$

Definition 2.8 (Wang et al., 2005) The density of a SVNG $G = (A, B)$ of $G^* = (V, E)$, is $D(G) = (D_T(G), D_I(G), D_F(G))$, where

$$D_T(G) \textit{ is defined by } D_T(G) = \frac{2\sum_{u,v\in V} T_B(u,v)}{\sum_{(u,v)\in V} T_A(u)T_A(v)}, \textit{ for } u, v \in V,$$

$$D_I(G) \textit{ is defined by } D_I(G) = \frac{2\sum_{u,v\in V} I_B(u,v)}{\sum_{(u,v)\in V} I_A(u) \vee I_A(v)}, \textit{ for } u, v \in V \textit{ and}$$

$$D_F(G) \textit{ is defined by } D_F(G) = \frac{2\sum_{u,v\in V} F_B(u,v)}{\sum_{(u,v)\in V} F_A(u) \vee F_A(v)}, \textit{ for } u, v \in V$$

Definition 2.8 (Wang et al., 2005) A single valued neutrosophic graph $G = (A, B)$ is balanced if$D(H) \leq D(G)$, that is,$D_T(H) \leq D_T(G)$, $D_I(H) \leq D_I(G)$, $D_F(H) \leq D_F(G)$ for all sub-graphs H of G.

Definition 2.10 (Al-Hawary, 2011) A fuzzy graph $G = (V, E)$ is a self-complementary if $\mu(u,v) = \frac{1}{2}\big(\sigma(u) \bigwedge \sigma(v)\big)$ for all $u, v \epsilon V$. (Table 1).

Table 1 Some basic notations

Notation	Meaning
$G = (V, E)$	FG
$G = (P, Q)$	Fermatean NG
P	Fermatean Neutrosophic node Set
Q	Fermatean Neutrosophic link set
$T_p(v), I_p(v), F_P(v)$	Membership value of Authentic, ambiguous, and falsehood of the node v of $G = (P, Q)$
$T_Q(u, v), I_Q(u, v), F_Q(u, v)$	Membership value of Authentic, ambiguous, and falsehood of an edge (u, v) of $G = (P, Q)$
$\overline{G} = (\overline{A}, \overline{B})$	Complement of a Fermatean Neutrosophic graph
$\overline{T_Q(u, v)}, \overline{I_Q(u, v)}, \overline{F_Q(u, v)}$	Membership value of Authentic, ambiguous, and falsehood of an edge (u, v) of $\overline{G} = (\overline{P}, \overline{Q})$
$D_T(G), D_I(G), D_F(G)$	Density of authentic, ambiguous, and falsehood of $G = (P, Q)$
$D(G) = (D_T(G), D_I(G), D_F(G))$	Density of a Fermatean Neutrosophic graph $G =$ (P, Q)

3 Balanced Fermatean Neutrosophic Graphs

Definition 3.1 The density of a FNG $G = (P, Q)$ of $G^* = (V, E)$, is $DF(G) = (DF_T(G), DF_I(G), DF_F(G))$, where

$$DF_T(G)\, is\, defined\, by\, DF_T(G) = \frac{2\sum_{u,v\in P} T_Q(u,v)}{\sum_{(u,v)\in Q} T_P(u)T_P(v)},\ for\, u, v \in P,$$

$$DF_I(G)\, is\, defined\, by\, DF_I(G) = \frac{2\sum_{u,v\in P} I_Q(u,v)}{\sum_{(u,v)\in Q} I_P(u) \vee I_P(v)},\ for\, u, v \in P\, and$$

$$DF_F(G)\ is\, defined\, by\, DF_F(G) = \frac{2\sum_{u,v\in P} F_Q(u,v)}{\sum_{(u,v)\in Q} F_P(u) \vee F_P(v)},\ for\, u, v \in P$$

Definition 3.2 A FNG $G = (P, Q)$ is balance if$DF(H) \leq DF(G)$, that is,$DF_T(H) \leq DF_T(G)$, $DF_I(H) \leq DF_I(G)$, $DF_F(H) \leq DF_F(G)$ for all subnetworks H of G.

Example 3.1 Consider a FNG, $G = (P, Q)$, **such that** $P = \{(a, b, c, d)\}, Q = \{(a, b), (b, c), (c, d), (d, a)\}$.

$T-$Density.

$$DF_T(G) = 2\left(\frac{0.55 + 0.3 + 0.225 + 0.225}{0.6 + 0.4 + 0.3 + 0.3}\right) = 1.5$$

$I-$ density.

$$DF_I(G) = 2\left(\frac{0.55 + 0.33 + 0.77 + 0.77}{0.5 + 0..3 + 0.7 + 0..7}\right) = 2.2$$

$F-$ density.

$$DF_I(G) = 2\left(\frac{0.55 + 0.33 + 0.77 + 0.77}{0.5 + 0..3 + 0.7 + 0..7}\right) = 2.2$$

$$DF(G) = (DF_T(G), DF_I(G), DF_F(G)) = (1.5, 2.2, 2.4).$$

Let $H_1 = \{(a, b)\}$,$H_2 = \{(b, c)\}$,$H_3 = \{(c, d)\}$,$H_4 = \{(a, d)\}$,$H_5 = \{(a, b, c)\}$,$H_6 = \{(a, c, d)\}$,$H_7 = \{(a, b, d)\}$,$H_8 = \{(b, c, d)\}$,$H_9 = \{(a, c)\}$,$H_{10} = \{(b, d)\}$,$H_{11} = \{(a, b, c, d)\}$ be some subnetworks of G. Density $(DF_T(H), DF_I(H), DF_F(H))$ is $DF(H_1) = (1.5, 2.2, 2.4)$,$DF(H_2) = (1.5, 2.2, 2.4)$,$DF(H_3) = (1.5, 2.2, 2.4)$,$DF(H_4) = (1.5, 2.2, 2.4)$,$DF(H_5) = (1.5, 2.2, 2.4)$,$DF(H_6) = (1.5, 2.2, 2.4)$,$DF(H_7) = (1.5, 2.2, 2.4)$,$DF(H_8) = (1.5, 2.2, 2.4)$,$DF(H_9) = (0, 0, 0)$,$DF(H_{10}) = (0, 0, 0)$,$D(H_{11}) = (1.5, 2.2, 2.4)$. So $DF(H) \leq DF(G)$ for all subnetworks H of G. Hence G is balanced FNG (Fig. 1).

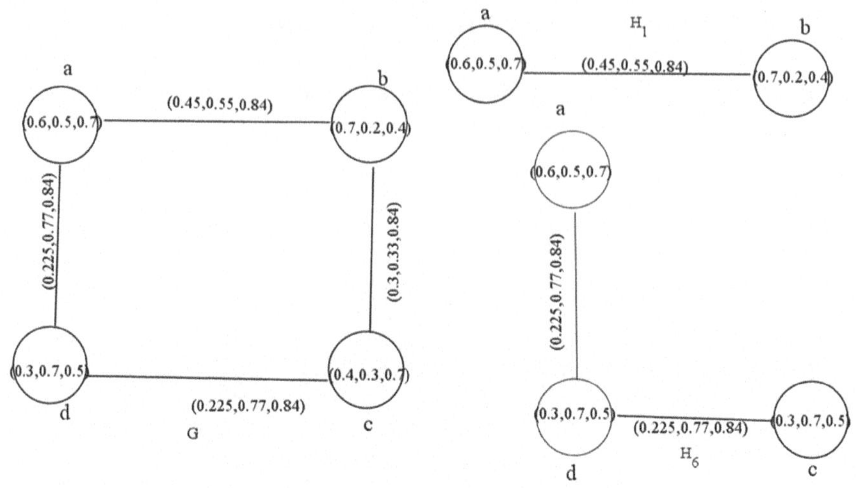

Fig. 1 Balanced fermatean neutrosophic graph

Definition 3.3 A FNG $G = (P, Q)$ is strictly balanced if for $u, v \epsilon V$, $DF(H) = DF(G)$ for all subnetworks H of G.

Example 2 Consider a FNG, $G = (P, Q)$, such that $P = \{(a, b, c)\}$,

$$Q = \{(a, b), (a, c), (b, c)\}.$$

$T-$ Density.

$$DF_T(G) = 2\left(\frac{0.39 + 0.325 + 0.325}{0.6 + 0.5 + 0.5}\right) = 1.3$$

$I-$ density.

$$DF_I(G) = 2\left(\frac{0.63 + 0.84 + 0.84}{0.6 + 0.8 + 0.8}\right) = 2.1$$

$F-$ density.

$$DF_F(G) = 2\left(\frac{1.05 + 1.05 + 0.6}{0.7 + 0.7 + 0.4}\right) = 3$$

$$DF(G) = (DF_T(G), DF_I(G), DF_F(G)) = (1.3, 2.1, 3).$$

Let $H_1 = \{(a, b)\}$,$H_2 = \{(a, c)\}$,$H_3 = \{(b, c)\}$,$H_4 = \{(a, b, c)\}$ be non-empty subnetworks of G. Density $(DF_T(H), DF_I(H), DF_F(H))$ is $DF(H_1) = (1.3, 2.1, 3)$,$DF(H_2) = (11.3, 2.1, 3)$, $DF(H_3) = (1.3, 2.1, 3)$,$DF(H_4) =$

(1.3, 2.1, 3). So $DF(H) = DF(G)$ for all subnetworks H of G. Hence G is strictly balanced FNG (Figs. 2, 3 and 4).

Theorem 3.4 *Every complete FNG G is balanced.*

Proof Let $G = (P, Q)$ be a completely FNG, then by the definition of completely, we have $T_Q(u, v) = \min\{T_p(u), T_p(v)\}$, $I_Q(u, v) = \max\{I_p(u), I_p(v)\}$ and $F_Q(u, v) = \max\{F_p(u), F_p(v)\}$ for each$u, v \in P$.

$$\therefore \sum_{u,v\epsilon P} T_Q(u, v) = \sum_{(u,v)\epsilon Q} T_P(u) \bigwedge T_P(v)$$

$$\sum_{u,v\epsilon P} I_Q(u, v) = \sum_{(u,v)\epsilon Q} I_P(u) \vee I_P(v) and$$

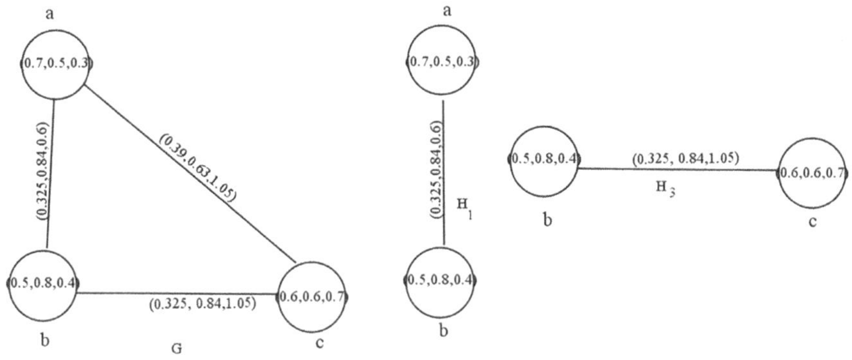

Fig. 2 Strictly balanced FNG

Fig. 3 Balanced but not complete FNG

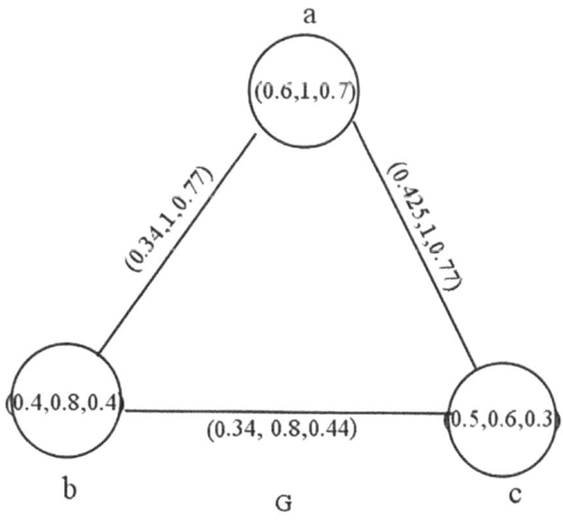

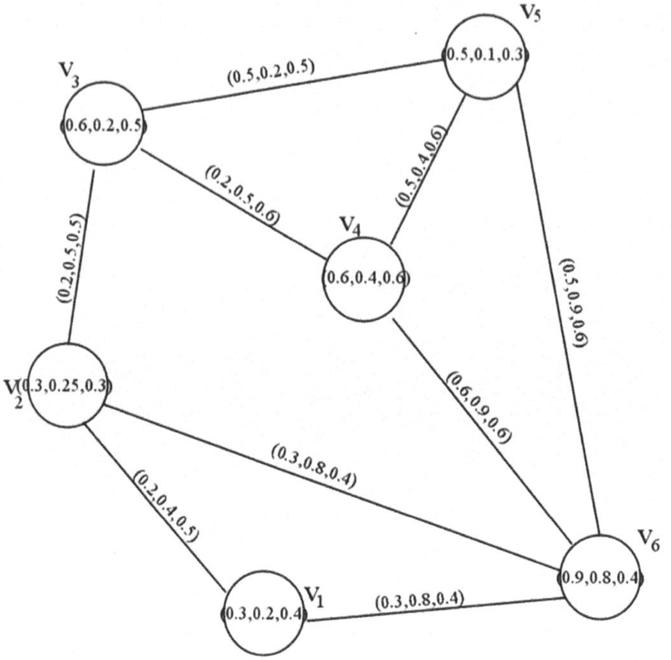

Fig. 4 Most populous cities in Karnataka

$$\sum_{u,v\epsilon V} F_Q(u, v) = \sum_{(u,v)\epsilon Q} F_P(u) \vee F_P(v).$$

Now $DF(G) = \left(\frac{2\sum_{u,v\epsilon P} T_Q(u,v)}{\sum_{(u,v)\epsilon Q} T_P(u) \bigwedge T_P(v)}, \frac{2\sum_{u,v\epsilon P} I_Q(u,v)}{\sum_{(u,v)\epsilon Q} I_P(u) \vee I_P(v)}, \frac{2\sum_{u,v\epsilon P} F_Q(u,v)}{\sum_{(u,v)\epsilon Q} F_P(u) \vee F_P(v)} \right)$

$$DF(G) = \left(\frac{2\sum_{(u,v)\epsilon Q} T_P(u) \bigwedge T_P(v)}{\sum_{(u,v)\epsilon Q} T_P(u) \bigwedge T_P(v)}, \frac{2\sum_{(u,v)\epsilon Q} I_P(u) \vee I_P(v)}{\sum_{(u,v)\epsilon Q} I_P(u) \vee I_P(v)}, \frac{2\sum_{(u,v)\epsilon Q} F_P(u) \vee F_P(v)}{\sum_{(u,v)\epsilon Q} F_P(u) \vee F_P(v)} \right)$$

$$DF(G) = (2, 2, 2).$$

Let H be non-empty subnetworks of G then, $DF(H) = (2, 2, 2)$ for every $H \subseteq G$. Hence G is balanced.

Note 3.5 The previous theorem's converse need not be true. Each balanced FNG does not have to be complete.

***Example** 3* Consider a FNG, $= (P, Q)$, such that $P = \{(a, b, c)\}$, $Q = \{(a, b), (a, c), (b, c)\}$.

$DF(G) = (DF_T(G), DF_I(G), DF_F(G)) = (1.7, 2, 2.2)$. Let $H_1 = \{(a, b)\}$,$H_2 = \{(a, c)\}$,$H_3 = \{(b, c)\}$,$H_4 = \{(a, b, c)\}$ be non-empty subnetworks of G. Density $(DF_T(H), DF_I(H), DF_F(H))$ is $DF(H_1) = (1.7, 2, 2.2)$,$DF(H_2) =$

(1.7, 2, 2.2), $DF(H_3) = (1.7, 2, 2.2)$,$DF(H_4) = (1.7, 2, 2.2)$ So $DF(H) \leq DF(G)$ for all subnetworks H of G. Hence G is balanced FNG.

From the above network easy to see that:

$T_Q(u, v) \neq \min\{T_p(u), T_p(v)\}$, $I_Q(u, v) = \max\{I_p(u), I_p(v)\}$ and $F_Q(u, v) \neq \max\{F_p(u), F_p(v)\}$ for every$u, v \in P$. Hence G is balanced, not complete.

Corollary 3.6 Every strongly Fermatean neutrosophic graph is balanced.

Theorem 3.7 *Let $G = (P, Q)$ be a self-complement FNG. Then* DF(G) = (1,1,1).

Proof Let $G = (P, Q)$ be a self-complement FNG, then

$$\sum_{u,v\epsilon P} T_Q(u, v) = \frac{1}{2}\sum_{(u,v)\epsilon Q} T_P(u) \bigwedge T_P(v)$$

$$\sum_{u,v\epsilon P} I_Q(u, v) = \frac{1}{2}\sum_{(u,v)\epsilon Q} I_P(u) \vee I_P(v) \, and$$

$$\sum_{u,v\epsilon P} F_Q(u, v) = \frac{1}{2}\sum_{(u,v)\epsilon Q} F_P(u) \vee F_P(v).$$

Now $DF(G) = \left(\frac{2\sum_{u,v\epsilon P} T_Q(u,v)}{\sum_{(u,v)\epsilon Q} T_P(u) \bigwedge T_P(v)}, \frac{2\sum_{u,v\epsilon P} I_Q(u,v)}{\sum_{(u,v)\epsilon Q} I_P(u) \vee I_P(v)}, \frac{2\sum_{u,v\epsilon P} F_Q(u,v)}{\sum_{(u,v)\epsilon Q} F_P(u) \vee F_P(v)}\right)$

$$DF(G) = \left(\frac{2\sum_{(u,v)\in Q} T_P(u) \bigwedge T_P(v)}{2\sum_{(u,v)\in Q} T_P(u) \bigwedge T_P(v)}, \frac{2\sum_{(u,v)\in Q} I_P(u) \vee I_P(v)}{2\sum_{(u,v)\in Q} I_P(u) \vee I_P(v)}, \frac{2\sum_{(u,v)\in Q} F_P(u) \vee F_P(v)}{2\sum_{(u,v)\in Q} F_P(u) \vee F_P(v)}\right)$$

Hence $DF(G) = (1, 1, 1)$.

Theorem 3.8 *Let $G = (P, Q)$ be a strictly balanced FNG and $\overline{G} = \left(\overline{P}, \overline{Q}\right)$ be its complement then* $DF(G) + DF(\overline{G}) = (2, 2, 2)$.

Proof Let $G = (P, Q)$ be a strictly balanced FNG and $\overline{G} = (\overline{P}, \overline{Q})$ be its complement.

Let H be a subnetwork of G which is non-empty. DF(G) = DF(H) for all H ⊆ G and u, v ∈ P since G is strictly balanced.

$$\text{In}\overline{G}, \overline{T_Q(u, v)} = \min\{T_p(u), T_p(v)\} - T_Q(u, v), \quad (1)$$

$$\overline{I_Q(u, v)} = \max\{I_p(u), I_p(v)\} - I_Q(u, v) \quad (2)$$

$$\text{and}\, \overline{F_Q(u, v)} = \max\left\{F_p(u), F_p(v)\right\} - F_Q(u, v) \text{ for every } (u, v) \in Q \quad (3)$$

Dividing (1) by $T_P(u) \bigwedge T_P(v)$

$$\frac{\overline{T_Q(u,v)}}{\min\{T_p(u),T_p(v)\}} = 1 - \frac{T_Q(u,v)}{\min\{T_p(u),T_p(v)\}}, \text{ for each } u,v \in P$$

Similarly dividing (2) by $I_p(u) \vee I_P(v)$

$$\frac{\overline{I_Q(u,v)}}{\max\{I_p(u),I_p(v)\}} = 1 - \frac{I_Q(u,v)}{\max\{I_p(u),I_p(v)\}}, \text{ for each } u,v \in P$$

and dividing (3) by $F_P(u) \vee F_P(v)$

$$\frac{\overline{F_Q(u,v)}}{\max\{F_p(u),F_p(v)\}} = 1 - \frac{F_Q(u,v)}{\max\{F_p(u),F_p(v)\}}, \text{ for each } u,v \in P$$

then

$$\sum_{u,v\in P} \frac{\overline{T_Q(u,v)}}{\min\{T_p(u),T_p(v)\}} = 1 - \sum_{u,v\in P} \frac{T_Q(u,v)}{\min\{T_p(u),T_p(v)\}}, \text{ for each } u,v \in P$$

$$\sum_{u,v\in P} \frac{\overline{I_Q(u,v)}}{\max\{I_p(u),I_p(v)\}} = 1 - \sum_{u,v\in P} \frac{I_Q(u,v)}{\max\{I_p(u),I_p(v)\}}, \text{ for each } u,v \in P$$

$$\sum_{u,v\in P} \frac{\overline{F_Q(u,v)}}{\max\{F_p(u),F_p(v)\}} = 1 - \sum_{u,v\in P} \frac{F_Q(u,v)}{\max\{F_p(u),F_p(v)\}}, \text{ for each } u,v \in P$$

Multiply the above equations by 2 on both sides

$$2\sum_{u,v\in P} \frac{\overline{T_Q(u,v)}}{\min\{T_p(u),T_p(v)\}} = 2 - 2\sum_{u,v\in P} \frac{T_Q(u,v)}{\min\{T_p(u),T_p(v)\}}, \text{ for each } u,v \in P$$

$$2\sum_{u,v\in P} \frac{\overline{I_Q(u,v)}}{\max\{I_p(u),I_p(v)\}} = 2 - 2\sum_{u,v\in P} \frac{I_Q(u,v)}{\max\{I_p(u),I_p(v)\}}, \text{ for each } u,v \in P$$

$$2\sum_{u,v\in P} \frac{\overline{F_Q(u,v)}}{\max\{F_p(u),F_p(v)\}} = 2 - 2\sum_{u,v\in P} \frac{F_Q(u,v)}{\max\{F_p(u),F_p(v)\}}, \text{ for each } u,v \in P$$

$DF_T(\overline{G}) = 2 - DF_T(G)$, $DF_I(\overline{G}) = 2 - DF_I(G)$ and $DF_F(\overline{G}) = 2 - DF_F(G)$

Now, DF(G) + DF($\overline{G}$) = $(DF_T(G), DF_I(G), DF_F(G))$ + $(DF_T(\overline{G}), DF_I(\overline{G}), DF_F(\overline{G}))$

$$\mathrm{DF(G)} + \mathrm{DF}(\overline{G}) = ((DF_T(G) + DF_T(\overline{G})), (DF_I(G) + DF_I(\overline{G})), (DF_F(G) + DF_F(\overline{G})))$$

Hence $\mathrm{DF(G)} + \mathrm{DF}(\overline{G}) = (2, 2, 2)$.

Theorem 3.9 *The complementary of a strictly balanced FNG is also strictly balanced.*

Proof Let $G = (P, Q)$ be a strictly balanced FNG and $\overline{G} = (\overline{P}, \overline{Q})$ be its complement.

Let H be a subnetwork of G which is non-empty. DF(G) = DF(H) for all H $\subseteq$ G and u, v $\in$ V since G is strictly balanced.

As G is strictly balanced by Theorem 3.8, $\mathrm{DF(G)} + \mathrm{DF}(\overline{G}) = (2, 2, 2)$

Since $\mathrm{DF(H)} + \mathrm{DF}(\overline{H}) = (2, 2, 2)$ for every $H \subseteq G$.

Which implies $\mathrm{DF}(\overline{H}) = \mathrm{DF}(\overline{G})$.

Hence $\overline{G}$ is strictly balanced.

Theorem 3.10 *The complementary of strong FNG is balanced.*

Proof Let $G = (P, Q)$ be a strong FNG and $\overline{G} = (\overline{P}, \overline{Q})$ be its complement.

Since G is strong, we have $T_Q(u, v) = \min\{T_p(u), T_p(v)\}$, $I_Q(u, v) = \max\{I_p(u), I_p(v)\}$ and $F_Q(u, v) = \max\{F_p(u), F_p(v)\}$ for every $(u, v) \in Q$.(1)

In $\overline{G}$, $\overline{T_Q(u, v)} = \min\{T_p(u), T_p(v)\} - T_Q(u, v)$,

$$\overline{I_Q(u, v)} = \max\{I_p(u), I_p(v)\} - I_Q(u, v)$$

and $\overline{F_Q(u, v)} = \max\{F_p(u), F_p(v)\} - F_Q(u, v)$ for every $(u, v) \in Q$.

Since G is strong, we have $\overline{T_Q(u, v)} = 0$, $\overline{I_Q(u, v)} = 0$ and $\overline{F_Q(u, v)} = 0$ by (1) for every

$(u, v) \in Q$ and

$$\overline{T_Q(u, v)} = \min\{T_p(u), T_p(v)\},$$

$$\overline{I_Q(u, v)} = \max\{I_p(u), I_p(v)\}$$

and $\overline{F_Q(u, v)} = \max\{F_p(u), F_p(v)\}$ for each $(u, v) \in \overline{Q}$.

$\Rightarrow \overline{G}$ is a strong FNG. Then by Corollary 3.6, $\overline{G}$ is balanced.

Theorem 3.11 *Let $G = (P, Q)$ be a FNG and $\overline{G} = (\overline{P}, \overline{Q})$ be its complement then* $\overline{\overline{G}}$= G.

Proof Let $G = (P, Q)$ be a FNG $\overline{G} = (\overline{P}, \overline{Q})$ be its complement. (1)

In $\overline{G}$, $\overline{T_Q(u, v)} = \min\{T_p(u), T_p(v)\} - T_Q(u, v)$, (1)

$$\overline{I_Q(u, v)} = \max\{I_p(u), I_p(v)\} - I_Q(u, v)$$

and $\overline{F_Q(u, v)} = \max\{F_p(u), F_p(v)\} - F_Q(u, v)$ for every$(u, v) \in Q$.

Taking complement for (1), we get $\overline{\overline{T_Q(u, v)}} = \min\{T_p(u), T_p(v)\} - \overline{T_Q(u, v)}$

Substitute $T_P(u) \bigwedge T_P(v) = T_Q(u, v) + \overline{T_Q(u, v)}$ from (1) we get, $= T_Q(u, v)$

Similarly, $= I_Q(u, v)$ and $\overline{\overline{F_Q(u, v)}} = F_Q(u, v)$

Hence $\overline{\overline{G}} = \text{G}$.

4 Balanced Neutrosophic Fermatean Graphs to Structure a Medical Treatment System in Indian Cities

Many private hospitals in Indian cities are well-known for their treatment and facilities, whereas there is a lack of treatment in government hospitals due to insufficient doctors and facilities. India is still a developing country, with many people relying on government hospitals. The population of India is growing, but the number of government hospitals is not increasing proportionally. In contrast to Western countries, the quality of government hospitals in India should improve over time and provide equal treatment to all citizens.

Every state capital has good government hospitals, but they are not always accessible to people who live outside of the state capital. In many cities, various treatments and facilities are not available in government hospitals, so many diseases are not identified at an early stage, resulting in more casualties. Suppose the disease is properly diagnosed at an early stage. In that case, the recovery rate will be higher, so it is beneficial to have multispecialty government hospitals with cutting-edge technology in every city across India. In this paper, we use balanced Fermatean neutrosophic graphs to create a structural framework for providing good treatment to all needy people in government hospitals. Let us consider Karnataka state and its major cities for our discussion.

Let $\{v_1, v_2, v_3, v_4, v_5, v_6\}$ represent the six most populous cities in Karnataka. The truth membership function T_A is the treatment and facilities available at a government hospital, indeterminacy membership function I_A is the population seeking for treatment in that hospital, and falsity membership function F_A is reachability and time duration for treatment. The truth membership value T_B of each edge is a set of people who prefer to take treatment either in two cities, indeterminacy edge membership I_B is the population seeking for treatment between two cities. Falsity edge membership function F_B is reachability and time duration for treatment between two cities.

Consider the cities; Mysore, Mangalore, Belgaum, Dharwad, Gulbarga, and Bangalore as vertices $v_1, v_2, v_3, v_4, v_5, v_6$ respectively. In a survey of 1000 people near each city, 300 prefer to take treatment in their city government hospital, 200 prefer to go to other government hospitals in their state, 400 people prefer due to reachability and time duration for the treatment, and their weightage (0.3,0.2,0.4) is assigned to v_1 and similarly (0.3,0.25,0.3) is assigned to v_2, and 200 people prefer to take treatment in either of two cities, 400 people prefer to go for treatment in a government hospital in two cities, 500 prefer due to reachability and time duration for treatment between two cities and their weightage (0.2, 0.4, 0.5) to the edge between $\{v_1, v_2\}$ and in a similar manner, the weightage is applied for all remaining vertices and edges given in Fig. 4.

The relative adjacency matrix $Adj(G)$ corresponds to the above network is

$Adj(G) =$

	v_1	v_2	v_3	v_4	v_5	v_6
v_1	(0, 0, 0)	(0.2, 0.4, 0.5)	(0, 0, 0)	(0, 0, 0)	(0, 0, 0)	(0.3, 0.8, 0.4)
v_2	(0.2, 0.4, 0.5)	(0, 0, 0)	(0.2, 0.5, 0.5)	(0, 0, 0)	(0, 0, 0)	(0.3, 0.8, 0.4)
v_3	(0, 0, 0)	(0.2, 0.5, 0.5)	(0, 0, 0)	(0.2, 0.5, 0.6)	(0.5, 0.2, 0.5)	(0, 0, 0)
v_4	(0, 0, 0)	(0, 0, 0)	(0.2, 0.5, 0.6)	(0, 0, 0)	(0.5, 0.4, 0.6)	(0.6, 0.9, 0.6)
v_5	(0, 0, 0)	(0, 0, 0)	(0.5, 0.2, 0.5)	(0.5, 0.4, 0.6)	(0, 0, 0)	(0.5, 0.9, 0.6)
v_6	(0.3, 0.8, 0.4)	(0.3, 0.8, 0.4)	(0, 0, 0)	(0.6, 0.9, 0.6)	(0.5, 0.9, 0.6)	(0, 0, 0)

Consider a subgraph $H_1 = \{(v_1, v_2)\}$ and $D(H_1) > D(G)$.

Here the above network is not balanced and many people in other cities prefer mostly Bangalore for their medical treatment. To have equivalent treatment, we must balance the network (Fig. 5).

Let us take $D(G) = (D_T(G), D_I(G), D_F(G)) = (1.3, 2.1, 3)$ and its corresponding adjacency matrix is

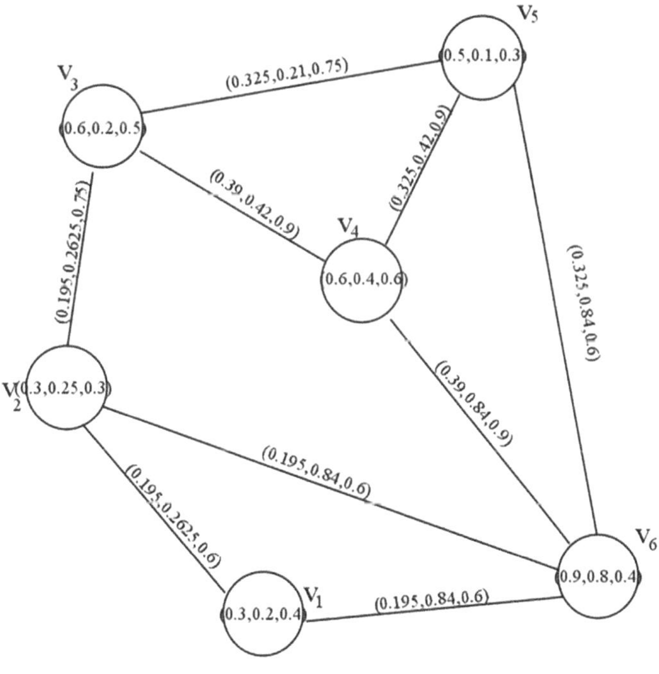

Fig. 5 Balanced fermatean neutrosophic network

$$Adj(G) = \begin{bmatrix} & v_1 & v_2 & v_3 & v_4 & v_5 & v_6 \\ v_1 & (0,0,0) & (0.195, 0.2625, 0.6) & (0,0,0) & (0,0,0) & (0.195, 0.84, 0.6) & (0.3, 0.8, 0.4) \\ v_2 & (0.195, 0.2625, 0.6) & (0,0,0) & (0.195, 0.2625, 0.75) & (0,0,0) & (0.195, 0.84, 0.6) & (0.3, 0.8, 0.4) \\ v_3 & (0,0,0) & (0.195, 0.2625, 0.75) & (0,0,0) & (0.39, 0.42, 0.9) & (0,0,0) & (0,0,0) \\ v_4 & (0,0,0) & (0,0,0) & (0.39, 0.42, 0.9) & (0,0,0) & (0.39, 0.84, 0.9) & (0.6, 0.9, 0.6) \\ v_5 & (0,0,0) & (0,0,0) & (0.39, 0.42, 0.9) & (0.325, 0.42, 0.9) & (0.325, 0.84, 0.6) & (0.5, 0.9, 0.6) \\ v_6 & (0.195, 0.84, 0.6) & (0.195, 0.84, 0.6) & (0,0,0) & (0.325, 0.84, 0.6) & (0,0,0) & (0,0,0) \end{bmatrix}$$

Here for any subgraph $H, D(H) \leq D(G)$. Hence G is a balanced Fermatean neutrosophic graph. When the network is balanced, all demographic groups will get timely medical treatment. The truth membership density of 1.3 stands for good treatment and facilities, indeterminacy membership function density of 2.1 population in that hospital, and falsity membership function density of 3 stands for reachability and time duration for treatment. So, if every city has a good multispecialty government hospital, then disease can be diagnosed at the early stage, and people prefer treatment in their neighboring cities, which is applicable to all the cities throughout the country.

5 Conclusion

The neutrosophic graph has a broad range of applications in medical diagnosis. We introduced the Balanced Fermatean neutrosophic graph and examined some of its properties in this paper. A Balanced Fermatean neutrosophic graph is modeled using density functions for providing medical care to all needy people at the right time in government hospitals in major cities of Karnataka. It concludes that if we have a multispecialty government hospital in all cities, people will arrive on time, the disease will be diagnosed at an early stage, and casualties will be reduced which is possible by balancing the system. The advantage of the proposed method is that it can be executed fast and even as the network gets larger utilizing a computer system that interprets networks as matrices.

Compliance with Ethical Standards

Conflict of Interest "The authors declare that they do not have any financial or associative interest indicating a conflict of interest in about submitted work."

References

Abdelfattah, W. (2019). Data envelopment analysis with neutrosophic inputs and outputs. *Expert Systems, 36*(6), e12453.

Adebisi, S., & Smarandache, F. (2023). On refined neutrosophic finite p-group. *Journal of Fuzzy Extension and Applications, 4*(2), 136–140.

Akram, M., & Waseem, N. (2018). Novel applications of bipolar fuzzy graphs to decision making problems. *Journal of Applied Mathematics and Computing, 56*, 73–91.

Akram, M., Karunambigai, M. G., Palanivel, K., & Sivasankar, S. (2014). Balanced bipolar fuzzy graphs. *Journal of Advanced Research in Pure Mathematics, 6*(4), 58–71.

Akram, M., Shah, S. M. U., Al-Shamiri, M. M. A., & Edalatpanah, S. A. (2022). Fractional transportation problem under interval-valued Fermatean fuzzy sets. *AIMS Mathematics, 7*(9), 17327–17348.

Al-Hawary, T. (2011). Complete fuzzy graphs. *International Journal of Mathematical Combinatorics, 4*, 26.

Batista, E., Figueiredo, G., & Prazeres, C. (2022). Load balancing between fog and cloud in fog of things based platforms through software-defined networking. *Journal of King Saud University-Computer and Information Sciences, 34*(9), 7111–7125.

Broumi, S., Nagarajan, D., Bakali, A., Talea, M., Smarandache, F., & Lathamaheswari, M. (2019b). The shortest path problem in interval valued trapezoidal and triangular neutrosophic environment. *Complex & Intelligent Systems, 5*, 391–402.

Broumi, S., Smarandache, F., Talea, M., & Bakali, A. (2016). Single valued neutrosophic graphs: degree, order and size. In *2016 IEEE international conference on fuzzy systems (FUZZ-IEEE)* (pp. 2444–2451). IEEE.

Broumi, S., Sundareswaran, R., Shanmugapriya, M., Bakali, A., & Talea, M. (2022b). Theory and applications of fermatean neutrosophic graphs. *Neutrosophic Sets and Systems, 50*, 248–286.

Broumi, S., Talea, M., Bakali, A., Smarandache, F., Nagarajan, D., Lathamaheswari, M., & Parimala, M. (2019a). Shortest path problem in fuzzy, intuitionistic fuzzy and neutrosophic environment: An overview. *Complex & Intelligent Systems, 5*, 371–378.

Broumi, S., Talea, M., Bakali, A., & Smarandache, F. (2016a). Single valued neutrosophic graphs. *Journal of New Theory, 10*, 86–101.

Broumi, S., Ajay, D., Chellamani, P., Malayalan, L., Talea, M., Bakali, A., & Jafari, S. (2022). Interval valued pentapartitioned neutrosophic graphs with an application to MCDM. *Operational Research in Engineering Sciences: Theory and Applications*, 5(3), 68–91.

Das, S. K., & Edalatpanah, S. A. (2022). Optimal solution of neutrosophic linear fractional programming problems with mixed constraints. *Soft Computing, 26*(17), 8699–8707.

Debnath, S. (2021). Neutrosophication of statistical data in a study to assess the knowledge, attitude and symptoms on reproductive tract infection among women. *Journal of Fuzzy Extension and Applications, 2*(1), 33–40.

Deng, Z., & Wang, J. (2022). New distance measure for Fermatean fuzzy sets and its application. *International Journal of Intelligent Systems, 37*(3), 1903–1930.

Edalatpanah, S. A. (2020). General non-square systems of linear equations in single-valued triangular neutrosophic number environment. *Neutrosophic Theories in Communication, Management and Information Technology*, pp. 157–172

Edalatpanah, S. A. (2020c). Systems of neutrosophic linear equations. *Neutrosophic Sets and Systems, 33*(1), 92–104.

Edalatpanah, S. A. (2020a). A direct model for triangular neutrosophic linear programming. *International Journal of Neutrosophic Science, 1*(1), 19–28.

Edalatpanah, S. A. (2018). Neutrosophic perspective on DEA. *Journal of Applied Research on Industrial Engineering, 5*(4), 339–345.

Ejegwa, P. A., & Zuakwagh, D. (2022). Fermatean fuzzy modified composite relation and its application in pattern recognition. *Journal of Fuzzy Extension and Applications, 3*(2), 140–151.

Gayen, S., Edalatpanah, S. A., Jha, S., & Kumar, R. (2023). On the characterization of antineutrosophic subgroup. *Advances in Mathematical Physics*, 2023.

Hobbs, A. M., Kannan, L., Lai, H. J., Lai, H., & Weng, G. (2010). Balanced and 1-balanced graph constructions. *Discrete Applied Mathematics, 158*(14), 1511–1523.

Huang, L., Hu, Y., Li, Y., Kumar, P. K., Koley, D., & Dey, A. (2019). A study of regular and irregular neutrosophic graphs with real life applications. *Mathematics, 7*(6), 551.

Karaaslan, F. (2017). Possibility neutrosophic soft sets and PNS-decision making method. *Applied Soft Computing, 54*, 403–414.

Karunambigai, M. G., Akram, M., Sivasankar, S., & Palanivel, K. (2017). Clustering algorithm for intuitionistic fuzzy graphs. *International Journal of Uncertainty, Fuzziness and Knowledge-Based Systems, 25*(03), 367–383.

Karunambigai, M. G., Sivasankar, S., & Palanivel, K. (2015). Some properties of a regular intuitionistic fuzzy graph. *International Journal of Mathematics and Computation, 26*(4), 53–61.

Kandasamy, V., Ilanthenral, K., & Smarandache, F. (2015). Neutrosophic graphs: a new dimension to graph theory. *Infinite Study*.

Kumar, R., Edalatpanah, S. A., Jha, S., & Singh, R. (2019). A novel approach to solve gaussian valued neutrosophic shortest path problems. *International Journal of Engineering and Advanced Technology, 8*(3), 347–353.

Liu, P., & Wang, Y. (2014). Multiple attribute decision-making method based on single-valued neutrosophic normalized weighted Bonferroni mean. *Neural Computing and Applications, 25*, 2001–2010.

Martin, N., & Edalatpanah, S. A. (2023). Application of extended fuzzy ISOCOV methodology in nanomaterial selection based on performance measures. *J. Oper. Strateg Anal, 1*(2), 55–61.

Mao, X., Guoxi, Z., Fallah, M., & Edalatpanah, S. A. (2020). A neutrosophic-based approach in data envelopment analysis with undesirable outputs. *Mathematical Problems in Engineering, 2020*, 1–8.

Mohanta, K. K., & Sharanappa, D. S. (2023). A novel method for solving neutrosophic data envelopment analysis models based on single-valued trapezoidal neutrosophic numbers. *Soft Computing*, 1–17.

Mohan, M., & Krishnaswamy, M. (2020). K-algebras on quadripartitioned single valued neutrosophic sets. *Journal of Fuzzy Extension and Applications, 1*(4), 325–339.

Mahapatra, R., Samanta, S., Pal, M., & Xin, Q. (2020). Link prediction in social networks by neutrosophic graph. *International Journal of Computational Intelligence Systems, 13*(1), 1699–1713.

Mahapatra, R., Samanta, S., Allahviranloo, T., & Pal, M. (2019). Radio fuzzy graphs and assignment of frequency in radio stations. *Computational and Applied Mathematics, 38*, 1–20.

Narayan, K. S., & Sunitha, M. S. (2012). Connectivity in a fuzzy graph and its complement. *General Mathematics Notes, 9*(1), 38–43.

Polymenis, A. (2021). A neutrosophic Student's t–type of statistic for AR (1) random processes. *Journal of Fuzzy Extension and Applications, 2*(4), 388–393.

Parvathi, R., & Karunambigai, M. G. (2006). Intuitionistic fuzzy graphs. In *Computational intelligence, theory and applications: international conference 9th fuzzy days in Dortmund, Germany, Sept. 18–20, 2006 Proceedings* (pp. 139–150). Springer Berlin Heidelberg

Patel, P. C., Fernhaber, S. A., McDougall-Covin, P. P., & Van der Have, R. P. (2014). Beating competitors to international markets: The value of geographically balanced networks for innovation. *Strategic Management Journal, 35*(5), 691–711.

Rani, P., Mishra, A. R., Deveci, M., & Antucheviciene, J. (2022). New complex proportional assessment approach using Einstein aggregation operators and improved score function for interval-valued Fermatean fuzzy sets. *Computers & Industrial Engineering, 169*, 108165.

Ruciński, A., & Vince, A. (1993). The solution to an extremal problem on balanced extensions of graphs. *Journal of Graph Theory, 17*(3), 417–431.

Saberhoseini, S. F., Edalatpanah, S. A., & Sorourkhah, A. (2022). Choosing the best private-sector partner according to the risk factors in neutrosophic environment. *Big Data and Computing Visions, 2*(2), 61–68.

Senapati, T., & Yager, R. R. (2020). Fermatean fuzzy sets. *Journal of Ambient Intelligence and Humanized Computing, 11*, 663–674.

Sivasankar, S., & Broumi, S. (2022). Balanced neutrosophic graphs. *Neutrosophic Sets and Systems, 50*, 309–319.

Shenggui, Z., Hao, S., & Xueliang, L. (2002). W-Density and w-balanced property of weighted graphs. *Applied Mathematics-A Journal of Chinese Universities, 17*(3), 355–364.

Smarandache, F. (2020). Generalizations and alternatives of classical algebraic structures to neutroAlgebraic structures and antiAlgebraic structures. *Journal of Fuzzy Extension and Applications, 1*(2), 81–83.

Smarandache, F. (2006). Neutrosophic set-a generalization of the intuitionistic fuzzy set. In *2006 IEEE international conference on granular computing* (pp. 38–42). IEEE.

Smarandache, F. (1999). A unifying field in logics. In *Neutrosophy: neutrosophic probability, Set and logic* (4 edn, pp. 1–141). American Research Press

Stanimirović, P. S., Ivanov, B., Stanujkić, D., Katsikis, V. N., Mourtas, S. D., Kazakovtsev, L. A., & Edalatpanah, S. A. (2023). Improvement of unconstrained optimization methods based on symmetry involved in neutrosophy. *Symmetry, 15*(1), 250.

Tapia, J. F. D. (2021). Evaluating negative emissions technologies using neutrosophic data envelopment analysis. *Journal of Cleaner Production, 286*, 125494.

Veeramani, C., Venugopal, R., & Edalatpanah, S. A. (2022). Neutrosophic DEMATEL approach for financial ratio performance evaluation of the NASDAQ Exchange. *Neutrosophic Sets and Systems, 51*, 766–782.

Veeramani, C., Edalatpanah, S. A., & Sharanya, S. (2021). Solving the multiobjective fractional transportation problem through the neutrosophic goal programming approach. *Discrete Dynamics in Nature and Society, 2021*, 1–17.

Ye, J. (2013). Multicriteria decision-making method using the correlation coefficient under single-valued neutrosophic environment. *International Journal of General Systems, 42*(4), 386–394.

Ye, J., & Cui, W. (2018). Neutrosophic state feedback design method for SISO neutrosophic linear systems. *Cognitive Systems Research, 52*, 1056–1065.

Woodall, W. H., Driscoll, A. R., & Montgomery, D. C. (2022). A review and perspective on neutrosophic statistical process monitoring methods. *IEEE Access*.

Wang, H., Smarandache, F., Sunderraman, R., & Zhang, Y. Q. (2005). interval neutrosophic sets and logic: theory and applications in computing: Theory and applications in computing (Vol. 5). Infinite Study.

Wang, Q., Huang, Y., Kong, S., Ma, X., Liu, Y., Das, S. K., & Edalatpanah, S. A. (2021). A novel method for solving multiobjective linear programming problems with triangular neutrosophic numbers. *Journal of Mathematics, 2021*, 1–8.

Zhan, J., Akram, M., & Sitara, M. (2019). Novel decision-making method based on bipolar neutrosophic information. *Soft Computing, 23*, 9955–9977.

TOPSIS-Based Entropy Measure for N-Valued Neutrosophic Trapezoidal Numbers and Their Application to Multi-Criteria Decision-Making Problems

Vakkas Uluçay and İrfan Deli

Abstract As an extension of the neutrosophic trapezoidal numbers, the N-valued neutrosophic trapezoidal numbers, which are special neutrosophic multisets on real numbers, are used to effectively solve the repetitive uncertainty of decision-makers in multi-criteria decision-making problems. The aim of the chapter is to develop a multi-criteria decision-making method under N-valued neutrosophic trapezoidal numbers. Therefore, we first propose some new generalized distance measures for N-valued neutrosophic trapezoidal numbers. Also, some desirable properties of these measures are shown, and some special cases of the measure are given. We second propose an entropy measure to construct a decision-making method, which is to find the weight of criterias. Then, we develop a multi-criteria decision-making method under N-valued neutrosophic trapezoidal numbers called TOPSIS-based entropy method. Furthermore, we apply it to a decision-making problem to illustrate the effectiveness of the developed method. Finally, a comparative analysis is initiated with the decision-making problem to show the advantages of our method.

Keywords Neutrosophic sets · Neutrosophic multisets · N-valued neutrosophic trapezoidal number · Generalized distance measure · Entropy measure · Multi-criteria decision-making

V. Uluçay (✉) · İ. Deli
Kilis 7 Aralık University, 79000 Kilis, Turkey
e-mail: vakkas.ulucay@kilis.edu.tr

İ. Deli
e-mail: irfandeli@kilis.edu.tr

© The Author(s), under exclusive license to Springer Nature Singapore Pte Ltd. 2024

S. A. Edalatpanah et al. (eds.), *Analytical Decision Making and Data Envelopment Analysis*, Infosys Science Foundation Series in Mathematical Sciences,
https://doi.org/10.1007/978-981-97-6972-8_19

1 Introduction

Since decision-making problems which contain uncertainty are difficult to model and solve, it is a need for us to develop some mathematical theories. In recent years, fuzzy set theory by using only one degree of membership proposed by Zadeh (1965) and intuitionistic fuzzy set theory by using two degree of membership introduced by Atanassov (1986) have received great attention in solving various decision-making problems. These theories can better solve the fuzziness of the uncertain decision-making therefore the theories are all very successfully studied by Narayanamoorthy et al. (2019), Liu et al. (2021), and Hu et al. (2018).

By using truth-membership function, indeterminacy-membership function, and falsity-membership functions, in 1998, Smarandache (1998) proposed the concept of neutrosophic sets (N-sets), which is a generalization of the concept of fuzzy set Zadeh (1965) and intuitionistic fuzzy sets Atanassov (1986). In 2013, Smarandache (2013) generalized the classical neutrosophic logic to neutrosophic refined logic which has more than one with the possibility of the same or different membership functions. Moreover, Ye and Ye (2014), Chatterjee et al. (2015) and Ye and Smarandache (2016) introduced the concept single-valued neutrosophic multisets as a further generalization of that of neutrosophic sets based on both the neutrosophic refined logic and multisets of Yager (1986). The multisets and single-valued neutrosophic multisets have received more and more attention since their appearance in Broumi and Deli (2015), Deli (2016), Deli et al. (2021), Pramanik (2016), Sahin et al. (2018), Ulucay et al. (2018), Ulucay (2021). Furthermore, they are widely used in decision-making field Basset et al. (2018), Batool (2018), Karaaslan (2018), Khatter (2021), Ejegwa et al. (2013), Ejegwa (2015), Mondal (2018), Miyamoto (2001, 2004), Rajarajeswari and Uma (2013a, 2013b, 2013a, 2014), Sebastian and Rajarajeswari (2010, 2011, 2011a), Shinoj and John (2012, 2013, 2015), Syropoulos (2012), Ulucay et al. (2018, 2019a), Adak and Kumar (2022), Da Silva et al. (2021), Mohan et al. (2020), Rayappan and Krishnaswamy (2020), Rayappan and Mohana (2021), Salimi and Edalatpanah (2020).

In order to use the concept of single-valued neutrosophic multisets to define an uncertain quantity or a quantity difficult to quantify, Deli et al. (2021), the authors put forward the concept of continuous N-valued neutrosophic trapezoidal numbers (NVNT-numbers). They developed a TOPSIS method by giving some operational laws of NVNT-numbers and some aggregation operators of NVNT-numbers.

Distance measure is an important information measure in the study of single-valued neutrosophic multisets but there are few distance formulas for NVNT-numbers proposed in studies. There, this paper will first propose some new generalized distance measures for NVNT-numbers then use them to develop a decision-making method based on an entropy measure which find the weight of criterias. The paper is organized as follows. Section 2 briefly reviews the basic concepts related to N-valued neutrosophic trapezoidal number. In Section 3, some new generalized distance measures for N-valued neutrosophic trapezoidal numbers are defined. And, some properties of the new generalized distance measures are also analyzed. Section 4, uses the new generalized distance measures to solve real-world problems as well as illustrative with a numerical example. Section 5 summarizes the main results and conclusions of the paper.

2 Preliminary

This section firstly introduces several known definitions and propositions that would be helpful for a better study of this chapter.

Definition 2.1 (Wang, 2010) Assume that E is the universe. Then, a single-valued neutrosophic set (N-set) A in E defined as

$$A = \{< x, T_A(x), I_A(x), F_A(x) > : x \in E\} \tag{1}$$

where $T_A(x), I_A(x), F_A(x) \in [0,1]$ for each point x in such that $0 \le T_A(x) + I_A(x) + F_A(x) \le 3$.

Tanim 2.1 (Ye, 2014) For two N-sets A and B in a universe of discourse $E = \{x_1, x_2, \ldots x_n\}$, which are denoted by $A = \{< x_i, T_A(x_i), I_A(x_i), F_A(x_i) > : x_i \in E\}$ and $B = \{< x_i, T_B(x_i), I_B(x_i), F_B(x_i) > : x_i \in E\}$ with weight w_i (i = 1, 2,…,n) of an element x_i (i = 1, 2,…,n), with $w_i \ge 0$ (i = 1, 2,…,n) such that $\sum_{i=1}^{n} w_i = 1$. Then, generalized single-valued neutrosophic weighted distance measure for $p > 0$, is defined as;

$$d_p(A, B) = \frac{1}{3}.(\sum_{i=1}^{p} w_i[|T_A(x_i) - T_B(x_i)|^r + |I_A(x_i) - I_B(x_i)|^r + |F_A(x_i) - F_B(x_i)|^r]^{\frac{1}{r}} \tag{2}$$

when $p = 1,2$ generalized single-valued neutrosophic weighted distance measure is reducing to the Hamming distance and Euclidean distance, respectively.

Definition 2.2 (Smarandache 2013; Ye and Ye 2014) Let E be a universe. A_1 neutrosophic multiset set A_1 on E can be defined as follows:

$$A_1 = \{< x, (T^1_{A_1}(x), T^2_{A_1}(x), \ldots, T^P_{A_1}(x)), (I^1_{A_1}(x), I^2_{A_1}(x), \ldots, I^P_{A_1}(x)),$$
$$(F^1_{A_1}(x), F^2_{A_1}(x), \ldots, F^P_{A_1}(x)) >: x \in E\},$$

where

$$T^1_{A_1}(x), T^2_{A_1}(x), \ldots, T^P_{A_1}(x), I^1_{A_1}(x), I^2_{A_1}(x), \ldots, I^P_{A_1}(x),$$
$$F^1_{A_1}(x), F^2_{A_1}(x), \ldots, F^P_{A_1}(x) : E[0, 1]$$

such that $0 \le supT^i_{A_1}(x) + supI^i_{A_1}(x) + supF^i_{A_1}(x) \le 3$ (i = 1,2,...,P) for any $x \in E$ is the truth-membership sequence, indeterminacy-membership sequence, and falsity-membership sequence of the element x, respectively.

Definition 7 (Ulucay et al. 2018) Let $w^i_{\bar{a}_i} \in [0,1]$, $a_i \le b_i \le c_i \le d_i$ such that $a_i, b_i, c_i, d_i \in R$, (i = 1,2,...,n). A trapezoidal fuzzy multi-number

$$\bar{a}_i = < (a_i, b_i, c_i, d_i); w^1_{\bar{a}_i}, w^2_{\bar{a}_i}, \ldots w^n_{\bar{a}_i} > (i = 1,2,\ldots,n) \tag{3}$$

is a special fuzzy multiset on the real number set R, whose membership functions $\mu^i_{\bar{a}_i} : R \to [0, w^i_a]$ can generally be defined as;

$$\mu^i_{\bar{a}_i}(x) = \begin{cases} \frac{(x-a_i)w^i_{\bar{a}_i}}{b_i - a_i}, & a_i \le x < b_i, \\ w^i_{\bar{a}_i}, & b_i \le x \le c_i, \\ \frac{(d_i - x)w^i_{\bar{a}_i}}{d_i - c_i}, & c_i < x \le d_i, \\ 0, & otherwise. \end{cases}$$

where $w^i_{\bar{a}_i} \in [0,1]$ is a constant, If $a_1, b_1, c_1, d_1 \in [0,1]$, then $\bar{a}_i$ is a normal trapezoidal fuzzy multi-number.

For $\overline{A_j} = (a_j, b_j, c_j, d_j); (\eta^1_{\overline{A_j}}, \eta^2_{\overline{A_j}}, \ldots, \eta^P_{\overline{A_j}}), (\vartheta^1_{\overline{A_j}}, \vartheta^2_{\overline{A_j}}, \ldots, \vartheta^P_{\overline{A_j}}), (\theta^1_{\overline{A_j}}, \theta^2_{\overline{A_j}}, \ldots, \theta^P_{\overline{A_j}})$ *for* $j \in \{1, 2\}$ the Euclidean distance measures between $\overline{A}_1$ and $\overline{A}_2$, are given below;

$$d(\overline{A}_1, \overline{A}_2) = \frac{1}{8p} \cdot \sum_{i=1}^{p} \Big[\Big|(1 + \eta^i_{\overline{A}_1})a_1 - (1 + \eta^i_{\overline{A}_2})a_2\Big| + \Big|(1 + \eta^i_{\overline{A}_1})b_1 - (1 + \eta^i_{\overline{A}_2})b_2\Big| + \Big|(1 + \eta^i_{\overline{A}_1})c_1 - (1 + \eta^i_{\overline{A}_2})c_2\Big| + \Big|(1 + \eta^i_{\overline{A}_1})d_1 - (1 + \eta^i_{\overline{A}_2})d_2\Big| \Big] \tag{4}$$

Definition 2.3 (Deli et al. 2021) Let $\eta^i_{A_1}, \vartheta^i_{A_1}, \theta^i_{A_1} \in [0,1]$ $(i \in \{1, 2, \ldots, p\})$ and $a, b, c, d \in \mathbb{R}$ such that $a \le b \le c \le d$. Then, an N-valued neutrosophic trapezoidal number (NVNT-number)

$\tilde{a} = \langle [a, b, c, d]; (\eta^1_{A_1}, \eta^2_{A_1}, \ldots, \eta^P_{A_1}), (\vartheta^1_{A_1}, \vartheta^2_{A_1}, \ldots, \vartheta^P_{A_1}), (\theta^1_{A_1}, \theta^2_{A_1}, \ldots, \theta^P_{A_1}) \rangle$ is a neutrosophic multiset on the real number set $\mathbb{R}$, whose truth-membership functions, indeterminacy-membership functions, and falsity-membership functions are defined as, respectively.

$$T^i_{\tilde{\alpha}}(x) = \begin{cases} \frac{(x-a)}{(b-a)}\eta^i_{\tilde{\alpha}}, & a \le x < b \\ \eta^i_{\tilde{\alpha}}, & b \le x \le c \\ \frac{(d-x)}{(d-c)}\eta^i_{\tilde{\alpha}}, & c < x \le d \\ 0, & otherwise, \end{cases}, \quad I^i_{\tilde{\alpha}}(x) = \begin{cases} \frac{(b-x) + \vartheta^i_{\tilde{\alpha}}(x-a)}{(b-a)}, & a \le x < b \\ \vartheta^i_{\tilde{\alpha}}, & b \le x \le c \\ \frac{(x-c) + \vartheta^i_{\tilde{\alpha}}(d-x)}{(d-c)}, & c < x \le d \\ 1, & otherwise, \end{cases}$$

and

$$F^{i}_{\tilde{\alpha}}(x) = \begin{cases} \frac{(b-x)+\theta^{i}_{A}(x-a)}{(b-a)}, & a \le x < b \\ \theta^{i}_{\tilde{\alpha}}, & b \le x \le c \\ \frac{(x-c)+\theta^{i}_{A}(d-x)}{(d-c)}, & c < x \le d \\ 1, & \text{otherwise}, \end{cases}$$

Note that the set of all NVNT-numbers on $\mathbb{R}$ will be denoted by Λ.

Definition 2.4 (Deli et al., 2021) Let $A_1 = \langle [a_1, b_1, c_1, d_1]; (\eta^1_{A_1}, \eta^2_{A_1}, ..., \eta^P_{A_1}), (\vartheta^1_{A_1}, \vartheta^2_{A_1}, ..., \vartheta^P_{A_1}), (\theta^1_{A_1}, \theta^2_{A_1}, ..., \theta^P_{A_1})\rangle$, $A_2 = \langle [a_2, b_2, c_2, d_2]; (\eta^1_{A_2}, \eta^2_{A_2}, ..., \eta^P_{A_2}), (\vartheta^1_{A_2}, \vartheta^2_{A_2}, ..., \vartheta^P_{A_2}), (\theta^1_{A_2}, \theta^2_{A_2}, ..., \theta^P_{A_2})\rangle \in \Lambda$Then

$$A_1 \le A_2 \Leftrightarrow a_1 \le a_2, b_1 \le b_2, c_1 \le c_2, d_1 \le d_2, \eta^1_{A_1} \le \eta^1_{A_2}, \eta^2_{A_1} \le \eta^2_{A_2}, \ldots, \eta^P_{A_1} \le \eta^P_{A_2}$$

$$\vartheta^1_{A_1} \ge \vartheta^1_{A_2}, \vartheta^2_{A_1} \ge \vartheta^2_{A_2}, \ldots, \vartheta^P_{A_1} \ge \vartheta^P_{A_2}, \theta^1_{A_1} \ge \theta^1_{A_2}, \theta^2_{A_1} \ge \theta^2_{A_2}, \ldots, \theta^P_{A_1} \ge \theta^P_{A_2}.$$

Definition 2.5 (Deli et al., 2021) Let $A_1 = \langle (a_1, b_1, c_1, d_1); (\eta^1_{A_1}, \eta^2_{A_1}, ..., \eta^P_{A_1}), (\vartheta^1_{A_1}, \vartheta^2_{A_1}, ..., \vartheta^P_{A_1}), (\theta^1_{A_1}, \theta^2_{A_1}, ..., \theta^P_{A_1})\rangle \in \Lambda$. If A_1 is not normalized NVTN-number($a_1, b_1, c_1, d_1 \notin [0,1]$), the normalized NVTN-number of A_1, denoted by $\overline{A}_1$ is given by;

$$\overline{A}_1 = \langle \left[\frac{a_1}{a_1+b_1+c_1+d_1}, \frac{b_1}{a_1+b_1+c_1+d_1}, \frac{c_1}{a_1+b_1+c_1+d_1}, \frac{d_1}{a_1+b_1+c_1+d_1} \right];$$

$$\left(\eta^1_{\overline{A}_1}, \eta^2_{\overline{A}_1}, ..., \eta^P_{\overline{A}_1}\right), \left(\vartheta^1_{\overline{A}_1}, \vartheta^2_{\overline{A}_1}, ..., \vartheta^P_{\overline{A}_1}\right), (\theta^1_{\overline{A}_1}, \theta^2_{\overline{A}_1}, ..., \theta^P_{\overline{A}_1})\rangle. \quad (5)$$

3 Entropy Measure for NVNT–Numbers Based on TOPSIS

This section first defines the concept of new generalized distance measures are called generalized distance measures under normalized NVNT-numbers and introduces some of its basic properties. The second one is that is to define an entropy measure to construct a decision-making. In the following, some definitions and propositions on other uncertain sets are defined by Narayanamoorthy et al. (2019), Liu et al. (2021), Hu et al. (2018), Ye (2014), Ulucay et al. (2018), and Deli et al. (2021) and extend/apply the definitions and propositions to NVNT-numbers

Definition 3.1 Let $\overline{\mathcal{A}} = \langle [a_1, b_1, c_1, d_1]; (\eta^1_{\bar{\mathcal{A}}}, \eta^2_{\bar{\mathcal{A}}}, \ldots, \eta^P_{\bar{\mathcal{A}}}), (\vartheta^1_{\bar{\mathcal{A}}}, \vartheta^2_{\bar{\mathcal{A}}}, \ldots, \vartheta^P_{\bar{\mathcal{A}}}), (\theta^1_{\bar{\mathcal{A}}}, \theta^2_{\bar{\mathcal{A}}}, \ldots, \theta^P_{\bar{\mathcal{A}}})\rangle$. and $\overline{\mathcal{B}} = \langle [a_2, b_2, c_2, d_2]; (\eta^1_{\overline{\mathcal{B}}}, \eta^2_{\overline{\mathcal{B}}}, \ldots, \eta^P_{\overline{\mathcal{B}}}), (\vartheta^1_{\overline{\mathcal{B}}}, \vartheta^2_{\overline{\mathcal{B}}}, \ldots, \vartheta^P_{\overline{\mathcal{B}}}), (\theta^1_{\overline{\mathcal{B}}}, \theta^2_{\overline{\mathcal{B}}}, \ldots, \theta^P_{\overline{\mathcal{B}}})\rangle$ be two normalized NVNT-numbers and $r > 0$. Then, the generalized distance measures between $\overline{\mathcal{A}}$ and $\overline{\mathcal{B}}$, denoted by $\mathrm{d_r}(\overline{\mathcal{A}}, \overline{\mathcal{B}})$, is given below;

$$\begin{aligned}
\mathrm{d_r}(\overline{\mathcal{A}}, \overline{\mathcal{B}}) = \frac{1}{16\mathrm{p}}\cdot\Bigg(\sum_{i=1}^{p}\Big[&\big(|(1+\eta^{\mathrm{i}}_{\overline{\mathcal{A}}} - \vartheta^{\mathrm{i}}_{\overline{\mathcal{A}}} - \theta^{\mathrm{i}}_{\overline{\mathcal{A}}})\mathrm{a}_1 - (1+\eta^{\mathrm{i}}_{\overline{\mathcal{B}}} - \vartheta^{\mathrm{i}}_{\overline{\mathcal{B}}} - \theta^{\mathrm{i}}_{\overline{\mathcal{B}}})\mathrm{a}_2|\big)^r + \\
&\big(|(1+\eta^{\mathrm{i}}_{\overline{\mathcal{A}}} - \vartheta^{\mathrm{i}}_{\overline{\mathcal{A}}} - \theta^{\mathrm{i}}_{\overline{\mathcal{A}}})\mathrm{b}_1 - (1+\eta^{\mathrm{i}}_{\overline{\mathcal{B}}} - \vartheta^{\mathrm{i}}_{\overline{\mathcal{B}}} - \theta^{\mathrm{i}}_{\overline{\mathcal{B}}})\mathrm{b}_2|\big)^r + \\
&\big(|(1+\eta^{\mathrm{i}}_{\overline{\mathcal{A}}} - \vartheta^{\mathrm{i}}_{\overline{\mathcal{A}}} - \theta^{\mathrm{i}}_{\overline{\mathcal{A}}})\mathrm{c}_1 - (1+\eta^{\mathrm{i}}_{\overline{\mathcal{B}}} - \vartheta^{\mathrm{i}}_{\overline{\mathcal{B}}} - \theta^{\mathrm{i}}_{\overline{\mathcal{B}}})\mathrm{c}_2|\big)^r + \\
&\big(|(1+\eta^{\mathrm{i}}_{\overline{\mathcal{A}}} - \vartheta^{\mathrm{i}}_{\overline{\mathcal{A}}} - \theta^{\mathrm{i}}_{\overline{\mathcal{A}}})\mathrm{d}_1 - (1+\eta^{\mathrm{i}}_{\overline{\mathcal{B}}} - \vartheta^{\mathrm{i}}_{\overline{\mathcal{B}}} - \theta^{\mathrm{i}}_{\overline{\mathcal{B}}})\mathrm{d}_2|\big)^r\Bigg)^{\frac{1}{r}}
\end{aligned} \tag{6}$$

For r = 1, the Eq. 6 is given as;

$$\begin{aligned}
\mathrm{d_1}(\overline{\mathcal{A}}, \overline{\mathcal{B}}) = \frac{1}{16\mathrm{p}}\cdot\sum_{i=1}^{p}\Big[&|(1+\eta^{\mathrm{i}}_{\overline{\mathcal{A}}} - \vartheta^{\mathrm{i}}_{\overline{\mathcal{A}}} - \theta^{\mathrm{i}}_{\overline{\mathcal{A}}})\mathrm{a}_1 - (1+\eta^{\mathrm{i}}_{\overline{\mathcal{B}}} - \vartheta^{\mathrm{i}}_{\overline{\mathcal{B}}} - \theta^{\mathrm{i}}_{\overline{\mathcal{B}}})\mathrm{a}_2| + \\
&|(1+\eta^{\mathrm{i}}_{\overline{\mathcal{A}}} - \vartheta^{\mathrm{i}}_{\overline{\mathcal{A}}} - \theta^{\mathrm{i}}_{\overline{\mathcal{A}}})\mathrm{b}_1 - (1+\eta^{\mathrm{i}}_{\overline{\mathcal{B}}} - \vartheta^{\mathrm{i}}_{\overline{\mathcal{B}}} - \theta^{\mathrm{i}}_{\overline{\mathcal{B}}})\mathrm{b}_2| + \\
&|(1+\eta^{\mathrm{i}}_{\overline{\mathcal{A}}} - \vartheta^{\mathrm{i}}_{\overline{\mathcal{A}}} - \theta^{\mathrm{i}}_{\overline{\mathcal{A}}})\mathrm{c}_1 - (1+\eta^{\mathrm{i}}_{\overline{\mathcal{B}}} - \vartheta^{\mathrm{i}}_{\overline{\mathcal{B}}} - \theta^{\mathrm{i}}_{\overline{\mathcal{B}}})\mathrm{c}_2| + \\
&|(1+\eta^{\mathrm{i}}_{\overline{\mathcal{A}}} - \vartheta^{\mathrm{i}}_{\overline{\mathcal{A}}} - \theta^{\mathrm{i}}_{\overline{\mathcal{A}}})\mathrm{d}_1 - (1+\eta^{\mathrm{i}}_{\overline{\mathcal{B}}} - \vartheta^{\mathrm{i}}_{\overline{\mathcal{B}}} - \theta^{\mathrm{i}}_{\overline{\mathcal{B}}})\mathrm{d}_2|\Big]
\end{aligned} \tag{7}$$

$$\begin{aligned}
\mathrm{d_2}(\overline{\mathcal{A}}, \overline{\mathcal{B}}) = \frac{1}{16\mathrm{p}}\cdot\sum_{i=1}^{p}\Big[&\big((1+\eta^{\mathrm{i}}_{\overline{\mathcal{A}}} - \vartheta^{i}_{\overline{\mathcal{A}}} - \theta^{\mathrm{i}}_{\overline{\mathcal{A}}})\mathrm{a}_1 - (1+\eta^{\mathrm{i}}_{\overline{\mathcal{B}}} - \vartheta^{i}_{\overline{\mathcal{B}}} - \theta^{\mathrm{i}}_{\overline{\mathcal{B}}})\mathrm{a}_2\big)^2 + \\
&\big((1+\eta^{i}_{\bar{\mathcal{A}}} - \vartheta^{i}_{\bar{\mathcal{A}}} - \theta^{i}_{\bar{\mathcal{A}}})b_1 - (1+\eta^{i}_{\overline{\mathcal{B}}} - \vartheta^{i}_{\overline{\mathcal{B}}} - \theta^{i}_{\overline{\mathcal{B}}})b_2\big)^2 + \\
&\big((1+\eta^{i}_{\bar{\mathcal{A}}} - \vartheta^{i}_{\bar{\mathcal{A}}} - \theta^{i}_{\bar{\mathcal{A}}})c_1 - (1+\eta^{i}_{\overline{\mathcal{B}}} - \vartheta^{i}_{\overline{\mathcal{B}}} - \theta^{i}_{\overline{\mathcal{B}}})c_2\big)^2 + \\
&\big((1+\eta^{i}_{\bar{\mathcal{A}}} - \vartheta^{i}_{\bar{\mathcal{A}}} - \theta^{i}_{\bar{\mathcal{A}}})d_1 - (1+\eta^{i}_{\overline{\mathcal{B}}} - \vartheta^{i}_{\overline{\mathcal{B}}} - \theta^{i}_{\overline{\mathcal{B}}})d_2\big)^2\Big]^{\frac{1}{2}}
\end{aligned} \tag{8}$$

Example 3.2 Let $\overline{\mathcal{A}}$=$\langle [0.2, 0.3, 0.5, 0.8]; (0.1, 0.3, 0.6, 0.8), (0.2, 0.5, 0.4, 0.3), (0.5, 0.6, 0.3, 0.1)\rangle$ and $\overline{\mathcal{B}} = \langle [0.1, 0.4, 0.6, 0.7]; (0.4, 0.5, 0.7, 0.8), (0.1, 0.2, 0.3, 0.5), (0.2, 0.3, 0.4, 0.5)\rangle$ be two normalized NVNT-numbers then, the measure $\mathbf{d}_2(\overline{\mathcal{A}}, \overline{\mathcal{B}})$ between $\overline{\mathcal{A}}$ and $\overline{\mathcal{B}}$ are found below;

$$d_2(\overline{\mathcal{A}}, \overline{\mathcal{B}}) = \frac{1}{64}.\Big[((1+0.1-0.2-0.5)0.2-(1+0.4-0.1-0.2)0.1)^2 + ((1+0.3-0.5-0.6)0.2$$

$$((1+0.3-0.5-0.6)0.2$$

$$-(1+0.5-0.2-0.3)0.1)^2 + ((1+0.6-0.4-0.3)0.2-(1+0.7-0.3-0.4)0.1)^2$$

$$((1+0.8-0.3-0.1)0.2-(1+0.8-0.5-0.5)0.1)^2 + ((1+0.1-0.2-0.5)0.3$$

$$-(1+0.4-0.1-0.2)0.4)^2 + ((1+0.3-0.5-0.6)0.3-(1+0.5-0.2-0.3)0.4)^2 +$$

$$((1+0.6-0.4-0.3)0.3-(1+0.7-0.3-0.4)0.4)^2 + ((1+0.8-0.3-0.1)0.3-$$

$$(1+0.8-0.5-0.5)0.4)^2 + ((1+0.1-0.2-0.5)0.5-(1+0.4-0.1-0.2)0.6)^2 +$$

$$((1+0.3-0.5-0.6)0.5-(1+0.5-0.2-0.3)0.6)^2 + ((1+0.6-0.4-0.3)0.5-$$

$$-(1+0.7-0.3-0.4)0.6)^2 + ((1+0.8-0.3-0.1)0.5-(1+0.8-0.5-0.5)0.6)^2 +$$

$$((1+0.1-0.2-0.5)0.8-(1+0.4-0.1-0.2)0.7)^2 + ((1+0.3-0.5-0.6)0.8-$$

$$-(1+0.5-0.2-0.3)0.7)^2 + ((1+0.6-0.4-0.3)0.8-(1+0.7-0.3-0.4)0.7)^2$$

$$((1+0.8-0.3-0.1)0.8-(1+0.8-0.5-0.5)0.7)^2\Big]^{1/2}$$

$$= 0.1599$$

Theorem 3.3 Let $\bar{\mathcal{A}} = \left\langle (a_1, b_1, c_1, d_1); \left(\eta^1_{\bar{\mathcal{A}}}, \eta^2_{\bar{\mathcal{A}}}, \ldots, \eta^P_{\bar{\mathcal{A}}}\right)\left(\vartheta^1_{\bar{\mathcal{A}}}, \vartheta^2_{\bar{\mathcal{A}}}, \ldots, \vartheta^P_{\bar{\mathcal{A}}}\right), \left(\theta^1_{\bar{\mathcal{A}}}, \theta^2_{\bar{\mathcal{A}}}, \ldots, \theta^P_{\bar{\mathcal{A}}}\right)\right\rangle, \bar{\mathcal{B}} = (a_2, b_2, c_2, d_2); \left(\eta^1_{\bar{\mathcal{B}}}, \eta^2_{\bar{\mathcal{B}}}, \ldots, \eta^P_{\bar{\mathcal{B}}}\right), \left(\vartheta^1_{\bar{\mathcal{B}}}, \vartheta^2_{\bar{\mathcal{B}}}, \ldots, \vartheta^P_{\bar{\mathcal{B}}}\right), \left(\theta^1_{\bar{\mathcal{B}}}, \theta^2_{\bar{\mathcal{B}}}, \ldots, \theta^P_{\bar{\mathcal{B}}}\right)$ and $\bar{\mathcal{C}} = (a_3, b_3, c_3, d_3); \left(\eta^1_{\bar{\mathcal{C}}}, \eta^2_{\bar{\mathcal{C}}}, \ldots, \eta^P_{\bar{\mathcal{C}}}\right), \left(\vartheta^1_{\bar{\mathcal{C}}}, \vartheta^2_{\bar{\mathcal{C}}}, \ldots, \vartheta^P_{\mathcal{C}}\right),, \left(\theta^1_{\bar{\mathcal{C}}}, \theta^2_{\bar{\mathcal{C}}}, \ldots, \theta^P_{\bar{\mathcal{C}}}\right)$ be three normalized NVNT-numbers. Then, $d_r(\overline{\mathcal{A}}, \overline{\mathcal{B}})$ satisfies the following properties:

i. $0 \leq d_r(\overline{\mathcal{A}}, \overline{\mathcal{B}}) \leq 1$,
ii. $\overline{\mathcal{A}} = \overline{\mathcal{B}} \Rightarrow d_r(\overline{\mathcal{A}}, \overline{\mathcal{B}}) = 0$,
iii. $d_r(\overline{\mathcal{A}}, \overline{\mathcal{B}}) = d_r(\overline{\mathcal{B}}, \overline{\mathcal{A}})$,
iv. $d_r(\overline{\mathcal{A}}, \overline{\mathcal{B}}) \leq d_r(\overline{\mathcal{A}}, \overline{\mathcal{C}}) + d_r(\overline{\mathcal{C}}, \overline{\mathcal{B}})$.

Proof $\bar{\mathcal{A}} = \left\langle (a_1, b_1, c_1, d_1); \left(\eta^1_{\bar{\mathcal{A}}}, \eta^2_{\bar{\mathcal{A}}}, \ldots, \eta^P_{\bar{\mathcal{A}}}\right), \left(\vartheta^1_{\bar{\mathcal{A}}}, \vartheta^2_{\bar{\mathcal{A}}}, \ldots, \vartheta^P_{\bar{\mathcal{A}}}\right), \left(\theta^1_{\bar{\mathcal{A}}}, \theta^2_{\bar{\mathcal{A}}}, \ldots, \theta^P_{\bar{\mathcal{A}}}\right)\right\rangle$, $\overline{\mathcal{B}} = \left\langle (a_2, b_2, c_2, d_2); \left(\eta^1_{\bar{\mathcal{B}}}, \eta^2_{\bar{\mathcal{B}}}, \ldots, \eta^P_{\bar{\mathcal{B}}}\right), \left(\vartheta^1_{\bar{\mathcal{B}}}, \vartheta^2_{\bar{\mathcal{B}}}, \ldots, \vartheta^P_{\bar{\mathcal{B}}}\right), \left(\theta^1_{\bar{\mathcal{B}}}, \theta^2_{\bar{\mathcal{B}}}, \ldots, \theta^P_{\bar{\mathcal{B}}}\right)\right\rangle$ and $\overline{\mathcal{C}} = \left\langle (a_3, b_3, c_3, d_3); \left(\eta^1_{\bar{\mathcal{C}}}, \eta^2_{\bar{\mathcal{C}}}, \ldots, \eta^P_{\bar{\mathcal{C}}}\right), \left(\vartheta^1_{\bar{\mathcal{C}}}, \vartheta^2_{\bar{\mathcal{C}}}, \ldots, \vartheta^P_{\mathcal{C}}\right), \left(\theta^1_{\bar{\mathcal{C}}}, \theta^2_{\bar{\mathcal{C}}}, \ldots, \theta^P_{\bar{\mathcal{C}}}\right)\right\rangle$ be three normalized NVNT-numbers. Then,

i. It is obvious from the above Definition 3.1 that $0 \leq d(\overline{\mathcal{A}}, \overline{\mathcal{B}}) \leq 1$ for all NVNT−numbers.

ii. When $\overline{\mathcal{A}}$ and $\overline{\mathcal{B}}$ are equal then $a_1 = a_2$, $b_1 = b_2$, $c_1 = c_2$, $d_1 = d_2$, $\eta^i_{\bar{\mathcal{A}}} = \eta^i_{\bar{\mathcal{B}}}$, $\vartheta^i_{\bar{\mathcal{A}}} = \vartheta^i_{\bar{\mathcal{B}}}$, and $\theta^i_{\overline{\mathcal{A}}} = \theta^i_{\overline{\mathcal{B}}}$.

$$d_r(\overline{\mathcal{A}}, \overline{\mathcal{B}}) = \frac{1}{16p}\cdot\sum_{i=1}^{p}\Big[\big(\big|(1+\eta^i_{\bar{\mathcal{A}}}-\vartheta^i_{\bar{\mathcal{A}}}-\theta^i_{\bar{\mathcal{A}}})a_1-(1+\eta^i_{\bar{\mathcal{B}}}-\vartheta^i_{\bar{\mathcal{B}}}-\theta^i_{\bar{\mathcal{B}}})a_2\big|\big)^r+$$
$$\big(\big|(1+\eta^i_{\bar{\mathcal{A}}}-\vartheta^i_{\bar{\mathcal{A}}}-\theta^i_{\bar{\mathcal{A}}})b_1-(1+\eta^i_{\bar{\mathcal{B}}}-\vartheta^i_{\bar{\mathcal{B}}}-\theta^i_{\bar{\mathcal{B}}})b_2\big|\big)^r+$$
$$\big(\big|(1+\eta^i_{\bar{\mathcal{A}}}-\vartheta^i_{\bar{\mathcal{A}}}-\theta^i_{\bar{\mathcal{A}}})c_1-(1+\eta^i_{\bar{\mathcal{B}}}-\vartheta^i_{\bar{\mathcal{B}}}-\theta^i_{\bar{\mathcal{B}}})c_2\big|\big)^r+$$
$$\big(\big|(1+\eta^i_{\bar{\mathcal{A}}}-\vartheta^i_{\bar{\mathcal{A}}}-\theta^i_{\bar{\mathcal{A}}})d_1-(1+\eta^i_{\bar{\mathcal{B}}}-\vartheta^i_{\bar{\mathcal{B}}}-\theta^i_{\bar{\mathcal{B}}})d_2\big|\big)^r\Big]^{\frac{1}{r}}$$

$$= \frac{1}{16\mathrm{p}}\cdot\sum_{i=1}^{\mathrm{p}}\Big[\Big(\big|(1+\eta^i_{\bar{\mathcal{A}}}-\vartheta^i_{\bar{\mathcal{A}}}-\theta^i_{\bar{\mathcal{A}}})a_2-\big(1+\eta^i_{1\bar{\mathcal{A}}}-\vartheta^i_{\bar{\mathcal{A}}}-\theta^i_{\bar{\mathcal{A}}}\big)a_2\big|\Big)^r+.$$
$$\big(\big|(1+\eta^i_{\bar{\mathcal{A}}}-\vartheta^i_{\bar{\mathcal{A}}}-\theta^i_{\bar{\mathcal{A}}})\mathrm{b}_2-(1+\eta^i_{\bar{\mathcal{A}}}-\vartheta^i_{\bar{\mathcal{A}}}-\theta^i_{\bar{\mathcal{A}}})\mathrm{b}_2\big|\big)^r+$$
$$\big(\big|(1+\eta^i_{\bar{\mathcal{A}}}-\vartheta^i_{\bar{\mathcal{A}}}-\theta^i_{\bar{\mathcal{A}}})\mathrm{c}_2-(1+\eta^i_{\bar{\mathcal{A}}}-\vartheta^i_{\bar{\mathcal{A}}}-\theta^i_{\bar{\mathcal{A}}})\mathrm{c}_2\big|\big)^r+$$
$$\big(\big|(1+\eta^i_{\bar{\mathcal{A}}}-\vartheta^i_{\bar{\mathcal{A}}}-\theta^i_{\bar{\mathcal{A}}})\mathrm{d}_2-(1+\eta^i_{\bar{\mathcal{A}}}-\vartheta^i_{\bar{\mathcal{A}}}-\theta^i_{\bar{\mathcal{A}}})\mathrm{d}_2\big|\big)^r\Big]^{\frac{1}{r}}=0$$

iii. Assume that $\mathrm{d}_2(\overline{\mathcal{A}}, \overline{\mathcal{B}})$ be a generalized distance measure between $\overline{\mathcal{A}}$ and $\overline{\mathcal{B}}$. then

$$\mathrm{d_r}(\bar{\mathcal{A}}, \bar{\mathcal{B}}) = \frac{1}{16\mathrm{p}}\cdot\sum_{i=1}^{\mathrm{p}}\Big[\big(\big|(1+\eta^i_{\bar{\mathcal{A}}}-\vartheta^i_{\bar{\mathcal{A}}}-\theta^i_{\bar{\mathcal{A}}})\mathrm{a}_1-(1+\eta^i_{\bar{\mathcal{B}}}-\vartheta^i_{\bar{\mathcal{B}}}-\theta^i_{\bar{\mathcal{B}}})\mathrm{a}_2\big|\big)^r+$$
$$\big(\big|(1+\eta^i_{\bar{\mathcal{A}}}-\vartheta^i_{\bar{\mathcal{A}}}-\theta^i_{\bar{\mathcal{A}}})\mathrm{b}_1-(1+\eta^i_{\bar{\mathcal{B}}}-\vartheta^i_{\bar{\mathcal{B}}}-\theta^i_{\bar{\mathcal{B}}})\mathrm{b}_2\big|\big)^r+$$
$$\big(\big|(1+\eta^i_{\bar{\mathcal{A}}}-\vartheta^i_{\bar{\mathcal{A}}}-\theta^i_{\bar{\mathcal{A}}})c_1-(1+\eta^i_{\bar{\mathcal{B}}}-\vartheta^i_{\bar{\mathcal{B}}}-\theta^i_{\bar{\mathcal{B}}})c_2\big|\big)^r+$$
$$\big(\big|(1+\eta^i_{\bar{\mathcal{A}}}-\vartheta^i_{\bar{\mathcal{A}}}-\theta^i_{\bar{\mathcal{A}}})\mathrm{d}_1-(1+\eta^i_{\bar{\mathcal{B}}}-\vartheta^i_{\bar{\mathcal{B}}}-\theta^i_{\bar{\mathcal{B}}})\mathrm{d}_2\big|\big)^r\Big]^{\frac{1}{r}}$$

$$= \frac{1}{16p}\cdot\sum_{i=1}^{p}\Big[\big(\big|(1+\eta^i_{\bar{\mathcal{B}}}-\vartheta^i_{\bar{\mathcal{B}}}-\theta^i_{\bar{\mathcal{B}}})a_2-(1+\eta^i_{\bar{\mathcal{A}}}-\vartheta^i_{\bar{\mathcal{A}}}-\theta^i_{\bar{\mathcal{A}}})a_1\big|\big)^r+$$
$$\big(\big|(1+\eta^{\mathrm{i}}_{\overline{\mathcal{B}}}-\vartheta^{\mathrm{i}}_{\overline{\mathcal{B}}}-\theta^{\mathrm{i}}_{\overline{\mathcal{B}}})\mathrm{b}_2-(1+\eta^{\mathrm{i}}_{\overline{\mathcal{A}}}-\vartheta^{\mathrm{i}}_{\overline{\mathcal{A}}}-\theta^{\mathrm{i}}_{\overline{\mathcal{A}}})\mathrm{b}_1\big|\big)^r+$$

$$\left(\left|(1+\eta^{i}_{\overline{\mathcal{B}}}-\vartheta^{i}_{\overline{\mathcal{B}}}-\theta^{i}_{\overline{\mathcal{B}}})c_2-(1+\eta^{i}_{\overline{\mathcal{A}}}-\vartheta^{i}_{\overline{\mathcal{A}}}-\theta^{i}_{\overline{\mathcal{A}}})c_1\right|\right)^r+$$

$$\left(\left|(1+\eta^{i}_{\overline{\mathcal{B}}}-\vartheta^{i}_{\overline{\mathcal{B}}}-\theta^{i}_{\overline{\mathcal{B}}})d_2-(1+\eta^{i}_{\overline{\mathcal{A}}}-\vartheta^{i}_{\overline{\mathcal{A}}}-\theta^{i}_{\overline{\mathcal{A}}})d_1\right|\right)^r\Bigg]^{\frac{1}{r}}=d_r(\overline{\mathcal{B}},\overline{\mathcal{A}})$$

iv.

$$d_r(\overline{\mathcal{A}},\overline{\mathcal{B}})=\frac{1}{16p}\sum_{i=1}^{p}\left[\begin{pmatrix}\left(1+\eta^{i}_{\overline{\mathcal{A}}}-\vartheta^{i}_{\overline{\mathcal{A}}}-\theta^{i}_{\overline{\mathcal{A}}}\right)a_1-\left(1+\eta^{i}_{\overline{\mathcal{C}}}-\vartheta^{i}_{\overline{\mathcal{C}}}-\theta^{i}_{\overline{\mathcal{C}}}\right)a_3+\\\left(1+\eta^{i}_{\overline{\mathcal{C}}}-\vartheta^{i}_{\overline{\mathcal{C}}}-\theta^{i}_{\overline{\mathcal{C}}}\right)a_3-(1+\eta^{i}_{\overline{\mathcal{B}}}-\vartheta^{i}_{\overline{\mathcal{B}}}-\theta^{i}_{\overline{\mathcal{B}}})a_2\end{pmatrix}^r\right.$$

$$\begin{pmatrix}\left(1+\eta^{i}_{\overline{\mathcal{A}}}-\vartheta^{i}_{\overline{\mathcal{A}}}-\theta^{i}_{\overline{\mathcal{A}}}\right)b_1-\left(1+\eta^{i}_{\overline{\mathcal{C}}}-\vartheta^{i}_{\overline{\mathcal{C}}}-\theta^{i}_{\overline{\mathcal{C}}}\right)b_3+\\(1+\eta^{i}_{\overline{\mathcal{C}}}-\vartheta^{i}_{\overline{\mathcal{C}}}-\theta^{i}_{\overline{\mathcal{C}}})b_3-(1+\eta^{i}_{\overline{\mathcal{B}}}-\vartheta^{i}_{\overline{\mathcal{B}}}-\theta^{i}_{\overline{\mathcal{B}}})b_2\end{pmatrix}^r+$$

$$\begin{pmatrix}\left(1+\eta^{i}_{\overline{\mathcal{A}}}-\vartheta^{i}_{\overline{\mathcal{A}}}-\theta^{i}_{\overline{\mathcal{A}}}\right)c_1-\left(1+\eta^{i}_{\overline{\mathcal{C}}}-\vartheta^{i}_{\overline{\mathcal{C}}}-\theta^{i}_{\overline{\mathcal{C}}}\right)c_3+\\\left(1+\eta^{i}_{\overline{\mathcal{C}}}-\vartheta^{i}_{\overline{\mathcal{C}}}-\theta^{i}_{\overline{\mathcal{C}}}\right)c_3-(1+\eta^{i}_{\overline{\mathcal{B}}}-\vartheta^{i}_{\overline{\mathcal{B}}}-\theta^{i}_{\overline{\mathcal{B}}})c_2\end{pmatrix}^r+$$

$$\left.\begin{pmatrix}\left(1+\eta^{i}_{\overline{\mathcal{A}}}-\vartheta^{i}_{\overline{\mathcal{A}}}-\theta^{i}_{\overline{\mathcal{A}}}\right)d_1-\left(1+\eta^{i}_{\overline{\mathcal{C}}}-\vartheta^{i}_{\overline{\mathcal{C}}}-\theta^{i}_{\overline{\mathcal{C}}}\right)d_3+\\(1+\eta^{i}_{\overline{\mathcal{C}}}-\vartheta^{i}_{\overline{\mathcal{C}}}-\theta^{i}_{\overline{\mathcal{C}}})d_3-(1+\eta^{i}_{\overline{\mathcal{B}}}-\vartheta^{i}_{\overline{\mathcal{B}}}-\theta^{i}_{\overline{\mathcal{B}}})d_2\end{pmatrix}^r\right]^{\frac{1}{r}}$$

$$\le\frac{1}{16p}\sum_{i=1}^{p}\Big[\left((1+\eta^{i}_{\overline{\mathcal{A}}}-\vartheta^{i}_{\overline{\mathcal{A}}}-\theta^{i}_{\overline{\mathcal{A}}})a_1-(1+\eta^{i}_{\overline{\mathcal{C}}}-\vartheta^{i}_{\overline{\mathcal{C}}}-\theta^{i}_{\overline{\mathcal{C}}})a_3\right)^r+$$

$$\left((1+\eta^{i}_{\overline{\mathcal{A}}}-\vartheta^{i}_{\overline{\mathcal{A}}}-\theta^{i}_{\overline{\mathcal{A}}})b_1-(1+\eta^{i}_{\overline{\mathcal{C}}}-\vartheta^{i}_{\overline{\mathcal{C}}}-\theta^{i}_{\overline{\mathcal{C}}})b_3\right)^r$$

$$\left((1+\eta^{i}_{\overline{\mathcal{A}}}-\vartheta^{i}_{\overline{\mathcal{A}}}-\theta^{i}_{\overline{\mathcal{A}}})c_1-(1+\eta^{i}_{\overline{\mathcal{C}}}-\vartheta^{i}_{\overline{\mathcal{C}}}-\theta^{i}_{\overline{\mathcal{C}}})c_3\right)^r$$

$$+\left((1+\eta^{i}_{\overline{\mathcal{A}}}-\vartheta^{i}_{\overline{\mathcal{A}}}-\theta^{i}_{\overline{\mathcal{A}}})d_1-(1+\eta^{i}_{\overline{\mathcal{C}}}-\vartheta^{i}_{\overline{\mathcal{C}}}-\theta^{i}_{\overline{\mathcal{C}}})d_3\right)^r\Big]^{\frac{1}{r}}$$

$$+\frac{1}{16p}\sum_{i=1}^{p}\Big[\left((1+\eta^{i}_{\overline{\mathcal{C}}}-\vartheta^{i}_{\overline{\mathcal{C}}}-\theta^{i}_{\overline{\mathcal{C}}})a_3-(1+\eta^{i}_{\overline{\mathcal{B}}}-\vartheta^{i}_{\overline{\mathcal{B}}}-\theta^{i}_{\overline{\mathcal{B}}})a_2\right)^r$$

$$+\left((1+\eta^{i}_{\overline{\mathcal{C}}}-\vartheta^{i}_{\overline{\mathcal{C}}}-\theta^{i}_{\overline{\mathcal{C}}})b_3-(1+\eta^{i}_{\overline{\mathcal{B}}}-\vartheta^{i}_{\overline{\mathcal{B}}}-\theta^{i}_{\overline{\mathcal{B}}})b_2\right)^r$$

$$\left((1+\eta^{i}_{\overline{\mathcal{C}}}-\vartheta^{i}_{\overline{\mathcal{C}}}-\theta^{i}_{\overline{\mathcal{C}}})c_3-(1+\eta^{i}_{\overline{\mathcal{B}}}-\vartheta^{i}_{\overline{\mathcal{B}}}-\theta^{i}_{\overline{\mathcal{B}}})c_2\right)^r$$

$$+\left((1+\eta^{i}_{\overline{\mathcal{C}}}-\vartheta^{i}_{\overline{\mathcal{C}}}-\theta^{i}_{\overline{\mathcal{C}}})d_3-(1+\eta^{i}_{\overline{\mathcal{B}}}-\vartheta^{i}_{\overline{\mathcal{B}}}-\theta^{i}_{\overline{\mathcal{B}}})d_2\right)^r\Big]^{\frac{1}{r}}$$

$$\le d_r(\overline{\mathcal{A}},\overline{\mathcal{C}})+d_r(\overline{\mathcal{C}},\overline{\mathcal{B}}).$$

Definition 3.4 Let $\bar{A}=\langle[a_1,b_1,c_1,d_1];(\eta^1_{\bar{\mathcal{A}}},\eta^2_{\bar{\mathcal{A}}},\ldots,\eta^P_{\bar{\mathcal{A}}}),(\vartheta^1_{\bar{\mathcal{A}}},\vartheta^2_{\bar{\mathcal{A}}},\ldots,\vartheta^P_{\bar{\mathcal{A}}}),(\theta^1_{\bar{\mathcal{A}}},\theta^2_{\bar{\mathcal{A}}},\ldots,\theta^P_{\bar{\mathcal{A}}})\rangle$ and $\overline{\mathcal{B}}=\langle[a_2,b_2,c_2,d_2];(\eta^1_{\overline{\mathcal{B}}},\eta^2_{\overline{\mathcal{B}}},\ldots,\eta^P_{\overline{\mathcal{B}}}),(\vartheta^1_{\overline{\mathcal{B}}},\vartheta^2_{\overline{\mathcal{B}}},\ldots,\vartheta^P_{\overline{\mathcal{B}}}),$

$\left(\theta^1_{\overline{\mathcal{B}}}, \theta^2_{\overline{\mathcal{B}}}, \ldots, \theta^P_{\overline{\mathcal{B}}}\right)\rangle$ be two normalized NVNT-numbers then, respectively, the weighted Hamming and Euclidean distance measures between $\overline{\mathcal{A}}$ and $\overline{\mathcal{B}}$ are given below;

$$\begin{aligned} d_r^w(\overline{\mathcal{A}}, \overline{\mathcal{B}}) = \frac{1}{16p}.(\sum_{i=1}^{p}\Big[\Big(|w_{\overline{\mathcal{A}}}\Big(1+\eta^i_{\overline{\mathcal{A}}}-\vartheta^i_{\overline{\mathcal{A}}}-\theta^i_{\overline{\mathcal{A}}}\Big)a_1 - w_{\overline{\mathcal{B}}}\Big(1+\eta^i_{\overline{\mathcal{B}}}-\vartheta^i_{\overline{\mathcal{B}}}-\theta^i_{\overline{\mathcal{B}}}\Big)a_2|\Big)^r + \\ \Big(|w_{\overline{\mathcal{A}}}(1+\eta^i_{\overline{\mathcal{A}}}-\vartheta^i_{\overline{\mathcal{A}}}-\theta^i_{\overline{\mathcal{A}}})b_1 - w_{\overline{\mathcal{B}}}(1+\eta^i_{\overline{\mathcal{B}}}-\vartheta^i_{\overline{\mathcal{B}}}-\theta^i_{\overline{\mathcal{B}}})b_2|\Big)^r + \\ \Big(|w_{\overline{\mathcal{A}}}(1+\eta^i_{\overline{\mathcal{A}}}-\vartheta^i_{\overline{\mathcal{A}}}-\theta^i_{\overline{\mathcal{A}}})c_1 - w_{\overline{\mathcal{B}}}(1+\eta^i_{\overline{\mathcal{B}}}-\vartheta^i_{\overline{\mathcal{B}}}-\theta^i_{\overline{\mathcal{B}}})c_2|\Big)^r + \\ \Big(|w_{\overline{\mathcal{A}}}(1+\eta^i_{\overline{\mathcal{A}}}-\vartheta^i_{\overline{\mathcal{A}}}-\theta^i_{\overline{\mathcal{A}}})d_1 - w_{\overline{\mathcal{B}}}(1+\eta^i_{\overline{\mathcal{B}}}-\vartheta^i_{\overline{\mathcal{B}}}-\theta^i_{\overline{\mathcal{B}}})d_2|\Big)^r\Big])^{\frac{1}{r}} \end{aligned} \tag{9}$$

For r = 1, the equation 9 is given as;

$$\begin{aligned} d_1^w(\overline{\mathcal{A}}, \overline{\mathcal{B}}) = \frac{1}{16p}.\sum_{i=1}^{p}[|w_{\overline{\mathcal{A}}}(1+\eta^i_{\overline{\mathcal{A}}}-\vartheta^i_{\overline{\mathcal{A}}}-\theta^i_{\overline{\mathcal{A}}})a_1 - w_{\overline{\mathcal{B}}}(1+\eta^i_{\overline{\mathcal{B}}}-\vartheta^i_{\overline{\mathcal{B}}}-\theta^i_{\overline{\mathcal{B}}})a_2| + \\ |w_{\overline{\mathcal{A}}}(1+\eta^i_{\overline{\mathcal{A}}}-\vartheta^i_{\overline{\mathcal{A}}}-\theta^i_{\overline{\mathcal{A}}})b_1 - w_{\overline{\mathcal{B}}}(1+\eta^i_{\overline{\mathcal{B}}}-\vartheta^i_{\overline{\mathcal{B}}}-\theta^i_{\overline{\mathcal{B}}})b_2| + \\ |w_{\overline{\mathcal{A}}}(1+\eta^i_{\overline{\mathcal{A}}}-\vartheta^i_{\overline{\mathcal{A}}}-\theta^i_{\overline{\mathcal{A}}})c_1 - w_{\overline{\mathcal{B}}}(1+\eta^i_{\overline{\mathcal{B}}}-\vartheta^i_{\overline{\mathcal{B}}}-\theta^i_{\overline{\mathcal{B}}})c_2| + \\ |w_{\overline{\mathcal{A}}}(1+\eta^i_{\overline{\mathcal{A}}}-\vartheta^i_{\overline{\mathcal{A}}}-\theta^i_{\overline{\mathcal{A}}})d_1 - w_{\overline{\mathcal{B}}}(1+\eta^i_{\overline{\mathcal{B}}}-\vartheta^i_{\overline{\mathcal{B}}}-\theta^i_{\overline{\mathcal{B}}})d_2|] \end{aligned} \tag{10}$$

For r = 2, the Eq. 9 is given as;

$$\begin{aligned} d_2^w(\overline{\mathcal{A}}, \overline{\mathcal{B}}) = \frac{1}{16p}.\sum_{i=1}^{p}\Big[\Big(w_{\overline{\mathcal{A}}}(1+\eta^i_{\overline{\mathcal{A}}}-\vartheta^i_{\overline{\mathcal{A}}}-\theta^i_{\overline{\mathcal{A}}})a_1 - w_{\overline{\mathcal{B}}}(1+\eta^i_{\overline{\mathcal{B}}}-\vartheta^i_{\overline{\mathcal{B}}}-\theta^i_{\overline{\mathcal{B}}})a_2\Big)^2 + \\ \Big(w_{\overline{\mathcal{A}}}(1+\eta^i_{\overline{\mathcal{A}}}-\vartheta^i_{\overline{\mathcal{A}}}-\theta^i_{\overline{\mathcal{A}}})b_1 - w_{\overline{\mathcal{B}}}(1+\eta^i_{\overline{\mathcal{B}}}-\vartheta^i_{\overline{\mathcal{B}}}-\theta^i_{\overline{\mathcal{B}}})b_2\Big)^2 + \\ \Big(w_{\overline{\mathcal{A}}}(1+\eta^i_{\overline{\mathcal{A}}}-\vartheta^i_{\overline{\mathcal{A}}}-\theta^i_{\overline{\mathcal{A}}})c_1 - w_{\overline{\mathcal{B}}}(1+\eta^i_{\overline{\mathcal{B}}}-\vartheta^i_{\overline{\mathcal{B}}}-\theta^i_{\overline{\mathcal{B}}})c_2\Big)^2 + \\ \Big(w_{\overline{\mathcal{A}}}(1+\eta^i_{\overline{\mathcal{A}}}-\vartheta^i_{\overline{\mathcal{A}}}-\theta^i_{\overline{\mathcal{A}}})d_1 - w_{\overline{\mathcal{B}}}(1+\eta^i_{\overline{\mathcal{B}}}-\vartheta^i_{\overline{\mathcal{B}}}-\theta^i_{\overline{\mathcal{B}}})d_2\Big)^2\Big]^{\frac{1}{2}} \end{aligned} \tag{11}$$

Theorem 3.5 Let $\overline{\mathcal{A}} = \langle(a_1, b_1, c_1, d_1); \left(\eta^1_{\overline{\mathcal{A}}}, \eta^2_{\overline{\mathcal{A}}}, \ldots, \eta^P_{\overline{\mathcal{A}}}\right), \left(\vartheta^1_{\overline{\mathcal{A}}}, \vartheta^2_{\overline{\mathcal{A}}}, \ldots, \vartheta^P_{\overline{\mathcal{A}}}\right), \left(\theta^1_{\overline{\mathcal{A}}}, \theta^2_{\overline{\mathcal{A}}}, \ldots, \theta^P_{\overline{\mathcal{A}}}\right)\rangle$, $\overline{\mathcal{B}} = \langle(a_2, b_2, c_2, d_2); \left(\eta^1_{\overline{\mathcal{B}}}, \eta^2_{\overline{\mathcal{B}}}, \ldots, \eta^P_{\overline{\mathcal{B}}}\right), \left(\vartheta^1_{\overline{\mathcal{B}}}, \vartheta^2_{\overline{\mathcal{B}}}, \ldots, \vartheta^P_{\overline{\mathcal{B}}}\right), \left(\theta^1_{\overline{\mathcal{B}}}, \theta^2_{\overline{\mathcal{B}}}, \ldots, \theta^P_{\overline{\mathcal{B}}}\right)\rangle$and $\overline{\mathcal{C}} = \langle(a_3, b_3, c_3, d_3); \left(\eta^1_{\overline{\mathcal{C}}}, \eta^2_{\overline{\mathcal{C}}}, \ldots, \eta^P_{\overline{\mathcal{C}}}\right), \left(\vartheta^1_{\overline{\mathcal{C}}}, \vartheta^2_{\overline{\mathcal{C}}}, \ldots, \vartheta^P_{\overline{\mathcal{C}}}\right),$

$\left(\theta^1_{\overline{C}}, \theta^2_{\overline{C}}, \ldots, \theta^P_{\overline{C}}\right)\rangle$ be three normalized NVNT- numbers. Then, $d^w_r(\overline{\mathcal{A}}, \overline{\mathcal{B}})$ satisfies the following properties:

i. $0 \leq d^w_r(\overline{\mathcal{A}}, \overline{\mathcal{B}}) \leq 1$,
ii. $\overline{\mathcal{A}} = \overline{\mathcal{B}} \Rightarrow d^w_r(\overline{\mathcal{A}}, \overline{\mathcal{B}}) = 0$,
iii. $d^w_r(\overline{\mathcal{A}}, \overline{\mathcal{B}}) = d^w_r(\overline{\mathcal{B}}, \overline{\mathcal{A}})$,
iv. $d^w_r(\overline{\mathcal{A}}, \overline{\mathcal{B}}) \leq d^w_r(\overline{\mathcal{A}}, \overline{\mathcal{C}}) + d^w_r(\overline{\mathcal{C}}, \overline{\mathcal{B}})$.

Proof By similar proof manner of Theorem 3.3, we can prove $d^w_r(\overline{\mathcal{A}}, \overline{\mathcal{B}})$ which is not repeated here.

Definition 3.6 A real-valued function $\mathcal{E}_r : \boldsymbol{\mu} \rightarrow [0, 1]$ is called an entropy on NVNT-numbers if it satisfies the following properties:

$$\mathcal{EP}1.\mathcal{A} = \begin{cases} \langle [a, b, c, d]; (1,1, ..., 1), (0,0, ..., 0), (0,0, ..., 0)\rangle \\ \langle [a, b, c, d]; (0,0, ..., 0), (0,0, ..., 0), (1,1, ..., 1)\rangle \end{cases} \Rightarrow \mathcal{E}_r(\mathcal{A}) = 0;$$

$\mathcal{EP}2$. $\mathcal{E}_r(\mathcal{A}) = \mathcal{E}_r(\mathcal{A}^c)$ for all $\mathcal{A} \in$ NVNT-numbers, where

$$\mathcal{A}^c = \langle [a, b, c, d]; \left(\theta^1_{\mathcal{A}}, \theta^2_{\mathcal{A}}, \ldots, \theta^P_{\mathcal{A}}\right), \left(1 - \vartheta^1_{\mathcal{A}}, 1 - \vartheta^2_{\mathcal{A}}, \ldots, 1 - \vartheta^P_{\mathcal{A}}\right), \left(\eta^1_{\mathcal{A}}, \eta^2_{\mathcal{A}}, \ldots, \eta^P_{\mathcal{A}}\right)\rangle$$

$\mathcal{EP}3$. $d_r(\mathcal{A}, \mathcal{A}^-) = d_r(\mathcal{A}, \mathcal{A}^+) \iff \mathcal{E}_r(\mathcal{A}) = 1$ for all $\mathcal{A} \in$ NVNT-numbers, where $d_r(\mathcal{A}, \mathcal{A}^+)$ is a distance from $\mathcal{A}$ to $\mathcal{A}^+$ and $d_r(\mathcal{A}, \mathcal{A}^-)$ is a distance from $\mathcal{A}$ to $\mathcal{A}^-$;

$\mathcal{EP}4$. For all $\mathcal{A}, \mathcal{B} \in$ NVNT-numbers, if

$$\left|\frac{d_r(\mathcal{A}, \mathcal{A}^-)}{d_r(\mathcal{A}, \mathcal{A}^+) + d_r(\mathcal{A}, \mathcal{A}^-)} - \frac{1}{2}\right| \geq \left|\frac{d_r(\mathcal{B}, \mathcal{B}^-)}{d_r(\mathcal{B}, \mathcal{B}^+) + d_r(\mathcal{B}, \mathcal{B}^-)} - \frac{1}{2}\right| \tag{12}$$

then $\mathcal{E}(\mathcal{A}) \leq \mathcal{E}(\mathcal{B})$, where $d_r(\mathcal{B}, \mathcal{B}^+)$ is a distance from $\mathcal{B}$ to $\mathcal{B}^+$ and $d_r(\mathcal{B}, \mathcal{B}^-)$ is a distance from $\mathcal{B}$ to $\mathcal{B}^-$, where

$$\mathcal{A}^+ = \langle [a, b, c, d]; (1,1, ..., 1), (0,0, ..., 0), (0,0, ..., 0)\rangle$$

and

$$\mathcal{A}^- = \langle [a, b, c, d]; (0,0, \ldots, 0), (1,1, \ldots, 1), (1,1, \ldots, 1)\rangle.$$

Theorem 3.7 Assume that d_r is a distance measure for NVNT-numbers. Then, for any $\mathcal{A} \in$ NVNT-numbers,

$$\mathcal{E}_r(\mathcal{A}) = 1 - 2\left|\frac{d_r(\mathcal{A}, \mathcal{A}^-)}{d_r(\mathcal{A}, \mathcal{A}^+) + d_r(\mathcal{A}, \mathcal{A}^-)} - \frac{1}{2}\right| \tag{13}$$

is the entropy of NVNT-numbers based on TOPSIS.

Proof It is straightforward to prove that $\mathcal{E}_r(\mathcal{A})$ satisfies the four conditions $\mathcal{EP}1$-$\mathcal{EP}4$ in Definition 3.4.

i. If $\mathcal{A}$ is crisp set, that is,

$$\mathcal{A} = \begin{cases} \langle[\text{a, b, c, d}];\ (1,1,\ ...,\ 1),\ (0,0,\ ...,\ 0),\ (0,0,\ ...,\ 0)\rangle \\ \langle[\text{a, b, c, d}];\ (0,0,\ ...,\ 0),\ (0,0,\ ...,\ 0),\ (1,1,\ ...,\ 1)\rangle \end{cases} \Rightarrow \mathcal{E}_r(\mathcal{A}) = 0;$$

by using (7) equation, then we have;

$$\frac{\mathrm{d_r}(\mathcal{A}, \mathcal{A}^-)}{\mathrm{d_r}(\mathcal{A}, \mathcal{A}^+) + \mathrm{d_r}(\mathcal{A}, \mathcal{A}^-)} = 1\text{or}\frac{\mathrm{d_r}(\mathcal{A}, \mathcal{A}^-)}{\mathrm{d_r}(\mathcal{A}, \mathcal{A}^+) + \mathrm{d_r}(\mathcal{A}, \mathcal{A}^-)} = 0$$

so, $\mathcal{E}_r(\mathcal{A}) = 0$.

ii. $$\mathrm{d}_r\left(\mathcal{A}^c, \mathcal{A}^-\right) == \frac{1}{16p}\cdot\sum_{i=1}^{p}\Big[\left((1 + \theta^i_{\mathcal{A}} - 1 + \vartheta^i_{\mathcal{A}} - \eta^i_{\mathcal{A}})a - (1 + 0 - 1 - 1)a\right)^r +$$

$$\left((1 + \theta^i_{\mathcal{A}} - 1 + \vartheta^i_{\mathcal{A}} - \eta^i_{\mathcal{A}})\mathrm{b} - (1 + 0 - 1 - 1)\mathrm{b}\right)^r +$$

$$\left((1 + \theta^i_{\mathcal{A}} - 1 + \vartheta^i_{\mathcal{A}} - \eta^i_{\mathcal{A}})\mathrm{c} - (1 + 0 - 1 - 1)\mathrm{c}\right)^r +$$

$$\left((1 + \theta^i_{\mathcal{A}} - 1 + \vartheta^i_{\mathcal{A}} - \eta^i_{\mathcal{A}})\mathrm{d} - (1 + 0 - 1 - 1)\mathrm{d}\right)^r\Big]^{\frac{1}{r}}$$

$$= \frac{1}{16\mathrm{p}}\cdot\sum_{i=1}^{p}\Big[\left((1 + \eta^i_{\mathcal{A}} - \vartheta^i_{\mathcal{A}} - \theta^i_{\mathcal{A}})\mathrm{a} - (1 + 1 - 0 - 0)\mathrm{a}\right)^r +$$

$$\left((1 + \eta^i_{\mathcal{A}} - \vartheta^i_{\mathcal{A}} - \theta^i_{\mathcal{A}})\mathrm{b} - (1 + 1 - 0 - 0)\mathrm{b}\right)^r +$$

$$\left((1 + \eta^i_{\mathcal{A}} - \vartheta^i_{\mathcal{A}} - \theta^i_{\mathcal{A}})\mathrm{c} - (1 + 1 - 0 - 0)\mathrm{c}\right)^r +$$

$$\left((1 + \eta^i_{\mathcal{A}} - \vartheta^i_{\mathcal{A}} - \theta^i_{\mathcal{A}})\mathrm{d} - (1 + 1 - 0 - 0)\mathrm{d}\right)^r\Big]^{\frac{1}{r}}$$

$$= \mathrm{d_r}(\mathcal{A}, \mathcal{A}^+)$$

Similarly, $\mathrm{d_r}(\mathcal{A}^c, \mathcal{A}^-)$ and $\mathrm{d_r}(\mathcal{A}, \mathcal{A}^+)$ are also equal. From here, If $\mathrm{d_r}\left(\mathcal{A}^c, \mathcal{A}^+\right) = \mathrm{d_r}(\mathcal{A}, \mathcal{A}^-)$ and $\mathrm{d_r}\left(\mathcal{A}^c, \mathcal{A}^-\right) = \mathrm{d_r}(\mathcal{A}, \mathcal{A}^+)$, then

$$\left|\frac{d_r(\mathcal{A}^c, \mathcal{A}^-)}{d_r(\mathcal{A}^c, \mathcal{A}^-) + d_r(\mathcal{A}^c, \mathcal{A}^+)} - \frac{1}{2}\right| = \left|\frac{d_r(\mathcal{A}, \mathcal{A}^-)}{d_r(\mathcal{A}, \mathcal{A}^-) + d_r(\mathcal{A}, \mathcal{A}^+)} - \frac{1}{2}\right|.$$

As a result, $\mathcal{E}_r(\mathcal{A})and\mathcal{E}_r(\mathcal{A}^c)$ are equal.

iii. Obviously, $d_r(\mathcal{A}, \mathcal{A}^-) = d_r(\mathcal{A}, \mathcal{A}^+) \iff \mathcal{E}_r(\mathcal{A}) = 1$ for all $\mathcal{A} \in$ NVNT-numbers.

iv. If $\mathcal{A}$and$\mathcal{B} \in$ NVNT-numbers, then

$$\left|\frac{d_r(\mathcal{A}, \mathcal{A}^-)}{d_r(\mathcal{A}, \mathcal{A}^+) + d_r(\mathcal{A}, \mathcal{A}^-)} - \frac{1}{2}\right| \geq \left|\frac{d_r(\mathcal{B}, \mathcal{B}^-)}{d_r(\mathcal{B}, \mathcal{B}^+) + d_r(\mathcal{B}, \mathcal{B}^-)} - \frac{1}{2}\right|$$

$$\Rightarrow 1 - 2\left|\frac{d_r(\mathcal{A}, \mathcal{A}^-)}{d_r(\mathcal{A}, \mathcal{A}^+) + d_r(\mathcal{A}, \mathcal{A}^-)} - \frac{1}{2}\right| \leq 1 - 2\left|\frac{d_r(\mathcal{B}, \mathcal{B}^-)}{d_r(\mathcal{B}, \mathcal{B}^+) + d_r(\mathcal{B}, \mathcal{B}^-)} - \frac{1}{2}\right|$$

$$\Rightarrow \mathcal{E}_r(\mathcal{A}) \leq \mathcal{E}_r(\mathcal{B}).$$

4 A Method for MCDM Problems with NVNT–Numbers

In this section, we give a multi-criteria decision-making method with normalized NVNT-numbers.

Assume that $K = \{K_1, K_2, \ldots, K_m\}$ be the set of alternatives and $G = \{g_1, g_2, \ldots, g_n\}$ be the set of criterias. In Deli et al. (2021), the normalized NVNT-numbers decision matrix is given as;

$$(K_{kj})_{mxn} = \begin{pmatrix} K_{11} & K_{12} & \cdots & K_{1n} \\ K_{21} & K_{22} & \cdots & K_{2n} \\ \vdots & \vdots & \ldots & \vdots \\ \vdots & \vdots & \ldots & \vdots \\ K_{m1} & K_{m2} & \cdots & K_{mn} \end{pmatrix}$$

such that

$K_{kj} = \langle [a_{kj}, b_{kj}, c_{kj}, d_{kj}], \left(\eta^1_{kj}, \eta^2_{kj}, \eta^3_{kj}, \ldots, \eta^p_{kj}\right), \left(\vartheta^1_{kj}, \vartheta^2_{kj}, \vartheta^3_{kj}, \ldots, \vartheta^p_{kj}\right), \left(\theta^1_{kj}, \theta^2_{kj}, \theta^3_{kj}, \ldots, \theta^p_{kj}\right)\rangle$, (k=1,2,...,m) and (j=1,2,...,n).

It carried out the following algorithm to get the best choice:

Algorithm:

Step 1: Create an evaluation matrix $(K_{kj})_{mxn}$, (k = 1,2,...,m; j = 1,2,...,n)

Step 2: Find the weights of the criteria vector $w = \{w_1, w_2, \ldots, w_n\}$ by using the equation in Theorem 3.3 as;

$$w_j = \frac{m - \sum_{k=1}^{m} \mathcal{E}_{kj}}{m.n - \sum_{k=1}^{m} \sum_{j=1}^{n} \mathcal{E}_{kj}}, \ (j = 1,2, \ldots, n).$$

where the entropy matrix $(\mathcal{E}_{kj})_{mxn}$ (k = 1,2,...,m; j = 1,2,...,n) of the decision matrix $(K_{kj})_{mxn}$ and where

$$\mathcal{E}_{kj} = 1 - 2\left|\frac{d_r\left(K_{kj}, K_{kj}{}^{-}\right)}{d_r\left(K_{kj}, K_{kj}{}^{+}\right) + d_r\left(K_{kj}, K_{kj}{}^{-}\right)} - \frac{1}{2}\right|$$

$$(k = 1,2, \ldots, m;\ j = 1,2, \ldots, n).$$

Note that if the entropy matrix $(\mathcal{E}_{kj})_{mxn}$ (k = 1,2,...,m; j = 1,2,...,n) is not normalized then, the entropy matrix must be normalized as;

$$\overline{\mathcal{E}}_{kj} = \frac{\mathcal{E}_{kj}}{\max\left\{\mathcal{E}_{kj} : \mathcal{E}_{kj} \in (\mathcal{E}_{kj})_{mxn}, k = 1,2, \ldots, m \text{ and } j = 1,2, \ldots, n\right\}}.$$

Step 3: Determine the positive ideal solution r^+ and negative ideal solution r^-, respectively as;

$$r^+ = [a_{kj}^+, b_{kj}^+, c_{kj}^+, d_{kj}^+]; (\eta_{kj}^{1+}, \eta_{kj}^{2+}, \eta_{kj}^{3+}, \cdots, \eta_{kj}^{p+}), (\vartheta_{kj}^{1+}, \vartheta_{kj}^{2+}, \vartheta_{kj}^{3+}, \cdots, \vartheta_{kj}^{p+}), (\theta_{kj}^{1+}, \theta_{kj}^{2+}, \theta_{kj}^{3+}, \ldots, \theta_{kj}^{p+})$$

$$= \left[\max_k\{a_{kj}\}, \max_k\{b_{kj}\}, \max_k\{c_{kj}\}, \max_k\{d_{kj}\}\right];$$

$$\left(\max_k\left\{\eta_{kj}^1\right\}, \max_k\left\{\eta_{kj}^2\right\}, \max_k\left\{\eta_{kj}^3\right\}, \ldots, \max_k\left\{\eta_{kj}^p\right\}\right)$$

$$\left(\min_k\left\{\vartheta_{kj}^1\right\}, \min_k\left\{\vartheta_{kj}^2\right\}, \min_k\left\{\vartheta_{kj}^3\right\}, \ldots, \min_k\left\{\vartheta_{kj}^p\right\}\right),$$

$$\left(\min_k\left\{\theta_{kj}^1\right\}, \min_k\left\{\theta_{kj}^2\right\}, \min_k\left\{\theta_{kj}^3\right\}, \ldots, \min_k\left\{\theta_{kj}^p\right\}\right)$$

and

$$r^{-} = [a_{kj}^{-}, b_{kj}^{-}, c_{kj}^{-}, d_{kj}^{-}]; (\eta_{kj}^{1-}, \eta_{kj}^{2-}, \eta_{kj}^{3-}, \cdots, \eta_{kj}^{p-}), (\vartheta_{kj}^{1-}, \vartheta_{kj}^{2-}, \vartheta_{kj}^{3-}, \cdots, \vartheta_{kj}^{p-}), (\theta_{kj}^{1-}, \theta_{kj}^{2-}, \theta_{kj}^{3-}, \ldots, \theta_{kj}^{p-})$$

$$= \left[\min_k\{a_{kj}\}, \min_k\{b_{kj}\}, \min_k\{c_{kj}\}, \min_k\{d_{kj}\}\right]; \left(\min_k\left\{\eta_{kj}^{1}\right\}, \min_k\left\{\eta_{kj}^{2}\right\}, \min_k\left\{\eta_{kj}^{3}\right\}, \ldots, \min_k\left\{\eta_{kj}^{p}\right\}\right)$$
$$\left(\max_k\left\{\vartheta_{kj}^{1}\right\}, \max_k\left\{\vartheta_{kj}^{2}\right\}, \max_k\left\{\vartheta_{kj}^{3}\right\}, \ldots, \max_k\left\{\vartheta_{kj}^{p}\right\}\right), \left(\max_k\left\{\theta_{kj}^{1}\right\}, \max_k\left\{\theta_{kj}^{2}\right\}, \max_k\left\{\theta_{kj}^{3}\right\}, \ldots, \max_k\left\{\theta_{kj}^{p}\right\}\right)$$

for all (k = 1,2,…,m) and (j = 1,2,…,n).

Step 4: According to Eq. (9), positive value of $V^{+}(K_k)$ based on positive ideal solution r^{+} and negative value of $V^{-}(K_k)$ based on negative ideal solution r^{-} of alternative K_k (k = 1,2,…,m) calculated as follows:

$$V^{+}(K_k) = \frac{1}{n}\sum_{j=1}^{n} d_r^{w}(K_{kj}, r^{+})$$

$$= \frac{1}{16.n.p}\cdot\sum_{j=1}^{n}\sum_{k=1}^{p}\Big[\Big(w_{K_{kj}}(1+\eta_{kj}^{i}-\vartheta_{kj}^{i}-\theta_{kj}^{i})a_{kj} - w_{r^{+}}(1+\eta_{kj}^{i\ +}-\vartheta_{kj}^{i\ +}-\theta_{kj}^{i\ +})a_{kj}\Big)^{r}$$
$$+\Big(w_{K_{kj}}(1+\eta_{kj}^{i}-\vartheta_{kj}^{i}-\theta_{kj}^{i})b_{kj} - w_{r^{+}}(1+\eta_{kj}^{i\ +}-\vartheta_{kj}^{i\ +}-\theta_{kj}^{i\ +})b_{kj}\Big)^{r}+$$
$$\Big(w_{K_{kj}}(1+\eta_{kj}^{i}-\vartheta_{kj}^{i}-\theta_{kj}^{i})c_{kj} - w_{r^{+}}(1+\eta_{kj}^{i\ +}-\vartheta_{kj}^{i\ +}-\theta_{kj}^{i\ +})c_{kj}\Big)^{r}+$$
$$\Big(w_{K_{kj}}(1+\eta_{kj}^{i}-\vartheta_{kj}^{i}-\theta_{kj}^{i})d_{kj} - w_{r^{+}}(1+\eta_{kj}^{i\ +}-\vartheta_{kj}^{i\ +}-\theta_{kj}^{i\ +})d_{kj}\Big)^{r}\Big]^{\frac{1}{r}}$$

and

$$V^{-}(K_k) = \frac{1}{n}\sum_{j=1}^{n} d_r^{w}(K_{kj}, r^{-})$$

$$\frac{1}{16.n.p}\cdot\sum_{j=1}^{n}\sum_{k=1}^{p}\Big[\Big(w_{K_{kj}}(1+\eta_{kj}^{i}-\vartheta_{kj}^{i}-\theta_{kj}^{i})a_{kj} - w_{r^{-}}(1+\eta_{kj}^{i\ -}-\vartheta_{kj}^{i\ -}-\theta_{kj}^{i\ -})a_{kj}\Big)^{r}$$
$$\Big(w_{K_{kj}}(1+\eta_{kj}^{i}-\vartheta_{kj}^{i}-\theta_{kj}^{i})b_{kj} - w_{r^{-}}(1+\eta_{kj}^{i\ -}-\vartheta_{kj}^{i\ -}-\theta_{kj}^{i\ -})b_{kj}\Big)^{r}+$$

$$\left(w_{K_{kj}}(1+\eta_{kj}^{i}-\vartheta_{kj}^{i}-\theta_{kj}^{i})c_{kj}-w_{r^-}(1+\eta_{kj}^{i^-}-\vartheta_{kj}^{i^-}-\theta_{kj}^{i^-})c_{kj}\right)^{r}+$$

$$\left(w_{K_{kj}}(1+\eta_{kj}^{i}-\vartheta_{kj}^{i}-\theta_{kj}^{i})d_{kj}-w_{r^-}(1+\eta_{kj}^{i^-}-\vartheta_{kj}^{i^-}-\theta_{kj}^{i^-})d_{kj}\right)^{r}\Big]^{\frac{1}{r}}$$

where $w_{r^+} = \max\{w_j : j = 1,2,\ldots,n\}$ and $w_{r^-} = \min\{w_j : j = 1,2,\ldots,n\}$.

Step 5: Calculate the relative closeness degree CC_k of each alternative K_k (k = 1,2, ..., m) as;

$$CC_k = \frac{V^-(K_k)}{V^-(K_k)+V^+(K_k)},\ k = 1,2, ..., m. \tag{12}$$

Step 6: Rank all alternatives according to $CC_k(k = 1,2, ..., m)$ in decreasing order and determine the best alternatives.

4.1 Examples and Comparative Analysis

Example 4.1.1 Assume that a company's board of directors tries to choose the best investment vehicle for investing in the stock market. For this, he has five different investment vehicles and three craters. That is, the company, uses investment instruments which is the set of alternatives as $K = \{K_1, K_2, \ldots, K_5\}$ and according to three criteria determined $G = \{g_1 =$ very risky investment, $g_2 =$ medium risk investment, $g_3 =$ low risky investment. Then we try to choose and rank all alternatives K_k for all $k = 1,2,\ldots,5$ by using the following algorithm.

Algorithm

Step 1: The evaluation matrix $(K_{kj})_{5x3}$ is given by an expert as;

$$(K_{kj})_{5x3} = \begin{matrix} k_1 \\ k_2 \\ k_3 \\ k_4 \\ k_5 \end{matrix}\begin{pmatrix} \langle[0.32,0.44,0.51,0.69]; (0.3,0.5,0.7,0.8), (0.1,0.3,0.2,0.3), (0.6,0.3,0.5,0.6)\rangle \\ \langle[0.23,0.25,0.41,0.45]; (0.4,0.2,0.3,0.5), (0.2,0.5, 0.7,0.6), (0.7,0.5,0.6,0.8)\rangle \\ \langle[0.66,0.72,0.79,0.83]; (0.7,0.6,0.4,0.8), (0.5,0.5,0.5,0.6), (0.4,0.3,0.4,0.5)\rangle \\ \langle[0.52,0.63,0.76,0.91]; (0.8,0.7,0.5,0.6), (0.4,0.3,0.7,0.5), (0.1,0.5,0.7,0.7)\rangle \\ \langle[0.13,0.35,0.41,0.58]; (0.7,0.8,0.9,0.9), (0.2,0.7,0.5,0.6), (0.1,0.7,0.8,0.4)\rangle \end{pmatrix}$$

$$\begin{matrix} \langle[0.28,0.32, 0.38,0.43]; (0.5,0.3,0.4,0.6), (0.2,0.1,0.5,0.4), (0.4,0.6,0.5,0.7)\rangle \\ \langle[0.12,0.15,0.18,0.23]; (0.3,0.7,0.9,0.9), (0.1,0.2,0.3,0.7), (0.3,0.4,0.7,0.5)\rangle \\ \langle[0.65,0.66,0.72,0.75]; (0.6,0.8,0.9,0.8), (0.2,0.5,0.4,0.3), (0.2,0.3,0.6,0.6)\rangle \\ \langle[0.08,0.15,0.27,0.37]; (0.3,0.9,0.8,0.4), (0.8,0.7, 0.6,0.5), (0.1,0.1,0.4,0.3)\rangle \\ \langle[0.09,0.13,0.19,0.69]; (0.2,0.5,0.7,0.9), (0.1,0.3,0.5,0.4), (0.6,0.7,0.8,0.8)\rangle \end{matrix}$$

$$\left.\begin{matrix} \langle[0.12,0.27,0.60,0.65]; (0.2,0.7,0.8,0.9), (0.4,0.3,0.8,0.5), (0.2,0.5,0.6,0.4)\rangle \\ \langle[0.22,0.48,0.43,0.73]; (0.3,0.8,0.9,0.7), (0.5,0.7,0.7,0.6), (0.1,0.4,0.8,0.6)\rangle \\ \langle[0.14,0.33,0.43,0.83]; (0.1,0.6,0.9,0.5), (0.8,0.5,0.6,0.7), (0.1,0.3,0.5,0.8)\rangle \\ \langle[0.63,0.73,0.83,0.93]; (0.4,0.5,0.7,0.6), (0.2,0.6,0.8,0.3), (0.3,0.6,0.7,0.2)\rangle \\ \langle[0.41,0.43,0.68,0.74]; (0.5,0.7,0.8,0.3), (0.1,0.2,0.6,0.4), (0.4,0.2,0.9,0.7)\rangle \end{matrix}\right)$$

Step 2: Since the normalized entropy matrix is

$$(\mathcal{E}_{kj})_{5\times 3} = \begin{pmatrix} 0.561587 & 0.869281 & 0.848676 \\ 0.621053 & 0.506173 & 0.900990 \\ 0.739696 & 0.403579 & 0.936975 \\ 0.789368 & 0.714889 & 0.394178 \\ 0.609610 & 0.966851 & 0.760479 \end{pmatrix}_{5\times 3}$$

we have calculated the weights of the criteria $w = (w_1, w_2, w_3)$ as;

$$\begin{aligned} w_1 &= \frac{5-(\mathcal{E}_{11}+\mathcal{E}_{21}+\mathcal{E}_{31}+\mathcal{E}_{41}+\mathcal{E}_{51})}{15-(\mathcal{E}_{11}+\mathcal{E}_{12}+\mathcal{E}_{13}+\mathcal{E}_{21}+\mathcal{E}_{22}+\mathcal{E}_{23}+\mathcal{E}_{31}+\mathcal{E}_{32}+\cdots+\mathcal{E}_{42}+\mathcal{E}_{43}+\mathcal{E}_{51}+\mathcal{E}_{52}+\mathcal{E}_{53})} \\ &= \frac{5-(0.561587+0.621053+0.739696+0.789368+0.609610)}{15-(0.561587+0.869281+0.848676+0.621053+\cdots+0.60961+0.966851+0.760479)} \\ &= 0.383558117 \end{aligned}$$

similarly, we have $w_2 = 0.35169353$, and $w_3 = 0.264748353$.

Step 3: The positive ideal solution r^+ and negative ideal solution r^-, respectively calculated as;

$$r^+ = \langle[0.66,0.73,0.83,0.93]; (0.8,0.9,0.9, 0.9), (0.1,0.1,0.2,0.3), (0.1,0.1,0.4,0.2)\rangle$$

and

$$r^- = \langle[0.08,0.13,0.18,0.23]; (0.1,0.2,0.3,0.3), (0.8,0.7,0.8,0.7), (0.7,0.7,0.9,0.8)\rangle.$$

Step 4: According to Eq. (9) positive value of $V^+(K_k)$ based on positive ideal solution r^+ and negative value of $V^-(K_k)$ based on negative ideal solution r^- of alternative K_k (k = 1,2,…,5) calculated as follows:

$$V^+(K_1) = 0.107,\ V^+(K_2) = 0.127, V^+(K_3) = 0.067, V^+(K_4) = 0.114, V^+(K_5) = 0.110$$

$$V^-(K_1) = 0.044, V^-(K_2) = 0.122, V^-(K_3) = 0.055, V^-(K_4) = 0.084, V^-(K_5) = 0.047$$

Step 5: We calculated the relative closeness degree CC_k of each alternative K_k (k = 1,2, ..., 5) as;

$$CC_1 = 0.1716,\ CC_2 = 0.3650,\ CC_3 = 0.3518,\ CC_4 = 0.3183,\ CC_5 = 0.1749$$

Step 6: Based on the index values $CC_k(k = 1,2, ..., 5)$ the ranking of alternatives $K_k(k = 1,2, ..., 5)$ are shown in Figs. 1 and 2 and given as;

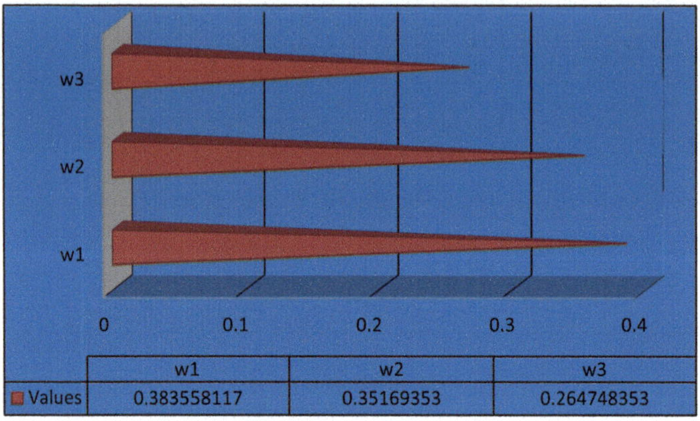

Fig. 1 Weights of the criteria by normalized NVNT–numbers

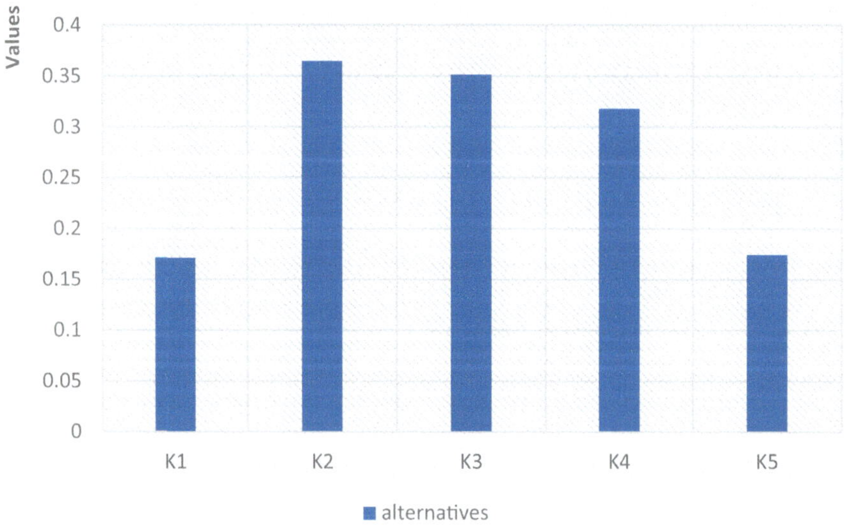

Fig. 2 The ranking of alternatives K_k based on CC_k (k = 1,2, ..., 5)

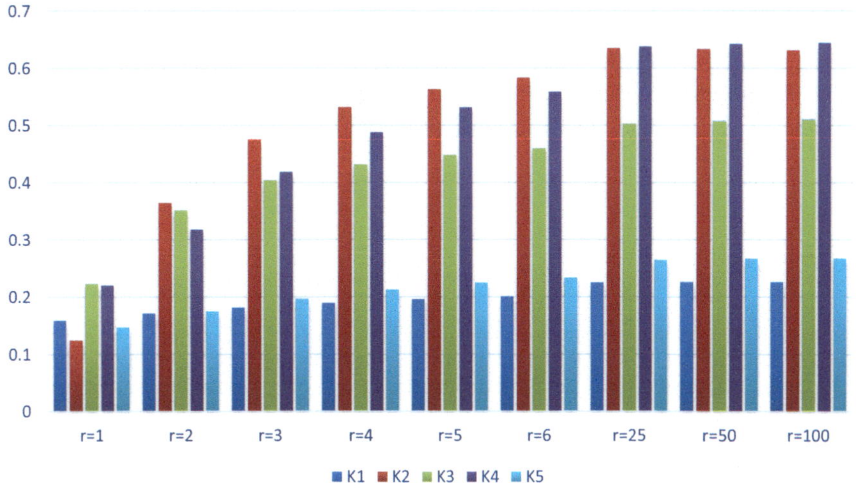

Fig. 3 The results from the different distance measures

$$K_2 > K_3 > K_4 > K_5 > K_1.$$

Finally, the best alternative is K_2.

The results from the different distance measures used to resolve the MCDM problem in Sect. 4 are shown in Fig. 3

5 Conclusions

Based on the special function, this chapter redefines a kind of entropy measure, which not only includes other forms of entropy but also sorts the alternatives and selects the optimal scheme according to the multi-attribute decision-making method of TOPSIS with distance measures based on NVNT-numbers. Finally, this chapter illustrates the feasibility of the entropy measure, compares and analyzes it with other decision-making methods of entropy measure, obtains the results consistent with this chapter, and further explains the effectiveness of the method proposed in this chapter. Later, we will continue to study the other neutrosophic sets and corresponding decision-making methods, and apply them to practical problems.

Acknowledgments This study was supported by Kilis 7 Aralik University Scientific Research Projects Coordination Unit (KIYU, BAP, Project Number: 21-12131).

Abbreviations

NVNT-numbers	N-valued neutrosophic trapezoidal numbers
MCDM	Multi-criteria decision-making

References

Atanassov, K. (1986). Intuitionistic fuzzy sets. *Fuzzy Sets Syst, 20*, 87–96.

Adak, A. K., & Kumar, D. (2023). Spherical Distance Measurement Method for Solving MCDM Problems under Pythagorean Fuzzy Environment. *Journal of fuzzy extension and applications, 4*(1), 28–39.

Basset, M. A., Mohamed, M., & Sangaiah, A. K. (2018). Neutrosophic AHP-Delphi Group decision making model based on trapezoidal neutrosophic numbers. *Journal of Ambient Intelligence and Humanized Computing, 9*(5), 1427–1443.

Batool, B., Ahmad, M., Abdullah, S., Ashraf, S., & Chinram, R. (2018). Entropy based Pythagorean probabilistic hesitant fuzzy decision-making technique and its application for fog-haze factor assessment problem. *Entropy, 22*(318), 1–18.

Broumi, S., & Deli, I. (2015). Correlation measure for neutrosophic refined sets and its application in medical diagnosis. *Palestine Journal Of Mathematics, 5*(1), 135–143.

Chatterjee, R., Majumdar, P., & Samanta, S. K. (2015). Single valued neutrosophic multisets. *Annals of Fuzzy Mathematics and Informatics, 10*(3), 499–514.

Da Silva, I. A., Bedregal, B., Bedregal, B., & Santiago, R. H. N. (2021). An interval-valued Atanassov's intuitionistic fuzzy multi-attribute group decision making method based on the best representation of the WA and OWA operators. *Journal of Fuzzy Extension and Applications, 2*(3), 239–261.

Deli, I., Broumi, S., & Smarandache, F. (2015). On neutrosophic refined sets and their applications in medical diagnosis. *Journal of New Theory, 6*, 88–98.

Deli I,, Uluçay V., Polat Y., (2021).N-valued neutrosophic trapezoidal numbers with similarity measures and application to multi-criteria decision-making problems, Journal of Ambient Intelligence and Humanized Computing, https://doi.org/10.1007/s12652-021-03294-7.

Deli I (2016) Refined neutrosophic sets and refined neutrosophic soft sets: theory and applications. In:John SJ (ed) Handbook of Research on Generalized and Hybrid Set Structures and Applications for Soft Computing. IGI Global, pp 321–343

Ejegwa, P. A., & Awolola, J. A. (2013). Some Algebraic Structures of Intuitionistic Fuzzy Multisets (IFMSs). *International Journal of Science and Technology, 2*(5), 373–376.

Ejegwa, P. A. (2015). New Operations on Intuitionistic Fuzzy Multisets. *Journal of Mathematics and Informatics, 3*, 17–23.

Karaaslan, F. (2018). Gaussian Single-valued neutrosophic number and its application in multi-attribure decision making. *Neutrosophic Sets and Systems, 22*, 101–117.

Hu, J., Yang, Y., Zhang, X., & Chen, X. (2018). Similarity and entropy measures for hesitant fuzzy sets. *International Transactions in Operational Research, 25*(3), 857–886.

Liu, P., Shen, M., Teng, F., Zhu, B., Rong, L., & Geng, Y. (2021). Double hierarchy hesitant fuzzy linguistic entropy-based TODIM approach using evidential theory. *Information Sciences, 547*, 223–243.

Narayanamoorthy, S., Geetha, S., Rakkiyappan, R., & Joo, Y. H. (2019). Interval-valued intuitionistic hesitant fuzzy entropy based VIKOR method for industrial robots selection. *Expert Systems with Applications, 121*, 28–37.

Khatter, K. (2021). Interval valued trapezoidal neutrosophic set: multi-attribute decision making for prioritization of non-functional requirements. *Journal of Ambient Intelligence and Humanized Computing, 12*(1), 1039–1055.

Miyamoto S (2001). Fuzzy multisets and their generalizations. In Multiset Processing, Springer Berlin Heidelberg 225–235

Miyamoto, S. (2004). Data Structure and Operations for Fuzzy Multisets. *Transactions on Rough Sets II, Lecture Notes in Computer Science, Springer-Verlag, Berlin, 3135*, 189–200.

Mohan, S., Kannusamy, A. P., & Samiappan, V. (2020). A new approach for ranking of intuitionistic fuzzy numbers. *Journal of fuzzy extension and applications, 1*(1), 15–26.

Mondal K, Pramanik S, Giri BC (2018) Multi-criteria group decision making based on linguistic refined neutrosophic strategy. In: Smarandache F, Pramanik S (eds) New trends in neutrosophic theory and applications. 2rd edn. Pons Editions Brussels, Belgium, pp 125–139

Pramanik S, Banerjee D, Giri BC (2016) TOPSIS approach for multi attribute group decision making in refined neutrosophic environment. In: Smarandache F, Pramanik S (Eds) New trends in neutrosophic theory and applications. Pons Editions Brussels, Belgium, pp 79–91

Rayappan, P., & Krishnaswamy, M. (2020). Some similarity measures of spherical fuzzy sets based on the Euclidean distance and their application in medical diagnosis. *Journal of fuzzy extension and applications, 1*(3), 244–251.

Rayappan, P., & Mohana, K. (2021). Spherical fuzzy cross entropy for multiple attribute decision making problems. *Journal of Fuzzy Extension and Applications, 2*(4), 355–363.

Rajarajeswari, P., & Uma, N. (2013). On Distance and Similarity Measures of Intuitionistic Fuzzy Multi Set. *IOSR Journal of Mathematics, 5*(4), 19–23.

Rajarajeswari P, Uma N (2013a) Intuitionistic fuzzy multi similarity measure based on cotangent function. In International Journal of Engineering Research and Technology 2(11), ESRSA Publications

Rajarajeswari, P., & Uma, N. (2014). Correlation measure for intuitionistic fuzzy multi sets. *International Journal of Research in Engineering and Technology, 3*(1), 611–617.

Sahin, M., Deli, I., & Ulucay, V. (2018). Extension principle based on neutrosophic multi-sets and algebraic operations. *Journal of Mathematical Extension, 12*(1), 69–90.

Sebastian, S., & Ramakrishnan, T. V. (2010). Multi-Fuzzy sets. *International Mathematical Forum., 5*(50), 2471–2476.

Sebastian, S., & Ramakrishnan, T. V. (2011). Multi-fuzzy extension of crisp functions using bridge functions. *Annals of Fuzzy Mathematics and Informatics, 2*(1), 1–8.

Sebastian, S., & Ramakrishnan, T. V. (2011). Multi-fuzzy Subgroups. *Int. J. Contemp. Math. Sciences, 6*(8), 365–372.

Shafi Salimi, P., & Edalatpanah, S. A. (2020). Supplier selection using fuzzy AHP method and D-Numbers. *Journal of fuzzy extension and applications, 1*(1), 1–14.

Shinoj, T. K., & John, S. J. (2012). Intuitionistic fuzzy multisets and its application in medical diagnosis. *World Academy of Science Engineering and Technology, 6*(1), 1418–1421.

Shinoj, T. K., & John, S. J. (2013). Intuitionistic Fuzzy Multisets. *International Journal of Engineering Science and Innovative Technology (IJESIT), 2*(6), 1–24.

Shinoj, T. K., & John, S. J. (2015). Intuitionistic Fuzzy Multigroups. *Annals of Pure and Applied Mathematic, 9*(1), 131–143.

Smarandache F (1998) A Unifying Field in Logics. Neutrosophy: Neutrosophic Probability, Set and Logic, Rehoboth: American Research Press

Smarandache, F. (2013). N-Valued Refined Neutrosophic Logic and Its Applications in Physics. *Progress in Physics, 4*, 143–14.

Syropoulos, A. (2012). On generalized fuzzy multisets and their use in computation. *Iranian Journal Of Fuzzy Systems, 9*(2), 113–125.

Ulucay, V., Deli, I., & Şahin, M. (2018). Trapezoidal fuzzy multi-number and its application to multi-criteria decision making problems. *Neural Computing and Applications, 30*(5), 1469–1478.

Ulucay, V., Kılıç, A., Sahin, M., & Deniz, H. (2019). A new hybrid distance-based similarity measure for refined neutrosophic sets and its application in medical diagnosis. *Matematika, 35*(1), 83–96.

Ulucay, V., Deli, I., & Şahin, M. (2019). Intuitionistic trapezoidal fuzzy multi-numbers and its application to multi-criteria decision-making problems. *Complex and Intelligent Systems, 5*(1), 65–78.

Ulucay, V. (2020). Some concepts on interval-valued refined neutrosophic sets and their applications. *Journal of Ambient Intelligence and Humanized Computing, 1–16*,. https://doi.org/10.1007/s12652-020-02512-y

Wang, H., Smarandache, F., Zhang, Y. Q., & Sunderraman, R. (2010). *Single valued neutrosophic sets. Multispace Multistruct, 4*, 410–413.

Yager, R. R. (1986). On the theory of bags (Multi sets). *Int Joun Of General System, 13*, 23–37.

Ye, S., & Ye, J. (2014). Dice similarity measure between single valued neutrosophic multisets and its application in medical diagnosis. *Neutrosophic Sets and Systems, 6*, 48–52.

Ye, J., & Smarandache, F. (2016). Similarity measure of refined single-valued neutrosophic sets and its multicriteria decision making method. *Neutrosophic Sets and Systems, 12*, 41–44.

Zadeh, L. A. (1965). Fuzzy Sets. *Information and Control, 8*, 338–353.

A New Decision-Making Analysis Model Based on the Transformation of Picture Fuzzy Sets into Fuzzy Sets

Taiwo O. Sangodapo, Nasreen Kausar, and Mohammad Y. Chreif

Abstract In today's era of data analysis and decision-making, the concept of picture fuzzy sets has emerged as a valuable tool for addressing uncertain real-life problems. Picture fuzzy sets uniquely consider neutral answers and accommodate choices beyond the typical binary yes or no, including the neutral option. However, the application of artificial intelligence, machines, and software is predominantly optimized for traditional fuzzy sets. In this chapter, we propose an innovative approach that transforms picture fuzzy sets into conventional fuzzy sets. This transformation bridges the gap between these two mathematical frameworks, empowering industries to harness the precision of fuzzy logic and control by providing exact fuzzy values for more accurate results. This work contributes to the integration of picture fuzzy sets into the broader landscape of fuzzy logic, enhancing their applicability in various industrial contexts.

Keywords Fuzzy set · Picture fuzzy set · Mathematical methods · Fuzzy value · Fuzzy logic and control

1 Introduction

The evolution of set theory, from classical sets to fuzzy sets introduced by Zadeh in (1965), has significantly enriched our ability to handle and represent uncertainty in various domains such as home appliances (Chen et al., 2020), distribution network

T. O. Sangodapo · N. Kausar
Department of Mathematics, University of Ibadan, Ibadan, Nigeria
e-mail: to.ewuola@ui.edu.ng; toewuola77@gmail.com

N. Kausar (✉)
Department of Mathematics, Yildiz Technical University, 34220 Istanbul, Turkey
e-mail: nkausar@yildiz.edu.tr

M. Y. Chreif
Department of Mathematics, Lebanese International University, Beqaa Valley, Lebanon
e-mail: mohamad.chreif@liu.edu.lb

© The Author(s), under exclusive license to Springer Nature Singapore Pte Ltd. 2024

S. A. Edalatpanah et al. (eds.), *Analytical Decision Making and Data Envelopment Analysis*, Infosys Science Foundation Series in Mathematical Sciences,
https://doi.org/10.1007/978-981-97-6972-8_20

(Adabavazeh et al., 2022), portfolio management (Kaviani & Fakhrehosseini, 2020), scheduling (Zanjani et al., 2021), psychopathology (Alayande et al., 2021), design concepts (Olabanji 2020), risk assessment (Khodadadi-Karimvand & Shirouyehzad, 2021), Corona prognosis (Arora et al., 2021), transportations (El-Shorbagy et al., 2020), budgeting (El-Morsy, 2022), accounting (Imeni, 2020), human resource development (Heravi et al., 2023; Kannan et al., 2024; Gazi et al., 2024), etc. Fuzzy sets, characterized by their membership functions that capture the degree of belongingness of elements to a particular class, have been instrumental in managing vagueness and imprecision inherent in real-world data. However, as the field of fuzzy sets progressed, it became apparent that some essential aspects were absent from the traditional fuzzy set framework (Hussain & Ullah, 2024). Notably, the notions of non-membership and hesitation were notably absent. This realization led to the formulation of Intuitionistic Fuzzy Sets (IFS) by Atanassov in (1986). Intuitionistic fuzzy sets extended the original fuzzy set concept by incorporating the degree of non-membership along with a hesitation margin. This addition enabled a more nuanced representation of uncertainty and became a pivotal development for researchers and mathematicians (Szmidt & Szmidt, 2014; Bhattacharya, 2021; Asif et al., 2024; Imran et al., 2024).

Despite the fact that intuitionistic fuzzy set is a generalization of fuzzy set at conveying cloudy and unclear data, the theory still lacks a very crucial parameter which is the degree of neutrality. This degree of neutrality is essential in situations such as voting systems, medical diagnosis, personal selection, and many others. For example, in a voting system, a voter might not only choose to vote for or against a proposition but could also abstain or refuse to vote. Similarly, in medical diagnosis, symptoms like fever and headache may have varying degrees of influence on the diagnosis of disorders like chest pain or stomach pain. To address these nuanced scenarios, Cuong and Krepinevich (2013) introduced and studied picture fuzzy sets in 2013, representing a novel generalization encompassing both intuitionistic fuzzy sets and traditional fuzzy sets. Picture fuzzy sets introduce the concept of three degrees: positive membership, neutral membership, and negative membership, allowing for a more comprehensive modeling of uncertainty and neutrality; for more details see (Khan et al., 2019; Roan et al., 2020; Akram et al., 2021; Mohammad Kamrul et al., 2022; Sangodapo, 2022; Sahoo et al., 2024).

The crux of this chapter lies in the transformation of picture fuzzy sets into conventional fuzzy sets, achieved through mathematical methods. This transformation serves a pivotal role in harnessing the advantages of both frameworks, enabling industries to employ fuzzy logic and fuzzy control with the precision of exact fuzzy values. In the following sections, we delve into the methodology of this transformation and its potential applications in real-world decision-making processes. By doing so, we bridge the gap between the innovative concept of picture fuzzy sets and the established power of fuzzy logic and control, facilitating more accurate and informed decisions in various industrial contexts.

The organization of this chapter is designed for a coherent flow of ideas. It commences with Sect. 2, where we lay the groundwork by presenting fundamental preliminaries, including essential definitions and concepts. In Sect. 3, we delve into the profound importance of the transformation, elucidating its relevance in real-world decision-making scenarios. Section 4 is dedicated to the presentation of meticulously chosen mathematical methods, emphasizing the necessity of accounting for the refusal part, irrespective of its value, to ensure the integrity of the results. Finally, Sect. 5 brings the chapter to a close, offering valuable conclusions and insights derived from this transformative process, encapsulating its practical implications and advantages.

2 Preliminaries

This section gives basic definitions and preliminaries that are needed in the sequel (Zadeh, 1965; Atanassov, 1986; Cuong & Kreinovich, 2013).

Definition 2.1 (Zadeh, 1965) A fuzzy set $\tilde{Q}$ of a nonempty set $\mathcal{Y}$ is defined by

$$\tilde{Q} = \{< a, \tilde{\sigma}(a) >, mathcalligraa \in \mathcal{Y}\},$$

where $\tilde{\sigma}$ is a function from $\mathcal{Y}$ to the interval [0, 1] called the membership function.

Example 2.1 Let $\mathcal{Y} = \{a, b\}$ and $\tilde{Q} = \{< a, 0.8 >, < b, 0.3 >\}$. Then $\tilde{Q}$ is a fuzzy set of $\mathcal{Y}$.

Fuzzy sets are used to modelise and solve real-life problems characterized with ambiguity and uncertainty. Here is an example of representing a realistic situation through the fuzzy sets concept.

Example 2.2 Consider the set $\mathcal{S}$ of students defined by $\mathcal{S} = \{s_1, s_2, s_3, s_4, s_5, s_6\}$. Let $\tilde{Q}$ be the fuzzy set of "smart" students given by

$$\tilde{Q} = \{< s_1, 0.2 >, < s_2, 0.3 >, < s_3, 1 >, < s_4, 0.5 >, < s_5, 0.9 >, < s_6, 0.3 >$$

Here,$\tilde{Q}$ indicates that the smartness degree of s_1 is 0.2 while the smartness degree of s_5 is 0.9.

In example 2.2, rather than categorizing students into binary groups of smart or non-smart, this concept introduces a nuanced scale that enables us to assess the degree of smartness of each student. Additionally, it facilitates comparisons among multiple students based on their respective smartness levels. Indeed, when utilizing fuzzy sets to represent a specific case, the focus traditionally revolves around the degree of membership, often overlooking other crucial factors. However, in 1983, Atanassov (1986) introduced the concept of intuitionistic fuzzy sets as an extension of fuzzy sets, offering a more comprehensive perspective by incorporating the degree of non-membership. Instead of assigning a membership value alone to each element within the fuzzy set, intuitionistic fuzzy sets provide both a degree of membership and a degree of non-membership for each element.

The significance of this generalization has captivated the attention of researchers over the years, leading to extensive exploration of its properties and practical applications in real-world contexts, as detailed in (Atanassov, 2012; Bhattacharya, 2016), and (Gu et al., 2022). Furthermore, recognizing its vital role in modeling, there have been several endeavors to transform intuitionistic fuzzy sets into conventional fuzzy sets, as documented in (Ansari et al., 2004).

Definition 2.2 (Bhattacharya, 2021; Atanassov & Atanassov, 1999) Let $\mathcal{Y}$ be a nonempty set. An intuitionistic fuzzy set $\tilde{Q}$ of $\mathcal{Y}$ is an object of the form

$$\tilde{Q} = \{\langle a, \tilde{\sigma}(a), \tilde{\tau}(a)\rangle, a \in \mathcal{Y}\},$$

where $\tilde{\sigma} : \mathcal{Y} :\rightarrow [0, 1]$ and $\tilde{\tau} : \mathcal{Y} :\rightarrow [0, 1]$ are called the membership and non-membership functions of a in $\mathcal{Y}$ respectively satisfying $0 \leq \tilde{\sigma}(a) + \tilde{\tau}(a) \leq 1$.

Example 2.3 Let $\mathcal{Y} = \{a, b\}$ and $\tilde{Q} = \{< a, 0.6, 0.2 >, < b, 0.3, 0.4 >\}$. Then $\tilde{Q}$ is an intuitionistic fuzzy set of $\mathcal{Y}$.

Many real-world scenarios demand responses that go beyond simple binary options of yes or no. Instead, they encompass responses such as abstaining and refusal. In recognition of this complexity, Cuong proposed a division of the hesitancy membership into two distinct components: neutral membership and refusal membership. This innovative approach not only enhances the precision with which uncertain situations can be addressed but also paves the way for the development of novel decision-making algorithms, as exemplified in (Sangodapo, 2022) and (Singh & Ganie, 2022). Consequently, Cuong introduced the concept of a picture fuzzy set, defined as follows:

Definition 2.3 (Cuong & Kreinovich, 2013, 2014; Cuong & Pham, 2015) A picture fuzzy set $\tilde{Q}$ of $\mathcal{Y}$ is an object of the form

$$\tilde{Q} = \{< a, \tilde{\sigma}(a), \tilde{\tau}(a), \tilde{\gamma}(a) >, a \in \mathcal{Y}\},$$

where $\tilde{\sigma}$, $\tilde{\tau}$ and $\tilde{\gamma}$ are functions from $\mathcal{Y}$ to the interval $[0, 1]$ satisfying $0 \leq \tilde{\sigma}(a) + \tilde{\tau}(a) + \tilde{\gamma}(a) \leq 1, \forall a \in \mathcal{Y}$.

These functions are called the positive, neutral, and negative membership functions of a in $\mathcal{Y}$, respectively.

We define, $\mathcal{S}_{\mathcal{Y}}(a) = 1 - (\tilde{\sigma}(a) + \tilde{\tau}(a) + \tilde{\gamma}(a)) \forall a \in \mathcal{Y}$. $\mathcal{S}_{\mathcal{Y}}(a)$ is called the refusal membership function of a in $\mathcal{Y}$.

Example 2.4 Let $\mathcal{Y} = \{a, b\}$ and $\tilde{Q} = \{< a, 0.6, 0.2, 0.1 >, < b, 0.3, 0.4, 0.2 >\}$. Then $\tilde{Q}$ is a picture fuzzy set of $\mathcal{Y}$.

Picture fuzzy sets represent an advancement in the realm of fuzzy and intuitionistic fuzzy sets, marking a recent innovation deserving closer examination to unveil their unique properties and characteristics. Valuable insights into these attributes can be found in references such as Khan et al. (2019), Akram et al. (2021), and Si et al. (2021).

Furthermore, the applications of picture fuzzy sets are gaining momentum across diverse domains, piquing the interest of numerous authors who recognize the potential of this approach for attaining well-informed decisions and precise results. To delve deeper into these burgeoning applications, consider references (Mohammad Kamrul et al., 2022; Si et al., 2021; Kumar et al., 2022; Zhao et al., 2023) for additional insights and information.

3 The Importance

The concept of picture fuzzy sets represents a novel approach in the realm of fuzzy logic and decision analysis, with emerging applications in various industrial contexts, as evidenced by references (Dutta & Ganju, 2018; Ganie, 2023; Yildirim & Yıldırım, 2022; Sahu et al., 2021). Additionally, the majority of industrial machinery and software systems rely on fuzzy set data for effective implementation, given the confidence in the accuracy of results generated by these systems using such data. Hence, it becomes imperative to develop a tool for the transformation of picture fuzzy sets into equivalent fuzzy sets, as explored in reference (Ejegwa, 2015).

One prevalent and highly regarded method for data collection involves soliciting the insights of experts. When these perspectives are gathered in a manner that accounts for the hesitancy inherent in the opinions and ideas of the population, they yield picture fuzzy set values instead of traditional fuzzy set or intuitionistic fuzzy set values.

4 Methods

In transforming picture fuzzy sets into fuzzy sets, it is possible to neglect the refusal part irrespective of its value, but this will yield incorrect results. Thus, some mathematical methods which are effective in obtaining fuzzy sets from picture fuzzy sets are presented.

Consider the set $\mathcal{Y} = \{a\}$. Let $\tilde{Q}$ be the picture fuzzy set given by

$$\tilde{Q} = \{< a, 0.55, 0.21, 0.15 >\}.$$

This implies that

$$\tilde{\sigma}(a) = 0.55,\ \tilde{\tau}(a) = 0.21 \text{ and } \tilde{\gamma}(a) = 0.15$$

Method 1

In this method, we decompose the refusal value into three equal parts and add them equally to $\tilde{\sigma}(a)$, $\tilde{\tau}(a)$ and $\tilde{\gamma}(a)$.

We find

$$\mathcal{S}_{\mathcal{Y}}(a) = 1 - (\tilde{\sigma}(a) + \tilde{\tau}(a) + \tilde{\gamma}(a))$$

Thus

$$\mathcal{S}_{\mathcal{Y}}(a) = 1 - (0.55 + 0.21 + 0.15) = 0.09$$

Then, we divide the refusal value into three equal parts. We get $\frac{0.09}{3} = 0.03$. The modified membership functions are

$$\tilde{\sigma}_{new}(a) = 0.55 + 0.03 = 0.58$$

$$\tilde{\tau}_{new}(a) = 0.21 + 0.03 = 0.24$$

$$\tilde{\gamma}_{new}(a) = 0.15 + 0.03 = 0.18$$

Hence, the equivalent fuzzy set to picture fuzzy set is

$$\tilde{Q}_{\mathcal{F}} = \{< a, 0.58 >\}$$

Method 2

In this method, the refusal value is added to the greatest value among $\tilde{\sigma}(a)$, $\tilde{\tau}(a)$ and $\tilde{\gamma}(a)$.

The positive membership degree is the greatest among all of the membership functions. Thus, the modified positive membership function is $\tilde{\sigma}_{new}(a) = 0.55 + 0.09 = 0.64$, where $\mathcal{S}_{\mathcal{Y}}(a) = 0.09$.

Therefore, the equivalent fuzzy set to picture fuzzy set is

$$\tilde{Q}_{\mathcal{F}} = \{< a, 0.64 >\}$$

Remark 4.1 If it happens that the positive membership degrees are equal, i.e., $\tilde{\sigma}(a) = \tilde{\tau}(a) = \tilde{\gamma}(a)$, then the refusal value is added arbitrarily to either $\tilde{\sigma}(a)$ or $\tilde{\tau}(a)$ or $\tilde{\gamma}(a)$ or we adopt method 1.

Method 3

In this method, we calculate the percentage of each of the membership degrees with respect to the sum of all of them, ignoring the refusal value. Then, we find the amount of these percentages from the refusal value. Finally, we add each of these amounts to the specific membership degree.

First, we calculate the percentage of each of the membership degrees with respect to their sum:

$$\% \, of \, \tilde{\sigma}(a) = \frac{\tilde{\sigma}(a)}{\tilde{\sigma}(a) + \tilde{\tau}(a) + \tilde{\gamma}(a)} = \frac{0.55}{0.91} \times 100 = 60.4396$$

$$\% \, of \, \tilde{\tau}(a) = \frac{\tilde{\tau}(a)}{\tilde{\sigma}(a) + \tilde{\tau}(a) + \tilde{\gamma}(a)} = \frac{0.21}{0.91} \times 100 = 23.0769$$

$$\% \, of \, \tilde{\gamma}(a) = \frac{\tilde{\gamma}(a)}{\tilde{\sigma}(a) + \tilde{\tau}(a) + \tilde{\gamma}(a)} = \frac{0.15}{0.91} \times 100 = 16.4835$$

Second, we compute the amount of these percentages from the refusal membership degree and add each of these amounts to the specific membership value.

$$60.4396\% \text{ of } 0.09 = 0.0544, \text{ then } \tilde{\sigma}_{new}(a) = 0.55 + 0.0544 = 0.6044,$$

$$23.0769\% \text{ of } 0.09 = 0.0208, \text{ then } \tilde{\tau}_{new}(a) = 0.21 + 0.0208 = 0.2308, \textit{ and}$$

$$\tilde{\gamma}_{new}(a) = 1 - (0.6044 + 0.2308) = 0.1648$$

Therefore, the equivalent fuzzy set is $\tilde{Q}_{\mathcal{F}} = \{< a, 0.6044 >\}$.

Example 2.5 Four students did a mathematics exam. After the exam is finished, each student declares his/her hesitated answers. The following table represents the grades taken by each of them:

a_i	$< \tilde{\sigma}(a_i), \tilde{\tau}(a_i), \tilde{\gamma}(a_i) >$
a_1	$< 0.4, 0.1, 0.2 >$
a_2	$< 0.4, 0.01, 0.4 >$
a_3	$< 0.4, 0.2, 0 >$
a_4	$< 0.39, 0, 0 >$

where,

$\tilde{\sigma}(a_i)$ represents the grades gained from the true answers of the student a_i,
$\tilde{\tau}(a_i)$ represents the grades gained from the hesitated answers of the student a_i,
and $\tilde{\gamma}(a_i)$ represents the grades lost from the wrong answers of the student a_i.

Using method 3, we transform the picture fuzzy set data into fuzzy set ones and we get the following results:

a_i	$<\tilde{\sigma}(a_i), \tilde{\tau}(a_i), \tilde{\gamma}(a_i)>$	$\tilde{\sigma}_{new}(a_i)$
a_1	$< 0.4, 0.1, 0.2 >$	0.57
a_2	$< 0.4, 0.01, 0.4 >$	0.549
a_3	$< 0.4, 0.2, 0 >$	0.66
a_4	$< 0.39, 0, 0 >$	1

Therefore, the equivalent fuzzy set of the given picture fuzzy set is:

$$\tilde{Q}_{\mathcal{F}} = \{< a_1, 0.57 >, < a_2, 0.549 >, < a_3, 0.66 >, < a_4, 1 >\}$$

5 Conclusion

The transformation of picture fuzzy sets into conventional fuzzy sets emerges as a significant and contemporary endeavor, offering a bridge between innovative concepts and practical applications. With well-established effectiveness in data analysis and decision-making processes, fuzzy sets play a crucial role in industrial contexts. This chapter has examined three distinct transformation methods, presenting a streamlined approach for users of fuzzy logic and fuzzy control in diverse industrial applications. Notably, Method 3 stands out as the most suitable choice, ensuring the acquisition of precise fuzzy values essential for accurate decision-making. As the applications of picture fuzzy sets continue to expand, this transformation process serves as a vital link, enhancing the practical utility of fuzzy sets and furthering their relevance in an ever-evolving technological landscape.

References

Adabavazeh, N., Amindoust, A., & Nikbakht, M. (2022). A Fuzzy BWM approach to prioritize distribution network enablers. *International Journal of Research in Industrial Engineering, 11*(4), 349–365.

Akram, M., Bashir, A., & Edalatpanah, S. A. (2021). A hybrid decision-making analysis under complex q-rung picture fuzzy Einstein averaging operators. *Computational and Applied Mathematics, 40*, 1–35.

Alayande, S., Akande, E., & Egere, A. (2021). Application of fuzzy algebraic model to statistical analysis of neuro-psychopathology data. *Journal of Fuzzy Extension and Applications, 2*(2), 156–162.

Ansari, A. Q., Siddiqui, S. A., & Alvi, J. A. (2004). Mathematical techniques to convert intuitionistic fuzzy sets into fuzzy sets. *Note on IFS, 10*(1), 13–17.

Arora, S., Vadhera, R., & Chugh, B. (2021). A decision-making system for Corona prognosis using fuzzy inference system. *Journal of Fuzzy Extension and Applications, 2*(4), 344–354.

Asif, M., Ishtiaq, U., & Argyros, I. K. (2024). Hamacher Aggregation Operators for Pythagorean Fuzzy Set and its Application in Multi-Attribute Decision-Making Problem. *Spectrum of Operational Research, 2*(1), 27-40. https://doi.org/10.31181/sor2120258

Atanassov, K. T. (1986). Intuitionistic fuzzy sets. *Fuzzy Sets and Systems, 20*, 87–96.

Atanassov, K. T. (2012). *On intuitionistic fuzzy sets theory* (Vol. 283). Springer.

Atanassov, K. T., & Atanassov, K. T. (1999). *Intuitionistic fuzzy sets* (pp. 1-137). Physica-Verlag HD.

Bhattacharya, J. (2016). A few more on intuitionistic fuzzy set. *Journal of fuzzy set valued analysis, 3*, 214–222.

Bhattacharya, J. (2021). Some results on certain properties of intuitionistic fuzzy sets. *Journal of Fuzzy Extension and Applications, 2*(4), 377–387.

Chen, T., Karimov, I., Chen, J., & Constantinovitc, A. (2020). Computer and fuzzy theory application: review in home appliances. *Journal of Fuzzy Extension and Applications, 1*(2), 133–138.

Cuong, B. C., & Kreinovich, V. (2013). Picture fuzzy sets-a new concept for computational intelligence problems. In *2013 third world congress on information and communication technologies (WICT 2013)* (pp. 1–6). IEEE.

Cuong, B. C., & Pham, V. H. (2015). Some fuzzy logic operators for picture fuzzy sets. In *2015 seventh international conference on knowledge and systems engineering (KSE)* (pp. 132–137). IEEE.

Cuong, B. C., & Kreinovich, V. (2014). Picture fuzzy sets. *Journal of computer science and cybernetics, 30*(4), 409–420.

Dutta, P., & Ganju, S. (2018). Some aspects of picture fuzzy set. *Transactions of A. Razmadze Mathematical Institute, 172*(2), 164–175.

Ejegwa, P. A. (2015). Mathematical techniques to transform intuitionistic fuzzy multisets to fuzzy sets. *Journal of Information and Computing Science, 10*(2), 169–172.

El-Morsy, S. (2022). Optimization of fuzzy zero-base budgeting. *Computational Algorithms and Numerical Dimensions, 1*(4), 147–154.

El-Shorbagy, M. A., Mousa, A. A. A., ALoraby, H., & Abo-Kila, T. (2020). Evolutionary algorithm for multi-objective multi-index transportation problem under fuzziness. *Journal of Applied Research on Industrial Engineering, 7*(1), 36–56.

Ganie, A. H. (2023). A picture fuzzy distance measure and its application to pattern recognition problems. *Iranian Journal of Fuzzy Systems, 20*(1), 71–85.

Gazi, K. H., Raisa, N., Biswas, A., Azizzadeh, F., & Mondal, S. P. (2024). Finding the most important criteria in women's empowerment for sports sector by pentagonal fuzzy DEMATEL methodology. *Spectrum of Decision Making and Applications, 2*(1), 28–52. https://doi.org/10.31181/sdmap21202510

Gu, X. B., Ma, Y., Wu, Q. H., & Liu, Y. B. (2022). The application of intuitionistic fuzzy set-TOPSIS model on the level assessment of the surrounding rocks. *Shock and Vibration*. https://doi.org/10.1155/2022/4263276

Heravi, A., Zamani Moghadam, A., Hashemi, S. A., Vakil Alroaia, Y., & Sajadi Jagharg, A. (2023). Evaluation of the influential factors in human resource development in state-owned enterprises using a mixed method. *Journal of Applied Research on Industrial Engineering, 10*(2), 238–255.

Hussain, A., & Ullah, K. (2024). An intelligent decision support system for spherical fuzzy Sugeno-Weber aggregation operators and real-life applications. *Spectrum of Mechanical Engineering and Operational Research, 1*(1), 177–188. https://doi.org/10.31181/smeor11202415

Imeni, M. (2020). Fuzzy logic in accounting and auditing. *Journal of Fuzzy Extension and Applications, 1*(1), 66–72.

Imran, R., Ullah, K., Ali, Z., & Akram, M. (2024). A Multi-Criteria Group Decision-Making Approach for Robot Selection Using Interval-Valued Intuitionistic Fuzzy Information and Aczel-Alsina Bonferroni Means. *Spectrum of Decision Making and Applications, 1*(1), 1–32. https://doi.org/10.31181/sdmap1120241

Kannan, J., Jayakumar, V., & Pethaperumal, M. (2024). Advanced Fuzzy-Based Decision-Making: The Linear Diophantine Fuzzy CODAS Method for Logistic Specialist Selection. *Spectrum of Operational Research, 2*(1), 41–60. https://doi.org/10.31181/sor2120259

Kaviani, M., & Fakhrehosseini, S. (2020). Application of fuzzy logic in portfolio management: evidence from Iranian researches. *Journal of Fuzzy Extension and Applications, 1*(2), 108–111.

Khan, M. J., Kumam, P., Ashraf, S., & Kumam, W. (2019). Generalized picture fuzzy soft sets and their application in decision support systems. *Symmetry, 11*(3), 415.

Khodadadi-Karimvand, M., & Shirouyehzad, H. (2021). Well drilling fuzzy risk assessment using fuzzy FMEA and fuzzy TOPSIS. *Journal of Fuzzy Extension and Applications, 2*(2), 144–155.

Kumar, S., Arya, V., Kumar, S., & Dahiya, A. (2022). A new picture fuzzy entropy and its application based on combined picture fuzzy methodology with partial weight information. *International Journal of Fuzzy Systems, 24*(7), 3208–3225.

Mohammad Kamrul, H., Md. Yasin, A., Abeda, S., & Nirmal Kanti, M. (2022). Some picture fuzzy mean operators and their applications in decision-making. *Journal of Fuzzy Extension and Applications, 3*(4), 349–361.

Olabanji, O. M. (2020). Fuzzified synthetic extent weighted average for appraisal of design concepts. *International Journal of Research in Industrial Engineering, 9*(2), 183–201.

Roan, N., Coll, S., Alonso, M., Rubio, J. M., López, P., Andujar, F., Le, S., Vu, M., & Smarandache, F. (2020). The picture fuzzy distance measure in controlling network power consumption. *Journal of Fuzzy Extension and Applications, 1*(3), 139–158.

Sahoo, S. K., Choudhury, B. B., & Dhal, P. R. (2024). A bibliometric analysis of material selection using MCDM methods: Trends and insights. *Spectrum of Mechanical Engineering and Operational Research, 1*(1), 189–205. https://doi.org/10.31181/smeor11202417

Sahu, R., Dash, S. R., & Das, S. (2021). Career selection of students using hybridized distance measure based on picture fuzzy set and rough set theory. *Decision Making: Applications in Management and Engineering, 4*(1), 104–126.

Sangodapo, T. (2022). Some notions on convexity of picture fuzzy sets: convexity of picture fuzzy sets. *Journal of the Nigerian Mathematical Society, 41*(2), 83–103.

Si, A., Das, S., & Kar, S. (2021). Picture fuzzy set-based decision-making approach using Dempster-Shafer theory of evidence and grey relation analysis and its application in COVID-19 medicine selection. *Soft Computing*, 1–15.

Singh, S., & Ganie, A. H. (2022). Applications of a picture fuzzy correlation coefficient in pattern analysis and decision-making. *Granular computing*, 1–15.

Szmidt, E., & Szmidt, E. (2014). Intuitionistic Fuzzy Sets as a Generalization of Fuzzy Sets. *Distances and Similarities in Intuitionistic Fuzzy Sets, 307*, 7–38.

Taiwo, O. S., & Onasanya, B. O. (2022). Some characteristics of picture fuzzy subgroups via cut set of picture fuzzy set. *Ratio Mathematica, 42*, 341.

Yildirim, B. F., & Yıldırım, S. K. (2022). Evaluating the satisfaction level of citizens in municipality services by using picture fuzzy VIKOR method: 2014–2019 period analysis. *Decision Making: Applications in Management and Engineering, 5*(1), 50–66.

Zadeh, L. A. (1965). Fuzzy sets. *Information and Control, 8*, 338–353.

Zanjani, B., Amiri, M., Hanafizadeh, P., & Salahi, M. (2021). Robust multi-objective hybrid flow shop scheduling. *Journal of Applied Research on Industrial Engineering, 8*(1), 40–55.

Zhao, R. R., Luo, M. X., Li, S. G., & Ma, L. N. (2023). A parametric similarity measure between picture fuzzy sets and its applications in multi-attribute decision-making. *Iranian Journal of Fuzzy Systems, 20*(1), 87–102.

An Enhanced Score Function for Quadripartitioned Single-Valued Neutrosophic Sets

Akanksha Singh, Said Broumi, S. Krishna Prabha, Assia Bakali, and Mohamed Talea

Abstract The concept of the fuzzy neutrosophic soft matrix (NSM) has advanced by integrating the neutrosophic set (NS) with a soft set to manage uncertain data. The recently introduced theory of fuzzy quadripartitioned NSM generalizes the NSM. Within this quadripartitioned single-valued (QSV) NS, the indeterminacy function's partition is categorized into contradiction and ignorance values. This study introduces an enhanced score function (SF) and accuracy function (AF) for the QSVNS, addressing existing limitations. Their properties are explored and verified through specific cases. Additionally, an example demonstrates the proposed multi-criteria decision-making method, emphasizing the importance of ranking orders in determining optimal outcomes. A comparative analysis showcases the efficacy of the new SF and AF against traditional methods.

Keywords Neutrosophic set · Quadripartitioned single-valued neutrosophic numbers · Score function · Accuracy function · Multi-criteria decision-making

---

A. Singh
Chandigarh University, Mohali, Punjab, India
e-mail: akanksha.e10462@cumail.in

S. Broumi (✉) · M. Talea
Laboratory of Information Processing, Faculty of Science Ben M'Sik, University of Hassan II, Casablanca, Morocco
e-mail: broumisaid78@gmail.com

S. Broumi
STIE Team, Regional Center for the Professions of Education and Training, Casablanca–Settat, Morocco

S. K. Prabha
Department of Mathematics, PSNA College of Engineering and Technology, Dindigul, Tamil Nadu, India

A. Bakali
Ecole Royale Navale-Boulevard Sour Jdid, B.P 16303 Casablanca, Morocco

© The Author(s), under exclusive license to Springer Nature Singapore Pte Ltd. 2024
S. A. Edalatpanah et al. (eds.), *Analytical Decision Making and Data Envelopment Analysis*, Infosys Science Foundation Series in Mathematical Sciences,
https://doi.org/10.1007/978-981-97-6972-8_21

1 Introduction

Zadeh in (1965), established a fuzzy set (FS), allowing components to have varying strength of membership value in the collection. The strength of membership falls within the range of real-closed interval [0, 1]. Atanassov in (1986), proposed the intuitionistic fuzzy set (IFS) and suggested membership, and non-membership value to the elements in the collection. By expanding IFS and commencing the truth, indeterminacy, and falsities, Samrandache in (1999), established the ideology of NS. Wang et al. in (2010), propounded the idea of a single-valued neutrosophic (SVN) set, which is a generalization of the classical set, FS, the spacing value fuzzy set, and the IFS. A new hybrid model of the SVN model was proposed by Yang in (2017). Edalatpanah (2020), introduced the concept of the neutrosophic structured element (NSE) as an advancement in neutrosophic sets (NS), establishing operational laws, a score function, and several aggregation operators specific to NS; for more models and applications of NS, see (Bhat, 2023; Dhar, 2021; Duran et al., 2021; Edalatpanah & Smarandache, 2023; Edalatpanah et al., 2023a, 2023b; Hosseinzadeh & Tayyebi, 2023; Ihsan et al., 2023; Kumar et al., 2019; Kumari et al., 2023; Mohanta & Toragay, 2023; Nagarajan et al., 2023; Polymenis, 2021; Stanimirović et al., 2023; Veeramani et al., 2022; Wang et al., 2021).

Chatterjee et al. in (2016) commenced the concept of QSVNS which is entirely built on Belnap's (1977) four-valued logic and Smarandache's (1999) "four-digit neutrosophic logic", which suggests that if the uncertainty element of an NS is disposed into two proportions: "contradiction" (both true and false) and "unknown" (neither true nor false), then four elements are obtained, denoted as T, C, U, and F, that interpret a new set called QSVNS. By combining the theory of rough sets and QSVNS, Mohana and Mohanasundari in (2018), introduced a new hybrid model of the QSVN rough set. Mohana and Mohanasundari in (2019), studied various similarity measures (SMs) of SVN rough sets; see also (Mohan & Krishnaswamy, 2020; Radha & Arul Mary, 2021; Radha et al., 2023a, 2023b).

Dombi in (1982), invented Dombi Bonferroni mean operators, and because of their excellent exhibits with a generic parameter, they are often employed in multi-attribute group decision-making (MGDM) situations. Ye in (2014), utilized aggregation operators for the MGDM method for simplified neutrosophic sets (NSs). Hamacher aggregation operators and their application to MGDM in some generalized neutrosophic numbers are studied by Liu et al. in (2014). The application of interval NSs in MGDM problems was presented by Zhang et al. in (2014). Sun et al. (2015) proposed the interval neutrosophic numbers Choquet integral operator for MGDM. Interval neutrosophic prioritized ordered weighted aggregation operator and its application to MGDM was discussed by Liu and Wang (2016). Wu et al. in (2016) discussed the applications of MGDM problems in simplified NSs environments using cross-entropy and prioritized aggregation operators. Some SVN Dombi weighted aggregation operators for MGDM problems were researched by Chen and Ye in (2017).

Innovative perceptions on QSVN Graph with real-life is proposed by Hussain et al. in (2022). In 2020 Chatterjee et al. (2020) discussed quadripartitioned neutrosophic (QN) weighted aggregation operators using QN numbers in an interval-valued possibility QSVN soft set environment. In 2020, SMs of SVN bipolar NSs was presented by Roy et al. (2020). The application of QN cross-entropy in MGDM was discussed by Mohanasundari and Mohana in (2021).

This chapter introduces two types of QSVNNs Dombi T-norm and T-Conorm operators, focusing on the QSVN environment. We present the quadripartitioned SVN Dombi weighted arithmetic (QSVNDWAA) and geometric (QSVNDWGA) aggregation operators, analyzing their properties. To determine the optimal choice among available options, we propose a modified score function (SF) and accuracy function (AF) for QSVNSs, aiming to rank QSVNS alternatives effectively.

The manuscript is organized as per Sect. 1. Introduction of the proposed work Sect. 2. Basic preliminaries are discussed. Section 3. The proposed SF and AF for QSVNSs and their properties Sect. 4. Methodology is described Sect. 5. Comparison Analysis from the existing literature is discussed with an illustration of the novel ranking method with the best procedure for choosing a superior alternative Sect. 6. Finally, the work is concluded.

2 Preliminaries

Some important requisites of the single-valued neutrosophic set (SVNS), and QSVNSs for real-life problems in De–M.

Definition 2.1 Let X be a non-empty set. A set $\tilde{\mathcal{A}}^{\mathrm{N}}$ is a neutrosophic set (NS) (Smarandache, 1999) defined over a real non-standard unit interval $\left]0^{-}, 1^{+}\right[$, and is expressed as

$$\tilde{\mathcal{A}}^{N} = \left\{ \begin{array}{l} x,\ \lambda_{\tilde{\mathcal{A}}^{N}}(x),\ \mu_{\tilde{\mathcal{A}}^{N}}(x), \nu_{\tilde{\mathcal{A}}^{N}}(x) | \ x \in X,\ 0^{-} \leq \lambda_{\tilde{\mathcal{A}}^{N}}(x),\ \mu_{\tilde{\mathcal{A}}^{N}}(x), \\ \nu_{\tilde{\mathcal{A}}^{N}}(x) \leq 1^{+},\ \lambda_{\tilde{\mathcal{A}}^{N}}(x) + \mu_{\tilde{\mathcal{A}}^{N}}(x) + \nu_{\tilde{\mathcal{A}}^{N}}(x) \leq 3^{+} \end{array} \right\},$$

whereas, a set $\tilde{\mathcal{A}}^{\mathrm{N}}$ is a single-valued neutrosophic set (SVNS) (Wang et al., 2010), defined over a real standard unit interval $[0, 1]$, and is expressed as

$$\tilde{\mathcal{A}}^{\mathrm{N}} = \left\{ \begin{array}{l} \mathrm{x}, \lambda_{\tilde{\mathcal{A}}^{\mathrm{N}}}(\mathrm{x}), \mu_{\tilde{\mathcal{A}}^{\mathrm{N}}}(\mathrm{x}), \nu_{\tilde{\mathcal{A}}^{\mathrm{N}}}(\mathrm{x}) | \ \mathrm{x} \in \mathrm{X}, 0 \leq \lambda_{\tilde{\mathcal{A}}^{\mathrm{N}}}(\mathrm{x}) \leq 1, \\ 0 \leq \mu_{\tilde{\mathcal{A}}^{\mathrm{N}}}(\mathrm{x}) \leq 1, 0 \leq \nu_{\tilde{\mathcal{A}}^{\mathrm{N}}}(\mathrm{x}) \leq 1, \lambda_{\tilde{\mathcal{A}}^{\mathrm{N}}}(\mathrm{x}) + \mu_{\tilde{\mathcal{A}}^{\mathrm{N}}}(\mathrm{x}) + \nu_{\tilde{\mathcal{A}}^{\mathrm{N}}}(\mathrm{x}) \leq 3 \end{array} \right\}$$

In an NS $\tilde{\mathcal{A}}^{\mathrm{N}}$, $\lambda_{\tilde{\mathcal{A}}^{\mathrm{N}}}(\mathrm{x})$, $\mu_{\tilde{\mathcal{A}}^{\mathrm{N}}}(\mathrm{x})$, and $\nu_{\tilde{\mathcal{A}}^{\mathrm{N}}}(\mathrm{x})$ characterize the truth value, the indeterminacy value, and the false value of the element x in $\tilde{\mathcal{A}}^{\mathrm{N}}$.

Definition 2.2 Let X be a non-empty set. A set

$$\tilde{Q}^N = \Big\{x, t_{\tilde{Q}^N}(x),\ c_{\tilde{Q}^N}(x),\ u_{\tilde{Q}^N}(x), f_{\tilde{Q}^N}(x)|x \in X, 0 \le t_{\tilde{Q}^N}(x), c_{\tilde{Q}^N}(x), u_{\tilde{Q}^N}(x),$$

$$f_{\tilde{Q}^N}(x) \le 1, t_{\tilde{Q}^N}(x) +\ c_{\tilde{Q}^N}(x) + u_{\tilde{Q}^N}(x) + f_{\tilde{Q}^N}(x) \le 4\Big\},$$

is said to be a quadripartitioned single-valued neutrosophic set (QSVNS) (Chatterjee et al., 2016), where, $t_{\tilde{Q}^N}(x), c_{\tilde{Q}^N}(x), u_{\tilde{Q}^N}(x)$, and $f_{\tilde{Q}^N}(x)$ are the true value, the contradiction value, ignorance value, and the false value respectively of the element x in $\tilde{Q}^N$. Also, when X is discrete, then the set $\tilde{Q}^N$ is represented as $\tilde{Q}^N = \{\sum_{i=1}^{n} \langle t_{\tilde{Q}_k^N}(x_i), c_{\tilde{Q}^N}(x_i), u_{\tilde{Q}^N}(x_i), f_{\tilde{Q}^N}(x_i)\rangle / x_i, x_i \in X\}$. For convenience in this article, QSVNS is written as $\tilde{Q}^N = \langle t_{\tilde{Q}_k^N}, c_{\tilde{Q}^N}, u_{\tilde{Q}^N}, f_{\tilde{Q}^N}\rangle$.

Definition 2.3 (Chatterjee et al., 2016) Let X be a non-empty set. The complement of a QSVNS $\tilde{Q}^N$ is denoted by $\left(\tilde{Q}^N\right)^c$ and is mathematically expressed as

$$\left(\tilde{Q}^N\right)^c = \left\{\sum_{i=1}^{n} f_{\tilde{Q}^N}(x_i), u_{\tilde{Q}^N}(x_i), c_{\tilde{Q}^N}(x_i), t_{\tilde{Q}^N}(x_i)/x_i, x_i \in X,\right\}$$

i.e.,$t_{\left(\tilde{Q}^N\right)^c}(x_i) = f_{\tilde{Q}^N}(x_i)$,$c_{\left(\tilde{Q}^N\right)^c}(x_i) = u_{\tilde{Q}^N}(x_i), u_{\left(\tilde{Q}^N\right)^c}(x_i) = c_{\tilde{Q}^N}(x_i)$,$f_{\left(\tilde{Q}^N\right)^c}(x_i) = t_{\tilde{Q}^N}(x_i)$,$x_i \in X$.

Definition 2.4 (Chatterjee et al., 2016) Consider two QSVNSs $\mathcal{A}$ and $\mathcal{B}$ over a non-empty set X, then a set $\mathcal{A}$ is said to be contained in $\mathcal{B}$, i.e., $\mathcal{A} \subseteq \mathcal{B}$, iff $t_{\mathcal{A}}(x) \le t_{\mathcal{B}}(x), c_{\mathcal{A}}(x) \le c_{\mathcal{B}}(x), u_{\mathcal{A}}(x) \le u_{\mathcal{B}}(x) \text{and} f_{\mathcal{A}}(x) \le f_{\mathcal{B}}(x)$.

Definition 2.5 (Chatterjee et al., 2016) Let $\mathcal{A}$ and $\mathcal{B}$ be two QSVNSs defined over a non-empty set X. The union of two QSVNSs $\mathcal{A}$ and $\mathcal{B}$ is defined as $\mathcal{A} \cup \mathcal{B} = \sum_{i=1}^{n} \langle t_{\mathcal{A}}(x_i) \vee t_{\mathcal{B}}(x_i), c_{\mathcal{A}}(x_i) \vee c_{\mathcal{B}}(x_i), u_{\mathcal{A}}(x_i) \vee u_{\mathcal{B}}(x_i), f_{\mathcal{A}}(x_i) \vee f_{\mathcal{B}}(x_i)\rangle / x_i, x_i \in X$.

Definition 2.6 (Chatterjee et al., 2016) Let $\mathcal{A}$ and $\mathcal{B}$ be two QSVNSs defined over a non-empty set X. The intersection of two QSVNSs $\mathcal{A}$ and $\mathcal{B}$ is defined as $\mathcal{A} \cap \mathcal{B} = \sum_{i=1}^{n} \langle t_{\mathcal{A}}(x_i) \wedge t_{\mathcal{B}}(x_i), c_{\mathcal{A}}(x_i) \wedge c_{\mathcal{B}}(x_i), u_{\mathcal{A}}(x_i) \wedge u_{\mathcal{B}}(x_i), f_{\mathcal{A}}(x_i) \wedge f_{\mathcal{B}}(x_i)\rangle / x_i, x_i \in X$.

Definition 2.7 (Chatterjee et al., 2020) An element of $[0,1]^4$, denoted by $\tilde{Q}^N = \langle t_{\tilde{Q}^N}, c_{\tilde{Q}^N}, u_{\tilde{Q}^N}, f_{\tilde{Q}^N}\rangle$ is called a quadripartitioned single-valued neutrosophic number (QSVNN), and the collection of all quadripartitioned single-valued neutrosophic numbers (QSVNNs) are represented by $\mathcal{QNN}$.

Definition 2.8 (Chatterjee et al., 2020) Let $\rho, \sigma \in \mathcal{QNN}$, and $k \in \mathbb{N}$ then the following basic operational laws hold:

(i) $\rho \oplus \sigma = \langle \rho_{t_{\tilde{Q}^N}} + \sigma_{t_{\tilde{Q}^N}} - \rho_{t_{\tilde{Q}^N}}\sigma_{t_{\tilde{Q}^N}}, \rho_{c_{\tilde{Q}^N}} + \sigma_{c_{\tilde{Q}^N}} - \rho_{c_{\tilde{Q}^N}}\sigma_{c_{\tilde{Q}^N}}, \rho_{u_{\tilde{Q}^N}}\sigma_{u_{\tilde{Q}^N}}, \rho_{f_{\tilde{Q}^N}}\sigma_{f_{\tilde{Q}^N}}\rangle$,

(ii) $\rho \odot \sigma = \left\langle \rho_{t_{\tilde{Q}^N}}\sigma_{t_{\tilde{Q}^N}}, \rho_{c_{\tilde{Q}^N}}\sigma_{c_{\tilde{Q}^N}}, \rho_{u_{\tilde{Q}^N}} + \sigma_{u_{\tilde{Q}^N}} - \rho_{u_{\tilde{Q}^N}}\sigma_{u_{\tilde{Q}^N}}, \rho_{f_{\tilde{Q}^N}} + \sigma_{f_{\tilde{Q}^N}} - \rho_{f_{\tilde{Q}^N}}\sigma_{f_{\tilde{Q}^N}} \right\rangle$,

(iii) $(\rho)^k = \langle \left(\rho_{t_{\tilde{Q}^N}}\right)^k, \left(\rho_{c_{\tilde{Q}^N}}\right)^k, 1 - \left(\rho_{u_{\tilde{Q}^N}}\right)^k, 1 - \left(\rho_{f_{\tilde{Q}^N}}\right)^k \rangle,$

(iv) $k\rho = \langle 1 - \left(\rho_{t_{\tilde{Q}^N}}\right)^k, 1 - \left(\rho_{c_{\tilde{Q}^N}}\right)^k, \left(\rho_{u_{\tilde{Q}^N}}\right)^k, \left(\rho_{f_{\tilde{Q}^N}}\right)^k \rangle.$

Definition 2.9 SF and AF for Ranking QSVNS Let X be a non-empty set and a set $\tilde{Q}^N = \left\{\langle x, t_{\tilde{Q}^N}(x), c_{\tilde{Q}^N}(x), u_{\tilde{Q}^N}(x), f_{\tilde{Q}^N}(x)\rangle | x \in X\right\}$ be a QSVNS, then SF and AF in the existing literature for QSVNS are defined as,

(i) Existing QSVNS SF and AF (Mohanasundari & Mohana, 2020) are defined in Eqs. (1) and (2) as follows:

$$E_S\left(\tilde{Q}^N\right) = \frac{3 + t_{\tilde{Q}^N}(x) - c_{\tilde{Q}^N}(x) - u_{\tilde{Q}^N}(x) - f_{\tilde{Q}^N}(x)}{4}, \text{ where } E_S\left(\tilde{Q}^N\right) \in [0,1], \quad (1)$$

$$H_A\left(\tilde{Q}^N\right) = t_{\tilde{Q}^N}(x) - f_{\tilde{Q}^N}(x), \text{ where } H_A\left(\tilde{Q}^N\right) \in [-1,1]. \quad (2)$$

(ii) Existing QSVNS SF and AF (Debnath, 2022) are defined in Eqs. (3) and (4) as follows:

$$S\left(\tilde{Q}^N\right) = \frac{t_{\tilde{Q}^N}(x) + c_{\tilde{Q}^N}(x) - u_{\tilde{Q}^N}(x) - f_{\tilde{Q}^N}(x)}{2}, \text{ where } S\left(\tilde{Q}^N\right) \in [0,1], \quad (3)$$

$$H\left(\tilde{Q}^N\right) = \frac{t_{\tilde{Q}^N}(x) + c_{\tilde{Q}^N}(x) + u_{\tilde{Q}^N}(x) + f_{\tilde{Q}^N}(x)}{2}, \text{ where } \tau_A\left(\tilde{Q}^N\right) \in [-1,1] \quad (4)$$

(iii) Existing QSVNS SF and AF (Chatterjee et al., 2020) are defined in Eqs. (5) and (6) as follows:

$$S_S\left(\tilde{Q}^N\right) = \frac{2 + t_{\tilde{Q}^N}(x) + c_{\tilde{Q}^N}(x) - u_{\tilde{Q}^N}(x) - f_{\tilde{Q}^N}(x)}{4}, \text{ where } S_S\left(\tilde{Q}^N\right) \in [0,1] \quad (5)$$

$$S_{A_1}\left(\tilde{Q}^N\right) = (t_{\tilde{Q}^N}(x) + c_{\tilde{Q}^N}(x)) - (u_{\tilde{Q}^N}(x) + f_{\tilde{Q}^N}(x)),$$

$$S_{A_2}\left(\tilde{Q}^N\right) = \frac{\left(t_{\tilde{Q}^N}(x) - c_{\tilde{Q}^N}(x)\right)}{2}, \text{ where } S_A\left(\tilde{Q}^N\right) \in [-1, 1] \quad (6)$$

$$S_{A_3}\left(\tilde{Q}^N\right) = \frac{(u_{\tilde{Q}^N}(x) - f_{\tilde{Q}^N}(x)}{2}$$

Definition 2.10 (Debnath, 2022) **Average operator for QSVNSs**. Since $\tilde{Q}^N = \left\{\langle x, t_{\tilde{Q}^N}(x), c_{\tilde{Q}^N}(x), u_{\tilde{Q}^N}(x), f_{\tilde{Q}^N}(x)\rangle | x \in X\right\}$ is a QSVNS, then let $\tilde{Q}^N_k (k = 1,2, \ldots, n)$ be n numbers of QSVNSs.

(i) The n-dimensional QN weighted arithmetic aggregation operator ($QSVN_{WAA}$) is a mapping $QSVN_{WAA}$: $QSVNN^n \rightarrow QSVNN$ defined as, $QSVN_{WAA} = \tilde{Q}_k^N (k = 1,2, \ldots, n) = \oplus_{k-1}^{n} w_k \tilde{Q}_k^N$, where $w = (w_1, w_2, \ldots, w_n)^T = w_k$ denotes the weight vector of QSVNSs $\tilde{Q}_k^N (k = 1,2, \ldots, n)$ and satisfies the constraint, $w_k \in [0, 1]$and $\sum_{k=1}^{n} w_k = 1$. The general expression for $QSVN_{WAA}$ is given as:

$$QSVN_{WAA} = \left\langle 1 - \prod_{k=1}^{n} \left(1 - t_{\tilde{Q}_k^N}\right)^{w_k}, 1 - \prod_{k=1}^{n} \left(1 - c_{\tilde{Q}_k^N}\right)^{w_k}, \prod_{k=1}^{n} \left(u_{\tilde{Q}_k^N}\right)^{w_k}, \prod_{k=1}^{n} \left(f_{\tilde{Q}_k^N}\right)^{w_k} \right\rangle \tag{7}$$

(ii) The n-dimensional QN weighted geometric aggregation operator ($QSVN_{WGA}$) is a mapping $QSVN_{WGA}$: $QSVNN^n \rightarrow QSVNN$ defined as, $QSVN_W GA = \tilde{Q}_k^N (k = 1, 2, \cdots, n) = \odot_{(k-1)}^{n} (\tilde{Q}_k^N)^{(w_k)}$, where $w = (w_1, w_2, \ldots, w_n)^T = w_k$ denotes the weight vector of QSVNSs $\tilde{Q}_k^N (k = 1,2, \ldots, n)$ and satisfies the conditions such that $w_k \in [0, 1]$and $\sum_{k=1}^{n} w_k = 1$. The general expression for $QSVN_{WGA}$ is given as:

$$QSVN_{WGA} = \left\langle \prod_{k=1}^{n} \left(t_{\tilde{Q}_k^N}\right)^{w_k}, \prod_{k=1}^{n} \left(c_{\tilde{Q}_k^N}\right)^{w_k}, 1 - \prod_{k=1}^{n} \left(1 - u_{\tilde{Q}_k^N}\right)^{w_k}, 1 - \prod_{k=1}^{n} \left(1 - f_{\tilde{Q}_k^N}\right)^{w_k} \right\rangle \tag{8}$$

The examples given below show that the existing SF and AF (Chatterjee et al., 2020; Debnath, 2022; Mohanasundari & Mohana, 2020) exhibit certain limitations and are not able to lead to the preferable solution in making a selection between any two QSVNNs.

Example 2.1 Let $\tilde{Q}_1^N = \langle 0.38, 0.50, 0.29, 0.62 \rangle$, and $\tilde{Q}_2^N = \langle 0.44, 0.65, 0.14, 0.68 \rangle$ be any two QSVNNs, then by using the existing SF Eq. (1) and AF, Eq. (2) (Chatterjee et al., 2016), the obtained SF and AF is:

$$E_S\left(\tilde{Q}_1^N\right) = 0.4925 \text{ and } E_S(\tilde{Q}_2^N) = 0.4925,$$

$$H_A\left(\tilde{Q}_1^N\right) = -0.24 \text{ and } H_A\left(\tilde{Q}_2^N\right) = -0.24,$$

which states that both the QSVNNs $\tilde{Q}_1^N$ and $\tilde{Q}_2^N$ are equal but in actuality, these 'QSVNNs are not the same numbers so no conclusion can be drawn using the existing SF, Eq. (1) and AF Eq. (2) (Mohanasundari & Mohana, 2020).

Example 2.2 Let $\tilde{Q}_1^N = \langle 0.3, 0.7, 0.4, 0.5\rangle$, and $\tilde{Q}_2^N = \langle 0.4, 0.6, 0.5, 0.4\rangle$ be any two QSVNNs, then by using the existing SF, Eq. (3) and AF Eq. (4) (Debnath, 2022), the obtained SF and AF is:

$$\mathrm{S}(\tilde{Q}_1^N) = 0.025 \text{ and } S(\tilde{Q}_2^N) = 0.025,$$
$$\mathrm{H}(\tilde{Q}_1^N) = 0.475 \text{ and } \mathrm{H}(\tilde{Q}_2^N) = 0.475,$$

which states that both the QSVNNs $\tilde{Q}_1^N$ and $\tilde{Q}_2^N$ are equal but in actuality, these 'QSVNNs are not the same numbers, so no conclusion can be drawn using the existing SF, Eq. (3) and AF Eq. (4) (Debnath, 2022).

Example 2.3 Here the same Example 2.2 is evaluated by using the existing SF, Eq. (5) (Chatterjee et al., 2020), then the obtained score value is

$$S_S(\tilde{Q}_1^N) = 0.5250 \text{ and } S_S(\tilde{Q}_2^N) = 0.5250.$$

Since by using the existing SF Eq. (5) (Chatterjee et al., 2020), the obtained score value ranks both the QSVNNs $\tilde{Q}_1^N$ and $\tilde{Q}_2^N$ as equal numbers, therefore no conclusion can be drawn.So, now the accuracy value for the QSVNNs $\tilde{Q}_1^N$, and $\tilde{Q}_2^N$ is determined by using the existing AF, $\mathrm{S}_{A_1}\left(\tilde{\mathrm{Q}}^{\mathrm{N}}\right)$, and $\mathrm{S}_{A_3}\left(\tilde{\mathrm{Q}}^{\mathrm{N}}\right)$ of Eq. (6) (Chatterjee et al., 2020) and it is observed that,

$$S_{A_1}(\tilde{Q}_1^N) = S_{A_1}(\tilde{Q}_2^N) = 0.1,$$

$$S_{A_3}(\tilde{Q}_1^N) = S_{A_3}(\tilde{Q}_2^N) = -0.05,$$

indicating no conclusion can be drawn. But on applying the $\mathrm{S}_{A_2}\left(\tilde{\mathrm{Q}}^{\mathrm{N}}\right)$ AF of Eq. (6) (Chatterjee et al., 2020), the obtained accuracy value suggests that

$$S_{A_2}(\tilde{Q}_1^N) = -0.2$$

, and

$S_{A_2}(\tilde{Q}_2^N) = -0.1$, that implies $S_{A_2}(\tilde{Q}_2^N) > S_{A_2}(\tilde{Q}_1^N)$, henceforth $\tilde{Q}_2^N > \tilde{Q}_1^N$.

It is noted that the existing AF Eq. (6) (Chatterjee et al., 2020) poses more computational efforts to deduce an optimal solution, if the data is huge then it would require more time and cost and still at some point it may or may not lead to the conclusion.

Thus, from Example 2.1, Example 2.2, and Example 2.3, it is observed that there may exist several QSVNNs which could be ranked equally by using Eqs. (1)-(6) and hence makes it difficult to choose a superior QSVNN among all the present alternatives by using the existing SF and AF (Chatterjee et al., 2020; Debnath, 2022; Mohanasundari & Mohana, 2020), therefore a new SF and a new AF are required to make a better judgment in a De-M problem and to reduce computational efforts.

3 Suggested SF and AF for QSVNSs

This section presents a novel SF and AF to determine the highest QSVNSs among all the available alternatives.

3.1 Suggested SF for QSVNSs

Let $\tilde{Q}^N = \left\{ \langle x, t_{\tilde{Q}^N}(x), c_{\tilde{Q}^N}(x), u_{\tilde{Q}^N}(x), f_{\tilde{Q}^N}(x) \rangle | x \in X \right\}$ be a QSVNS, then an SF in terms of the truth value, the contradiction value, ignorance value, and the false value respectively for QSVNS, is defined as:

$$\psi_S(\tilde{Q}^N) = \frac{3 - t_{\tilde{Q}^N} + 2\,c_{\tilde{Q}^N} - 2\,u_{\tilde{Q}^N} - f_{\tilde{Q}^N}}{4}, \text{ where } \psi_S(\tilde{Q}^N) \in [0, 1]. \quad (9)$$

To support the claim of the suggested SF (Eq. (9)), Example 2.1, Example 2.2, and Example 2.3 are solved again by using the suggested SF (Eq. (9)) as follows:

Example 3.1.1 On applying the new proposed SF $\psi_S(\tilde{Q}^N)$ given in Eq. (9) to Example 2.1, then the score values are obtained as follows:

$$\psi_S(\tilde{Q}_1^N) = 0.7950 \text{ and } \psi_S(\tilde{Q}_2^N) = 0.9450$$

Therefore, as shown below in Fig. 1, $\tilde{Q}_2^N > \tilde{Q}_1^N$ by using the proposed SF $\psi_S(\tilde{Q}^N)$ given in Eq. (9).

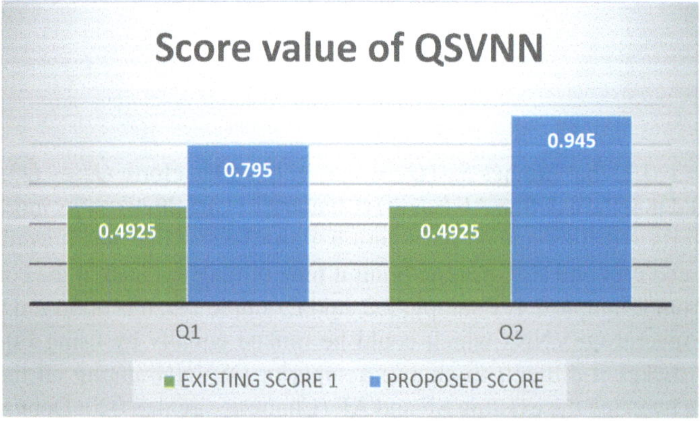

Fig. 1 Score value of Example 2.1

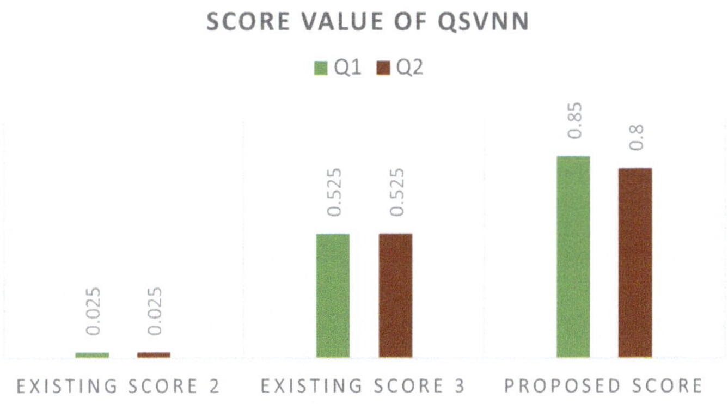

Fig. 2 Score value of Examples 2.2, 2.3 and 3.1.2

Example 3.1.2 On applying the new proposed SF $\psi_S(\tilde{Q}^N)$ given in Eq.(9) to Example 2.2, then the score values are obtained as follows:

$$\psi_S(\tilde{Q}_1^N) = 0.85 \text{ and } \psi_S(\tilde{Q}_2^N) = 0.8$$

Therefore, as shown below in Fig. 2, $\tilde{Q}_1^N > \tilde{Q}_2^N$ by using the proposed SF $\psi_S(\tilde{Q}^N)$ given in Eq. (9).

Thus, from Sect. 2, Examples 2.1, 2.2, and 2.3 it is observed that there may exist several QSVNNs which could be ranked equally by using Eqs. (1)-(6) and hence makes it difficult to choose a superior QSVNN among all the present alternatives, but from Sect. 3.1, the suggested SF (Eq. 9) is providing a reasonable result as shown in Examples 3.1.1 and 3.1.2 respectively. Hence, it claims the superiority of the suggested SF Eq. (9), which states its effectiveness.

Since we do not live in an absolute world, there may exist certain ambiguous data that could be expressed as a QSVNS, but which may or may not sometimes fail the suggested SF (Eq. (9)) as stated in the example given.

Example 3.1.3 Let $\tilde{Q}_1^N = \langle 0.7, 0.2, 0.1, 0.2\rangle$, and $\tilde{Q}_2^N = \langle 0.8, 0.6, 0.3, 0.5\rangle$ be any two QSVNNs, then by using the proposed SF Eq. (9), we get

$$\psi_S(\tilde{Q}_1^N) = 0.575 \text{ and } \psi_S(\tilde{Q}_2^N) = 0.575,$$

which concludes that the two QSVNNs are equal, i.e., $\tilde{Q}_1^N = \tilde{Q}_2^N$ Hence, in such cases when the QSVNN are equal, then we require a better metric function like a new AF to rank them uniquely since the existing AF (Chatterjee et al., 2020; Debnath, 2022; Mohanasundari & Mohana, 2020) has certain limitations. Thus, to overcome such indecision due to equal QSVNNs it is essential to propose a new and valid AF.

3.2 Suggested AF for QSVNSs

In Sect. 3.1, from Example 3.1.3, it is observed that there may exist several QSVNNs where the new suggested SF (Eq. (9)) might give equal ranking for the QSVNNs, then the suggested SF, Eq. (9) may or may not be able to rank the QSVNNs uniquely, hence a new AF has been suggested in this section to measure such equal QSVNNs.

Let $\tilde{Q}^N = \left\{ \langle x, t_{\tilde{Q}^N}(x), c_{\tilde{Q}^N}(x), u_{\tilde{Q}^N}(x), f_{\tilde{Q}^N}(x) \rangle | x \in X \right\}$ be a QSVNS, then a new AF in terms of the truth value, the contradiction value, ignorance value, and the false value respectively for QSVNS, is defined as follows:

$$\varphi_A(\tilde{Q}^N) = t_{\tilde{Q}^N} - c_{\tilde{Q}^N}\left(1 - t_{\tilde{Q}^N}\right) + u_{\tilde{Q}^N}\left(1 - t_{\tilde{Q}^N}\right) - f_{\tilde{Q}^N}\left(1 - c_{\tilde{Q}^N}\right) - f_{\tilde{Q}^N}(1 - u_{\tilde{Q}^N}), \tag{10}$$

where $\varphi_A(\tilde{Q}^N) \in [-1, 1]$,

Now we shall determine the ranking of equal QSVNNs, of Example 3.1.3 by using the suggested AF $\varphi_A(\tilde{Q}^N)$, Eq. (10) as follows:

Example 3.2.1 On applying the suggested AF $\varphi_A(\tilde{Q}^N)$ given in Eq. (10) to Example 3.1.3, the accuracy values are obtained as follows:

$$\varphi_A(\tilde{Q}_1^N) = 0.3300 \text{ and } \varphi_A(\tilde{Q}_2^N) = 0.1900.$$

Therefore, the QSVNN $\tilde{Q}_1^N > \tilde{Q}_2^N$ by using the suggested AF $\varphi_A(\tilde{Q}^N)$ given in Eq. (10).Also, the suggested AF $\varphi_A(\tilde{Q}^N)$ given in Eq. (10) is applied to Examples 2.1, 2.2, and 2.3 of Sect. 2, and the obtained accuracy values are as follows:

Example 2.1 $\varphi_A(\tilde{Q}_1^N) = -0.5004$ and $\varphi_A(\tilde{Q}_2^N) = -0.6684$, i.e., the QSVNN $\tilde{Q}_1^N > \tilde{Q}_2^N$.

Example 2.2 $\varphi_A(\tilde{Q}_1^N) = -0.3600$, and $\varphi_A(\tilde{Q}_2^N) = -0.0200$, i.e., the QSVNN $\tilde{Q}_2^N > \tilde{Q}_1^N$.

Hence, as shown above, in Fig. 3, Example 3.2.1, asserts the validity of the suggested accuracy function that it provides a reasonable and effective solution to De-M problems when the various existing SF and AF (Chatterjee et al., 2020; Debnath, 2022; Mohanasundari & Mohana, 2020) are exhibiting limitations.

3.3 Suggested MGDM Method for QSVNSs Using Suggested SF and AF

Based on the suggested SF $\psi_S(\tilde{Q}^N)$ and the suggested AF $\varphi_A(\tilde{Q}^N)$ given in Eqs. (9) and (10), of Sects. 3.1 and 3.2, an MCDeM method is proposed

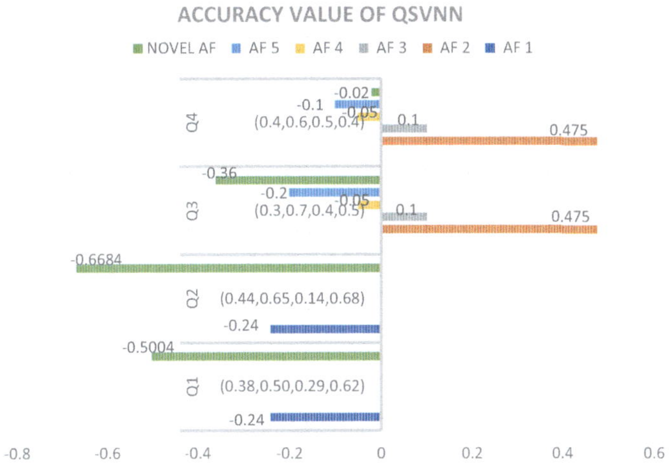

Fig. 3 Accuracy value of Examples 2.1, 2.2, 2.3 and 3.2.1

that provides a deliberate comparison technique to compare any two QSVNS $\tilde{Q}_1^N = \langle t_{\tilde{Q}_1^N}(x), c_{\tilde{Q}_1^N}(x), u_{\tilde{Q}_1^N}(x), f_{\tilde{Q}_1^N}(x)\rangle$ and $\tilde{Q}_2^N = \langle t_{\tilde{Q}_2^N}(x), c_{\tilde{Q}_2^N}(x), u_{\tilde{Q}_2^N}(x), f_{\tilde{Q}_2^N}(x)\rangle$ as follows:

- If $\psi_S(\tilde{Q}_1^N) > \psi_S(\tilde{Q}_2^N)$ then $\tilde{Q}_1^N > \tilde{Q}_2^N$.
- If $\psi_S(\tilde{Q}_1^N) < \psi_S(\tilde{Q}_2^N)$ then $\tilde{Q}_1^N < \tilde{Q}_2^N$.
- If $\psi_S(\tilde{Q}_1^N) = \psi_S(\tilde{Q}_2^N)$ then check $\varphi_A(\tilde{Q}^N)$ in the next step.
  - If $\psi_S(\tilde{Q}_1^N) < \psi_S(\tilde{Q}_2^N)$ then $\tilde{Q}_1^N < \tilde{Q}_2^N$.
  - If $\psi_S(\tilde{Q}_1^N) = \psi_S(\tilde{Q}_2^N)$ then check $\varphi_A(\tilde{Q}^N)$ in the next step.
  - If $\varphi_A(\tilde{Q}_1^N) > \varphi_A(\tilde{Q}_2^N)$ then $\tilde{Q}_1^N > \tilde{Q}_2^N$.

Thus, the suggested SF, Eq. (9), and the suggested AF, Eq. (10) can rank every QSVNN and hence, are efficient to provide an effective solution.

4 Properties of the Suggested SF and AF for QSVNSs

To support the suggested SF, Eq. (9), and the suggested AF, Eq. (10) stated in Sects. 3.1 and 3.2, a detailed analysis of their properties is presented below:

Property 4.1 *For QSVNS* $\tilde{Q}^N = \left\{\langle x, t_{\tilde{Q}^N}(x), c_{\tilde{Q}^N}(x), u_{\tilde{Q}^N}(x), f_{\tilde{Q}^N}(x)\rangle | x \in X\right\}$ *the value of the suggested* SF $\psi_S(\tilde{Q}^N)$, Eq. (9) *lies between* [0,1], i.e., $\psi_S(\tilde{Q}^N) \in [0,1]$.

Proof Let us consider QSVNS $\tilde{Q}^N = \left\{\langle x, t_{\tilde{Q}^N}(x), c_{\tilde{Q}^N}(x), u_{\tilde{Q}^N}(x), f_{\tilde{Q}^N}(x)\rangle | x \in X\right\}$.

(i) Suppose, $t_{\tilde{Q}^N}(x) = f_{\tilde{Q}^N}(x)$ and $c_{\tilde{Q}^N}(x) = u_{\tilde{Q}^N}(x)$, then according to the suggested SF, Eq. (9), we have $\psi_S(\tilde{Q}^N) \in [0.25, 0.75]$ as $t_{\tilde{Q}^N}(x) \in [0,1]$.
(ii) Since by the definition of QSVNS for each $x \in X$, $t_{\tilde{Q}^N}(x), c_{\tilde{Q}^N}(x), u_{\tilde{Q}^N}(x), f_{\tilde{Q}^N}(x) \in [0,1]$ and $0 \leq t_{\tilde{Q}^N}(x) + c_{\tilde{Q}^N}(x) + u_{\tilde{Q}^N}(x) + f_{\tilde{Q}^N}(x) \leq 4$, so let $\tilde{Q}^N = \langle 1,1,1,1 \rangle$, then according to the suggested SF, Eq. (9), we have

$$\psi_S(\tilde{Q}^N) = \frac{3 - 1 + 2(1) - 2(1) - 1}{4} = 0.25 \in [0,1]$$

Property 4.2 *For QSVNS* $\tilde{Q}^N = \left\{\langle x, t_{\tilde{Q}^N}(x), c_{\tilde{Q}^N}(x), u_{\tilde{Q}^N}(x), f_{\tilde{Q}^N}(x)\rangle | x \in X\right\}$ or QSVNN $\tilde{Q}^N = \langle t, c, u, f\rangle$ *(for convenience), the suggested SF, Eq.* (9) *relate with the existing SF,* $E_S\left(\tilde{Q}^N\right)$ *as follows:* $\psi_S(\tilde{Q}^N) = \frac{3-t+2c-2u-f}{4} = E_S\left(\tilde{Q}^N\right) - \frac{(2t+c+u)}{4} \in [0,1]$.

Property 4.3 *For QSVNS* $\tilde{Q}^N = \left\{\langle x, t_{\tilde{Q}^N}(x), c_{\tilde{Q}^N}(x), u_{\tilde{Q}^N}(x), f_{\tilde{Q}^N}(x)\rangle | x \in X\right\}$ or QSVNN $\tilde{Q}^N = \langle t, c, u, f\rangle$ *(for convenience), the suggested SF, Eq.* (9) *reduces to the existing SF, Eq.* (1) *in certain conditions only, i.e.,* $\psi_S(\tilde{Q}^N) = E_S\left(\tilde{Q}^N\right) = \frac{3-f}{4}$, *iff* $t = c = u = 0$, or $2t = -(c+u)$.

Property 4.4 *One property: If QSVNS* $\tilde{Q}^N = \left\{\langle x, t_{\tilde{Q}^N}(x), c_{\tilde{Q}^N}(x), u_{\tilde{Q}^N}(x), f_{\tilde{Q}^N}(x)\rangle | x \in X\right\}$ *is absolute, i.e.,* $\tilde{Q}^N = \langle 1,1,0,0\rangle$, *then* $\psi_S(\tilde{Q}^N) = 1$, *i.e., the maximum value of QSVNN* $\tilde{A}^N$ is 1.

Proof Let $\tilde{Q}^N = \langle 1,1,0,0\rangle$ be any QSVNN, then from Eq. (9), we have

$$\psi_S(\tilde{Q}^N) = \frac{3 - 1 + 2(1) - 2(0) - 0}{4} = 1.$$

Property 4.5 *Zero property:* If QSVNS $\tilde{Q}^N = \left\{\langle x, t_{\tilde{Q}^N}(x), c_{\tilde{Q}^N}(x), u_{\tilde{Q}^N}(x), f_{\tilde{Q}^N}(x)\rangle | x \in X\right\}$ *is null, i.e.,* $\tilde{Q}^N = \langle 0,0,1,1\rangle$, *then* $\psi_S(\tilde{Q}^N) = 0$, *i.e., the minimum value of QSVNN* $\tilde{A}^N$ *is* 0.

Proof Let $\tilde{Q}^N = \langle 0,0,1,1\rangle$ be any QSVNN, then from Eq. (9), we have

$$\psi_S(\tilde{Q}^N) = \frac{3 - 0 + 2(0) - 2(1) - 1}{4} = 0.$$

Property 4.6 *For any subset of QSVNS* $\tilde{Q}^N = \left\{\langle x, t_{\tilde{Q}^N}(x), c_{\tilde{Q}^N}(x), u_{\tilde{Q}^N}(x), f_{\tilde{Q}^N}(x)\rangle | x \in X\right\}$ *or* QSVNN $\tilde{Q}^N = \langle t, c, u, f\rangle$ *(for convenience), the value of* $\psi_S(\tilde{Q}^N) = \frac{1}{2}(1 + c - u)$.

Proof Let $\tilde{Q}^N = \langle t, c, u, f \rangle$ be any subset of QSVNS.

(i) Let $\tilde{Q}^N = \langle t, c, u, 1 - t \rangle$, then from Eq. (9), we have

$$\psi_S\left(\tilde{Q}^N\right) = \frac{3 - t + 2\,\mathrm{c} - 2\,\mathrm{u} - (1 - t)}{4} = \frac{1}{2}(1 + c - u).$$

(ii) Let $\tilde{Q}^N = \langle 1 - f, c, u, f \rangle$, then from Eq. (9), we have

$$\psi_S\left(\tilde{Q}^N\right) = \frac{3 - (1 - f) + 2\,\mathrm{c} - 2\,\mathrm{u} - f)}{4} = \frac{1}{2}(1 + c - u).$$

Property 4.7 *For QSVNS* $\tilde{Q}^N = \left\{\langle \mathrm{x}, t_{\tilde{Q}^N}(\mathrm{x}), \mathrm{c}_{\tilde{Q}^N}(\mathrm{x}), \mathrm{u}_{\tilde{Q}^N}(\mathrm{x}), \mathrm{f}_{\tilde{Q}^N}(\mathrm{x})\rangle | \mathrm{x} \in \mathrm{X}\right\}$ or QSVNN $\tilde{Q}^N = \langle t, c, u, f \rangle$ (for convenience), the value of the suggested AF $\varphi_A\left(\tilde{Q}^N\right)$, Eq. (10) *lies between* $[-1,1]$ i.e., $\varphi_A\left(\tilde{Q}^N\right) \in [-1,1]$.

Proof Let us consider QSVNS $\tilde{Q}^N = \left\{\langle \mathrm{x}, t_{\tilde{Q}^N}(\mathrm{x}), \mathrm{c}_{\tilde{Q}^N}(\mathrm{x}), \mathrm{u}_{\tilde{Q}^N}(\mathrm{x}), \mathrm{f}_{\tilde{Q}^N}(\mathrm{x})\rangle | \mathrm{x} \in \mathrm{X}\right\}$.

(i) Since by the definition of QSVNS for each $x \in X$, $t_{\tilde{Q}^N}(\mathrm{x}), \mathrm{c}_{\tilde{Q}^N}(\mathrm{x}), \mathrm{u}_{\tilde{Q}^N}(\mathrm{x}), \mathrm{f}_{\tilde{Q}^N}(\mathrm{x}) \in [0,1]$ and $0 \le t_{\tilde{Q}^N}(\mathrm{x}) + \mathrm{c}_{\tilde{Q}^N}(\mathrm{x}) + \mathrm{u}_{\tilde{Q}^N}(\mathrm{x}) + \mathrm{f}_{\tilde{Q}^N}(\mathrm{x}) \le 4$, so let $\tilde{Q}^N = \langle 1,1, 1,1 \rangle$, then according to the suggested AF, Eq. (10), we have

$$\begin{aligned}\varphi_A\left(\tilde{Q}^N\right) &= t_{\tilde{Q}^N} - \mathrm{c}_{\tilde{Q}^N}\left(1 - t_{\tilde{Q}^N}\right) + \mathrm{u}_{\tilde{Q}^N}\left(1 - t_{\tilde{Q}^N}\right) - \mathrm{f}_{\tilde{Q}^N}\left(1 - \mathrm{c}_{\tilde{Q}^N}\right) - \mathrm{f}_{\tilde{Q}^N}\left(1 - \mathrm{u}_{\tilde{Q}^N}\right) \\ &= 1 \in [-1, 1]\end{aligned}$$

(ii) *One property*: If QSVNS $\tilde{Q}^N = \left\{\langle \mathrm{x}, t_{\tilde{Q}^N}(\mathrm{x}), \mathrm{c}_{\tilde{Q}^N}(\mathrm{x}), \mathrm{u}_{\tilde{Q}^N}(\mathrm{x}), \mathrm{f}_{\tilde{Q}^N}(\mathrm{x})\rangle | \mathrm{x} \in \mathrm{X}\right\}$ is absolute, i.e., $\tilde{Q}^N = \langle 1,1, 0,0 \rangle$, then $\varphi_A\left(\tilde{Q}^N\right) = 1$, i.e., the maximum value of QSVNN $\tilde{A}^N$ is 1

Proof Let $\tilde{Q}^N = \langle 1,1, 0,0 \rangle$ be any QSVNN, then according to the suggested AF Eq. (10), we have

$$\varphi_A\left(\tilde{Q}^N\right) = 1 - (1 - 1) + 0(1 - 1) - 0(1 - 1) - 0(1 - 0) = 1 \in [-1,1].$$

(iii) *Zero property*: If QSVNS $\tilde{Q}^N = \left\{\langle \mathrm{x}, t_{\tilde{Q}^N}(\mathrm{x}), \mathrm{c}_{\tilde{Q}^N}(\mathrm{x}), \mathrm{u}_{\tilde{Q}^N}(\mathrm{x}), \mathrm{f}_{\tilde{Q}^N}(\mathrm{x})\rangle | \mathrm{x} \in \mathrm{X}\right\}$ is null, i.e., $\tilde{Q}^N = \langle 0,0, 1,1 \rangle$, then $\varphi_A\left(\tilde{Q}^N\right) = 0$, i.e., the minimum value of QSVNN $\tilde{A}^N$ is 0.

Proof Let $\tilde{Q}^N = \langle 0,0, 1,1 \rangle$ be any QSVNN, then according to the suggested AF Eq. (10), we have

$$\varphi_A\left(\tilde{Q}^N\right) = 0 - 0(1 - 0) + 1(1 - 0) - 1(1 - 0) - 1(1 - 1) = 0 \in [-1,1]$$

5 Methodology

From Sects. 3.1 and 3.2, we utilize the suggested SF $\psi_S(\tilde{Q}^N)$, and the suggested AF $\varphi_A(\tilde{Q}^N)$ given in Eqs. (9) and (10) for QSVNSs in practical MGDM problems to illustrate the application of the suggested method.

5.1 MGDM Method Using Novel SF and AF for QSVNNs

Let us examine an MGDM situation having m number of options, i.e., $\tilde{A}^N = \{\tilde{A}_1^N, \tilde{A}_2^N, \ldots, \tilde{A}_m^N\}$ which is rated on n number of criteria, i.e., $\tilde{C}^N = \{\tilde{C}_1^N, \tilde{C}_2^N, \ldots, \tilde{C}_n^N\}$. Suppose an expert assigns the weights to each criterion such that $w_k \in [0, 1]$and $\sum_{k=1}^{n} w_k = 1$, where the information of options $\tilde{A}_i^N (i = 1,2, \ldots, m)$ per criterion $\tilde{C}_j^N (j = 1,2, \ldots, n)$ are given by QSVNSs, $\tilde{Q}^N = \{x, t_{\tilde{Q}^N}(x), c_{\tilde{Q}^N}(x), u_{\tilde{Q}^N}(x), f_{\tilde{Q}^N}(x) | x \in X,\ 0 \leq t_{\tilde{Q}^N}(x), c_{\tilde{Q}^N}(x), u_{\tilde{Q}^N}(x), f_{\tilde{Q}^N}(x) \leq 1,\ t_{\tilde{Q}^N}(x) + c_{\tilde{Q}^N}(x) + u_{\tilde{Q}^N}(x) + f_{\tilde{Q}^N}(x) \leq 4\}$ for all $i = 1 to m$ and $j = 1 to n$, for convenience, it is written here as $\tilde{Q}^N = \langle t_{\tilde{Q}^N}, c_{\tilde{Q}^N}, u_{\tilde{Q}^N}, f_{\tilde{Q}^N} \rangle$. The quadripartitioned single-valued neutrosophic decision matrix (QSVNDM) taken from the gathered quadripartitioned SVN information available for m alternatives concerning the n number of the criterion is represented as follows:

$$D = (\Lambda_{ij})_{m\times n} = \left(t_{\tilde{Q}^N}, c_{\tilde{Q}^N}, u_{\tilde{Q}^N}, f_{\tilde{Q}^N}\right)_{m\times n}, i.e.,$$

$$D = \begin{array}{c} \\ A_1 \\ A_2 \\ \vdots \\ A_m \end{array} \begin{array}{c} \begin{array}{cccc} \tilde{C}_1^N & \tilde{C}_2^N & & \tilde{C}_n^N \end{array} \\ \begin{bmatrix} \langle t_{11}, c_{11}, u_{11}, f_{11} \rangle & \langle t_{12}, c_{12}, u_{12}, f_{12} \rangle & \cdots & \langle t_{1n}, c_{1n}, u_{1n}, f_{1n} \rangle \\ \langle t_{21}, c_{21}, u_{21}, f_{21.} \rangle & \langle t_{22}, c_{22}, u_{22}, f_{22} \rangle & \cdots & \langle t_{2n}, c_{2n}, u_{2n}, f_{2n} \rangle \\ \vdots & \vdots & \ddots & \vdots \\ \langle t_{m1}, c_{m1}, u_{m1}, f_{m1} \rangle & \langle t_{m2}, c_{m2}, u_{m2}, f_{m2} \rangle & \cdots & \langle t_{mn}, c_{mn}, u_{mn}, f_{mn} \rangle \end{bmatrix} \end{array}$$

For determining the MGDM problem for QSVNSs we suggested a general step-wise procedure with the help of $QSVN_{WAA}$ and $QSVN_{WGA}$ operator (Chatterjee et al., 2020) as follows:

Step 1: Determine whether all the criteria of the QSVNDM, D are of the same type or not, i.e., cost or benefit type.

Case (i) If all are of the same type, then go to Step 2.
Case (ii) If some criteria are varying then normalize the QSVNDM by transforming the cost criterion into the benefit criterion, as follows: If the pth criterion is the cost criterion, then replace all the elements $\langle t_{ip}, c_{ip}, u_{ip}, f_{ip} \rangle$ of the pth column of the decision matrix, D with $\langle 1 - f_{ip}, 1 - u_{ip}, c_{ip}, t_{ip} \rangle$.

Step 2: First aggregate all the sub-criteria $C_{ki}(k = 1,2,3,4; i = 1,2,3)$ given as QSVNSs in the decision matrix, D for each $\tilde{A}_i^N$ into criteria's $C_k(k = 1,2,3,4)$ using QSVN_{WAA} operator, Eq. (7), or the QSVN_{WGA} operator, Eq. (8) (Chatterjee et al., 2020).

Step 3: Now aggregate all the criteria $C_k(k = 1,2,3,4)$ obtained in Step 2 given as QSVNSs in the decision matrix, D into a QSVNNs $\left(\tilde{Q}_k^N\right)$ for each $\tilde{A}_i^N$ using QSVN_{WAA} operator, Eq. (7), or the QSVN_{WGA} operator, Eq. (8) (Chatterjee et al., 2020).

Step 4: After aggregation (by applying either of the approaches, i.e., QSVN_{WAA} or QSVN_{WGA} operator) as stated in Step 3, each $\tilde{A}_i^N$ is now a QSVNN. To acquire the crisp value of each alternative $\tilde{A}_i^N$ we can evaluate the score value or accuracy value by using the suggested SF $\psi_S\left(\tilde{Q}^N\right)$, Eq. (9), or AF $\varphi_A\left(\tilde{Q}^N\right)$, Eq. (10).

Step 5: After Step 4, obtain the ranking of all the alternatives as per the obtained score value of $\psi_S\left(\tilde{Q}^N\right)$, Eq. (9) or AF $\varphi_A\left(\tilde{Q}^N\right)$, Eq. (10), and choose the best alternative.

5.2 *Real-Life Application of the MGDM Method for QSVNS*

Here a problem from the education sector has been considered, where the most suitable candidate has to be selected among the 04 competing candidates $\tilde{A}_i^N(i = 1,2,3,4)$ for admission to the university under the meritorious scholarship. Hence, a scientific approach is required for the assessment scope of college students' scholarship selection, for which a scholarship assessment system has been developed based on the required criteria in different categories at Level 1, like- student attitude, academic performance, physical and psychological well-being, and practical activity. Again, these criteria at Level 1 requirement have some further sub-criteria at Level 2 that have to be satisfied as shown in Table 1 given.

Table 1 College scholarship assessment system

	Level 1	Level 2
C_1	Student's attitudes (scientifically and ethically)	• c_{11} Discipline • c_{12} Competitive award and innovative • c_{13} Rapport in peers and teachers
C_2	Academic performance	• c_{21} Score in Computer and English • c_{22} Any professional qualification • c_{23} General academic score
C_3	Physical and psychological well-being	• c_{31} Physical fitness • c_{32} Sports experience • c_{33} Cognitive and affective health
C_4	Practical activity	• c_{41} Activity participation • c_{42} Management skills • c_{43} Regional/National award

In Table 1, all the mentioned criteria at Level 1 and Level 2 have different weight vectors as per the requirement of the college scholarship assessment system that satisfies the conditions such as $w_k \in [0, 1]$and $\sum_{k=1}^{n} w_k = 1$. In the considered MGDM problem let us assume that all the criteria $C_k(k = 1,2, 3,4)$ are given the same weightage, i.e., $w = (w_1, w_2, w_3, w_4)^T = \langle 0.5, 0.5,0.5,0.5\rangle$, and all the sub-criteria's $C_{ki}(k = 1,2, 3,4; i = 1,2, 3)$ weight vectors are given as, $\langle 0.37, 0.4, 0.23\rangle$, $\langle 0.5, 0.25, 0.25\rangle$, $\langle \frac{1}{3}, \frac{1}{3}, \frac{1}{3}\rangle$, and $\langle 0.5, 0.4, 0.1\rangle$ respectively. To find a suitable candidate $\tilde{A}_i^N(i = 1,2, 3,4)$ among the 04 competing candidates after assessing them based on all the criteria $C_k(k = 1,2, 3,4)$ the MGDM problem can be depicted in the form of a decision matrix $D = (\Lambda_{ij})_{m\times n}$ on $\mathcal{QNN}$.

5.2.1 Illustrative Example 5.2 Using the Algorithm 5.1 with QSVN_{WAA} Operator

By applying the suggested MGDM problem approach for QSVNSs given in Sect. 5.1 we can determine the best candidate among all the competing candidates by using the step-wise procedure with the help of the QSVN_{WAA} operator as follows:

Step 1: The QSVNDM, $D = (\Lambda_{ij})_{m\times n}$ is represented in Table 2.

Since all the sub-criteria's $C_{ki}(k = 1,2, 3,4; i = 1,2, 3)$ are of the same type, we can move to Step 2.

Step 2: Using Step 2 of Sect. 5.1 reduce the QSVNDM $D = (\Lambda_{ij})_{m\times n}$ for each $\tilde{A}_i^N(i = 1,2, 3,4)$ with the sub-criteria $C_{ki}(k = 1,2, 3,4; i = 1,2, 3)$ into the QSVNDM $D = (\Lambda_i)_{m\times n}$ of criteria $C_k(k = 1,2, 3,4)$ where the weight vectors are, $\langle 0.37, 0.4, 0.23\rangle$, $\langle 0.5, 0.25, 0.25\rangle$, $\langle \frac{1}{3}, \frac{1}{3}, \frac{1}{3}\rangle$, and $\langle 0.5, 0.4, 0.1\rangle$, respectively. Now, using the QSVN_{WAA} operator, Eq. (7) (Chatterjee et al., 2020) the QSVNDM $D = (\Lambda_i)_{m\times n}$ is obtained in Table 3, as given:

Step 3: Using Step 3 of Sect. 5.1, reduce the QSVNDM $D = (\Lambda_j)_{m\times n}$ for each $\tilde{A}_i^N(i = 1,2, 3,4)$ into QSVNN $(\tilde{Q}_k^N, k = 1, 2,3, 4)$ using QSVN_{WAA} operator, Eq.(7) (Chatterjee et al., 2020), where the weights are taken as $w = \langle 0.5, 0.5,0.5,0.5\rangle$ respectively. Hence, the obtained QSVNNs for each alternative are given:

$$\tilde{A}_1^N(\tilde{Q}^N) = \langle 0.5749, 0.4914, 0.0, 0.0\rangle,$$

$$\tilde{A}_2^N(\tilde{Q}^N) = \langle 0.3553, 0.3849, 0.2667, 0.2454\rangle,$$

$$\tilde{A}_3^N(\tilde{Q}^N) = \langle 0.4139, 0.3443, 0.0, 0.0\rangle,$$

$$\tilde{A}_4^N(\tilde{Q}^N) = \langle 0.5762, 0.4073, 0.2100, 0.0\rangle.$$

Table 2 QSVNDM $\boldsymbol{D} = \left(\boldsymbol{\Lambda}_{ij}\right)_{m \times n}$

		$\tilde{A}_1^N$	$\tilde{A}_2^N$	$\tilde{A}_3^N$	$\tilde{A}_4^N$
	C_{11}	⟨0.7,0.5,0.2,0.1⟩	⟨0.4,0.2,0.5,0.8⟩	⟨0.9,0.2,0, 0⟩	⟨0.5,0.1,0.6,0.2⟩
	C_{12}	⟨0.2,0.6,0.1,0.5⟩	⟨0,0.25,0.7,0.6⟩	⟨0.01,0.1,0.2,0.1⟩	⟨0.1,0.7,0.2,0.5⟩
	C_{13}	⟨0.5,0.2,0.7,0.1⟩	⟨0.5,0.5,0.3,0.1⟩	⟨0.1,0.2,0.5,0.7⟩	⟨0.8,0.5,0.2,0.4⟩
	C_{21}	⟨0.7,0.5,0.2,0.1⟩	⟨0.5,0.6,0.1,0.1⟩	⟨0.01,0.1,0.5,0.1⟩	⟨0.45,0.2,0.1,0.3⟩
$\tilde{C}_1^N$	C_{22}	⟨0.9,0.2,0, 0⟩	⟨0.2,0.5,0.3,0.5⟩	⟨0.5,0.4,0.2,0.01⟩	⟨0.4,0.4,0.01,0⟩
$D =$ $\tilde{C}_2^N$	C_{23}	⟨0.4,0.2,0.2,0.3⟩	⟨0.5,0.2,0.7,0.1⟩	⟨0.2,0.1,0.3,0.5⟩	⟨0.5,0.3,0.4,0.4⟩
$\tilde{C}_3^N$	C_{31}	⟨0.56,0.8,0, 0⟩	⟨0.45,0.4,0.11,0.05⟩	⟨0.6,0.7,0.01,0⟩	⟨0.4,0.5,0.2,0.6⟩
$\tilde{C}_4^N$	C_{32}	⟨0.6,0.5,0.3,0.2⟩	⟨0.35,0.2,0.35,0.45⟩	⟨0.5,0.5,0.4,0.2⟩	⟨0.8,0.5,0.3,0.4⟩
	C_{33}	⟨0.4,0.4,0.5,0.6⟩	⟨0.45,0.3,0.2,0.2⟩	⟨0.3,0.2,0.5,0.6⟩	⟨0.9,0.2,0.7,0.3⟩
	C_{41}	⟨0.4,0.5,0.1,0.5⟩	⟨0.3,0.6,0.1,0.4⟩	⟨0.2,0.6,0.3,0.2⟩	⟨0.4,0.2,0.1,0.1⟩
	C_{42}	⟨0.6,0.5,0.6,0.7⟩	⟨0.1,0.1,0.6,0.3⟩	⟨0.4,0.2,0.7,0.6⟩	⟨0.6,0.6,0.5,0.5⟩
	C_{43}	⟨0.4,0.1,0.1,0.1⟩	⟨0.5,0.3,0.4,0.2⟩	⟨0.4,0.4,0.4,0.5⟩	⟨0.5,0.5,0.8,0.1⟩

Table 3 QSVNDe-M $\boldsymbol{D} = (\mathbf{A}_i)_{m\times n}$ using $\mathbf{QSVN_{WAA}}$

$\tilde{A}_1^N$	$\tilde{A}_2^N$	$\tilde{A}_3^N$	$\tilde{A}_4^N$

$$D = \begin{matrix} \tilde{C}_1^N \\ \tilde{C}_2^N \\ \tilde{C}_3^N \\ \tilde{C}_4^N \end{matrix} \begin{bmatrix} \left\langle \begin{matrix} 0.5005, 0.4905, \\ 0.2022, 0.1904 \end{matrix} \right\rangle & \left\langle \begin{matrix} 0.2942, 0.3003, \\ 0.5086, 0.4420 \end{matrix} \right\rangle & \left\langle \begin{matrix} 0.5853, 0.1614, \\ 0, 0 \end{matrix} \right\rangle & \left\langle \begin{matrix} 0.4877, 0.4934, \\ 0.3003, 0.3384 \end{matrix} \right\rangle \\ \left\langle \begin{matrix} 0.7289, 0.3675, \\ 0, 0 \end{matrix} \right\rangle & \left\langle \begin{matrix} 0.4377, 0.4970, \\ 0.2141, 0.1495 \end{matrix} \right\rangle & \left\langle \begin{matrix} 0.2087, 0.1868, \\ 0.3500, 0.0841 \end{matrix} \right\rangle & \left\langle \begin{matrix} 0.4511, 0.2800, \\ 0.0795, 0 \end{matrix} \right\rangle \\ \left\langle \begin{matrix} 0.5273, 0.6085, \\ 0, 0 \end{matrix} \right\rangle & \left\langle \begin{matrix} 0.4185, 0.3048, \\ 0.1975, 0.1651 \end{matrix} \right\rangle & \left\langle \begin{matrix} 0.4808, 0.5068, \\ 0.1260, 0 \end{matrix} \right\rangle & \left\langle \begin{matrix} 0.7711, 0.4152, \\ 0.3476, 0.4160 \end{matrix} \right\rangle \\ \left\langle \begin{matrix} 0.4898, 0.4697, \\ 0.2048, 0.4870 \end{matrix} \right\rangle & \left\langle \begin{matrix} 0.2516, 0.4149, \\ 0.2352, 0.3326 \end{matrix} \right\rangle & \left\langle \begin{matrix} 0.3072, 0.4504, \\ 0.4333, 0.3402 \end{matrix} \right\rangle & \left\langle \begin{matrix} 0.4990, 0.4215, \\ 0.2344, 0.1904 \end{matrix} \right\rangle \end{bmatrix}$$

Step 4: Now using Step 4 of Sect. 5.1, the crisp value of each $\tilde{A}_i^N\,(i = 1{,}2, 3{,}4)$ is obtained by applying the suggested SF $\psi_S\big(\tilde{Q}^N\big)$, Eq. (9) as follows:

$$\psi_S\big(\tilde{A}_1^N\big(\tilde{Q}^N\big)\big) = 0.8520,\ \psi_S\big(\tilde{A}_2^N\big(\tilde{Q}^N\big)\big) = 0.6589,\ \psi_S\big(\tilde{A}_3^N\big(\tilde{Q}^N\big)\big) = 0.8187,$$
$$\text{and } \psi_S\big(\tilde{A}_4^N\big(\tilde{Q}^N\big)\big) = 0.7046.$$

Step 5: Using Step 5 of Sect. 5.1, the obtained ranking order using SF $\psi_S\big(\tilde{Q}^N\big)$, Eq. (9) is:

$$\tilde{A}_1^N > \tilde{A}_3^N > \tilde{A}_4^N > \tilde{A}_2^N$$

Hence, candidate $\tilde{A}_1^N$ is the best candidate to deserve the prestigious scholarship of the college based on all the criteria and sub-criteria.

Comparative Analysis

Here in this section, a systematic comparison of the above-considered MGDM problem is presented below in Table 4 by applying the existing SF (Chatterjee et al., 2020; Debnath, 2022; Mohanasundari & Mohana, 2020) and the suggested SF as follows:

From Table 4 and Figs. 4 and 5, it is visible that by each method, i.e., by the existing SF (Chatterjee et al., 2020; Debnath, 2022; Mohanasundari & Mohana, 2020) and the novel SF for finding the score value for QSVNNs the best alternative remains $\tilde{A}_1^N$ only. Hence, this validates our suggested SF for QSVNNs which is a useful tool for finding the solutions to real-life problems in MGDM.

Table 4 Systematic comparative analysis of the score values for $\tilde{A}_i^N$

Alternatives	Existing SF (Mohanasundari & Mohana, 2020)	Existing SF (Debnath, 2022)	Existing SF (Chatterjee et al., 2020)	Novel SF
$\tilde{A}_1^N$	0.7709	0.5332	0.7666	0.8520
$\tilde{A}_2^N$	0.6146	0.1140	0.5570	0.6589
$\tilde{A}_3^N$	0.7674	0.3791	0.6895	0.8187
$\tilde{A}_4^N$	0.7397	0.3868	0.6934	0.7046
Ranking order	$\tilde{A}_1^N > \tilde{A}_3^N > \tilde{A}_4^N > \tilde{A}_2^N$	$\tilde{A}_1^N > \tilde{A}_4^N > \tilde{A}_3^N > \tilde{A}_2^N$	$\tilde{A}_1^N > \tilde{A}_4^N > \tilde{A}_3^N > \tilde{A}_2^N$	$\tilde{A}_1^N > \tilde{A}_3^N > \tilde{A}_4^N > \tilde{A}_2^N$

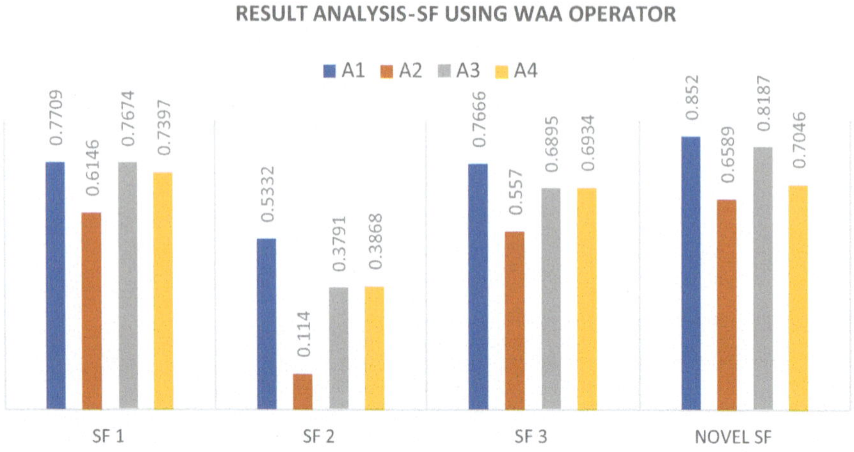

Fig. 4 Obtained Score value for the real-life application of Sect. 5.2.1

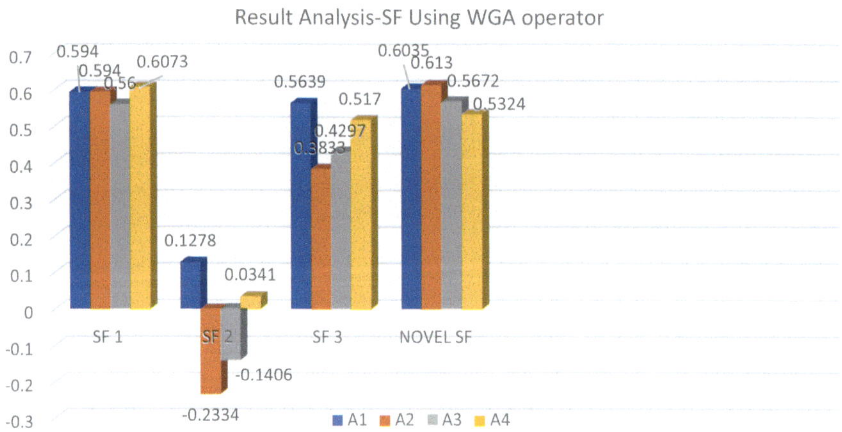

Fig. 5 Obtained Score value for the real-life application of Sect. 5.2.2

5.2.2 Illustrative Example 5.2 Using the Algorithm 5.1 with $QSVN_{WGA}$ Operator

By applying the suggested MGDM problem approach for QSVNSs given in Sect. 5.1 we can determine the best candidate among all the competing candidates by using the step-wise procedure with the help of the $QSVN_{WGA}$ operator (Chatterjee et al., 2020) as follows:

Step 1: The QSVNDM $D = \left(\Lambda_{ij}\right)_{m\times n}$ is represented in Table 2 given in above Sect. 5.2.1. Since all the sub-criteria $C_{ki}(k = 1,2,3,4;\ i = 1,2,3)$ are of the same type, we can move to Step 2.

Step 2: Using Step 2 of Sect. 5.1, reduce the QSVNDM $D = (\Lambda_{ij})_{m\times n}$ for each $\tilde{A}_i^N (i = 1,2,3,4)$ with the sub-criteria $C_{ki}(k = 1,2,3,4; i = 1,2,3)$ into QSVNDM $D = (\Lambda_i)_{m\times n}$ of criteria $C_k(k = 1,2,3,4)$ where the weight vectors are, $\langle 0.37, 0.4, 0.23\rangle$, $\langle 0.5, 0.25, 0.25\rangle$, $\langle \frac{1}{3}, \frac{1}{3}, \frac{1}{3}\rangle$, and $\langle 0.5, 0.4, 0.1\rangle$, respectively. Now, using the QSVN$_{\text{WGA}}$ operator, Eq.(8), the QSVNDM $D = (\Lambda_i)_{m\times n}$ is obtained in Table 5 as given:

Step 3: Using Step 3 of Sect. 5.1, reduce the QSVNDM $D = (\Lambda_j)_{m\times n}$ for each $\tilde{A}_i^N (i = 1,2,3,4)$ into QSVNN $(\tilde{Q}_k^N, k = 1,2,3,4)$ using QSVN$_{\text{WGA}}$ operator, Eq. (8) (Chatterjee et al., 2020) where the weights are taken as $w = \langle 0.5, 0.5, 0.5, 0.5\rangle$ respectively. Hence, the obtained QSVNNs for each alternative are given:

$$\tilde{A}_1^N(\tilde{Q}^N) = \langle 0.4976, 0.4397, 0.2862, 0.3956\rangle,$$

$$\tilde{A}_2^N(\tilde{Q}^N) = \langle 0.0, 0.3103, 0.3914, 0.3858\rangle,$$

$$\tilde{A}_3^N(\tilde{Q}^N) = \langle 0.1590, 0.2393, 0.3712, 0.3084\rangle,$$

$$\tilde{A}_4^N(\tilde{Q}^N) = \langle 0.4519, 0.3194, 0.3540, 0.3492\rangle.$$

Step 4: Now using Step 4 of Sect. 5.1, the crisp value of each $\tilde{A}_i^N (i = 1,2,3,4)$ is obtained by applying the suggested SF $\psi_S(\tilde{Q}^N)$, Eq. (9) as follows:

$\psi_S(\tilde{A}_1^N(\tilde{Q}^N)) = 0.6035$, $\psi_S(\tilde{A}_2^N(\tilde{Q}^N)) = 0.6130$, $\psi_S(\tilde{A}_3^N(\tilde{Q}^N)) = 0.5672$ and $\psi_S(\tilde{A}_4^N(\tilde{Q}^N)) = 0.5324$

Step 5: Using Step 5 of the suggested method, the obtained ranking order using score function $\psi_S(\tilde{Q}^N)$, Eq. (9) is: $\tilde{A}_2^N > \tilde{A}_1^N > \tilde{A}_3^N > \tilde{A}_4^N$.

Table 5 QSVNDM $D = (\Lambda_i)_{m\times n}$ using **QSVN$_{\text{WGA}}$**

		$\tilde{A}_1^N$	$\tilde{A}_2^N$	$\tilde{A}_3^N$	$\tilde{A}_4^N$
$D =$	$\tilde{C}_1^N$	$\langle 0.3925, 0.4356, 0.3308, 0.2886\rangle$	$\langle 0.0, 0.2700, 0.5596, 0.6270\rangle$	$\langle 0.0898, 0.1516, 0.2202, 0.2732\rangle$	$\langle 0.2926, 0.3154, 0.3810, 0.3796\rangle$
	$\tilde{C}_2^N$	$\langle 0.6481, 0.3162, 0.1541, 0.3656\rangle$	$\langle 0.3976, 0.4356, 0.3578, 0.2230\rangle$	$\langle 0.0562, 0.1414, 0.3883, 0.2043\rangle$	$\langle 0.4486, 0.2632, 0.1671, 0.2636\rangle$
	$\tilde{C}_3^N$	$\langle 0.5122, 0.5429, 0.2953, 0.3160\rangle$	$\langle 0.4138, 0.2884, 0.2236, 0.2523\rangle$	$\langle 0.4481, 0.4121, 0.3328, 0.3160\rangle$	$\langle 0.6604, 0.3684, 0.4482, 0.4482\rangle$
	$\tilde{C}_4^N$	$\langle 0.4704, 0.5000, 0.3493, 0.5677\rangle$	$\langle 0.2034, 0.2734, 0.3752, 0.3432\rangle$	$\langle 0.2828, 0.3713, 0.5089, 0.4215\rangle$	$\langle 0.4810, 0.3402, 0.3879, 0.2886\rangle$

Table 6 Comparative analysis of the score values for $\tilde{A}_i^N$

Alternatives	Existing score function (Mohanasundari & Mohana, 2020)	Existing score function (Debnath, 2022)	Existing score function (Chatterjee et al., 2020)	Suggested score function
$\tilde{A}_1^N$	0.5940	0.1278	0.5639	0.6035
$\tilde{A}_2^N$	0.5940	−0.2334	0.3833	0.6130
$\tilde{A}_3^N$	0.5600	−0.1406	0.4297	0.5672
$\tilde{A}_4^N$	0.6073	0.0341	0.5170	0.5324
Ranking order	$\tilde{A}_4^N > \tilde{A}_3^N > \tilde{A}_2^N = \tilde{A}_1^N$	$\tilde{A}_1^N > \tilde{A}_4^N > \tilde{A}_3^N > \tilde{A}_2^N$	$\tilde{A}_1^N > \tilde{A}_4^N > \tilde{A}_3^N > \tilde{A}_2^N$	$\tilde{A}_2^N > \tilde{A}_1^N > \tilde{A}_3^N > \tilde{A}_4^N$

Hence, candidate $\tilde{A}_2^N$ is the best candidate to deserve the prestigious scholarship of the college based on all the criteria and sub-criteria.

Comparative Analysis

Here in this section, a systematic comparison of the above-considered MGDM problem is presented below in Table 6 by applying the existing SF (Chatterjee et al., 2020; Debnath, 2022; Mohanasundari & Mohana, 2020) and the suggested score function as follows:

From Table 6 it is visible that by the suggested SF for finding the score value for QSVNNs, the best alternative obtained is $\tilde{A}_2^N$ whereas $\tilde{A}_1^N$ is the second-best candidate whereas the results of the existing SF (Chatterjee et al., 2020; Debnath, 2022; Mohanasundari & Mohana, 2020) are varying. Also, as the suggested SF $\psi_S(\tilde{Q}^N)$, Eq. (9) and AF $\varphi_A(\tilde{Q}^N)$, Eq. (10) satisfies all the properties, therefore, their applicability and the results are reasonable and reliable. Hence, this validates the suggested SF and AF for QSVNNs which is a useful tool for finding the solutions to real-life problems in MGDM.

6 Conclusions

In this chapter, we critically examined existing QSVNNs along with their associated Score Functions (SF) and Accuracy Functions (AF), highlighting some of their inherent limitations through relevant examples. To address these shortcomings, we introduced innovative SF and AF, which demonstrate enhanced capabilities. The practicality and effectiveness of these new approaches were validated using a real-world multi-group decision-making (MGDM) problem from the education sector. A comprehensive comparative analysis juxtaposed our proposed methods against existing ones, solidifying the superiority and applicability of our introduced MGDM method for QSVNSs, especially when employing the new SF and AF. Given the adeptness of QSVNS in handling extensive and intricate data, its applications in real-world scenarios are vast and varied. Looking ahead, we aim to expand the proposed SF and AF for QSVNS into other neutrosophic set environments, such as pentapartitioned NSs, Plithogenic NSs, and hypersoft NSs.

References

Atanassov, K. T. (1986). Intuitionistic fuzzy sets. *Fuzzy Sets and Systems, 20*, 87–96.

Belnap, N. D., Jr. (1977). A useful four valued logic. *Modern uses of multiple-valued logic* (pp. 5–37). Springer.

Bhat, S. A. (2023). An enhanced AHP group decision-making model employing neutrosophic trapezoidal numbers. *J. Oper. Strateg Anal, 1*(2), 81–89.

Chatterjee, R., Majumdar, P., & Samanta, S. K. (2016). On some similarity measures and entropy on quadripartitioned single valued neutrosophic sets. *Journal of Intelligent & Fuzzy Systems, 30*(4), 2475–2485.

Chatterjee, R., Majumdar, P., & Samanta, S. K. (2020). A multi-criteria group decision making algorithm with quadripartitioned neutrosophic weighted aggregation operators using quadripartitioned neutrosophic numbers in IPQSVNSS environment. *Soft Computing, 24*(12), 8857–8880.

Chen, J., & Ye, J. (2017). Some single-valued Neutrosophic Dombi weighted aggregation operators for multiple attribute decision-making. *Symmetry, 9*(6), 82.

Debnath, S. (2022). Fuzzy quadripartitioned neutrosophic soft matrix theory and its decision-making approach. *Journal of Computational and Cognitive Engineering, 1*(2), 88–93.

Dhar, M. (2021). Neutrosophic soft matrices and its application in medical diagnosis. *Journal of Fuzzy Extension and Applications, 2*(1), 23–32.

Dombi, J. (1982). A general class of fuzzy operators, the demorgan class of fuzzy operators and fuzziness measures induced by fuzzy operators. *Fuzzy Sets and Systems, 8*, 149–163.

Duran, V., Topal, S., & Smarandache, F. (2021). An application of neutrosophic logic in the confirmatory data analysis of the satisfaction with life scale. *Journal of Fuzzy Extension and Applications, 2*(3), 262–282.

Edalatpanah, S. A. (2020). *Neutrosophic Structured Element. Expert Systems, 37*(5), e12542.

Edalatpanah, S. A., Smarandache, F., & Garg, H. (2023a). Guest editorial: Preface to the special issue on the neutrosophical approach: Applications in management decision and organizational research methods. *Management Decision, 61*(2), 357–362.

Edalatpanah, S. A., Pamučar, D., & Zhang, L. T. (2023b). Preface to the special issue on numerical simulations and optimization under uncertainty. *Advances in Mechanical Engineering, 15*(3), 16878132231161484.

Edalatpanah, S. A., & Smarandache, F. (2023). Introduction to the Special Issue on Advances in Neutrosophic and Plithogenic Sets for Engineering and Sciences: Theory, Models, and Applications. *Computer Modeling in Engineering and Sciences, 134*(2), 817–819.

Hosseinzadeh, E., & Tayyebi, J. (2023). A compromise solution for the neutrosophic multi-objective linear programming problem and its application in transportation problem. *Journal of Applied Research on Industrial Engineering, 10*(1), 1–10.

Hussain, S.S., Durga, N., & Hossein, R. et al. (2022). New concepts on quadripartitioned single-valued neutrosophic graph with real-life application. *International Journal of Fuzzy Systems.* https://doi.org/10.1007/s40815-021-01205-8-2022

Ihsan, M., Saeed, M., & Rahman, A. U. (2023). Optimizing hard disk selection via a fuzzy parameterized single-valued neutrosophic soft set approach. *J. Oper. Strateg Anal, 1*(2), 62–69.

Kumar, R., Edalatpanah, S. A., Jha, S., & Singh, R. (2019). A novel approach to solve gaussian valued neutrosophic shortest path problems. *International Journal of Engineering and Advanced Technology 8*(3), 347–353

Kumari R. S., Kalayathankal, S., George, M., & Smarandache, F. (2023). On some related concepts n-cylindrical fuzzy neutrosophic topological spaces. *Journal of Fuzzy Extension and Applications, 4*(1), 40–51.

Liu, P. D., & Wang, Y. M. (2016). Interval neutrosophic prioritized OWA operator and its application to multiple attribute decision making. *Journal of Systems Science and Complexity, 29*, 681–697.

Liu, P. D., Chu, Y. C., Li, Y. W., & Chen, Y. B. (2014). Some generalized neutrosophic number Hamacher aggregation operators and their application to group decision making. *Journal of Intelligent and Fuzzy System, 16*, 242–255.

Mohan, M., & Krishnaswamy, M. (2020). K-algebras on quadripartitioned single valued neutrosophic sets. *Journal of Fuzzy Extension and Applications, 1*(4), 325–339.

Mohana, K., Mohanasundari, M. (2018). *Quadripartitioned single valued neutrosophic rough sets.* Nirmala Annual Research Congress (NARC-2018), ISBN-978–93–5321–859–1, 3, 165.

Mohana, K., & Mohanasundari, M. (2019). On some similarity measures of single valued neutrosophic rough sets. *Neutrosophic Sets and Systems, 24*, 10–22.

Mohanasundari, M., & Mohana, K. (2021). Multicriteria decision-making based on quadripartitioned neutrosophic cross-entropy. In: Smarandache, F., Abdel-Basset, M. (eds.), *Neutrosophic operational research.* Springer. https://doi.org/10.1007/978-3-030-57197-9_2

Mohanasundari, M., & Mohana, K. (2020). Quadripartitioned single valued neutrosophic Dombi weighted aggregation operators for multiple attribute decision making. *Neutrosophic Sets and Systems, 32*(1), 9.

Mohanta, K. K., & Toragay, O. (2023). Enhanced performance evaluation through neutrosophic data envelopment analysis leveraging pentagonal neutrosophic numbers. *J. Oper. Strateg Anal, 1*(2), 70–80.

Nagarajan, D., Kanchana, A., Jacob, K., Kausar, N., Edalatpanah, S. A., & Shah, M. A. (2023). A novel approach based on neutrosophic Bonferroni mean operator of trapezoidal and triangular neutrosophic interval environments in multi-attribute group decision making. *Scientific Reports, 13*(1), 10455.

Polymenis, A. (2021). A neutrosophic Student's t –type of statistic for AR (1) random processes. *Journal of Fuzzy Extension and Applications, 2*(4), 388–393.

Radha, R., & Arul Mary, A. S. (2021). Quadripartitioned neutrosophic pythagorean lie subalgebra. *Journal of Fuzzy Extension and Applications, 2*(3), 283–296.

Radha, R., Mary, A. S. A., Broumi, S., Jafari, S., & Edalatpanah, S. A. (2023). Effectiveness on impact of COVID vaccines on correlation coefficients of pentapartitioned neutrosophic pythagorean statistics. In *Cognitive intelligence with Neutrosophic statistics in bioinformatics* (pp. 335–356). Academic Press

Radha, R., Mary, A. S. A., Broumi, S., Jafari, S., & Edalatpanah, S. A. (2023). Improved correlation coefficients in neutrosophic statistics for COVID patients using pentapartitioned neutrosophic sets. In *Cognitive intelligence with Neutrosophic statistics in bioinformatics* (pp. 237–258). Academic Press.

Roy, S., Lee, J. G., Pal, A., & Samanta, S. K. (2020). Similarity measures of quadripartitioned single-valued bipolar neutrosophic sets and its application in multi-criteria decision making problems. *Symmetry, 12*(6), 1012. https://doi.org/10.3390/sym12061012

Smarandache, F. (1999). A unifying field in logics. Neutrosophy: Neutrosophic probability, set and logic, 1–141, 4th (eds.). American Research Press

Stanimirović, P. S., Ivanov, B., Stanujkić, D., Katsikis, V. N., Mourtas, S. D., Kazakovtsev, L. A., & Edalatpanah, S. A. (2023). Improvement of unconstrained optimization methods based on symmetry involved in neutrosophy. *Symmetry, 15*(1), 250.

Sun, H. X., Yang, H. X., Wu, J. Z., & Yao, O. Y. (2015). Interval neutrosophic numbers Choquet integral operator for multi-criteria decision making. *Journal of Intelligent and Fuzzy System, 28*, 2443–2455.

Veeramani, C., Venugopal, R., & Edalatpanah, S. A. (2022). Neutrosophic DEMATEL approach for financial ratio performance evaluation of the NASDAQ exchange. *Neutrosophic Sets and Systems, 51*, 766–782.

Wang, H., Smarandache, F., Zhang, Y. Q., & Sunderraman, R. (2010). Single valued neutrosophic sets. *Multispace and Multistructure, 4*, 410–413.

Wang, Q., Huang, Y., Kong, S., Ma, X., Liu, Y., Das, S. K., & Edalatpanah, S. A. (2021). A novel method for solving multiobjective linear programming problems with triangular neutrosophic numbers. *Journal of Mathematics, 2021*, 1–8.

Wu, X. H., Wang, J. Q., Peng, J. J., & Chen, X. H. (2016). Cross-entropy and prioritized aggregation operator with simplified neutrosophic sets and their application in multi-criteria decision-making problems. *Journal of Intelligent and Fuzzy System, 18*, 1104–1116.

Yang, H.L. (2017). A hybrid model of single vsalued neutrosophic sets and rough sets: single valued neutrosophic rough set model. *Soft Computing., 21*, 6253–6267.

Ye, J. (2014). Correlation coefficient of dual hesitant fuzzy sets and its application to multiple attribute decision making. *Applied Mathematical Modelling, 38*, 659–666.

Zadeh, L. A. (1965). Fuzzy sets. *Information and Control, 8*, 338–353.

Zhang, H.Y., Wang, J.Q., & Chen, X.H. (2014). Interval neutrosophic sets and their application in multicriteria decision making problems. *Scientific World Journal*, 645–953.

SPRINGER NATURE

GPSR Compliance

The European Union's (EU) General Product Safety Regulation (GPSR) is a set of rules that requires consumer products to be safe and our obligations to ensure this.

If you have any concerns about our products, you can contact us on ProductSafety@springernature.com

In case Publisher is established outside the EU, the EU authorized representative is:

Springer Nature Customer Service Center GmbH
Europaplatz 3
69115 Heidelberg, Germany

The manufacturer's authorised representative in the EU is Springer Nature Customer Service Centre GmbH, Europaplatz 3, 69115 Heidelberg, Germany. If you have any concerns regarding our products, please contact ProductSafety@springernature.com

Printed and bound by CPI Group (UK) Ltd, Croydon, CR0 4YY
01/10/2026
02225915-0017